DISCOURSES WE LIVE BY

Photo by Tom Perkins, CC-BY 4.0

Discourses We Live By

Narratives of Educational and Social Endeavour

Edited by
Hazel R. Wright and Marianne Høyen

OpenBook Publishers

ISBN Paperback: 978-1-78374-851-8
ISBN Hardback: 978-1-78374-852-5
ISBN Digital (PDF): 978-1-78374-853-2
ISBN Digital ebook (epub): 978-1-78374-854-9
ISBN Digital ebook (mobi): 978-1-78374-855-6
ISBN XML: 978-1-78374-856-3
DOI: 10.11647/OBP.0203

Cover design by Anna Gatti.
Cover image, and photographs on pages ii, xxii, 22, 114, 206, 284, 378, 460, 544, 620, 634, by Tom Perkins, CC-BY 4.0.

Contents

Acknowledgements   ix
Organization of the Book   xi
Notes on Contributors   xiii

Narrative, Discourse, and Biography: An Introductory Story   1
Marianne Høyen and Hazel R. Wright

**I.   DISCOURSES WE LIVE WITHIN: FRAMEWORKS THAT   23
       STRUCTURE**

1.   Truth and Narrative: How and Why Stories Matter   27
      Janet Dyson

2.   From Experience to Language in Narrative Practices in   53
      Therapeutic Education in France
      Hervé Breton

3.   Narratives of Fundamentalism, Negative Capability and   73
      the Democratic Imperative
      Alan Bainbridge and Linden West

4.   Understandings of the Natural World from a   91
      Generational Perspective
      Hazel R. Wright

II. DISCOURSES WE WORK WITHIN: OF THE WORKPLACE   115

5.   Opposing Cultures: Science and Humanities Teaching in   119
      Danish Schools
      Marianne Høyen and Mumiah Rasmusen

6.   Shaping 'the Good Teacher' in Danish and Kenyan   141
      Teacher Education
      Kari Kragh Blume Dahl

7.   Irish Adult Educators Find Fulfilment amid Poor   163
     Employment Conditions
     Sarah Bates Evoy

8.   Nurture Groups: Perspectives from Teaching Assistants   185
     Who Lead Them in Britain
     Tristan Middleton

III. DISCOURSES WE WORK THROUGH: CHALLENGES TO   207
**   OVERCOME**

9.   Punishment Discourses in Everyday Life   211
     Khum Raj Pathak

10. Irish Students Turning First-Year Transition Obstacles into   225
     Successful Progression
     Vera Sheridan

11. Care Leavers in Italy: From 'Vulnerable' Children to   245
     'Autonomous' Adults?
     Laura Formenti, Andrea Galimberti and Mirella Ferrari

12. What Game Are We Playing? Narrative Work that   269
     Supports Gamblers
     Micaela Castiglioni and Carola Girotti

IV. DISCOURSES WE WORK AROUND: MANAGING   285
**   CONSTRAINING CIRCUMSTANCES**

13. A Danish Prisoner Narrative: The Tension from a   289
     Multifaceted Identity During (Re-)Entry to Society
     Charlotte Mathiassen

14. Inclusion and Exclusion in Colombian Education,   311
     Captured Through Life Stories
     Miguel Alberto González González

15. Navigating Grades *and* Learning in the Swedish Upper   333
     Secondary School Where Neoliberal Values Prevail
     Patric Wallin

16. Adult Education as a Means to Enable Polish Citizens to   353
     Question Media Coverage of Political Messages
     Marta Zientek

V.	**DISCOURSES THAT EXPLORE OR REVEAL DIVERSITY: FACING CHOICE AND CHANGE**	**379**
17.	Examining a Kazakh Student's Biographical Narrative and the Discourses She Lives By *Rob Evans*	383
18.	The Needs of Low-Literate Migrants When Learning the English Language *Monica Mascarenhas*	403
19.	Uncovering Habitus in Life Stories of Muslim Converts *Simone R. Rasmussen*	425
20.	Participatory Approaches in Critical Migration Research: The Example of an Austrian Documentary Film *Annette Sprung*	445
VI.	**DISCOURSES TO SUPPORT DIVERSITY: PROJECTS THAT EMPOWER**	**461**
21.	Decolonizing and Indigenizing Discourses in a Canadian Context *Adrienne S. Chan*	465
22.	Embedding Feminist Pedagogies of Care in Research to Better Support San Youth in South Africa *Outi Ylitapio-Mäntylä and Mari Mäkiranta*	485
23.	From Defender to Offender: British Female Ex-Military Re-Joining Civilian Society *Linda Cooper*	501
24.	UK Senior Citizens Learn Filmmaking as a Creative Pathway to Reflection and Fulfilment *Teresa Brayshaw and Jenny Granville*	517
VII.	**DISCOURSES THROUGH A SELF-REFLEXIVE LENS: THOUGHTS FROM RESEARCHERS**	**545**
25.	Diversifying Discourses of Progression to UK Higher Education Through Narrative Approaches *Laura Mazzoli Smith*	549

26. Using Journaling and Autoethnography to Create   569
    Counter-Narratives of School Exclusion in Britain
    Helen Woodley

27. Reflections on a Creative Arts Project to Explore the   587
    Resilience of Young Adults with a Muslim Background in
    Finland
    Helena Oikarinen-Jabai

28. Discourses, Cultural Narratives, and Genre in   609
    Biographical Narratives: A Personal Overview
    Marianne Horsdal

Learning from Narratives, Discourses and Biographical   621
Research: An Afterword
    Hazel R. Wright and Marianne Høyen

List of Illustrations   633
Index   635

Acknowledgements

As editors, we would like to thank the thirty-five authors whose work appears in this volume for their collective efforts in making this a successful publication and their patience during the lengthy preparatory stages prior to publication. They have provided us with interesting and well-thought-out chapters, and those whose native tongue is other than English, have translated not only their own texts and their narrative data, but also the literature that they cite, making their material readily accessible in a common language to all our readers. For this, also, we are grateful.

We thank Alessandra Tosi and her team of editors and IT experts at Open Book Publishing — particularly Lucy, Luca, Laura and Anna — for helping us to create and disseminate this varied and lengthy coverage of the narratives around discourses in private and professional spaces. Doing this successfully has been a challenging but worthwhile process, and we hope that you will find it a stimulating read.

Special thanks are due to Tom Perkins (https://tomperkins.info) for taking and editing the photographs that introduce each section, which, as some of you may recognize, pursue a European theme in keeping with the spatial range of the book. We are grateful, too, for permission to use another of his photographs on the cover. Thanks also to Katie Wright for creating the graphic illustrations from the authors' originals. We are very grateful to AUFF (the funding arm of Aarhus University, Denmark) for providing financial support for this open access publication.

Organization of the Book

The personal and professional narratives in this book are grouped into seven sections that each takes a different slant on everyday discourses.

There are four distinctive but complementary chapters in each section, and these are preceded by introductory notes that provide an overview and rationale for the section and describe the content and purpose of the individual narrative accounts placed within it.

However, each chapter is fully referenced and complete and can be read independently from those with which it is associated, or alongside other chapters in the book. The sectional structure of the book is laid out below, with further information available in the first chapter, 'Narrative, Discourse, and Biography: An Introductory Story'. Consider, too, the final chapter, 'Learning from Narratives, Discourses and Biographical Research', that draws attention to the new knowledge to be gleaned from a comprehensive reading of the different chapters.

The seven sections are:

I. Discourses We Live Within: Frameworks that Structure

II. Discourses We Work Within: Of the Workplace

III. Discourses We Work Through: Challenges to Overcome

IV. Discourses We Work Around: Managing Constraining Circumstances

V. Discourses that Explore or Reveal Diversity: Facing Choice and Change

VI. Discourses to Support Diversity: Projects that Empower

VII. Discourses Through a Self-Reflexive Lens: Thoughts from Researchers

Notes on Contributors

Alan Bainbridge is a Chartered Psychologist, Doctor of Clinical Science and Senior Lecturer in Education at Canterbury Christ Church University, UK, having previously taught in secondary schools for eighteen years. He is interested in the contested space between psychoanalytic thought and practices to education in its widest sense and is a co-coordinator of the European Society for Research on the Education of Adults (ESREA) Life History and Biography Network. His recent writing focuses on the impact of the fetish in education and how learning and the 'natural world' are interconnected and includes the monograph *On becoming an education professional* (2015).

Sarah Bates Evoy is a Lecturer and Researcher at Waterford Institute of Technology, Ireland, where she works in the School of Lifelong Learning and Education. Sarah has had a diverse and varied career as a Social Care Worker, Adult Guidance Counsellor and Further Education teacher. Her current research interests include Adult and Further Education and Training, in particular practitioner identities, and innovative research and teaching methods. Recent papers and publications include work on further education training and open space technologies in teaching.

Teresa Brayshaw is Principal Lecturer in Performing Arts at Leeds Beckett University, UK, and works freelance as a Feldenkrais Teacher, Theatre Practitioner and Personal Development Coach in a range of international contexts. Her research centres upon creating environments in which people can learn through movement and awareness, to develop their innate potential and become happier and healthier as a result. She is co-editor of both the *Twentieth century performance reader* (2016) and *The twenty first century performance reader* (2020).

Hervé Breton is Associate Professor of Adult Education at the University of Tours, France. His research investigates and examines the effects of the narrative and descriptive experience on lifelong learning processes and on the formalization of experiential knowledge. Author of many articles and chapters, he was coordinator of a special issue on Autobiographical research in Asia in the *Brazilian Journal of (Auto)Biographical Research* (2019).

Micaela Castiglioni is Associate Professor of Adult Education and Education of the Elderly at the University of Milano-Bicocca, Italy. Her research and training interests focus on the fragility and vulnerability of contemporary adults, transitions in adulthood, and the use of narrative and writing practice in the care relationship. She deals with the training of professionals in medical care using narrative and reflexive approaches. She is the author of numerous articles and publications, including *Il posto delle fragole* (2019).

Adrienne S. Chan is a Professor at the University of Fraser Valley, Canada. Her research has a social justice orientation — community-based research with Indigenous peoples, child welfare in immigrant and minority populations, race, gender, diversity, anti-oppression and equity issues. She has been awarded national research grants for social justice, child welfare, and suicide prevention among Indigenous youth. Recent publications include a co-authored paper, 'Burdens felt by child protection workers serving immigrant families with limited English proficiency', in *The International Journal of Community Diversity* (2019).

Linda Cooper is a Senior Research Fellow in the Veterans & Families Institute for Military Social Research (VFI) at Anglia Ruskin University in Chelmsford, UK. Her main research interests are veterans in the criminal justice system, military transition and access to education. Previously, Linda was a Course Leader for an Education & Childhood Studies degree with an interest in women in higher education after a period as an educational researcher at the University of Cambridge. She has published on the military and education and continues to supervise and teach on PhD programmes.

Kari Kragh Blume Dahl is an Associate Professor at the Danish School of Education, Aarhus University, Denmark. She is a Licensed Psychologist with a PhD in Education and her research interests are teacher education, teachers' school practice, organizational learning and communality in teaching, which she explores through comparative, cultural analytical and critical psychological perspectives. Having published widely, her latest and third monograph is *With the best of intentions: Becoming somebody in Kenyan teacher education* (2017).

Janet Dyson, a teacher-educator, researcher and writer affiliated to the Billericay Teaching School Alliance, specializes in teaching reflective practice through creative writing. She has explored the processes with her students and gathered and analysed examples of their work for many years before synthesizing this material for her doctoral study at Anglia Ruskin University. Her chapter, 'Four seasons of composing stories to live by' (written with Clare Smith), recently appeared in Hanne & Kaal, *Narrative and metaphor in education* (2019).

Rob Evans, born in London, studied Russian and History at Leeds and Tübingen. After working in adult, further and higher education as a freelancer he taught Academic English at the University of Magdeburg, Germany until 2019. His main research interests include biography research methods, the language of narrative, conversation analysis and discourses of learning. Publications include chapters, journal articles, and edited books, most recently *Before beside and after (beyond) the biographical narrative* (2016).

Mirella Ferrari carries out research and training activities for numerous companies in Italy. Her research interests range from adult education to corporate training. She pursues three key areas: the processes of learning art through advanced technologies, social inclusion and the training of migrants, and the sociology of education. She has curated museum displays and published with Franco Angeli, Ledizioni, Aracne and Guerini, including *Sociologia dei contesti di apprendimento. Scuola, musei e formazione continua* (2018).

Laura Formenti is a Professor at the University of Milano-Bicocca, Italy; Chair of the Italian Universities' Network for Lifelong Learning, and Convenor of ESREA's Life History and Biography Network. She was Chair of ESREA from 2014 to 2019. Her research areas are educators' professional competence and identity, family pedagogy, and the development of child and family welfare services in a systemic, aesthetic, and collaborative perspective. *Transforming perspectives in lifelong learning and adult education. A dialogue* (2018) (co-authored with Linden West) was awarded the American Association for Adult and Continuing Education (AAACE) 2019 Cyril O. Houle prize for outstanding literature on adult education.

Andrea Galimberti is researcher at the Department of Human Sciences for Education, University of Milano-Bicocca, Italy. He is interested in researching systemic and constructionist approaches across the areas of adult education, lifelong learning, higher education and work-based learning. With Barbara Merrill, Adrianna Nizinska and José Gonzàlez Monteagudo he recently edited the book *Continuity and discontinuity in learning careers: Potentials for a learning space in a changing world* (2018).

Carola Girotti is a Pedagogue at Grandangolo, a Social Cooperative in North Italy and a Community Manager and Fundraiser for a Community Welfare and Social Innovation Project. With Social Services and Health, she is responsible for designing and managing educational and intercultural projects to support the integration of foreign families. As a teaching assistant at University of Milano-Bicocca, since 2016 she has been working on medical graphics for adult education, narrative medicine and medical humanities with Professor Micaela Castiglioni, writing articles about the use of comics in health contexts.

Miguel Alberto González González is a Lecturer and Senior Researcher at the Universidad de Manizales, Colombia, with PhDs in Educational Sciences and Latin American knowledge and culture. Education, diversity and power languages are his research interests. Miguel presents and publishes over a broad national and international spectrum. In 2017 he edited the collected papers of the 5th international symposium *Horizontes Humanos, Toledo, Spain 2017: Diversidades e inclusiones* (2018).

Jennifer Granville retired as Principal Lecturer at Leeds Beckett University, UK, in 2018 returning to full-time practice as performer, writer and producer. Her practice focuses on adaptation — enabling and facilitating the members of the communities to which she belongs to learn new skills and create new methodologies to tell their stories. She is adapting her graphic novel, *Prime suspects* (2019), based around a mathematical theorem, into a live performance piece.

Marianne Horsdal, Professor Emerita at the University of Southern Denmark, is a key international specialist in the study of narratives and has written widely on the subject in both Danish and English. Introducing her seminal work, *Telling lives: Exploring dimensions of narratives* (2012), she reveals how through examining family memorabilia and having an academic background in Literature, she developed an interest in life history, later embracing identity research and cultural studies in a desire to increase both theoretical and methodological understanding.

Marianne Høyen is an Associate Professor at Aarhus University, Denmark with significant experience in teaching adults, particularly those who work in educational settings. She is a Bourdieu specialist with an interest in the sociology of the professions and, particularly, the various views on nature that different professionals hold. An interdisciplinary academic (her PhD was situated within the philosophy of science and addressed professionals' self-understanding), Marianne's chapter 'Teaching about nature across generations' (in Formenti & West, *Stories that make a difference*, 2016) combined both these interests.

Mari Mäkiranta, a Senior Lecturer at the University of Lapland, Faculty of Art and Design, and Adjunct Professor at the University of Jyväskylä, Department of Music, Art and Culture Studies, is interested in autobiographical and self-portrait photography art, specializing in socially engaged visual arts, feminist theories and arts-based research. She has curated national and international exhibitions and served on a number of editorial boards. Her latest work, co-edited with Brusila and Nikula, is *Visual thinking: Theories & practices* (2019); her latest project is called Floating Peripheries: Mediating the Sense of Place.

Monica Mascarenhas is an ESOL teacher who has worked with refugees and asylum seekers in the UK and Europe. Monica was born in Brazil and lived in several countries, thereby acquiring relevant experiences and languages. When asked for an affiliation she replied, 'I consider myself a citizen of the world with a little bit of every refugee and/or asylum seeker I have had the privilege to work with'. Strongly committed to supporting a fairer global society, she pursues two research areas: language, communication and literacy; and teaching English to adults who do not have literacy in their own language.

Charlotte Matthiassen, Associate Professor at Aarhus University, Denmark, is a registered Clinical Psychologist who has worked with children and families, and with adults in prisons, now her primary field of research. She remains interested in school bullying and its consequences in adult life, as well as its possible links to later offending. Charlotte's work is informed by cultural historical frameworks and anthropological psychology, so it fits well with narrative and life history approaches. Her chapter, 'Being a woman in mixed-gender prisons' (in Smith & Ugelvik, *Scandinavian penal history, culture and prison practice*) in English, appeared in 2017.

Laura Mazzoli Smith is Assistant Professor in the School of Education at Durham University, UK. Her research interests are in adult education, out-of-school learning and barriers to education. Methodologically her research uses interpretive participatory methods including narrative inquiry and digital storytelling. She has published widely in the field of education, most recently an article, 'Conceptualising poverty as a barrier to learning through "poverty proofing the school day"', in conjunction with Liz Todd (*British Educational Research Journal*, 2019).

Tristan Middleton is Senior Lecturer in Education and Joint Course Leader for the MA Education suite at the University of Gloucestershire, UK. He is a key player (and researcher) in the field of Special Education Needs / and Disability (SEN/D) and Chair of Directors of Leading Learning for SEND CiC which oversees the work of the National SENCo Award Partnership. He is Associate Editor of the *International Journal of Nurture in Education* and the author of *Using an inclusive approach to reduce school exclusion* (2020).

Helena Oikarinen-Jabai is a researcher, a freelance writer, an educator and a psychologist, *inter alia* interested in different ways of knowing, embodied spaces, diversity and decolonization. In her transdisciplinary research she explores arts-based and performative approaches as means of producing creative spaces, dialogue, participation and action. She has published widely, generating both art productions and professional academic outputs, including a recent article 'Young Finnish people of Muslim background: Creating 'spiritual becomings' and 'coming communities' in their artworks' (*Open Cultural Studies*, 2019).

Khum Raj Pathak is an auto/biographical educational researcher interested in how violence during childhood may contribute to political extremism, conflict, crime, spiritual fragmentation and economic stagnation. He examined the barriers to education in Nepal (2013) and later the life-long effects of corporal punishment in schools there (2017). He now teaches mathematics in Kent to children in SEN and alternative educational settings and is currently working on a book entitled *DAMAGE!* This is a worldwide study of the effects of corporal punishment, focusing on learners from nine countries.

Mumiah Rasmusen works as a schoolteacher at an inner-city school in Copenhagen, Denmark, with children who live in socio-economically marginalized and multicultural areas, a role enriched by his Education (BA) and Sociology of Education (MA) degrees. This work has inspired research interests in equality and diversity issues, such as sociocultural, multicultural, racial/ethnic, representation and gender equity studies from educational perspectives. For his Master's thesis, Mumiah studied the recruitment and retention of Danish teachers.

Simone R. Rasmussen works as coordinator and teacher within the field of second language acquisition and is affiliated to CLAVIS — Language and Competence, Aarhus, Denmark. She has a BA in Arabic and Islamic studies and an MA in Educational Sociology from Aarhus University. Her main interest lies in the different perceptions and understandings of Islam and Islamic education and formation in the West. Simone's research is mainly founded in the Bourdieusian approach and in narrative methodology. Her chapter in this book, 'Uncovering habitus in life stories of muslim converts', is her first publication.

Vera Sheridan is an Associate Lecturer in the School of Applied Language and Intercultural Studies, Dublin City University, Ireland, where she lectured previously in English language, linguistics and contemporary culture and society. Research areas include student experience of higher education, identity in organisations and nations, and refugee resettlement. She co-edited a report on LGB identity in the Irish police force and a book on life in post-communist Eastern Europe after EU membership. Vera's 2019 article, 'Disclosing the self: 1956 Hungarian student refugees creating autobiographies for university scholarships in the USA' (in *Life Writing*), indicates her current focus.

Annette Sprung is Professor of Migration and Education at the University of Graz/Educational Sciences (A), Austria. Her research focuses on (adult) education in migration societies, racisms, diversity, social inequality and citizenship education. She is a convenor of the ESREA Network on Migration, Transnationalism and Racisms. Recent publications focus on solidarity with refugees and transformative learning processes in volunteering. 'Refugees welcome? Active citizenship and political learning through volunteering', co-written with Brigitte Kukovetz, appeared in *Zeitschrift für Wirtschaftsgeographie (ZfW)* in 2018.

Patric Wallin is an Associate Professor in the Department of Education and Lifelong Learning at the Norwegian University of Science and Technology (NTNU) in Trondheim. He uses critical pedagogy and transformative learning as entry points to research personal development, dialogue, and learning environments. His 2019 publication 'Challenging spaces: Liminal Positions and Knowledge Relations in Dynamic Research Partnerships', *International Journal for Students as Partners (IJSaP)* (2019), co-written with Liselott Aarsand, explores how to create educational spaces that enable students to make meaningful contributions to society and how to challenge traditional student-teacher positions through partnership.

Linden West is Professor of Education at Canterbury Christ Church University, UK. His key research interests are adult and popular education, struggles for dialogue and recognition in zones of conflict, and opportunities for and resistance to transformative experience; they are grounded in interdisciplinary sensibilities. A widely published author, his recent book *Transforming perspectives in lifelong learning and adult education* (with Laura Formenti, 2018) won the 2019 AAACE Cyril O. Houle Award for outstanding literature in adult education.

Helen Woodley is a Senior Lecturer at the University of Northumbria, UK. She teaches on the Primary Education BA and the Postgraduate Diploma in Mental Health and Emotional Wellbeing Studies in the Education Environment. A former teacher, her research interests include teacher wellbeing, alternative education and the use of autoethnography and fictionalized narratives in education. Her most recent publication *Toxic schools* (with R.M. McGill) focuses on teacher wellbeing in challenging school cultures (2018).

Hazel R. Wright is a Visiting Fellow at Anglia Ruskin University in Cambridge, UK, where she was a Senior Lecturer in Education following an earlier publishing career. She pursues three key research areas using narrative methods when possible: adult (and particularly women's) education; childhood, which she accesses through contemporary children and memory work with adults; nature, space and sustainability from a human perspective. Author of many articles and chapters, she has also written two monographs, most recently *The child in society* (2015).

Outi Ylitapio-Mäntylä, an Adjunct Professor of gender studies, is working as a Senior Lecturer in the Faculty of Education at the University of Oulu, Finland. Initially ascertaining how gender and power are constructed in everyday pedagogical practices by collecting the childhood memories and stories of early childhood education teachers, Outi began to combine narrative, memory-work and feminist research methods, as here, and in her chapter (with Mari Mäkiranta) 'Engaging ethics of care in socially responsible design and in research projects with Indigenous communities', in Miettinen & Sarantou, *Managing complexity and creating innovation through design* (2019).

Marta Zientek is an active English (and more recently, Spanish) teacher in Poland. Early in her career she worked with teenage students but sometimes with adults as in her doctoral study within the Department of Pedagogy, Sociology and Psychology at the University of Zielona Góra. This researches the social capital and the non-formal, everyday learning of adults, most of whom are social activists in two localities in Poland. As a sociologist and economist, Marta applies an andragogical perspective to the concepts of lifelong learning and social capital. A recent publication in English considers 'adult learning as a permanent fixture in non-formal community' (in *Sino-US English Teaching*, 2017).

Photo by Tom Perkins, CC-BY 4.0

Narrative, Discourse, and Biography

An Introductory Story

Marianne Høyen and Hazel R. Wright

Who Writes About Whom?

Contributors to this book, who come from countries across Europe and sometimes further afield, share a common interest in narrative research about people's lives, thoughts and actions. Contributors have a common interest, too, in the education of adults and thus ongoing contact with those who are 'other' than themselves. This potentially enables their access to the lives, thoughts and practices of a wide and disparate range of social groupings, broadening the scope of research subjects and topics. As researchers, they encourage people to share their life stories and experiences in order to make better sense of the world in which they live; telling such stories sometimes triggers the urge to go out and change lives. Narrative research is an interactive process. It uses words, images, activities or artefacts to ask people — either individually or collectively within their social groupings — to examine, discuss, portray or otherwise make public their place in the world, their sense of belonging to and identity within the physical and cultural space they inhabit. The contributors come together in this publication to present their recent findings from explorations within specific contexts and perspectives. Prompted by our focus on 'narratives, discourses, biography', they analyse their work to find the factors that influence how people view their worlds,

   https://doi.org/10.11647/OBP.0203.30

the embedded values and practices that underpin the way people think and act (often without even realizing why); in short, the 'discourses by which they live'.

Beyond these common interests, the contributors come from a range of backgrounds. They represent a number of different academic disciplines within the humanities and social sciences and professional practices, a range of countries and cultures. They span a broad spectrum of age, status and outlook, and differently employ a variety of research methods. This diversity itself supports our endeavour, as editors, to deploy the concept of discourse as a means to identify and challenge inequality and prejudice in everyday lives and to unpick the assumptions that serve to maintain an unthinking acceptance of the status quo. For, like Hall (2001, p. 72), we believe that discourse '"rules in" certain ways of talking about a topic, defining an acceptable and intelligible way to talk, write or conduct oneself' while it '"rules out", limits and restricts other ways of talking, of conducting ourselves in relation to the topic or constructing knowledge about it'. Yet the authors walk towards the book's themes from different starting places, as the meanings that inhere to narrative, discourse and biography have mutated over time, and are interpreted in different ways depending on the cultural and disciplinary background of the scholar.

Why and Where Our Story Starts

We, Hazel and Marianne, the instigators and editors of this book, have in common a long-standing interest in narrative and life history research, and a shared sociological background. Given the opportunity to organize a conference within the field of adult education, we thought that an exploration of the discourses that shape people's personal and collective worldviews would lead to some interesting findings and debates — which it did! At the conference, many new and interesting research processes and findings were presented, and we determined to put together a book that would take some of this material to a broader audience. To create a coherent publication, we developed an overall structure and contacted individuals (both conference presenters and other academic colleagues) and asked them to contribute research-based chapters to fit one of a set of themes.

We selected authors who explore a range of professional and personal situations to consider what shapes these contexts, ever mindful that the focus is on adults and their education whether formal, informal, non-formal or incidental (Foley, 1999). We sought to craft a book that, through its very authorship and content, would inject a diversity of ideas and approaches into the field. Our authors come from diverse backgrounds, different cultures, nations and political systems, and this represents a shift away from the often-dominant Anglocentric worldview. This diversity has a bearing, too, on the literatures to which authors make reference; some very few move easily between sources in different languages but many stay within their linguistic boundaries. We have asked for an English translation of titles where possible, as this is the language of publication. We observe also that there are different traditions in the way literature is used. In the English-speaking world there is a tendency to evidence every claim made, whereas in some other European cultures, new research is more narrowly embedded within core literature, creating another level of variance. Authors come from a range of academic disciplines that focus differently on theory, praxis, rhetoric and case work. They occupy different epistemological positions, are at different stages of their careers, and have varied prior experience of publication. We have welcomed all who had an interesting tale to share rather than cherry-picking those who could work most autonomously. We believe that it is important to include voices from the margins, and surely it is better to tell a story imperfectly than not at all. Like parenting (Winnicott, 1971) stories can be 'good enough'.

Some of our authors research alone or in partnership; others are part of significant collaborative ventures, on occasion limited in what they can write about outside official project reports and specified articles. They use a range of methodological approaches but for reasons of space this is rarely the focus of the chapters, as authors were asked to foreground discourse and narrative. We wanted just 'enough' detail of methods to demonstrate credibility (Polkinghorne, 1995, p. 20) unless this was an important aspect of their work. Like Erben (1998, p. 4), we believe that 'too much emphasis on research techniques can limit an understanding of the connection between the method and purpose of the study'. However, we also acknowledge that this approach is still contested and may raise questions of 'adequacy' or 'quality' for some (Roberts, 2002, p. 6).

In terms of analysis, interpretation may be loosely framed, with references to 'grounded' approaches that imply a 'general stance' (Roberts, 2002, p. 10) rather than a set of procedural steps. As Roberts states earlier (2002, p. 6): 'The study of biographical research rests on a view of individuals as creators of meanings which form the basis of their everyday lives' and, in our view, 'creators of meanings' cannot imply a search for a single truth. Creation is important and implies imaginative analysis. Seeking understanding, most authors go beyond just 'giving voice' to avoid the possibility that 'little is added to [...] perceptions of the world, which may in turn reflect dominant discourses' (Sparkes, 1994, p. 108).

Authors use verbal and visual media; they create texts, reflexive accounts, life histories and films. Some use formal structures to shape their telling; some embrace a more open multi-source approach; others choose an oral history approach, recognizing the idea that 'it might be possible to render oneself invisible or non-interfering [...] as mythical and certainly not desirable' (Bornat, 2008, p. 351). We believe that these differences add power to the tellings, for they suggest authenticity and challenge the reader to focus anew on each chapter.

In short, this is an edited, themed collection of twenty-eight research texts with an intriguing diversity of content and perspective. It is also a source book for narrative and education that shows some of the many things that can be done under the rubric of *Discourses We Live By*. Chapters are grouped and linked to create sections that have a degree of coherence, but the structures imposed on the book are deliberately fluid; at times a chapter may have as many links across sections as it does within its section — but we believe that the texts selected for inclusion fit within the frameworks we have chosen without significant dissonance. We are mindful that the texts are studies of real lives; many rely on life stories or histories, and life is messy and complicated. Yet, who would deny that the individual life has a shape and pattern that makes it both recognizable and unique, even as it runs parallel to others, sometimes intertwining with them? So, too, the chapters in this book.

However, we would like to be a little more helpful, by talking more generally about the key common aspects — narrative, discourse, biography — and offering some shared understanding of what these terms mean within this book. In doing this, we recognize that 'when we talk about sharing we implicitly or explicitly engage with a set of values' (John, 2017, p. 4) and recognize that we cannot assume that all our authors subscribe to them in totality, or at all, or that they will be acceptable to the reader. We hope they will be.

A Narrative on Narrative

The research data within the chapters was customarily collected through narratives (whether as interviews, art, film or other modalities, as justified by Barthes in 1977) and recounted in a narrative style. In doing this, our authors have made a choice; but within pre-literate societies, visual, physical and spoken narratives were often the only way to record and share the historical account, to impart important information or describe dramatic events, those planned and those that had already taken place. Witness the cave paintings, ritual dances and the sagas, ballads and legends that are traceable through to modern times. In a much-quoted paragraph, Barthes set out his claim that 'narrative is international, transhistorical, transcultural: it is simply there, like life itself' (1977, p. 79) for he saw it to be both universal and fundamental to human existence.

Rather than view this statement in isolation, we should note that it headed a chapter that dealt purely with the structural analysis of narrative, seeking the means to understand its commonalities and reach an abstract sense of what narrative is. Barthes delineated the breadth of narrative form to make the case that a deductive approach was essential, as was a focus on how narratives work, arguing that these together would enable a clarification of divergence and understanding of its diversity. Drawing on linguistic theory he then proposed a tentative 'system of narrative' that was both multi-layered and horizontally segmented to capture variety. However, his overall conclusion was that narrative must be divorced from representation, a point that may be contested but surely leaves space for creative interpretations and multiple means of dissemination within the field.

Despite the relevance of other modalities, language remains a central feature of much narrative research and our own experience, quite apart from our pan-European interactions, has made us especially sensitive to the complexities of understanding what is being communicated across differences of time and place. Linguistic fluency, the ability to translate a story from one tongue to another, can be a taxing process but one that may be overcome by careful annunciation, changes of speed of delivery, efforts to translate key words or phrases into another language. Within a conference session, the presence of multi-lingual speakers who can actually paraphrase the content to suit a range of listeners' ears may help a little. In a book, we have to assume our readership in advance and hope that ideas travel. However significant, content constitutes only a part of the problem when communicating across cultural divides. We find the conceptual (mis)understandings when a simple label conceals a wealth of associated meanings more difficult to grasp and convey. Drawing purely on our own experience of working across the English and Danish cultures, we are constantly finding new terms and ideas that are difficult to explain to each other, and we give some examples here.

On one occasion Marianne was puzzled by an English colleague's talk of his working-class origins, as these seemed to imply a very different set of circumstances than the literal translation into Danish would suggest. Conversely, Hazel found it difficult to grasp that moving from Copenhagen to the provinces or vice versa was deemed a change that, to a Dane, required significant social adjustment. (We had asked a class of Masters students to identify someone who had experienced a significant life event and to interview this person for a practice assignment, and Hazel was astounded that for a number of the students this urban-rural transfer was deemed an important area to investigate.) Insignificant in a UK context, the shift from the capital to a rural area involves a degree of adaptation, even culture shock, in Denmark, where spatial divisions are more marked than class ones. These examples show that to understand a phenomenon might require a historical-epistemological analysis if one is really to grasp meanings within their cultural spheres (Bachelard, 1968/1940; Canguilhem, 1988/1968) but also that we need to view phenomena as constructs (Latour & Woolgar, 1986) to enable multiple interpretations and applications.

Within education itself, we have had similar debates around the different cultural interpretations of vocational education, and indeed of adult education itself. In the UK these terms convey different meanings.

Adult education has evolved from a long liberal tradition of provision for the workers, to stand for a form of non-compulsory education with a distinctive ethos. It usually caters for somewhat older students who are seeking a second chance to gain necessary qualifications in an attempt to move up a level or two, or across into another field (if vocational), or maybe wanting a new hobby or better social understanding (if not vocational). In Denmark, on the other hand, adult education refers to the teaching of lower-level practical skills suitable for the workplace: it is firmly vocational and sits in contrast to an academic education. Even more confusing is the British Further Education (FE) sector in which non-academic studies are grouped; the like of which does not exist in many European countries. We have also brushed up against other concepts that do not travel well. Hazel finds the Danish suffix *tøj* (and its German equivalent *zeug*) really hard to grasp. These words refer to something that extends the bodily ability to do a task by being 'present-at-hand'. Following Heidegger (1927), a tool such as a hammer is both a thing when it is lying on a table, but an 'interpretation' when held ready for use. A water mill makes visible an interpretation of a river as a force; a clock encapsulates an interpretation of time as mathematics. In Denmark the suffix '*tøj*' can be attached to a whole of range of actions to make composite nouns: Stentøj refers to ceramics fired into stone (or more accurately stoneware pottery in English) but a *legetøj* is a toy, or something to play with, yet tøj on its own stands for clothes. *Zeug*, often translated as 'stuff' (although 'thing' might be a closer equivalent) is similarly connectable to a range of other words. So, an aeroplane is a flying tool or thing, a *Flugzeug*. Similarly, *Feuerzeug* ('fire tool') is a lighter, a *Fahrzeug* (driving thing) is a vehicle, a *Werkzeug* a (work) tool.

There are significant discussions around narrative style that have some bearing on our book so, drawing on White's seminal article of 1984, they are briefly mentioned here. White (himself, drawing on the works of Mink and Ricœur to support his argument) sought to challenge the traditional historian to think beyond the atheoretical chronological text, the descriptive account that moves forward through a set of logical steps 'and then... and then... and then... and then...' (to paraphrase Mink). Instead, they might create coherent accounts that weave a range of modes together, cleaving neither to the literary tradition (poesis) nor the knowledge tradition (noesis) but inhering symbolization to achieve a form of 'realism' that is neither representational nor factual but, perhaps, emotionally credible (as valued by Ricœur). This approach broadens the scope of narrative, allowing possibilities for emplotment (storying) and contextualization. Such arguments for variety leave a legacy from which this book benefits, as they sanction the use of a range of approaches supporting the diversity that we highly value.

White's article also provides a framework through which to recognize, and thereby to understand further, the innate diversity that emanates from the different cultural traditions the authors inhabit, for he sets out a sequence of four major influences on narrative thinking that shaped its theoretical development and acceptance over more than thirty years. Firstly, White identifies how Anglo-American analytical philosophers (like Dray, Gardiner, Mink) examined the epistemological status of narrativity. Secondly, he discusses the historians with a social science orientation (like the French Annales group comprising, for example, Braudel, Furet, Le Goff) who wished to free the historical tradition from such ideological methods of representation. Thirdly, he identifies those with a semiotic bent (like Barthes, Foucault, Derrida, Kristeva), who, perhaps more tolerantly, accepted narrative as one 'code' among many, to be used when appropriate. And finally, he mentions philosophers of the hermeneutic tradition (like Gadamer and Ricœur), who see narrative as a means of structuring and foregrounding a consideration of time. To White these four 'strains' offer consecutive challenges to those holding traditional perspectives. To our authors, they represent a range of influences that, with a greater or lesser degree of consciousness, shape the way they construe the term 'narrative' and how they work within the field. To the editors, they leave the term narrative as one that is difficult to define should one want to so constrain it; narrative research characterized as a methodology with various forms, each of which develops its own sense of coherence and flow.

Yet we have a shared view of narrative, and like our colleague, José González Monteagudo (2011), this stems from the seminal works of Bruner, from his key writings of the mid-80s during the 'narrative turn' and his 'search for integration between different approaches' (ibid., p. 299). Bruner made a determined effort to connect across disciplines and challenge simplistic approaches to the processing of information, recognizing the human capacity for continual transformation of both self and society, and the role of stories as a means to create possible worlds and therefore possibilities for change (Bruner, 1986). Bruner recognized distinctive narrative (storied) and paradigmatic (logical) cognitive modes of construing reality and valued both. Some of the chapters in this book reflect Polkinghorne's (1995) suggestion that data collected in one tradition can be usefully subjected to the other: the story analysed for significance, the logical account (or collection of data) shaped into a single story. However, we are ever mindful of the arguments our colleague, Linden West, makes for avoiding 'fragmenting' the data. As he states, 'medium and message, narrative and experience, reality and representations, self and story, are not easily prized apart' (West, 1996, p. 10), hence our acceptance that the performing arts chapters adopt an open format that encourages the reader to make his/her own interpretations. Citing Lea (1995), West also claims that 'narrative structures [...] may themselves organize and give meaning to experience rather than being simply reflective of it' (West, 1996, p. 11). Narrative is a powerful medium.

Like Clandinin (2013, p. 11), we recognize that the term narrative can be applied in very different ways, to:

> anything that uses, for example, stories as data, narrative as story as representational form, narrative as content analysis, narrative as structure, and so forth

but unlike her we are not trying to define, or especially focus on, a particular methodology, Narrative Inquiry. For the purposes of this book it is discourses and diversity that matter. Temporality, space and sociality are important but not constraining factors. Narrative need not be 'both the phenomenon under study and the methodology for its study' but it is 'how we understand human experience' (p. 216).

For similar reasons, the work represented here straddles distinctions between big and small stories (Baynham & Georgakopoulou, 2006) for many are collected through interviews and often the interview starts with a broad and open invitation to 'tell me about X', but few of the texts appearing in this volume represent a lengthy attempt to build a complete life history; even the long-term projects with which some authors are involved have a different focus. Chapters often describe episodes that could be labelled 'small stories' in the sense that they appear or are constructed through 'ordinary conversational exchanges' (and sometimes from a talk-in-action perspective). However, as editors we would be unwilling to attribute either label to the chapters within this book, seeing such distinctions as potentially limiting, and perhaps as a continuation of Polkinghorne's (1995) belief that storied data should be analysed into taxonomies and categories, while material with diverse origins should be shaped into a narrative explanation.

In our desire to support diversity this book avoids strong framings (Bernstein, 1971) and instead groups chapters within sections that loosely define boundaries. It includes chapters that embrace narratives in many ways and we believe that the experimental, the interdisciplinary, the not-quite-formulated and those projects that morph part way through are important. The chapters include the tidier retrospective accounts and the narratives that are 'good enough' — maybe because they discuss work-in-progress — but still offer valuable insights. When selecting contributions, we did not strive for perfection or a strong sense of direction when the processes were still developing, the author's narratives still unfolding and taking shape; just clear communication and something interesting to say.

Thus, we see that narrative is a complex and creative force that changes over time and place and is capable of multiple styles of application, formation, interpretation and dissemination. Discourse, too, is a difficult term to pin down and define for those with that intention, so now it seems appropriate to consider why this is a core theme within the individual texts and the book as a whole.

Why Discourse?

It was our attempts to make sense of the linguistic complexities encountered that led us, through our mutual interest in sociology, to begin to question the ways of thinking that guide people's actions as well as their thoughts and conversations; the embedded, often tacit rules that govern how humans act and understand other people's actions; the rules by which they live. Such discourses develop insidiously within societies and social groups. Even when hidden, such discourses will work to maintain the status quo, creating subtle barriers to change, excluding those — often the newcomers — who do not know how matters 'work' and thereby transgress social norms and expectations.

Like narrative, the term discourse can be used in different ways and at different levels, depending on where and when it is encountered, and how specialist the usage. At a basic level, discourse can mean no more than 'speech'; the act of holding a conversation through which two people start a dialogue (although not limited to an engagement of two); the linking of language and practice (Fairclough, 1993; Foucault, 1970). But it has more sophisticated connotations, too, and these, too are commonly associated with Foucault. In his inaugural lecture of December 1970 at the Collège de France, Foucault spoke of a 'kind of gradation between different discourses' (p. 12), suggesting that as a concept it has multiple layers and also multiple iterations, for there are many things said in everyday interaction that are ephemeral, quickly forgotten by both speaker and listener but endlessly re-created in new contexts. Foucault argues that this hierarchy enables discourse to be both permanent and endlessly constructed, creating both an ordering framework and possibilities for change. Foucault believed that discourses are created through both exterior and interior processes. Exterior processes comprise systems of exclusion, and he named three: forbidden speech (what cannot be said); the division of madness (that represses the unwanted voice); and the will to truth (that determines what we can know and the practices whereby we create new knowledge). Foucault explains how, with the internal processes, discourse 'exercises its own control' (p. 12). These comprise: the principles of commentary (the interplay between influential texts that underpin our ways of thinking and acting and everyday conversation); of discipline (which specify methods, rules and definitions within a field); and rarefaction among speaking subjects (ways of limiting access to commentary and disciplinary power by, for example, specifying threshold qualifications that only a minority possess).

In the continual reconstruction of new discourses, the detail and context changes but the purposes are repeated, creating a sense of endless repetition of ideas that are never directly stated. It is this process, one he terms commentary, that:

> gives us the opportunity to say something other than the text itself, but on condition that it is this text itself which is uttered, and in some ways finalised. (p. 13)

These are complex arguments, in themselves made clear only through statements that are somewhat paradoxical. In application at the local level they are made more difficult to discuss when the people in the room come from multiple backgrounds, disciplinary and cultural. For discourse is a term that has undergone change: as time passes, ideas travel. Ideas are formed, found, and adopted by others to meet their needs in ways that do not necessarily align with the intentions of earlier users. Meanings become more narrowly or more broadly focused, possibly even changed as a usage more appealing than the original becomes embedded. In effect, meanings can be adapted or duplicated (or both).

Concepts similarly undergo change. They emerge initially to enable discussion of specific phenomena within contemporary texts, and on further examination and application may be found to be insufficiently precise, perhaps ambiguous. When a concept moves into general written usage, it becomes detached from its origins, unfettered by the thinking of its original author. Made available to any reader (Ong, 1982) it gathers nuances as each one interprets it to fit with his or her personal cultural and disciplinary baggage. Occasionally, a reader will take up a concept and deliberately re-shape it for his or her individual purposes, which may be somewhat different than those intended by its creator. As knowledge grows, concepts may be appropriated to explain newly developing ideas, as happened with the concept of 'postmodernism' This was conceived in the French-speaking world by Lyotard (1984) but later taken up in America to explain visible trends in contemporary society, embellished to carry new meanings. In turn, this newly coined notion of postmodernism was fed back into European consciousness, and consequently connotes in more than one way (Sestoft, 1999).

Postmodern thinking challenged the beliefs of modernism; trust in the Grand Narrative that scientific progress would solve the world's problems, and as a result, eventually enable a more utopian society. The overturning of the Grand Narratives made space for what Lyotard termed 'small narratives', empowering assertions that multiple perspectives had validity and that plurality and complexity were acceptable, in a refutation of claims to access a single overarching universal truth. Thus, Lyotard's concept became a descriptor for an ongoing change that was tearing apart the Western ideal of universality, making way for greater plurality, and (perhaps) to the hearing and valuing of a wider range of voices within society; the diversity valued here.

So now to consider our shared understanding of discourses within this book, and again we turn to Foucault to show how discourses can be controlling and exclusionary, and can lead to prejudice at individual and social levels, often operating tacitly. In *The Archaeology of Knowledge* (1972) he explains that discourse is steeped in status and power: it is the frame for what it is possible even to think in a given period. To identify a discourse, analysis focuses on practices and ideas that demarcate and marginalize. As such, a discourse is a culturally constituted means of representing reality that is used to determine what it is possible to talk about and do within a society. Thus, discourses establish social 'norms' that then go unquestioned, perpetrating existing patterns of control and behaviour. Even, in contemporary society, people often conform to 'norms' accepting them as 'truths' rather than questioning their provenance, validity or applicability to different contexts.

In this book, authors seek to explore, and often to challenge these norms, through theorizing and/or through examining practice. The aim is to disrupt the 'one-world thinking' that can overwrite diversity, concealing how the 'universal' process of globalization affects us differently depending on our place in the world (Standing, 2016). So, the authors quite often (but not always) study disadvantaged and/or minority groups — such categories are often intersectional (Crenshaw, 2019) — and do so in a variety of contexts. They look within education itself or other professional caring contexts, or turn to those whom society marginalizes, such as migrant groups, ex-offenders, addicts, troublesome pupils, the elderly. When writing their chapters, we tasked our authors to question their own assumptions by examining the suppositions and frameworks that underpin their thinking and their practices: the discourses they live by. We asked them too — to use the words of the Danish anthropologist, Kirsten Hastrup (2012, p.ix) — to remember that individuals all live 'differently in the world'.

As editors, we also sought diversity. We sought chapters relating to discourses within an adult educational context, whatever the background of the researcher, to extend the disciplinary reach. In doing this, we accepted that the authors' decisions on what they would do and how they would do it would differ, welcoming a diversity of approach. Within that variety, many would be collecting data using biographical methods, seeking the life stories of people who worked within the field they chose to investigate.

Biography as a Means of Enquiry

The intention in this section is not to focus on how to implement biographical methods; rather to consider how biography relates to the theme of this book overall. The writing of biographies can be traced back to the late Middle Ages and is often considered a historical pursuit because it deals with the past (but only in relation to making an account of an individual's life). Traditionally, the formal biographer is seeking more than a chronological listing, and in the ways that he or she seeks to create an illusion of the life-as-lived must select what to include and exclude to craft a story, so placing the activity within the field of literature (*Encyclopedia Britannica*, 2017). Biography as a means of enquiry within qualitative research is undertaken at a much smaller scale, perhaps equating more to Tonkin's term 'representations of pastness' (1992, p. 2), but its use has grown exponentially, leading to what Bornat (2008, p. 343) describes as 'a vast and constantly changing and expanding ferment of creative work' across a range of disciplines. At its broadest scope the researcher wants to understand a person's life events, so he or she gathers sufficient information to create a timeline for this person and seeks, through conversation and gentle questioning, to understand their feelings and motivations, as well as 'what' they do 'when'. Increasingly 'individual life experience is generated, analysed and drawn on to explain the social world' (Bornat, 2008, p. 343). So, the researcher studies individuals who represent a specific grouping, and the research focuses more on how they think and feel and are involved in shared activities rather than excavating their entire life histories. But there is usually a desire to fit the findings into a broader frame; to understand how each persons' beliefs and actions are shaped by their prior experiences, their childhoods and schooling; perhaps by traumatic events that occurred in their pasts. In this case, biography is akin to personal history but it is more of a pen portrait than an entire volume.

This focus on the individual as a research 'subject' with a context and opinions belongs to the qualitative tradition, whereby the analysis is an interpretative one. That this is deemed acceptable as research stems from significant changes of paradigms within this field, particularly what is referred to as 'the biographic turn' by Rustin (2000) who sees this as a reaction to 'the prescriptive conceptions of scientific method' (p. 35). Like White before him, he identifies multiple sites of unrest through which this change was channelled: German and French philosophers, American Interactionists, and early pioneers (like Dilthey and Weber) within the new discipline of sociology. This biographical 'turn' required an ontological acceptance of the agentive individual but also an acceptance of inductive methods, a belief 'that biographies *make* society and are *not merely made by it*' (our emphasis) (Rustin, p. 46). Without refuting the reverse move from theory to real lives that is also present, Rustin clearly advocates the types of inductive approaches that are found within this book, making it clear that justification requires effort; description alone will not suffice:

> What has to be demonstrated is that sociological theory can be developed from the study of individual cases, in contrast to the usual sociological practice by which individual lives are shown to have meaning by their framing within previously established sociological categories. (Rustin, p. 45)

However, in this book, the contributors are not primarily seeking new theory. Nor are they tasked to clarify the meaning of narrative, discourse or biography, terms that we acknowledge originated in other fields (linguistics, history and literature, for example); terms that are used in different ways and whose meanings converge, diverge and overlap at times.

In this book, our shared understanding of biographical research is a broad one, akin to Roberts' (2002, p. 1) explanation in his book of that name. The term is used:

> to indicate various, often interrelated, approaches to the study of individuals. Biographical research is an exciting, stimulating and fast-moving field which seeks to understand the changing experiences and outlooks of individuals in their daily lives, what they see as important, and how to provide interpretations of the accounts they give of their past, present and future.

We concur with Roberts that biographical research is 'intentionally interdisciplinary' (p. 2), and often takes a pragmatic stance (p. 7) recognizing 'that stories or accounts by individuals are central but that they are collected and used in different ways for different methodological and theoretical purposes' (p. 8).

The purpose of this book is to excavate, examine and question assumptions that humans accept and respond to without asking why — the discourses that underpin our lives. This, too, requires work, but work with a different focus; and, inevitably, as with all inductive research, the outcomes are sometimes other than those intentionally sought, introducing a welcome degree of diversity. In focusing on discourse, many of the authors tend to look away from the literary narrative tradition (but some embrace it). Nor is narrative seen 'primarily as a tool for meaning-making' in both individual and group life: rather it is a communicatory device that can deal with 'sociological questions about power, solidarity, equality and social change' (Poletta et al., 2011, p. 113). Narratives tell a story and storying is a powerful communicative tool that can be strategically deployed; here, it is one that connects to individual biographies. Even the simplest story can influence public opinion. A diverse range of stories has the potential to be inclusive, encouraging diversity within the social sphere, and again reinforcing the importance that a work like this one should encompass a variety of themes and the voices of a breadth of groups and individuals from differing backgrounds, cultures and disciplines.

Imposing a Structure on Diverse Elements

To understand diversity as something more than an assemblage of disparate entities their arrangement needs to be managed, particularly when the chosen form of communication is a book, a format that requires a sequential arrangement of distinctive texts.

It is for the Readers to decide how to approach their task but, as Editors, we felt that a description of the content — the themes addressed — might make it easier to choose whether to read from start to finish or select by chapter or thematic grouping. With a multi-voiced and multi-chaptered volume like this there is no simple linear progression we can impose, nor would we want to do this were it possible. However, the book is crafted to provide a route through our collective offerings; to give the book a sense of flow and direction, an unevenly stitched and knotted narrative thread. To this end, our knots — the twenty-eight chapters that form the book — are strung in groups of four within seven sections that each take a specific stance towards discourses. In this way, we manage — and assiduously place — our diverse texts.

Mindful of the vital narrative thread, it is time to examine the stitches that determine it, so inevitably we now sew a straight seam through the fabric of the book, briefly considering each section in turn and outlining the commonality of purpose that governs the selection of its four constituent chapters. The book starts with texts that offer a broad sweep, the discourses we live 'within' as humankind; and next turns to discourses that shape the workplace, as many of the contributions (and indeed, their authors) straddle both academic and professional fields. In the book we then consider how professionals work to mediate (work through) or outwit (work around) constraining discourses, before turning to possible ways of exposing / exploring / revealing (sometimes repressed) diversity, and of empowering (supporting diversity among) marginalized groups. Finally, the texts consider internality as, in the last section authors reflect on their own relationships with their research topics and the conditions through which they encounter them.

Section I. Discourses We Live Within: Frameworks that Structure

The discourses that frame and shape human lives — the big frames like truth and its telling, language and emotion, society and culture and the natural environment — are addressed in this section.

Section II. Discourses We Work Within: Of the Workplace

Here the chapters address the discourses that shape the workplace from both academic and professional perspectives, considering the customs and boundaries that shape working life.

Section III. Discourses We Work Through:
Challenges to Overcome

These chapters examine socially embedded discourses that constrict lives, demonstrating ways in which individuals and/or professionals, while working within the system, can support better outcomes.

Section IV. Discourses We Work Around:
Managing Constraining Circumstances

Chapters here address how groups and individuals (with differing degrees of success) strive to expose, to circumvent, even 'outwit', constraining discourses, to achieve outcomes other than those commonly anticipated.

Section V. Discourses that Explore or Reveal Diversity:
Facing Choice and Change

The repression and achievement of diversity, and how individuals (both researched and researchers) find personal ways of exploring or challenging social norms, form the content of this section.

Section VI. Discourses to Support Diversity:
Projects that Empower

Chapters placed here address ways in which marginalized groups (represented collectively or individually) are empowered through support provided in a range of ways, some traditional others more radical in approach.

Section VII. Discourses Through a Self-Reflexive Lens:
Thoughts from Researchers

The chapters in this section draw on personal reflections to make sense of discourses in people's personal and professional worlds. This is a two-way process, and some researchers achieve new insights they can apply more broadly, others a better understanding, maybe confirmation, of their preferred ways of working.

Now Readers, the choices are yours. It is time to twist your own narrative threads.

References

Bachelard, G. (1968/1940). *La philosophie du non* (Philosophy of no: A philosophy of the new scientific mind). Orion Press: New York.

Barthes, R. (1977). Introduction to the structural analysis of narratives. In: *Image-Music-Text*. London: Fontana.

Baynham, M. & Georgakopoulou, A. (2006). *'Big' stories and 'small' stories: Reflections on methodological issues in narrative research.* https://nanopdf.com/download/big-stories-and-small-stories_pdf

Bernstein, B. (1971). On the classification and framing of educational knowledge. In: Young, M. (ed), *Knowledge and Control*. London: Collier-Macmillan.

Bornat, J. (2008). Biographical methods. In: Alasuutari, P., Bickman, L. & Brannen, J. (eds), *The Sage Handbook of Social Research Methods*. London: Sage.

Bruner, J. (1986). *Actual minds, possible worlds*. Cambridge, MA: Harvard University Press.

Canguilhem, G. (1988/1968). *L'objet de l'histoire des sciences* (Ideology and rationality in the history of the life sciences). Cambridge, MA: MIT Press.

Clandinin, D.J. (2013). *Engaging in narrative inquiry*. Abingdon: Routledge.

Crenshaw, K. (2019). *On intersectionality: Essential writings*. New York, NY: New Press.

Encyclopedia Britannica (2017). Biography. *Encyclopaedia Britannica, Inc.* https://www.britannica.com/art/biography-narrative-genre

Erben, M. (1998). Biography and research method. In: Erben, M. (ed), *Biography and education: A reader*. London: Falmer Press.

Fairclough, N. (1993). Critical discourse analysis and the marketization of public discourse: The universities. *Discourse & Society*, 4(2): 133–68. https://doi.org/10.1177/0957926593004002002

Foley, G. (2004). Introduction: The state of adult education and learning. In: Foley, G. (ed), *Dimensions of adult learning: Adult education and training in a global era*. Maidenhead: Open University Press.

Foucault, M. (1970). Orders of discourse (inaugural lecture). *Social Science Information*, 10(2): 7–30, April 1971. https://10.1177/053901847101000201

Foucault, M. (1972). *The archaeology of knowledge*. London: Tavistock.

González-Monteagudo, J. (2011). Jerome Bruner and the challenges of the narrative turn: Then and now. *Narrative Inquiry*, 21(2): 295–02. https://10.1075/ni.21.2.07gon

Hall, S. (2001). Foucault: Power, knowledge and discourse. In: Wetherell, M., Taylor, S. & Yates, S.J. (eds), *Discourse theory and practice: A reader*. London: Sage.

Hastrup, K. (2004). Religion in context: A discussion of ontological dumping. In: Antes, P., Geertz, A.W. & Warne, R.R. (eds), *New approaches to the study of religion: 1, Regional, critical and historical approaches*. New York: Walter De Gruyter.

Heidegger, M. (1927/2008). *Being and time*. New York: HarperPerennial.

John, N.A. (2017) *The age of sharing*. Cambridge: Polity Press.

Latour, B. & Woolgar, S. (1986). *Laboratory life: The construction of scientific facts*, 2nd edn. Princeton, NJ: Princeton University Press.

Lea, M. (1995). Published as Lea, M. (1996). Narratives and identity: Adults negotiating higher education. *Scottish Journal of Adult Education*, 3(2): 5–18.

Lyotard, J.-F. (1979/1984). *The postmodern condition: A report on knowledge*. Minneapolis, MN: University of Minnesota Press.

Mink, L.O. (1978). Narrative form as a cognitive instrument. In: Canary, R.H. & Kozicki, H. (eds), *The writing of history: Literary form and historical understanding*. Madison: University of Wisconsin Press.

Ong, W.J. (1982). *Orality and literacy, the technologizing of the word*. London: Methuen.

Polkinghorne, D.E. (1995). Narrative configuration in qualitative analysis. *International Journal of Qualitative Studies in Education*, 8(1): 5–23. https://doi.org/10.1080/0951839950080103

Poletta, F., Chen, P.C.B., Gardner, B.G. & Motes, A. (2011). The sociology of storytelling. *Annual Review of Sociology*, 37:109–30. https://10.1146/annurev-soc-081309-150106

Roberts, B. (2002). *Biographical research*. Buckingham: Open University Press.

Rustin, M. (2000). Reflections on the biographical turn in social science. In: Chamberlayne, P., Bornat, J. & Wengraf, T. (eds), *The turn to biographical methods in social science*. London: Routledge. https://doi.org/10.4324/9780203466049

Sestoft, C. (1999). Hvad et begreb gør (u)begribeligt: Postmodernisme-begrebets historier (What a concept makes (in)comprehensible: The concept of postmodernisms' stories). *Kritik*, 32(139): 1–23.

Sparkes, A.C. (1994). Self, silence, and invisibility as a beginning teacher: A life history of lesbian experience. *British Journal of Sociology of Education*, 15(1): 83–118. https://doi.org/10.1080/0142569940150106

Sparkes, A.C. (1997). Ethnographic fiction and representing the absent other. *Sport, Education and Society*, 2(1): 25–40. https://doi.org/10.1080/1357332970020102

Standing, G. (2016). *The precariat: The new dangerous class*, 2nd edn. London: Bloomsbury.

Tonkin, E. (1992). *Narrating our pasts: The social construction of oral history.* Cambridge, Cambridge University Press.

West, L. (1996). *Beyond Fragments: Adults, motivation and higher education.* Abingdon: Taylor & Francis.

White, H. (1984). The question of narrative in contemporary historical theory. *History and Theory*, 23(1): 1–33.

Winnicott, D.E. (1971). *Playing and reality.* London: Tavistock Publications.

Photo by Tom Perkins, CC-BY 4.0

I.

DISCOURSES WE LIVE WITHIN: FRAMEWORKS THAT STRUCTURE

Together the chapters in this section address some of the discourses through which we humans give our lives structure: the big frames like truth and fiction, language, health and ill-health, beliefs and socio-political groupings, cultures of knowing and acting in relation to the natural world, appear within the four chapters placed here.

Firstly, in 'Truth and Narrative: How and Why Stories Matter' (Ch1) Janet Dyson examines the potency of literature and poetry in capturing and conveying truth(s). She draws on a long-term interest in the 'truthfulness' of fiction developed during a career as a teacher trainer with a specialism in reflective practice. Janet encourages her trainees to write descriptive factual accounts of their experiences and later reflect on them but also to write and think *with* stories and poems to gain new perspectives and broader and deeper understanding(s). This chapter sets out the theoretical and practical framework for her approach (including her commitment to the narrative inquiry tradition set out by Clandinin and Connelly) and its benefits as a pedagogic practice, illustrating claims with evidence from published literature and story-work with trainees.

Secondly, situated within a French theoretical framework, we have 'From Experience to Language in Narrative Practices in Therapeutic Education in France' (Ch2). This study, by Hervé Breton, explores ways of sharing patients' experiences verbally in a health context as a contribution to making such services more democratic. Making medical practitioners more aware of patients' needs and feelings acts to redress power imbalances between patients and professionals. The study shows how formulating experiences as stories makes them 'sayable' and worthy of attention in an account that highlights new practical uses for narratives. This is a beautifully crafted chapter, thoroughly supported by a range of French academic literature. To assist those for whom this may not be accessible, some English texts are added in the chapter.

In the next chapter, 'Narratives of Fundamentalism, Negative Capability and the Democratic Imperative' (Ch3), Linden West and Alan Bainbridge together explore politics, religion, economics and ideology through a case study of fundamentalism (and, indirectly exclusion and poverty) in a post-industrial city in the north of England, ironically the home of the Workers' Educational Association, which was founded in 1908. The chapter offers a wide-ranging discussion of its subjects through a psychological lens, drawing on John Keats' notion of negative capability to theorize fundamentalism as a determination to 'grab' at new belief systems, or remain securely within established ones, rather than risk more nuanced understandings or change as these can appear threatening.

Lastly, 'Understandings of the Natural World from a Generational Perspective' (Ch4) collects the views of members from four generations of the same family in order to ascertain their knowledge of nature (meaning, here, plants and animals) and the ways in which this was acquired. Hazel Wright is interested in examining the extent to which residual learning stems from family practices, schooling or from other everyday experiences. She later compares her findings with 'grand narratives' around nature, reflecting on how such discourses become embedded within society.

Together, these chapters offer ideas that underpin our interpretations of human life. Truth, communication, political and cultural contexts and the human relationship with the natural environment resonate with most people, so these chapters may provide the sequential reader with ideas to take forward into later chapters. They also offer a taste of the different styles and literatures underpinning national research traditions, since they exemplify the philosophical, the praxeological, the rhetorical and social-constructivist approaches.

However, none of these chapters claim to offer more than a single exploration among many 'potentialities'. A broader, yet personal perspective on narrative methodology can be found in Horsdal (Ch28), who looks back on a long engagement in the field. For readers interested in forms of expression, Evans' work with conversation analysis (Ch17); Formenti and colleagues' study of children leaving care (Ch11); and

Pathak's rhetorical discussion of punishment (Ch9) may be useful, among others. Dyson's focus on trainee teachers relates to Dahl's work (Ch6), and her interest in reflexivity is relevant to the work of Mazzoli Smith (Ch25) and Woodley (Ch26). Aspects of Breton's work also resonate with Castiglioni and Girotti's discussion of the power of narrative in work with gamblers (Ch12). Readers of Bainbridge and West (Ch3) may choose to look at the González González (Ch14) and Zientek (Ch16) chapters, as both work within highly politicized contexts, or glean different facets of Islam from the work of Rasmussen (Ch19) and Oikarinen-Jabai (Ch27). Like Wright, Mazzoli Smith (Ch25), Høyen and Rasmusen (Ch5), and Mascarenhas (Ch18) consider how prior experiences shape future learning and learning choices.

1. Truth and Narrative
How and Why Stories Matter

Janet Dyson

Janet Dyson explores forms of, and the importance of, narrative truth embodied in acts of storytelling. Calling on philosophers, published authors and her own research and teaching experience, she shows how fictional accounts can divulge deeper (if less universal) truths in ways that engage the imagination of the reader, becoming memorable. When training student teachers, Janet encourages them to adopt creative approaches as they reflect on their school experiences and, here, demonstrates how such a story can capture both an event and the emotions it engenders.

'The truth about stories is that that's all we are.' (King, 2003, p. 153)

We are living at a time when the postmodern rise of relativism and the reluctance to challenge the validity of any asserted truth has reached the public consciousness. The discourses around absolute and relative truth(s), heavily contested during the 'qualitative revolution' (see Wertz, 2011) have given way to what is perhaps a more sinister state, a growing culture of 'fake news', conspiracy and denial (D'Ancona, 2017) in which there is a real danger of the public accepting all truths as equally valid without question.

This chapter makes no attempt to revisit the arguments around the plausibility of an absolute truth. Like Frank (2004, p. 439) I accept that 'postmodern truth sees too many perspectives to accept the closure of explanation'. Nor does this chapter engage with the *distinction* between the descriptive chronological account (White, 1984; Mink, 1978) and the 'realism' of texts that are neither representational nor factual, but interpretable, as we move away from what they say to what they talk about (Ricœur, 1976). Instead it enters Bruner's (1986) 'possible worlds', turning to the role that stories and storied accounts can play in capturing and communicating the 'reality' as 'lived' and 'experienced' by the narrator and/or protagonist(s); accepting the impossibility of purely objective truth and the power of stories to illuminate fundamental issues as claimed by Gadamer in *Truth and Method* (2004/1960). It is accepted that narrative can still support 'understanding' of 'specifically human truth' (White, 1984, pp. 25, 33) and acknowledges it to be 'an imaginary discourse about real events that may not be less true for being imaginary' (op.cit. p. 33). To cite Frank again (op.cit., p. 439), through embracing complexity 'we gain a power to see what is and to say what is'. These multiple notions of truth and narrative are examined, challenged, theorized and exemplified within this chapter, and I draw particularly on ideas expressed by Hans-Georg Gadamer and Wolfgang Iser and the views of more contemporary writers.

My Research Context

White (1984) claimed a space for using narrative in history that I acknowledge, but for me there are further questions around the value of 'stories', and I am inspired continually to (re)explore Rushdie's rhetorical question 'What is the use of stories that aren't even true?' (Rushdie, 1990, p. 20). This key question has served me well in a long career as a teacher-trainer in England, where I have been able to encourage my student trainees to reflect on their experiences in school and put them into words — as stories, dialogues, poems, if they were willing to risk the move away from the linear factual account. Over many decades I have collected such 'fictional' narratives with a view to later analysis, and as a reflective tool to work alongside these trainees to capture their changes of viewpoint and perspective as incidents arise and their careers unfold.

This chapter draws on my experience of encouraging story-writing with trainee teachers through reflective journals in which they seek to examine the value of stories as a means of conveying 'truths'. It is part of more extensive studies (Dyson, 2018; Dyson & Smith, 2019) and ongoing work that use a narrative inquiry approach, the study of experiences as story (after Clandinin & Connelly, 2000). Narrative inquiry spaces are places of belonging for both researchers and participants, marked always by ethical responsibility, attitudes of openness, mutual vulnerability, reciprocity, and care. The empowerment that stories bring to tellers and listeners is emphasized, as are the ways in which stories have the power to direct and change our lives, disturbing and puzzling us. Bruner talks about the narrative power and possibilities that reside in texts — which are 'all we have' — and which are not reliant on the 'ontology of verification' (1994, p. 34). A decade earlier (1986, pp. 12–14) he identified two distinctive ways of thinking: the *argument* that seeks to convince people through a series of logical steps and evidence, and the *story* that seeks to be lifelike and draw people into a world that resembles the 'real'; valuing the story as a form that engages the imagination. Like Bruner (reflecting, in his Millennium lectures, 2002[1]), I believe that stories have a vital role in helping us to make sense of the world.

It is frequently the case that, when I tell or read a story in the context of teaching about reflective story writing, the first question asked is 'But is it true?' There is often a sense that, like the reader of Wallace Stevens' poem, *The House Was Quiet and the World Was Calm*, the inquirer wants desperately to hear that the story is true, recognizing instinctively that the imagination is our 'necessary angel' (Stevens, 1942–1951); an antidote to the pressures of reality with the capacity to transcend what *is* and see a different, better version of what *could be*. Often, I will qualify my answer with 'It depends what you mean by *true*' before drawing on a number of writers who have contributed to my understanding of the nature of truth in fiction and how this relates to reflective storytelling.

Salman Rushdie has consistently demonstrated his understanding of fiction as truth-telling in his own fictional work. Talking about his (then) new novel *Two Years Eight Months*, Rushdie (2015, in interview with Franklin) explains that this is a story about the act of storytelling. 'It's a story that's crowded with stories on purpose [...] It has stories nested inside of stories, stories breaking off in order to tell other stories [...]'. He believes that fictional writing can 'intensify our perceptions

---

1   Bruner's Millennium lectures, published as *Making Stories: Law, Literature, Life* (2002), include endnotes that provide a comprehensive overview of how humans use, and have used, stories to better understand the world in which they live.

and perhaps our understanding of the world' and describes how literary devices can 'make something happen in the reader's head'. For Rushdie, fiction is 'another way of getting at the truth', through a process that makes beautiful even 'the darkest truths' (ibid.). He believes, too, that when factual and fictional discourses 'collide' the outcomes are interesting. Both gain from association (ibid.).

Together these sources set the scene for what follows: a text that is fundamentally focused on demonstrating the power of the storied narrative tale. In writing this chapter I am breaking the habit of a lifetime in allowing theory and context to precede the actual stories themselves. Invariably, for me, it has been the story that comes first, as is almost always the case in reflective writing of the kind I encourage in my students and practise for myself. It is the story that wants to be told that we 'find', the one that cannot be suppressed but makes its presence felt. It is rare for someone to write a story about what a good day they have had at school. Stories are prompted by trouble of some kind, things that go awry; there's a dilemma, an unexpected turn of events, a sense of compulsion to tell the story. Just as in literary fiction, for a story to be worth telling, something unexpected has to happen. There is disruption. Questions are raised. 'Stories are possible because some initial order has been disrupted' (Eagleton, 2013, p. 104). 'Something goes awry, otherwise there's nothing to tell about' (Bruner, 2002, p. 17). As Aristotle (Poetics, c.335 BCE/2013) recorded there must be *peripeteia* (reversal); a point where an unexpected event occurs; a twist in the plot becomes apparent.

Framing My Research

My storied work with students sits in the overlapping spaces of reflection and narrative inquiry, adhering broadly to the framework established by Clandinin and Connelly (2006), which, they claim, owes its influence to Dewey's belief that in order to have meaning, experience must be subjected to reflection. Clandinin and Connelly (in Schön, 1991, pp. 258–9) explain '[...] if we take the view that the storied quality of experience is both unconsciously re-storied in life and consciously re-storied and lived through the processes of reflection, then the rudiments of method are born in the phenomenon of narrative'. Here it can be seen that both narrative inquiry and reflective inquiry have their roots in Dewey's philosophy of experience. I recognize this as the way the reflective process has worked for those who have been prompted to write the stories and poems that I have collected over my career.

Dewey saw experience as grounded in continuity: '[...] every experience both takes up something from those which have gone before and modifies in some way the quality of those which come after' (1938, p. 35). His understanding of experience also included the notions of situation and interaction: 'An experience is always what it is because of a transaction taking place between an individual and what at the time constitutes his environment' (ibid., p. 43). These attributes form the basis for the three commonplaces of temporality, sociality and place developed by Clandinin and Connelly (2006). Thus, the connection between reflective inquiry and narrative inquiry is made more explicit and the overlaps and tensions — indeed, the possibilities — between these two approaches have been explored by Downey and Clandinin (2010). Schön (1983) built on Dewey's thinking and developed the practice of deliberate and systematic reflection in a range of professional contexts, identifying and distinguishing between reflection *on* and reflection *in* action. Bolton (2010) viewed reflection and reflexivity as cognitive states of mind, which she linked to pedagogical practices in education, health and social care. Furthermore, she asserted that any narrative is inevitably fiction, in that events are reconstructed or recreated from a perspective' (p. 93), meaning that each individual will tell the story differently. The stories in my inquiry, because of their subject matter, turn out to be not simply reflections on teaching but reflections on the social, and cultural conditions that have an impact on teaching (van Manen, 1991; Zeichner & Liston, 1987). Subjects that have prompted reflective story writing have included issues relating to equality and diversity of race, culture and gender; inclusion and exclusion; child protection; online safety; and social and political issues such as child poverty. Several of these themes intersect in Etta's story, which I shall share later in this chapter.

First, however, I wish to clarify that the focus of *my* research is the ways that stories can be written as a means of reflection on practice and are the *results* of reflection on practice. They represent the action of reflecting and the outcomes of that reflection. They have been explored through a narrative inquiry with attention to the three commonplaces and using the strategy of thinking *with* rather than *about* the stories (Morris, 2002; Estefan, Caine & Clandinin, 2016). The commonplaces of time, place and sociality, and the continuity that is established as we relive and retell stories over time follow the practice explained here by Clandinin and Connelly (2000): 'Through stories humans create coherence through time, between the personal and the social, and across situations. Stories are not just about experience itself; we live and learn in, and through, the living, telling, retelling and reliving of our stories' (p. 387).

Blurring the Boundaries of Truth and Fiction

The borders between truth and fiction become increasingly permeable during the twentieth century, attracting the attention of philosophers, theorists and fiction writers alike. In *Truth and Method* (2004/1960), Hans-Georg Gadamer argued that we can never reach a totally objective perspective because we cannot stand outside history and culture/tradition. He attacked the view that only science held a vision of truth and argued that the truth conveyed by art is necessary for human life — through interpreting texts, we educate the imagination and develop our ability to envisage things differently. Maxine Greene (1995, p. 15) concurs, claiming that 'it is disruptive to look at things as if they could be otherwise. There is tension in this looking; there is a blank resistance for a while. But then resistance, imagination, open capacities, inventiveness, and surprise are shown to be joined somehow.'

Gadamer further argued that the inability to imagine things differently leads to simplistic entrenchment in received truths and to a fearful defence of what has always been — lack of imagination often leads to fundamentalism. He suggested that to achieve deeper understanding we must integrate something unfamiliar into our familiar way of seeing things and engage our imaginations. Through reading literature and poetry our existing perspectives are altered, both enlarged and deepened; our prejudices and biases are highlighted and begin to shift — in what Gadamer calls 'the fusion of horizons'. Gadamer stresses that in both the sciences and the humanities only a well-trained imagination can see things otherwise (Lawn, 2006, p. 69), providing support for my decision to introduce the creative and expressive arts whenever possible within teacher-training programmes, as I do through reflective practices.

Foucault, when questioned about 'truth and fiction' with regard to his first volume of *The History of Sexuality*, asserted, 'I am well aware that I have never written anything but fictions. I do not mean to say, however, that truth is therefore absent. It seems to me that the possibility exists for fiction to function in truth, for a fictional discourse to include effects of truth' (Gordon, 1980, p. 193). He seeks not 'proof' but to offer ideas to see how they attract and withstand criticism; in effect, truth is set aside to establish levels of acceptance and credibility.

At the start of his book *The Fictive and the Imaginary*, Wolfgang Iser (1993) similarly challenges the fact/fiction dichotomy when he poses the question: 'Are fictional texts truly fictions, and are nonfiction texts truly without fictions?' (p. 1). He describes literary texts as 'a mixture of reality and fictions' that bring about 'an interaction between the given and the imagined' (ibid.). He proposes to replace the duality of fiction and reality with a triad: 'the real, the fictive and what we shall henceforth call the imaginary' (ibid.). I am, perhaps, over-simplifying Iser's complex argument here but I believe he is identifying imagination as essential for the act of fictionalizing to take place. This triadic relationship is very clear to me in the kinds of stories that have been generated through the reflections of the participants I have studied, where 'real' events and experiences have been fictionalized through the exercise of imagination. And this is a strategy deliberately employed by narrative researchers like Peter Clough, who fictionalizes participant profiles to avoid compromising anonymity.

> [...] stories can provide a means by which those truths, which cannot otherwise be told, are uncovered. The fictionalization of educational experience [...] [is] thus providing the protection of anonymity to the research participants without stripping away the rawness of real happenings. (Clough, 2002, p. 8)

This century, philosopher Richard Kearney (2002) tells us that: 'Telling stories is as basic to human beings as eating. More so, in fact, for while food makes us live, stories are what make our condition human' (p. 3). He argues that stories give us agency in our own history: '[...] [it is] only when haphazard happenings are transformed into story, and thus made *memorable* over time, that we become full agents in our history' (ibid.). Kearney reminds us that when someone asks us who we are, we tell our stories: '[...] you recount your present condition in the light of past memories and future anticipations. You interpret where you are now in terms of where you have come from and where you are going to. And so doing you give a sense of yourself as a *narrative identity* that perdures and coheres over a life time' (p. 4). He says that every story 'regardless of differences in style, voice, plot, genre, shares the common function of *somebody telling something to somebody about something*' (p. 5).

Within the literary tradition, Barthes (1966) stated that: 'The narratives of the world are without number [...] The narrative is present at all times, in all places, in all societies: the history of the narrative begins with the history of mankind; there does not exist, and never has existed, a people without narratives,' (p. 14). He also states that: 'narrative is simply there like life itself, international, trans-historical and trans-cultural' (Barthes, 1977, p. 79). If you share the view that all life is story, then the perspective of the narrative inquirer that we live storied lives on storied landscapes becomes a way of life, a way of understanding the world and our place in it. Novelist E.L. Doctorow claimed that: 'There is no longer any such thing as fiction or non-fiction, there is only narrative' (cited in Denzin, 1997, p. 126), and for Laurel Richardson (2000) the difference between fiction and non-fiction is simply 'the claim the author makes for the text' (p. 926). King (2003) asserts more boldly that: 'The truth about stories is that that's all we are' (p. 153). Making a claim that is very relevant to my work and to this book on *Discourses We Live By*, Robert Eaglestone (2013) writes that: 'Literature is where ideas are investigated, lived out, explored in all their messy complexity [...] Literature is how we make ourselves intelligible to ourselves' (p. 1), a very strong claim for the role of literature in shaping the biographical narrative.

For Lore Segal, however, philosophers and storytellers should keep fact and truth apart. In the Afterword to her fictionalized account of her escape from Nazi Germany as a child on the *Kindertransport* (2018/1964, p. 279), she writes:

> As a novelist writing autobiographically I get impatient with the reader who wants to know what 'really' happened [...] It takes a philosopher to define reality, and to differentiate between fact and truth; the novelist

wants to do it with story [...] Why did I choose to fictionalise my personal history? Because I experience and remember and understand like a storyteller rather than a historian. Story chooses me.

How Stories Negotiate Truth(s)

F or John Berger, both critic and author, other aspects of stories hold significance. In his essay, *Another Way of Telling* (1982), he reminds us of the centrality of the story's main characters between whose 'actions and attributes and reactions [...] the unstated connections are being made' (p. 172). He claims that: 'Stories walk like animals or men. And their steps are not only between narrated events but between each word. Every step is a stride over something not said' (op.cit., ibid.). For Berger, stories are discontinuous, their authority dependent on a tacit agreement that what is not said is acceptable to the listener, and that its discontinuities make sense. This became really clear to me when I watched three-year-old Eva listening to the story *I Want My Hat Back* (Klassen, 2017). This picture book has minimal text and little character development but, through simple dialogue and images, poses an ethical question. Eva is sure she knows who stole the hat and is indignant on behalf of the hat's owner, entering into the tacit agreement that stealing the hat is wrong, understanding implicitly what is not said. Berger argues that what makes a story worthy of being told is the extent to which it 'invests with authority its characters, its listeners' past experience and its teller's words' (ibid.). He calls this fusing of teller, listener and protagonists 'the story's reflecting voice,' going on to explain that: 'The story narrates on behalf of the subject, appeals to it and speaks in its voice. This fusing occurs within the discontinuities and the silent (but commonly agreed) connections, which allow the listener to enter the narration and become part of its reflecting subject' (ibid.). Eva implicitly understood these processes at the age of three, supporting Berger's further argument that the 'truth' of stories is not as relevant as their impact. For her, and those who watched her, the issue of 'truth' was not in question. Eva demonstrated the magical experience of being told a story. As she listened, she was able to put herself into the story, to understand what was not said, to respond on behalf of the characters and to engage with its ethical questions.

To respond to a story, as Eva did, arguably requires a blending of cognitive and emotional understandings. Indeed, a good story quickly captures the reader's attention. The best stories are memorable; they make a powerful impression; they prompt an emotional response; they stay with you and inform your view of the world. As Emihovich (1995) writes: 'Stories do not pretend to be objective because they deal with emotions, the irrational part of behaviour, they tap into the qualities of imagination and fantasy' (p. 39/40). For Grumet (1988), in her analysis of stories of women and teaching: 'Fidelity rather than truth is the meaning of these tales' (p. 66), a view echoed by qualitative researcher Kim (2015), who sees fidelity as one of the characteristics that distinguishes a story as research from a story that is read for leisure. However, the term fidelity implies 'something to be trusted' (ibid., p. 111), and I interpret this to indicate that the reader regards the storyteller as trustworthy. Blumenfeld-Jones (1995, p. 33), also discussing the idea of fidelity, suggests that the 'believability' of the story is a key factor, and that the story should resonate with the audience's experiences, something I have heard described by readers and listeners as 'ringing true'. Barone (2000) who has elegantly addressed the issue of trust and mistrust in educational storytelling, emphasizes the significance of intention. He considers that it depends on what is being attempted by the writer and what claims are being made about the truth of those attempts. We saw earlier that, for Gadamer, the truthfulness of a text lies in its 'power to throw light on fundamental matters at issue' (Lawn, 2006, p. 50), connoting truth-seeking as illumination or examination. All are useful views when considering my main concern.

To return to Rushdie, I ask, is it not a key role of fiction to contribute to answering the questions about the meaning of truth, when addressing the use of 'stories that aren't even true' (1990, p. 20). And, moreover, should we not now consider how storied narratives have the power to influence, even change, the viewpoints of individuals and groups?

The Power of Stories and Fictional Truth

Stories are never neutral. They may be viewed as subversive, as threatening, or as agents of moral teaching, depending on their nature and on how they are perceived and used (Rushdie, 2008; Squire et al, 2014). King tells us that: 'Stories are wondrous things. And they are dangerous' (2003, p. 9); and novelist Amanda Craig asserts that: 'People are much more frightened of novelists than they are of journalists or researchers' (Craig, 2013). Here, Craig is echoing Plato's much earlier belief in the power of stories to influence for good or ill. Plato saw them as soul shapers, to be treated with caution, allowing only certain types of stories and promoting censorship of others; an example of stories as a means of social control.

> Then we must first of all, it seems, supervise the storytellers. We'll select their stories whenever they are fine or beautiful and reject them when they aren't. And we'll persuade nurses and mothers to tell their children the ones we have selected, since they will shape their children's souls with stories much more than they shape their bodies by handling them. Many of the stories they tell, however, must be thrown out. (Republic 3776)

Some writers have used stories to comment on real life. Charles Dickens, for example, used fictional writing as a means of critiquing Victorian values and exposing social injustices. He wrote with a clear social purpose in mind, creating stories to raise awareness of cultural, political and social issues. In his novel *Hard Times* (1854) his character, Mr Thomas Gradgrind, represents Victorian utilitarianism in its most intransigent forms. Gradgrind is deeply threatened by stories and expresses horror at what he terms 'fancy', that is the power of imagination. He fears the ability to see one thing in terms of another, the imaginative power to create metaphors, to see a thing 'beyond us, yet ourselves' (Stevens, 1965). Gradgrind insists that: 'In this life, we want nothing but Facts, sir; nothing but Facts' (Dickens, op.cit., p. 9). He is determined to protect his children from the threat posed by what he calls 'idle storybooks' (ibid.) seeing such books as a risk to the political economy, as they could engender different ways of seeing the world. He feels threatened by the possibility that the world could be imagined in a new way, and perhaps changed as a result of fictional engagement. Other classic examples of stories with a social purpose include Harriet Beecher-Stowe's novel *Uncle Tom's Cabin* (1852), Mary Gaskell's *North and South* (1855) and John Steinbeck's *The Grapes of Wrath* (1939). Such writings offer what Barone (1992, p. 172) calls 'experience-based critiques that challenge conventional, politically comfortable descriptions of social phenomena'.

In their different ways and at different points in history, Plato, Dickens and Craig have all shown that fiction poses a threat for some, a view shared by Nussbaum who describes literature and the literary imagination as 'subversive' (1995, p. 2). Nussbaum argues that it is novels, rather than histories and biographies, which 'engender the ability to imagine what it is like to live the life of another person who might, given changes in circumstances, be oneself or one of one's loved ones' (p. 5). She suggests that literature has the power to prompt its readers to 'wonder about themselves' (p. 5) and that it is disturbing because it 'summons powerful emotions, it disturbs and puzzles' (ibid.). Stories raise questions about self and others. They promote identification and sympathy in the reader and they unsettle, prompting questioning of the status quo. Nussbaum suggests that good literature 'inspires distrust of conventional pieties and exacts a frequently painful confrontation with one's own thoughts and intentions' (ibid).

In the case of Plato, Dickens and Craig the social purpose is directed towards others, but this need not be the case. Ralph Ellison, writing his novel *Invisible Man* (first published in America in 1952) was very much an 'insider'. In November 1981, composing an introduction to a thirtieth-anniversary edition of his book, he looked back on the writing process and highlighted some interesting perceptions of the workings of truth and fiction. Ellison describes his task as a novelist as 'revealing the human universals hidden within the plight of one who was both black and American [...] gambling with the reader's capacity for fictional truth, to reveal the human complexity which stereotypes are intended to conceal' (Ellison, 1982, p.xl). Ellison considers that, despite the seriousness of the subject matter, there was enjoyment in writing it: 'a great deal of fun along the way', claiming that 'I knew that I was composing a work of fiction that would allow me to tell the truth while actually telling a "lie" which is the Afro-American term for an improvised story' (ibid., p.xl).

Further seeking the chance of 'letting stories breathe', like Frank (2010, p. 2 of prologue) I have paid attention 'as carefully as I can to what storytellers say about stories', those like Ellison who wrote about the process, but also more directly. Grasping the opportunity to talk to a contemporary author, Ali Smith, at a conference in 2017, I questioned the extent to which writers of fiction see their work as a means of telling truths that are difficult to accept, unpopular, unpalatable. She responded by writing this aphorism in my copy of her book, *Artful*: 'Truth will always out and fiction will always be a way in', leading me to further consider how fiction is used as 'a way in', or — in Gadamer's terms — as a means to actively highlight 'fundamental matters at issue' (Lawn, 2006, p. 50). I now examine how a story can offer 'a way in' to address 'fundamental matters' through a sequence of interim texts (Clandinin, 2013) that tell and examine a story I collected from Etta, a trainee teacher.

A Story that Confronts and Conveys Truth(s)

This is an appropriate point to exemplify how reflective story-writing works. In the following extracts from her *Reflective Journal*, Etta creates a story as a means of critical reflection on her experiences when visiting a Pupil Referral Unit (PRU) (a specialist educational unit for English children excluded from mainstream provision, often for behavioural reasons).

Etta's entry for November 9th begins with seven lines from a song written for Nina Simone that includes the salient line: 'Oh Lord, please don't let me be misunderstood' and goes on to claim good intentions even when these fail under duress. These song lyrics are followed by Etta's story about 'Tyrone'.

> Sometimes music is the only thing that keeps me sane. I rap lyrics in my head. Over and over, and over and over again. Justine always shouts at me for tapping to the beat but I can't help it. Tap, tap, tap, tap, tap, tap, tap. I don't like it when she tells me off and I rarely listen because she isn't my real Mum. My real Mum gave me up when I was born, apparently she was addicted to drugs... should I say 'Gave me up'? Perhaps 'Gave up on me' would be better. Justine is alright, to be fair. She bought me an ipad for Christmas last year so I'm always on youtube listening to music.
>
> People don't get it. People don't get me. All the teachers at my old school had the same reaction — they all 'gave up on me'. I'm a smart cookie and they knew that, which is why they were reluctant to hand me over at first. I could have really boosted their statistics with my cleverness. But when I punched the Headteacher, they all gave up on me. I was sorry after, but I found out years ago sorry doesn't make everything alright. So, I got sent to this other place instead of school. It's where the 'naughty kids' go. It's in the middle of a housing estate about twenty minutes from

my house. I only go in the mornings and just learn about maths and English. The other boys are alright, but I'm much cleverer than them and it's frustrating learning about things I already know.

That's when I get angry. It's boring going over and over and over the same thing. That's when I start tapping to the rap music in my head. Tap, tap, tap, tap, tap, tap, tap. Until Miss Smee says: 'Tyrone will you stop that tapping' and BHAM! Like a firework, I explode. They know to leave me alone when I'm like this. I sit on the green beanbag in the hallway and dig my nails into the carpet. I continue my tapping and rapping, more aggressively. I say through my teeth, my whole face tense. It releases the tension and eventually I'm feeling more calm. I stand up, hood goes up, I stroll back into class. 'Tyrone, you're back just in time for a biscuit.' I wonder how long it will be 'til Miss Smee gives up on me too?

Etta followed the story with a more formal reflection drawing on her background in psychology and exploring and theorizing some of the issues raised by her experiences at the Pupil Referral Unit (PRU). Etta explained how she was prompted to write the story and her feelings about writing it:

> This story was written from the point of view of a boy I met at the PRU. He was very able, having already passed his 11 plus exam[2] and was working on KS3[3] (Secondary level) work. I worked closely with him and talked to his teachers during my visit. I thought about him a lot afterwards. I actually felt sadder following writing this reflection. Writing from the point of view of this child made me realize how it must be to have an unstable home life, to feel unwanted at home and again at school.

In her story Etta demonstrates her ability to go beyond reflection to the deeper process of reflexivity. This process allows us to distance ourselves from ourselves so that, like Alice passing through the looking glass,[4] we find that the view from the other side is 'as different as possible'. Taking the reflexive turn allows us to be both inside and outside ourselves and able to look both ways, to move back and forth between two worlds. When Etta stands back and reflects on her story, examining her feelings on writing it, she is demonstrating the 'doubleness' that reflexivity involves. Beyond this there is another dimension as Etta theorizes what

---

2   Examination traditionally governing admission to grammar schools in England and Northern Ireland.

3   Formal educational stage for 11–14-year-olds in England and Wales.

4   Lewis Carroll (1872). *Through the Looking-Glass*. (London: Macmillan, 2015) p. 12.

she has observed and experienced. She is showing how understanding our own personal connection with the writing process can deepen and enrich our writing. The extent to which our 'characters' act like real human beings depends on the power of our imagination, the depth of our insight, and also our ability to empathize with them. Etta's reflective journal entries demonstrate a well-developed capacity to reflect critically on her experiences and to create fiction that reflects truth. Through the writing of Tyrone's story she is able to stand in his shoes, and in reading this story we are also enabled to try them on to see what they feel like.

Framing Etta's Story

Clandinin and Connelly (2000) identified a three-dimensional inquiry space in which we, as researchers, are situated with our participants. The three dimensions are temporality, place and sociality. *Temporality* refers to the past, present and future of events and people. *Place* refers to the location where the inquiry takes place. *Sociality* refers to the relationship between researcher and participants. These are the relational spaces that provide the setting for the diversity of people and experiences in different contexts and relationships as they travel through the landscape, the scene of the inquiry. Clandinin (2013) shows how the three dimensions are 'interconnected and interwoven' (p. 50) explaining that: 'Temporality is threaded into place and into events and emotions [...] we cannot understand a person's experience of place without understanding temporality' (p. 50). The researcher is located within this space, always attending to how the three dimensions have shaped their own experiences. Understanding the three-dimensional inquiry space enables clarification of research puzzles, justifies a study and helps the researcher to understand his/her place within it. As the inquiry progresses, moving towards a final research text, continuing to draw on the three-dimensional narrative inquiry space enables a deeper understanding of the narratives, stories and poems and of the conversations with participant(s). In Clandinin's words, such reflection enables the researcher to be 'in relation' with the participants (2016, p. 25).

Clandinin refers back to her earlier work with Michael Connelly to re-emphasize this relational nature of narrative inquiry:

> Narrative inquiry is the study of experience, and experience, as John Dewey taught, is a matter of people in relation contextually and temporally. Participants are in relation, and we as researchers are in relation to participants. Narrative inquiry is an experience of the experience. It is people in relation studying with people in relation. (Clandinin & Connelly, 2000, p. 189)

In terms of the three-dimensional inquiry space, Etta and I are travelling companions on this particular journey. We are in relation as tutor/researcher and trainee/participant, sharing the time and place in which this experience has taken place. We are both inquiring into our experiences and our practice through the use of stories.

In their critique of the design of narrative inquiries that focus on teachers' and teacher educators' own practices (Clandinin, Pushor & Murray Orr, 2007), the writers emphasize that narrative inquiry is 'much more than telling stories' (p. 21). They suggest that part of the attraction of narrative inquiry may be 'the comfort that comes from thinking about and telling stories' (ibid.). They underline the importance of the researcher establishing a relationship to and interest in the inquiry and of justifying the research practically, identifying how it will lead to insights that will prompt changes in the researcher's practices or those of others. They also point out that the researcher should consider the larger social and educational issues that the study might address, and what the responses might be to the questions: *'So what?'* and *'Who cares?'* (p. 25). These questions embrace the personal dimension of the inquiry and the practical implications; in my case prompting me to ask what have the stories revealed and what differences will this make to my own practice and that of my participants? How might this research contribute to theoretical understanding or to making situations more socially just? Considering these questions in relation to Etta's story, it is clear that through travelling to his world and writing the story of Tyrone, she has highlighted a number of social and political questions relating to the way schools provide for vulnerable pupils, who are able, but whose behaviour challenges their teachers. Writing the story may not have solved this problem for Etta as a teacher at the beginning of her career but it has raised her awareness of the complexity of the situation and allowed her to empathize with Tyrone's situation. I believe it will make her a better teacher.

Seeing Things Differently

E tta's story shows the importance of imagination in enabling people to see things differently. She has taken the reflexive turn that enables her to put herself into the shoes of Tyrone and view the world from his perspective, asking 'What might it be like to be you?' In doing this she has demonstrated her ability to engage in 'world-travelling' (Lugones, 1987, p. 17):

> The reason why I think that travelling to someone's 'world' is a way of identifying with them is because travelling to their 'world' we can understand *what it is to be them and what it is to be ourselves in their eyes*. Only when we have travelled to each other's 'worlds' are we fully subjects to each other.

Her imaginative leap is shareable with others through the process of storying. Depending on their standpoint, readers may be troubled, puzzled, challenged, made curious or angry by what they have read. There is disruption. Questions are raised. Mindful of Eagleton (2013: p. 104), we can see how Etta's story was possible as 'some initial order has been disrupted'. In Bruner's terms, there was 'something to tell about' (2002, p. 17).

In turn, stories such as Etta's have the power to disturb the reader into asking important questions about the nature of teaching, the role of the teacher, the meaning and purpose of education. Or, as a specific response to Etta's story, ask: 'How can schools provide the support needed for vulnerable pupils like Tyrone?' Etta's story is memorable in ways that an objective factual account could never be and it is not just the reader who is affected by its emotions, for she also highlights the power of stories to move the author, when she notes the sadness she felt after writing the story. She is thinking through her story and, like Toni Morrison, finds a means of resolution: 'Writing is really a way of thinking, not just feeling but thinking about things that are disparate, unresolved, mysterious, problematic or just sweet' (Morrison, cited in *Guardian*, 2019). The words of Margot Ely also resonate: 'We write to know. We write to learn. We write to discover' (2007, p. 570).

Concluding Thoughts

From undertaking my larger study, I learned that reflexivity is a crucial element of reflection. Meta-reflection requires that we return to our assumptions and expectations and question them in the light of experience, engaging in critical reflection. Our critical reflections may lead us to question previously held beliefs and ideas, not least about ourselves and our identity. Such reflection can lead to discomfort. We are provoking, disturbing ourselves who used to be one way and are now another (Dyson & Genishi, 1994); prompted to see things otherwise (Greene, 1995) and to explore the implications of our new perceptions both professionally and personally, as Etta exemplifies. In acting in these ways, we are using our narrative imagination (Nussbaum, 1995; Greene, 1995) to play a tune beyond us, yet finding for ourselves that 'things as they are, are changed upon the blue guitar' (Stevens, 1965). Perhaps something totally unexpected emerges from a story — something we didn't know before, something we hadn't thought about, something that gives us a different way of seeing, a new perspective, a different point of view; seeing something in a new light.

In another research conversation, Ben — a trainee teacher and a former journalist used to reporting 'facts' — identified the significance of imagination when writing fictionalized accounts from the perspectives of pupils:

> It comes back to empathy because if you're striving to understand someone and then simply reporting — you're making no attempt, so you write 'this happened, then this happened' you're just simply reporting. Using your imagination means you're at least making an attempt, not merely to observe, but to understand.

In the literature, Walker (2007, p. 296) considers that: 'Above all good stories help us to think well about practice [...] Once any story is told, ways of seeing are surely altered?'. Other writers consider the role of the reader more directly. Barone (1995, p. 66) asserts that, 'the aim of storytellers is not to prompt a single, closed, convergent reading but to persuade readers to provide answers to the dilemmas they pose'. He sees this as a feature of the 'storysharing contract between reader and writer' (ibid., p. 250). And Iser (1974, p. 113) writes that: 'Such story form invites the reader to join in, solve the problem — the reader fills the gaps, the blanks'. As Okri (1997, p. 34) says, 'it is readers who make the book. A book unread is a story unlived'. This brief discussion of the role of readers highlights that stories can be used well but also badly. In stories used as a means of control, to promote a particular view of history, for example, or to embed political or religious ideologies, there is no thinking 'with', no asking back, no expectation that the reader will have an interpretive role. Okri (1997, p. 49) makes this clear: 'Writers are dangerous when they tell the truth. Writers are dangerous when they tell lies'. Kearney (2002, p. 148) argues strongly that truth is not the sole prerogative of the so-called exact sciences: 'There is also a truth, with its corresponding understanding, that we may properly call 'narrative'. We need both'. For Gadamer (2004/1960) meaning is not subjectively determined. He identifies a process of coming to understanding *with the text*. I perceive this as thinking *with* rather than *about* stories, a hermeneutic practice that makes me ask not only what a story means to me, but how I can understand what it means to the teller and to other readers or listeners.

Furthermore, I consider that reflective story-telling can be seen as a critical pedagogical practice in that it confronts both writers and readers with questions, challenges curriculum, highlights social and cultural issues at individual and institutional levels and may contribute to change, allowing us to see the world in new ways. Nussbaum (1995) does not claim that reading fiction *per se* will solve all social justice problems but that it 'can be a bridge both to a vision of justice and to the social enactment of that vision' (ibid., p. 12). Counter-stories can be created that act subversively against dominant stories (Nelson, 1995) and thus provide access to the benefits of the dominant society to those who are marginalized; such ideas are explored further in the narrative inquiry work of Clandinin, Murphy et al. (2009).

Stories such as the one written by Etta, and many other stories written by trainee teachers that I collected over time, have become an integral part of my pedagogy in teaching about reflective story writing. In *Living by Fiction* (1982) Annie Dillard explores the question: 'Can fiction interpret the world?' (p. 145). She suggests that, by its very nature, fiction lends itself to the interpretive process: 'Fiction elicits an interpretation of the world by being itself a world-like object for interpretation. It is a subtle pedagogy' (p. 155). This is an idea that I have carried into my teaching.

The idea of fiction as a means of teaching readers subtly about the world is pertinent to my inquiry question about the 'use' of stories that aren't even true, and particularly the value of the teachers' stories as learning tools for themselves and for others. The trainee teachers' responses exposed the feelings and emotions that emerged in the telling of the stories, surprising the writers/tellers and memorable to the listeners/readers. Reflecting on the power of her stories to bring about personal learning, one teacher, Evelyn, commented: 'On the way I stopped and looked differently', thus exemplifying the claim of Thomas King, the Canadian First Nations writer and storyteller quoted at the beginning of this chapter who stated that: 'The truth about stories is that that's all we are' (King, 2003, p. 153). He writes that stories have the capacity to be both 'wondrous' and 'dangerous' and, reminds us that: 'Once a story is told it cannot be called back. Once told it is loose in the world' (ibid., p. 10). Etta's and Tyrone's stories, and indeed my own viewpoints have been let loose here, lightly tethered within this chapter, but starting a life of their own.

Coda

It seems appropriate to follow Bruner and end this chapter with a coda, 'a retrospective evaluation of what it all might mean... an invitation to problem solving'; to focus on 'what comes after the story' (2002, p 20); to codify my thoughts on the power of narrative truth on tellers and listeners, writers and readers, and where stories stand in relation to the factual account that presents evidence in logical steps to reach an (apparently) irrefutable conclusion. Like Bruner (1986, p. 43), I find that the power of stories lies in their ability to 'create a reality of their own' and to draw others into it. Engagement with the story that has to be told requires us to exercise our imagination, allowing us to become world-travellers, to be both inside and outside ourselves and see things differently. Stepping into the shoes of others prompts us to ask the question 'What might it be like to be you?' In fiction we have the possibility to create stories that are memorable and compelling, that draw the reader in to share our space. I will never hear Nina Simone singing 'Please don't let me be misunderstood' without remembering Etta's story about Tyrone. And each time I think of Tyrone, I will be provoked to re-engage with the social and political questions regarding vulnerable children in schools, demonstrating how the powerful story can lead to action. Etta's story, my own stories and those of many other writers have the capacity to do what the most powerful stories do: to surprise, perhaps even shock us and disrupt our view of the world; to challenge us to think differently, give us new ways of seeing, and, perhaps, new ways of acting.

When we tell a story, we draw our audience in to share an experience that is profoundly memorable; one that captures our imagination and engages our emotions; one that shows us how others feel and how they perceive the problems they encounter; one that provokes us to search for resolution. We think *with* rather than *about* the stories and *retell* them to others to share their impact and this, I believe, is the power of narrative truth; *my* understanding of how and why stories matter.

Acknowledgements

T he author thanks all the trainee teachers who agreed to be involved in her research, especially those who are cited in this chapter.

References

Aristotle (c.335BCE/2013). *Poetics* (translated by Anthony Kenny). Oxford: Oxford University Press.

Barone, T. (1992). Beyond theory and method: A case of critical storytelling. *Theory into Practice*, 31(2): 142–46.

Barone, T. (1995). Persuasive writings, vigilant readings, and reconstructed characters: the paradox of trust in educational story-sharing. In: Hatch, J.A. & Wisniewski, R. (eds), *Life history and narrative*. London: Routledge Falmer.

Barone, T. (2000). *Aesthetics, politics and educational inquiry: Essays and examples*. New York: Peter Lang.

Barthes, R. (1966). *Introduction to the structural analysis of the narrative*. Occasional paper for Contemporary Cultural Studies, University of Birmingham.

Barthes, R. (1977). *Image, music, text: Essays selected and translated by Stephen Heath*. London: Fontana Press.

Beecher-Stowe, H. (1852). *Uncle Tom's cabin*. (2008, Oxford: Oxford University Press).

Berger, J. (1982). Stories. In: McQuillan, M. (ed) (2000). *The narrative reader.* Abingdon: Routledge.

Blumenfeld-Jones, D. (1995). Fidelity as a criterion for practicing and evaluating narrative inquiry. In: Hatch, J.A. & Wisniewski, R. (eds). *Life history and narrative.* Abingdon: Routledge Falmer.

Bolton, G. (2010). *Reflective practice: Writing and professional development*, 3rd edn. London: Sage.

Bruner, J. (1986). *Actual minds, possible worlds.* Cambridge, MA: Harvard University Press.

Bruner, J. (1994). Life as narrative. In: Dyson, A.H. & Geneshi, C. (eds) *The need for story: Cultural diversity in classroom and community.* Illinois: National Council of Teachers of English.

Bruner, J. (2002). *Making stories: Law, literature, life.* Harvard: Harvard University Press.

Clandinin, D.J. & Connelly, M. (2000). *Narrative inquiry: Experience and story in qualitative research.* New York: Jossey-Bass.

Clandinin, D.J., Pushor, D. & Murray Orr, A. (2007). Navigating sites for narrative inquiry. *Journal of Teacher Education*, 58(1): 21–35. https://doi.org/10.1177/0022487106296218

Clandinin, D.J. & Murphy, M.S. (2009). Relational ontological commitments in narrative research. *Educational Researcher*, 38(8): 598–602.

Clandinin, D.J. (2013). *Engaging in narrative inquiry.* Walnut Creek, CA: Left Coast Press.

Clandinin, D.J., Steeves, P. & Caine, V. (2013). *Composing lives in transition: A narrative inquiry into the experiences of early school leavers.* Bingley, UK: Emerald.

Clough, P. (2002). *Narratives and fictions in educational research.* Buckingham, UK: Open University Press.

Craig, A. (2013). *Guardian* Master Class, November. Kings Place, London N1.

D'Ancona, M. (2017). *Post truth: The new war on truth and how to fight back.* London: Ebury Press.

Dewey, J. (1938). *Experience and education.* New York: Touchstone.

Dickens, C. (1854). *Hard times.* (2003, London: Penguin Books).

Dillard, A. (1982). *Living by fiction.* New York: HarperCollins.

Denzin, N.K. (1997). *Interpretive ethnography: Ethnographic practices for the twenty-first century.* Thousand Oaks, CA: Sage.

Downey, C.A. & Clandinin, D.J. (2010). Narrative inquiry as reflective practice: Tensions and possibilities. In: Lyons, N. (ed). *Handbook of reflection and reflective inquiry: Mapping a way of knowing for professional reflective inquiry.* New York: Springer.

Doyle, W. & Carter, K. (1993). Narrative and learning to teach: Implications for teacher education curriculum. *Journal of Curriculum Studies*, 35(2): 129–37.

Dyson, A.H. & Genishi, C. (eds) (1994). *The need for story: Cultural diversity in classroom and community*. Illinois: National Council of Teachers of English.

Dyson, J. (2019). *'What's the use of stories that aren't even true?' (Rushdie, 1990): A narrative inquiry into reflective story writing with trainee teachers*. Unpublished Thesis, Anglia Ruskin University, Cambridge, UK.

Dyson, J. & Smith, C. (2018). Four seasons of composing stories to live by. In: Hanne, M. & Kall, A. (eds). *Metaphor and narrative in teaching, learning and research strategies in teacher education*. Abingdon: Routledge.

Eaglestone, R. (2013). *Contemporary fiction: A very short introduction*. Oxford: Oxford University Press. https://doi.org/10.1093/actrade/9780199609260.003.0001

Eagleton, T. (2013). *How to read literature*. New Haven: Yale University Press.

Ellison, Ralph (1982). *Invisible Man*, 30th anniversary edn. (2001, London: Penguin Books) (originally 1952, New York: Random House).

Ely, M. (2007). In-forming re-presentations. In: Clandinin, D.J. (ed). *Handbook of narrative inquiry: Mapping a methodology*. Thousand oaks, CA: Sage.

Emihovitch, C. (1995). Distancing passion: Narratives in social science. In Hatch, J.A. & Wisniewski, R. (eds). *Life histories and narrative*. London: Falmer Press.

Estefan, A., Caine, V. & Clandinin, D.J. (2013). A Return to methodological commitment: Reflections on narrative inquiry. *Scandinavian Journal of Educational Research*, 57(6): 574–86, https://doi.org/10.1080/00313831.2013.798833

Frank, A.W. (2004). After methods, the story: From incongruity to truth in qualitative research. *Qualitative Health Research*, 14(3): 430–40. https://doi.org/10.1177/1049732303261955

Frank, A.W. (2012). *Letting stories breath: A socio-narratology*. Chicago: University of Chicago Press.

Gadamer, H-G. (2004/1960). *Truth & method* (2nd rev. edn). London: Continuum.

Gaskell, M. (1855). *North and South*. (2008, Oxford: Oxford University Press).

Gordon, C. (ed) (1980). Michel Foucault, The history of sexuality, an interview with Lucette Finas. In: *Power/Knowledge*. New York: Pantheon Books.

Greene, M. (1995). *Releasing the imagination: Essays on education, the arts, and social change*. San Francisco: Jossey Bass.

Grumet, M. (1988). *Bitter milk: Women and teaching*. Massachusetts: University of Massachusetts Press.

Hatch, J.A. & Wisniewski, R. (1995). *Life history and narrative: Questions, issues and exemplary works*. Abingdon: Routledge Falmer.

Iser, W. (1974). *The implied reader*. Baltimore: Johns Hopkins University Press.

Iser, W. (1993). *The fictive and the imaginary: Charting literary anthropology*. Baltimore: Johns Hopkins University Press.

Kearney, R. (2002). *On stories*. Abingdon: Routledge.

Kim, J-H. (2016) *Understanding narrative inquiry*. Thousand Oaks, CA: Sage.

King, T. (2003). *The truth about stories*. Toronto: House of Anansi Press.

Klassen, J. (2012). *I want my hat back*. Massachusetts: Candlewick Press.

Lawn, C. (2006). *Gadamer: A guide for the perplexed*. London: Continuum.

Lugones, M. (1987). Playfulness, 'world'-travelling and loving perception. *Hypatia*, 2(2): 3–19.

Mink, L.O. (1978). Narrative form as a cognitive instrument. In: Canary, R.H. & Kozicki, H. (eds). *The writing of history: Literary form and historical understanding*. Madison: University of Wisconsin Press.

Morris, D.B. (2002). Narrative, ethics and pain: Thinking with stories. In Charon, R. & Montello, M.(eds). *Stories matter: The role of narrative in medical ethics*. New York: Routledge.

Guardian (2019) Morrison, T. *'Love is never any better than the lover': Toni Morrison — a life in quotes*, 6 August. https://www.theguardian.com/books/2019/aug/06/toni-morrison-author-life-in-quotes

Nelson, L.H. (1995). Resistance and insubordination. *Hypatia*, 10(2): 23–43.

Nussbaum, M. (1995) *Poetic justice: The literary imagination and public life*. Boston: Beacon Press.

Okri, B. (1997). *A way of being free*. London: Phoenix House

Plato (360 BCE). *The Republic*. (2007, Penguin Classics Edition. London: Random House).

Richardson, L. (1990). *Writing strategies: Reaching diverse audiences*. Newbury Park: Sage.

Richardson, L. (2000). Writing: A method of inquiry. In: Denzin, N.K. & Lincoln, Y.S. (eds). *Handbook of qualitative research*, 2nd edn. Thousand Oaks: Sage.

Ricœur P. (1976). Explanation and understanding. Essay 4 in: *Interpretation theory: Discourse and the surplus of meaning*. Fort Worth, TX: Texas Christian University Press.

Rushdie, S. (1990). *Haroun and the sea of stories*. London: Granta Books in association with Penguin.

Rushdie, S. (2008). Salman Rushdie tells stories of oppression, freedom and the fatwa. Reported by Cynthia Haven, *Stanford Report*, May 14, https://news.stanford.edu/news/2008/may14/rushtwo-051408.html

Rushdie, S. (2015). Salman Rushdie talks fiction, fairy tales and 'the problem of an interesting life', in interview with M.J. Franklin, 8 September, https://mashable.com/2015/09/08/salman-rushdie-two-years-eight-months-interview/?europe=true (on 07/03/20).

Rushdie, S. (2015). *Two years eight months and twenty-eight nights*. London: Vintage Books.

Schön, D.A. (1983). *The reflective practitioner: How professionals think in action*. New York: Basic Books.

Schön, D.A. (1991). *The reflective turn, case studies in and on reflective practice*. Colombia University, NY: Teachers' College Press.

Segal, L. (2018/1964). *Other people's houses*. London: Sort of Books.

Steinbeck, J. (1939) *The grapes of wrath*. (2000, London: Penguin Classics).

Stevens, W. (1942–1951). *The necessary angel: Essays on reality and the imagination*. New York: Vintage Books.

Stevens, W. (1965). *Poems*. London: Faber & Faber.

Squire, C., Davis, M., Cigdem, E., Andrews, M., Harrison, B., Hyden, L-C., & Hyden, M. (2014). *What is narrative research?* London: Bloomsbury.

Van Manen, M. (1991). *Researching lived experience: Human science for an action sensitive pedagogy*. New York: State University of New York Press.

Walker, M. (2007). Action research and narratives: 'Finely aware and richly responsible'. *Educational Action Research*, 15(2): 295–303.

Wertz, F. (2011). The qualitative revolution and psychology science, politics, and ethics. *The Humanistic Psychologist*, 39: 77–104. https://doi.org/10.1080/08873267.2011.564531

White, H. (1984). The question of narrative in contemporary historical theory. *History and Theory*, 23(1): 1–33.

Zeichner K.M. & Liston, D.R. (1987). Critical pedagogy and teacher education. *Journal of Education*, 169(3): 117–37.

2. From Experience to Language in Narrative Practices in Therapeutic Education in France

Hervé Breton

Hervé Breton presents a clear exposition of a process that can make patients' lived experiences of illness visible to both themselves and the medical community. He reveals the stages of selecting, verbalizing and storying and — focusing on a patient account — enables the reader to grasp the theoretical approach, how to put this into practice, and what the stages might look like.

This chapter examines processes that assist patients to make their lived experiences of ill health audible, to enable medical practitioners to better understand the consequences of their approaches and interventions. It presents a way of working that facilitates the expression of the experience of enduring into language. It uses the dynamics of biographical inter-comprehension to help patients to express particular life experiences, and to enable others to receive their stories. This approach, which transforms lived experience over time into existential and expressible content, may enable improvements to guidelines for the facilitation of therapeutic education, resulting in an enhanced complementarity between experiential and experimental approaches. In these ways it complements and extends existing work in the Anglo-American tradition[1] in looking at ways to do this.

---

1   For example: Hurwitz, B. & Charon, R. (2013 Jun 1). A narrative future for health care. *Lancet*, 381(9881): 1886–87; Bradby, H., Hargreaves, J. & Robson, M. (2009). Story in health and social care. *Health Care Anal.* 17(4): 331–44.

https://doi.org/10.11647/OBP.0203.02

The Motivational Context

O n the occasion of the 2016 colloquium of the French high commission on health (Haute Autorité en Santé, HAS),[2] Professor Agnès Buzyn (who was named health minister in 2017) stated in her conference opening speech: 'The experience of the patient adds a perspective that is complementary to that of the health professionals. It has to be taken into consideration, if our health system is to evolve towards more democracy.'[3] More than merely expressing a political will to take the patient's experience into account, Professor Buzyn reflected on ways forward:

> We can no longer rely only on the analyses of patients' complaints and undesirable events to improve the quality of health care. We must go further. Patients are the ultimate beneficiaries of the HAS' commitment to quality care. We therefore we need their guidance as to the methods, service delivery and the way forward.

In this chapter I shall attempt to look at the concrete challenges this raises. Which methods may be used to foster acceptance of the patient's experience in a care setting? What really is at issue in counselling and in the facilitation of the expression of the patient's experience? In which ways can patients' stories, and the things they express, help make medical practices more pertinent? How can narrative approaches in healthcare and experimental medical sciences be complementary?

We will start with the quest for a definition of the patient's unique experience. This will provide the 'cornerstone' for studying narrative practices, the stakes they raise, their processes and methods. We will then examine the narrative forms that are at work by looking at two 'passages': one from the experience to its expression; and one that takes place as the stories are being shared in a group context. We will first study these transitions by examining a story written in the first person during a period in which its author received the diagnosis of the onset of a rare illness. After this example of an inaugural moment of a challenging experience, we will look at the processes by which the expression of an experience into words can transform it into a story, and

---

2   The author has translated French sources into English for this chapter.
3   HAS Website: https://webzine.has-sante.fr/portail/jcms/c_2728261/fr/patients-et-soignants-vers-un-necessaire-partenariat.

then into a story to be told in a joint storytelling session that aims to foster biographical inter-comprehension. The understanding of the processes by which lived experiences are shaped into existential and 'narratable' form helps to develop guidance that may enhance counselling and facilitation practices in therapeutic education, as well as new forms of complementarity between experiential and experimental approaches.

The Patient Experience: Elements of a Definition

T hat I stress the necessity of listening to the experience of a patient in care may surprise you: it suggests that the patient may become forgotten by a medical practice supposed to be entirely dedicated to him or her. This possible oblivion may originate in the will to increase what Illich (critically) names 'the efficacy of the medical act' (1975, p. 15) whereby patients have to learn to make themselves available, so that the gestures of medical intervention can be dispensed in an orderly way on their bodies, which are thereby reduced to passive matter. Forgetting the subject legitimizes a process of naturalization whereby the patient is merely the bearer of an autonomous phenomenon, personal experience a residual phenomenon in a medical practice, in which his or her reified body is merely altered material, the passive terrain of processes of decay and contamination. An alternative and non-competing view to that verbalized by Illich is to consider that the medical professions have a limited capacity to make space for the expression of patient experience, as this is not defined in medical sciences. Narrative work, story-*writing* and story*telling* are viewed as strange, with a distant theoretical possibility to become an add-on during the treatment, or useful for interviews aiming to establish an 'educational diagnosis'.[4]

When the health sector shows interest in the expression of the patient experience, it signifies a change in its positioning. Indeed, seeking to understand 'from the viewpoint of the sick person' presents difficulties and constraints: it takes time and requires reciprocal engagement. It is complex as individuals will find the onset of an illness very different in terms of the depth of the experience, the forms of endurance, their

---

4   HAS guidance: *Recommandations. Education thérapeutique du patient. Définitions, finalités et organisation*: https://www.has-sante.fr/portail/jcms/c_1241714/fr/education-therapeutique-du-patient-etp

duration and intensity. In his conference with psychiatrists in 1992, the philosopher Paul Ricœur thematized a link between the notions of 'acting-enduring', which helps us to think through the question of suffering in the course of an illness:

> As to the powerlessness to act, the gap between wanting and being in a position to act is, at the start, common to pain and suffering. This explains the partial overlapping of the two. The meaning of the old word 'to suffer' reminds us, that suffering first means enduring. Thus, the passivity of suffering contains a minimal degree of agency. (Marin & Zaccaï-Reyners, 2013, p. 20)

Beyond its physical manifestations, perhaps even beyond pain, illness gives rise to a suffering that includes bodily experiences without it being exhausted by them:

> thus, we shall reserve the term 'pain' to affects perceived as localized in particular organs of the body or in the whole body, and the term 'suffering' to affects that are open to reflexivity, language, relationship to self, relationship to others, relationship to the senses and to questioning. (ibid., p. 14)

These experiences of endurance and suffering impact on the life of the subject as it occurs, and on the life history as it occurs in daily life, given the new constraints linked to the illness and/or its treatment: the waiting times, the daily uncertainty, the pain in the organs. These are all phenomena that the subject endures and needs to negotiate. The illness impacts on the subject's history, because the characteristic reduction of agency in the experience of enduring originates in the lessening of physical abilities and in the deterioration of temporal structures that enable the person to perform and act in certain ways, and in the dependence on medical expertise. Undertaking narrative work to try to make sense of, and to bring into dialogue, the various forms of 'enduring/suffering' that result from extended dependence (on the medical world, the expertise of medical and nursing staff, the treatments and the manifestations of the illness) can contribute to the preservation and rehabilitation of the subject's agency.

The expression of the patient's experience, its crafting into a story and its reception by others (peers and medical staff) thus represents a dimension of the health journey, as we shall endeavour to show. This activity of transforming the event of illness into a story takes time. Benaroyo (2013) stresses this when he identifies the phases through which the experience of illness presents itself, first in unspeakable forms that reduce the person to silence, sometimes to complaint, and then gradually evolving towards forms of expression that take the form of a story. Ricœur's enlightening thesis (1983) brings to light the processes of reciprocity between the temporalization of the experience (putting it into a meaningful timeline) and the story writing. The opening up of spaces in which the experience becomes 'sayable' represents a vital process that cannot be ignored in the health journey. From a biographical perspective, the fact that the experience of illness is being welcomed supports the endeavour of working on the experience, of passing it into language and making it 'speakable' and 'tellable'. Such a process is a condition for the patient to retain agency and to find the strength of empathy in order to endure the illness. One of the values of narrative practices in healthcare is their capacity to support the maintenance of a sense of self through the opening up of spaces that allow endurance to be expressed, and to become known and recognized by communities of loved ones, peers, medical staff and perhaps even by the medical world. By becoming tellable, the experience can be shared with a view to a collective elaboration and formalization of knowledge acquired in the process. This can potentially complement knowledge constituted by experimental science.

Expressing the Lived Experience of Suffering: Expressibility and Wording

U nderstanding the process of expressing and then narrating the lived experience of a patient, and its being received by others, requires paying attention to transformative processes that take place during the activities of wording, meaning-making and storytelling. Composing one's story takes time. The story needs to take shape, to develop, to configure itself, and to turn into a story for others. The study of these gradual changes, as processes and as phenomena that unfold over time, provides a way of understanding what represents, to the patient, a transformation of his or her relationship with his or her lived experience and illness.

Expressibility of Suffering:
Grasping the Experience and the Gradual Process of Wording

T he passage from experience to language is the result of a journey: it starts with the evocation of a moment to be explored 'in the living flesh' and involves bodily sensations, impressions, anticipations and inferences. This experience is stratified (Petitmengin, 2010) and needs to find its way via wording into language. This journey transforms the experience itself and arises thetically for the subject in the act of narration and then becomes something that can be put into words, even in the form of speech. This change can be studied in the first person, notably with the help of the techniques of self-explicitation (auto-explicitation). Pierre Vermersch (2000b, 2007) modelled this, starting with the notion of 'reference experience' and then focusing on the selection of words by which to 'say and tell' the experience.

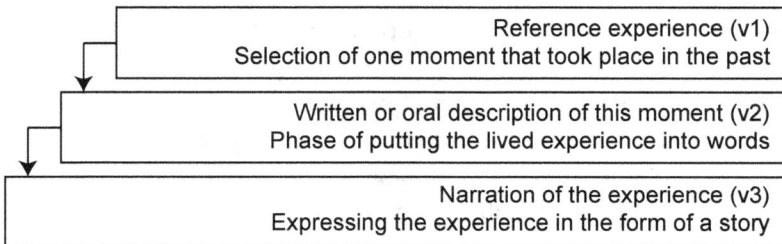

| Reference experience (v1)
Selection of one moment that took place in the past |
| Written or oral description of this moment (v2)
Phase of putting the lived experience into words |
| Narration of the experience (v3)
Expressing the experience in the form of a story |

Fig. 2.1 Phases of the passage from experience into language.
Source: Breton, 2017a.

The diagram identifies three phases: choosing a singular moment to evoke (v1), wording it in a descriptive form (v2) and putting it into the form of a story (v3). To explore an event such as the onset of an illness and situating it in the course of a life begins with identifying its inaugural moment – of which the span is as yet to be determined. This first phase consists of the identification of this 'primordial' moment and its evocation. It is followed by a second process: that of the detailed description of its unfolding and its various aspects. The description of the aspects of this experience is part of the process of wording. It forms the basis for the third phase, which consists of configuring the experience within a storyline that holds its component parts together in an 'experiential unity' that is meaningful to the subject. This process in three phases structures the gradual journey of the experience entering into language as description. This activity transforms the experience and renders it sayable. It thus creates the requisite conditions for the illness-event to become integrated into a biographical story.

A First-Person Story of a Journey of Diagnostic Delay

L et us put the question of the expressibility or sayability of the experience of enduring to the test, by looking at a story about a long journey of diagnostic delay in a case of a diagnosis of lupus, a rare illness. It is a story 'radically in the first person' (Berger, 2016, p. 105), that had been written up in the context of a research project undertaken by the working group on biographical research in health at CIRBE.[5] It covers the inaugural moment of receiving a diagnosis from a GP, who diagnosed lupus after a quick examination. This 'reference experience' is a pivot in the patient's life with the illness-event. It was put into words retrospectively, twelve months after the diagnosis was made.

> On 31 December 2013, I went to see a countryside GP because I had two red blotches on my cheeks. The skin was inflamed. In spite of having applied a hydrating cream that I had found in a drawer and that had been used by my son a few years ago while he had bouts of eczema, things seemed to be getting worse. It was about 09h30 when I arrived at the doctor's, accompanied by my spouse. After waiting for half an hour in a crowded room, I walk into the doctor's surgery and sit down on a chair to the left of the room. The doctor is completing the medical file on his computer without saying a word. Then he turns towards me and asks: what brings you here?
>
> Somewhat surprised that he'd ask me this question given the highly visible eruption on my skin, I reply: 'I have been having two red blotches on my face for two weeks. I would like a cream to calm the eruptions.' Without getting up and without examining me, the doctor responds: 'You have got lupus. I will give you a cream to apply to your face. You can get it from the pharmacy next to the dispensary.' A wee bit surprised, I ask him what a lupus is, gathering that it is a particular kind of eczema. He replies, that I need to see a specialist consultant close to my home after the Christmas holidays to get the diagnosis confirmed and the treatment adjusted. Back at home, I read up the notice for the cream and look up 'lupus' on google. That's the beginning of six months of diagnostic delay.

---

5   The International College of Biographical Research in Education.

When the patient received the news in December 2013, the impact was massive. Getting to know a diagnosis of a chronic, potentially serious and disabling illness 'first person' represents a challenge to anticipatory structures and to the way of projecting oneself into one's existential and professional future. It is worthwhile to note that the events as they happened represent an unusual account of a subject being 'diagnosed with lupus' when compared to existing research into the announcement of rare illnesses. The fact, that these illnesses are rare, that their symptoms are frequently systemic (which is the case with lupus), that they are gradual and come with changing levels of intensity, usually results in difficulty when it comes to diagnosis, which can in turn result in a process of diagnostic wandering for the patient.

Boucand (2010, p. 313) reveals for example that in a survey on 'Ehlers-Danlos' syndromes, 'one person in four affected by the illness had to wait for more than 30 years before being given an accurate diagnosis and that 40% of the survey sample had been given the wrong diagnosis before being given the correct one'. Such a situation leads patients to doubt the ability of the medical world to listen to and understand their experiences and troubles, and to take them into account in their health journeys. Boucand notes that, in addition, this situation creates forms of dependence on the few medical experts in a given field, who are seen by the patients as the keepers of the expertise that can help their recovery. The story just presented illustrates a reverse situation. The 'lupus' diagnosis was established during the first consultation. The patient was given the task to have it confirmed by a specialist dermatologist. In the meantime, the patient had been prescribed treatment based on the conclusions of a first diagnosis, which can be quantified as 'reliable, though not certain'. The historicization of the experience then requires biographical work on temporalization, by which this specific event finds its place within the duration of the journey. As this happens, the event becomes 'thinkable' as a trying period in a life journey.

The conditions for putting this moment into the shape of a story — and making it sayable — deserve attention. The text presented above was written thirty-six months after the event had taken place. It had shown itself to be the inaugural moment of the storyline and its power remained intact. In other words, the way in which the experience presents itself in the course of the storytelling process can be considered a gauge of what still remains to be understood in it. As the experience becomes speakable, it reveals itself to the subject, or as Ricœur says: 'The experience can be told, it asks to be told. To bring it into the realm of language does not mean changing it into something else, but in articulating and in developing it, it becomes itself' (Ricœur, 1986, p. 62). There are experiences that need to be reflected on to find their place in a story. Their sayability takes time. It is a process of maturation that can be envisaged under three aspects: one, the possibility of reflecting on and of understanding different aspects of the experience that became an event; two, a gradual attempt at grasping the silent transformations happening in the 'living now'; three, a reconstitution of the temporal horizons of a given period of life that make it possible to situate the illness-event in the duration of a life story.

The Temporalization of the Experience: From the Pre-Figuration of the Experience to its Expression in the Form of a Story

The historicization of the illness-event proceeds from a complex temporality. Its study requires differentiating 'reflexivity in the course of the experience' and 'reflexivity after the experience'. Regarding the development of a storyline, Ricœur underlines the combination 'in variable proportions of two temporal dimensions: a chronological dimension and one that isn't. The first constitutes the episodic dimension of the story: it characterizes the story as being composed of events. The second is the "configuring" dimension proper, thanks to which the plot transforms the events into a story' (1983, p. 129). Seen from this perspective, the episodic dimension of the story arises from the chronological sequencing of salient moments of a period in life, while the configuring dimension confers duration and narrative unity to the story. The temporalization presents the storyline of the events situated on a timeline. Conversely, the narrative weaving harnesses the process of temporalization to explore and configure these moments together, and transforms the (linear) narrative regime of succession into a more integrated one of continuity. The creation of a story proceeds thus from an extension: triggered by the description of the reference experience (a moment), the narration then covers a period in one's life that may last from a few months to a few years. In other words, the activity of the temporalization of the experience transforms the story with something like a 'change of scale'. What happens here transforms the narrative work by letting it move from a regime of description / aspectualization (Adam, 2015) to one of periodization / historicization. This is illustrated in Figure 2.2 below, which follows on from and develops the expression, in the form of a story, of the experience of being given a diagnosis of 'lupus'. In this example, the extension of the duration of the experience transforms the content of what is being narrated: the story of the inaugural moment, which includes this moment, is titled 'Story of a period of diagnostic delay'.

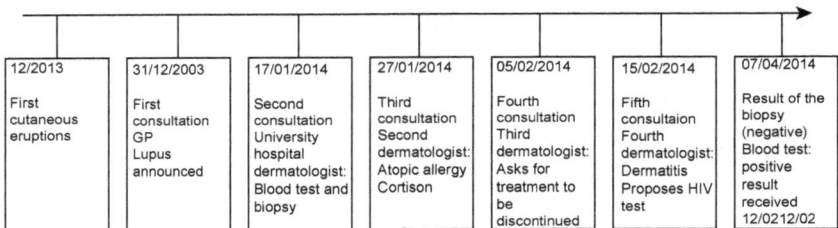

12/2013	31/12/2003	17/01/2014	27/01/2014	05/02/2014	15/02/2014	07/04/2014
First cutaneous eruptions	First consultation GP Lupus announced	Second consultation University hospital dermatologist: Blood test and biopsy	Third consultation Second dermatologist: Atopic allergy Cortison	Fourth consultation Third dermatologist: Asks for treatment to be discontinued	Fifth consultaion Fourth dermatologist: Dermatitis Proposes HIV test	Result of the biopsy (negative) Blood test: positive result received 12/0212/02

Fig. 2.2 Periodization of the experience of the patient between being given a first diagnosis and having it confirmed.

The above diagram sequences and punctuates particular moments in a journey of diagnostic delay by ordering them chronologically and making them appear in succession. The temporalization of the journey, which spanned a period of six months, makes seven salient moments apparent. The expression of these experiences into a story now needs to integrate each of these moments as a unity in themselves, and then, to explore the links existing between these moments together. It is indeed the configuration of these moments taken together that makes a stretch of experience (a period in life) appear, the scope and structure of which enable the identification of different themes of the first story: the erosion or loss of agency of the patient along a timeline, a variety of lived temporal experiences (waiting, inertia, stuckness, urgency...), daily acts and gestures to stay the course and to keep being engaged at work, the rehabilitation of anticipatory structures, knowledge of the illness acquired in the course of time, transformation of the modes of attention to oneself and to bodily sensations... A correlation can be envisaged between the duration of the experiences explored and the thematic work, that developed in the context of the patient-carer relationship or through the patients' attempts to formalize knowledge acquired during their experience of illness. This observation highlights the forms of co-dependence between the temporal scales of the experience that is taken into account in the narrative work, and the processes of understanding that result from that work, for oneself, for peers (other patients) or for the medical professions. ·

From Expression of the Experience to the Reception of the Stories

A t this stage, we have identified a first passage: the passage from experience to language, which has its own temporality that varies according to: the relationship the 'subject' has with his or her experience; the events experienced; and the domains and dimensions of existence that the experience touches. This passage also has a micro-dynamic that combines and alternates the activity of temporalizing the experience with the task of configuring it through wording and developing a story. Language transforms experience, owing to the thetic work that underlies it. This qualitative transformation of the experience is also that of the subject, who gives form to his or her existence by expressing it in the form of a story and who becomes a reflective and historical subject, who can think of him- or herself in time and tell his or her story. Putting experience into narrative form shapes and transforms the experience. The capacity to express experience arises from this process. We shall now examine the second passage, which allows the story to be re-viewed through the circulation of its modes of expression.

Reflecting on the Time of Passing the Story On to a Community

T he expression of the story in a group context opens up to participants the possibility of a singular experience: the reception of the story. This process is the subject of particular attention for, and during, the sessions in which life stories are developed. The story of diagnostic delay outlined earlier could, for example, be shared and socialized during a session of expressing and writing life histories (Lainé, 2004). During this phase, the stakes change. The presentation of stories in a group context requires a re-view of the story first written 'in first person' in order for it to be received by 'others than oneself'. Conversely, one requires narrative abilities to make oneself available to listen to patient's stories (Charon, 2015). These can be practiced as part of the experience of doing biographical work in a group. The patients, as well as the health professionals who engage with this process, experience the story as they articulate different levels of enunciation of the experience of the illness, when they narrate 'in the first person' (illness) and bring the different stories into dialogue (disease), when the collective thematization (in the third person) is likely to make new categories emerge, destined to support knowledge creation and medical science (sickness) (for further context see: Laplantine, 1992; Depraz, 2014). The circulation of these narrative modes starts in the training workshops on life stories and the lived experience of the subject and moves to the gradual facilitation of putting experience into words, for oneself first and then for others.

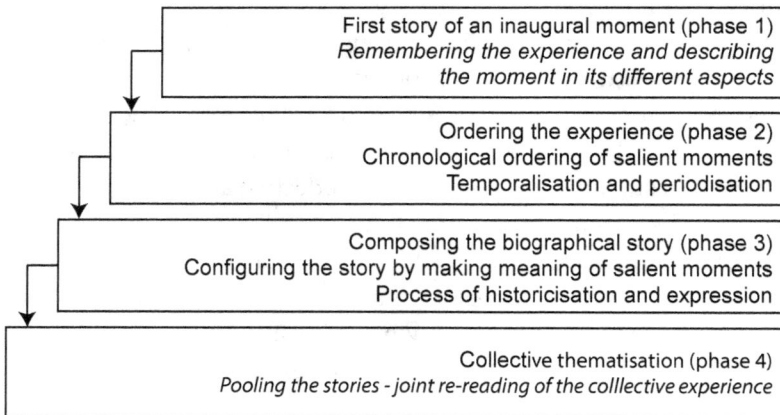

Fig. 2.3 Expressing experience in a story in sessions of expressing and writing life histories.

The approach presented here has four distinct phases:

Phase 1: the subject becomes involved in identifying and remembering a salient moment that s/he tells 'in first person' (Depraz, 2013). This phase of working on one's own includes choosing a moment, remembering and describing it.

Phase 2: the subject presents the story to a sub-group. The interactions that take place following the first narration support the ongoing work of the narrator, remembering the moments that took place during the inaugural experience from which the plot originates. The successive remembrances of an event are chronologically ordered on a timeline that defines the event's place in a sequence of lived experiences.

Phase 3: the temporal plot that lists experiences chronologically prefigures the activity of composing the story. The narrative work is being initiated by the subject, with an exploration of the relationship that connects the different events that occurred during the temporalization of the experience and that has remained in part tacit. In other words, the historicization of the experience proceeds from an activity of configuration by which the different moments that constitute, for the subject, a period in his or her life 'hold together'.

Phase 4: the activity of shaping experience into the form of a story with a biographical dimension takes place at home. The fourth phase of the sessions of expressing and writing life histories is one of socialization. The experience happens in the community through work in a group and the reception of the story in a group, first in the first person, during the telling of the story or parts of it by everyone and in the processes of inter-comprehension that arises from it.

Reciprocity of Levels of Enunciation:
First, Second and Third Person

The expression of experience during a biographical interview, or, as is the case here, during sessions of developing live stories, involves a second transformation of the experience, which occurs when stories are shared with a community. A set of processes take part in this transformation. We will present these succinctly while paying particular attention to the connections between the different modes of expressing stories. There are three modes with three distinct processes and effects:

In first person: in the course of his or her narrative work activity in the first person, the subject is immersed and existentially engaged, searching for propitious words to 'get as close as possible' to what s/he has gone through and felt in the course of the event to be narrated. As mentioned earlier, this work presupposes access to these memories, and requires the person taking time to put them in the form of words through a reflexive grasp of the different moments and by historicizing the events within a duration or a journey. To become tellable, the experience needs to have been expressed in ways the subject considers to be true. This mode of expression is thus strongly infused with subjectivity. What is told contains the various dimensions of the felt experience of the subject, as well as what stands out in it or what has been understood about it. The interpretation of the experience expressed in this way reflects a way of seeing, of signifying and configuring a period of life with a view to making it tellable to loved ones, to peers, to the medical world. Stories shaped in this way become tellable and open possibilities for re-viewing the experience *as* it is brought into dialogue by others *or* owing to the reflexive reciprocity arising during the listening to and receiving of a life story from someone else.

In second person: the socialization of the story opens up different possibilities for re-viewing the story. The meaning-making in the story-making process follows on from bringing the experience into dialogue with others, e.g., during inter-personal meetings, in small or large groups. Dialogue may arise from an exchange of testimonials. This format opens up the possibility of mutual recognition and makes visible the unique nature of the stories, as well as the inter-comprehension of the dimensions of these stories that bring forth our shared humanity: anthropological dimensions of the course of life, the sharing of major historical events, the intrinsic vulnerability of the human condition (illness-events, grief, life-crisis, search for meaning...). The work in the second person thus transforms 'what is considered as true by the subject'. The exchanges and the reception of the story by others open up hitherto unconsidered perspectives for interpreting one's history and integrating social dimensions into the subject's comprehension of life.

In third person: work in the third person consists of the thetic, existential analysis of what appears as the fabric of 'humanity', beyond the uniqueness of everyone's stories. Here, there is potential for defining the recognition of experiential knowledge acquired in situations of vulnerability (Zaccaï-Reyners, 2006), for improving practices and frameworks for facilitation (Jouet, Flora & Las Vergnas, 2010; Jouet

& Flora, 2010) and for upgrading training in healthcare (Thievenaz & Tourette-Turgis, 2015). The third-person mode thus takes as an object what has been told and experienced by the group during the socialization phase, without referring to any specific story. The analysis of the experience thus takes place in the third person, and it includes all who take part in the training or in the 'recognition of experiential learning' sessions (Breton, 2017b).

The diagram below offers a model through which to cross-analyse the narrative modes of the story in the course of the biographical activity, when expressing and writing down experiences in life history sessions:

Phases of passage / The narrative modes	From experience to language: composing the story	Expressing the story : circulation of modes of expression	Socialising the stories: unicity of experiences and reciprocity of the stories
Work "in the first person"	Remembering, temporalising and putting experience into words	Selecting passages of the story with a view to experiencing their expression	Reflexive activity linked to the reception of the experiences: joint and reciprocal attention
Work "in the second person"	First form of socialisation of the story with close ones (friends, family…)	Processes of inter-comprehension through bringing different stories into dialogue	Reflexive reciprocity owing to reception of the stories: processes of inter-comprehension
Work "in the third person"	Suspending generic forms (already there) of the translation of the experience	Collective experience of alternating expression and reception of stories	Collective thematisation owing to the reception of the stories: recognition of solidarity between the stories

Fig. 2.4 Narrative modes and transformations of experience during biographical activity.

The processes of understanding that take place in the course of biographical activity have several results, including the alternation of the modes of expression of experience (the diagram above attempts to visualize this). Bringing experience into dialogue on the other hand proceeds from co-reflexivity. Through this alternation of the narrative modes, the unique experience receives recognition as a singular experience. Understood by the group, which symbolizes the community of peers, it then integrates what Husserl calls 'the life world' (Bégout, 2007) and Dilthey 'vital wholeness' (Zaccaï-Reyners, 1995).

Facilitation Strategies in Therapeutic Education

T he pertinence of narrative work, as seen from this perspective in therapeutic education, can be envisaged in two ways: the first relates to its contribution to the rehabilitation of the agency of the patient; the second concerns the possibilities opened up by the emergence and renewal of medical know-how and expertise. With regard to the question of 'contribution', the development of narrative work requires that the strategic and methodological dimensions of care practices that integrate narrative approaches are clarified. The story told in this chapter has been drawn from Colinet & Avenel (2017), who named it 'a situation of announcing the diagnosis of a rare disease' which they describe in the following way: 'the doctor's practice includes the task of announcing the rare disease, but also and above all, at a medical level, to accompany the patient in the decision-making process s/he needs to go through'. Seen in this way, the narrative work of the patient can contribute to the understanding of the things that support the taking of enlightened decisions in the course of his or her life.

I have tried to show that this work of recognition and rehabilitation of the patient's identity may necessitate the combination of different forms and phases of expression: for oneself (putting experience into the form of a story in the first person); in the patient-carer relationship (bringing stories into dialogue, involvement of a second person); transformations of the experiences (in a group, as the third person). I have also tried to show that the narration of a lived experience proceeds by successive stages that require time: firstly, for the experience to pass into language; secondly, for the story to configure itself; thirdly, for it to be expressed (making time available for this during the patient-carer relationship is then a matter of planning); and fourthly, for a dialogue to develop with a view to recognizing the experiential knowledge that has been acquired.

Describing the dimensions of narrative work, its processes and temporalities does have some implications for healthcare practices. The expression of lived experience does not take place in the organized and orderly fashion of standard practices described in manuals. Welcoming and listening to the patient's lived experience is an immersion in the 'singular' life with the risk of feeling involved:

> [...] person-centered health care cannot be translated into a grammar of
> accountability indispensable for accreditation. The taking into account of
> the particular, on which health care is founded, finds itself diminished at
> the expense of the standardization of practices construed as a guarantee
> of quality, efficiency, throughput and productivity. And that means the
> death knell of much needed creativity. Thus, the possibility of a clinician
> trained in practical wisdom gets eroded. (Weber, 2017, p. 19)

The expression of a patient's lived experiences requires that the
practitioner pay attention to the pain of the 'speaking subject', but also
to his or her suffering, which is often expressed at the beginning in terms
that are close to the intimacy of private language. Remaining sensitive
to what is being said, while facilitating the activity of expressing, with
the aim of individualizing the health journey (*parcours de soins*) requires
from health professionals the ability to be close to the patient without
identifying with the suffering contained in the stories.

In Conclusion:
Towards a Narrative Science in Medical Care?

In this chapter, I have tried to formalize concepts and methods with the
aim of identifying the stakes and the process of narrative work in care
settings. Further work is needed to define the conditions under which
these approaches may become recognized by medical science. One
important task is to research and/or substantiate the complementarities
existing between experiential approaches that involve narrative
practices (Depraz, 2009; Pineau & Legrand, 1993) and experimental
approaches in biomedical science (Lemoine, 2017). A body of research
already undertaken in the biographical domain exists. Many research
papers, in the domain of the expression and writing of life histories
and biographical research in education, interrogate the place allowed
for the lived experience of the patient in medical practice (Dominicé &
Waldvogel, 2009; Delory-Momberger & Tourette-Turgis, 2014; Jouet &
Flora, 2010). A range of research projects have been carried out in the
domain of alcohology (Niewiadomski, 2000; Pentecouteau, 2013) and,
for example, in the field of chronical illnesses.

More recently, innovative work has been published in the field of
micro-phenomenology. This has made it possible to lay the foundations

of a 'science of lived experience' (Petitmengin, Bitbol, & Ollagnier-Beldame, 2015) and to reflect on its uses and potential contribution to healthcare (Petitmengin, 2005). These three authors respond to criticism addressed to introspective approaches in the first person (such as biographical approaches and micro-phenomenology), labelled as 'subjective' and 'mentalist' in experimental science. The authors defend and argue the case for a paradigm of a science of the singular (Vermersch, 2000a & 2003) by seeking to trace a 'middle path' between fragmentary and private subjectivism and reified and entrenched objectivism. Several criteria have been defined for advancing towards a science of the description of lived experience. They include the study of methods of collecting descriptions of lived experience, categories of analysis that allow the formalization of the structures of lived experiences to be recognized in singular stories, and the circulation between first-person and third-person expression. These research projects contribute to strengthen the validation of experiential approaches in health, while at the same time shifting the boundaries of power that organize the legitimacy of knowledge (Foucault, 1969). It is our belief, that this shift is needed for patient experience to become recognized as 'the locus' around which inter-disciplinary work in healthcare is organized.

References

Benaroyo, L. (2013). Le sens de la souffrance. In: Marin, C. & Zaccaï-Reyners, N. (ed), *Souffrance et douleur. Autour de Paul Ricœur*. Paris: Presses Universitaires de France.

Berger, E. (2016). Dans mon corps se fait jour de manière non loquace que quelque chose se prépare..., *Intellectica*, 66: 103–24.

Boucand, M-H. (2010). Le diagnostic d'une maladie rare... perçue comme nomination, au risque d'une identification: Une position fragile du malade. In: Hirsch, E. (ed), *Traité de bioéthique*, Paris: Eres.

Breton, H. (2017a). Expérience du temps et récit de soi au cours de l'activité biographique en formation d'adultes. *Chemins de Formation*, 21: 45–57.

Breton, H. (2017b). Interroger les savoirs expérientiels via la recherche biographique. *Le Sujet dans la Cité*, 8: 25–41.

Charon, R. (2015/2006). *Médecine narrative. Rendre hommage aux histoires de malades*. Oxford: Oxford University Press (*Narrative medicine: Honoring the stories of illness*, 2006 in English).

Colinet, S. & Avenel, C. (2017). Vécus croisés des médecins et des patients. Le cas de l'annonce diagnostique de la maladie rare. *Éducation et socialisation.* http://edso.revues.org/2146

Delory-Momberger, C. & Tourette-Turgis, C. (eds) (2014). Vivre avec la maladie. Expériences Épreuves Résistances. *Le sujet dans la cité.* Paris: LF'Harmattan.

Depraz, N. (2009). *Plus sur Husserl. Une phénoménologie expérientielle.* Paris: Atlande.

Depraz, N. (2013). D'une science descriptive de l'expérience en première personne: pour une phénoménologie expérientielle. *Studia Phaenomenologica,* 13(1): 387–402.

Depraz, N. (ed) (2014). *Première, deuxième, troisième personne.* Bucharest: Zeta books.

Dominicé, P. & Waldvogel, F. (2009). *Dialogue sur la médecine de demain.* Paris: Presses Universitaires de France.

Foucault, M. (1969). *L'archéologie du savoir.* Paris: Gallimard (*The archaeology of knowledge,* 1972, in English).

Illich, I. (1975). *Némésis médicale. L'expropriation de la santé.* Paris: Seuil (*Medical nemesis,* 1975, in English).

Jouet E. & Flora L. (2010). Usagers — experts: La part du savoir des malades dans le système de santé? *Pratiques de Formation — Analyse*: 58–59.

Jouet E., Flora L. & Las Vergnas O. (2010). Construction et reconnaissance des savoirs expérientiels des patients: Note de synthèse. *Pratiques de Formation — Analyse,* 58–59: 13–94.

Lainé, A. (2004). *Faire de sa vie une histoire.* Paris: Desclée de Brouwer.

Laplantine F. (1992). *Anthropologie de la maladie.* Paris: Payot.

Lemoine, M. (2017). *Introduction à la philosophie des sciences médicales.* Paris: Hermann.

Marin, C. & Zaccaï-Reyners, N. (eds) (2013). *Souffrance et douleur. Autour de Paul Ricœur.* Paris: Presses Universitaires de France.

Niewiadomski, C. (2000). *Histoires de vie et alcoolisme.* Paris: Seli Arslan.

Petitmengin, C. (2005). Un exemple de recherche neuro-phénoménologique: L'anticipation des crises d'épilepsie. *Intellectica,* 2005/1(40): 85–92.

Petitmengin, C. (2010). La dynamique pré-réfléchie de l'expérience vécue. *Alter,* 18: 63–89.

Petitmengin, C., Bitbol, M. & Ollagnier-Beldame, M. (2015). Vers une science de l'expérience vécue. *Intellectica,* 2015/2(64): 53–76.

Pentecouteau, H. (2013). *Un anonyme alcoolique: Autobiographie d'une abstinence.* Rennes: Presses Universitaires de Rennes.

Pineau, G. & Legrand, J-L. (1993). *Les histoires de vie*. Paris: Presses Universitaires de France.

Ricœur, P. (1983). *Temps et récit. 1. L'intrigue et le récit historique*. Paris: Seuil.

Ricœur, P. (1986). *Du texte à l'action*. Paris: Seuil.

Ricœur, P. (1992/2013). La souffrance n'est pas la douleur. In: Marin. C. & Zaccaï-Reyners. N. (eds), *Souffrance et douleur. Autour de Paul Ricœur*. Paris: Presses Universitaires de France.

Thievenaz, J. & Tourette-Turgis, C. (2015). *Penser l'expérience du soin et de la maladie: Une approche par l'activité*. Paris: De Boeck.

Vermersch, P. (2000a). Approche du singulier. In: *L'analyse de la singularité de l'action*. Paris: ESF Éditeur.

Vermersch, P. (2000b). *L'entretien d'explicitation*. Paris: ESF Éditeur.

Vermersch, P. (2003). Psycho-phénoménologie de la réduction. *Alter*, 11: 229–55.

Vermersch, P. (2007). Bases de l'auto-explicitation. *Expliciter*, 69. https://www.grex2.com/assets/files/expliciter/bases_de_l_autoexplicitation_un_expliciter_69_mars_2007.pdf

Weber, J-C. (2017). *La consultation*. Paris: Presses Universitaires de France.

Zaccaï-Reyners, N. (1995). *Le monde de la vie. 1. Dilthey et Husserl*. Paris: Cerf.

Zaccaï-Reyners, N. (2006). Respect, réciprocité et relations asymétriques. Quelques figures de la relation de soin. *Esprit*, 321: 95–108.

3. Narratives of Fundamentalism, Negative Capability and the Democratic Imperative

Alan Bainbridge and Linden West

Alan Bainbridge and Linden West offer a theoretical discussion of (mainly) contemporary British society with particular reference to Stoke-on-Trent, the home of the Workers' Education Association and a city still struggling to adjust following the decline of the pottery industry. They posit the growth of fundamentalism as a search for certainties and propose that Keats' notion of negative capability (the ability to accept uncertainty) may offer an alternative lens.

The Starting Point: Fundamentalism Is Ordinary

The notion that 'we', as individuals, whole groups or cultures, possess the truth and nothing but the truth, unlike the other and otherness, seems to be a universal discursive tendency, colonizing diverse minds and hearts, across different historical times and geographical spaces. The truth and nothing but the truth of politics, religion, economics, and of myth and diverse ideologies — here lies the province of the fundamentalist; and maybe the fundamentalist lurking in every one of our psychologies and cultures. Fundamentalism, we argue, is quite ordinary.

The word fundamentalism was coined in California and its origins lie in Protestant movements in nineteenth-century America. These movements consisted of people who wanted to assert the inerrancy of the

https://doi.org/10.11647/OBP.0203.03

Bible — the direct creation of the world and humanity *ex nihilo* by God as opposed to Darwinian evolution — and the authenticity of miracles and the Virgin birth. But fundamentalism and related discourses of absolute truth encompass very different phenomena (Ruthven, 2007). Following Wittgenstein, the word, heuristically, is helpful in a search for discursive similarities across different forms. Of course, not every person whom we call a fundamentalist reaches for a Kalashnikov or pipe bomb. But, broadly speaking, fundamentalism can be thought of as a retreat from engagement with others and otherness, rooted, perhaps, in feelings of disrespect, marginalization and or psychological or even cultural vulnerability. It works at the level of discourse or metanarrative, colonizing inner space: the other — whether Jew, 'White trash', 'people of colour', Muslims, working class people, etc. — is to blame for a range of ills. Fundamentalism also presents itself as beyond contestation, that there is simply no alternative available, as in the kind of market fundamentalism pervading the contemporary world. In the case of racism and Islamism, people turn to those who think like themselves and hostility develops towards the different other, or ideas and experiences that challenge their view of the world. Fundamentalism among some men, for instance, can represent a reaction to the terror of seeming feminine and unmanly — as in extreme fascistic organizations (Flemmen, 2014).

The dynamics of fundamentalism can encompass processes we might recognize in ourselves, at least at times: when stress and uncertainty seem overwhelming, when we feel out of our depth and can't cope, and when we may grab at facts or certainties to help manage anxiety. Traits such as dogmatism, rigidity and a need for order and power, can underpin a wide psycho-political spectrum of people and groups. The need for external sources of absolute authority or truth, or for discourses of complete certainty — for the mythical texts of Communism, Islamism or Catholicism — may be a kind of defence against not knowing, as well as being a widespread human phenomenon. So is the tendency, individually and collectively, to split off parts of ourselves that we fear or don't like, such as the capacity for violence or greed, and to project these onto others.

We can factor 'market fundamentalism' into our wordplay, with its dogmatism, its tendency towards absolute truths and its disparagement of the poor as deviant and wholly responsible for their own condition. According to academic and psychoanalyst Paul Verhaeghe (2014), this way of thinking casts the unsuccessful as deficient in some way, embedding and exacerbating feelings of confusion and despair engendered by disadvantage. Turning inwards, people feel increasingly isolated and this insularity extends into institutional life. When educational and care establishments function as businesses and financial reward depends on performance, team spirit and cooperative endeavour are replaced by competition and personal enterprise. This individualism penetrates wider society making it harder to develop and sustain deep, even loving, relationships and, thus, our lives are colonized by the performative imperative.

Verhaeghe's main concern is how social change has led to what he calls a psychic crisis and altered the way we think about ourselves. He has investigated the effects of neoliberal fundamentalism for more than thirty years, concluding that the context in which we live heavily influences who we become, and that neoliberal practices have negative consequences on mental health, for example, the development of narcissistic tendencies.

He claims that 'dependence is spineless' and believes that we must make our mark, stand up for ourselves and do our own thing (Verhaeghe, 2014, p. 13). Such individualism and the disintegration of collective notions of well-being can exact a terrible price in suffering and distress. So too might the tendency to blame the poor for their condition and the negative stereotyping of whole communities. Some turn in response to the racist gang or extreme Islamist group: having a gang and mythic narrative of our own is one response to anomie and alienation (West, 2016).

We suggest that an important antidote to fundamentalist tendencies, of whatever kind, lies in what the English poet John Keats called 'negative capability'. This is the capacity to live in doubt and not knowing, as part of a process of coming to know and being open to what may be more truthful, worthwhile, even beautiful. Such capability, we argue, is grounded in the quality of our relationships, which encompass educational settings as well as families, communities and those closest to us. We explore one manifestation of negative capability in a form of liberal workers' education that emerged in the United Kingdom at the end of the nineteenth and early twentieth centuries. But we also suggest, paradoxically, that we might have need of our fundamentalisms, at times, in biographical trajectories, as a means to escape restrictive and stifling cultures of conformity. Adolescent flirtations with various forms of extreme politics is one example. However, we regard this as part of the difficult business of growing up, and as a stage in the struggle for more open, reflexive and dialogical ways of knowing.

Distress in a City

Our central argument is the outcome of historical reappraisal and in-depth, auto/biographical narrative research into racism and fundamentalism in a post-industrial city, Stoke-on-Trent, in the English Midlands, where Linden was born and raised (West, 2016). The research included in-depth narrative interviews with autodidacts, schooled in workers' education and the wider Labour movement. He revisited the history of workers' education, including his own writing (West, 1972), in the light of the city's post-industrial distress, encompassing racism on the public housing estate where he had lived. The process was stimulated by Jonathan Rose's reassessment of workers' education (Rose, 2010) and its place in the development of British social democracy, alongside the insights of the historian Lawrence Goldman (1995; 2013). Rose drew on diverse personal testimonies and forms of life writing in his re-evaluation of the Workers' Educational Association (WEA) while Goldman interrogated the historical interpretation of historians like Roger Fieldhouse and Stuart Macintyre. Linden was once modishly dismissive of forms of workers' education. But then he was a child of the 1960s, when space opened for critical thinking alongside new forms of fundamentalism, hubris and dismissiveness towards previous generations. This is a central theme of his recent book (West, 2016).

The basic contention of the chapter is that we are all prone, at times, to cling to what we conceive to be the truth and nothing but that truth, which can be illuminated through auto/biographical and historical enquiry. In the history of workers' education, for instance, in the United Kingdom, non-conformist autodidacts could sometimes be dogmatic, rooted in religion or hard, structuralist readings of Marxism. Their questioning was paradoxical: challenging conventional wisdoms but inflexible in their response to others. They might quote texts with quasi-religious fervour in workers' classes. Their Marxism could involve an extremely mechanical version of the materialist conception of history, in which human activity was controlled by economic forces independent of human volition (Macintyre, 1980).

Workers' education in the UK was characterized by a mix of Enlightenment idealism, the aspirations of democratic socialism, as well as Marxism, and for many, a religious belief in the potential divinity in everyone. It was a social as much as an educational movement. Jonathan Rose (2010) argues that it played a key role in creating the welfare state after the Second World War. Workers' education could model, in microcosm, the good, fraternal and equal dialogical and democratic society. These adult classes represented a social and educational experiment open to the marginalized, with an equality of status between students that encouraged freedom of expression and enquiry, tolerance and respect, alongside the turbulence generated in the clash of ideas and difference. But difference and dispute did not, in general, degenerate into 'I-it' objectification, at least in any permanent way. At their best the classes were communities of imaginative, caring, committed and thoughtful students, in which all could be teachers as well as learners.

Workers' education, in the form of tutorial classes, once thrived in Stoke. The first ever university workers' tutorial class took place there in 1908 sponsored by the University of Oxford. Thirty or so worker-students met on Friday evenings for two hours, over a period of years, with their tutor, R. H. Tawney, subsequently a distinguished economic historian. The tutorial classes constituted an alliance, unusual in European popular education, between progressive elements in universities and workers' organizations. The classes were free from prescribed curricula and members were encouraged to explore issues in their working lives from the perspectives of history, politics, economics and literature. Fortnightly essays were required, and the standard of some of these was high (Goldman, 1995; West, 1972, 2017). There were no formal examinations or qualifications due to a desire to eliminate competition and vocationalism from the classroom (Rose, 2010; West, 1972).

The first students met in the pottery town of Longton that was to become part of the new city of Stoke-on-Trent. They were potters, miners, clerks, shop assistants and elementary school teachers, women as well as men (West, 1972). Many came from nonconformist backgrounds, from families that encouraged them to think for themselves. The Marxist Social Democratic Federation (SDF) made up the nucleus of the first class. The Social Democratic Federation was formed in 1883 under the leadership of Henry Hyndman, who was the son of a businessman and became a journalist and political agitator (Macintyre, 1980). The Federation was strongly opposed to the British Liberal Party of the time, and its programme was progressive, calling for a forty-eight-hour working week, the abolition of child labour, compulsory free secular education, equality for women and the nationalization of the means of production, distribution and exchange. Some members of the SDF, according to Stuart Macintyre, held an extremely 'mechanical version of the materialist conception of history' in which the whole of human experience was controlled by economic forces independent of human agency (Macintyre, 1980, p. 17). Education, politics and consciousness were mere epiphenomena of the techniques and relations of production. Such students could be rigid in their economic doctrines (ibid.), and this rigidity played out in the tutorial classes.

However, Tawney (1917) thought the tutorial class 'movement' and the WEA a successful 'experiment in democratic education' (Taylor & Steele, 2011, pp. 32, 30). According to him, it was founded on three core principles. First, the opposition to revolutionary violence: 'one may not do evil that good should come', in Cobbett's dictum of a century before. Second, no institution, however perfect in conception, could be made to work effectively by individuals whose morality was inadequate. Third, where a sound morality was lacking, this could be forged in a community of scholars seeking truth and the common good (Dennis & Halsey, 1988). There was an Aristotelian ideal at work, as well as Oxford idealism (Goldman, 1995): notions of the fully developed person living in communities, building and sustaining virtue in relationship — communities cultivating not self- but other-regardedness — directing themselves to higher aims than the purely egotistic or narcissistic (Dennis & Halsey, 1988). The idealists at Oxford who influenced Tawney were opposed to individualism, utilitarianism and social atomism and drew on German philosophers, especially Kant and Hegel, and the notion that individuals are best understood and can best realize their potential in the collective. Men and women were part of webs of social and political, as well as economic relationships from which they could not be divorced for analytic or practical purposes. They were linked together by values, institutions and diverse patterns of association rather than economics alone.

Tawney himself had doubts about the tutorial classes, not least the intellectual and emotional effort required from the worker students. Tawney was also far from a naïve idealist and there were 'limits to his moralising', as Lawrence Goldman notes (Goldman, 1995, p. 160). He was aware that the same spirit of non-conformity that drove some of the worker students could also narrow viewpoints and bring the tendency to over-proselytize, making it difficult to engage in dialogue and be respectful to difference.

Breakdown, and Taking Tea

It is interesting that many of the worker-students admired tutors like Tawney, who remained steadfast as well as respectful even when harangued by a fundamentalist student. Leftist fundamentalists, sometimes from the Social Democratic Federation and later the Communist Party, though not exclusively so, might quote from texts like *Das Capital* with religious fervour. The other students noted how Tawney remained steadfast in the face of provocation. One recalled a particular Marxist — the SDF could dominate the early tutorial classes — challenging point after point and referring to classic Marxist texts. Tawney took it in his stride but insisted that there were other points of view. The student accused the tutor of hopping around like a bird, from twig to twig, and a sense of bad temper pervaded the room. However, Tawney insisted that everyone, including his challenger, take tea together afterwards and tell stories, read poetry and sing songs. A shared humanity and a spirit of fraternity were restored (Rose, 2010, p. 266; West, 2017). The class stayed together despite the local secretary of the SDF demanding that his members leave for fear of contamination (Goldman, 2013).

John Holford (2015) usefully reminds us that these were classes, not lectures, and ideas were explored and developed in discussion. The processes of education were democratized — students engaged in research and discovery through using original source material, like historical documents, rather than simply relying on secondary texts. The fundamental aim of the tutorial classes was to make university education available to all people in their localities, in pedagogically democratic and dialogical ways. The movement was about building social solidarities rather than the contemporary obsession with social mobility. Humanity, risk taking, and engagement with otherness, and challenges to fundamentalism, of whatever kind, constituted a cultural as well as collective challenge to the seductions of omniscience.

The Seductions of Fundamentalism

We are suggesting that a long, never-to-be-completed struggle is to be fought against fundamentalism, in ourselves as well as others. Psychoanalyst Adam Phillips (2012) has considered the relationship between the internal world and the appeal of fundamentalism. Drawing on clinical work, over many years, he discusses the problems of 'not getting it' in intimate or wider social life. Not 'getting it', feeling confused, misunderstood or inadequate can have devastating effects in early life. We don false mantles in the hope of gaining the other's attention and regard. 'Getting it' — feeling understood by a powerful other — means potentially not feeling humiliated or diminished. 'Not getting it', however — not understanding what is going on and feeling lost and frantic, like the child who struggles to understand a mother's depression — is a widespread human experience. What we may then long for, as mentioned above, is a gang and a mythic narrative of our own. A dream of like-mindedness is the dream in which the possibility of not getting it disappears. We can be attracted to groups of the like-minded because the issue of not getting it is resolved in the abolition of complexity. The defence against not getting it, or not knowing, evokes the seduction of certainty. Hannah Arendt (1958) observed how opinion can solidify into ideology and fundamentalism, which demand assent and certainty. There are fundamentalisms of the left as well as of the political and ideological right.

The process involves creating rigid boundaries between 'us' and 'them', and between our self of present understanding and a potential self of a different way of seeing. Fundamentalist groups offer compelling 'truths' of how the other is to blame — whether in the 'moral corruption' of the West or the 'greedy Jew' — and how 'our' group is good. The trouble is that this involves splitting into an idealized self or selves, and the projection onto the other of aspects we most dislike in ourselves. No hard work is required in this anti-education, because the fault lies elsewhere. The turn to fundamentalism, old and new, brings for its disciples the feeling of getting it, of belonging, of recognition in a grand if delusional way. We are made to feel part of something that is essential to creating a purified world. Education, however, as in the workers' tutorial classes, gives us choice — to decide whether or not we love the world enough to wish to seek to understand and take responsibility for it, as well as to engage with the other in humane and open ways (Nixon, 2015).

Therefore, we suggest there are psychosocial patterns across fundamentalism in its many guises. Wittgenstein thought it important to play with similarities in the use of a word: a word such as 'games', for instance, in its various guises. Ball games, word games, Olympic Games are all different but there can be family resemblances (Ruthven, 2007). There may be resemblances between market and Islamic fundamentalism, or between the zealots in a tutorial class and (only occasionally we hope), our own behaviour. Islamic fundamentalism may, like forms of leftist ideology, exploit the power of trauma and myth in the processes of radicalization. If Islam is full of narratives of mercy and tolerance, as Christianity and socialism are, all too have a darker side (Hassan & Weiss, 2015). The dark side is revealed in the worship of violence, the degeneration of the ideals of the French Revolution into slaughter, and the grotesque narcissism of small difference that continues to haunt the progressive imagination.

Market fundamentalism might appear to be different with regards to violence. But it too employs powerful mythology, grounded in social Darwinism and the cult of success, in ways that have penetrated to the heart of modern Western societies. The market is sovereign and can provide for all human needs: consumption is crucial, as is the consumer (rather than the citizen). It works through appealing, via instruments of persuasion, to a desire for status, triumph, power, sexual success and transcendental performance (Verhaeghe, 2014). It may also, in its manipulation of images, employ violence in video games or social media to sell products, using heroes, myths and triumphal sexual conquest to make its pitch. Thus Mirowski (2013), drawing on Hayek's free market ideas, argues that neoliberalism is profoundly anti-educational in its assumptions and practices: encouraging the prioritization of the market and consumption as the only good. Too much education of a questioning kind is antithetical to the efficient functioning of markets and the cultivation of desire, discontent and materialistic illusions on which conspicuous consumption depends.

We suggest that the importance of the open, diverse social and educational group for human flourishing mirrors the psychoanalytic stress on the cosmopolitan, democratic psyche or Biesta's normative subjectification (Biesta, 2011). Andrew Samuels (1993) has written that the cultural diversity of the population is not a disaster, but a challenge and opportunity for healthy internal life. How to remain open to others and acknowledge and learn from difference, rather than seeing it as a threat, becomes the central issue for us all. The metaphor of the psyche as a theatre helps us to comprehend this idea: internal worlds are constituted and peopled by varied 'objects' drawn from intersubjective relationships — objects that encourage or constrain and enable us to take risks with the unknown and the other.

But, as indicated, there can be a more positive and developmental dimension to our relationship with fundamentalism. An insight into this emerged in a discussion on the social unconscious at the ESREA Triennial Conference in 2017 (Salling Olesen et al., 2017). Lynn Froggett, in response to Linden's paper, described how she embraced the Socialist Workers Party, at one stage in her life, as a kind of antidote to the stifling narrowness of a provincial background. She used its discursive forms, however 'fundamentalist' these might have been, as a good object, in psychoanalytic terms, to break free from certain kinds of conformity and to play with new discourses. We might need a more sympathetic educational reading of fundamentalist tendencies, one that can be biographically developmental. The capacity for negative capability might, in such terms, be a lifelong struggle.

Negative Capability and the Unconscious

I t is worth returning to Keats' emblematic consideration of the struggle to remain engaged with the verisimilitude of beauty. He refers to this in a letter (Keats, 1817/2018) to his brothers and offers a helpful metaphor, especially when combined with psychoanalytic understandings of the interplay between internal and external worlds. Keats introduces the principle of negative capability as his letter ends — it seemingly emerges from a discussion on the qualities required for 'achievement' in literature. Yet the narrative of the letter is initially less whimsical, indeed, rather prosaic, as tales are told of endless dining out while bemoaning such conviviality ('for I have been out too much lately'). Keats is critical of a painting he had recently seen that offered 'nothing to be intense on', arguing that the excellence of art is in its intensity. 'I imagine a painting, that in common-parlance, is what it is'; there being no depth of hidden meaning, no salacious seduction, for Keats, 'no women one feels mad to kiss'. The painting disappoints on all levels as it has an 'unpleasantness without momentous depth of speculation excited, in which to bury its repulsiveness'. There appears to be a disconnect between the realness of the painting and the emotion it could, should evoke, if it were good. Despite being an actual painting, existing in an actual world, there is for Keats something viscerally lacking in it, and it is this something that can make a painting 'intense'.

There is a similar story told in the same letter, not of painting, or literature, but of how to enjoy the company of others. Keats acknowledges that he has dined out too much, and maybe has become weary of company. He complains to his brothers how tiresome it is to be subjected to 'wit' and not 'humour'. The witty say things 'that make one start, without making one feel' and are overly concerned with fashion and etiquette. There is a superficiality in Keats' description of these dining partners and he would much rather be in 'low company' where humorous conversation predominated, not fashion and clever verbal games. For Keats, an enjoyable meal is one where the company is unpretentious and less likely to be persuaded by the continuing ephemerality of fashion. The illustrations provided in Keats' letter represent the interplay between an encounter with the external world, the painting or these companions, in conjunction with an internal/emotive response. It is at this stage of the letter that Keats introduces negative capability, and at this stage of our chapter we return to psychoanalysis to make links between such negative capability, Klein's theory of mental positions and fundamentalism.

Unlike Freud, Klein (1998) assumed that the ego and its defences were active in the infant from birth, and that mature mental development equated to a resolution of internal desires with external realities. Klein proposed two mental positions that corresponded to the developing relationship between the internal self and the external other: the early paranoid-schizoid, and a latter, more mature depressive position. The very young paranoid-schizoid infant has the experience of hunger, or the desire to be cuddled, but as yet no symbolic way of communicating this to an 'other'. As a result, there is a conflict between the individual's internal experience and the reality of an 'other'-dominated external world. The infant also cannot distinguish between the self and other and inhabits a frustrating world, with feelings, without memory, which are unknown and seemingly unknowable. It is this paranoid-schizoid mode of functioning with which Keats' negative capability struggles, staying with uncertainty, doubt and myth without access to fact or reason. What is significant is that the infant does not stay stuck in paranoid-schizoid thinking, and can be enabled, with the help of an empathic other, to move towards a depressive, more integrated position where needs can be satisfied, if always provisionally, and where the world is a mix of nurture and frustration.

The achievement of the human infant is the creative act of successfully negotiating the paranoid-schizoid position, in relationship, informed by the symbols and metaphors offered by language, to be able to inhabit the psychic reality of the depressive position. From the perspective of the depressive position the infant can utilize language, alongside feelings, to think about a world previously experienced through feelings alone, and importantly to distinguish between the needs of self and other. Therefore, the shift from paranoid-schizoid to depressive thinking is a move from selfish frustration, with the creative use of language, to a position where metaphor and abstract thinking can be used to integrate the needs of the self and others. Despite Klein locating her description of the paranoid-schizoid position in very early infant experience, it is largely assumed (see Bion, 1963) that this and the depressive position are two mental states that exist across the lifespan; and can be thought about as normative as well as pathological (Britton, 1998, cited in Harrang, 2012). The thinking characteristic of both the paranoid-schizoid and depressive positions provides insight into unconscious processes that may help us theorize the nature of fundamentalism, as against an emotional and intellectual openness in the history of workers' education.

As we have suggested, paranoid-schizoid thinking is a frustrating state, without memory, waiting for meaning to evolve, during which the infant or the adult experiences feelings that are as yet unarticulated. For the adult, negative capability — where unknowns are sensed and thought about with others in the right environment — needs time to emerge. Bion (1970, cited in Harrang, 2012) argues that this is the space in which creativity emerges, leading to the depressive position, and it is a normal part of thinking throughout the lifespan. Britton (1998, cited in Harrang, 2012) acknowledges that each of Klein's positions can also be experienced pathologically: for example, if the frustrations inherent within paranoid-schizoid thinking, or the experience of negative capability, are not resolved, then the adult will exaggerate good and bad feelings. Unconscious defences operate to protect the self, resulting in primitive 'splitting', where good feelings are introjected, and bad feelings projected outwards onto external objects. Therefore, the self is experienced as good and the other as bad, and a fundamentalist, black and white/right and wrong splitting predominates. Interestingly, Britton also recognizes a potential pathology when the more thoughtful, mature depressive position is used to defend against uncertainty, as well as the anxiety of the paranoid-schizoid position. Again, the fundamentalist can be seen to inhabit such positions and to hold on, in an extreme and exaggerated manner, to the security of established belief system(s), or to grab at new ones, without properly internalizing and digesting their complex qualities and discursive potential.

The fundamentalist is not therefore to be seen as simply 'stuck' in a primitive paranoid-schizoid position, unable to access and use negative capability; for it is equally possible that certainty in more mature depressive thinking provides sufficient motivation to defend against the potential uncertainty of negative capability. Keats' letter contains both possibilities: the depressive certainty of the witty fashionable bore, and the painting that, despite being accurate, does not evoke deep emotion. He also references Coleridge's attempt to describe beauty 'pursed through Volumes' that ultimately 'obliterates all consideration' and it is in the lines before this that Keats introduces negative capability. It is here that Keats appreciates the creative accomplishments that can be achieved, if only artists or dinner companions could stay with uncertainty and allow thoughts to emerge in a world that is complex as well as psychically and psychosocially real, satisfying and frustrating.

Conclusion: Negative Capability

Notwithstanding, being colonized by the truth and nothing but a truth denotes the opposite of certainty or epistemological substance — it represents a fragile and uncertain subjectivity in need of externally derived authority, whether of Marxism, religion or whatever. But 'liberal' workers' education provided a cultural and educational space to engage with fundamentalisms in various guises, including racism and bigotry, and to move towards what Melanie Klein (1998) called the depressive position. This involves some acceptance of the good and not so good in every one of us, and thus greater openness to the other and otherness (see Nancy Dobrin, 1990, for instance, for one compelling account). Here was a cultural space of sufficient equality, respectfulness (including towards the bigot), dialogue and truth-seeking. At best the process generated what critical theorist Axel Honneth (2007; 2009) calls self/other recognition, including the capacity to recognize the other by being fully recognized oneself. Through life writing and auto/biographical narrative research, we bear witness to how educators like Tawney and the worker-students created a good-enough space to question and transcend discursive assumptions and engage in the eclectic symbolic world, and its otherness, in emotionally, intellectually and discursively liberating ways.

How best to conclude our discussion of negative capability? Stephen Hebron (2009, 2017) writes of how, in December 1817, Keats' letter to his brothers talked of returning from a Christmas pantomime and discussed various subjects: several thoughts dovetailed in his mind, Keats said, and he wondered about the qualities that went to form great and satisfying achievement especially in literature. Shakespeare possessed such qualities in abundance, but less so with Coleridge, he thought. Keats concluded that negative capability was at the core of this quality: when a person can stay in uncertainties, or mysteries and doubts, without irritably reaching after fact, reason or certainty. His language, although not immediately clear, is suggestive and idiosyncratic. Obviously, the word 'negative' is not used pejoratively but to communicate a notion that a person's potential is defined by what he or she does not possess. Essential to literary achievement, Keats insists, is a certain passivity, a willingness to wait and let what is mysterious or doubtful remain just that. It might in short be best to break off from a relentless search for knowledge, and instead contemplate something beautiful and true, in the Romantic spirit; 'a fine verisimilitude'. The experience and intuitive appreciation of the beautiful, or of the potential beauty of a different idea or way of seeing, is central to poetic talent, but also to democratic educational sensibilities (Hebron, 2009; 2017).

Moreover, such an idea finds deep traction in psychoanalytic thinking about struggles for profounder forms of change. Any new idea presents itself as an emotional experience, which can be beautiful but also threatening. Pleasure and pain — of losing cognitive certainty — may co-exist (Meltzer & Harris Williams, 1988). In the workers' tutorial classes, as well as in other creative struggles in literature or in therapeutic settings, negative capability might just thrive, sufficiently, to enable a person to live in doubt, and then to experience, over time, a fundamental change in a way of seeing and feeling, despite how unsettling the process might be. The culture of learning groups matters in such a process: a spirit of fraternity, and the capacity of a teacher to live in uncertainty, matter greatly. Such cultures were at the heart of Tawney's successful experiment in democratic education and may lie at the core of all good-enough, inclusive and dialogical learning groups.

References

Arendt, H. (1958). *The human condition.* Chicago: University of Chicago Press.

Biesta, G. (2011). *Learning democracy in school and society: Education, lifelong learning and the politics of citizenship.* Boston: Sense.

Bion, W.R. (1963). *Elements of psycho-analysis.* London: Heinemann.

Dennis, N. & Halsey, A.H. (1988). *English ethical socialism; from Thomas More to R.H. Tawney*. Clarendon Press: Oxford.

Dobrin, N. (1980). *Happiness*. Kings Langley: Sacombe Press.

Fieldhouse, R. (1995). Conformity and contradiction in English responsible body adult education, *Studies in the Education of Adults*, 17(2): 123.

Fieldhouse, R. (1996). The Workers' Educational Association. In: Fieldhouse, R. and Associates, *A history of modern British adult education*. Leicester: NIACE.

Flemmen, H. (2014). Fundamentalism, Nazism and inferiority. In: Auestad, L. (ed), *Nationalism and the body politic*. London: Karnac. https://doi.org/10.4324/9780429477522

Goldman, L. (1995). *Dons and workers: Oxford and adult education since 1850*. Oxford: Clarendon Press.

Goldman, L. (2013). *The life of R.H. Tawney: Socialism and history*. London: Bloomsbury Academic.

Harrang, C.E. (2012). Printing poppies: On the relationship between concrete and metaphorical thinking. In: Frosch, A. (ed), *Absolute truth and unbearable psychic pain: Psycho-analytic perspectives on concrete experiences*. London: Karnac.

Hassan, H. & Weiss, M. (2015). *ISIS: Inside the army of terror*. New York: Regan Arts. https://doi.org/10.1111/1468-2346.12426

Hebron S. (2009). *John Keats, a poet and his manuscripts*. London: The British Library.

Hebron, S. (2017). *John Keats and 'negative capability'*. https://www.bl.uk/romantics-and-victorians/articles/john-keats-and-negative-capability#sthash.dpuf

Holford, J. (2015). Adult and higher education in the early work of R.H. Tawney. At the Standing Conference of University Teachers and Researchers in the Education of Adults (SCUTREA). It's all Adult Education. The University of Leeds, 7–9 July.

Honneth, A. (2007). *Disrespect: The normative foundations of critical theory*. Cambridge: Polity Press.

Honneth, A. (2009). *Pathologies of Reason: On the legacy of critical theory*. New York: Columbia University Press.

Keats, J. (1817/2018). On Negative Capability: Letter to George and Tom Keats, 22 December 1817. https://www.poetryfoundation.org/articles/69384/selections-from-keatss-letters

Klein, M. (1998). *Love, guilt and reparation and other works, 1921–1945*. London: Virago.

Macintyre, S. (1980). *A proletarian science: Marxism in Britain, 1917–1933*. Cambridge: Cambridge University Press.

McIlroy, J. (1993). The Unknown Raymond Williams. In: McIlroy, J. & Westwood, S. (eds), *Border country, Raymond Williams in adult education*. Leicester: NIACE.

Meltzer, D. & Harris Williams, M. (1988). *The apprehension of beauty: The role of aesthetic conflict in development, art and violence*. London: The Clunie Press with the Roland Harris Trust.

Mirowski, R. (2013). *Never let a serious crisis go to waste*. London: Verso.

Nixon, J. (2015). Hanna Arendt: Thinking versus evil. *Times Higher Education*, 25 February.

Rose, J. (2010). *The intellectual life of the British working classes*, 2nd edn. New York: Yale University Press.

Ruthven, M. (2007). *Fundamentalism: A very short introduction*. Oxford: Oxford University Press.

Phillips, A. (2012). *Missing out: In praise of the unlived life*. London: Hamish Hamilton.

Salling Olesen, H. (2017). The socially unconscious and the sources for social change, a symposium in honour of Kirsten Weber, ESREA Triennial Conference. Maynooth, September.

Samuels, A. (1993). *The political psyche*. London: Routledge.

Tawney, R.H. (1914). An experiment in democratic education, *Political Quarterly*, cited in Taylor, R. & Steele, T. (2011) *British labour and higher education, 1945–2000: Ideologies, policies and practice*. London: Continuum.

Taylor, R. & Steele, T. (2011). *British labour and higher education, 1945–2000: Ideologies, policies and practice*. London: Continuum.

Verhaeghe, P. (2014). *What about me? The struggle for identity in a market-based society*. London: Scribe.

West, L. (1972). The Tawney legend re-examined. *Studies in Adult Education*, 4(2): 105–19.

West, L. (2016). *Distress in the city; racism, fundamentalism and a democratic education*. London Trentham/UCL Books.

West, L. (2017). Resisting the enormous condescension of posterity: Richard Henry Tawney, Raymond Williams and the long struggle for a democratic education. *International Journal of Lifelong Education*, 36(1–2), January-April: 129–44.

4. Understandings of the Natural World from a Generational Perspective

Hazel R. Wright

Hazel R. Wright uses a recall approach to gather and compare the distinctive views of nature held by four members of different generations within the same family. The narratives collected are examined for evidence of residual learning, to judge the respective importance of formal schooling, real experiences and family practices when forming individual worldviews of nature.

In this chapter, I consider how humans relate to the natural world in which they live. To do this, I first present a brief overview of the classic discourses of nature that were dominant in different historical periods. I then examine data I collected through a small contemporary empirical study in an English context. This study sought personal views of nature, to see how these were formed and whether they reflect the historical discourses. To capture changing time frames, I talked to people from different generations. Assuming that individual viewpoints will be mediated by everyday encounters — with social discourses, educational opportunities and within the family and local environment — I chose members of four generations of the same family, seeking to identify how their funds of knowledge came into play (Vélez-Ibáñez & Greenberg, 1992).

Nature is present in everyone's life, even in the most urbanized contexts there is 'unofficial countryside', marginal sites of wasteland

 https://doi.org/10.11647/OBP.0203.04

where wildlife thrives (Lorimer, 2008, p. 2042), so, as a topic, nature allowed the possibility of different types of learning, within schools, homes and the community. However, the family grouping offered an element of geographical congruence as all members lived in similar rural environments in the south-west of England. As data collection relied on retrospection and recall, the process created a space in which to consider residual learning and whether understandings of nature developed from formal, non-formal, informal or incidental learning opportunities (Foley, 2004). I was interested to see whether ideas about nature were predominantly passed down through family practices, learned in school or simply absorbed through contact with the natural world. At the analysis stage Bamberg's (2014) distinction between Capital-D and small-d discourses merited attention, as will become clear.

Classic Discourses on Nature

T he geographer Noel Castree (2005, p.xvii) claims nature to be 'one of the most widely talked about and investigated things there is', and one that 'continues to be understood in a multitude of ways, many of them incompatible'. Yet it is also 'one of the most important topics in our lives' (p.xix). In practice it is 'a portmanteau word or what social scientists call a "chaotic concept"' (p. 36). Despite this chaotic characteristic, I sought an overview for nature discourses (in the sense of plants and animals) and found a starting point in Glacken's (1999) work; a framework around which I could assemble a partially chronological account.

In his *Reflections on the History of Western Attitudes to Nature*, Glacken (1999, p. 1) identified four underpinning discourses that developed over time but still have currency. First, he describes an historical focus on the interrelationships between humans and other life forms, more easily termed the Supremacy discourse. Next, he identifies a desire to clarify connections within the natural world, which I refer to as the Classificatory discourse. He then considers the position whereby human influences effect changes to the natural world, for brevity the Exploitative discourse, and finally, discusses 'subjective, emotional and [a]esthetic reactions to nature' (ibid., p. 15) for simplicity, the

Appreciative discourse. These discourses were dominant in different periods through history but linger on in different guises even now.

The Supremacy Discourse

T his discourse is belief based. It unequivocally places a divine being in a superior position and views humankind as the embodiment of celestial power. Living things have a natural order. Although Glacken acknowledges that such ideas were modified as time passed, he sees anthropocentric conceptualizations as clearly rooted in the classical world and in line with biblical interpretations of nature where the human is unequivocally positioned at the apex, answerable only to an omnipotent deity. A variation of this belief, Creationism, sees God as the absolute creator of heaven and earth and all living things (Ruse, 2018) and interprets the Bible literally to attribute the development of the world to a six-day period (Numbers, 1992). Despite being 'a commonly and loosely used term' (Emerson & Hartman, 2006, p. 128), religious fundamentalism, as 'a militant truth claim which derives its claim to power from non-disputable, higher revelation, people, values, or ideologies' (Schirrmacher, 2013, p. 13) is a contemporary belief system that attributes absolute power to a supreme deity. It may also be a protest against the secularity of modernist societies (Emerson & Hartman, 2006, p. 128) for it can be seen as 'the rational response of traditionally religious peoples to social, political and economic changes that downgrade and constrain the role of religion in the public world' (Bruce, 2000, p. 117).

The Classificatory Discourse

G lacken's second discourse is knowledge based. It also builds on ideas established in Greek, and possibly earlier, civilizations' desires to rank life forms, but came to the fore in the European Renaissance of the seventeenth century, with Francis Bacon a keen protagonist (Pyenson & Sheets-Pyenson, 1999, p. 251). Knowledge of nature had its roots in natural theology (immanent in the first, supremacy, discourse) — the descriptive works of Ray, White, Paley and Muir — but also in the classificatory activities of Linnaeus, Humboldt, and Darwin, for example.

Darwin's *On the Origin of Species* (1859/2009) is based on empirical observation and, with its evolutionary stance, explains both change over time (tracing the origins of humankind to their ancestors, the apes) and variations within species according to genetic mutation (Desmond, 2019). The formal learning of plant and animal names and labels continued within education throughout the modern period, ensuring a 'solid and unchallengeable foundation' for precise communication among new generations of scientists (Phillips, 1989, p. 59).

The Exploitative Discourse

This discourse has a functional basis. The intention to harness nature to the service of mankind, named by Worster (1994/1977) the Imperialist discourse, is also attributed to Francis Bacon, although, again, such ideas stem from classical times (Bunnin & Yu, 2004), and his objective was simply to encourage nature to 'yield to us her fruits' (More, 1943, p. 492). However, this pursuit of greater productivity gave the natural sciences dominance (Serjeantson, 2014), feeding modernist beliefs that progress can be fuelled by continual advances in scientific knowledge, and leading ultimately to environmental crisis (Norgaard, 2006), as mechanization, modification and materiality increasingly challenge the earth's ability to replenish its resources (McKibben, 1990).

The Appreciative Discourse

This fourth discourse, named by Worster (1994/1977) the Arcadian viewpoint, refers to subjective, emotional and aesthetic reactions to nature, so implies that any discussion will be individualized. Indeed, selectivity is inevitable due to the breadth of possible content: the aesthetic alone includes a range of art forms. The label 'Romanticism' applies to an 'efflorescence' of responses to nature (through art, music, poetry and literature) from the mid-eighteenth to the mid-nineteenth century, as the sensitive sought refuge from the industrial revolution (Grout, 1973, p. 543) but continued well beyond that period and into new art forms as technology progressed (Sanders & Albers, 2010). Relevant too, is Edward Wilson's notion of biophilia, defined as 'the innately emotional affiliation of human beings to other living organisms' (Wilson, 1993, p. 31).

The Crisis Discourse

N one of Glacken's categories adequately lead to the contemporary 'environmental crisis' discourse, although the exploitative and appreciative discourses point this way. This is a discourse that dominates news broadcasts but it is a contested topic: the message is not entirely negative. Even the nature expert Castree (2005, p. 6) raises doubts about whether we are witnessing 'the end of nature' (McKibben, 1990) while stressing the need to protect our planet. Also the UK *State of Nature* report (Hayhow et al, 2016), a publication produced by more than seventy organizations, supports a positive outlook. In its Foreword, Attenborough recognizes that nature 'needs our help as never before' but also draws attention to the number of innovative conservation projects that are underway, believing that if we 'all pull together, we can provide a brighter future for nature and for people'.

To summarize, in major Discourses, nature is seen as a gift from 'God', as comprehensible when systematized, as a resource for mankind, as a source of pleasure, and as a habitat in crisis.

The Empirical Study

N ow, I turn to my own research with a small sample of people from different generations of a single family, and to data collected prior to learning about these conceptualizations, but first I present some relevant frameworks.

Theoretical Frameworks

Forms of Learning

F oley (2004) acknowledges that learning is embedded in all aspects of living before identifying four dimensions of adult learning relevant to this study. *Formal* education takes place in a classroom or a workplace training session. It has specific curricular goals and often leads to a qualification. *Non-formal* education is more sporadic but still systematic, maybe one-off sessions to serve a specific purpose. *Informal* applies to learning that is deliberate but not taught, like individual and group reflection or a review of a situation. *Incidental* is unplanned (experiential) learning occurring naturally through engagement in other activities. It may be tacit rather than directly acknowledged by the learner. I would argue, therefore, that family learning is often incidental but could be non-formal or informal if instruction is planned or intentional.

Funds of Knowledge (FoK)

FoK refers to existing knowledge upon which people can draw in new situations. This may have been acquired through any of the learning practices that Foley lists but, like incidental learning, often remains tacit until needed (or excavated during the interview process). Moll and colleagues (1992) used this concept in home-school studies in Mexico, establishing the 'accumulated bodies of knowledge of the households' (Vélez-Ibáñez & Greenberg, 1989) to enable researchers to better understand learning processes within families and their potential for classroom utility. FoK is frequently used in planning environmental education for young children (Edwards et al, 2016) and more widely, and is useful when considering family learning in this study.

Types of Discourse

Bamberg's discussion of Capital-D and small-d discourses raises some interesting points for the analysis of the data. Bamberg (2014) labels Capital-D discourses as those that 'reflect' existing concepts, beliefs and ideologies and small-d discourses as those that 'constitute' current assumptions (p. 132). He associates these, respectively, with dominant (master) narratives or everyday forms of talk (small stories) (p. 133), seeing Discourses as accepting language as transparent, and discourses as using language to shape and change the world; a toolbox for sense-making (p. 133). Furthermore, Bamberg views this discursive differentiation as equating to different goals: Discourses aim to 'scrape out the implicit worldviews that individuals propagate through the stories they tell about their lives' and discourses interactively navigate 'a sense of who-they-are' and having 'two-directions of fit', leads them to choose to adopt a role at one end of the spectrum, to act agentively at the other (p. 134).

Bamberg acknowledges that both types of discourse share a similar constructivist orientation initially as they are part of a 'language-based, discursive narrative framework' (pp. 132–3). Importantly, too, he recognizes that both lenses matter as 'people are both agentive and influenced by pre-existing discourses and master narratives for the construal of self and others' (p. 133). More problematically for my study, Bamberg sees each type as calling for different methodological approaches. The exploration of Discourses needs methods that 'try to tap into these concepts' through questionnaires, experimental design, or as in my case, interviews. Whereas discourses are developed through 'talk' (p. 133), reflecting the small-stories concept (Bamberg, 2007; Georgakopoulou, 2007; Bamberg & Georgakopoulou, 2008), and earlier work on talk-in-interaction (Psathas, 1995). Bamberg's divisions identify the potential for dissonance when research starts out to explore viewpoints through interviews and finds the participants agentively constructing their own meanings, perhaps worldviews, even if unconsciously; a point that will be further explored later.

Taken together these frameworks capture the processes through which people may develop a concept of nature. They offer ways to distinguish between learning that is taught and that which is gained from 'merely' living, and to identify that which is passed down through the generations from that which is individually, maybe even randomly, acquired. The notion of D- and d-discourses offers a means to distinguish between established and individual viewpoints, making a space for original thought, for personal interpretation and agency when considering how people 'see' nature.

Methodological Approaches

Participants

The family members from four generations all happened to be female, setting the inquiry within a series of cascading mother-daughter relationships, and offering an opportunity to capture possible learning through family practices, albeit down the female line. Taking a historicist stance, the intention was to capture instances of change and continuity by talking to people who knew each other intimately, who shared a common (if evolving) social background and whose views might be expected to display similar cultural threads. As the participants lived in locations that were geographically distant, I elected to carry out the interviews by telephone, writing copious field notes to capture ideas and phrases of speech and transcribing immediately afterwards to optimize accuracy.

From the outset the participants were given pseudonyms (Jo, Vera, Stacy, Harriet) to maintain anonymity and protect their identities. To assist the reader, the chosen names lengthen in inverse proportion to age, so the shortest name refers to the oldest participant.

Jo, aged eighty-nine, was born in the late 1920s, so, for her, schooling was something to be valued, as only elementary education was compulsory. However, she was able to 'stay on' at school and studied biology at the height of the modernist paradigm when 'scientific' objectivity (Phillips, 1989) was dominant.

For Vera, Jo's daughter, aged fifty-eight, schooling was compulsory until fifteen and influenced by the child-centric movement that 'made it impossible to derive an effective pedagogy' (Simon, 1999/1981, p. 42), in a system that divided children at eleven into an academic minority and the rest who, like her, attended secondary-modern schools where teaching had a practical orientation.

Stacy, aged thirty-four, a child of the early 'eighties, entered primary school shortly before the government introduced a National Curriculum (in 1988), regular testing and school inspection, seriously stressing teachers who resorted to desk-based methods (Chitty, 2004, p. 126) that alienated many of their pupils.

Harriet, aged twelve, attends secondary school. The repeated changes affecting the teaching profession, its methods of teaching and its curriculum, have slowed down as naming and shaming practices have supposedly been effective in eradicating poor provision (Bevan & Wilson, 2013). Schools are beginning to find their own ways forward and teachers to teach more creatively, albeit within restrictive frameworks.

Data Collection

A biographical approach (Roberts, 2002), starting with an open invitation to talk about nature, presented participants with an opportunity to articulate what nature stood for in their daily lives before any attempt was made to steer the conversation. However, this was an active listening process that saw meaning-making as a participatory practice (Holstein & Gubrium, 1995) and I continually monitored progress in a pragmatic attempt to ensure adequate coverage of the topic, introducing specific questions relating to experiences, contexts and to species when necessary.

The accounts relied on memory, specifically declarative memory, 'where information is consciously recalled and can be articulated' (Sutton et al, 2010, p. 211) and this will always be subjective and selective. Invoking memories suited the purposes of this study, because it allowed me to access the views of people of different ages and enabled me to tap into residual learning; that which remains long after the event. Memory is an active process 'forging its pasts to serve present interests' and 'memory's activities in the present belie the apparently simple, reified, and knowable past evoked by the call to remember' (Radstone & Schwarz, 2010, p. 3). Although it can be selective, autobiographical memory seeks to be 'coherent' and to have 'correspondence' with reality (Sutton et al, 2010, p. 215), so what one is told is more likely to have validity than not; a reassuring claim.

The overall research approach was exploratory, an inductive one, as is common within qualitative research. I sought to collect spontaneous narratives mediated by questioning, and then examine and analyse the material, looking both within and across the interviews to establish what could be learned.

Data Analysis

The preliminary data analysis was carried out by creating synthetic narratives that brought the specific detail, the actions, events and happenings related, together in a single story (a pen portrait for each individual), as suggested by Polkinghorne (1995). Such portraits are essentially descriptive and lengthy so are not reproduced within this chapter. However, they can be and were analysed further to establish the individual's view(s) of nature and to examine the insights they provided into the types of learning that each family member experienced and valued.

Discussion and Findings

T he synthesizing process drew my attention to the worldviews of nature that each individual held. The processes of analysis involved a consideration of the relationship between individual worldviews and established Discourses. The evidence of individuals learning in distinctive ways enabled me to establish what forms of learning had a lasting (residual) impact.

A meta-analysis of all four portraits revealed the power of human agency, for each participant constructed a personal view of nature in keeping with social cognitive theory that 'accords a central role to cognitive, vicarious, self-reflective, and self-regulatory processes' (Bandura, 1989). It is noteworthy that the individual worldviews of nature did not directly reflect the dominant Discourses of times past or present but were individually constructed. I had collected a series of small d-discourses of nature, despite starting from a broader biographical direction and then asking specific questions. In this study, Bamberg's (2014) polarities didn't remain as neatly distinctive as the literature claims, but on reflection it may be that in engaging the participant in a dialogue it was I who breached the distinctive approaches. My initial intention had been to examine the significance of forms of learning and funds of knowledge, so my questioning had not been devised to 'scrape out' particular Discourses on nature. Indeed, I had neither studied them in advance nor thought to find coherent and individualized worldviews, so for me, their unanticipated emergence made them all the more credible. However, despite this blurring of boundaries, the notion of small d-discourses remains a useful concept for describing the findings from this research.

Modes of Learning and Meaning-Making

I n terms of Foley's categories of learning, no non-formal processes were evident and informal learning was only visible in occasional references to using books or watching television. Formal and incidental learning were commonplace, the significance of each varying between participants.

Formal Learning: The Lasting Influence of Learning at School

D ata about schooling was both freely offered and specifically requested at interview.

Jo claims nature as the 'most important subject', one she studied formally as botany and zoology, but only at secondary school — where this involved dissection (which she disliked), classification and the naming of parts — inculcating a knowledge of Latin names and identification by species that Jo can still recall and use in everyday situations. Her range of contact with nature is broad. She can name many flora and fauna, including relatively rare species, and is familiar with wildlife that lives in unusual habitats. Her interest is both active and academic, for she talks about observing and collecting specimens, pressing wildflowers and taking photographs, but also about plant identification and collecting old textbooks about wildlife that present individual plants and animals in detail. Her knowledge remains current, suggesting that when a student commits to learning and the pedagogy is both demanding and interesting, knowledge and practices formally learned can be retained and recalled for ongoing use over the life-course.

However, for her daughter, Vera, schooling made little impact. Her learning about nature is clearly rooted in adulthood and often relates to her roles as parent and childminder. Discussing nature, she claims to learn in order to 'pass information on to children'. Vera mentions examples rather than concepts, which again suggests that her learning has little formal basis. She admits she is 'not good on names' and her discussion of the environment is very generalized. Vera suggests we 'keep it going as best we can' and recommends 'being very vigilant with our surroundings', offering 'keeping everything as it should be' and preventing 'damage by chemicals' when pushed to add detail. Nor does she choose to look things up in books, although she will watch programmes on, say, volcanoes or glaciers (and *Countryfile*). Vera's narrative reveals little evidence of residual learning from school, perhaps a consequence of a schooling system that offered her few opportunities for academic learning (Simon, 1999/1981). Frequently staff were only qualified to teach practical subjects: the domestic science, woodwork, metalwork intended to enable entry into vocational employment. Vera chose the first, domestic, option.

Nor does Stacey refer to schooling when talking about nature. She is dismissive when asked about individual species and never reads books about nature. There is a touch of excitement when she talks of exotic species encountered on holiday in Mexico, Cuba and the Dominican Republic; toucans, dolphins and palm trees. These are still unusual holiday locations and may evidence educational influences as Stacey studied Tourism at college after leaving school at sixteen. She gets annoyed at 'how humans treat nature, leave litter, not caring for it or tidying up for ourselves' and states very strongly that nature was 'here before us' and it matters for survival: 'it feeds us, keeps us going', 'we eat off the land — what nature produces'. It is possible that these opinions have a formal origin, as residual learning from schooling, but overall the passive learning processes then practiced in education seem to have made little lasting impact.

Harriet is still at school and appears to enjoy formal learning. She can recall what she has studied and explain why it matters. Her primary school offered opportunities to explore woodland and pondlife, and to learn names for leaves, trees and fossils. Harriet talks at length and has clearly retained a good deal of information about a recent project on bees and their habitat, an active-learning programme involving visits to a nature reserve and contact with beekeepers. She is knowledgeable about nature, is curious, and is learning the names of species within a curriculum that also provides opportunities to get outside and experience nature. She names a range of species and often adds contextual information. Her language is peppered with technical terms, indicative of formal learning, and she demonstrates a broad knowledge of how the natural world is harnessed to support human life. She talks about habitat, crops and milling wheat; she uses insects as a collective term. Disliking 'anything poisonous — sharp — anything that can harm you' she gives a number of specific examples, demonstrating an ability to link the general to the particular. Harriet also mentions looking things up in books independently and sees learning as an 'adventure' rather than a task. Whether her interests will continue and deepen in adult life or whether they are foregrounded here because they relate to an immediate past is uncertain, but they are important now and learning is enjoyable. Active learning processes at least engage the student.

The narratives reveal very different levels of residual learning directly attributable to school experiences. Jo and Harriet clearly enjoyed formal learning: Jo retained significant school knowledge, for her learning was memorable; Harriet's recall of detail might reflect improved pedagogies over the intervening period, for the limited recall of Vera and Stacy reveal the inadequacies of education prior to and during its reform, through the introduction of a National Curriculum, student assessment strategies and a dedicated inspection service. Certainly, they both left school for vocational training at the earliest opportunity. However, it is important to be aware, too, that other — unacknowledged — factors will have influenced residual learning from schooling.

Incidental Learning: Instances of Learning Through Everyday Life

D ata that informs this section derives from generalized conversation about childhood, life and interests.

Jo had the freedom to roam the countryside with friends and experience a range of habitats near to where she lived: seashore and dunes, pine woods, heathland, low-lying peat moss, and, a cycle trip away, the Pennine hills. She was encouraged to attend and submit entries to the local flower show and continued to press flowers throughout adulthood. As a Girl Guide and later with her husband and children, she enjoyed the outdoors and camping, and nostalgically recalls holidays in Scotland, a place she describes as her 'spiritual' home. She had many opportunities to live close to the land and get to know the wildlife. Her memories of this are vivid.

Vera knows about nature and mentions common species of flower, tree and animal, but largely in relation to her garden. She has a basic functional knowledge of growing things, how to care for them, the role of birds in disseminating seeds and bees in pollination, the rules of the countryside, knowing that there are plants 'you aren't allowed to dig up any more when you see them in the countryside' and feeding birds 'but never with bread'. She is aware of seasonal changes and the interdependency of natural life but explains this through examples, offering common soundbites when prompted to generalize. Perhaps this knowledge stems from watching *Countryfile*. Vera is recalling memories but only over a recent past; she is building a nature narrative from incidental learning and makes no mention of childhood experiences of the natural world.

When Stacy discusses nature, her knowledge is both local and exotic. The exotic stems from holiday travel; she twice chose to swim with dolphins abroad. She likes to be in nature, to be outside and to be active but she, too, watches *Countryfile* on television. With her new boyfriend, who 'scavenges for horseradish and wild garlic', she learns to identify plants she can eat. She goes 'swimming in the mill pond in warm weather' and for walks with her father — who presumably knows about geology, as she talks enthusiastically about the Jurassic coast but is only incidentally interested in the fossils that are found there. But she has fond memories of how she 'ran up and down hills on walks'. She talks of movement: 'rivers, they flow', trees 'falling down', storms as 'nature out of control', and spiders that 'move very fast and bite; my friend was bitten'. The focus is on physical aspects. Even her comment about cows is about activity thwarted; she is irritated 'waiting for them to cross roads'.

For Harriet horse-riding is a great passion, so, like her mother, she is enjoying nature actively. Riding also gives her freedom to explore the countryside with friends and to visit her (paternal) grandparents' farm where she picks blackberries, 'feeds cows with horseradish by hand', sees 'wheat being grown and harvested'. She likes learning about nature and being in it and, very strikingly, there is a strong aesthetic undercurrent to Harriet's narrative that is often descriptive. She defines nature as 'outdoors, wild'; learning metaphorically as 'like a little adventure'. Lilies are not simply listed but described as 'red, pink' and the roses grow 'wild and have their own designs'. The cows' tongues are 'hard and bumpy' and horses are enthusiastically admired for their strength and build: 'they have loads of muscle in them. How strong they are and how they jump. How they react differently'. Harriet rejoices in nature's richness, it has 'a lot of feeling to it — colourful and different'. Her local and practical knowledge is boosted by watching television; *Countryfile* is mentioned as regular viewing.

Family Learning: Aspects of Transmission Through the Generations

Mostly the data that informs this section was collected from incidental comments, connections made by the researcher rather than the participants. The sequential interviewing of family members, though this is limited to mothers and daughters, offers some insight into the funds of knowledge that exist to be passed down through the generations. This generational process captures knowledge transmission but also its absence, for there are opportunities for transfer that are not taken, necessitating a consideration of what is not mentioned as well as what is talked about.

As the eldest participant, Jo has no one to corroborate her potential learning from elder family members, so we must rely on her own recall. It is clear that Jo's parents valued education as they managed to pay to send their five children to 'better' schools. However, they were reluctant to do this beyond the compulsory level and insisted Jo could only 'stay on' if she achieved high grades, making education a privilege to be earned. We learned, too, that Jo joined her mother in submitting entries to local flower shows. We know that Jo had a formal and thorough grounding in nature subjects, collected specimens and could name many species: she had considerable personal funds of knowledge. When Jo was a mother, most family holidays were spent under canvas in the countryside, especially in the Scottish Highlands, a naturally 'wild' environment.

Yet there is little evidence that Vera learned about nature from her mother, Jo. She will have shared those family holidays in Scotland, but they form no part of her conversation. When she mentions trips, they are to entertain children; her own and later those she cares for as a childminder (a form of work that locates her within her own home and garden). She appears not to share her mother's interests. Indeed, Vera's focus on the garden and the domesticated could even be a reaction against 'wild' environments. She does value rural England — 'if we didn't have the countryside it would be a very boring place' — but her contact beyond the garden wall is mainly indirect. Now her children are adult she is 'done' with the beach but with her husband she is happy to 'drive through woods', taking 'country routes if we can'; it is he who goes for long walks. However, Vera learns from television documentaries and it is she who starts a tradition of watching *Countryfile*, a programme liked by both Stacy and her daughter Harriet. Vera is aware of the countryside code (how to behave appropriately in the countryside to protect other living things) but she relates more to gardens.

Stacy scarcely mentions gardens. She expresses surprise that a palm tree her parents bought at a garden centre (something she has seen in its natural habitat abroad) is now 'big as the house' and states that she has no houseplants as they 'die too easily'. We saw her annoyance when people leave litter, and here she is possibly echoing her mother's teaching of the countryside code. We have seen that Stacy's knowledge is a mix of the exotic and the local and there is evidence that she learns from others — she recalls walking with her father and scavenging with her boyfriend — but little evidence that she has learned about nature from either mother or grandmother. There may well be a mismatch between Vera's love of the domestic and Stacy's liking to be active within nature, possibly just evidence again of an individual developing a personal worldview.

With Harriet, the emphasis is on school where she enjoys active forms of learning, but this is the reality of being a schoolgirl. Similarly, when we glimpse her mother's influence, this could be because she is still a minor. For instance, when Harriet mentions the palm tree, her interest could be independent or due to her mother. She also talks about rainforests, and this could stem from school, books, or her mother's interest in the exotic. At best, such connections are incidental. Like Mum and Grandma Vera, Harriet watches *Countryfile* but unlike them she likes 'discovering' new 'plants and things' and will choose factual books on nature in the library to find things out for herself (like Great Grandma Jo). Through horse-riding she is actively enjoying nature, like her mother, who supports this interest by paying for her lessons. Harriet also benefits from visiting her paternal grandparents' farm. This sits outside of the mother-daughter relationship, as her parents have separated, but is still evidence of learning across generations.

Overall, the interviews do not elicit many instances of shared family practices, but I cannot claim that they do not occur, only that they are not foregrounded or easily traced within the data. They may, of course, relate to topics other than nature. A shared interest in *Countryfile* is passed down through three generations but the only viewpoint common to all four is a dislike of spiders, and this could be learned or individually acquired. Overall, this lack of shared practices lends some support to the view that the relationship with nature is individualized.

Individual Constructions of Nature

On completing the analysis, I was struck by the very different ways that each family member related to nature, subsequently realizing that this was suggestive of active knowledge formation in a social cognitive sense (Bandura, 1989). Learning was influenced by schooling, experience and family practices but each individual presented a nature narrative that was individual and resonated with a particular way of thinking. Essentially, each individual had developed a personal worldview of nature, although reactions to school, everyday life, and family interests surely mediated these.

When asked why nature matters, Jo talks about the survival of the planet, the role of trees in the oxygen cycle and the significance of the food chain. This is a knowledgeable standpoint; hers is a scientific discourse involving taught and self-taught knowledge of names, parts and purposes, as well as rarity, causes, connections and consequences.

Vera's relationship with nature is habitual, it is 'part of our way of being'. It is bound up in her garden and with making sure that children treat it with respect and don't dig up plants or snap twigs off trees. It is essentially a domestic discourse.

Stacy, however, describes nature in terms of activity and movement, something to be 'in' and engage with bodily. She presents a physical discourse: perhaps in reaction to the increasingly formalized and sedentary style of learning she experienced in school.

Harriet's relationship with nature is complex; partially utilitarian ('bees for honey, trees can produce wood, gives animals a home — habitat'); partly something to be studied but also something to be actively explored. Harriet's nature narrative is unique within the family because of the language that she uses. This is descriptive even when it is factual, and she continually demonstrates her admiration for the natural world and aesthetic appreciation of its assets in the way that she talks about it. So, again, we have a worldview of nature that cannot be said to derive directly from either the education system or the practices within the family. Nature is ultimately something pleasurable and worthy of observation. Hers is predominantly an aesthetic and emotional discourse.

Classic and Personal Worldviews

There is little evidence that the participants' views are shaped by the prevailing Discourse on nature. Environmental crisis is scarcely raised in the interviews: Jo discusses a few specific problems, and Vera briefly repeats commonplace views. At most, Stacy refers to the rules of the countryside, defining her caring as everyday acts like clearing up litter, and Harriet makes no mention at all.

The Arcadian view that humans should live in harmony with nature is implicit in all the individual stories; it is explicit in Vera's view that we 'keep it going as best we can', in Stacey's that it was 'here before us'. There is also an understanding that nature supports human life in comments such as Stacey's 'we eat off the land' and Harriet's mention of habitat, crops and milling wheat. However, these are far from Imperialist; there is no suggestion that humans should dominate nature. Arguably, Vera's domestic discourse is slightly exploitative: in that gardening involves a shaping of nature to the gardener's ends. Stacy's enjoyment of being in nature, swimming with dolphins, is again a form of 'using' nature for one's own purposes but to describe this as exploitative would be an overstatement.

There is no sign of religiosity; neither echoes of the ancient belief in the Order of Nature with a deity in supreme authority (Glacken, 1991) nor of its revival as Creationism (Numbers, 2002). This is scarcely surprising as teaching creationism is banned in the UK, while the theory of evolution is mandatory (Hafiz, 2014), although there are claims that some faith schools are flaunting this legislation (Mortimer, 2016). The closest comment is Jo's claim that Scotland is her 'spiritual home' but this is a way of justifying her attachment rather than a reference to religion or divine order.

Jo's interests in labelling and species align with the long-practiced Classificatory discourses (of John Ray in the seventeenth, Carl Linnaeus in the eighteenth, and Charles Darwin in the nineteenth centuries) (Pyenson & Sheets-Pyenson, 1999) but she was only ever 'learning and using' rather than 'creating' hierarchies and connections. Her scientific discourse is in keeping with the modernist views that prevailed when she was in formal education.

It is Harriet's viewpoint that most clearly fits into a bigger worldview, for, making allowances for her immaturity, her aesthetic pleasure in nature has something in common with the Appreciative viewpoint (Glacken, 1991). However, her views are expressed in terms of a more robust physicality, unlike the poetic, artistic and musical outpourings of the mid-eighteenth to mid-nineteenth centuries. Also, my interpretation is based on her choice of examples and ways of describing things; she is neither engaging in creative activities nor reacting to external changes within society of the scale of the industrial revolution, as were the Romantics; the circumstances differ.

What is interesting about this research is the evidence that each individual, whatever her education and role in the family, unconsciously builds a personal worldview of nature, suggesting that this construction is an embedded process. It is me, the researcher, who listens to the narratives and identifies the different viewpoints through ideas expressed in a variety of ways and contexts. It would be an overstatement to claim that the research reveals a common 'passionate love' of 'all that is alive' (Fromm, 1973) but there are indications of an affiliation to nature in keeping with Wilson's work set out in *Biophilia* (1984): nature matters, and this appears to be intrinsically the case.

Conclusions

O n reflection, the 'recall' nature of the biographical approach may predispose the participants to create coherent worldviews. In reality, however, the conversations were too fragmented to allow auto-analysis during the actual interviews, so this is unlikely. The participants were being asked in the present day to talk about nature throughout their lives, and it may be that their current concerns are shaping the way in which they create their contemporary accounts. Perhaps they already hold personal worldviews of wider import and these are extended to embrace their views of nature? Jo describes her school days with great nostalgia and there is evidence that her interest in collecting and naming species continued into adult life, so her 'scientific' discourse may have greater application. For Vera, the family, home and garden, were all-important, so a broader 'domestic' discourse makes sense, and for Stacy being active is evidently fundamental to her view of nature, but also a lifestyle choice. Harriet is still learning and growing and may be developing an interest in the expressive arts that will stay with her for life — we cannot know. I wonder, could this small-scale study actually be capturing the process of discourse formation as it happens?

Surely at an individual level the process mirrors major Discourse formation in society, where the dominant needs and interests that prevail at any time, as well as a collective set of shared values, shape the social frameworks that become embedded. If we consider similar processes operating within contemporary society, it is very clear that discussions about nature arise in connection to the prevalent Discourse of environmental concern, a Discourse that is increasingly one of 'sustainability'. Yet such Capital-D discourses are not reflected significantly in the interview material either directly or as associated small-d discourses. The participants are agentive, creating their own understandings, their individual discourses, rather than echoing the major Discourses that prevail in the literature and in real life in relation to nature.

In terms of engaging future generations to adopt conservational measures, this 'individualization' process implies that choice and freedom are important. It may be better to make the natural environment accessible to people to enjoy as they choose, thereby giving them a 'stake' in their local communities, than to proselytize about the crises that surround them. In schools, lasting and enthusiastic learning was evidenced from two contrasting pedagogies: Jo's formal study, by teaching the fundamental physical processes and the names and terms, enabled her future and ongoing application of what she had learned; Harriet's active project work generated an interest in nature and its systems, enabling deeper learning. Probably both approaches have a role to play in future educational practices.

Such insights are neither exceptional nor unique but might need to be regularly restated in a neoliberal culture where success is measured statistically as improvements to narrowly defined and short-term outputs.

References

Bamberg, M. (2007). Stories: Big or small: Why do we care? In: Bamberg, M. (ed), *Narrative — State of the art*. Amsterdam: John Benjamins Publishing.

Bamberg, M. (2014). Invited commentary: Narrative practices versus Capital-D Discourses: Ways of investigating family. *Journal of Family Theory & Review*, 6: 132–36. https://doi.org/10.1111/jftr.12033

Bamberg, M. & Georgakopoulou, A. (2008). Small stories as a new perspective in narrative and identity analysis. *Text & Talk*, 28(3): 377–96. https://doi.org/10.1515/TEXT.2008.018

Bandura, A. (1989). Human agency in social cognitive theory. *American Psychologist*, 44(9): 1175–84.

Bevan, G. & Wilson, D. (2013). Does 'naming and shaming' work for schools and hospitals? Lessons from natural experiments following devolution in England and Wales. *Public Money & Management*, 33(4): 245–52. https://doi.org/10.1080/09540962.2013.799801

Bruce, S. (2000). *Fundamentalism*. Maiden, MA: Blackwell.

Bunnin, N. & Yu, J. (2004). *Blackwell dictionary of Western philosophy*. Oxford: Blackwell.

Castree, N. (2005). *Nature*. Abingdon: Routledge.

Chitty, C. (2004). *Education policy in Britain*. Basingstoke: Palgrave Macmillan.

Darwin, C. (1859/2009). *On the origin of species*. London: Penguin.

Desmond, A.J. (2019). Charles Darwin: British naturalist. *Encyclopedia Britannica*. https://www.britannica.com/

Edwards, S., Skouteris, H., Cutter-Mackenzie, A. & 5 others (2016). Young children learning about well-being and environmental education in the early years: A funds of knowledge approach, *Early Years*, 36(1): 33–50. https://doi.org/10.1080/09575146.2015.1064099

Emerson, M.O. & Hartman, D. (2006). The rise of religious fundamentalism. *Annual Review of Sociology*, 32: 127–44. https://doi.org/10.1146/annurev.soc.32.061604.12314

Foley, G. (2004). *Dimensions of adult learning*. Maidenhead: Open University Press.

Fromm, E. (1973). *The anatomy of human destructiveness*. New York: Holt, Rinehart & Winston.

Georgakopoulou, A. (2007). Thinking big with small stories in narrative and identity analysis. In: Bamberg, M. (ed), *Narrative — State of the art*. Amsterdam: John Benjamins Publishing.

Glacken, C.J. (1999). Reflections on the history of Western attitudes to nature. In: Buttimer, A. & Wallin, L. (eds), *Nature and identity in cross-cultural perspective*. Dordrecht: Kluwer.

Grout, D.J. (1973). *A history of Western music*, 2nd edn. London: Dent.

Hafiz, Y. (2014). Creationism banned from UK schools. *The Huffington Post*, 25 June. https://www.huffingtonpost.co.uk/entry/creationism-banned-uk-schools_n_5529693

Hayhow, D.B., Burns, F., Eaton, M.A. & 46 others (2016). *State of nature 2016*. The State of Nature partnership. https://www.rspb.org.uk/globalassets/downloads/documents/conservation-projects/state-of-nature/state-of-nature-uk-report-2016.pdf

Holstein, J.A. & Gubrium, J.F. (1995). *The active interview*. Thousand Oaks, CA: Sage.

Lorimer, J. (2008). Living roofs and brownfield wildlife: Towards a fluid biogeography of UK nature conservation. *Environment and Planning A*, 40: 2042–60. https://doi.org/10.1068/a39261

McKibben, R. (1990). *The end of nature*. New York, NY: Vintage.

Moll, L., Amanti, C., Neff, D. & Gonzalez, N. (1992). Funds of knowledge for teaching: Using a qualitative approach to connect homes and classrooms. *Theory into Practice*, 31(2): 132–41.

More, L.T. (1943). Newton's philosophy of nature. *The Scientific Monthly*, 56(6): 491–504.

Mortimer, C. (2016). Creationist views 'risk going unchallenged in schools' due to counter-terror measures, headteacher says. *Independent*, 29 January. https://www.independent.co.uk/news/education/education-news/creationist-views-risk-going-unchallenged-in-schools-due-to-governments-counter-terrorism-measures-a6840711.html

Norgaard, R. (2006). *Development betrayed: The end of progress and a co-evolutionary revisioning of the future.* Abingdon: Routledge. https://doi.org/10.4324/9780203012406

Numbers, R.L. (1992). *The creationists: The evolution of scientific creationism.* New York, NY: Knopf.

Phillips, D.C. (1989). Subjectivity and objectivity: An objective inquiry. In: Hammersley, M. (1993/2003) *Educational Research, 1.* London: Paul Chapman.

Polkinghorne, D.E. (1995). Narrative configuration in qualitative analysis. *International Qualitative Studies in Education*, 8(1): 5–23.

Psathas, G. (1995). *Conversation Analysis: The study of talk-in-interaction.* Thousand Oaks, CA: Sage.

Pyenson, L. & Sheets-Pyenson, S. (1999). *Servants of nature.* London: HarperCollins.

Radstone, S. & Schwarz, B. (2010). Introduction: Mapping memory. In: Radstone, S. & Schwarz, B. (eds), *Memory: Histories, theories, debates.* Fordham University.

Roberts, B. (2002). *Biographical research.* Buckingham: Open University Press.

Ruse, M. (2018). Creationism, *The Stanford Encyclopedia of Philosophy*, Winter 2018 Edition, Zalta,E.N. (ed). https://plato.stanford.edu/archives/win2018/entries/creationism/

Sanders, J. & Albers, P. (2010). Multimodal literacies: An introduction. In: Albers, P. & Sanders, J. (eds), *Literacies, the arts, and multimodality.* Urbana: National Council of Teachers of English.

Schirrmacher, T. (2013). *Fundamentalism: When religion becomes dangerous* (Trans. R. McClary). Bonn: Verlag für Kultur und Wissenschaft.

Serjeantson, R. (2014). Francis Bacon and the 'interpretation of nature' in the late Renaissance. *Isis*, 105(4): 681–705. https://doi.org/10.1086/679419

Simon, B. (1999/1981). Why no pedagogy in England? In: Leach J. & Moon, B. (eds), *Learners & Pedagogy.* London: Paul Chapman.

Strauss, A.L. & Corbin, J. M. (1990). *Basics of qualitative research.* Newbury Park: Sage.

Sutton, J., Harris, C.B. & Barnier, A.J. (2010). Memory and cognition. In: Radstone, S. & Schwarz, B. (eds), *Memory: Histories, theories, debates.* Fordham University.

Vélez-Ibáñez, C., & Greenberg, G. (1992). Formation and transformation of Funds of Knowledge among US-Mexican households. *Anthropology and Education Quarterly,* 23(4): 313–35.

Wilson, E.O. (1984). *Biophilia.* Boston, MA: Harvard University Press.

Worster, D. (1994/1977). *Nature's economy: A history of ecological ideas,* 2nd edn. Cambridge: Cambridge University Press.

Photo by Tom Perkins, CC-BY 4.0

II.

DISCOURSES WE WORK WITHIN: OF THE WORKPLACE

C ollectively, the chapters in this section explore discourses that shape the workplace, which, in this book, is normatively an educational and/or professional centre or context. Issues are addressed from both academic and professional perspectives, in order to consider the customs and boundaries that influence working practices. Here we have two chapters from Danish researchers, one from an Irish and one from an English colleague, but the scope of the material extends to include information on Kenya, too. We also span educational sectors: looking at the recently qualified teacher in Denmark, teacher education students in Denmark and Kenya, adult educators in Ireland, and then at teaching assistants in England working with children deemed to be 'difficult'.

In chapter five, 'Opposing Cultures: Science and Humanities Teaching in Danish Schools', Marianne Høyen and Mumiah Rasmussen examine the cultural divide between the expectations and practices of humanities (culture) and science (nature) teachers in Denmark, whose different learning is mandated within the state curriculum, possibly permitting a derogatory discourse around cultural subjects. They collect and analyse the life stories of newly qualified teachers, seeking to understand what informs their choice to work within these distinctive traditions and the extent to which this is due to family, schooling or external influences. Are their decisions culturally embedded or determined by opportunity at a later career stage?

Chapter six, 'Shaping "the Good Teacher" in Danish and Kenyan Teacher Education', uses ethnographic material and quantitative data to compare practices in two very different countries where the author, Kari Kragh Blume Dahl, has lived and worked. She questions what informal, institutional norms look like in both contexts and how these impinge on the student group, and she examines the links between institutional discursive power and individual identification, seeking an understanding of what promotes a sense of identity and belonging in students. Her chapter also provides useful contextual data on schooling in each country.

Next we have a chapter, which considers Irish systems. 'Irish Adult Educators Find Fulfilment amid Poor Employment Conditions' (Ch7). Sarah Bates Evoy studies the working conditions of part-time lecturers in Further Education and Training by interviewing the practitioners in person, seeking to establish why they tolerate their conditions of work and whether they are even aware that they are disadvantaged compared to other sectors in education. The chapter uses Margaret Archer's (2000, 2003) work on identity, agency and structure as an effective framework for analysis, considering wellbeing in terms of natural, practical and social factors.

Tristan Middleton, a former headteacher and author of the final chapter in this section, 'Nurture Groups: Perspectives from Teaching Assistants Who Lead Them in Britain' (Ch8) turns to the English primary stage (ages four to eleven) and examines with teaching assistants how they deal with critical incidents when running Nurture groups for children with challenging behavior. As an insider researcher who has worked with Nurture groups himself, Tristan is keen to capture the reality of the work and encourages the practitioners to talk freely in order to explore both negative and positive aspects. Carried out alongside supervisory sessions, the study coincidentally encouraged reflective practice, creating additional layers of benefit.

Taken together, these chapters offer a range of insights into the spaces where the personal and official narratives meet, and therefore, the ways that the teachers/practitioners (when prompted) perceive themselves as belonging to the educational culture in which they reside. The approaches are very different, even within national boundaries, but it could be argued that the ways of working and literature that underpin each chapter might influence the reading of the others in the section. There are certainly shared glimpses of the reasons behind decisions to choose and to stay within a particular career, and, in the case of the Irish and English chapters, evidence that practitioners are doing this even when the tangible rewards are less than ideal.

Given the overall educational focus of this book, many other chapters will be relevant to these topics. Those that may be of particular interest include Janet Dyson's exploration of fictional writing as a pedagogic practice for reflection and truth-telling (Ch1); Vera Sheridan's research on students in Irish higher education encountering and overcoming the failure of first year examinations (Ch10); Patric Wallin's study of students negotiating the transition to university in Sweden (Ch15); and Laura Mazzoli Smith's reflective discussion of such a progression in a UK context from a lecturer's perspective (Ch25). Helen Woodley's study of school exclusion in Britain (Ch26) lays out what might happen next if initiatives like Nurture groups are not in place to turn children's behaviour around early in the schooling process.

5. Opposing Cultures
Science and Humanities Teaching in Danish Schools

Marianne Høyen and Mumiah Rasmusen

Marianne Høyen and Mumiah Rasmusen explore C.P. Snow's 'two cultures' perspective of education through interviews with four newly qualified teachers about to enter the profession for the first time. They ask what professionalism means within their disciplines and examine how childhood and family influences shape the desire to teach. It is clear that disciplinary cultures are firmly embedded, because the humanity students offer 'why' responses to questions, the scientists 'how' responses.

In his 1959 Rede lecture, the British scientist and physician C.P. Snow introduced the concept of 'two cultures' to describe the divide separating the classical humanities and the modern technical and science-based cultures within English society; a division that, he argued, would have unfortunate global consequences. That the human and physical sciences rely on fundamentally different ways of thinking and knowing was not a new discovery; it was recognized in the Renaissance, but at that time polymaths were able to work with both natural and cultural ideas. However, the division grew more problematic as science became more sophisticated. In 1924, seeking to assert the characteristics of the humanities, Dilthey (1924, in Gundem, 1992) clearly articulated the division that Snow saw in his daily contact with Cambridge academics in the UK: 'We explain nature but understand human life', is how he clarified the division.

It is clear today that disciplinary boundaries separate the natural sciences and humanities, but difficult to ascertain whether this amounts

https://doi.org/10.11647/OBP.0203.05

to 'two cultures' as other dichotomies cross-cut these distinctions: theory / practice, disciplinarity / interdisciplinarity, mode one / mode two knowledge,[1] objective truth / social constructs, just to mention a few. However, the notion of 'two cultures' seems a valuable concept, even if it fails to stand up to closer examination. Certainly, the idea of 'us and them' within the sciences is far from dead.

In this chapter, we turn to the unified school system in Denmark (comprised of grades 0 to 9) to see if 'two cultures' thrive here, too. If, as Snow believed, 'two cultures' present a challenge with potential global consequences, it makes sense to analyse school provision, as it is here that the mindset of young students is shaped. Thus, in this chapter the aim is to see if and how schoolteachers identify with the notion of two cultures, and to do so by considering subjects rooted in the humanities as cultural, and those rooted in science and mathematics as nature-related.

Within the education system, several factors signal that such a division exists. Firstly, it is supported in legal texts and explicitly stated in political-administrative documents relating to grades 0–9 and the three-year upper secondary school system. Mandatory school subjects are grouped thematically into cultural and natural subjects, plus practical-musical subjects, and, until recently, this division was used throughout the academic upper secondary school (Undervisningsministeriet, 2016b; 2017). Secondly, in public debate, especially that initiated by the professional bodies for trade and industry and liberal political-economic bodies, it is frequently argued that too many young students are interested in the humanities. Provocatively, those studying for cultural degrees have been described as seeking a 'master's in uselessness' when a natural-science or technology focus would lead to employment (Wiegand, 2014). The humanities are derided as 'whipped-cream' disciplines, for science and technology are what are needed in the 'competition state' — a Danish version of neoliberalism (Campbell, 2006). Behind these points of view, we can identify the struggle related to *bildung* (self-cultivation) and what the future generation should learn. Politicians point to science

---

1   Distinguishes traditional objective disciplinary scientific research (mode one) from the more applied practical and often transdisciplinary research that generates knowledge for a social purpose (mode two). Terminology coined by Gibbons et al (1994).

as the answer, not the humanities, even though it is often said that it is difficult, even impossible, to predict the qualifications needed in the future (Malchow-Møller et al., 2017) and that the 'knowledge society' will require knowledge as yet unknown (Johansen, 2002) together with insight into innovation and entrepreneurship.

Within general society, a discursive division between the humanities and sciences clearly exists, so now we ask if newly qualified teachers share similarly polarized views and, potentially, the inclination to promote this division within schools. If yes, we seek to discover how the differences are expressed as, to some extent, we share Snow's belief that a division into two cultures is fundamentally inappropriate. The challenges the world faces (as outlined in the UN's sustainable development goals of 2017) are better met through flexible ontological positions and a cooperative will. Childhood influences impact strongly on future educational and career plans: it would be both unfortunate and undesirable if the school contributes to socialization into the division into two cultures, and thus cements it.

Background and Context

With the adoption of the Danish constitution in 1849, the school held a position as a unifying and culture-bearing institution (Appel et al., 2013). Shedding its earlier religious associations, teaching became an altruistic vocation focused on the care of the individual. Teachers were to educate and mould the young, preparing them to enter society (Braad, 2005). After World War Two, the educational process became more democratic. Rather than merely transmitting accepted knowledge to children, teachers developed more child-centred approaches, based on a knowledge of child development and the science of learning and rooted in dialogue with both pupils and their parents. In Denmark, teacher education was influenced by Grundtvigian folk high-school ideas[2] and, later, the working-school tradition focusing

---

2   Philosopher and philanthropist, N.F.S. Grundtvig (1783–1872) believed that education should be life enlightening, supporting individual and group development and community cohesion through active and practical engagement with others in lively dialogue relevant to the real world. His beliefs underpinned the establishment of a Folk High School scheme that offers alternative educational experiences to anyone over seventeen-and-a-half. More information @ https://www.danishfolkhighschools.com/about-folk-high-schools/what-is-a-folk-high-school/

on self-efficacy.[3] The 1970s saw an emphasis on equality through education (Telhaug et al., 2006), and since the 1990s the teacher has been construed as a resource in the global market economy, with a role to play in creating the knowledge society (OECD, 2005). Throughout this period the humanities have dominated in schools, as the aim of education was itself humanist (religious upbringing, self-efficacy and democracy). These general aspects of education are normally assigned to the school subject Danish Language and Literature, but, despite more than twenty-five years of endeavour, little progress has been made in giving natural science subjects a similar status. Formally the possibilities exist but internally they are obstructed. Across the two cultures, there is little cooperation, either practically or symbolically, in furthering a mutual understanding (Høyen, 2016).

Teacher education takes place in teaching colleges, institutions with a strong and distinctive culture established in the late 1700s, which, until recently, enjoyed independent status. These colleges reflected the state's efforts to establish a well-educated corpus of teachers who would function as role models to inspire local societies to aim higher — as until the early 1900s Denmark was dominated by a peasant culture. It was only in 2007, as part of the unification of the system for higher education, that these teaching colleges became part of university colleges (professional institutions to educate nurses, social workers, and early childhood pedagogues). Previously, such professionals underwent 'medium length, higher educations' with a significant element of practical work experience, but after restructuring they enrolled on professional Bachelor degrees, part of a general academization of all medium-length educational programmes.

Until 1997 the view that any educated teacher should be able to teach all subjects at all levels was prevalent in teaching colleges, but this is no longer the case, as international OECD tests revealed the reading levels of Danish students to be lower than expected for a country of its standing. As a consequence, there is now a strong focus on teaching competence and student teachers must focus on either Danish Literature and Language or Maths (specializing in either the older or younger age

---

3   The 'education for living' philosophy underpins Danish practice and is rigorously defended. When writing about teachers, reference is always to teacher 'education' rather than the Anglicized term 'training'.

group) and select a small number of additional subjects. Symbolically this maintains a notion of two cultures, but in practice, within schools (especially smaller ones) teachers often take subjects they are not qualified to teach.

In schools generally, there is often a shortage of teachers of nature-related subjects, so pupils are taught either by teachers who are qualified in other subjects, or by those with a non-teaching degree, for example, a Master's degree. In order to work on equal terms with the dedicated schoolteachers, such differently educated teachers must study for up to three more years. They enrol on 'supplementary education' courses, but these focus on pedagogy — 'teachers' foundational competence' — not subject knowledge.

Teachers' foundational competence sits within a German-Scandinavian didactic tradition that is fundamentally humanistic and where the question of 'why' is absolutely central. Dilthey's hermeneutics underpins this didactic tradition, placing the emphasis on praxis, and observing four key rules:

1. Because understanding of life can only be gained through lived experience, the practice of education should have priority.

2. Development of educational theory and/or concepts as well as educational phenomena must be examined within the practices of schooling and teaching: theory and practice cannot be separated.

3. When reflecting on educational practice, one must take historicity into account and deal with the context — the past, present and future.

4. One should be always aware of the complexities embedded in the relations between schooling, teaching and learning.

A central aspect of this didactical thinking is the ideal of *bildung*, the goal of human autonomy. Hence, teaching should be seen as a meeting between an autonomous teacher, autonomous students and content (Willbergh, 2015). The teacher's job is to be the professional interpreter: the teacher should constantly reflect on which teaching content would make sense to the pupils, be of importance in the concrete/actual context and enable greater connectivity. The paramount aim of education is the cultivation of 'self-determination', 'co-determination', and solidarity (Klafki, 2000). An understanding of the children at school as learners is different from the thinking related to curriculum and competences, where educators with an overarching objective plan the steps necessary to reach that goal. Furthermore, it places the responsibility for learning with the individual learner, referred to as a student. The difference is especially significant in relation to teachers' choice of content. The aim of teaching should be to give pupils the possibility to discuss and develop their views on current themes that are relevant to their worlds. This offers the possibility for personal growth (Willbergh, 2015).

It is expected that a teacher's professional competence will draw on a narrative where the thinking of *bildung* dominates. Today this is challenged — at least on the surface — by a counter-narrative dominated by thinking around set competences. Since the millennium, schools have been subject to external forces linked to neoliberal ideas and the 'knowledge society', as well as a subsequent focus on prescriptions, tests, and assessment of competences. In our interviews, carried out to examine the possibility of identifying two cultures, we have to search for explanations at several levels, as a subject-related narrative as well as a didactical narrative, for both may play a part.

Method

To address our research question, we interviewed four newly educated teachers, who all had specific teaching experience (as private home tutors or as supply teachers) before commencing their studies. We chose to interview teachers situated on the boundary between teacher education and a professional job, in order to catch them at a time when the teacher-education culture was still strong in their minds but they were not yet embedded into a job at a school and influenced by its specific organizational culture. Two of the informants, Carina and Carl, chose Danish Language and Literature as their primary teaching subject together with History and Music, so are deemed as aligning with the humanistic tradition. The other two, Nico and Nina, chose Mathematics as their primary subject together with Physics and are therefore seen to be part of the scientific tradition. All four teachers are given pseudonyms and these are chosen to reflect their alignment, the Cs working with cultural [humanities] subjects, the Ns with natural science subjects.

The interviews were carried out in Danish[4] in 2016 and lasted about one-and-a-half hours each. The interviewer was Mumiah Rasmusen, a qualified teacher of a similar age to the informants. We were adopting an open approach that encourages narrative and avoids inappropriately shaping or narrowing the space for meaning (Horsdal, 2016), so our starting point was the question 'Why did you choose to become a teacher within [the informant's principal teaching subject]?'. The interviews were conversational in style, aiming to reveal the informant's understanding of his or her profession described from his or her viewpoint. Logically, this meant that each interview developed slightly differently, making direct comparisons impossible, but we kept faith with the view that a teacher's understanding of his or her role emerges narratively from the subjective interpretation of his or her life (Goodson, 2003).

We wanted to avoid reproducing the 'discourse of defect' related to teachers' professionalism that prevails, especially amongst those with a peripheral relation to contemporary school (parents, politicians, previous students) so our starting point was that the teachers were able to do 'everything needed in order to be a good teacher', and we strove to maintain a neutral position rather than to privilege our own ideas about what the informants should stress in relation to our research question. Consequently, when we began to analyse the research data we had to draw on explorative and reflective approaches (Hammersley & Atkinson, 1995) aware that we were covering new ground in analysing teachers' understanding from a 'two-cultures' perspective and therefore must proceed with an open mind.

Our process was inspired by techniques from Grounded Theory (Charmaz, 2000). Within the emerging main themes, we searched for indications of coherent narratives (Clark & Rossiter, 2008), postulating that their coherence might reveal embedded lines of thought relating to Snow's two cultures. Within the interviews we found various layers of narratives:

- From what we were told directly, we could clearly identify the two cultures. The informants understood themselves through

---

4   Interviews translated by authors.

associated trappings and practices, and clearly distanced themselves from the opposite culture.

- Within each of the two academic traditions we could trace threads that identified a collective, fundamental narrative related to teachers' professional reflections.

- We could also identify narratives that related to the broader discourses in society about the role of the school. The teachers' narratives showed a deterministic compliance with correct or acceptable feelings, thoughts, ideas and actions.

The interviews also offer narratives that run transversally across the three levels: about their childhood and youth, about their relation to school, and about making the decision to work as a teacher. At the immediate descriptive level, there were a lot of stories about their childhood years in school, successes and failures, experiences and reflections — tales shaped into stories, which, once constructed, can be told over and over again (Polkinghorne, 1995). The transcripts clearly show that in their 'tellings' all four informants make use of such stories, especially when the dialogue touches upon their own childhood, youth and schooling. But it is also clear that, often, when the informants talk about their relationships to the teaching profession, the relationship goes beyond what is traditionally voiced in political discourses relating to the educational system.

The Stories: Why Choose to Become a Schoolteacher Within One of These Traditions?

When explaining their choice of a primary teaching subject, all four spontaneously claimed that an interest had developed during childhood and adolescence. This was especially the case for the two science teachers, Nico and Nina. For Nico, school science was legitimized through association with his parents' work. The nature-related subjects also offered the opportunity to finish homework quickly and proceed to other more interesting pursuits, such as family sporting activities. In contrast, Nico found literary analysis impossible to complete quickly and confidently, as there were no right answers.

He remembers the culture-related subjects as senseless. For Nina, nature-related subjects also enabled connection to her family; they investigated things together nearly every day, sometimes motivated by Nina's homework but often just through everyday life. Nina's father was a self-taught computer scientist and often brought examples of his work home with him. Examination and experimentation played a central role in Nina's upbringing.

The humanities teachers told similar stories of learning and interest embedded in childhood and adolescence. Carina grew up in a tight-knit community with shared values (one that she later realized mildly excluded those who did not embrace the same beliefs). Her parents came from different European cultures, both with strong traditions that they upheld; one rooted in the Danish folk high-school tradition, the other in a southern European artisan-family tradition where arts and crafts provided a shared livelihood. In contrast, Carl's parents worked 'with numbers', so his early childhood was not particularly orientated towards the humanities, but, growing up in the capital, his friends introduced him to various sporting and musical communities and through these he became aware of an 'emerging' multiculturalism (at that time a relatively new phenomenon in Denmark). They also enabled him to experience the processes that underpin democracy. His parents firmly believed that everyone should find the way in life that suits them best and Carl did just this, for after training as a Maths teacher for a year, he switched to teaching education.

Though they followed different paths, all four participants developed a sense of community through childhood and engagement with youth groups that encouraged individual participation (in sport or music, for example) within a broader shared framework. These social collectives were supportive environments enabling the individual to develop a sense of 'I' can do this and 'we' can do that together, but not a sense of groups with distinct goals (as found in a political party, for example). For all four participants, the experience that 'we are able to do something together' and especially the personal realization of the value of participating and belonging, was a driving force for becoming a teacher. They wanted to guide others to participate in similar communities.

Narrative Understandings

A ccording to the literature, when asked what inspired them to teach, teachers often mention a teacher they met as a pupil (Lortie, 2002). However, this is not the case with our informants: we have seen that instead they pointed to their membership of communities. Family practices and friendships seemed to be more significant than school experiences, something that Lortie (ibid.) did not find surprising.

Now we ask: which narratives do the informants draw on in relation to their understanding of their role as a teacher? We will see that they embrace the culture of their primary discipline, drawing on an embedded narrative that exists in its own right at the same time as the other culture appears as a counter-narrative (Bamberg & Andrews, 2004). Next, we examine the larger professional narrative of teaching that the informants also draw on, one that is acquired through their recently completed degrees, setting expectations for what they will find in their future jobs as qualified teachers. From a political-administrative perspective, a teacher's job is to fulfil professional expectations laid out in the legal framework for schools (Undervisningsministeriet, 2016a) but in reality, the informants talk far beyond the political framework, offering strong professional and institutional narratives. Finally, we turn towards the social discourses which shape both the school and the teachers' roles.

The Narrative About the Teaching Subject

I n the stories told in the dialogue between interviewer and informant, we find that the participants make reference to and distinguish between their 'own' and the 'other' culture.

From the humanities teachers, we find two dominating themes related to the core of the subject and the thinking related to it. Most significant is the understanding that the humanities offer pupils insight into the diversity of human perspectives on existence. Through acquaintance with literature, claim the informants, we learn to know and understand that humans have different backgrounds, roles, interests and difficulties. This, they argue, provides pupils with material to inform their own reflections about the world, and, irrespective of age and background, makes humans more tolerant, insightful and critical in their own lives. The informants further stress that language, not just spoken and written but also that of art and music, teaches pupils to communicate — to converse, to enter a dialogue, to argue and thereby make an imprint on the world.

It is striking that the humanities teachers are so occupied by their own subjects that their relationship to the other culture, science, is minimal; subjects related to nature are simply of no interest and they cannot be bothered to engage with them. The counter-narrative is apparent as passive resistance: Carina says that no one in her family is involved with numbers or nature-related subjects, and she herself is 'mega-bad' with these themes. However, she does reflect that she holds a formless but significant antagonism towards science and wonders if there is something wrong with her brain, circling around the concept of dyscalculia without specifying the term. For Carl, his engagement with the humanities is such that he simply has no room for the sciences. His ideas about being a teacher are amply fulfilled within the humanities frame, but he mentions science as a possible counterbalance to faith and religion. In principle he is open to including some nature aspects in his teaching, but then the mere nature association makes him unsure. He considers the possibility of an interdisciplinary approach and reflects on the idea of producing a story with his pupils: '[...] add some nature-related concepts, such as beech leaves or what-the-hell-is-their-names, or something — eh, something about the food chain or something about that the birds eats the larvae which makes the larvae afraid of the birds and then they become the enemies in the story'. Thus he muses, but he uses vocabulary from the humanities, not from the sciences.

The informants working with science subjects are similarly engaged in their field, but for them the idea of the 'aha moments' these subjects provide is dominant. Without addressing this directly, the informants take for granted that the world exists and is awaiting man's discoveries. Both informants are preoccupied with being able to participate in this discovery, capture its elements and, as a teacher, pass this experience on to their pupils. For these informants, science subjects seem to offer an underlying security as, unlike the humanities, science offers logical methods to follow. In this way, science offers possibilities for agency to independent- and knowledge-seeking individuals. It implies independence from the school and escape from the whims of colleagues and reduces possible failures of competence. The natural scientists reveal a distinct opposition to the humanities. In Nico's eyes, they hold nothing of interest, either intrinsically as subjects or for society in general. He states several times that he cannot understand that 'poems or Swedish texts' (the latter a mandatory component of the Danish curriculum) make sense or are compelling. In contrast to Nico's clear opposition, Nina shows less resistance. She sees Mathematics as a form of language, and has carried out observations of dialogues between Maths teachers and pupils, but her reflections are personal; she makes no attempt to seek explanatory frameworks within the humanities. However, she does see science as 'liberating' and would like more girls to engage with it.

In their portrayal of their own and the opposing subject's cultures, the informants demonstrate that Snow's division is relevant within schools and that it is the culture and mindsets of the teachers that constitute the divide. Yet, and paradoxically, the teachers describe their enthusiasm for their subjects as emanating from family and leisure activities rather than from school *per se*, but this is challenged by their description of their own teachers' enjoyment of the subjects they taught, as well as by their accounts of their teachers' recognition of the informants' interest in their subject: they talk about feeling successful in class after 'being noticed' by their teachers, and conversely of distancing themselves from subjects where this did not happen. However, for the informants, by far the most important aspect determining their choice of teaching subject is their belief about how their subject can educate their pupils. Hence, the informants see their students' opportunities for *bildung* as essential and focus on how they can support this.

The Narrative About *Bildung*

This emphasis on the possibilities for fostering *bildung* can best be understood through a general discussion of this concept. As already stated, it has been central to teacher education historically and it has connections with practical philosophy, especially the work of Kold and Grundtvig in Denmark (Hall et al., 2015; Korsgaard & Wiborg, 2006; and for a more historical account, Martin, 2018). Academization pushed discussions about *bildung* aside in favour of a more application-oriented competence perspective, leading to ideological infighting in university colleges about the aim of teacher education. Thus, within teacher education the informants experienced polarized viewpoints divided along ideological and cultural lines.

Like adjusting to the workplace, to be educated within a profession necessitates embracing a specific understanding of practice (Schön, 1983). For the teaching profession this is a practice that, at its core, involves debates about practical and philosophical questions that are marked by ideological fights. If, inspired by work on 'social movements' (Benford, 2002), we view teacher education as the carrier of a collective but contested narrative, and teacher education as the place where this narrative is negotiated and re-shaped by student teachers in their attempts to attain professional skill, we can find traces of these fights in the informants' stories. When we focus our analysis on what the informants tell us about teachers' knowledge base in relation to the question, 'what should be taught?', we see that the discussion about 'why' stands in opposition to 'how'.

It is noticeable that when asked about professional practice, 'why' responses are dominant within the humanities, 'how' responses within the natural sciences. Carina focuses on the atmosphere in the classroom and on collective wellbeing in a broad sense, and literature is her starting point to achieve this. She sees it as her task to enable all students to prosper by creating an understanding that there are many ways to be 'normal'. She gives children opportunities to reflect on the habits and views that they bring from home, to grasp that these can be different for other children. For example, in relation to religion, she finds it important to show her pupils that girls from an Islamic background have things in common with girls from a Christian background. As a teacher, Carina says, it is your duty to promote diversity; all else is futile: 'Learning happens in situations where you feel accepted and where everybody is okay with each other, doesn't it?'. Carl is keen to get his pupils to imagine things, and to express themselves, and he would like them to communicate their ideas in story form. He explains that he likes to present the pupils with all sorts of universes and then ask the pupils to fill them, visually and with text. It can be an everyday universe (such as the family room they remember from childhood) or a world described in literature (prompting Carl to discuss the author's life, and the social and cultural context underpinning the text, to make the text meaningful to the pupils). He wants to teach his pupils that things can 'speak', to encourage them to use their imaginations and to be creative in order to understand literature, language and the world around them.

Within the science subjects, the question of 'how' is more distinct. Nico says that as an adult he has realized that not everybody finds science as fun and interesting as he does. He demands that teaching must be fun — that is what he wanted in his own schooldays and this informs his reflections on his teaching: 'I have realized that a lot of pupils find Maths boring when the answers are fixed [...] therefore I try to open up the subject a bit to appeal to pupils who reject what I think is cool'. Nico's solution is to make his teaching problem-oriented, because then he thinks that he can attract the bored pupils by showing that there is more than one way to find the correct answer. However, as a new teacher Nico finds that he lacks the experience to do what he wants with the pupils. He clearly reflects back to his own schooldays when he says 'it might be that I think something is cool but if I have to teach others, then I have to respect that they have other opinions than I have — I have to find a way to cope with that'. In Nico's time as a pupil, he encountered humanities teachers that failed to do this, and he does not want to be such a teacher himself. Nina's reflections circle around encouraging her pupils to develop curiosity and engagement with science. She finds that many pupils are afraid of interacting with scientific ideas and she wants to tear that barrier down. 'Just making a start' is something Nina knows from her childhood, when it was customary for the entire family to dive together into something that they found exciting, until they figured out how it worked — it was highly satisfying when they experienced an 'aha moment'. Nina follows the same principle with her pupils in school and with children who participate in courses she teaches for free; these courses are offered by voluntary organizations to encourage more young people to engage in science. Nina is also interested in exploring what pupils or students do not understand. She has noticed that teachers' answers often go over their heads, perhaps because a common scientific language has not yet been established. Overall, the 'two cultures' are apparent in the didactic thinking that underpins the informants' discussions of their teaching subjects.

Within social-movement narratives, a great deal of effort is expended on maintaining a narrative that is distinctively different to that of opposing movements (Benford, 2002). In relation to the *bildung* aspect, we see that there are two tendencies that to some extent travel in the same direction. Firstly, within the humanities the informants are focused on the individual pupil and his or her place within the class as a collective; within the sciences, informants also claim that they are interested in the individual pupil but have no intention of incorporating their teaching into a more general curriculum, as some scholars within science have argued should be the case (Sjøberg, 1998). Secondly, within the ideologically riven teacher colleges, didactically the humanities traditionally create 'why' narratives while the sciences create 'how' narratives. 'How' is anything but a new question, but today it aligns seamlessly with the application of evaluation criteria for usefulness, which creates new baggage that weighs these narratives down.

Finally, all four informants stress that, to be an effective teacher, it is imperative that they can engage personally in the development of their teaching; they can only teach subjects they are passionate about. Whatever their disciplinary background, their views echo traditional thinking around *bildung*: they see the professional teacher as one who orchestrates the interplay between the teaching subject and the needs of the actual class — an endeavour termed 'the pedagogical meeting' by the German existential philosopher Bollnow (Koerrenz & Friesen, 2017). But nowadays, schools increasingly buy 'fixed packages' from commercial publishers who specialize in teaching materials, or 'communication-optimized courses' from external organizations (private companies, NGOs, semi-public cultural institutions). Despite this trend, the informants see developing their own (or adapting existing) teaching materials as a significant part of their professional identity.

Thus, through these interviews, the informants demonstrate that they have absorbed the disciplinary values embedded in their teacher education but that this hasn't yet been challenged, possibly because of their short professional careers. As a teaching student, one's position is that of an agent who will be edged into the profession through an education and a degree qualification. In order to qualify, the student teachers have to learn the disciplinary culture from the teaching institution and then re-orient themselves to fit into the practical and collaborative work ethos they find in schools on gaining employment. The ethos within the teaching profession no longer naturally augments that of teacher education, a finding that leads to discussion of the role of the school in society.

The School in Society

T o reiterate, the idea of *bildung* is a strong element of the informants' stories about their subjects, and in the collective professional narrative about teaching. However, we also learned that this narrative differs between the sciences and humanities.

When the informants talk about the schools in which they currently work, they all make reference to broader society. Their stories swing between stressing their opposition to what they see as the contemporary discourse within education (one which values competences and tests) and their desire to be the teacher they want to be. Carina highlights this dilemma:

> [...] instead of giving space and time to the immersion education should be [...] to me, there is a huge discrepancy between how we really think we should educate children and what we actually educate them into. As teachers we think it is immersion, reflection, citizenship and democracy. But what we really do in class and during the lessons, that is much more goal-oriented and 'teach-to-the-test'-like...

Is the reason for Carina's conflict simply the fact that humanities teachers 'hold on' to the democratic discourse embedded in welfarism and hence to an understanding which provided the individual teacher with better conditions for fulfilling their vocation? This is often the claim made by politico-administrative voices. But are other matters at stake?

Let us return to our earlier claim that the globalized knowledge society needs more people to work in the natural sciences and technology, and hence not in disciplines that cannot be directly converted into economic growth. This view, of course, influences views of the role of schools in society and thus discourses about schools, too. The question is: have neoliberal discourses merely superseded those of social welfarism, with the result that the question about the school's role has been changed from a traditional 'why' to a newer 'how'? Or are other aspects related to the idea of globalization and a knowledge-intensive society relevant?

A closer look at changes in the teacher's role and the notion of *bildung* may shed some light here.

From the mid-twentieth century, teachers were no longer the authority for knowledge in Danish society. No longer local role models or part of the local cultural elite, the teacher was cast as a carer whose role was pedagogic (Schmidt, 1999). At the same time, the growing population, the increased educational achievements of the parental generation, and consequent greater critique of authorities and regimes of authority, resulted in the status of teachers in society being challenged. Rather than rely on their collective role as knowledgeable authorities, teachers had to assert their own personal value as individual and pedagogical power became the ideal. Furthermore, it became increasingly difficult to establish general ideals for education within society. Scholars in the field argue that the globalized world entails a broadening of the traditional idea of *bildung* (Hammershøj, 2009) but we need to consider the historical perspective here. In earlier times, people were born into specific social groups where styles of upbringing maintained group coherence, but today, as Giddens argues, we believe in individualism, and settled social groups have been replaced by volatile communities who share the same tastes (Giddens, 1991). Referring to the French sociologist, Alain Ehrenberg, we could argue that the former division between the legal and the forbidden is today replaced by a conflict between the possible and the impossible. Therefore, *bildung* is now about having experiences that relate to the kind of person we want to be (Hammershøj, 2009).

We can, therefore, argue that the schools that informants will work within are characterized by two somewhat conflicting discourses. One demands that teachers as individuals provide a knowledge space where pupils can learn, but that teachers should do this mindful of the knowledge society's educational ideal, according to which experiences gained in loosely-knit communities are central. The second focuses on application and usefulness to the economy, and relates to the idea that globalization is linked to knowledge as the basis for financial growth.

If we were to identify a collective narrative that informs teachers how to be good at what they do, this would draw on a fundamental understanding that best corresponds to the narrative from the humanities. These teachers, talked about understanding various perspectives, and introducing students to different communities to extend what they already know. Engaging in didactical thinking related to 'why', the teacher might be guided to seek as yet unknown communities, not just the ones that they already know through their own experience. The science teachers conformed less to this collective narrative; they seemed to identify more closely with their personal school experiences, and are apparently more attracted toward individual learning, employing practices that appeal more to the individual pupil and the possibilities for providing 'aha' experiences. These informants draw on science as their knowledge base but accept that not everyone finds science subjects 'cool'. Their didactic interests are directed against the methodological 'how', and they do not consider the benefits of learning science subjects within a community, failing to see communities as open to such possibilities.

Thus, the informants relate differently to the contradictory discourses that shape society's views on the role of the school: science and humanities teachers appear to incline towards different aspects of those discourses.

Conclusion

The point of departure for this chapter was to discuss whether 'two cultures' exist amongst schoolteachers, akin to those within academia.

'Two cultures' do exist, not just in relation to ways of thinking within the teaching subjects themselves but also in relation to the teachers' professionalism and didactic thinking. We learned that the informants value different things when reflecting on their teaching, but they all have specific ideas about their teaching subject related to the school and to their pupils. Furthermore, they draw from different elements in the discourses that shape the school's role in society, finding aspects that best fit with their embedded ways of thinking.

Altogether, the 'two cultures' remain relevant and actively articulated and may well continue to be so. Broadly speaking, humanities teaching supports society's cultural development and its changing community structures, and science teaching supports application, immediacy and utility.

Snow warned that the division between the two is unfortunate and even dangerous, and for society it still is. Some politicians claim that science never has and never will be able to be part of general education, or *bildung*, even if scientists want it to be (Sjøberg, 1998) but perhaps the two traditions could learn from each other, even though their ontological background differs. Learning about each other's way of understanding, being more explicit about values, paying attention to a social gathering of any kind as not just an entity but as a place for being together might benefit both. The survival of future communities and the need for workable (useful) solutions present challenges to both humanistic and scientific cultures.

References

Appel, C., & Coninck-Smith, et al. (2013). *Dansk skolehistorie.* Aarhus: Aarhus Universitetsforlag.

Bamberg, M.G.W. & Andrews, M. (2004). Considering counter narratives: Narrating, resisting, making sense. *Studies in narrative, 4.* Amsterdam: J. Benjamins. https://doi.org/10.1075/sin.4

Benford, R.D. (2002). Controlling narratives and narratives as control within social movements. In: Davis, J.E. (ed), *Stories of change — narrative and social movement.* New York: State University of New York.

Braad, K.B. (2005). *For at blive en god lærer: Seminarier i to århundreder.* Helsinge: Selskabet for Skole- og Uddannelseshistorie.

Charmaz, K. (2000). Grounded theory: Objectivist and constructivist methods. In: Denzen, N.K. & Lincoln, Y.S. (eds), *Handbook of qualitative research.* Thousand Oaks, CA: Sage.

Clark, M.C. & Rossiter, M. (2008). Narrative learning in adulthood. *New Directions for Adult and Continuing Education,* 2008: 61–70. https://doi.org/10.1002/ace.306

Dilthey, W. (1924). *Einleitung in die Philosophie des Lebens, 1. Hälfte: Abhandlungen zur Grundlegung der Geisteswissenschaften.* Leipzig: B.G. Teubner.

Gibbons, M., Limoges, C., Nowotny, H., Schwartzman, S., Scott, P., & Trow, M. (1994). *The new production of knowledge: The dynamics of science and research in contemporary societies.* London: Sage Publications, Inc.

Giddens, A. (1991). *Modernity and self-identity. Self and society in the late modern age.* Stanford: Stanford University Press.

Goodson, I. (2003). *Professional knowledge, professional lives. Studies in education and change*. Buckingham: Open University Press.

Gundem, B.G. (1992). Notes on the development of Nordic didactics. *Journal of Curriculum Studies*, 24: 61–70.

Hall, J.A., Korsgaard, O.F. & Pedersen, O.K.F. (eds) (2015). *Building the nation: N.F.S. Grundtvig and Danish national identity*. Copenhagen: DJØF.

Hammershøj, L.G. (2009). The social pathologies of self-realization: A diagnosis of the consequences of the shift in individualization. *Educational Philosophy and Theory*, 41: 507–26. https://doi.org/10.1111/j.1469-5812.2007.00383.x

Hammersley, M. & Atkinson, P. (1995). *Ethnography*. London & New York: Routledge.

Horsdal, M. (2016). The narrative interview — method, theory and ethics: Unfolding a life. In: Goodson, I. (ed), *The Routledge international handbook on narrative and life history*. London: Taylor & Francis.

Høyen, M. (2016). Teaching about nature across generations. In: Formenti, L. & West, L. (eds), *Stories that make a difference*. Milan: Pensa Multimedia.

Johansen, M.B. (2002). *Dannelse*. Aarhus: Aarhus Universitetsforlag.

Klafki, W. (2000). The significance of classical theories of bildung for a contemporary concept of allgemeinbildung. In: Westbury, I., Riquarts, K. & Hopmann, S.T. (eds), *Teaching as a reflective practice: The German Didaktik tradition*. Mahwah, NJ: Lawrence Erlbaum Associates.

Koerrenz, R. & Friesen, N. (2017). *Existentialism and education: An introduction to Otto Friedrich Bollnow*. Basingstoke: Palgrave Macmillan. https://doi.org/10.1007/978-3-319-48637-6

Korsgaard, O. & Wiborg, S. (2006). Grundtvig, the Key to Danish Education? *Scandinavian Journal of Educational Research*, 50: 361–82.

Lortie, D.C. (2002). *Schoolteacher: A sociological study*. Chicago: University of Chicago Press.

Malchow-Møller, N. et al (2017). *Danmarks Kvalifikationsbalance*. København: Gyldendal.

Martin, C.J. (2018). Imagine all the people: Literature, society, and cross-national variation in education systems. *World Politics*, 70: 398–442. https://doi.org/10.1017/S0043887118000023

OECD (2005). *Teachers matter: Attracting, developing and retaining effective teachers*. Paris: OECD. https://doi.org/10.1787/19901496

Polkinghorne, D.E. (1995). Narrative configuration in qualitative analysis. *International Journal of Qualitative Studies in Education*, 8(1): 5–23.

Schmidt, L.-H.F. (1999). *Diagnosis*. København: Danmarks Pædagogiske Institut.

Schön, D.A. (1983). *The reflective practitioner: How professionals think in action.* New York: Basic Books.

Sjøberg, S. (1998). *Naturfag som allmenndannelse: En kritisk fagdidaktikk.* Oslo: Gyldendal akademisk.

Snow, C.P. (1959). *Two cultures and the scientific revolution.* London: Cambridge University Press.

Telhaug, A.O., Mediås, O.A. & Aasen, P. (2006). The Nordic model in education: Education as part of the political system in the last 50 years. *Scandinavian Journal of Educational Research,* 50: 245–83. https://doi.org/10.1080/00313830600743274

Undervisningsministeriet (2016a). Bekendtgørelse af lov om folkeskolen. In: *Folketinget* LBK nr 747. København: Undervisningsministeriet.

Undervisningsministeriet (2016b). Lov om de gymnasiale uddannelser — LOV nr 1716 af 27/12/2016. In: *Folketinget.* København: Folketinget.

Undervisningsministeriet (2017). Bekendtgørelse af lov om folkeskolen — LBK nr 1510 af 14/12/2017 In: *Folketinget.* København: Folketinget.

Wiegant, B. (2014). 5 metoder der gør stud.ubrugelig til cand.alt. In: *Mandag Morgen,* 8. december 2014. www.mm.dk/artikel/5-metoder-goer-studubrugelig-candalt

Willbergh, I. (2015). The problems of 'competence' and alternatives from the Scandinavian perspective of Bildung. *Journal of Curriculum Studies,* 47: 334–54. https://doi.org/10.1080/00220272.2014.1002112

6. Shaping 'the Good Teacher' in Danish and Kenyan Teacher Education

Kari Kragh Blume Dahl

Kari Kragh Blume Dahl makes a widely theorized comparison of teacher education in Denmark and Kenya, seeking to show how institutions establish the notion of a 'good' teacher, how they convey this notion to their students and how students conform to expectations publicly whilst flouting them in private.

This chapter examines informal discourses of teacher education in two diverse contexts, Denmark and Kenya, and considers what they mean for the students'[1] professional 'becoming', the process whereby students begin to think and act like a teacher. Specifically, the chapter explores how local, moral worlds, using Kleinman's conceptualization (1992), produce different contexts of shared experience in these teacher education settings,[2] how students negotiate their everyday lives at college in relation to these two contexts, and what this means for their sense of belonging in the teaching profession. The chapter raises two significant questions about discursive life and becoming in institutional education contexts: firstly, what do informal, institutional norms look

---

1   'Students' means 'student teachers' throughout this chapter.
2   'Teacher education' in this chapter refers to all formal and informal notions of studying teaching. However, though the term is widely used in a Danish context, in other contexts such as the Kenyan — and the English — the more customary term is 'teacher training'.

https://doi.org/10.11647/OBP.0203.06

like in Danish and Kenyan teacher education institutions regarding professional standards and behaviour; and secondly, do these norms and practices influence student teachers' professional becoming, for instance in relation to their sense of belonging in the teaching profession? The process of becoming refers to a constructionist way of understanding human change as something that is varied, multiple, unstable and thus always in process, as opposed to more traditional understandings of concepts of learning and development.

The teaching profession is not a 'value-free' entity, but arises within teacher education institutions with distinctive cultural identities and local systems of beliefs, attitudes, understandings and meanings that shift over time, and where existing power and knowledge hierarchies are sometimes challenged and/or reinforced (Cochran-Smith & Boston College Evidence Team, 2009; Ladson-Billing, 2006). Seeking to better understand how identities are formed, the chapter explores linkages between institutional discursive power and individual identification. It does this by examining how students develop a sense of belonging in the teaching profession, as it is performed in diverse teacher education institutions. 'Identification' in relation to the teaching profession is taken as a culturally constructed and performed issue rather than an external, static and constant determinant (Levinson & Holland, 1996). Identification and belonging are seen as the results of a complex interplay between several concurrent conditions at the teacher education institution, whose physical forms, lively materialities (Jones, 2011) and norm formations also play a part in the bonds that exist and are negotiated between students and the institution.

The study draws on different theoretical perspectives to match the complexity of the social processes, and includes discourse theory, cultural analysis and social anthropology to explore how different values and virtues embedded in the different institutional discourses produce human intentionality and belonging. Foucault's (1989/1969) definition of discourse as a system of representations is useful to articulate meaning and the forms of social practice that are embedded in the two different institutional fields. According to a Foucauldian view, discourse constitutes knowledge and, together with social practices, it establishes forms of subjectivity and power relations that inhere in such knowledge and social relations (Weedon, 1987). Together with conceptualizations of morality and local moral worlds (Kleinman 1992; Lakoff & Johnson, 1999) discourse may expand our understanding of how students conceive of, negotiate and perform everyday practices in discursive teacher education fields. Local moral worlds are contexts of shared experience, which mediate macro-social forces and shape specific local effects, so they are particular, intersubjective and constitutive of the lived flow of experience in the micro-contexts of daily life (Kleinman, 1992). They may help us to see students' learning as a pathway that does not have a beginning or an end; and as a process of becoming that is not only cognitive and resource-oriented but also socio-culturally and discursively produced.

Conceptualizing teacher education institutions as distinct local moral worlds can shed light on the significance and changing form of morality in different social contexts, based on, for instance, socio-cultural environments and the historical-political context of the different settings of Danish and Kenyan teacher education. Finally, this study is informed by Bourdieu (1977, 1986), whose conceptualizations of habitus may shed light on how human life and meaning are produced within the objective structures of teacher education, as institutional structures and processes are negotiated by student teachers. The study draws on material from ethnographic fieldwork conducted in Denmark 2017 in two university colleges (UC) and in Kenya 2009–2011 in three teacher-training colleges (TTC), and quantitative data for Kenya. Participants' names are changed to protect their anonymity.

Conceptualizing 'Discursive Becoming'

Some studies suggest that the teacher profession and teacher education (Dahl, 2014; Moos, 2017) are entangled in discursive practices. Drawing on conceptualizations such as categorization and positioning (Davies, 1990; Davies & Harré, 1990), discourse (Foucault, 1977), habitus (Bourdieu, 1977, 1986), and morality (Kleinman, 1992), this chapter addresses relational, dynamic and partly unstable processes of professional becoming — becoming as something that changes and is difficult to locate (Khawaja, 2013). Social categories can be defined as something a person does, not something a person is or has. They are 'not the *cause* of certain behavior but rather the *effect* of certain behavior'

(Staunæs, 2003, p. 104). Categories therefore become tools for selecting and ordering, for inclusion and exclusion, and for positioning and making hierarchies, hence they can be spoken of as 'shaping' the student body and determining what constitutes professionalism in college. Exploring categories makes it possible to discuss what is regarded as appropriate in different fields; by adopting the perspective of Bourdieu (1986) and employing a cultural analytical view of human agency as embedded, intentional and directed (Levinson & Holland, 1996) we can acknowledge that students actively negotiate institutionally produced categories in relation to their daily lives.

Davies (1990) argues that being an individual person in the modern world involves taking on the discursive practices through which a person is constituted. This resonates with Foucault's (1977) concept of self-technology, which describes how people internalize external power technologies and how institutions exercise power over individuals through their own self-surveillance, thereby becoming an agent of their own subjectification. In other words, people take up discursive practices as their own, rather than seeing them as external and coercive (Davies, 1990). According to this perspective, becoming is a process of positioning and locating oneself within different categories that are made available to one; it is associated with learning to participate in the discursive practices that give meaning to those categories, for instance in relation to the local moral worlds of teacher education. People take up their subject position (Davies & Harré, 1990) and make it their own within discursive fields.

Subjectivity is the post-structural concept that describes a person's sense of self, and it can be used to grasp, for instance, stability as well as change and rupture (Staunæs, 2003). From a post-structural perspective, this means that a person is a subject who has been categorized and positioned (by others) and therefore changed, for instance in relation to their sense of belonging. Students' sense of belonging in the teaching profession thus also depends on historical, political and cultural categorizations, which are also objects of analysis. Categorization may be viewed as a kind of positioning that is an ongoing and dynamic process (Davies & Harré, 1990). In relation to institutional categorization, this means exploring students' use of the positions and categories made available to them. Douglas (1966) highlights the fundamental role played by conceptual boundaries in constructing ideas of Self against those of the Other. In relation to institutional becoming and categorizations, this means exploring boundaries for students' control and examining how transgressing the social order might construct or tear down the sense of belonging that comes with being a teacher. Institutional frames demarcate spaces of individual people's possibilities (Douglas, 1986), and thus give rise to different versions of morality, gender, class, ethnicity and professionalism, which emerge and become cultivated in the daily life of teacher education college.

Professionalism and the Sense of Belonging

As a concept, 'belonging' has been addressed through different theoretical perspectives, for instance psychodynamic theory (Yuval-Davies, 2006) and social anthropological and postcolonial research (Khawaja, 2013). Belonging is a term that contains 'longing' (Khawaja, 2013), which addresses a kind of 'drive' towards or desire for something. Belonging has been conceptualized through its emotional aspects, by Yuval-Davies (2006), who sees it as being about emotional attachment, feeling at home and feeling safe, and by Davies (1990, p. 506) who describes it as about becoming emotionally committed to a category of membership and to an experience of 'belonging or not belonging in moral terms'. In relation to communalities such as teacher education institutions, morality addresses contexts of shared experience that shape local effects (Kleinman, 1992), for instance the morality of student teachers. This means that student teachers' morality may be seen as linked to a sense of belonging to (or longing for) being a member of a certain community, or longing for, or desiring teaching professionalism in specific ways.

According to Yuval-Davies, people can 'belong' in many different ways and to many different objects of attachment; belonging can vary between particular people in a concrete or abstract way, or be an act of self-identification or identification by others, in a stable, contested or transient way (Yuval-Davies, 2006). In a social anthropological view, morality might involve the things that are considered good in specific contexts (Kleinman, 1992; Lakoff & Johnson, 1999) and how these are related to ideas about teaching and professionalism. In terms of student teachers' 'longing for belonging' (Davies, 2000, cited in Khawaja, 2013, p. 533) in the teaching profession, this means exploring students' desires for belonging and being acknowledged and recognized as teachers and professionals. It also means examining the different hegemonic forms of local moralities and norms that are associated with the teaching profession in a specific setting, for instance, as they are communicated in different teacher education institutions. Finally, it means exploring the changing forms of the morality of professionalism in teaching, as it is discursively produced.

Morality and belonging are echoed in the professional literature that particularly employs the psychological perspectives of identity and identification as important categories of professionalism. Feelings of belonging or alienation may thus arise when student teachers become interwoven 'into the fabrics of others' lives' (Beardwood & O'Shea, 2011, p. 36), i.e., when they identify with, become rejected by or reject the social groups surrounding them.

Professional ideals are categorizations of what is considered 'good', for instance, regarding teaching. In Denmark and Kenya, professional ideals about teaching focus on promoting social equality, respect and independence (MOEST, 2002; Danmarks Lærerforening, 2002), yet they are negotiated differently by student teachers in the two national contexts (Dahl, 2018). In addition, 'professionalism' is an imprecise concept, but it can reflect an understanding of human agency and knowledge as contextual, embedded and directed, when linked with related concepts such as habitus, discourse and belonging. Teaching professionalism has been conceptualized as a matter of having a 'mission' (Korthagen, 2004) or feeling a 'calling' (Hansen, 1995) for teaching, which means that professionalism is also something that individuals may desire. Exploring teaching professionalism as a matter of professional longing therefore means addressing students' aspirations to become teachers, and how their categories of a 'good teacher' correspond with those of the institution.

Context: Teacher Education in Denmark and Kenya

D anish and Kenyan teacher education share many similarities: both draw on a curriculum focusing on subject matter and pedagogical practical training, and include specific sets of professional ideals which explicitly concern democratic classroom values (Danmarks Lærerforening, 2002; MOEST, 2004). In both settings, the teaching profession has lost prestige and is less attractive. In Denmark, it is difficult to recruit students for teacher education, and dropout rates are high (Nordic Council of Ministers, 2010). In Kenya, less than two-thirds of student teachers have teaching as their primary career aspiration (Dahl, 2017). This section explores the historical and socio-cultural contexts of teacher education in the two settings in order to locate discursive and institutionally embedded local moral worlds of teacher professionalism.

Denmark: Teacher Education as Civil Emancipation in a Neoliberal State

D anish teacher education started in 1791, when the first teacher-training college offered a four-year pedagogical and theoretical training course (Laursen, 2011). In teacher education today, two political trends can be identified: teacher education as civil emancipation (see Brandt & Böwadt, 2009) and as neoliberalism (see Andersen et al., 2017). With the latest teacher education reforms in 2013, teacher-specific regulations were revoked, and teaching subsumed within a more generic set of requirements for professional education. Danish teacher education is presently decentralized in accordance with common legislation (Rasmussen & Bayer, 2014), and is a four-year professional Bachelor's degree. The traditional division into subjects has been abolished and the content incorporated into four areas: professional aspects, teaching subjects, pedagogical training and Bachelor's project (Uddannelses- og Forskningsministeriet, 2012).

In 2007, teacher-training colleges merged with other professional Bachelor's education institutions into seven university colleges (UCs). From 2013, the new UCs were built as large complexes each serving around 10,000 students and 1,500 student teachers (Danske Professionshøjskoler, 2017). General education focusing on formative experiences was intended to 'permeate the whole education', so that the school could 'prepare pupils for participation, co-responsibility, rights and obligations in a society with freedom and democracy' (Uddannelses- og Forskningsministeriet, 2012, p. 1). For instance, one of the aims of UC Capital, the largest Danish UC with 10,087 students and 2,504 student teachers, is to educate teachers with 'a strong professional identity who are critical and constructive in relation to the pedagogical and educational political practice', so that teachers acquire 'a professional approach to the school's role as formative and educative institution' (Professionshøjskolen UCC, 2017, pp. 3–4). Values that embrace the formative role of teacher education in the emancipation of civil society can be traced to the 1940s, when a teacher-training-college rector wrote that the school 'through its whole atmosphere must educate for civil life and cooperation [...] that is democracy' (Christensen, 1945, p. 106, translated by author). Within this 'formative discourse', teachers' professional experiences and knowledge, among other things, are seen as legitimizing a widespread autonomy (Moos, 2017, p. 55). By organizing teacher education institutions in today's inclusive UCs, comprising teaching and research, UCs could appear consolidated and distinctive, and target development of a strong teacher identity (Hansén & Forsman, 2009; Andersen et. al., 2017). Yet, concerns have been raised that Danish teacher education during recent history appears to have been damaged and broken down by the many reforms and strict, detailed regulation that have been imposed on it, which have diminished its autonomous status and reduced the opportunity for self-definition (Andersen et al., 2017).

Many of today's UCs appear to be all-encompassing villages, with supermarkets, pharmacies, cafés, hotels, receptions, large cafeterias, social spaces and 'base camps' where staff work behind information desks from which they both advise students about their studies and physically direct them to other sites, on impersonal campuses characterized by 'hard functionalism' (Kirkeby, 2006, cited in Tanggaard & Szulewicz, 2013, p. 80). Spaces, and their usages, are clearly defined in ways that do not encourage flexibility or requests for alteration. In spite of an increased interest in relational and class-managerial competencies (Nordenbo et al., 2008), teaching studies have become more academic, with subject specializations and augmented admission criteria despite recruitment problems. It is easier for courses to adapt to market demands, due to the decentralized regulation of the UCs. Each of the seven UCs has the mandate to develop a distinctive profile; UCs can in many ways be seen as neoliberal institutions, created by the state as enterprising and competitive entrepreneurs (Olssen, 2003) practising freedom.

Kenya: Teacher Education as British Missionary History in Eastern Africa

U ntil 1911, British missionaries controlled education in Kenya with the declared purpose of enlightening Africans 'so that they could read the Bible and assist in spreading Christianity and western civilization to fellow Africans' (Eshiwani, 1993, p. 17). Colonial African schooling has been described as 'tools for colonial powers to educate and civilize the savage black population to become a submissive local workforce' (Sifuna & Otiende, 2006, p. 192). By the beginning of the 1920s, teacher training was carried out as 'training on the job' (Sifuna & Otiende, 2006) by the Christian Church; however, the Phelps-Stoke Commission visited East Africa in 1924 and recommended a uniform education system with adequate teacher-training centres focusing on agricultural and industrial programmes to meet local needs. Moral concerns about how teachers were to be role models for the population were expressed in the Binns Commission's worries about the 'lack of dignity in the teaching profession' (Sifuna & Otiende, 2006, p. 225) in 1952.

Consequently, a plan to re-organize teacher training was initiated by the Christian Council of Kenya in 1956. Still, there were too few teachers and most of them were untrained when Kenya gained independence in 1963 (Eshiwani, 1993). Shortly after independence, the Kenyan government consolidated teacher education into the present eighteen public teacher-training colleges (TTCs) with a capacity of about 600 students each (Sifuna & Otiende, 2006). In addition, Kenya today has about 100 private TTCs. The stated aims for teacher education formally stress emancipation for civil society, since student teachers are meant to learn to 'foster nationalism, and promote national and individual development, sound moral and religious values, social equality and responsibility, respect for and development of Kenya's rich and varied culture, international consciousness, positive attitudes towards other nations, good health, and environmental protection' (MOEST, 2004, pp. vi–viii).

Teacher education today in Kenya is a two-year residential course, where students obtain the Primary Teacher Education (PTE) certificate based on a final exam prepared by the Kenya National Examination Council (KNEC). The PTE exam consists of eighteen different subjects, most of which are studied during the student's second year at college, and assessment is conducted in the form of written, multiple-choice tests, emphasizing detailed, core-subject knowledge. The content of subjects and topics in the core curriculum and the PTE exam at the public and private TTCs is theoretically similar, but teacher-training institutions communicate value differently. Formally, Kenyan TTCs are regulated through the Education Act of 1980, which outlines the education system in general terms only (Republic of Kenya, 2012). At present, there is neither a policy paper nor act governing the primary sector specifically but the area is regulated by a locally appointed Board of Governors, many of whose members have a religious background. Strong Christian religious influence on local management committees has probably led to what has been termed informal, moralistic education in Kenyan public TTCs (Dahl, 2015).

Categorizing 'the Good Student' in Diverse Institutions

This section explores how social order and moral boundaries in the two settings were maintained or transgressed (see Douglas, 1966) as the institutions promoted, and students negotiated, categories of being a 'good student'. Discussing categories may inform us about how the different kinds of institution provide different possibilities for interaction and positioning, which students take up and make their own.

Good students in Danish UCs displayed appropriate moral behaviour by attending classes with their homework done, not being late, and being active and critically engaged in class discussions initiated by the teacher. After the first semester, students' attendance during class dropped dramatically so a class with thirty students could shrink to a handful of students. Students reported that tutors would often comment during classes on students who were late or did not come to class. Tutors, on the other hand, felt that it was difficult to maintain a coherent programme of study when the student population in a specific class was not consistent due to the irregular turnout. However, students claimed that many tutors did not read and correct their homework, leaving them without guidance regarding their academic performance. Tutors articulated the role of teacher education enabling students to develop independence and critical consciousness so they could locate and 'identify with their own special teacher profile'. Yet many students found this a difficult task, since they felt they were left to their own devices to figure out what 'kind of teacher' they were. In many ways, the institutional demands from the tutors about developing professionalism did not match the students' opportunities for doing so, as the following interview extract with a female student-teacher illustrates:

> It was because I did not really participate in classes, so I was not 'seen' by my classmates. So, I think half a year passed by before I realized that this is not going to be easy. I had totally underestimated this [...] It became hard, and I was also forced to find out, or to put my feelings into words on which kind of teacher I would like to become. It was a question we got quite fast. So, you were kind of, 'I don't know, I just want to become a teacher'. [...] We were told over and over again that we should find out what was important for us so we could argue for why we did one thing instead of another. (Melissa, 28-year-old female student)

Though students were aware of the institutional demands facing them, these demands appeared in an 'empty' space, where there seemed no reference points such as written guidance or concrete feedback to guide them in future. Tutors were busy and did not interact with individual students. Students, who had fewer fixed interactions with their peers, had difficulties in understanding what was appropriate student behaviour. At a first glance, the space for 'becoming' at Danish UCs appeared ungoverned; a place where 'anything goes' in a kind of 'laissez-faire pedagogy' (Jacobsen & Kristiansen, 2001, p. 112). Laissez-faire is a personal morality that builds on a conception of value nihilism (ibid., 2001) in a context of minimal state intervention and control. However, Danish teacher education was not a value-free entity without structures and rules, since classes, pedagogical training and exams were conducted according to strict regulations, albeit with a minimal effort by many of the students who, in return, often found that their homework was not marked by the tutor. In spite of tutors' annoyance about late and unprepared students, many students felt left to their own devices by busy teachers and subsequently thought of the course as 'an easy task'.

According to Dean (2002), liberalism is not freedom, but another form of 'conduct of conduct' and government. In Dean's view, the institutional government of students became self-government. Davies and Bansel for instance argue (2010, p. 5) that the single most important feature of a neoliberal government is 'that it systematically dismantles the will to critique, thus potentially shifting the very nature of what a university is and the ways in which academics understand their work'. This means that the market becomes the singular discourse through which individual and institutional acceptability is recognized (Davies & Bansel, 2010). The market in this case being the audit technologies that 'standardize and regularize expert knowledge so that they can be used to classify and diagnose populations of workers' (Davies & Bansel, 2010, p. 7), such as students and tutors depending on how they deliver academic performance standards in the form of, for instance, pass percentages and academic achievements. Free will and choice seemingly did not result in more democracy but instead in institutional moulding, where new hierarchies regarding physical presence and the delivery of output on time became dominant categories for how 'a good student' was perceived.

'Good students' in Kenyan TTCs displayed appropriate 'moral' behaviour, which included obeying the Ten Commandments and keeping friendships with the opposite gender at a platonic level (see Dahl, 2014). 'Immoral' behaviour, however, on the other hand, included engaging in intimate relationships, partying during weekends, drinking alcohol and dressing in Western clothes, such as short dresses and tight jeans, all of which purportedly led to achieving low marks. However, it was the majority of students — and most of them female students — who were perceived as 'spoilers', 'romantic ladies' and 'naughty ones', as college staff and students categorized those students who behaved in what were considered immoral ways, illustrated in this male student's account (as discussed in Dahl, 2017, p. 157):

> It [immoral behaviour] lowers your dignity, because people could judge you, they say something must be wrong with you because we [male and female students] are not meant to relate in a cordially [sic] manner. [...]
> It means bad reputation for you. It spoils your name. It makes people hate you [...] If you have got that Biblical kind of brought up [sic] then it can help you, because the readings in the Bible are always very clear that if you fail to follow this, then retributions are there. Like the Bible

says, the remedy for sin is death. So if you sin, you die. But if you do according to the commandment [...] life is there. (Martin, 25-year-old male student)

Achieving good marks also mattered, but much more importance was attached to moral behaviour. Immoral behaviour, such as engaging in intimate relations with students of the opposite gender, was sanctioned severely and meant that 'The Dean's eyes will now be on you', as a student explained. Since many students secretly engaged in intimate premarital relations and had boyfriends or girlfriends, they all became 'Other' (Collins, 1998) in relation to the dominant matrix. Most students followed practices outside the norms of the civilized order of teacher training; practices considered illegitimate and inappropriate. Yet, many students seemingly took up the subject positions (Davies & Harré, 1990) available for them within the institutional space and made them their own. Students apparently internalized the dominant matrix and discipline as bodily gestures and would, for instance, appear in the public college space with lowered heads and voices, physically separated from one another according to gender. The institutional discipline was maintained without overt violence, and the controlled persons had in some ways become the source of their own control (Foucault, 1977).

Generally, teacher education in the two contexts seems characterized by boundaries between what is considered 'good' and 'pure' student behaviour and what is considered dangerous and beyond the margins of teacher education, and probably teacher professionalism, paraphrasing Douglas (1966). In the Danish context, these boundaries are drawn by indefinite claims in relatively empty spaces for students' self-preservation, and in the Kenyan context by a stricter boundary separating illicit and permitted student behaviour. Subjects, however, often handle their social realities in more complex ways than institutions think. Deterministic analyses of institutional power as something standardized and one-way must be transgressed (Staunæs, 2007) to include an empirical analysis of students' lives. Danish Melissa's and Kenyan Martin's accounts of being student teachers illustrate how values and moralities became an integral part of the way they thought of themselves as teachers — Melissa in the way she became frustrated as she sensed the institutional pressure of navigating in an ungoverned yet controlled space, and Martin in the form of fear of diverging from the institutionally legitimized student behaviour and being positioned as an inappropriate 'Other' (see Collins, 1998). Overall, morality appeared to be an important aspect of students' learning in both settings; students' learning at teacher education institutions was in other words not only intellectual and cognitive but also recognized 'underlying principles of ethics and moralities' (LeVine & White, 1986), meaning that students' professionalization had a socially constructed nature (see Phoenix, 2008).

Appropriating Categories and Achieving a Sense of Professional Belonging

I n Danish teacher education, value formation took place as informal learning (Eraut, 2004) in Kristendomskundskab, Livsoplysning og Medborgerskab (KLM, Religious Education, Life Education and Citizenship). The purpose of KLM was that students should gain a 'critical sense of relation to their outlooks on life and value orientation', focusing on strengthening the teaching profession by studying the meaning of Christianity for European values (Brandt & Böwadt, 2009, p. 5).

Many students thought of KLM as a benchmark for their subsequent studies, since tutors continually referred to it during teacher education. In an informal way, the organization of classes as group work seemed to underline the institutional demands that students should be active, self-defining and skilled in argument. A female student described how the organization of tuition as group work was central to the students' ability to gain recognition in the institution as 'good students' who were continually confronted by other students to learn to speak up as part of a civil emancipatory project, pressurizing them to reconsider their recognition of being teachers:

> We started quite early during the studies being placed in groups to do group work. I never took the lead. In the beginning, I was the quiet mouse who sat in the corner and said nothing, unless I was asked. So when I came home I would think, 'It's annoying I didn't say this or that'. [...] [But tuition] was totally varied. There was never really anything of the same (no cohesion) [...] It was very much running like with lectures,

exercises, up and walk, walking around with exercises, brainstorm and then talk. (Laura, 27-year-old female student)

Though the values of KLM were continuously referred to during subsequent classes, this only took place during class hours, initiated by tutors, so many students felt that their sense of belonging in the civil emancipatory project faded as they completed their studies. Though students felt that formal teaching in the first semester was permeated by explicit value formation, forcing them to reflect on their own values in relation to the teaching profession, they also felt the lack of social 'glue' in the institution, and this made them stick together to overcome feelings of isolation. Students felt that the former 'spirit' from teacher education in the smaller colleges, where tutors and students knew each other, had disappeared and they were left with the large, impersonal complexes, 'which did not make sense to me as a human being', as a female student explained. Yet traces of the students' development of professional belonging remained, since KLM initiated reflections on what kind of teacher they wanted to be. Their sense of belonging in college was mostly linked to relations with student peers, and many students' relationships with their colleges were reduced to attending classes; youth life and peer identification replaced the values of the civil emancipatory project ingrained in the institution. So, student teachers avoided the institutional control and stigma by constructing normative communalities of 'kindred spirits' with other students (see Jones, 2011). However, 'good students' received additional attention from tutors and, as a consequence, put more effort into relating to the teaching profession.

In Kenyan TTCs, informal education, such as teaching with moralistic content (see Dahl, 2015) seemed highly characteristic of students' spaces of becoming. During teacher education, students were subjected to a mix of different informal learning discourses that intermingled and represented complex spaces for students' possible orientation. Informal education with moralistic content seemed to be the dominant discourse of meaning, meant to coerce students to become puritan, obedient subjects. Yet, the analysis demonstrates that though moral discipline conveyed by the institution impacted students' meaning-making, so some students conformed to 'biblical' values and refrained from engaging in intimate relationships, many other students actively negotiated the categories intended to dominate them, creating new meaning. The institutional discipline of students was most successful when institutions also provided space for social and emotional attachment between students and the institution. In most TTCs, for instance, the deputy principal had the unpopular role of disciplining and controlling students. Consequently, the head of the institution, the principal, seldom criticized or scolded students, but was able to interact with them in a more friendly and symmetrical fashion and demonstrate a more forgiving way of handling their 'misconducts'. This was, for instance, visible in TTCs who had institutionalized their surveillance of students into emotional 'relationing', asking older students to become 'student mothers' and 'student fathers', and appointing a specific lecturer to each student, a 'personal' lecturer, who through emotional attachment could closely monitor the specific student's conduct.

Following Bourdieu (1997), the personal charisma of tutors or more experienced students was therefore used to transform relations of dominance into emotional relations, thereby casting an emotional spell that controlled students in different ways. Power worked subtly, as tutors assisted students with 'motherly advice', lent them pocket money for travel home during the holidays, and in other ways sought to be 'close' to students. Students in these teacher education cultures felt devotion and connectedness to the persons who were appointed to be responsible for their studies, and came to appreciate that owing somebody something was to be understood as a feeling, and thereby perceived as a longer-lasting trait of the person who executed the generous action (Bourdieu, 1997). Relations of dominance and suppression were sometimes turned into emotional relations using charm and charisma; in these cases, the symbolic violence was gentler, and more hidden forms of violence (Bourdieu, 1977) were inflicted on students.

A questionnaire distributed to 3,145 Kenyan student teachers found that though the vast majority of students entering TTC were seeking an education rather than to become a teacher, 64% of first-year students and 65% of second-year students indicated that given a second chance, they would still choose teaching as a career (Dahl, 2017). This indicates that a sense of professional belonging had developed in students during their teacher education. However, research also indicates that the sense of belonging was dependent on the kind of institutional culture the students belonged to. Since a sense of belonging contains both cognitive and affective elements in a person's evaluation of his or her role in relation to a specific group, belonging also results in affective responses (Hurtado & Carter, 1997). Students' sense of belonging was thus associated with receiving positive feedback, for instance in informal 'relationing' with tutors and fellow students. Institutional cultures that provided such spaces aroused positive emotions and thus a sense of belonging in the place and the teaching profession in students. Kenyan TTCs were, in spite of being overall spaces for communicating morality, also spaces for positive, social interaction between students and institutionally legitimized personnel such as tutors. This could possibly explain why students, in spite of their negative evaluations of the bodily and mental disciplining they experienced, developed a sense of belonging to the teaching profession during their stay at the TTC, since they also received moral instruction that increased their feeling of being professionally responsible (see Solbrekke & Englund, 2011).

Conclusion

T his chapter has discussed what it means to be a student teacher in diverse teacher education contexts, and how institutional moralities categorize and shape students' identification and sense of belonging in the teaching profession through their being subjected to different spaces of becoming, cultivated in the two institutions. Findings suggest that, in both Denmark and Kenya, teacher education is not a totally open and power-neutral carrier of history and tradition, but rather informs future students' stories about what it means to be a schoolteacher. Students in both settings are subjected to discursive practices that constitute them in different ways; yet the findings suggest that informal moralization emphasizing values such as democratic emancipation (in Danish teacher education) and Christian, religious education (in Kenyan teacher education) are present in both settings, and that students do become categorized according to their moral values in both settings. However, it appears that, compared to Kenya, Danish teacher education practices impacted on students' professional becoming in different, rather than less pervasive, ways. In Kenya, value disciplining for some students remained external, since students' peer culture critically negotiated and resisted the biblical messages conveyed by the institutions; in Denmark, value disciplining worked in more subtle ways, probably since students had a greater say in their student life and spare time compared to their Kenyan peers. However, being subjected to a seemingly empty space of 'laissez-faire' (Jacobsen & Kristiansen, 2001), with minimal intervention, systematically deconstructed students' will to critique (see Dean, 2002). The very nature of the university as a reflective space disappeared.

Having finished their teaching studies, Danish students subsequently struggled with their professional identities and many had difficulty in finding a sense of belonging in the profession. In contrast, the Kenyan students occupied a tight institutional space where values were clearly set out. Yet these values only partly penetrated students' ideas about what a good teacher is, probably as the biblical and highly moralistic values sharply contrasted with their everyday lives, where independence and modern lifestyles were possible. Kenyan students and their Danish peers used student communities to negotiate categories of professionalism, and their sense of belonging was therefore created in relation to peer communities rather than solely the institution. Perhaps, through continually visualizing and reflecting on moral education in the institutional space, students can be enabled to develop their own version of professionalism and through this a sense of belonging in the profession.

References

Andersen, F.Ø., Wiskerchen, M. & Honoré, C.L. (2017). *Finsk læreruddannelse — i et dansk perspektiv*. Aarhus University: Danish School of Education.

Beardwood, R. & O'Shea, R. (eds) (2011). *Exploring issues of identity and belonging*, 4th edn. Victoria, Australia: Insight.

Bourdieu, P. (1977). *Outline of a theory of practice*. Cambridge: Cambridge University Press.

Bourdieu, P. (1986). *Distinction*. London: Routledge.

Bourdieu, P. (1997). *Af praktiske grunde*. Copenhagen: Hans Reitzels Forlag.

Brandt, A.K. & Böwadt, P.R. (2009). *Citizenship in teacher education. Report to the Ministry of Education*. https://backend.folkeskolen.dk/~/Documents/154/59354.pdf

Christensen, G. (1945). Social-pædagogisk Forenings og Frit Danmarks Lærergruppes skoleplaner. *Pædagogisk Psykologisk Tidsskrift*, V: 105–36.

Cochran-Smith, M. and Boston College Evidence Team. (2009). 'Re-culturing' teacher education: Inquiry, evidence, and action. *Journal of Teacher Education*, 60(5): 458–68.

Collins, P.H. (1998). It's all in the family: Intersections of gender, race and nation. *Hypatia*, 3(3): 62–82.

Dahl, K.K.B. (2014). 'Paradoxical health education': Learning about health in Kenyan teacher training colleges. *Compare*, 44(4): 634–54. https://doi.org/10 .1080/03057925.2013.800784

Dahl, K.K.B. (2015). Informal, moralistic health education in Kenyan teacher education and how it influences the professional identity of student-teachers. *Research in Comparative and International Education*, 10(2): 167–84. https://doi. org/10.1177/1745499915571705

Dahl, K.K.B. (2017). *With the best of intentions. Becoming somebody in Kenyan teacher education*. Copenhagen: Roskilde University Press.

Dahl, K.K.B. (2018). Mo(ve)ments in professional identification. Achieving professional identity and becoming a teacher in Denmark and Kenya. *Compare: A Journal of Comparative and International Education*. https://doi.org /10.1080/03057925.2018.1508333

Danmarks Lærerforening (Danish Union of Teachers) (2002). *Professionsideal for Danmarks Lærerforening*. Copenhagen: Danmarks Lærerforening. http:// www.dlf.org/media/974300/profesionsideal_endelige-version.pdf

Danske Professionshøjskoler (Danish University Colleges) (2017). *Tal og Fakta*. http://danskeprofessionshøjskoler.dk/tal-fakta/

Davies, B. (1990). The problem of desire. *Social Problems*, 37(4): 501–16.

Davies, B. (2000). (In)scribing body/landscape relations. Walnut Creek: AltaMira Press. Cited in: Khawaja, I. (2013). Fællesskab som fællesgørende bevægelse? — Muslimskhed, fælleshed og belonging. *Psyke & Logos*, 34: 510–39.

Davies, B. & Bansel, P. (2010). Governmentality and academic work. *Journal of Curriculum Theorizing*, 26(3): 5–20.

Davies, B. & Harré, R. (1990). Positioning: The discursive production of selves. *Journal for the Theory of Social Behaviour*, 20(1): 43–63.

Dean, M. (2002). Powers of life and death beyond governmentality. *Cultural Values*, 6: 119–38.

Douglas, M. (1966). *Purity and danger*. New York: Frederick A. Praeger.

Douglas, M. (1986). *How institutions think*. New York: Syracuse University Press.

Eraut, M. (2004). Informal learning in the workplace. *Studies in Continuing Education*, 26(2): 247–73.

Eshiwani, G.S. (1993). *Education in Kenya since independence*. Nairobi: East African Educational.

Foucault, M. (1977). *Discipline and punish: The birth of the prison*. London: Penguin Books.

Foucault, M. (1989/1969). *The archaeology of knowledge*. London: Routledge.

Hansen, D.T. (1995). *The call to teach*. New York: Teachers College Press.

Hansén, S.-E. & Forsman, L. (2009). Design and dilemmas — Experiences from Finnish teacher education. *Didacta Varia*, 14(1): 3–23.

Hurtado, S. & Carter, D.F. (1997). Effects of college transition and perceptions of the campus racial climate on Latino college students' sense of belonging. *Sociology of Education*, 70(4): 324–45.

Jacobsen, M.H. & Kristiansen, S. (2001). *Farligt feltarbejde*. Aalborg: Aalborg University Press.

Jones, O. (2011). Materiality and identity: Forests, trees and senses of belonging. In: Ritter, E. & Dauksta, D. (eds) *New perspectives on people and forests: World forests*, 9. Dordrecht: Springer.

Khawaja, I. (2013). Fællesskab som fællesgørende bevægelse? — Muslimskhed, fælleshed og belonging. *Psyke & Logos*, 34: 510–39.

Kirkeby, I.M. (2006). Skolen finder sted (Hørsholm: Statens Byggeforskningsinstitut), cited in: Tanggaard, L. & Szulevicz, T. (2013). Sociale læreprocesser som analytisk begreb. *Psyke & Logos*, 34: 69–82.

Kleinman, A. (1992). Pain and resistance: The delegitimation and relegitimation of local worlds. In: Good, M.-J.D.V., Brodwin, P.E., Good, B.J., & Kleinman, A. (eds), *Pain as human experience*. Los Angeles, CA: University of California Press.

Korthagen, F.A.J. (2004). In search of the essence of a good teacher. *Teaching and Teacher Education*, 20: 77–97. https://doi.org/10.1016/j.tate.2003.10.002

Ladson-Billing, G. (2006). It's not the problem of poverty, it's the poverty of culture: The problem with teacher education. *Anthropology & Education Quarterly*, 37(2): 104–09. https://doi.org/10.1525/aeq.2006.37.2.104

Lakoff, G. & M. Johnson. (1999). Morality. In: Lakoff, G. & Johnson, M. (eds), *Philosophy in the flesh*. New York: Basic Books.

Laursen, P.F. (2011). Teori og praksis. In: Kristensen, H.J. & Laursen, P.F. (eds), *Gyldendals Pædagogikhåndbog*. Copenhagen: Gyldendal.

LeVine, R.A. & White, M.I. (1986). *The human conditions*. New York: Routledge.

Levinson, B.A. & Holland, D.C. (1996). The cultural production of the educated person. In: Levinson, B.A., Foley, D.E. & Holland, D.C. (eds), *The cultural production of the educated person*. New York: Albany.

Moos, L. (2017). Professionerns fire diskurser. *Tidsskrift for Professionsstudier*, 13(25): 54–63.

MOEST (Ministry of Education, Science &Technology) (2002). *Primary education syllabus*. Nairobi: MOEST.

MOEST (2004). *Primary teacher education syllabus*. Nairobi: MOEST.

Nordenbo, S.E., Larsen, M.S., Tiftikçi, N., Wendt, R.E. & Østergaard, S. (2008). *Lærerkompetencer og elevers læring i barnehage og skole*. Copenhagen: Danish Clearinghouse.

Nordic Council of Ministers (2010). *Rekrutteringsproblematikken på nordiske læreruddannelser*. Copenhagen: Nordic Council of Ministers. http://norden. diva-portal.org/smash/get/diva2:701429/FULLTEXT01.pdf

Olssen, M. (2003). Structuralism, post-structuralism, neoliberalism. *Journal of Education Policy*, 18(2): 189–202.

Phoenix, A. (2008). Racialised young masculinities: Doing intersectionality at school. In: Seemann, M. (ed), *Ethnische Diversitäten, Gender und Schule*. Oldenburg: BIS Verlag.

Professionshøjskolen UCC (University College UCC) (2017). *Profil af læreruddannelsen*. Copenhagen: University College Capital. https://ucc.dk/ sites/default/files/170307_profilpapir.pdf

Rasmussen, J. & Bayer, M. (2014). Comparative study of teaching content in teacher education programmes in Canada, Denmark, Finland and Singapore. *Journal of Curriculum Studies*, 46(6): 798–818.

Republic of Kenya (2012). *Education Act*. Nairobi: National Council for Law Reporting.

Sifuna, D.N. & Otiende, J.E. (2006). *An introductory history of education*. Nairobi: University of Nairobi Press.

Solbrekke, T.D., & Englund, T. (2011). Bringing professional responsibility back in. *Studies in Higher Education*, 36(7): 847–61. https://doi.org/10.1080/03075 079.2010.482205

Staunæs, D. (2003). Where have all the subjects gone? Bringing together the concepts of intersectionality and subjectification. *NORA — Nordic Journal of Feminist and Gender Research*, 11(2): 101–10. https://doi. org/10.1080/08038740310002950

Staunæs, D. (2007). Subversive analysestrategier. In: Koefoed, J. and Staunæs, D. (eds), *Magtballader*. Copenhagen: Danish University of Education Press.

Uddannelses- og Forskningsministeriet (Ministry of Education and Research) (2012). *Reform af læreruddannelsen — Aftaletekst*. https://ufm.dk/lovstof/ politiske-aftaler/reform-af-laereruddannelsen

Weedon, C. (1987). *Feminist practice and poststructuralist theory*. Oxford: Basil Blackwell.

Yuval-Davies, N. (2006). Belonging and the politics of belonging. *Patterns of Prejudice*, 40(3): 197–214. https://doi.org/10.1080/00313220600769331

7. Irish Adult Educators Find Fulfilment amid Poor Employment Conditions

Sarah Bates Evoy

Sarah Bates Evoy examines the views of six part-time tutors in Irish Further Education selected from a larger project. She explains the poor employment conditions within which the tutors work, but shows that they enjoy their jobs and motivate themselves to continue because they see their work as valuable. The narratives are subject to within- and across-analysis, using Archer's framework of identity, structure and agency.

This chapter considers what motivates educated and experienced individuals with a variety of different employment options to choose to work with part-time adult programmes within the Irish Further Education and Training (FET) sector, especially when this part of the sector is characterized by poor employment conditions. It also examines how Irish FET practitioners balance the insecure nature of their job roles, with their desire for a wage, consistent working conditions and job satisfaction. It does this by exploring what motivates six FET practitioners who find fulfilment in their teaching and training roles despite the unsatisfactory employment conditions that prevail in the sector, drawing on the findings of a larger research project ('Practitioner Identities and Sector Reform in Contemporary Further Education and Training in Ireland') which examined the impact of major reforms since 2013.

https://doi.org/10.11647/OBP.0203.07

Firstly, the reader is introduced to the Irish Further Education and Training Sector, particularly its part-time programmes, and briefly shown how the material in this chapter fits within the larger research project. Then, in the second half of the chapter, the interviewees' own words are used to both reveal issues related to employment conditions and to demonstrate the practitioners' awareness of them. The key motivations of the six interviewees who choose to work with part-time FET programmes, despite experiencing unfavourable employment conditions, are examined using both within-narrative and across-narrative approaches and Margaret Archer's (2000, 2003) work on identity, agency, and structure as a framework.

Introduction to the Irish Further Education and Training Sector

In 2013 the Irish FET Sector became a distinct and official sector of the national education system, one that provides for those learners who seek *more* rather than *higher* education, and typically courses with a vocational rather than an academic focus. The Irish FET sector is a result of the amalgamation of a range of different education and training bodies, providing programmes and learning opportunities to individuals typically over the age of 16. FET is distinct from the mainstream Primary, Secondary and Tertiary Education Sectors and offers both accredited and non-accredited education and training, which can take place in both formal and informal contexts, with full-time or part-time learners. Accredited FET programmes lead to awards between Levels 1 and 6 on the Irish National Framework of Qualifications (NFQ), which is equivalent to Levels 1 to 5 on the European Qualifications Framework (EFQ) (McGuinness et al., 2014; SOLAS, 2014).

The newly amalgamated Irish FET sector brought together numerous and diverse learning and teaching environments and contexts, all of which had developed separately and somewhat organically over a long period (McGuinness et al., 2014; SOLAS, 2014). This diversity is evident, for example, even in the ways that educators are named. Teacher, tutor, trainer, facilitator, instructor and lecturer are used in different settings, necessitating my use of the more inclusive term 'FET practitioners'. Diversity is also evident in FET practitioners' own education, training, professional qualifications, career goals, values and beliefs about learning and teaching, and workplace contexts and ethos. This has led to much confusion about what FET is supposed to be, what FET actually is, and what constitutes a professional FET practitioner. The scenarios currently playing out in the Irish context are not unique in the international context and the complexity of Irish FET mirrors that found in comparable sectors internationally. Equivalent sectors and activities exist in various other countries, but may be described by different terms, including Adult, Vocational, Technical, and Continuing Education and Training.

Part-Time FET Programmes

T he six FET practitioners who taught on part-time FET programmes, and whose interviews underpin this chapter, all work with Education and Training Boards (ETBs, the main statutory providers of FET) within the South-East of Ireland. They all have experience of Back to Education Initiatives: part-time accredited courses, typically two years in duration, for learners aged sixteen and over, many of whom have not completed mainstream education. Four of the six also have experience working with ETB Adult Literacy Services and on Community Education programmes, teaching both accredited and non-accredited courses.

Conditions of Employment for Those Working on Part-Time Programmes

P art-time FET programmes cater for part-time learners, and the hours that individual FET practitioners spend engaging with these programmes are extremely varied; many work with a number of programmes. Even if practitioners have contracts of employment, they are not generally entitled to sick pay or pay outside of term-time. Currently ETBs have a variety of different employment types, which vary in entitlements, and 'annual leave, sick pay and maternity pay are subject to variation across this range of employment types' (CMETB, 2014, p. 27).

ETB terms and conditions of employment are generally the result of 'collective agreements negotiated and agreed between Trade Unions,

Staff Associations, managerial authorities and the [Government's] Department of Education & Skills' (CMETB, 2014, p. 27). At the time of writing (early 2018), the Teachers Union of Ireland (TUI) was in negotiations with the Department of Education & Skills and the Workplace Relations Commission to improve the employment conditions of FET practitioners working in 'non-mainstream Further Education' which included practitioners working with part-time FET programmes (TUI, 2017). The union was advocating that all practitioners with four years of successive service be given so called CIDs (Contracts of Indefinite Duration) which would set out the minimum number of teaching/ tutoring hours for which individual practitioners would be paid on an annual basis (TUI, 2017). In addition, the TUI was campaigning for the 'establishment of a common, sector-wide incremental salary scale and terms of employment for adult education tutors' as well as 'access to leave schemes and paid leave,' which would include maternity leave and paid sick leave (TUI, 2017). That this was happening, exemplifies the claim that existing conditions were poor.

Researching Further Education and Training Practitioners

Research Design

The methodological design was underpinned by a critical realist position and the theoretical approach was informed by the work of Margaret Archer in relation to identity, agency and structure. The study applied an inductive approach to the investigation of the research issues to allow the research and the findings to be firmly rooted in the opinions, experiences, perspectives and narratives of Irish FET practitioners themselves.

The larger research project consisted of three stages: a scoping exercise, a wider context-building exercise utilising an online survey, and a more in-depth examination of twelve individual FET practitioners' identities through narrative interviews. This chapter discusses six of the twelve interviewees, selecting those who worked with part-time FET programmes including Back to Education Initiatives, Adult Literacy and Community Education.

The research data generated were analysed through a process of content analysis, a form of qualitative data analysis involving a set of flexible, systematic techniques which guide researchers in analysing the qualitative, informational content of textual research data. Qualitative content analysis aims to achieve a deep level of description and understanding of the phenomenon or group being researched within their unique context (Forman & Damschroder, 2008; Schreier, 2014).

With the aid of a computer programme (Nvivo) data were categorized into themes/codes. Codes were established inductively, directly from the transcripts, as was the case with the 'motivation' code which was drawn upon for this chapter, and deductively, based on themes that emerged from the academic literature. Descriptive reports were then created based on individual codes and small collections of related codes. These reports were then analysed and interpreted, which re-contextualized the data and created an overall story. The reports were also viewed and analysed through a conceptual lens based on Archer's theories on identity and structure and agency. This was done in an attempt to better identify and understand the various factors that influenced the formation of interviewees' professional identities, and reach tentative explanations regarding the interaction and relationships between structure, culture and agency shown in the research data.

Profile of Interviewees

Of the six interviewees, three are female (Mary, Lucy, Maggie) and three male (Fergus, Luke, Peter). At the time of the interviews, two were aged between thirty-six and forty-five and the other four were aged between forty-six and fifty-five. All the interviewees had more than 10 years' experience of delivering education and training, though not all of the interviewees' teaching experience related to the FET sector. One had trained apprentices, two had worked in early education and three had worked in higher education.

Conceptualizing Personal Identity

As already stated, Margaret Archer's theories formed a conceptual lens through which to view the professional identities of FET practitioners, and this chapter discusses the aspect of Archer's theories that relates to the formation of personal identities.

Archer (2000, p. 9) asserts that individual personal identities are an expression of reflective, considered engagement with the 'three orders of reality': natural (our physical wellbeing), practical (our performative achievements) and social (our sense of self-worth). She explains that within each order of reality we will have concerns, things we want to have happen for us. The expression of our personal identities is reflected in how we prioritize our concerns: 'it is the distinctive patterning of these concerns which is held to give people their unique personal identities' (Archer, 2000, p. 9). As humans, our overall wellbeing depends on us attending to our various concerns within the three orders, 'to strike a balance between our trinity of inescapable human concerns' (Archer, 2000, p. 10). Archer (2000, 2003) further explains that, through a process of 'internal conversation', individuals identify and sort subordinate concerns from ultimate concerns, and through prioritizing and compromising, create a set of commitments that they feel they can live with (Archer, 2000, p. 10).

What follows is based on the six narrative interviews with practitioners who had recent experience working with part-time FET programmes.

Findings from the Narrative Interviews

Interviewees' Reflections on their Employment Conditions

Analysis across the six interviews showed that employment conditions were a key theme among the interviewees, though their individual situations differed. Their comments demonstrate that problems were both 'real' and 'felt'.

> Unpaid holidays and lack of security re: hours from one academic year to the next is the real downside of the job. (Lucy)

One of the interviewees works twenty-two hours per week (the equivalent hours to a full-time, recognized teacher) tutoring with the Back to Education Initiative and claims social welfare benefits during the summer months. Another of the interviewees has a high number of tutor hours across various part-time programmes and his timetable changes from term to term and year to year. He compensates for not having a year-round wage by working in his previous role in between term times.

The other four practitioners have part-time tutoring hours. Two have taken on part-time, permanent resource positions within their education centres. Resource positions involve supporting co-ordinators and usually involve significant administrative duties. These positions pay less than tutoring, but guarantee regular hours and benefits such as sick pay. Of the remaining two practitioners, one is a stay-at-home parent when she is not teaching and the other has a permanent part-time post in another sector of the education system.

As stated, four of the six interviewees have additional jobs as well as their tutoring/teaching posts, which compensate for the lack of security associated with working with part-time FET programmes.

> I do part-time resource as well as teaching, so if I have a sick day on my part-time resource, it's fine, I get paid for it. But if I have a sick day when I'm teaching, I don't. That's why I took the part-time resource job for a bit of security. (Maggie)

The interviewees spoke about several issues that negatively impacted on their experiences and perceptions of their employment conditions and contracts. All commented on the lack of contracts with guaranteed hours, even though contracts had been promised to several of the interviewees for many years.

> I was being promised, 'Oh yeah, there'll be a full-time contract now or a CID coming', and they only came last year. So, you know, they had been promised for years, for as long as I had been there they had been promised and they didn't come. (Luke)

In 2016, some of the interviewees received CIDs (contracts of indefinite duration), which guaranteed them a specific number of hours yearly, but which failed to give them additional benefits such as sick leave. Other interviewees, who work in different ETB areas, have yet to receive any contracts.

> Back to Education Initiative; it's brilliant for learners, because it is learner-centred but it's appalling and atrocious to the teachers, the people who are actually delivering the course. Because you have no future, you've

no fixed income, you've no pension, you've no sick pay. That's hopefully changing very soon. But I'm ten years at this. (Fergus)

The interviewees were also aware that they as 'tutors' were treated and paid differently to full-time Further Education 'teachers' who were often delivering the same modules as them.

I have an issue with tutors being seen as less than teachers and I don't think that's right and I think there should be the same terms and conditions and contracts across the board. (Luke)

We work alongside fully contracted teachers who get paid over all holiday periods while we have to 'sign on'. (Fergus)

The interviewees also spoke about the lack of clear communication between Human Resources departments and FET practitioners. They found it very hard to get accurate information, or at times, to get any response to concerns.

We have issues, so we email, and she [HR Personnel] doesn't even get back to you. You feel you're non-existent. (Maggie)

It's pointless really ringing somebody to ask questions, because they don't know the answers and it's different all over the country. (Peter)

While interviewees were largely dissatisfied with their current employment conditions, a belief that change was slowly happening and the sector was moving in the right direction engendered a sense of hope.

They are improving now, with the CIDs we have some comfort because we know we have so many hours when we go back in September [...] I do think we are finally going in the right direction. (Maggie)

Motivating Factors and Individual FET Practitioners

A nalyses within the individual narratives provide an insight into the key motivating factors for each of the six interviewees.

Mary

F rom the Archerian perspective, Mary's professional identity is reflective of concerns linked with the social order of reality. Her purpose, her sense of self-worth, is associated with her ability to provide safe, welcoming, learning spaces, particularly for adult women returning to education.

Mary was an early school leaver who engaged in part-time adult education as a young adult. It was within this educational setting that she discovered a love of learning that has never left her. One of the key motivating factors in Mary's current FET practitioner role, and an ultimate concern that informs her life's work, is to create safe spaces for other adult women to have similar opportunities to those that she was given as a young adult woman. Through Mary's own experiences, she can relate to the difficulties associated with returning to education, particularly for married women or mothers, but can also testify to the great satisfaction she got from adult education.

> I'm a happy person, I'm very satisfied with my life. I'm satisfied with the achievements that I have myself and I'd love people to go from, like myself, being unaware of what they can do into an awareness of what is possible. If I could help a couple of people to do that, I think that is really worthwhile.

Mary believes that FET can fill the gap which has been left in the educational, and indeed overall, lives of those who did not complete primary or secondary schooling or of those for whom the experience of primary or secondary school did not inspire self-confidence or any form of love or desire for learning. She believes that as a FET practitioner, one can awaken within learners a love of learning, an increased awareness of their own capabilities and potential, and a better understanding of how the world works, and could work.

> You [as a FET practitioner] have to be interested in education. You have to be interested in what that does to a person, what moving from the unknown into the known, whatever the topic [...] Once you're aware, you're never unaware again.

Mary feels strongly that there has been, and remains, a lack of role models for women. She believes that, in her FET practitioner role, she can act as a role model for women who want to return to education as adults and she believes she can awaken such women to the possibilities of lifelong learning. She wants to enable women to carve out a space for themselves that is separate from their families and their roles as daughter, wife or mother. This space, she believes, can be found in education and training. She wants women to invest time and energy in themselves, in their own personal development which may also include or lead onto further professional development.

> They need to be trained into how to support themselves [...] you need to say, 'I'm a mother, I'm a carer, I'm a shop assistant and I may be a cleaner as well', all those things [but] in order for you to get this qualification that you're looking for, you need to just give time to yourself.

Mary prefers the term facilitator to any other term that could be used for a FET practitioner. While she works within an accredited, part-time FET programme, her core aim, which she hopes to achieve alongside her learners gaining accreditation, is to facilitate her learners' personal growth. While Mary speaks mainly about female learners in her interview, she acknowledges that her approach is similar when she is working with all-male groups or mixed groups. Her personal objectives, of which only a few are reflected in the specific learning outcomes of the accredited modules she teaches, involve facilitating learners to feel more empowered and to build their self-esteem and self-confidence to the point where they can advocate for their own needs and desires and that of their communities and future clients. Mary, while reflecting on a learner who shared in class how she had gained the confidence through her course to ask a question at a public meeting, stated: 'Now that to me is as important as the woman that went off and got her doctorate.'

Mary is adamant that a successful and fulfilling life does not necessarily equate to being highly educated or having a well-paying job.

> You can be in the pursuit of success in your life, not in your job or in your earning power, just in your life. I think some people have to be told that. Sit them down and say, 'You know you can be very successful and never work a day in your life. You can have a successful life'.

She encourages her learners to find out what gives them satisfaction, and to pursue these things in their lives: 'Whether that's keeping hens and chickens or whether that is going off and getting a job.' She tries to instil a desire in her learners to pursue the life they want along with the belief that they can achieve it by taking it one step at a time.

Mary now, as a middle-aged woman, has a life she never could have predicted as a young girl, teenager or young wife. She has found much joy in both her own further education and training, and in that of others, both children and adults. One of her key motivations, in life and in her role as a FET practitioner, is to encourage women to value their roles in society and to open up their minds to the endless possibilities that further education and training can hold for them, as it has done and continues to do for Mary herself.

Lucy

In Archerian terms, Lucy is concerned with the practical order of reality, in particular the performative abilities of her learners and her past occupational area. She is attempting to improve the Irish Childcare Sector by preparing her learners to be effective childcare workers and advocates of change.

Lucy has had two previous careers prior to 'falling into' teaching within the FET sector. The vast majority of her teaching (she refers to herself as a teacher) has been with Back to Education Initiatives (part-time, accredited FET programmes) where she teaches on courses related to her previous occupational areas, one of which is childcare.

In the past, while working as a practitioner, supervisor and manager within the childcare sector, Lucy had grown disheartened at the lack of respect shown towards childcare workers and the challenging work they do. She felt the general public often believed that childcare workers 'play' all day and that 'the assumption is you must be stupid if you're doing childcare'. What concerned her even more was what she perceived to be the lack of respect childcare workers often showed towards themselves and their occupation, through the acceptance of poor wages and low status within their workplace and society. Lucy wants to help counteract this through her teaching role: 'I feel I can do more to change things as a teacher then I could have done while working in childcare.'

One of Lucy's key motivations in her role as a FET practitioner is to increase the status of her previous occupational area (childcare) by increasing the confidence and skill levels of her learners (trainee childcare workers) and helping them to understand why things work the way they do.

> My thinking is, if you can instil more confidence in the people working with the kids that will actually bring the whole status up which I think badly needs to happen. So that will impact on the children as well.

Lucy endeavours in her teaching role to ensure her learners understand the reality of working in the childcare sector at present, so that they avoid entering the profession in the naïve belief that it operates as described in policy documents and childcare texts. She also wants to ensure that they are equipped with enough knowledge and skill to deal with situations they will face in real life childcare contexts. Lucy explained that often this requires her to teach about topics that are not covered by the specific learning outcomes specified in the modules she teaches.

> We spend an awful lot of time talking about child protection issues, behaviour issues, dealing with parents and that's not going to be assessed but that's actually what they need to know.

Ultimately Lucy wants her learners to be critical of the childcare sector they are entering into or already working within. She wants them always to question what they encounter and strive for a better future for themselves, their sector and the children that are cared for within their sector.

> Topics will come up in class and it makes people question, and if enough people question consistently enough, surely things will change at some point.

Maggie

From the Archerian perspective, Maggie is heavily influenced by concerns relating to the social order of reality. She finds fulfilment and meaning in her working life by supporting her learners to have opportunities for learning and growth. She is motivated by wanting in some way to re-balance the inequitable distribution of opportunity that exists in Irish society.

During her childhood and adolescence, Maggie found school relatively easy and she attributes this to having a good memory. After completing second-level schooling, she then successfully completed a university degree.

> If you have a good memory you can fly through your Leaving Cert, fly through your degree, even your Masters. You can get through it a lot easier than other people, if you can remember stuff.

After university Maggie went on to work in private industry for over ten years. She then chose to have children and work in the home for a number of years before looking for part-time employment that would suit the lifestyle and routine of a family with young children. It was at this point that Maggie, like many other FET practitioners, 'fell into' working within FET. She saw an advertisement looking for tutors in her subject areas: 'So I said "Ah sure I'll apply" [...] I was testing the water.'

Maggie has worked across numerous part-time FET programmes, both accredited and non-accredited, including a substantial amount of work with adult literacy learners. She refers to herself as a tutor. The key motivation and ultimate concern expressed in her interview is her desire to support adults who have not had the same opportunities and good fortune she has had in relation to her natural academic ability and access to opportunities in higher education.

Maggie was raised by her parents to believe that we, as human beings, are all equally worthy but that, unfortunately, some people are disadvantaged along the way — by the situations they are born into, the lack of opportunities made available to them, their inability to adapt effectively to the social situations that they find themselves in, such as the Irish mainstream schooling system: 'Some people don't get the advantages everybody else does, but it [having a degree] doesn't make any of us, in my eyes, better than anyone else.' Maggie finds a sense of worth and purpose in her working life, by striving to give opportunities to people she considers equal to herself but less fortunate. She aims to support her learners to succeed, which requires her to adapt her approach to suit their needs.

> The student is the most important person, not you. I had to adapt [...] I had to realize this isn't going to work with this particular person.

When Maggie reflects on the first part of her working life, she questions how much this really mattered compared to what she does now.

> Did it really matter at the end of the day if the company could produce more efficiently because of what I wrote? Not really. But if a person (learner) could do those things that they couldn't before, that's great. You know that to me is the most important thing.

Maggie gains huge satisfaction from watching her learners improve, particularly within an Adult Literacy context, and from seeing them being able to operate competently within their social worlds.

> Now she [Maggie's learner] knows if she goes into a shop, if she's going to have change or whatever, she can tell. It mightn't seem a lot to us but it makes a huge difference to people's lives. I think that's what I like, the fact that you can see the students' competence, from when they come in to when they leave. You can even tell we're at a stage now where they won't be back next year, you can tell when they've got to that level that they are ready to go back out in the real world and work away. I find that that for me is one of the most important things. I suppose the job satisfaction is very high in what we do.

Fergus

Fergus, like Maggie, is motivated by concerns relating to the social order of reality. His mission is to create the type of learning spaces he wishes for his son, who has a disability. In the years before Fergus became a FET practitioner, he had his own business and was lecturing part-time in higher-education institutions in his area of expertise. Then his son was born with special needs and everything changed for him and his young family. Fergus and his family completely re-evaluated their priorities and decided to move to an area in the south-east of Ireland where his son would have access to a school that could support his needs and where they would have family close by. Fergus reflects that, when his family was moving, the last thing on the list was a job for Fergus.

When his family were settled in their new home, Fergus started looking for work and chose to focus on education, as he no longer wanted the level of work that accompanied being self-employed. It was at this point that Fergus started working with several adult-education centres and part-time FET programmes.

Fergus now has over ten years' experience working with FET and one of his key motivations is to provide learning opportunities for what he terms 'compromised people', people who have ability but are also limited in some way. He reflects from his own experience that 'the majority of people that come back to education are compromised somehow'. Fergus' life changed dramatically when he had a son with a disability and this appears to greatly impact on his working role.

> Having a child with a disability focuses your life tremendously; it makes
> you look at the world a lot different than you used to. It's changed my life
> in a lot of different ways.

Fergus favours a community education approach where possible, where
the focus is on participation as opposed to certification, even though
certification may still be offered. He works with various groups of
people who have limiting conditions or disabilities, such as people who
have a fear of computers, people on the autistic spectrum, people with
acquired brain injuries, mental health issues, dexterity issues or people
who are blind. His personal mission is to continuously re-design his
module materials so that the people in his current groups can participate
as fully as possible from within their own limitations and the limitations
of certified modules with specific learning outcomes: 'it's taking people
on board and recognizing their abilities and also their disabilities.'

Fergus wants to create learning situations where people of all
abilities can be supported to express themselves through various media
and to build their own skills. He aims to provide a level of instruction
and guidance that is facilitative and encouraging, while still offering
learners a high level of freedom in how they choose to engage with their
learning.

> I love teaching, especially working with special-needs adults, because of
> my son, and I love helping people and showing people how to do things
> and giving them the skillset to be independent.

Luke

In Archerian terms, Luke is concerned with the practical order of
reality. He feels his effectiveness as a practitioner and the ability of
his learners to achieve is based on the quality of the relationships he can
form with them.

When Luke first started working with FET part-time programmes
he had a number of years' experience of full-time and part-time/night-
time lecturing in higher education (HE), as well as years of experience
working in private industry. Luke quickly increased his tutoring hours
by working across multiple part-time FET programmes on a weekly
basis and gave up his night-time lecturing hours. While Luke always
managed to get enough hours to 'pay the bills', he reflects that he worked

for years without a contract, and that while he was on high hours, he had no security.

Luke always had the option of returning to work for private industry or working as a lecturer in a higher education institution, but he chose to stay working in FET for well over a decade without a proper tutor/teacher contract. What is evident from Luke's interview is that it is his love of teaching that has kept him from returning to private industry. One of the reasons for staying in FET rather than returning to HE is that the FET approach to teaching more closely matches his values and beliefs system.

Luke holds that a trusting relationship between teachers and their learners sits at the core of good teaching and feels that this is often not present in HE but is encouraged and facilitated in many part-time FET contexts.

> I think for all good teaching and lecturing, the relationship is very important. I think in the Institutes of Technology and Higher Education perhaps it's not seen as important as it should be and sometimes lecturers come in and are just delivering and imparting knowledge [...] perhaps in Further Ed because of the smaller class sizes there's more scope for the relationship to be built.

Luke believes, and experiences, that it is from within this trusting relationship that FET practitioners can assist learners to break down the barriers that obstruct their learning. Luke associates certain approaches, as well as the positive ethos within part-time FET programmes, with the establishment of effective teacher-learner relationships. He makes reference to the flexibility of part-time FET services, which are learner-centred, not overly focused on a strict syllabus, and which encourage the creation of a teaching and learning environment that is relaxed, open, adaptive, supportive and empathetic. He also notes that within programmes such as Adult Literacy, learners are given the time to overcome past, negative experiences.

> After three years sometimes they all of a sudden just get it, and it can be difficult to understand why. And maybe it's just that they're now ready to learn, maybe the barriers that were there for whatever reason are now just gone and they've disassociated those bad experiences and they're now ready to learn.

Peter

P eter differs from the other five in that he is largely driven by concerns relating to the natural order of reality. He feared for his physical wellbeing in his previous job and thus ended up being attracted to a role that allowed him to look after his wellbeing while still pursuing his passion: working with food.

Peter has had a life-time love affair with food and cooking and has worked as a chef in Ireland and abroad since he was nineteen. After twenty years as a head chef, aware that very few chefs continue to work in kitchens until retirement age, he decided he needed to find an alternative job that suited the lifestyle of a family man but still involved working with people and food. Helping adults to learn how to cook or to improve their culinary skills allowed Peter to continue working in the field that he loved.

> The motivation was to keep doing what I'm doing but in a different way and something that I could keep doing until I'm sixty-five.

Peter's identity since becoming a FET practitioner has not altered greatly.

> I'm a chef. I don't really identify with the teacher role very much. People would say to me, 'But you're the teacher'. I say, 'I'm not a teacher, I'm a chef'. I would say my role, if I was to give it a name, would be to facilitate people to come together to produce something.

In Peter's interview, he reflected a lot about how teaching and training were also part of his past role as a head-chef. As an FET practitioner he is driven by the desire to pass on his love of cooking. He wants to get his learners interested in cooking. He strives to instil confidence in them to use their newly acquired or increased culinary skills at home and in their everyday lives.

On the occasion when he has a learner who wants to become a chef and work in the food industry, he is determined to teach them the skills and knowledge they need to succeed in a real kitchen. He finds that if the environment within adult education reflects that of a working kitchen, generally his learners are engaged: 'It's easy when you have people that are motivated and they're enthusiastic and they're interested.' He also gets to work with varied groups of people: 'a very diverse range of people come in to me, and I enjoy that.'

In his FET practitioner role, Peter has found a way to keep doing what he loves in a structured environment that suits the stage he is at in his life and with his young family. He has found a career that will sustain him: 'I love it. It's what I do now, it's what I intend to continue to do.'

Additional Motivating Factors Present

I n addition to the key personal motivating factors expressed above, several other common motivating factors were found when looking across the interview data.

Like most employees, several of the interviewees commented that having a wage was a motivating factor. While having enough money to provide for themselves and their families was important, the desire for more money via higher wages appeared not to be as important as other motivating factors.

All the interviewees stated that they experienced joy and a sense of fulfilment in their work and all spoke positively about the flexibility and variety associated with the part-time FET environment. Several of the interviewees with experience of working in Higher Education commented on how they preferred working with non-traditional, adult learners, and how they valued the focus that is often placed on personal and collective development within part-time FET contexts.

The opportunity to utilize knowledge and skills from their past occupations and to pass on their passions to their learners was important to interviewees. Also evident was an interest in people, which was reflected in the care and empathy interviewees had for their learners, their life experiences and situations. There was also a general realization of the potential power of education.

Striking a Balance Between Concerns

A s previously stated, Archer (2000) believes that peoples' wellbeing depends on them striking a balance between the concerns they prioritize in relation to the 'three orders of reality'; natural (our physical wellbeing), practical (our performative achievements) and social (our sense of self-worth).

Natural Order Concerns (Physical Wellbeing)

W hat is evident from the interviews is that the six interviewees have ensured that they and their families are provided for financially and can pay their bills. They have created a working situation, mainly through having a second position of employment, which compensates for the insecurity associated with teaching part-time FET programmes. The flexibility of part-time FET programmes has enabled the interviewees to construct weekly schedules that suit their lifestyles and that of their families. Having satisfied their concerns relating to the natural order of reality (physical wellbeing), they have placed other concerns above the desire for secure contracts and better conditions.

Practical Order Concerns (Performative Achievements)

A ll of the interviewees spoke about the approaches they take to working with their learners. They spoke of the need to be able to adapt and match their approaches and teaching style to the needs and abilities of individuals and groups, so that learners could discover their own capabilities and potential.

All were concerned to do a good job, which for them involved being effective communicators, creating safe learning environments and increasing the competences of their learners in their subject areas. It also involved successfully meeting the demands of certification, whilst providing learners with the skills and knowledge deemed necessary but not always reflected in the specific learning outcomes attached to certified modules. The interviewees often viewed their learners' successes as evidence of their own success.

Social Order Concerns (Sense of Self-Worth)

A ll the interviewees have alternative employment options, but are seeking a level of fulfilment, satisfaction and meaning from their work which they find in their FET-practitioner roles. The interviewees are aware that the FET sector fills a gap within the overall education system, and often provides an opportunity for adult learners to be compensated for past negative educational experiences. They understand that equal opportunity in relation to access to education and training involves providing additional supports, such as extended time periods and smaller class sizes, to individuals or groups who have been disadvantaged in some way.

The interviewees see the positive impact of their efforts on the lives of their learners and find fulfilment in the knowledge that they are helping to change lives for the better.

Conclusion

I n general FET practitioners working with part-time FET programmes seem to be disadvantaged by the poor employment conditions associated with this part of the Irish FET sector. They are choosing to continue working with these programmes due to strong personal motivations. These motivations are often linked with a powerful desire to create positive, empowering learning experiences for their learners who, practitioners hope, will be more competent and effective in their personal lives and in their potential future work roles as a result.

While employment conditions are slowly improving, stakeholders such as the Department of Education and Skills and the various Education and Training Boards need to work to provide FET practitioners with working conditions that offer a sense of security and parity with their counterparts in other parts of the FET sector and other mainstream education sectors. Not to do so is disrespectful towards the effort, care and talents displayed by FET practitioners and represents a failure to recognize the broader benefits to society from practitioners' work with adult learners, many of whom have not been well-served by the mainstream educational system.

References

Archer, M.S. (1982). Morphogenesis versus structuration: On combining structure and action. *The British Journal of Sociology*, 61: 225–52.

Archer, M.S. (2000). *Being human: The problem of agency.* Cambridge: Cambridge University Press.

Archer, M.S. (2003). *Structure, agency and the internal conversation.* Cambridge: Cambridge University Press.

CMETB. (2014). *Cavan and Monaghan education and training board staff handbook, 2014–2015*. http://www.cavanadulteducation.ie/images/uploads/CMETB_ Staff_Handbook_2014-15_(1).pdf

Forman, J. & Damschroder, L. (2008). Qualitative content analysis. In: Jacoby, L. & Siminoff, L. (eds), *Empirical methods for bioethics: A primer*. Bingley, UK: Emerald.

GOI (Government of Ireland) (2016). *Teaching Council (Registration) (Amendment) Regulations 2016* (on 07/11/17).

McGuinness, S., Bergin, A., Kelly, E., McCoy, S., Smyth, E., Whelan, A. & Banks, J. (2014). *Further education and training in Ireland: Past, present and future*. Dublin: The Economic and Social Research Institute.

Schreier, M. (2014). Qualitative content analysis. In: Flick, A., Scott, W. & Metzler, K. (eds), *The Sage handbook of qualitative data analysis*. London: Sage.

SOLAS (2014). *Further education and training strategy, 2014 — 2019*. Dublin: Department of Education and Skills.

TUI (2017). *TUI Survey of non-standard FE employment*. https://www.tui. ie/news-events/tui-survey-of-non-standard-fe-employment-deadline-extended-.10191.html

8. Nurture Groups
Perspectives from Teaching Assistants Who Lead Them in Britain

Tristan Middleton

Tristan Middleton, a former teacher, seeks the views of two teaching assistants who run nurture groups, to find out about their work and its implications for policy and practice. He examines a series of cyclical sessions set up with the aim of supporting the teaching assistants to cope with challenging pupil behaviour, for which he was both supervisor and insider researcher.

This chapter explains the role of nurture groups in supporting children who display challenging behaviours within the British school system and describes a small-scale narrative-inquiry research project undertaken with practitioners to better understand the issues that are relevant to their daily work. The researcher has 'insider' status so is able to carry this out alongside sessions that provide the teaching assistants who run the nurture groups with a level of support. Benefitting from the collaborative empathy that this way of working creates, the study enables the staff voices to be clearly heard, making the experience a transformative one that also has potential to influence future policy decisions.

Context of the Research

The study discussed within this chapter was informed by earlier work reported by Bennathan and Boxall in 1996, who described a specific approach — the Nurture Group — to provide for the needs

https://doi.org/10.11647/OBP.0203.08

of those learners in a school setting who find it difficult to learn in a mainstream classroom. The concept is underpinned by attachment theory (Ainsworth & Bowlby, 1991) and a psychosocial approach (Trenoweth & Moone, 2017) to understand the needs of children and young people who can often display challenging and violent behaviours towards both school staff and peers, and a range of negative attitudes to learning situations as a result of Social, Emotional and Mental Health (SEMH) challenges.

My research focused on one English primary school, with learners aged four to eleven, where there was a Nurture Group provision for approximately eight children, run by two teaching assistants (TAs).[1] The research used a narrative inquiry approach (Alleyne, 2015) to explore the impact of working with children with SEMH difficulties, who presented associated challenging behaviours, on both the personal and professional lives of the teaching assistants. The TAs constituted the research participants. The research also sought to identify supportive factors enabling Nurture-Group staff to navigate through these challenges.

A narrative inquiry approach was chosen as it is a methodology able to provide a space in which the research participants could examine and communicate their experiences and consider how they have impacted on their lives, a process with which they may not previously have consciously engaged.

Nurture Groups

Since their beginnings in the Inner London Education Authority in the 1970s, the prevalence, nature and location of Nurture Groups has gone through significant development. A Nurture Group, as initially defined by Bennathan and Boxall (1996), should be situated in a mainstream primary school, adhere to a clear structure of staffing and curriculum and run for a specified period of time. The current picture, following a decline towards the end of the twentieth century, is one of a growing number of school settings that have a Nurture-Group provision. The most recent census of 2015 identified 2,114 schools in the

---

1   TAs are variously termed learning support assistants, teaching aides, para-professional educators and education assistants in other contexts and places.

UK with Nurture Groups (NurtureUK, 2020) and examples of Nurture Groups are now found in Canada, Romania and New Zealand (Nurture Group Network, 2017). The structure and staffing guidelines, which were previously rather strict, are now more flexible, with guidance provided by the Nurture Group Network (Nurture Group Network, 2017) focusing on ethos and approach, rather than staffing and structures. In early iterations, Nurture Groups were led by a qualified teacher supported by a teaching assistant (Bishop, 2008). Later models have teaching assistants who run the Nurture Group without a teacher's direct, day-to-day involvement, possibly due to the funding challenges educational settings face. There are no comprehensive statistics to identify the prevalence of this way of staffing Nurture Groups.

The success of Nurture Groups in supporting the development of learners' social, emotional and mental health, as well as their academic learning, in a cost-effective way has been well documented by research literature (Cooper & Whitebread, 2007; Sloan et al., 2016) and also recognized by statutory school inspection bodies in England (Ofsted) and Wales (Estyn), as well as the Scottish Parliament (2017). There is a body of research which focuses on the interface between challenges, inclusion and resilience for teachers (Doney, 2013; Zee, de Jong & Koomen, 2016); however this is not the case for teaching assistants, who have been recognized as an under-researched group of educators (Sharples, Webster & Blatchford, 2015): likewise the Nurture-Group context is under-researched.

Whilst Scott Loinaz (2014) identifies some common behaviours exhibited by learners in Nurture Groups, there is little statistical or research evidence about the prevalence of emotionally distressing and physically violent behaviours carried out by learners and experienced by Nurture-Group practitioners. This area is rarely discussed either by practitioner groups or within forums, such as the charity NurtureUK. The reticence in discussing this significant area of practice (apart from private conversations between individuals) might be driven by a range of reasons, however, those that stand out to the author are: a sense of confidentiality combined with a desire to protect the individual children from criticism; a desire to protect the close relationship between the child / young person and the practitioner; but also a reluctance to revisit situations that the practitioner finds emotionally challenging. Whilst the researcher's approach sought to fill this gap in knowledge through a focus on the impact rather than the actual behaviours, it is important for the reader to understand the context and acknowledge that behaviours displayed by learners in Nurture Groups can be extremely violent, both physically and emotionally.

Discussion of Violence

T he research began from the position that it is not a violent act itself that has the significant impact, but the context, expectation and meaning-making of those involved. For example, when a rugby player pushes another player over, there is little emotional impact, but if a young person pushes their teacher to the ground, one might expect the teacher to experience significant emotional challenges. This interpretive viewpoint contributed to the choice of a narrative inquiry methodology, as this method enables the individual, contextual meaning-making that takes place during emotionally difficult situations to be explored openly, without the imposition of overt questions that may reflect the researcher's focus rather than that of the participants.

Layers of Discourse

M ethodological choices acknowledged the contextual, or social and interactive importance of the learning situation (Dewey, 1958) within the human experience of an educational setting (Webster & Mertova, 2007). The methodology adopted places the participants' subjective experience and their perceptions of the meanings of phenomena at the centre of the research (Mertens, 2015) within 'an emotive or emotional and expressive register' (Alleyne, 2015, p. 40). Furthermore, the ontological framework of the narrative construction of reality (Bruner, 1991) and the epistemological underpinning of the approach of exploring personal narratives to interpret the impact of experienced events, link closely with a narrative inquiry approach. This approach values the openness of interpretation and the ability to organize data around a narrative plot (Czarniawska, 2004, p. 7), as attempted here when I present a collection of complex layers of contextual meaning-making, based within the language defined by the particular values and beliefs of the individual.

The research cited here needs to be understood within the professional language of English primary-school practice, attachment-informed (Ainsworth & Bowlby, 1991) Nurture-Group theory, inclusive pedagogy (Nind, 2005) and relational ecologies (Warin & Hibbin, 2016). This context is further layered by the language of interpersonal professional relationships and both interpersonal and intrapersonal family relationships, which the research participants bring to the narrative. A further layer of context and language is introduced by the relationship enacted within the researcher/practitioner space (Clandinin, 2013) as the narrative is constructed. As the researcher interprets the data and communicates this in writing, a further layer of academic language is added. Finally, the reader will bring a personal contextual understanding and interpretation of the language, resulting in a potential discourse of meaning-making at this stage.

Researcher Intentions

As already indicated, within a narrative-inquiry approach, the context of the researcher — his/her identity, values and language — has a significant impact on the research relationship and the research data. Therefore, it is relevant to consider my own context as it is important to understand the researcher's value base in this interpretive relationship. I have a seven-year history of working as a teacher within a Nurture-Group setting, and also as a senior leader in a primary school. Furthermore, during my work as a Nurture-Group practitioner, I experienced significant professional and personal challenges related to my work including the physically and emotionally violent behaviours of children I worked with. Two important influences upon the research discourse can be seen to result from this. Firstly, as a researcher I was perceived by the participants to have a shared language, based upon common values and experiences. Secondly, my experiences enabled a shared understanding between researcher and participants (the two TAs).

These resulted in the creation of an honest and open narrative, where there were often shortcuts of understanding within shared frames of reference. We perceived each other to hold similar values, supporting my desire to create rapport. I wanted to influence policymaking related to Nurture Groups, by providing a way for practitioner voices to communicate the real impact of Nurture-Group work and for these voices to be heard. My aim was to use their voices to introduce discussions about the need for recognition and emotional support for Nurture-Group practitioners, to influence national policy within the context of layers of influence (Barth, 1994); this would then be an example of a local struggle and social movement having strong influences on policy change (Apple, 2014). As such, I hope that the research outputs, in addition to enabling positive changes at a 'micro' (Barth, 1994) or local level, may also influence 'median' and 'macro' levels (Barth, 1994) at a national scale.

Stages in the Research Process

My original intention was to carry out the actual research interviews with the two TAs (whose names are changed to ensure anonymity) as a series of 'research session cycles' (RSCs). However, a condition of researcher access was the introduction of 'supervision session cycles' (SSCs) to the process. The gatekeeper to the school setting insisted that I provide participants with a 'time and place to reflect on [their] work' (Bluckert, 2006, p. 109), a space to explore and express distress related to their work experiences (Hawkins & Shohet, 2006). Consequently, I scheduled a supervision session between each research session, taking care to separate the approach within the two. Possibly the research benefitted from this practice as the narrative space was less focused on the ideas that I as a researcher brought to the space; rather it was a place for the participants to explore their own issues and direct the foci of the sessions, resulting in a more iterative process to the emergence of the themes.

Findings of the Research

Difference

The overall experience of the participants' narrative was one of being separate from others who do not work within the context of nurture or support children with SEMH challenges. Their discourse described their work as something distinct and different to that of the other staff in the school:

> [...] they [mainstream staff] don't know what we were dealing with on a day-to-day basis. (Kerry, SSC1)

and described colleagues' reactions to Nurture-Group work as being:

> [...] quite closed to the whole thing. (Kerry, SSC1)

The difference was often framed within the language of nurturing and emotionally supporting children.

> I go in and I sit with him and I reassure him and we talk but it's not the same as going in and knowing exactly where I'm... or what's expected of me or what's needed of me and what he needs from me. (Lilly, SSC1)

The difference was further exemplified in their descriptions of conversations about their work with people they meet in their personal life:

> I usually just say, 'I'm a TA.' I don't tend to say about nurture because maybe people don't really know... (Lilly, SSC1)

Likewise with family members:

> He just doesn't get it, no matter how many times I explain it... (Lilly, RSC2)

This difference, discussed in terms of distance from other staff in the school, reflected a discourse of separateness and of others making decisions that go against their own views:

> I almost feel like I'm always railroaded, I'm always round the outside of it. (Kerry, RSC2)

The outcome of the nature of the work, combined with their sense of isolation, their difference and distance from other staff, is expressed through a discourse of intellectual and emotional challenge and frustration:

> Oh, it just frustrates me, it really frustrates me. (Kerry, RSC2)

> I just felt so het up and so anxious all the time. (Lilly, RSC3)

I am doing my best and trying to give him my all, I really am, but it's really difficult. (Kerry, RSC1)

Impact of Working Through Nurture Groups

T he initial research aims focused on the impact of working with children within a Nurture-Group context. Three themes emerge from the data: the physiological impact of the work, impact on motivation and impact upon personal relationships.

Physiological Impact

T he participants used a range of metaphors to describe the impact of their work with the children, some of which relate to physical impact:

I'd had so many buttons pressed... (Lilly, RSC3)

I was on my knees... (Lilly, SSC1)

The physical metaphor was also applied to exchanges with colleagues:

[...] my face hit the floor and it was that thing of like, okay, take it on the chin. You've got to take that on the chin... (Kerry, SSC1)

In the description of the impact of the permanent exclusion of one child with whom they both worked closely the metaphors included:

When he left it felt like losing an arm. (Kerry, SSC1)

I started to feel alright about him not being here and now it feels like the band aid has just been ripped off and I've started hurting all over again. (Kerry, SSC1)

The participants also included, within their narratives, actual physiological impact that they experienced. In the preliminary, pre-research discussions, Lilly described a recent critical incident. At the end of term, Lilly had allowed a child to bring his skateboard to school and she took him into the playground to use it. The child encouraged Lilly to try his skateboard and as she was attempting this, she fell off the skateboard. In spite of being injured, she then walked the child back into the school, including walking down a flight of stairs. When they reached another member of staff inside the building, Lilly sank to the floor. She was subsequently taken to hospital where she was diagnosed with a broken leg. In a more general sense, the physical impact of the work was clearly conveyed as part of the narrative:

It's draining as well, it's tiring. It's tiring. (Lilly, RSC3)

I was on my knees; I had nothing else to give at the end of the year and I was physically crying; it was my best year. (Lilly, SSC1)

Impact on Motivation

A very high level of commitment to, and emotional investment in, their nurture work in both a professional and personal sense was expressed in the narratives of both participants:

I love my Nurture Group; I love my job. (Lilly, RSC3)

That's what I love about the job, that is what gives me my drive, because I know by doing that sort of stuff, I'm hopefully supporting them and hopefully helping them to feel better about themselves, too, understanding themselves, too. (Kerry, RSC3)

In spite of this discourse of a deep commitment to a nurturing approach, a strong sense of their Nurture-Group work having a negative impact on their motivation was communicated:

I think within nurture, things are disclosed that are quite... that can be quite tricky and obviously sometimes we are told things... that are quite hard to deal with... (Lilly, RSC3)

[...] a couple of hours just sat and thought about it...that was me trying to... gee myself up to get in, a come on, come on, we can do this... (Kerry, RSC1)

I felt like I wasn't giving all the children 100% what they needed. [...] So, I think because I felt so frustrated, I was almost at a point where I thought, actually, I'm not even going to do it anymore. (Lilly, RSC1)

The practitioners' perceived 'differentness' in relation to other staff was a further factor with a negative impact on their motivation:

If you are butting heads with the teacher, it's really difficult to want to continue. (Lilly, RSC2)

So just personally I was sort of saying I don't want to go to work. For the first time in my life, I do not want to go. (Lilly, RSC1)

This negative impact even went so far as to prompt the consideration of a change of job:

I know both of us have been looking at other jobs too which is really bad. (Kerry, RSC1)

Impact on Personal Relationships

W ithin the contemporary professional context, where employers are visibly making more effort to address the wellbeing needs of their staff through a discourse of 'work-life balance', it may be expected that the practitioners compartmentalized their thoughts about work and did not allow thoughts about work into their 'non-work' time. However, the narrative pointed to thoughts about the nurture work dominating this personal time:

I mean, I've even dreamt of it before ... I was worried about him the whole time thinking, oh my God, what's happening to him at home and what's he doing, is he okay ... and yes, even dreamt about being in this room. (Kerry, RSC1)

It also revealed how tiredness prevented the practitioners from using their personal time, other than to recover from the nurture work:

[...] it does impact on your life because you're just going, 'Oh I'm so tired.' I said before, 'I've got nothing else to give.' I just want to sit here, drink tea and then just fall asleep on the sofa, which most of my Fridays are as exciting as that. (Lilly, RSC2)

The narrative also pointed to an impact on personal relationships, in relation to comments made by the participants' friends:

[...] one of my friends said to me 'God, is that all you do?' I said, 'What do you mean?' She said, 'All you've done is talk about work.' 'What?' She said 'That's all you do, isn't it?' (Kerry, SSC2)

The participants' home lives were also significantly highlighted within the narrative as being impacted:

I mean, I went home and I went, grrrrr, you know, screaming my head off. (Kerry, SSC1)

This was further described through the discourse around family members:

[...] it did feel like it became... he became almost an extension of my own children, he was then.... So, they're always there, always. (Kerry, RSC2)

[...] we take the dog for a walk every evening... most of that half an hour is me talking at my husband about the frustrations of my day to the point that eventually he says, 'Just stop. Just stop talking. You are doing it again'... there's so much going on in my own mind that I need to get out, that I can't focus on what he's saying to me. (Lilly, RSC2)

The TAs clearly recognize that nurture work impacts significantly on personal and family relationships. Lilly clearly described how her relationship with her son improved when a child with significant challenging behaviour left their setting:

We sort of talk to each other in the mornings and we have a bit of a giggle on the way to school now rather than me shouting at him and bellowing and being stressed. (Lilly, RSC2)

Emergent Findings on Successful Nurture-Group Practice

Whilst I, as researcher, had questions in mind, these were used as a guide rather than a destination (Kim, 2016) enabling the research to be collaborative. Since they were co-constructed, the findings were sometimes not as I anticipated (May, 1997). The three key factors that emerged through the narrative were: shared belief, friendship and leadership.

Shared Belief

As identified earlier, the participants evidenced strong beliefs in a nurture approach. The narratives demonstrated that the sharing of these deep beliefs played a key role in supporting staff when navigating the challenges that the work presented:

It's that connection, it's knowing somebody and obviously myself and
Kerry have both had the same training and we've both been in nurture
for quite a while now. (Lilly, RSC3)

The use of the personal pronoun 'we' in the following extract is further
evidence of the importance of a shared belief:

That opportunity and seeing their faces, it's like a toddler-like delight
isn't it? We looked at each other and said yes, this is why we do nurture.
(Lilly, SSC3)

Conversely, times when their work together was not positive also
provided evidence of the significance of the shared beliefs:

It feels like we are all disjointed. It doesn't feel like we are flowing. (Kerry,
RSC3)

Friendship

The importance of friendship, a relationship extending beyond
professional teamwork, was communicated as an important factor
for the participants in promoting successful work:

[...] we are really lucky and I think you've got to have that, you've got to
have a good working relationship and a good friendship to obviously be
able to co-lead a Nurture Group I think. (Lilly, RSC3)

Another important aspect of working together was physical proximity.
The TAs went on walks together during which

[they did] not even talk about nurture necessarily but just to sort of
wander. (Lilly, RSC3)

Leadership

The impact of the school leadership was a significant presence in
the narratives. Four key issues were communicated: being listened
to; feeling recognized, included and supported; not letting problems
escalate; and having a shared belief and involvement in leaders'
decisions.

Being Listened To

O ccurrences during which the participants perceived that members of the school leadership team had not listened to them were related within the discourse of significant negative impact:

> [...] that thing where you just know she's not really listening... it was almost like we weren't being listened to in a way... that really just makes you feel undervalued. (Lilly, RSC3)

> I've tried to discuss about the whole situation and how it was dealt with and how I felt about it, but I was shut down. (Kerry, RSC2)

Feeling Recognized, Included and Supported

B eyond being listened to, the participants identified the importance of their leaders acknowledging their work and the challenges they encountered:

> So, for me, it's the relief of being recognized. (Lilly, RSC3)

Where leaders' support is not clearly communicated or not perceived, this has a negative impact on the practitioners:

> [...] they don't trust me as much or they've lost confidence in me. (Kerry, RSC2)

> I'm doing the right thing by following procedures, policies, etc., but I'm not being backed up with it. (Kerry, RSC2)

In contrast, positive recognition is identified as having a positive impact:

> I think the realization that actually I must be doing something right is a good feeling. (Lilly, RSC2)

Not Letting Problems Escalate

F urther developing the theme of being listened to, recognized and supported, the need for this to happen in a timely way, as perceived by the practitioners, was highlighted:

[...] that thing of I feel like I'm doing everything I can but then not being able to talk to the correct person at that time. (Kerry, RSC2)

[...] it only seems to get to a proper meeting point when you go, 'Do you know what, I've had enough of this.' And I find that really strange... (Kerry, RSC2)

These comments point to the perception that unless practitioners have the opportunity to talk about challenges with their leaders, at the time that they are having an impact on them, the difficulties increase.

Shared Beliefs and Being Involved in Decision-Making

Within the narratives, a perceived gap between the participants and their managers when it came to beliefs and to involvement in the decision-making was identified as a key barrier to successful Nurture-Group practice:

I feel that actually there's so much more we could do and then if you want to do those things and then you're almost being cut off then you think eventually it will just be, 'well, you know what, you do it your way.' (Kerry, RSC2)

[...] how can we possibly make it a success if we're not all singing from the same hymn sheet? (Lilly, SSC2)

Summary of Findings

In summary, the research narratives highlighted the sense of difference the practitioners experienced between their role and practice and that of others in their professional and personal communities. The research identified that critical incidents related to the challenging behaviours of children impacted on the practitioners' physiological state, their motivation towards their Nurture-Group work and their personal relationships. The practitioners' ability to navigate these challenges varied according to their professional and personal relationships and was mediated by their beliefs and values. Their need to be listened to in a timely way by their leaders and to have a shared discourse with peers was an important theme.

Reflections upon the Discourse

Shared belief and friendship were present throughout the discourse and can be viewed as protective factors in supporting the practitioners' management of the challenges of their work. These themes may also be understood within the context of 'communitas' (Turner, 1997), that is, a form of comradeship that is based not only the homogeneity of setting and experience but also on shared beliefs. The creation of the liminal space of shared dialogue, between the researcher and the practitioners, highlighted this comradeship to the practitioners. Through having a sympathetic listener and a space in which to explore their own narratives, the practitioners' reflections led to them becoming more aware of these factors. The focus of the discourse on the impact of the senior leaders in the school was something that I had neither expected nor specifically sought, however the co-construction of the research dialogue allowed this unexpected finding to emerge. The factors identified by the practitioners as critical to the leadership they experienced could be viewed as ones which, if present, would lead to the development of a professional community in the setting based upon a more democratic and participatory model of shared values. This could be conceived as a desire on the part of the practitioners to develop a broader 'communitas' within their setting, and this has implications for both school leaders and Nurture-Group practitioners.

In order to support Nurture-Group practitioners to manage the challenges to their professional and personal lives that the nurture work presents, perhaps stakeholders should consider the potential value of developing shared value-systems and a shared paradigm of leadership, such as the approach of Distributed Leadership (Leemans, 2017) or 'soulful organisations' (Laloux, 2015).

Another enabling factor that practitioners identified as supportive was part of the research itself: the 'supervision' sessions. These were seen to be an important element of the discourse (Chappell, 1999), validating and supporting the practitioners (Hawkins & Shohet, 2006).

The practitioners' responses when asked to provide feedback on the research process included:

> I have become a more confident and effective practitioner, developed personally and become more self-aware. The process has made me

continuously self-evaluate. I have a deeper understanding of my beliefs
and boundaries. So much so, I felt encouraged to continue my exploration
of self-awareness and personal development. (Kerry, feedback)

The supervision has been vital this year as we have had our ups and
downs. I feel it has given me the reflection time I needed to make valuable
decisions and to recognize when it is okay to say no. (Lilly, feedback)

These reflections highlight the way in which the discourse of the
research facilitated practitioners to think reflectively. Furthermore, the
importance of the research dialogue taking place in the limbic space
of shared values and thinking was identified by the practitioners'
reflections:

I found talking to another professional [the researcher] who had been
a nurture practitioner themselves, easier to discuss situations that had
happened with children within the Nurture Group and staff. It put me at
ease, and I felt able to give my opinions, thoughts and feelings without
being judged. (Kerry, feedback)

It also gave me time to just talk to somebody who wasn't connected to
school but understands the importance of nurture coupled with the
importance of taking care of yourself to be the best person to do the job I
love (whilst maintaining my sanity). (Lilly, feedback)

The impact of this safe research space and the discourse that took place
within it could be considered as a transformative process for both the
participants and the researcher. The research space can be compared
with the safe human learning spaces described by Winnicott (1965).

I have been able to answer many questions in just one session as when I
am talking aloud or he [the researcher] is giving me feedback, I am able
to piece things together. Over time I have come to realize that my voice
is important and for the sake of the children in nurture and its success I
have to be prepared to challenge things that a year ago I would of [sic]
just nodded and smiled at. (Lilly, feedback)

This feedback emphasizes the empowering nature of the discourses,
which became apparent during the research. It could be considered that
the research process led to a change of habitus (Bourdieu, P., 1984). Before
the research process, the practitioners had a well-established view of
themselves and their capabilities. These were heavily influenced by the
contextual policy-led professional attitudes towards TAs and their own

views of their qualifications and roles within their own setting. Through being deeply heard (Rogers, 1967) in the context of the collaborative, transformative narrative inquiry (Webster & Mertova, 2007), the participants have experienced a level of 'biographical reconnaissance' through being awarded the time and space to walk towards themselves (West & Formenti, 2017).

> I think everybody is feeling more positive around me because I'm feeling more positive in myself. (Lilly, RSC2)

> And when you finally get that recognition that actually what you are saying is right... it is a relief. It's a relief everywhere. It's a relief at work, it's a relief at home. (Lilly, RSC3)

The recognition and validation identified by the participants provided a significant contrast to the disjoint of values and communication communicated in the data. It may be considered that the research process was part of the 'struggle, to reveal and undermine what is most invisible and insidious in prevailing practices' (Ball, 1995, p. 267) and that the discourse experienced within the research could contribute to developing the sense of agency and social power within the 'battle for truth' (Foucault, 1983).

In conclusion, the strength of the data which points towards the value of the layers of research discourse as a transformative and empowering experience could inform a way of conceiving the implementation of support for Nurture group practitioners. It suggests that we should consider an approach to leadership and management with a foundation of 'discourse as practice' (Foucault, 1972, p. 46). An approach which aims to develop a safe space for a discourse aiming to match shared values and to share experiences, within the context of being heard and validated, thereby supporting reflective practice.

The researcher acknowledges that the basis of this chapter is only one small-scale 'piece of research' situated within the 'complicated reality of academics and school people trying to work together' (Elbaz-Luwisch, 2007, p. 374), and as such there will be many limitations. Furthermore, the research did not address a range of other possible discourses, for example, the narrative of gender (Morissey et al., 2017), given the fact that the researcher identified as male and the two participants as female, or, within the context of the school setting, the narrative of the organization (Czarniawska, 2007). These, and other contexts can serve as ways to take the themes and findings of this research forward to further explore the truth and meanings of the subjectivities (West, 1996) explored here, through the creation of new authentically engaged research relationships (West, 1996), but for the present the story stops here.

References

Ainsworth, M.D.S. & Bowlby, J. (1991). An ethological approach to personality development. *American Psychologist*, 46: 331–41. http://dx.doi.org/10.1037/0003-066X.46.4.333

Alleyne, B. (2015). *Narrative networks: Storied approaches in a digital age*. London: Sage.

Apple, M.W. (2014). *Official knowledge: Democratic education in a conservative age*. Abingdon: Routledge.

Ball, S.J. (1995). Intellectuals or technicians? The urgent role of theory in educational studies. *British Journal of Education Studies*, 43(3): 255–71.

Barth, F. (1994). *Enduring and emerging issues in the analysis of ethnicity. The anthropology of ethnicity — Beyond ethnic groups and boundaries*. Amsterdam: Het Spinhuis.

Bennathan, M. & Boxall, M. (1996). *Effective intervention in primary schools: Nurture groups*. London: David Fulton. http://dx.doi.org/10.4324/9781315068992

Bishop, S. (2008). *Running a Nurture group*. London: Sage.

Bluckert, P. (2006). *Psychological dimensions to executive coaching*. London: McGraw-Hill Education.

Bourdieu, P. (1984). *Distinction: A social critique of the judgement of taste*. London, Routledge.

Bruner, J.S. (1991). The narrative construction of reality. *Critical Inquiry*, 18(1): 1–21. http://dx.doi.org/10.1086/448619

Clandinin, D.J. (2013). *Engaging in narrative inquiry*. Walnut Creek, CA: Left Coast Press. http://dx.doi.org/10.4324/9781315429618

Cooper, P. & Whitebread, D. (2007). The effectiveness of Nurture groups on student progress: Evidence from a national research study. *Emotional and Behavioural Difficulties*, 12(3): 171–90.

Czarniawska, B. (2004). *Narratives in social science research: Introducing qualitative methods*. London: Sage.

Czarniawska, B. (2007). Narrative inquiry in and about organizations. In: Clandinin, D.J. (ed), *Handbook of narrative inquiry: Mapping a methodology*. Thousand Oaks, CA: Sage. http://dx.doi.org/10.4135/9781452226552.n15

Dewey, J. (1958). *Democracy and education: An introduction to the philosophy of education*. New York: The Macmillan Company.

Doney, P.A. (2013). Fostering resilience: A necessary skill for teacher retention. *Journal for Science Teacher Education*, 24: 645–64.

Elbaz-Luwisch, F. (2007). Studying teachers' lives and experiences: Narrative inquiry into K-12 teaching. In: Clandinin, D.J. (ed), *Handbook of narrative inquiry: Mapping a methodology*. Thousand Oaks, CA: Sage.

Foucault, M. (1972). *The archaeology of knowledge*. London: Tavistock. http://dx.doi.org/10.4324/9780203604168

Foucault, M. (1983). *The culture of the self*. Lecture at University College, Berkeley. http://www.openculture.com/2014/08/michel-foucaults-lecture-the-culture-of-self.html

Hawkins, P. & Shohet, R. (2006). *Supervision in the helping professions*. Maidenhead: Open University Press.

Kim, J-H. (2016). *Understanding narrative inquiry: The crafting and analysis of stories as research*. London: Sage.

Laloux, F. (2015). How to become a soulful organisation. *RSA Journal*, 22 January.

Leemans, C. (2017). Distributed leadership: A powerful engine for organizational performance. *Leadership Excellence Essentials*, April.

May, T. (1997). *Social research: Issues, methods and process*, 2nd edn. Buckingham: Open University Press.

Mertens, D.M. (2015). *Research and evaluation in education and psychology*, 4th edn. Thousand Oaks, CA: Sage.

Morissey, D., Chant, D.A., Suart, R. & Stead, C. (2017). *Dominant narratives of gender, researching women's lives: Exploring the approaches and sensitivities that make this a distinctive genre*. Masterclass, ESREA/LHBN 2017 Life History and Biography Network Conference, 5 March, Aarhus University, Copenhagen, Denmark.

Nind, M. (2005). Inclusive education: Discourse and action. *British Educational Research Journal*, 31(2): 269–75.

Nurture Group Network (2017). *Nurture groups*. https://nurturegroups.org/sites/default/files/ngn_-_nurture_groups-2017-05web.pdf

NurtureUK (2020). *Nurture group census*. https://www.nurtureuk.org/research-evidence/ngn-commissioned-research/nurture-group-census

Rogers, C.R. (1967). *On becoming a person: A therapist's view of psychotherapy*. London: Constable & Company. http://dx.doi.org/10.1007/BF01560065

Scottish Parliament (2017). *Barnardo's Scotland, Nurture Week. Motion S5M-03336: Stuart McMillan, Greenock and Inverclyde, Scottish National Party,* Lodged 11/1/2017. http://www.parliament.scot/parliamentarybusiness/28877.aspx?SearchType=Advance&ReferenceNumbers=S5M-03336&ResultsPerPage=10

Scott Loinaz, E. (2015). *Pilot Study summary.* https://nurturegroups.org/evidence/ngn-commissioned-research/pilot-study-summary

Sharples, J., Webster, R. & Blatchford, P. (2015). *Making best use of teaching assistants. Guidance report — March 2015.* London: Education Endowment Fund. http://maximisingtas.co.uk/eef-guidance.php

Sloan, S., Winter, K., Lynn, F., Gildea, A. & Connolly, P. (2016). *The impact and cost effectiveness of Nurture groups in primary schools in Northern Ireland.* Belfast: Centre for Evidence and Social Innovation, Queen's University Belfast.

Trenoweth, S. & Moone, N. (eds) (2017). *Psychosocial assessment in mental health.* London: Sage.

Turner, V. (1997). *The ritual process: Structure and anti-structure.* New Brunswick: Aldine Transaction. http://dx.doi.org/10.4324/9781315134666

Warin, J. & Hibbin, R. (2016). A study of Nurture groups as a window into school relationships: Restorative justice and punishment in primary school settings. *International Journal of Nurture in Education,* 1(2): 7–14.

Webster, L. & Mertova, P. (2007). *Using narrative inquiry as a research method.* Abingdon: Routledge. http://dx.doi.org/10.4324/9780203946268

West, L. (1996). *Beyond fragments: Adults, motivation and higher education: A biographical analysis.* Exeter: Taylor Francis.

West, L. & Formenti, L. (2017). *Breakdown in Brussels, tension in Thessaly, and snow(!) in Tuscany: An intellectual auto/biography of the Network.* ESREA/LHBN 2017 Life History and Biography Network Conference. 5 March, Aarhus University, Copenhagen, Denmark.

Winnicott, D.W. (1965). *The maturational processes and the facilitating environment.* New York: International Universities Press.

Zee, M., de Jong, P.F. & Koomen, H.M.Y. (2016). Teachers' self-efficacy in relation to individual students with a variety of social-emotional behaviors: A multilevel investigation. *Journal of Educational Psychology,* 108(7): 1013–27. http://dx.doi.org/10.1037/edu0000106

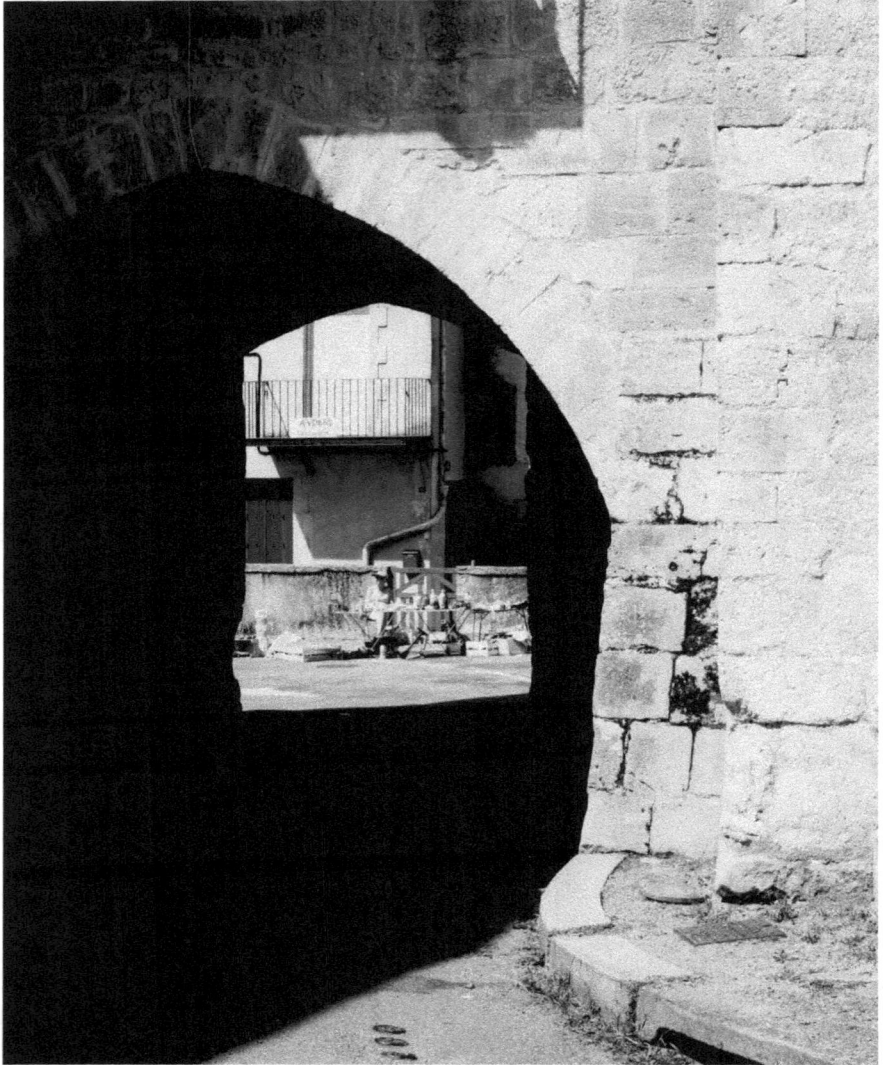

Photo by Tom Perkins, CC-BY 4.0

III.

DISCOURSES WE WORK THROUGH: CHALLENGES TO OVERCOME

The chapters in this section demonstrate how professionals in a range of contexts have found ways of working that mediate constraining discourses, whether through processes of endurance, through individual effort or through developing collaborative practices. The first chapter covers a difficult topic (punishment) in a Nepalese context; the second addresses failure within the Irish higher education system. The final two introduce Italian contexts, one focusing on overcoming the stigma and disadvantages inherent in growing up in care, the other studying the theoretical and practical frameworks for using narrative work with those addicted to gambling.

In chapter nine, 'Punishment Discourses in Everyday Life', Khum Raj Pathak is motivated by his insider knowledge as a student, then a teacher in Nepal to collect the stories of adults who suffered similar regimes of punishment. Working within a philosophical tradition he presents a powerful rhetorical argument about how violent language constructs punishment discourses, reminding us, through a flying visit to the British press, that such language is common in other cultures too, but may go unnoticed. In his narrative research he further explores the links between physical punishment and discourses of punishment and how together these disempower the individual who is punished.

Vera Sheridan's account (Ch10), of 'Irish Students Turning First-Year Transition Obstacles into Successful Progression', sits within the framework of academic retention and progression but focuses on students who overcome failure after being asked to write a reflective account of their situation for their repeat assessment. The professional input here (visible through the choice of strategy) is understated, but evidenced by the subsequent biographical interviews that capture the student's problems and the process of overcoming them. Despite its modest claims, this chapter actually presents an empathetic approach that scaffolds a transition from would-be to successful student.

'Care Leavers in Italy: From 'Vulnerable' Children to 'Autonomous' Adults?' (Ch11) makes appropriate use of its multiple authorship as Laura Formenti, Andrea Galimberti and Mirella Ferrari use different discursive frames to convey the problems associated with leaving care. Laura's tale is event-focused, looking at supportive relationships in different phases of her participant's life; Andrea's is relational, reflecting the interactive style of the interview; Mirella's fictionalized, creating meaning differently; so each researcher draws upon their individual strengths. In many respects this is a performative piece even though the medium is a written one, so little attempt is made to compare the merits of each approach. It is for you, the reader, to engage with the texts and decide how each approach works and what is useful to you and your research. Thus, the chapter avoids prescription and maintains its polyvocal stance, reaching out for interactive engagement.

Finally, in 'What Game Are We Playing? Narrative Work that Supports Gamblers' (Ch12), Micaela Castiglioni and Carola Girotti trace the notion of play back to its philosophical origins, as a pursuit that is important to adults and children alike and made up of games of competition, chance, simulation and vertigo. Drawing upon European theorizations (from, for example, Huizinga and Caillois) gambling is clearly situated in the category of chance (*Alea*), as the authors explain, and this very act helps to reduce the associated stigma, as it becomes play gone wrong. The authors discuss the usefulness of narratives in capturing the essence of difficulties with recovering addicts in two Italian contexts, although they keep the actual narratives confidential in order to maintain anonymity.

The chapters in this section cover troublesome issues in different ways, seeing them, in the case of punishment and gambling, as extreme versions of common behaviour patterns; in terms of student failure, as a temporary obstacle that can be overcome; and in the case of Italian care leavers, inviting the reader to consider the stories themselves and the act of telling, thus seeking to stimulate engagement with the issues.

They relate well to other chapters in the book in terms of content and approach. Particularly, we draw attention to the work of Linden West and Alan Bainbridge (Ch3) and Rob Evans' chapter for its interest in language (Ch17) in relation to Khum Raj Pathak's study of punishment; to the entire second section (Chs5–8) and Janet Dyson's (Ch1), Laura Mazzoli-Smith's (Ch25) and Helen Woodley's work in education (Ch27) with regard to Sheridan; to Teresa Brayshaw and Jennifer Granville's performative treatment of film-making with senior citizens (Ch24) and Matthiassen's (Ch13) and Cooper's (Ch23) studies of ex-offenders trying to rejoin civilian life in Denmark and Britain respectively in relation to the 'leaving care' text. The ex-offender texts (Chs13&23) can also be usefully read alongside that on gambling as all are seen as 'deviant' behaviours by general society even if treated more generously here.

9. Punishment Discourses in Everyday Life

Khum Raj Pathak

Khum Raj Pathak exposes the subliminal power of violence in controlling behaviour, drawing upon language from the workplace, politics and the media in Britain and narrative research in Nepal. He shows how violent language becomes embedded in a culture and how the experience of violence promotes conformity indirectly through fear, before challenging us to consider how educators and the whole of society might speak differently.

The normalization of punitive violence is aided and abetted by the normalization of violent language. I emerged from four years studying the damaging effects of corporal punishment in Nepalese schools with a heightened sensitivity to the language of threats and beatings, not least through the memories it reawakened from my own painful past, as both a pupil and a Maths teacher in Nepal. I recognize punishment discourses everywhere, from work to leisure; from the demands of citizenship to the private sphere of relationships. In particular, punishment discourses colonize global media, saturating our everyday lives and brutalizing our inner selves. The English language, honed and refined by generations of 'survivors' from public schools, is especially adept at incorporating violence into language. Such harsh disciplinarian discourses are slavishly reproduced by English language media everywhere, particularly in India, and in Nepal as it strives to appear modern, at the expense of gentler, reflective discourse traditions.

https://doi.org/10.11647/OBP.0203.09

What Are Punishment Discourses?

There is a language which is used to support the development of society's disciplinary rules: words which become a power in themselves. The movement from disciplinary concepts to physical power is explored by Foucault in *Discipline and Punish* (1995/1977). Foucault re-thinks Nietzsche's *On the Genealogy of Morals* (1887/1996) where Nietzsche exposes punishment discourses as merely 'signs indicating that a will to power has mastered something less powerful than itself and impressed the meaning of a function upon it in accordance with its own interests' (ibid., p. 58). Foucault analyses the genealogy of morality and punishment in the modern world as a gaze and a technology that are deliberately embedded in the human body. Such disciplinary processes impose norms and rules whose observance carries rewards. This framework underpins studies of punishment in the disciplines of criminology, education and sociology.

In this chapter, I discuss punishment as a discourse, a normalization of violent language, embedded in the language of everyday life especially by Nepalese schools. Here, I define punishment discourses as discourses that threaten (*do this or else*), use instrumental reason (*if you want x, then you must do y*), demand (*you are expected to*) or actually announce penalties. On one level, these hardly qualify as discourses, since they signify power and appropriation rather than communication based upon freedom and equality. They instantly create a dichotomy between the rule-maker and the 'other', who is ruled and punished.

The exposure of contingency could facilitate the possibility of change and transformation. Yet there is something about everyday punishment discourses that often invites acceptance and resignation rather than critique and resistance. One possible reason might be because they are used by people seen as 'only doing their jobs' — bureaucrats, law-enforcers, politicians, employers, managers, reporters — those responsible for organizing our thoughts and behaviours, apparently 'for our own good'. We seldom reflect upon the dangers of justifying behaviour on the basis of necessity alone, which could ultimately lead from the 'jobsworth' to a dimly sensed role in the Holocaust, as described by Zygmunt Bauman (1990, p. 133). In today's performativity-led economy, most criticism focuses on inefficiency and poor productivity rather than peaked-cap interventions, which were once overt, strict or bossy. Now we experience a subtle auto-domination which makes individuals flagellate themselves, terrified of not meeting their performance targets. In this way, any instincts of resistance to authoritarianism are diluted and diverted away from an unkind boss or other economic oppressor. Neoliberalism skilfully creates enough insecurity and financial dependency to make individuals punish themselves — with far greater efficiency and brutality than any state.

How Does Everyday Language Embed Violence Within Society?

V iolent language saturates everyday life in British culture to the extent that most people hardly recognize it as such. Once alerted, however, the number of examples seem almost overwhelming. The most superficial analysis of media content is sufficient to identify terms used to capture the reader's attention with brutalizing effects and the reckless propagation of aggression. In a seemingly innocuous newspaper article about football, we learn that a team has been 'thrashed' then 'laid into' by its managers. Public services face 'cuts' and 'cutbacks', budgets are 'slashed'. Governments deal out 'blows' and 'crackdowns' and 'short, sharp shocks'. In the UK general election of 2019, the opposition were said to have been 'massacred' (McKinstry, 2019).

In the world of work, employers write job descriptions in which they 'expect' employees to 'hit the ground running' and meet 'strict deadlines'. Physical pain and the threat of death lurk here by association. Teachers, in particular, must meet 'targets', a word derived from archery, or 'KPI', which stands for 'Key Performance Indicators'. Even everyday citizenship involves harsh language. Members of society are penalized for 'non-compliance', a terrifyingly normalized condemnation issued to describe crimes such as objecting to medication or failing to send off tax or pension documents (before a 'deadline'). In numerous contexts, our details must be sent online by clicking on the word 'submit'.

These terms not only carry violent and disciplinarian connotations but also involve reification, abstraction and constructions of 'necessity'. Under this terminology, human beings possess no intrinsic value that might protect them from these disrespectful verbal or written assaults.

Employees must 'perform' like engines or circus animals. Health service 'cuts' are mentioned as if they are a remote abstraction rather than the physical removal of specific life-saving treatments. Under the guise of discipline, the shifts in power heralded by these terms are widely accepted as a 'necessity'. If a government announced that it was going to take away the medicine from an individual cancer sufferer, there might be an outcry, but when it is just part of the 'general cuts', the public accept exactly the same consequences with merely a sigh of resignation.

Violent language has been especially favoured by the political right and by neoliberal ideologies of performativity and economization, which seek to punish by elimination the 'unproductive' or 'non-viable', creating a fear-conditioned 'precariat' (Standing, 2014; Moore & Robinson, 2015, p. 2776). But it is also used by authoritarian powers of all political hues seeking to exert control, suppress resistance or undermine the survival strategies of the most vulnerable. To give some more examples from English newspapers: we have 'crackdowns' on benefit cheats or illegal immigrants and failing schools 'whipped into shape'. Many violent words are apolitical and appeal to a widely accepted miserable way of working, a short-term repression for long-term survival recognized by Freud (Freud, 2010/1920, p. 185) and developed by Marcuse as the 'Reality Principle' (Marcuse, 1987/1956, pp. 12–13). Countless office workers say they must 'crack on', barely noticing that this is an association with a 'crack on the head' which causes us to furrow our brow. We all work to 'deadlines', for example, even though this word secretes an implicit threat of death for crossing a given timeline. Even non-violent resistance can involve 'strikes' and 'clashes'. Traffic violations can lead to culprits being 'slapped with a fine'; people may be 'shut down' by those who disagree with them. There is a peculiar thirst for the violent verbs that shock or excite us into buying tabloid newspapers following competitions or matches, and in computer games; almost as if violence enhances their fetish value.

This violent discourse makes it harder to introduce the language of compassion, sympathy or understanding, and those who try may rapidly be branded a 'snowflake' by alt-right trolls. As we learn from the history of genocide, 'vilifying rhetoric has contributed to mass violence' particularly among those predisposed to aggression (Kalmoe, 2018). The disrespect, reification and hardening of heart induced by violent language may lead swiftly to violence and killing, certainly to bullying and victimization.

Why Are Our Defences Against Punitive Language So Weak?

How does violent rhetoric manage to permeate our consciousness and influence our behaviour so successfully? My research suggests that the punishment discourses of everyday life impact especially upon those of us who have experienced corporal punishment. These power-laden discourses can yet inspire resistance, however, as much as they can induce submission.

My research in Nepal involved interviewing several adults who, like myself, had experienced corporal punishment during their school years. Through an auto/biographical methodology, my participants and I began to link our contemporary struggles in punitive contexts to past experiences of punishment. We each described difficulties that we faced in risk-taking, challenging authority and pursuing ambitions; impeded at every turn by discourses that seemed frightening and brought back memories of physical punishments in childhood. Eerily, my participants often actually repeated the disempowering words that could have been said to them as children, such as, 'you will never be good at anything'.

Mukunda's Story

Mukunda, a thirty-four-year-old from Devchuli, described various business ambitions that had never come to fruition. He had hoped to buy some land then open a school. Later, he planned to open a computer shop. Instead, he was held back by irrational fears. Mukunda feared that he 'did not have enough knowledge' (despite being the first person in his village to gain a Master's degree). He was scared that his business 'might make a big loss' — yet found himself bitterly regretting his indecision when friends of his opened successful computer shops and the land that he had viewed multiplied in value. Mukunda had even turned down a possible role as a community leader, saying:

> I worried I might not be able to fulfil people's expectations. I feel that if I fail to fulfil my promises to the people, they will have negative feelings

towards me. I am always afraid of that. Up till now society thinks I'm a good person but if I ever become a leader, then become unsuccessful, their opinion of me might change.

Where have these self-imposed restrictions come from? Mukunda traced them back to corporal punishment at school. Mukunda described two effects in particular. Firstly, a lack of creativity and innovation:

> All the while the teacher was using punishment in the classroom, we didn't try anything new. In fact, I never thought about new ideas. I just studied what the teacher told us to and how could any new ideas come from there? I did not have any new ideas at all.

Secondly, he voiced a fear that change or risk-taking could lead to punishment:

> They made us follow them dogmatically. They always insisted that students listen to them and copy them precisely. If someone tried to do [anything] different, then they would be beaten severely.

This 'NO' to change, reinforced by years of beatings and witnessing beatings, carries its echo into adult life. Mukunda does not describe the voices that led him to suppress his ideas and ambitions, so we do not know whether they were implanted by others around him, or from himself, or both. But it is easy to envisage how, for somebody with his background, dire warnings against change — from whatever source — could have an instant impact. How could he bear the pressure of 'targets' or his businesses 'crashing'?

Preeti's Story

For my twenty-six-year-old female participant, Preeti, corporal punishment led to confusion:

> I did exercise number three instead of number two or number four. I just got confused. Then I got beaten. Sometimes I used to ask my friends. [...] When the teachers saw that they used to bang our heads together.

She also described 'forgetting everything that she had just learnt' once she saw the teacher enter the classroom. In later life, this temporary amnesia was repeated. Preeti explained how she tends to 'forget what I believe and think' and abandon any of her own ideas as soon as her in-laws give her 'instructions'. Corporal punishment also affected her appetite and sleep, especially after one teacher began using a stick with thorns in it from the Sisau tree. Preeti said:

> Sometimes the beatings used to be quite a lot and my body could not bear it. I would have a fever and hotness in my body. I didn't want any food on that day. [...] I used to dream that the teacher was beating me after not memorizing the text and other very frightening dreams. [...] Some nights I used to wake up suddenly, shouting.

To this day, Preeti remains afraid that she might 'get punished' if she disobeys her in-laws and when her powerlessness makes her 'upset', she is unable to eat. Again, she does not describe the discourses around her literally but it is clear that they do not encourage dissent and debate, only obedience and conformity. Preeti said that she dreaded arguments and would do anything to avoid conflict — to the extent of leaving her teaching job. Preeti's housework, farm-work and shop-work 'deadlines' were so intense that she appeared baffled when I asked her about leisure time:

> Time for myself? I'm not sure what you mean. I can't study. Once I wake up at five, I am so worried about getting all my chores done in time. Every hour has its task or things go wrong.

This pressure was not countered by any alternative voice telling her to take it easy. Preeti's fears must be understood in the context of rural Nepal. We often do not have the choice to postpone jobs until tomorrow: our survival depends on a strict timetable and tasks such as feeding and milking the buffalo are unavoidable. Nevertheless, I had the impression that Preeti, like so many women in Nepal, was over-worked and overwrought by oppressive voices emanating from both her conscience and her family.

Krishna's Story

Krishna, a twenty-three-year-old farmer from Devchuli, had experienced the most severe corporal punishment, recalling how:

> They (teachers) used to thrash us, hang us upside down... make us walk through the playground on our knees; there would be blood while doing

that. They used to torture us a lot. [...] They beat us with nettles and with a long, bamboo stick.

Krishna described being beaten 'in every class, nearly every day' and finally, at the age of sixteen, in front of the whole school following allegations that he had a girlfriend. The beatings were accompanied by constant criticism, beginning with unfair attacks on his ability to master Nepali (Magar was his first language). Verbal and physical attacks from authority figures also occurred once he left school for a job in India:

> I cried at the beginning, as we had to wash up so fast and work such long hours compared to my life in Nepal. If we made any mistake, our bosses would beat us. They would swear at us with terrible words insulting our parents, saying that we worked too slowly.

Krishna then repeated as fact the words that his bosses might have said to him:

> It was boring work but India was full of unemployed young men waiting to fill our job and I had no qualifications to get anything better.

As time went on, he began to overreact to oppressive language. To this day, Krishna admitted, with a revealing mixture of tenses:

> If someone says something against me or tries to boss me about over something, I get very angry and wanted to fight with them. It became my habit.

Krishna described both his schooling and an attempted job as too difficult 'brain-wise', echoing the teachers who once labelled him as a weak student. For somebody with Krishna's experiences of violent punishment, discourses of gentle encouragement were essential to his survival, but these never came. His experiences of work abroad involved both verbal and physical abuse, leaving him so damaged that he would spring up in a rage at the slightest criticism.

My Story

My own experiences of violence have been masked to an extent by my academic persona. Yet I, too, struggle with what is almost a psychological allergy to punishment discourses. Perfectly reasonable demands for work to be 'submitted' within 'deadlines' fill me with sickening fears. This chapter itself was horrifically late. Threats of 'or else' seem to make me do the opposite and my creative ideas only seem to flow when I am in a peaceful atmosphere — such as the dead of night — free from pressure and punishment associations. Sometimes in public I stammer and forget what I was going to say, just as I used to in front of my most violent teachers. Similar difficulties are experienced by individuals who are already struggling to overcome violent memories from the past, exacerbated by punishment discourses in everyday life. Yet punishment discourses are seen as necessary and indispensable. In Britain they are fetishized, taboo, endowed with mystical properties, and difficult to challenge.

How Are Punishment Discourses Invested with Notions of Necessity?

Disciplining the workforce, increasing productivity, preventing idleness, corruption or inefficiency; many of us even try to frighten ourselves into a task (such as academic writing) that might require tremendous self-control. What can be done when polite requests are ignored? Moreover, punishment discourses are not necessarily chosen, but are often due to pressure from those above in the chain of command. An under-manager might berate and threaten her staff as she herself fears punishment for her team not meeting certain targets. The greater her fear, the harsher her language. Punitive language does not always indicate a metaphysically narrow focus; it might be due to temporary states of anxiety or feeling pressurized. It may be seen as a duty for a greater good. In Nepal, I remember using punitive discourses to prevent struggling pupils from having to drop down a class. At the time, I also believed that I had 'no choice' because I had seldom encountered non-punitive leadership.

This language is not unique to capitalism: many communist regimes have had demanding productivity targets, such as Stalin's Five-Year Plans. The punitive discourses of capitalism, however, are especially skilful at infiltrating consciousness through careful marketing. A threat of punishment is concealed within sales pitches that suggest 'can you afford NOT to buy this?' Consumers thus fear the terrible consequences that might ensue from not buying an item, which could be anything from a burglar alarm to a face cream. Neoliberal concerns about competitiveness, viability and comparative quality have intensified the pressure on companies to ensure that the productivity of each individual is squeezed to its maximum. There are also sado-masochistic elements in the public's passion for punitive headlines and bombastic rhetoric, currently demonstrated by intense reactions to racial and sexual politics.

Despite our saturation with punitive discourses, Foucault reminds us that the 'normalization' and 'naturalization' of 'disciplinary networks' is not necessary and eternal but, instead, historical, constructed and therefore changeable (Foucault, 1995/1977, pp. 303–06). Alternative styles of discourse, representing more egalitarian power structures, exist but are increasingly scrutinized for efficacy. The progressive teaching techniques of last century favoured encouragement over negative criticism (see Reese, 2001 on the discourse of child-centred learning) and the use of encouraging words such as: 'That is an interesting idea' rather than: 'You're wrong'. Results-centric educational policy research has tended to undermine praise, citing it as an example of 'ineffective practice' (Coe, et al, 2014, p. 22). Police services experimenting with interactive methods of community policing and research in America found that, on balance, encouraging dialogue with residents carries some success in reducing crime and disorder (Reisig, 2010) suggesting that threats are not the best way to enforce obedience. Sub-cultures such as Rastafarianism and hippy culture have long favoured discourses of gentleness, openness and tolerance, mirroring how the hippy might seek to literally 'drop-out' from the violent pressures of judgement, competition, acquisition and indeed, the force of interpretation itself (Hall, 1968). The word 'cool' is used to express approval, acceptance, open-heartedness and open-mindedness, in direct contrast to punitive language. Traditional etiquette, in many languages, also contains a phraseology that expresses sensitivity and sympathy rather than condemnation. As *Debrett's* puts it: 'The essence of good manners is to treat others as you would wish to be treated yourself, to show empathy, so that nobody feels confused, excluded or exposed' (Wyse, 2015). Where it does offer correction, the most polite language is tentative, respectful and minimalist. For example, saying 'Perhaps you might consider...', 'Could I suggest that...' or 'I wonder if it might be better to...', rather than more threatening direct language such as 'You can't do that'. Although in England, power-relations remain unchanged by polite language (indeed, the courtesy and *noblesse oblige* of the upper classes has been part of their survival strategy), at least human beings emerge from such encounters feeling less reified and more respected. Other areas of tolerance include mystical traditions, which stress love rather than punitive dogma (Cupitt, 1998, p. 83) and working-class idioms intended to reduce blame and fear, such as: 'Don't worry about it mate' and: 'We all make mistakes'.

For Krishna, working as a washing-up assistant in India, the manner in which he was addressed by his bosses could have made all the difference to his career and prevented his over-determined and self-destructive reaction to any criticism, which he associated with physical abuse. Punishment discourses also affect motivation. Preeti described how she would study in order to memorize rather than to understand, and out of sheer fear rather from any excitement or joy she took in studying. Finally, Mukunda felt unable to start a business or become a community leader because of performativity anxieties. Instead of being motivated by dedication or love or compassion for his community, his mind was tortured by worries about how he would perform and how this would affect his social image.

How Do We, as Educators, Overcome Dominant Punitive Discourses?

To overcome punitive discourses we should start with ourselves and try to make our communication less threatening and frightening. This means recognizing how punitive language in the classroom can limit learning by creating an alienated and alienating 'other'. Even so-called positive discipline, such as the awarding of stars, emerges from a punitive context (Kohn, 1999). A parallel may be made with competitive reality shows: contestants are degraded by the very fact that performances are judged and appraised by people holding up numbers. In education, as in the arts, how much more useful and fruitful are *specific* adjectives, engaged with *specific* aspects of an individual's work.

In everyday life, punishment discourses may be transformed through challenging bureaucracy and bureaucratic methods that prevent the recognition of the uniqueness of individuals and situations. Managers are seen to be managing properly if they provide a barrage of paperwork, containing quality control assessment forms, consumer feedback forms and Key Performance Indicators. However, the choices on such forms are usually limited by their reliance upon numbers or a few pre-determined answer options. Every week, for example, I have to rate my Tesco online shopping delivery driver on a scale of one to five. How can I 'sum up' another human being in the reifying language of the market? Grading itself contains punitive aspects that can be nonsensical, for example, in the way that reception-level children in Nepalese schools are condemned to streams, marked by numbers and letters, which withhold full approval for the majority of students. Bruner's ideal, a climate enabling pupils to 'experience success and failure not as reward and punishment, but as information' (Bruner, 1961, p. 26), is made more difficult by grading, according to Alfie Kohn (Kohn, 1994). It prevents the classroom being perceived as 'a safe place, where there is no fear of humiliation and punitive judgment' (ibid, p. 40) and therefore discourages learners from asking for help. These punitive effects of grading make it morally suspect and the darling of identitarian ideologies, attracted by its orgy of power, control and condemnation.

Punishment discourses can also be challenged by increasing our awareness of violent adjectives and metaphors. Our sensitivity to racism has led to changes in language: we no longer talk about 'blackening' somebody's character, for example. Similarly, we should reflect upon our use of words like thrash, cane, hit, and smash to describe everyday events, from sport to the economy. Are we right, for example, to embrace superhero cults that lead to the intrinsically violent word POW being used to decorate a pair of pants? The violence of words like 'cuts' can be beneficial as accurate reflections of the pain and suffering caused by the removal of funding for vulnerable people. Where 'cuts' become accepted as a general necessity, however, we appear to be desensitized to the suffering involved. To ban these violent words would also involve a degree of cruelty and violate the right to freedom of speech: would we really want to prosecute the pensioner for saying his football team was 'thrashed'? Unless we set our 'thinking against itself', to use Adorno's term (Adorno, 1973, p. 365), and admit the inadequacy of our conceptualization then we also become punishers. Nevertheless, reflecting upon a word's potential associations might help us to develop an aversion for normalized violent words and to understand why Adorno links conceptual condemnation to literal extermination (ibid., p. 362).

The removal of punitive discourses emanating from performativity ideologies is more difficult, since it challenges practices that feature frequently within economization and management strategies, deemed necessary for businesses to prove their efficiency and accountability to shareholders. Unions have worked to defend employees from the worst punitive discourses, but an increasing number of companies are replacing traditional reprimands with sinister forms of silent surveillance, including even embedding workers with microchips as part of their auto-quantification (Moore & Robinson, 2015, p. 2779). Such disciplinary strategies are no less aggressive and considerably more intrusive than the shouting and beatings of the past.

These wide-ranging examples show how punishment discourses are not merely an issue for the philosopher of education, but for the whole of human society. For my participants and for me, their prevalence forces us into a state of perpetual alertness: we constantly battle against their incapacitating effects upon every area of our private and collective lives.

References

Adorno, T. (1973/1966). *Negative dialectics*. London: Kegan Paul.

Bauman, Z. (1990). *Thinking sociologically*. Oxford: Blackwell. https://doi.org/10.1177/144078339202800117

Bruner, J.S. (1961). The act of discovery. *Harvard Educational Review*, 31: 21–32.

Coe, R., Aloisi, C., Higgins, S. & Major, L.E. (2014). *What makes great teaching? Review of the underpinning research*. https://www.suttontrust.com/wp-content/uploads/2014/10/What-Makes-Great-Teaching-REPORT.pdf

Cupitt, D. (1998). *Mysticism after modernity*. Oxford: Blackwell.

Foucault, M. (1995/1977). *Discipline and punish: The birth of the prison* (2nd English edn). New York: Vintage Books.

Freud, S. (2010/1920). *Beyond the pleasure principle*. In: S. Freud, *Collected works*. Seattle, WA: Pacific Publishing Studio.

Hall, S. (1968). *The Hippies — An American 'moment'*. Occasional Paper, 16. Centre for Contemporary Cultural Studies, University of Birmingham.

https://www.birmingham.ac.uk/Documents/college-artslaw/history/cccs/
stencilled-occasional-papers/1to8and11to24and38to48/SOP16.pdf

Kalmoe, N. (2018). Yes, political rhetoric can incite violence, *Politico*, October
30, 2018. https://www.politico.com/magazine/story/2018/10/30/
yes-political-rhetoric-can-incite-violence-222019

Kohn, A. (1994). Grading: The issue is not how but why? *Educational Leadership*,
52(2): 38–41.

Kohn, A. (1999). *Punished by rewards: The trouble with gold stars, incentive plans,
A's, praise and other bribes*. Boston, MA: Houghton Mifflin.

Marcuse, H. (1987/1956). *Eros and civilisation: A philosophical inquiry into Freud*.
London: Ark.

McKinstry, L. (2019). London's political bubble don't know what's hit
them — Labour and Corbyn were massacred. *The Sun*, 13 December 2019.
https://www.google.co.uk/amp/s/www.thesun.co.uk/news/10544543/
londons-political-bubble-dont-know-whats-hit-them-labour-and-corbyn-
were-massacred/amp/

Moore, P. & Robinson, A. (2015). The quantified self: What counts in the neoliberal workplace. *New Media & Society*, 2016, 18(11): 2774–92. https://doi.
org/10.1177/1461444815604328

Nietzsche, F. (1887/1986). *On the genealogy of morals*. Oxford: Oxford University
Press.

Pathak, K.R. (2017). *How has corporal punishment in Nepalese schools impacted upon
learners' lives?* PhD Thesis, Canterbury Christ Church University.

Reisig, M.D. (2010). *Community and Problem-Oriented Policing*. Crime and Justice,
39(1), pp. 1–53.

Standing, G. (2014). *The Precariat: The new dangerous class*. Bloomsbury Academic:
London.

Wyse, E. (2015). Preface to *Debrett's Handbook* (*British Style, Correct Form, Modern
Manners*). London: Debrett's Limited.

10. Irish Students Turning First-Year Transition Obstacles into Successful Progression

Vera Sheridan

Vera Sheridan provides a comprehensive overview of the literature on student retention and progression before discussing the narrative accounts of four Irish students who successfully continued their studies after failing in the first year, seeking to understand how this was achieved.

Significant levels of research into student progression during the first year of higher education exist internationally (James, Krause & Jennings, 2010; Tinto 1994, 2006; Yorke & Longden, 2008). A key theme to emerge from such studies is that there is no one single factor that affects the first-year student experience but a combination of academic, social, economic and personal factors that contribute to successful progression in higher education. Academic support (Leese, 2010) and social support, as from family and friends (Wilcox, Finn & Fyvie-Gauld, 2005), affect retention, as do economic factors (Bozick, 2007) including working while studying (Curtis & Shani, 2002). Particular student characteristics, such as social class and belonging (Ostrove & Long, 2007), being the eldest in the family (O'Shea, 2007), being a mature student (Reay, Crozier & Clayton, 2010) and coming from a minority (Carter, 2006) can also influence student outcomes and retention rates.

Retention and progression — these two terms are used together regularly — present as indicators of student success, often in large-scale institutional or national surveys. A limited, statistical definition of retention/progression rates, however, suggests a one-dimensional model, whereas for Ashby (2004) retention is multidimensional and contains institutional, student and employer aspects. The institutional dimension presents the indicators used to measure retention, and, with the expansion of higher education, high drop-out rates serve as indicators of institutional performance. The student dimension broadens the definition of retention as it includes the results of student feedback from withdrawal, course and satisfaction surveys. The employer dimension represents value for money, such as the contribution of skills to employability. The student dimension involves failing in first year, with failure here referring to not passing assignment/s. However, if the characteristics of retention/progression are multidimensional, failure to progress could equally be interpreted as being multidimensional, composed of academic, social, economic and personal factors. Consequently, the focus in this study is on the student dimension of retention and initial failure in first year, in a qualitative study of school leavers grounded in the Irish higher education context.

Intermittent research into retention or non-completion in Ireland has involved a single institution (Baird, 2002; Blaney & Mulkeen, 2008) or a particular higher-education sector, such as institutions of technology, which have experienced high dropout rates (Eivers, Flanagan & Morgan, 2002). The Higher Education Authority produced the first comprehensive study (Mooney et al., 2010) of retention/progression across the entirety of the Irish higher-level sector, followed by Frawley, Piggott & Carroll's (2017) report. In this report, on average fifteen per cent of new entrants are no longer present one year later across all higher education sectors. There is a rise in non-progression from nine per cent to eleven per cent across the universities from 2007–2015. A similar trend for university arts/social sciences is present in this period with non-progression rates rising from nine per cent to twelve per cent so that retention and non-progression warrant further investigation.

In the Irish context, academic performance is a greater indicator of successful progression from first year to second year than age, gender or social class and Mooney et al. (2010) point to the central role played by Leaving Certificate[1] results in progression by emphasizing the:

---

1   End-of-school examinations that enable entry to higher education.

importance of students' ability in meeting the academic demands of higher education. The results (of the Leaving Certificate) also highlight the importance of academic preparedness prior to entry and adequate learning supports on entry to higher education as students who fail first year and have to repeat are more likely not to progress to second year. (Mooney et al., 2010, p. 45)

Academic performance relates to the high percentage of students from the professional and managerial classes who are more likely to enrol in university than students from working-class backgrounds, for instance, despite the abolition of fees in 1997. Participation levels among students from highly professional families have reached a virtual saturation point while students from the other end of the social spectrum have not increased in numbers as significantly, despite the expansion of higher education from twenty per cent participation in the 1980s to fifty-four per cent by 2003 (McCoy & Smyth, 2011). Thus, further expansion relies on an increase in student participation from more disadvantaged groups. One of the aims for sectoral reform is to increase capacity 'while at the same time enhancing diversity' (HEA, 2016, p. 78) which would indicate ongoing concern with retention in a more diverse student body.

University entry procedures in Ireland link the number of course places to a points system: the results of the Leaving Certificate, the terminal secondary school examinations by subject, determine university entry through the number of points attained and the number of points required for a specific course. Mooney et al. (2010, p. 45) point to the central role of Leaving Certificate results 'in meeting the academic demands of higher education' and as 'academic preparedness prior to entry'. During the first year of a three-year undergraduate course, non-progression is due to factors such as making an uninformed decision regarding course choice (Mooney et al., 2010), a difficult transition (Sheridan & Dunne, 2012), assessment in university (Fleming & Finnegan, 2011) and the cost of living (McCoy & Smyth, 2011), particularly accommodation. Fleming and Finnegan (2011) advocate listening to students about their experiences as their narratives are not simple, one-dimensional accounts but are complex and multi-layered. They point towards an in-depth approach to retention, as in this qualitative study with first-year students who overcome obstacles to proceed to subsequent course years.

Theorizing Transition

T here is no one first-year experience, but rather a multiplicity of experiences (Harvey & Drew, 2006; Pitkethly & Prosser, 2001) which relate to the interactions between a higher-level institution and its students. Such interactions are themselves grounded in the particular sociocultural contexts of each university (Pitkethly & Prosser, 2001). Students begin the process of reconceptualizing the self in the break from home accompanied by homesickness and the weakening of old friendship ties leading to a realignment of friendships, including eventual break-up with boyfriends or girlfriends (Chow & Healey, 2008). A body of research has emerged which has shifted attention to Bourdieu and relates to the embodiment of social and cultural capital (Bourdieu, 1986) and of habitus or the 'sense of one's place' in social space (Bourdieu, 1989, p. 19). Such research has focused on institutional habitus (Reay, Crozier & Clayton, 2010: Sheridan, 2011), the role of habitus in retention (Thomas, 2002), social class (Reay, 1998; Quinn, 2004), gender (David et al., 2003) and cultural capital (Longden, 2004) in relation to early departure. Reay (2004) has critiqued what she considers to be an over-reliance on Bourdieu, particularly when research merely references habitus rather than working fully with the concept.

Higher education research has also turned to anthropology, to the concept of liminality as part of rites of passage (Turner, 1967; Van Gennep, 1960), which occurs as movement from membership of one group to another as from youth to adult status. This movement occurs across three stages: separation, transition and incorporation as an adult into society in accordance with its norms and beliefs. Each of these three stages involves different patterns of interaction between the individual and others where separation is the detachment, via decreasing interaction, with the group that is being left behind and where the individual is known. To enter a new group, a border is crossed, which includes a period of transition where the individual begins to act in new ways according to the norms of this new group. This second stage is critical as the individual is in the process of acquiring new knowledge to carry out the demands of the new role in the group but, simultaneously, is still a stranger who can feel isolated and untethered from the norms and beliefs of the past and future full membership of the new group. Consequently, this transitional stage carries all the dangers of departure from the group before achieving incorporation or full competency of group membership. Following incorporation, the individual can return to previous relationships with others having achieved the status of full member of the new group.

Turner (1967) considered the process of transition, the second phase of Van Gennep's (1960) rites of passage, to be transformative and termed the sociocultural properties of this second phase as 'margin' or 'limen'. The liminal individual is invisible by neither leaving nor fully becoming so that the individual has a physical but no social reality. The individual's condition 'is one of ambiguity and paradox' being 'neither one thing nor another' (Turner, 1967, p. 97). Turner characterizes the 'peculiar unity of the liminal: that which is neither this nor that, and yet is both' (ibid., p. 99) where an individual is in a position to think about society so that liminality becomes 'a stage of reflection' (ibid., p. 105) of this 'betwixt and between' period (ibid., p. 110). Studies on identity/ies in higher education draw on liminality in examinations of student-hood (Field & Morgan Klein, 2010), liminal identities in lifelong learning (Field, 2012), the positions of graduate teaching assistants (Winstone & Moore, 2017), doctoral students (Keefer, 2015), and teaching and learning (Cook-Sather & Alter, 2011). Liminality continues to inform education, such as the threshold concepts of student learning, according to which upsets to familiar understandings can open a portal to new ways of thinking, which subsequently lead to alterations in a learner's subjectivity or story of the self (Land, Rattray & Vivian, 2014). There are critiques of the ambiguous nature of the threshold concept resulting in different understandings of the theory (Rowbottom, 2007). The linear progression contained in the concept of liminality is also questioned, as liminality does not necessarily result in a simple transition from one status to another but can, instead, develop into a reconciliation of different cultural values as in biculturalism (Uttal, 2010).

Tinto (1988) applies a rites of passage approach to retention by focusing on a student's transition from school to university as it involves some separation from the past to result in successful incorporation into the new community of the university. Difficulties encountered in the transition process in the rites of passage:

are as much a reflection of the problems inherent in shifts of community membership as they are either of the personality of individuals or of the institution in which membership is sought. (Tinto, 1988, p. 442)

In effect, the transition is multi-layered in terms of relationships such as friends, family and home, and Tinto characterizes the physical and social parting from these relationships as painful or at least disorientating. Transition can involve stress, a sense of loss and bewilderment, and a student can withdraw from university early in first year without support. In the liminal space, Palmer, O'Kane & Owens (2009) view student transition as the transformative space betwixt and between home and university where students forge a sense of belonging to life at university. They critique theorizing of student first-year experience that omits the social aspect of transition and also ignores the student voice in the first few weeks of university, both of which are prominent in this research.

Method

The research poses the question: in what ways do students who fail in first year manage to resolve this experience to continue successfully with their studies?

This study focuses on the subjective understanding of life experience in the shifting story of the self (Bruner, 1990), in which narrative provides a meaningful sequence of events in a social context (Elliot, 2005). A small group of students, who failed a first-semester module, each wrote an essay reflecting on this failure for their repeat assessment. This assignment produced rich, autobiographical reflections on the issues these students considered significant to their lack of success in their first year. The interviews follow up four of these students who subsequently progressed successfully. Each interview revisited the concerns voiced in the reflective essay to see if and how these concerns, which had inhibited connecting with the academic and social life of the university, had been resolved. The interviews occurred in the first semester of either the second or third year, depending on progression. Consequently, the data spans a period of approximately two and a half years and presents an in-depth perspective on how students who did not begin well turned a negative experience into a successful navigation of their undergraduate course.

Out of six possible participants, three young women, Laoise, Caoimhe, Saoirse and one young man, Fiachra, gave permission to use their reflective essay as a source of data; they have been given atypical Irish names for anonymity. They can be considered an opportunistic sample (Onwuegbuzie & Leech, 2007) emerging from an ongoing study, approved by the university's Ethics Committee, on transition to higher-level education (see Sheridan & Dunne, 2012). My email request for participation came a year after the official promulgation of student results so that there was no pressure to participate and the four students gave permission for face-to-face interviews with one email interview.

Data Analysis

F ollowing West in Merrill & West (2009), a biography was created for each of the four participants from the reflective essays to provide the personal context for the stumbling blocks to progression. Secondly, taking a liminal perspective, each data set was analysed thematically (Plummer, 2001; Riessman, 2008) resulting in a table of themes and their categories for each data set. Overlapping themes were merged to create the set of themes that affect the transformation process from school leaver to successful first-year undergraduate and these are:

- Interpersonal relations: friendships, working with others.
- Personal development: being too young/maturity, responsibilities, motivation.
- Balancing competing demands: paid employment, balancing work and college, managing stress, values.
- Learning: autonomy, group work, presentations, timetable, difference between school and college, uncertainty in first semester.

The individual biographies detail how aspects of these themes coalesced in first year to produce failure, followed by the management of failure as it was transformed into successful progression.

Four Biographies

Laoise

L aoise had no other responsibility at school apart from working
to achieve the highest points possible in her Leaving Certificate
examination. She considered herself to be mature and discovered her
personal drive at the age of fifteen when she decided on a particular
university course following sensible advice provided by her school's
guidance counsellor. She successfully completed her Leaving Certificate
but decided that at seventeen she would be too young to go to university.
Instead, she gained another qualification through further education and
saved up money so that she was ready to leave home and set up on her
own in her first year at university. She would seem to possess qualities
to become a successful first-year undergraduate, but found that already
being in a relationship held her back to some extent in finding new
friends or engaging in campus activities. Laoise referred to a protracted
'in-between' stage regarding her friendships as she did not live on
campus or commute regularly:

> I think I was in that awkward limbo [...]. I still connected to my own
> friends but I still connected to my college friends and I was kind of
> in-between the two and obviously I'm still like that; I'm still talking to
> people from home but I definitely have made connections.

Laoise refers to being 'in-between' the old and the new with regard to
friends and feeling lonely as she drifted away from secondary-school
friends without having made new ones at university.

She had to contend with stress from trying to manage her personal
finances and finding accommodation to share with people she liked.
During her first year she moved regularly into different accommodation
as a cost-saving measure and worked at night as her parents were not
able to contribute towards university costs. As well as these upsets,
Laoise struggled with non-compulsory attendance and felt that she had
no routine. She found it hard to balance paid employment and living
costs with academic work and felt that the ensuing tension affected her
first year:

> It definitely did sacrifice first year, I can say it absolutely did, but it was
> just ... it was a solution that I came to, was to find somewhere with

cheaper rent and to not get myself into debt, and ... I'm still trying to find that now, where to find cheap rent ... First year I was working nights to try and get in eight hours and that wasn't a solution either and now I'm room sharing and that's still not a solution but I think again it's just a life experience; it's that difficult for a student, you know, scraping the money together.

Laoise prioritized leaving university debt-free so that financing her studies played a critical role in her life, despite entering first year with some savings, and regardless of its effect on her learning and assessment outcomes.

Caiomhe

Accommodation and interpersonal relations also affected Caiomhe as she went to school in a town where people knew each other; she enjoyed the closeness of being surrounded by family members living nearby, knowing her neighbours and having plenty of friends. She shared an apartment with friends in first year, but felt homesick, distanced herself from university social life and began to stay alone in the shared apartment watching television even as she saw her roommates go to classes regularly, make friends and enjoy academic life. She felt unsafe in the area of Dublin where she was living, and told family this when she returned home at weekends, resulting in Caiomhe travelling back to university on Monday mornings and missing classes. The more her friends began to enjoy college life, the more entrenched her distancing routine became: she did not even seek help for her dyslexia. She was not enjoying some of the modules she had chosen; she thought they were 'pointless', not 'proper' subjects and it appeared so easy to do well that it would be impossible to fail assignments.

Living away from home raised questions about her social values and sense of self:

... it was just a big shock I think because the place where I lived in first year I didn't get to know any of my neighbours, [...] when I was signing into the lift going up and down to my apartment I didn't talk to that person and have never in my life had that, even like when I'm walking along the streets in _____ when I see somebody I automatically say 'hello' and then go 'oh God, they don't know you, they think you're weird', but it's just the way that I've grown up with that and it stuck with me the whole way along.

Not being able to manage the changing nature of interpersonal relationships inter-linked with personal responsibility in her academic work, such as becoming involved with group-work assignments, so that each negative reaction reinforced the distancing from the academic and social life of the university. The lack of experience of working with others in group work became an impediment, and led to not being able to manage disagreements tactfully and to increasing absence:

> I kept dodging them and didn't go and then have people getting angry at me and then you fall into a cycle and keep continuing and then if people say 'oh, I don't want to work with Caiomhe because she's... She doesn't meet or she doesn't do what she has to do to pull her weight in the group', it really was a cycle and I had to work so hard to pull that around because I had got that image in first year.

Overall, interpersonal relationships presented immediate hurdles which appeared insurmountable and led to disengagement and withdrawal.

Caiomhe had felt 'untouchable' having gained her place at university but seriously underestimated the level of academic commitment she had to make. She realized that she had to change:

> I was just so lost; I was devastated and I remember telling my parents and them being so angry with me and me just covering it up and saying I didn't like my course but I'd never really given it a chance so I didn't know whether I liked it or not ... that day when I saw them [her results] I thought to myself 'you need to get your act together, you need one shot at this and you know you haven't given this course a chance'... those exams stuck with me for so long because I had to wait the whole summer, [...] it was constantly at the back of my mind so I just had to pull up my socks and I did in fairness, I did do it but knowing that those repeats were still coming I found that I didn't actually break free from it at all until I actually passed them and I got into second year.

At that point Caiomhe considered that her first year was not only about meeting academic challenges but that 'it has also given me an education on life'.

Fiachra

In school, Fiachra considered the careers guidance to be poor, particularly as he was not sure what he wanted to do, and he chose a college course solely because of its title without investigating further. He spent two months in his first college and, despite his parents' anger, he dropped out and then lived through some months of sheer boredom as he had nothing to do until he was offered an outdoor job. While working he began a thorough search for another course, found one of interest and even consulted a friend who had completed the same programme. Unfortunately, he had a relationship break-up in first year and withdrew into himself.

Fiachra prioritized the creation of friendships, which provides a reason for being on campus:

> if you don't make friends straightaway you're not as inclined to come in, cos you don't have someone to talk to cos even if you have friends coming in that are in other courses, you are more inclined if you make friends straightaway in your class you are more inclined to come in [...] instead of just being on your own.

Attendance affected the possibility to make friends as Fiachra, like Caoimhe fell into a cycle of non-attendance that became a self-fulfilling habit of absence:

> Even at first I think it was the thought of just 'ah I'll skip this class it's only one day, it's only a couple of hours' and then I'd made a habit of that so that was the worst part of it.

As material was available through Moodle, the virtual learning platform, Fiachra felt he could do everything on his own, but did not complete assignments on time as well as not attending classes. He failed core modules and said:

> Some of my funds for college that I saved up from work have to go towards exam repeats and I have learned a valuable lesson, that not going to class and handing mediocre assignments up end in disaster and unnecessary stress.

Consequently, he felt that he had paid the price for non-attendance in first year even if he had come to appreciate the social aspect of his university life where he 'enjoyed the night life without ever going too overboard like many other students usually do'.

Saoirse

S aoirse had made the transition from primary to secondary school with many of her friends and was anxious about beginning university life alone, as her friends had chosen other colleges. She made friends quickly by joining different societies so that 'the social life of college very quickly proved to be much busier and exciting than that of my school one'. She found the cost of college surprising — the expense of food and transport and the price of course books — as she was used to spending money only at the end of the school week. Saoirse considered herself fortunate that her parents could subsidize her, though she did work six hours a week and felt it 'was perfect for me, any more would have been overwhelming in my opinion'. She did find the commute to college difficult as she was used to strolling down the street to school, whereas travelling to university involved plenty of waiting around in between taking two forms of transport.

She struggled with the academic side of university life, as she had enjoyed a highly structured day in secondary school where her work was routinely checked. Her learning was based on how to answer a question to obtain the highest marks in her Leaving Certificate, an education practice of which she is now highly critical, as she no longer equates that type of learning with acquiring knowledge. Saoirse found a vast gap between school and university, particularly coping with independent study:

> This whole concept of having to do your own independent study is really something I found challenging, in contrast to school homework and that feeling of completion I would feel after a few hours of homework done. With college work I find this feeling of completion as such is a much harder or sometimes merely impossible emotion to reach.

She found constructing an essay problematic with regard to selecting sources, being unsure who to cite despite having reading lists for her modules. Saoirse felt 'weary' as she was unable to cope with the 'sheer volume of theorists and philosophers'.

Resolving Failure

C ommonalities in the factors impeding a successful first year and resolutions to the crisis of failure experienced by these four students arise in this study. Failure can be overturned to create a successful university experience, as Saoirse explains that she 'love(s) being in university, I loved my course, I didn't want to fail so I realized I had to get my act together'.

Contributing to this realization came an understanding of having to work to belong to a community rather than remaining on the sidelines, as Saoirse says:

> The importance of feeling like you belong, I feel in a big university a sense of belonging helps with your university work. After making friends I can remember making study groups.

The sense of belonging implies an emergence from the liminal state as each student worked through a combination of social, academic, economic and personal factors contributing to failure to transform failure into success. Personal development and interpersonal relations, planning — as in balancing competing demands — and developing autonomy as a learner contribute to this success.

Personal development, i.e., increasing maturity and a sense of responsibility, lead Fiachra to realize:

> It's up to yourself to go in whereas in school you're made go in and so I think that at the start just maybe the freedom was like too much because I just ended up staying in bed all day... but then as I got older, like this year, I think it was just a fact that it's well, it's up to me to do it obviously grow up a bit more instead of staying in bed all day.

Fiachra approaches his experience as part of 'growing up', in which motivation and maturity become ongoing processes, so that some aspects of the transformation process of liminality appear to extend into the future. Students like Laoise also emphasized the value of experience such as paid work while studying:

> I think that it's really important for people to work through college to develop as a person because if you go straight from primary school, secondary school to college and you haven't worked a day in your life, I think you'd be quite naïve to the real world.

The experience of failure transformed Caoimhe as she realized that her immature understanding of university life came from discourses shaped by fantasy:

> I pictured it like an American high school the way you see on TV shows and it's just so laid back and nobody cares and everyone is brainy anyway it doesn't matter, you made it to college so you have to be smart you know, but it's not like that at all.

Understanding does not, however, negate strong previously held values and attachments, so that Caoimhe, who had felt the separation from familiar surroundings so keenly, shared a house with friends in her second year and felt that she was 'at home away from home'. She had found a way to reconcile her value system in her new environment.

Planning and balancing competing demands do not always become easier over time. The pressure of having to self-fund does not disappear; rather the nature of such pressure changes over time and becomes manageable, as Laoise says:

> It's just a life experience, it's that difficult for a student, you know, scraping the money together. It would definitely be easier if I had more support from home of course, if they were able to fund me and my education, through a bit of cash here and there but it's not the way it is, and again [...] I have a lot more experience and it'll definitely stand to me but it's still a struggle.

Vestiges of liminality can remain as unfinished business as Laoise refers to never accomplishing 'one of those golden weeks where you've gone to every lecture; I still haven't; I'm in my final year and I've still always missed one here and there'. She does, however, attend sufficiently to be successful.

Finally, from engagement with and subsequent experience of academic approaches to learning, students like Caoimhe critique a secondary school system that did not foster learner autonomy:

> I think teachers need to let students do things by themselves because they look over your shoulder, they're constantly on your back, pushing you, you know to do the best you can which is great but people also need to learn for themselves and you're not going to do that because when you get to college you don't have that person behind you pushing you to do well all the time; you have to go out and do it by yourself.

Their critiques included the role of the Catholic Church in education, the quality of guidance counselling, the lack of interaction with male pupils so that they could articulate their feelings and a distressing lack of involvement with mental health issues. In effect, the lack of confidence of these students to approach lecturers or student support to help resolve a multiplicity of problems in first year becomes understandable if no one listened to their views at secondary level.

Discussion and Conclusion

Field and Morgan-Klein (2010) argue that liminality applies to the entire period of studenthood as it is a temporary state with a clearly defined entrance and exit where a student achieves the status of graduate and moves into the labour market. In this study, students emphasize community and belonging and have no enjoyment of being 'betwixt and between'. The liminal space, where transformation occurs, does not appear to be a fixed period, such as being restricted to first semester. The period of transformation extends beyond the boundary of the first year into the holiday period, when repeat examinations take place instead of satisfaction with progress. Only then is transformation complete, enabling successful progression to occur. Nor is incorporation achieved with a total success rate, such as achieving a hundred percent rate of attendance, as a student can succeed with less. Finally, while transformation in the liminal period implies progress towards a new state, the process involves an accommodation between the old and the new, such as reconciling the values of the 'home' place with those of the new environment. In this study the liminal phase does not appear to flow in a linear direction but rather appears to be an uneven process that produces change leading to success.

In this study, failure is not only an academic matter but is affected by a range of contributory factors, which points towards a definition of failure as being multidimensional. In the Irish context, academic preparedness has been stressed as being the most significant factor to affect retention and progression (Mooney et al., 2010). However, this qualitative study points towards a more complex situation involving guidance at secondary level, the effects of the Leaving Certificate on academic preparedness for higher-level education, financial support, as well as personal factors including the changing nature of friendships, relationship break-ups and making new friends. Mooney et al. (2010) emphasize the role of guidance counsellors in aiding students to make informed choices about future study and there is evidence in this research that there is variation in the quality of such counselling. Neither class nor gender formed part of this study, which was composed of school leavers, and Mooney et al. (2010) do not consider them to be as significant as academic preparedness with regard to progression.

Finally, Mooney et al. (2010) state:

> It is essential that all students leaving the second-level system are fully equipped for higher education in terms of academic preparatory, knowledge and understanding of course content and the requirements of the course, and an understanding of potential career paths. (Mooney et al., 2010, p. 45)

Evidently, this is not the case for the students in this study from their critique of teacher-centred learning focused on maximizing Leaving Certificate points. 71% of Irish higher-education academics consider students to be ill-prepared for higher-level study (Slowey, Kozina & Tan, 2014) and over half of academics find attendance is in decline. First year can confer anonymity instead of individuality (Pitkethly & Prosser, 2001) in institutions of mass education where fifty-nine per cent of academics teach in increasingly large classes (Slowey, Kozina & Tan, 2014). Academic-staff-to-student ratios increased from 1:15.6 to 1:20.6, while academic staff numbers have decreased since 2008 (HEA, 2016). Thus, there is pressure on the quality and funding of courses which can impact on future educational outcomes. At the same time there are policy recommendations that the higher-education sector should expand further because of the demand for skilled graduates: 'under-participating sectors of society can be mobilized to access education' (HEA, 2016, p. 10), which would indicate future deep engagement with a more diverse body of students with regard to retention and progression.

References

Ashby, A. (2004). Monitoring student retention in the Open University: Definition, measurement, interpretation and action. *Open Learning: The Journal of Open, Distance and e-Learning*, 19(1): 65–77. https://doi.org/10.1080/0268051042000177854

Baird, K. (2002). *An Inquiry into withdrawal from college: A study conducted at Trinity College Dublin, Ireland*. Dublin: Trinity College.

Blaney, C. & Mulkeen, S. (2008). *Student retention in a modular world, a study of student retention UCD entrants 1999–2007. Retention, modularisation, orientation, what's changed?* Dublin: UCD.

Bourdieu, P. (1986). The forms of capital. In: Richardson, J.E. (ed), *Handbook of theory of research for the sociology of education*. New York: Greenwood Press.

Bourdieu, P. (1989). Social space and symbolic power. *Sociological Theory*, 7(1): 14–25.

Bozick, R. (2007). Making it through the first year of college: The role of students' economic resources, employment, and living arrangements. *Sociology of Education*, 80: 261–85. https://doi.org/10.1177/003804070708000304

Bruner, J. (1990). *Acts of meaning*. Cambridge, MA: Harvard University Press.

Carter, D.F. (2006). Key issues in the persistence of underrepresented minority students. *New Directions for Institutional Research*, 130: 33–46. https://doi.org/10.1002/ir.178

Chow, K. & Healey, M. (2008). Place attachment and place identity: First-year undergraduates making the transition from home to university. *Journal of Environmental Psychology*, 28: 362–72. https://doi.org/10.1016/j.sbspro.2013.08.463

Cook-Sather, A. & Alter, Z. (2011). What is and what can be: How a liminal position can change learning and teaching in higher education. *Anthropology and Education Quarterly*, 42: 37–53. https://doi.org/10.1111/j.1548-1492.2010.01109.x

Curtis, S. & Shani, N. (2002). The effect of taking paid employment during term-time on students' academic studies. *Journal of Further and Higher Education*, 26(2): 129–38. https://doi.org/10.1080/03098770220129406

David, M.E., Ball, S.J, Davies, J. & Reay, D. (2003). Gender issues in parental involvement in student choices of higher education. *Gender and Education*, 15(1): 21–36. http://dx.doi.org/10.1080/0954025032000042121

Eivers, E., Flanagan, R. & Morgan, M. (2002). *Non-completion in institutes of technology: An investigation of preparation, attitudes and behaviours among first year students*. Dublin: Education Research Centre, St. Patrick's College, Drumcondra.

Elliot, J. (2005). *Using narrative in social research, qualitative and quantitative approaches.* London: Sage. https://dx.doi.org/10.4135/9780857020246

Field, J. (2012). Transitions in lifelong learning: Public issues, private troubles, liminal identities. *Studies for the Learning Society,* 2(2–3): 4–11. https://doi.org/10.2478/v10240-012-0001-6

Field J. & Morgan-Klein, N. (2010). Studenthood and identification: Higher education as a liminal transitional space. In: Leeds: Education-line / British Education Index. 40th Annual SCUTREA Conference, University of Warwick.

Fleming, T. & Finnegan, F. (2011). *Non-traditional students in Irish higher education: A research report.* http://www.dsw.edu.pl/fileadmin/www-ranlhe/files/Final_Copy_July_20_2011.pdf

Frawley, D., Pigott, V. & Carroll, D. (2017). *A study of progression in Irish higher education 2013/14 to 2014/15.* Dublin: Higher Education Authority. https://hea.ie/assets/uploads/2017/06/A-Study-Of-Progression-in-Irish-Higher-Education-201213-201314.pdf

Harvey, L., Drew, S. & Smith, M. (2006). *The first year experience: A review of literature for the Higher Education Academy.* London: The Higher Education Academy.

Higher Education Authority (2016). *Higher education system performance, first report 2014–2016.* Dublin: Higher Education Authority.

James, R., Krause, K. & Jennings, C. (2010). *The first year experience in Australian universities: Findings from 1994 to 2009.* Melbourne: Centre for the Study of Higher Education, University of Melbourne.

Keefer, J.M. (2015). Experiencing doctoral liminality as a conceptual threshold and how supervisors can use it. *Innovations in Education and Teaching International,* 52(1): 17–28. https://doi.org/10.1080/14703297.2014.981839

Land, R., Rattray, J. & Vivian, P. (2014). Learning in the liminal space: A semiotic approach to threshold concepts. *Higher Education,* 67: 199–217. https://doi.org/10.1007/s10734-013-9705-x

Leese, M. (2010). Bridging the gap: Supporting student transitions into higher education. *Journal of Further and Higher Education,* 34(2): 239–51. https://doi.org/10.1080/03098771003695494

Longden, B. (2004). Interpreting student early departure from higher education through the lens of cultural capital. *Tertiary Education and Management,* 10(2): 121–38.

McCoy, S. & Smyth, E. (2011). Higher education expansion and differentiation in the Republic of Ireland. *Higher Education,* 61: 243–60. https://doi.org/10.1007/s10734-010-9375-x

Merrill, B. & West, L. (2009). *Using biographical methods in social research.* London: Sage.

Mooney, O., Patterson, V., O'Connor, M., & Chantler, A. (2010). *A study of progression in Irish higher education, a report by the Higher Education Authority.* Dublin: Higher Education Authority.

Onwuegbuzie, A.J. & Leech, N.L. (2007). A call for qualitative power analyses. *Quality and Quantity*, 41: 105–21. https://doi.org/10.1007/s11135-005-1098-1

O'Shea, S.E. (2007). Well I got here… but what happens next? Exploring the early narratives of first year female students who are the first in the family to attend university. *Journal of Australian and New Zealand Student Services Association*, 29: 36–51.

Ostrove, J.M. & Long, S.M. (2007). Social class and belonging: Implications for college adjustment. *The Review of Higher Education*, 30(4): 363–89. http://dx.doi.org/10.1353/rhe.2007.0028

Palmer, M., O'Kane P. & Owens, M. (2009). Betwixt spaces: Student accounts of turning point experiences in the first year transition. *Studies in Higher Education*, 34: 37–54. https://doi.org/10.1080/03075070802601929

Pitkethly, A. & Prosser, M. (2001). The First Year Experience Project: A model for university-wide change. *Higher Education Research and Development*, 20: 185–98.

Plummer, K. (2001). *Documents of life, an invitation to a critical humanism.* London: Sage Publications Ltd.

Quinn, J. (2004) Understanding working-class 'drop-out' from higher education through a sociocultural lens: Cultural narratives and local contexts. *International Studies in Sociology of Education*, 14(1): 57–74. https://doi.org/10.1080/09620210400200119

Reay, D. (1998). 'Always knowing' and 'never being sure': Familial and institutional habituses and higher education choice. *Journal of Education Policy*, 13(4): 519–29.

Reay, D. (2004). 'It's all becoming a habitus': Beyond the habitual use of habitus in educational research. *British Journal of Sociology of Education*, 25(4): 431–44. https://doi.org/10.1080/0142569042000236934

Reay, D., Crozier, G., Clayton, J. (2010). 'Fitting in' or 'standing out': Working-class students in UK higher education. *British Educational Research Journal*, 36(1): 107–24. https://doi.org/10.1080/01411920902878925

Riessman, C.K. 2008). *Narrative methods for the human sciences.* Thousand Oaks, CA: Sage.

Rowbottom, D.P. (2007). Demystifying threshold concepts. *Journal of Philosophy of Education*, 41: 263–70. https://doi.org/10.1111/j.1467-9752.2007.00554.x

Sheridan, V. (2011). A holistic approach to international students, institutional habitus and academic literacies in an Irish third level institution. *Higher Education*, 62(2): 129–40. https://doi.org/10.1007/s10734-010-9370-2

Sheridan, V. & Dunne, S. (2012). The bigger picture: Undergraduate voices reflecting on academic transition in an Irish university. *Innovations in Education and Teaching International,* 49: 237–47. https://doi.org/10.1080/14 703297.2012.703019

Slowey, M., Kozina, E. & Tan, E. (2014). *Voices of academics in Irish higher education Perspectives on professional development.* Dublin: AISHE. https://doi.org/10.22554/ijtel.v2i1.11

Thomas, L. (2002). Student retention in higher education: The role of institutional habitus. *Journal of Education Policy,* 17(4): 423–42. https://doi.org/10.1080/02680930210140257

Tinto, V. (1988). Stages of student departure: Reflections on the longitudinal character of student leaving. *The Journal of Higher Education,* 59: 438–55.

Tinto, V. (1994). *Leaving college: Rethinking the causes and cures of student attrition.* Chicago: University of Chicago Press.

Tinto, V. (2006). Research and practice of student retention: What next? *Journal of College Student Retention,* 8(1): 1–19. https://doi.org/10.2190/4YNU-4TMB-22DJ-AN4W

Turner, V. (1967). *The forest of symbols, aspects of Ndembu ritual.* Ithaca: Cornell University Press.

Uttal, L. (2010). Liminal cultural work in family childcare: Latino immigrant family childcare providers and bicultural childrearing in the United States, 2002–2004. *Paedagogica Historica,* 46(6): 731–42. https://doi.org/10.1080/003 09230.2010.526333

Van Gennep, A. (1960). *The rites of passage.* Chicago: Chicago University Press.

Wilcox, P., Wynn, S. & Fyvie-Gauld, M. (2005). 'It was nothing to do with the university, it was just the people': The role of social support in the first-year experience of higher education. *Studies in Higher Education,* 30: 707–22. https://doi.org/10.1080/03075070500340036

Winstone, N. & Moore, D. (2017) Sometimes fish, sometimes fowl? Liminality, identity work and identity malleability in graduate teaching assistants. *Innovations in Education and Teaching International,* 54(5): 494–502. https://doi.org/10.1080/14703297.2016.1194769

Yorke, M. & Longden, B. (2008). *The first-year experience of higher education in the UK.* York: The Higher Education Academy.

11. Care Leavers in Italy
From 'Vulnerable' Children to 'Autonomous' Adults?

Laura Formenti, Andrea Galimberti
and Mirella Ferrari

Laura Formenti, Andrea Galimberti and Mirella Ferrari use data from their study of young people leaving the residential care system on reaching adulthood. They discuss the discourses around 'care' before offering three different ways to present narrative accounts. Each researcher demonstrates a distinctive approach – through realism, by focusing on a facet of interest, by fictionalizing the interview in order to go beyond it. Including the stories in full enables the reader to decide their relative utility.

This chapter is about care leavers, that is, young adults exiting the foster-care system whose lives and identities are shaped by dominant narratives and practices of 'vulnerability'. Our approach aims to deconstruct vulnerability and challenge master stories. We use discourse as a recursive and multiple concept — the discourse of discourses — to reflect on the perspectives of meaning in the foster care system, as well as in the researchers' view. We involved fostered people and professionals in participatory ways to discuss and dialogue with them about adulthood, learning and identity building, asking: what kind of life paths and struggles lead from foster care to adult life? What kind of learning is generated by the experience of fostering?

https://doi.org/10.11647/OBP.0203.11

These questions are illuminated by the notion of discourse and by the experience of care leavers as insiders. Narrative methods (Formenti & West, 2016; Merrill & West, 2009) focus on subjective experience and meaning, but a critical appraisal and the multiplication of perspectives are needed to avoid the naturalization of vulnerability, to overcome linear theories of care and education and to celebrate complexity. Thus, this study merges self-narration and cooperative inquiry in the pursuit of a more complex and thicker interpretation of the life trajectories of young 'vulnerable' adults, to be shared with professionals and decision makers in order to innovate socio-educational care practices.

Discourse: A Metaphor and Its Limits

W hat do we mean by 'discourse' in the framework of complexity theory and biographical studies? The discourse of discourse is a recursive way to interrogate this word that seems to overemphasize the role of propositional knowing (Heron, 1996), at risk of decontextualizing it and diminishing the embodied, presentational, emotional, or even spiritual ways to knowing. The linguistic origins of discourse studies highlight that parts can only be interpreted in relation to a whole. Isolated letters, words, or sentences are meaningless without a context. By context, we can mean the word in relation to letters, or the phrase in relation to words, or the conversation where they are produced, and so on. In communication, meaning is multiple and layered, often ambiguous, and requiring further contextualization. Briefly, discourse entails the whole layered system of communication, far beyond speech. The users of language, their bodies and actions, their webs of affiliation and, more generally, the practices of languaging (Maturana, 1990) in communities, form the meaning-full context.

Which discourse are we interested in? This manifold notion is used to interpret social interaction (microsociology, ethnomethodology), cultures (anthropology, ethnography), opinion making (social psychology), media, and so on. Discourse is disciplined by knowledge and power, to determine and shape our lives at the individual and collective levels (Foucault, 1969); normally accepted ideas become hegemonic (Gramsci, 1975) and their function is to legitimize and enforce power. The dominant discourse creates a medium where speakers are produced by, instead of making communication. Disciplinary structures inform our behaviour; the discourse of discourses reveals how established ideas and dominant narratives control creativity, freedom and self-positioning. Counter-hegemony (Gramsci, 1975) is discourse too, contrasting dominant assumptions, beliefs and established patterns of behaviour with alternative ones. Revelation is not exempt from discourse, hence from interpretation. From a systemic point of view, different levels or perspectives should not be reduced to one. The social, interactional and individual (macro, meso, micro) are separated, yet entangled. So, there is not one discourse, but different positions, actions and propositions. We interrogate them from a recursive perspective of complexity (Davis & Sumara, 2006; Formenti, 2018) and contextualization (Edwards, Biesta & Thorpe, 2009).

Our definition of discourse comes from its etymology: currere, that means 'to run' in Latin, is an embodied metaphor connecting languaging and enacting. The former is the ongoing process of coordination and co-evolution that builds a world together with self-consciousness (Maturana, 1990); the latter is the construction of meaning through action:

> ...knowledge depends on being in a world that is inseparable from our bodies, our language, and our social history — in short, from our embodiment. (Varela, Thompson & Rosch, 1991, p. 149)

So, discourse identifies an ongoing, and multi-layered, process (currere) of co-evolution. At the micro-level this process is about subjects within a system of interactions and interdependencies. At the meso-level there is a building of myths, artefacts, practices that influence the larger social system (the macro-level) where narratives and myths evolve with objects, spaces, images, institutions, media, in an ecological network of ideas, cultures and technologies. These entangled levels are always involved in learning, transformation and education. In his analysis of discourse in formal education, van Dijk identified three levels:

> [...] the structures of discourses used in education: style, contents, complexity, etc. [...] the processes of learning: the acquisition of knowledge, beliefs, opinions, attitudes, abilities, and other cognitive and emotional changes which are the goals of institutional education. Finally, the relationships between textual structures, textual processing and the structures of the socio-cultural contexts. (van Dijk, 1980)

Beyond this textual approach, we use a generative methodology of 'discursive multiplication' (multiplying narrations and their interpretations rather than fixing them) to explore structures, processes and contexts that may be hidden, unconscious, and embodied.

Foster Care: A Complex World

Foster care is a form of child protection where parents maintain their legal rights, but the child is temporarily separated from them. It takes different forms: foster family, family-like housing, residential centre, therapeutic unit, and others. The process is monitored by Social Services and entails a personalized socio-educational project. Custody ends with the re-insertion of the child in the original family, adoption, or adulthood. The latter is the most frequent case for institutionalized minors in Italy.

Foster care is a complex world, with its own dominant representations, metaphors and narrations. It is important to acknowledge that vulnerability is not inherent to these children or families, but the result of actions and communications. It is real though, and it structures meaning, identities and professional intervention.

The dominant narrative of vulnerability composes different ideas:

Multiple Problems

Children in this category are labelled and positioned within a frame of expectations about school under-achievement, behavioural problems and psychological symptoms. All of these are interpreted as signs and results of family problems. Life trajectories are qualified — forward and backward — by 'problems'.

Self-Fulfilling Prophecy

The problem-based definition becomes a predictor of future educational and professional failure, low-status careers and/or delinquency. The children's negative expectations and vulnerability justify official intervention. To correct and compensate for disadvantage dominates professional practices.

Control and Fragmentation

F ostered children are constantly accompanied, monitored and assessed by social workers, residential care workers, assistants, educators, psychotherapists, speech therapists, family tutors, etc. Their practices and perspectives are different. Psychologists and psychotherapists focus on mental and emotional aspects, leaving aside economic and practical issues, or the social context. Social workers aim to ensure legality, school attendance, fulfilment of basic needs, and protection from violence or trauma. Educators intervene in everyday life, to sustain formal and informal learning. Original families are stigmatized and silenced, while foster families may be over-idealized.

Starting from the — usually sudden and unexpected — forced extraction from their everyday context, these children are storied and categorized from their first entry into the foster-care system. There are many silenced stories of injustice, institutional carelessness, and symbolic violence, but they — or their parents — have no voice to speak aloud. Taking a child away from home, to place him or her in residence, is based on the assumption of his or her 'best interest'. In Italy, this means 12,400 (12 per thousand of overall minors) hosted in residential structures and 14,020 in foster families (in 2014). The law recommends family fostering, but data (unfortunately old, fragmentary and incoherent) show that institutionalization is growing. Available databases are focused on child protection and rights, dominated by quantitative data and categorization, hence blurring many relevant differences and obscuring the influence of context. Numbers do not tell much about meaning and lives; about becoming an adult in foster care and developing an identity, a life project, agency, freedom; about participation in education, work and public life — actions that could stop the spiral of violence and loneliness characterizing so many lives. The above-mentioned self-fulfilling prophecies are at risk of confirmation in linear deterministic studies, at best descriptive, not critical or transformative. Therefore, qualitative and participatory research is needed, in order to develop good theories and models to understand the social, political and educational factors at work in this phenomenon.

Biographical narratives bring nuances and embodied experience into the frame, allowing multiple perspectives and meanings and chronicling disorienting dilemmas and ways to overcome them — perhaps transformative ones (Mezirow, 1991). We are interested in the insider's self-positioning, that helps him or her achieve a distance from the dominant discourse. Thus, we multiply our levels of analysis and our settings for research.

Categorization and Meanings

W hat to call our subjects? Vulnerable? At risk? NEETs (Not in Education, Employment or Training), looked after, care leavers? Names are not neutral. They reflect discourse. Different words are used in literature; at first, we used them interchangeably, but a deeper reflection illuminated discourses of vulnerability and education, of which we are a part too.

From Vulnerable Children to NEETs: A Self-Fulfilling Prophecy?

A t the macro level, vulnerability offers a strong rationale for intervention based on the child's 'best interest'. Surveys map the main reasons that are referred to by the social agencies: relational problems within the family, addiction or neglectful conduct. Parental inadequacy is the dominant narrative. Negligent parents are stories of not loving, immorality or general incompetence, obscuring the role of poverty intensified by the economic crisis. Wealthy families are rarely referred to agencies. From databases, we can learn that single parents and foreign fathers are more highly represented than average; most mothers and more than forty per cent of fathers are unemployed. Yet poverty, unemployment and social problems should never be reasons for child removal in a democratic society where citizen's rights are respected. A distressed family should receive the best help in order to overcome a problematic situation; this is not always the case.

Gender and ethnic backgrounds are also relevant. Boys (unaccompanied foreign minors) are an increasing presence following migration fluxes; once from Romania and Morocco (Belotti, 2010), later Afghanistan, Bangladesh and Albania (ANCI, 2012), and recently, the Middle East and Central Africa. Institutionalization becomes a solution for adolescents (or undocumented young adults cheating on their real age) who are not 'vulnerable' in the ordinary sense; on the contrary they may be quite resilient and aware of their situation. After a difficult and perilous journey, they need to establish meaningful relationships and build some hope for the future. Migration is redefining the population in residential care, hence challenging established practices.

Age groups and length of time in care also vary. The number of adolescents and young adults is increasing, as well as the number who stay for a short period of time (under twenty-four months), while the average duration of stay is four years. When they become adults, these people disappear from records. No longer 'vulnerable children' needing protection, they are free to make their own lives, or more likely to enter another 'vulnerable' category, like NEETs, who are excluded from both formal education and the labour market. OECD[1] and EUROSTAT[2] use this category to measure the risks of social exclusion and to assess labour market dynamics. Italy scores highly in this group (Rosina, 2015), which is composed of different subgroups: highly qualified people looking for a job; a 'grey area' with low competence but open to learning possibilities; and a 'dark area' of people who despair of finding a job, stuck in complex situations and at risk of longer unemployment. Young adults who experienced fostering are more likely to fall into the dark category due to their lack of social capital and family support.

Looked-After People: The Reproduction of Care and Control

Literature uses another label, 'looked-after'; a passive verb with a connotation of care and attention. The 'looked-after' person is dependent, not competent enough or autonomous, and needing education, social care, psychotherapy, tutoring, and so on. Differently from 'vulnerability', this word focuses on a needs-based relationship with many connotations of education, care, and control. Life within foster houses can be extremely disciplined. This meso-level discourse shapes everyday practices, identities, and scripts enacted and internalized by professionals and youngsters. It conveys undisputed assumptions:

---

1   OECD: Organisation for Economic Co-operation and Development.
2   EUROSTAT: The Directorate-General of the EU responsible for statistical information.

- moving from a home to a residence (or foster family) is for the best, an opportunity to grow up in a better place;

- regular contact with parents and relatives is guaranteed, but needs to be monitored;

- conflict, tensions and difficulties must be erased from these children's lives, in order for them to learn different attitudes and to open possibilities for the future.

These are prejudicial ideas, suggesting that we do know, in fact, what is best. But systematic research on best practices is lacking; different models are implemented in Italy with substantial regional differences (Belotti, 2010), and in Europe. Comparative research (Eurochild, 2010) shows uneven results among EU countries (Thoburn, 2010). In France, child care intervention seems more akin to separation (nine per thousand). Great Britain has a similarly high rate of children in care (eight per thousand), Spain is lower (six per thousand), while Italy was reported at four per thousand. Data seem to offer evidence of a 'Mediterranean model' (Naldini & Saraceno, 2008) that insists on maintaining the original family ties, in contrast to northern Europe. However, no country among those considered by ANCI[3] (Germany, France, Britain, Italy, Belgium and Spain) produces regular statistics, let alone a shared model (ANCI, 2012).

We know from other studies (Carr & McAlister, 2016) that institutionalization may become repetitive and chronic. Once one has been entered into the system, it is difficult to be discharged, due in part to the lack of appropriate intervention in the family and social environments. The likelihood of further institutionalization increases; e.g., looked-after people enter the justice system at higher rates than average.

When you are 'looked after', the role of learning is weakened. Awareness, competence and autonomy may be developed in conflictual relationships, in struggles and even in relation to traumatic experiences. If adolescents, or young adults, are patronized and infantilized, this prevents them from learning what is needed to become an adult. Qualitative research can demonstrate that they are not really, or always, passive; they can position themselves in active ways and develop their own views of what they need; some may even develop a strong

---

3   Associazione Nazionale Comuni Italiani.

motivation to support their peers, even going so far as to choose a career in the helping professions (Melkman et al., 2015).

Care Leavers: Biographical Transitions and Challenging Transformations

The label of 'care leaver' shifts the focus from categories or relationships to transition: these subjects are moving, in the middle of identity development, to a new and evolving context. To leave care is a crucial moment of passage, highlighted by the active verb, in contrast with the passivity of 'being looked after'. This invites us to see the process, and hence also the interactions, challenges and transforming discourses that comprise it. This label focuses the transition from the care system to the external world, from institutionalization to freedom, and the challenges it brings. This is the moment in life when these people are asked, authorized, or forced to leave a protective environment and to take adult responsibilities; to behave and think like adults (or not). This transition can be excessively accelerated and compressed (Allen, 2003; Stein & Munro, 2008): care leavers are expected to make sudden and difficult changes with no previous experience and no time to elaborate a strategy. Several studies (Morgan, 2006; 2008; 2011; Pandolfi, 2015) show that most care leavers are not prepared for this step, and the lack of family support or other social networks adds to their difficulties.

In Italy, care leavers may volunteer to enter a period of 'administrative extension' and receive further aid for a short time (a maximum of three years). This entails rules, constraints, monitoring, and semi-autonomy, over a negotiated period. Here again, words are not neutral. This bureaucratic naming stresses the economic and structural dimensions of extension. It conceals the emotional, relational, and existential aspects, which require imagination and new forms of intervention.

We use biographies to address the transition (Field, Gallacher & Ingram, 2009; Field & Lynch, 2015) and investigate assumptions of care leavers and professionals that are revealed, maintained or transformed through conversations, not least in the research setting. It is a learning occasion for the whole system. Following Mezirow (1991), we expect to find disorienting dilemmas and disclose the frames of reference that structured a life, a world, and its truths. A dilemma is a learning moment in adult life, an occasion to take a reflective stance backwards and forwards and potentially trigger transformative learning (Formenti, 2016; Formenti & West, 2018). When care leavers take a stance towards their previous relationships and contexts, they develop their own ideas of adulthood and adult identity in continuity and/or discontinuity with previous discourses. Thanks to narration, they may position themselves in the proximal and larger system, revealing dominant discourses but also other dimensions and counter-narratives.

In order to think like an adult (Mezirow, 2012), we need to face disorienting dilemmas that question (often dramatically) our previous frames of meaning. Adaptation without dilemma can hardly bring us to adulthood. Being positioned and storied by social discourse (macro) and by the care system (meso) may lead fostered people to plain adaptation ('I'm what they say I am'), to counter dependence ('I'm different, I rebel'), and/or to a never-ending process of questioning ('I am confused'). Critical and reflexive questions illuminate these risks:

- Macro: Am I 'vulnerable' or NEET? Do these labels predict my future? Are they shaping my identity?

- Meso: Which stories did I receive and build with my family, the buddies in the residence centre, the educators and other professionals, schoolmates, teachers, and so on? Did I learn myths, representations, identity scripts? What was being 'looked after' for me? Can I unlearn it?

- Micro: How do I deal with my story? How do see myself, or relate to my experience? Am I becoming an adult, and how?

Stories show dilemmas. For example, between the institutional definition of successful practices in residential care and its subjective experience. Or, between autonomy and heteronomy, often polarized in taking decisions, e.g., between living on one's own or going back to family. Dilemmas are often expressed as questions: 'If I go back to my family home, will this be a failure? Will it ruin my future?' Biographical interviews show tensions between falling into clichés and/or developing a personal script, a different identity or theory, or a deeper understanding of social determinants. These need to be contrasted, somehow, in the pursuit of one's own meaningful life (a process called 'biographicity', see Alheit & Dausien, 2000).

Methodology

We started by interviewing a small sample of ten care leavers. Sampling itself was the result of a reflexive dialogic process with a group of professionals who coordinate residential units. They are involved in our research as co-researchers and insiders of the context that we want to illuminate by implementing a compositional method (Formenti, 2008), connecting different perspectives and allowing multiple descriptions (Bateson, 1979). More practically, we needed their collaboration to define the features of our sample and to get in touch with young adults whom we could interview. The first research meeting started a rich conversation that questioned previous ideas and hidden assumptions on both sides. For instance, those regarding 'administrative extension' programmes (from eighteen to twenty-one) which we interpreted as meant to sustain transition by creating a protected space for the unprepared. On the contrary, we found that the programme is suggested to the ones who have the best resources, the stronger and most motivated deemed most likely to keep on and 'make it up'. Our surprise revealed our hidden assumption that 'vulnerability' is a reason for intervention: we were unconsciously confirming that help is linked to fragility as compensation. Professionals applied, as they said, more realistic criteria linked to limited resources. Since the offer can be made only to a few, they choose the ones with better odds. So we ended up recognizing assumptions, perspectives and maybe prejudices on both sides. Our meetings in the project were not intended to build consensus. On the contrary, differences and curiosity were praised in the name of complexity.

Our sample of ten care leavers is not meant to be representative, but interesting (Merrill & West, 2009). It is a diverse group, in terms of gender and age (eighteen to twenty-seven), ethnic origins, religion, extension measures, work, living in the original family, with or without a partner, and having (or not having) problems with justice. Their unique voices can clarify the nature of the transition of leaving care better than any statistics. This sampling has a limit, as one professional said: 'It will be almost impossible to have the most interesting ones, those whom we have more in our hearts, that is, those who said no and choose their own way, since that is their own way and we have to respect it'.

The co-construction of a safe relationship during the interview was sustained by building a dialogical 'good-enough space' (Merrill & West, 2009) based on reciprocal learning and reflexivity. These subjects are expert interviewees who volunteered to participate, but we wanted to reduce the risk of an instrumental habitus learned in meetings with professionals, one of telling people what they want to hear. We assumed that participants were also able to position themselves in relation to received narrations during the interview (and this did happen). We wanted to listen to their personal theory and positioning expressed in their own terms. In questioning how stories influence the development of an adult identity in residential care, we were looking for clues of self-fulfilling prophecies, learning processes, and negotiations of meaning, or any sign of transition from vulnerability to agency, from protection to empowerment.

So, we started each interview with an open question: 'This interview is about your experience in residential care... where would you start in order to tell us about that?' We then let the narration flow, but we were also active, asking questions and giving feedback, both verbal and non-verbal. We had a guideline of four topics to inspire further questions:

- Present and future (How is life today? Do you have projects?);

- Education and training (Tell me about school. Any learning project in your future?);

- Relationships (Are you still in contact with those who looked after you? Was anyone, any relationship, particularly important for you?);

- Becoming an adult (Becoming an adult in foster care: what does it mean for you? Do you see yourself as an adult person?).

Our research goes beyond individual interviews, entailing further group meetings with participants and professionals. It involves using participatory inquiry to build a good-enough theory (Heron, 1996) by researching with rather than on people, connecting reflection and action, data and interpretation, and engaging participants in actions, observations and records of their own experience. This is an ethical choice, contrasting the discourse of vulnerability by treating others as adult partners.

Case Studies: Multiplying our Discursive Frameworks

We present here three stories to show the complexity of leaving care. We realized, as researchers, that we were enacting the discourses we live by, not least, in the ways we were analysing and interpreting our interviews. We are different: Andrea is an early-career researcher in adult education, previously an educator in the care system; Laura is an experienced academic with a long-standing relationship with care agencies and other stakeholders; Mirella has a double identity as an early-career researcher in sociology with a degree in literature. So, we wrote these case studies (and performed the interviews) from different postures, or discursive frames. Andrea took the stance of a researcher and educator who tries to be faithful to the interview as a relational event. Laura is guided by a question that came to her during the interview: how relevant are relationships in sustaining the transition? And what kind of relationships? Mirella fictionalizes her interview in order to celebrate interpretation as a process that can capture meaning beyond the individual story. This diversity reminds us that biographical research is not about objectifying people's lives or narrowing stories down to categories. As researchers, we take a responsibility — and in some measure we take 'care' — of the stories that we trigger, co-construct, and edit. We use these stories to enhance a complex understanding of life.

'Sheepdog or Alpha-Dog?': Andrea Describes Meeting Gabriel

At the start of the interview, Gabriel distances himself from his past — 'a bygone record' — and what could be my prejudice: 'I could tell you about old episodes but I will never tell them in anguish... if this is what is expected from me'. He refuses to indulge in the 'negative situation' at home, resulting in his outplacement at ten. He does not remember a lot, he claims, about living together with his mother (normally, coming home from school I found her plastered after an alcoholic morning [...] as it turns out, she wanted to commit suicide and she was going to kill me too'), father ('I remember fighting, the rare times he was there'), and sister ('she also had her slot in my memory but for a shorter time'). He describes it with a sort of detachment. 'Objectively, I had my problems, but I guess you do too, don't you?'

A dominant topic in our interview concerns what an educator should do in a child residence centre. Gabriel regrets that too many professionals seem not to be interested in listening; instead, their questions are aimed at interpreting or explaining a child's behaviour: 'sometimes for professional reasons they forget they are dealing with children, not with other professionals [...] I felt psychoanalysed more than listened to'. Professionalization bothers him: he believes educators should not have a degree but behave as an 'older brother' endowed with enough life experience to cope with distress. It is a matter of 'vocation', not profession.

Gabriel tells stories of young educators who were unprepared to face reality in a child residence, to meet someone like himself who 'stayed in hell and outlived it'. However, beside criticisms, the attention of professionals was highly desired, necessary, and sought out. This was a titanic endeavour: another seven young boys were living in the same place, crying out for attention, sometimes by breaking down doors or coming back late at night, stoned. How did he manage to get attention? 'I always tried to be part of you [the educators] and not the little one to be looked after. I still have the keys of the place; I knew all their shifts, the amounts of money that were given to the other boys... that was my way to get attention.' His efforts to create a horizontal connection with the adults around him often resulted in violent quarrels: 'Sometimes I provoked the other [the educator] just for the taste of it, just to face up to him and hold my head high, just to prove that I am not a young boy but *your* equal, even if I wasn't like that. I felt myself growing up through this feeling of being equal with adults.'

Gabriel's self-narrative is mostly centred on his capacity to face up to other people, namely adults, and to know how they should help the children in such situations. But he is able to reflect on and criticize his own behaviour: 'I was so focused on myself and the need to show my iron hand... that I forgot those standing in front of me... those persons deserving my attention...'. He does not feel ready to be an educator: 'I know that I am not ready to take care of another person... it is probably related to my experience... I still feel like the one to be taken care of.' And 'I was never taught to take care of others'.

Now, aged twenty-five, seven years after leaving care, Gabriel is engaged to a man of forty-three: 'for me this is the best choice as he is youngish, we do the same identical things, and at the same time he has those past experiences that allow him to be my mentor and my guide'. He makes a connection between the way his partner relates to him and the way a good educator should behave: 'I am happy when he simply hugs me. But the little one in the care centre feels the same desire... he's just not interested in someone sitting on the other side of a desk and trying to understand him'.

Before meeting his partner, Gabriel had to learn how to survive outside the care centre. It was difficult and painful: 'when you go back home you receive everything at once...'. He realized that he had lived in a 'bell jar', not preparing him for the future, for going back to his father, disconnected from relationships, in a new territory, unable to find a job, poor. And very naive about 'paying the bills', 'what you should and should not buy', or how to 'manage your time, your rhythms of working and living'. He worked these things through, however, thanks to significant others who were helpful: his grandparents, who bought a car for him to enable him to move, and a neighbour, who found him a job to help him keep going.

The complexities of this transition made him critical of the way he had been looked after: 'you have this place with eight young troubled boys and do nothing but keep them in check? You are a sheepdog and not the alpha dog! You are keeping us at bay; you are managing! That's not how it should be! You do not make sure that I don't jump over the fence. You teach me what is there outside the fence and how to manage the fence itself'.

Towards the end of the interview, when asked, Gabriel says that he does not feel like an adult now, as he 'is not yet facing the world all alone'. Living with an older partner and his mother, he does not need to care about fundamental things: 'I still have to learn how to manage with bills and rent payments...' This is an advantage with a drawback: 'after twenty-five years, I still don't have a place that I consider my own'. However, he feels different now, when considering his life: 'I'm really proud that I didn't let my life break me up... I didn't defeat my life and was not defeated by it... I just made it a part of myself... I might live it coldly, but I remember it warmly. I don't see my life as a tragedy; I see it as neither happy nor sad. It is the route I made to get to be myself, as I am now.'

Gabriel positioned himself actively during the interview, in many regards. He is very clear in defining our relationship: 'This is not a dialogue; it's me telling you, totally one-sided'. He is able to criticize the discourses and, even more so, the practices he lived by. He is developing his own ideas about the transition from being looked after — in a way he considers inadequate today — to adult life. He is able to recognize his feeling of being unprepared to live alone, to take care of others, and his dependence on his partner about practical things. He also regrets that many of his 'brothers' failed somehow. His interview is a gold mine for educators and professionals working in fostering.

'No Bed of Roses, If You Go Against the Tide': Laura and Issa's Story

When I meet Issa, I get a surprise: I expected an Egyptian or Moroccan Muslim but the person in front of me is a tall Black Ivorian with a strong handshake, direct gaze and unlikely accent from Bergamo, the city where he has lived for half of his twenty-seven years. He has a rich vocabulary and the eloquence of an educated person. I know that he works in a bakery, so I find myself wondering about his education. I then discover that he has talked about his experiences on previous occasions, e.g., when he was invited to do so by the University of Bergamo, and this could have fixed his narrative as a polished master story. Regardless, his reflectiveness is amazing. He has developed a clear view of himself, of the many tensions and dilemmas he has had to face, and the trajectory towards the person he is becoming.

His story contains many plots but one emerges with more force: it is the story of an ordeal, of many and difficult challenges, and literal struggles for life. It is a story of redemption, but with no sign of mythical build-up or a hero story. It is also a story of violence. Our contact person described him as a difficult boy when he was looked after. 'Once, he sent an educator to the hospital with a broken arm'.

'Going against the tide' is a frequent expression he uses to describe himself as a difficult adolescent with a complicated family, featuring 'quarrels, disease'. 'They did not realize ... for them I was a little boy ... but I understood and lived those experiences on my skin. When I saw my mother crying, I rebelled.' He was a rebel but 'for an adolescent, it's normal'. At eighteen, Issa decided to leave care and refused the administrative extension programme. He expected 'to have the world at his feet, a job, a car' but soon realized that 'out there, there were no more educators, I had no reference points'. Nowadays, Issa defines as 'tantrums' his outbursts in the children's home, prior to meeting 'real facts', which was a 'devastating experience'.

When you become 'legally adult' after fostering, you have to 'restart from zero'. So, when Issa realized that his family was stuck in the same situation that had brought about his institutionalization five years previously, he decided to transfer to another city:

> I went back home. I thought the situation would be different. During the meetings with social workers I had seen my parents close ranks but all of it was about staging things and lying... I was grown enough at that point and able to understand the situation and the only solution for me was to go off. Distance myself from this situation, which had hurt me so much in the past. Find a job... leave the school...

He was alone, with no frameworks but a well-paid job. 'I thought I was filthy rich. Only a few months ago I had fights with my educators for the 20-euros handouts they gave to me, and now I come to take 1200 euros with no one there to say how I should spend them or do like this or like that.' He soon lost his job, due to his unreliability. Then, the financial crisis limited the job opportunities in the region: 'a sort of catastrophe. I didn't even know where to go. I stayed around at friends' places for at least 3–4 months ... they hosted me very kindly, then I got away... I enrolled in the Foreign Legion'.[4]

Laura: 'How come?' The pitch of my voice, its register, reveals my astonishment. Decidedly, this is a man of surprises!

'I felt useless... I was very young and very naïve and I had nobody to answer to.' These words reveal what may happen to a young man who is alone, who finds no recognition or love in the eyes of the 'other' (Honneth, 1996) and is overwhelmed by a feeling of unworthiness: Issa found an extreme solution. If this was happening today, he might embrace some form of radicalization or even terrorism (West, 2016). Hopelessness and solitude lead you to search for meaning and often you can find it in communities where you belong. But in the Foreign Legion, Issa met brutality: 'The idea of hurting or killing someone for

---

4   Military unit of the French army staffed by foreign volunteers.

money', 'that world, so manly and brutal at the same time', 'they change your life, you lose your identity, if you die nobody cares, you are a name on a list'. His comrades were stragglers and losers with stories of failure, escaped from war. 'I understood immediately, that world was not mine', but it was impossible to leave as he had signed a contract for five years. He feared that he would not make it, but, unexpectedly, he received help within the Legion — 'they took me under their wing', 'it's like brotherhood' — and eventually found a diplomatic way out, one year after recruitment. Italy was the only place in the world where he had once felt a sense of home. So, he came back. But he had lost everything. He was homeless and desperate.

Issa reflects: 'That experience was of service, indeed, since prior to that... I was an overheated boy, almost violent, but that world changed me, since I met people who were far more violent than me, far more [he heaves a sigh] it's a human experience that cannot be cancelled'.

The details of his story are difficult to bear but he does not over-emphasize them. He appears calm and reflective while he tells me about the brainwashing, the extreme control and severe punishments: 'so tough and devastating that you could lose your life'. It is evident to me that he has thought a lot about those times. Eventually — he says — he took a position: 'if something doesn't kill you, it fortifies you'. He grew wiser: 'in such a context, you reason, since you could end up dead'.

Then another phase in his life began, characterized by nights at the train station and charity soups, until someone recognized him, and it was a punch 'like an arrow in my heart'. 'Is it you, Issa?' 'Well, I had a long beard, I was so different...'. She was a schoolmate, volunteering at the charity centre. A long time ago, Issa had wanted to become an educator, like her. He was ashamed. But this encounter brought hope in his life and drove him to look for solutions; he carved his path, he asked for help, from the educators and social workers who had once looked after him. 'From time to time, I went there to talk'. The unravelled fabric of his life, slowly but steadily, was re-woven. Relationships were reactivated. He began to work: 'I rolled up my sleeves'. He liked making bread. His patron did not know, for months, that he was still homeless. Then he was put forward to enter a social housing project. In the residence, many young Africans kept arriving and he offered to help with translating paperwork for asylum seekers — and he talked. He knew that talking was important.

Multiple transitions, crises and relational factors emerge from Issa's story: they form a complex picture that illuminates the power of relationships and lucky circumstances in creating possibilities, but also Issa's capacity to think, his sensitivity and force. Immediately after leaving care, he was left alone and without any reference points. The crises arrived unexpectedly and Issa had no resources to turn to. Bad choices left him homeless, literally at a dead end, his possibilities dramatically narrowed down. Relationships helped him to find a way out, but he had to decide that he could trust them. He found people who cared for him, who saw the good in him (even in the Foreign Legion) and recognized him as worthy. He used his knowledge and previous experience of the care system to rebuild his life: a life where solidarity and a new paternal role are crucial now. As he says: 'I like the person that I have become!'

'I Smile but It's No Smiling Matter': Mirella Re-Telling Nello's Story

Nello is not used to the beauty of the countryside. Grace, balance and harmony are new to his life. He loves his solitary strolls and the feelings in his body: embryonic emotions, hardly discernible at the threshold of his twenty-four years, after a story of conflict, violence, loneliness. Walking to the underground, headed home, memories come to his mind.

> I remember that day, one like any other, I got a swollen eye and her ankle was bruised. It was not normal; it was not an argument between teenagers looking for trouble. That was the usual mess with my mother. I punched her; she punched me. Day after day, things went on in disarray. Since birth, my parents always beat me. When I grew up, I did the same. I rebelled, making the most of my imagination, using knives and other tools, anything I could get. And any excuse was good to start.
>
> Police often came in. That day, they swooped home in the thick of it, when I had just got heated. I was sixteen, and there were no more excuses. A rigmarole of denunciations began. I reported my mother and she reported me. We liked to denounce each other, until that damned and lucky day, when I had to choose. I was eighteen and I had already been

reported so many times to social services. I was found guilty, so I had to choose — jail or residence? I chose the latter. Happy choice. If I had not, I would not be the person I am now. My brothers followed a different path: neither of them was removed from our home. Nevertheless, my sister Daniela is fragile and too keen to abandon herself to her own weaknesses. Gigi, my brother, is the pride of our family, with a degree in agronomy and working in some gardening centre.

I was the one who went to a children's residence. But it worked for me! I was living in the midst of threats, shouts and quarrels, and — incredible to say — I saw the gleam of quiet. I feel so lucky; my family come from the old school: they always believed in solving problems with beatings. They were inflexible and old-fashioned, and I was violent.

Nello walks to the subway. A deafening noise catches his attention. It comes from a building site: people cutting marbles to pave the square. The screech of the sawblade on stone is ear-splitting. The sun heats his neck and the jumper that his brother gave to him itches. Inexpressible impatience drives him downstairs to the subway. He thinks back to adolescence and psychological treatment, those Tuesday afternoons spent in the company of the lady. A friendly presence; she was quiet; he could tell her everything. Her house had a cocoon-like atmosphere. 'When I grew up, I realized that I had told her so much! I really like that kind of job!'

The metro stops. While getting off, Nello's eye is caught by black-blue stripes: an advert for his favourite soccer team, Atalanta. A passion, 'like falling in love for someone. That takes me back!' He climbs the stairs. Gets in the elevator. Sticks the key in the lock. He is in now. Memories are gone. A comfortable silence washes the house.

Conclusions

W hat is discursive multiplication? How does it work? In this chapter, we introduced different discursive levels to explore leaving care and the transition to adult life.

At a macro level, institutional discourse tends to define, categorize, offer solutions, make previsions. It is structured by professional expertise, rules, laws, hierarchy. Welfare agencies make their decisions based on categorization (diagnosis, assessment) and the available resources are always deemed insufficient (for what, you might ask?). This level is blind to meaning, emotions and perceptions. As our participants told us, they were put into residential care because of difficult family relationships (as we said, this is not always the case). Their families were stigmatized as inappropriate environments for them to live in.

The discourse at a meso level touches family myths and scripts, attitudes and behaviours among peers, the role of mentors and educators, as multiple voices that define reality, that offer listening or recognition or solutions in a way that is always coherent with the context and the reciprocal definition of identities within the ongoing relationship. These processes may be inadequate, hopeless, or stigmatizing. Yet, they are always relevant, for better or worse. Our case studies explore how relationships and interactions shape lives, offer models, open possibilities, sometimes on purpose, but in most cases working at the edges of consciousness. These relationships need special care and attention, since a child or an adult can be unprepared to ask for help, to accept love, or to invest energy in them. This is the level and role of education and good educators.

The participant's voice, at a micro level, struggles to find a way forward, drifting among different discourses. Voice is local, unique; it changes over time, with emotions, even during an interview. It must be clear that we have a version of the stories here: some of their aspects might have crystallized beforehand, while others are co-created during the interview. They are changing.

The researchers' gaze brings forth another level of discourse. In our analysis, we tried to show that our interpretation is not neutral: as a re-storying of the interview it is a selective process, a (re)presentation of the researcher as well as the subject. We are three, and more interpreters will be involved in cooperative phases of this research. The multiplication of perspectives never ends.

A meta-discourse is also present in our study: the conventional perspective proper to western culture demands an adult to be autonomous. The 'cybernetics of Self' (Bateson, 1972, pp. 309–37) that dominates our epistemology is a sort of addiction hindering our capability to surrender and accept vulnerability. Our case studies show that, at some point, being able to ask for help, to accept one's own limits and trust dialogue are necessary to cope with transition (in this case, from care to adult life). Our stories describe the struggles of three young men to become 'relatively adult' in a world where employment, housing, well-being, worthiness, and meaning depend on relationships with significant others. All of them described being alone, left with no reference points, lacking crucial experience, learning and competences, or receiving misplaced help, and yet finding the inner and outer resources to keep on keeping on. They experienced significant danger, literally risking death, or killing people, or embracing fundamentalist ideas; the most dangerous discourses of our times. Any practice of education with care leavers should take into account these risks and multiply discourses to overcome them.

References

Alheit, P. & Dausien, B. (2000) 'Biographicity' as a basic resource of lifelong learning. In: Alheit, P., Beck, J., Kammler, E., Salling Olesen, H. & Taylor, R. (eds) *Lifelong learning inside and outside schools*, 2. Roskilde: Roskilde University.

Allen, M. (2003). *Into the mainstream: Care leavers entering work, education and training*. York: Joseph Rowntree Foundation.

ANCI (2012). *I minori stranieri non accompagnati. Roma: IV Rapporto Fondazione Anci*. http://www.cittalia.it/index.php/welfare

Bateson, G. (1972). *Steps to an ecology of mind*. New York: Ballantine Books.

Bateson, G. (1979). *Mind and nature: A necessary unity*. New York: Bantam Books.

Belotti, V. (2010). *Bambine e bambini temporaneamente fuori dalla famiglia di origine*. Firenze: Istituto degli Innocenti, Centro Nazionale Documentazione e Analisi per l'Infanzia e l'Adolescenza.

Carr, N. & McAlister, S. (2016). The double-bind: Looked after children, care leavers and criminal justice. In: Mendes, P. & Snow, P. (eds), *Young people transitioning from out-of-home-care: International research, policy and practice*. Rotterdam: Springer. https://doi.org/10.1057/978-1-137-55639-4_1

Davis, B. & Sumara, D. (2006). *Complexity and education. Inquiries into learning, teaching and research*. Mahwah, NJ: Lawrence Erlbaum.

Edwards, R., Biesta, G. & Thorpe, M. (2009). *Rethinking contexts for learning and teaching*. Abingdon: Routledge.

Field, J. & Lynch, H. (2015). Getting stuck, becoming unstuck: Agency, identity and transition between learning contexts. *Journal of Adult and Continuing Education*, 21: 3–17. https://doi.org/10.7227/JACE.21.1.2

Field, J., Gallacher, J. & Ingram, R. (2009). Learning transitions: Research, policy, practice. In: *Researching transitions in lifelong learning*. Abingdon: Routledge.

Formenti, L. (2008). La composition dans/de l'autobiographie. *Pratiques de formation/Analyses*, 55: 171–91.

Formenti, L. (2016). Learning to live. The pattern which connects education and dis/orientation. In: Formenti, L. & West, L. (eds), *Stories that make a difference. Exploring the collective, social and political potential of narratives in adult education research*. Lecce: Pensa Multimedia.

Formenti L. (2018). Complexity, adult biographies and co-operative transformation. In: Milana M. et al. (eds), *The Palgrave international handbook on adult and lifelong education and learning*. Basingstoke: Palgrave Macmillan. https://doi.org/10.1057/978-1-137-55783-4

Formenti, L. & West, L. (eds) (2016). *Stories that make a difference. Exploring the collective, social and political potential of narratives in adult education research*. Lecce: Pensa Multimedia.

Formenti, L. & West, L. (2018). *Transforming perspectives in lifelong learning and adult education: A dialogue*. Basingstoke: Palgrave Macmillan.

Foucault, M. (1969). *L'archéologie du savoir*. Paris: Éditions Gallimard.

Gramsci, A. (1975). *Prison notebooks*. New York: Columbia University Press.

Heron, J. (1996). *Co-operative inquiry: Research into the human condition*. London: Sage.

Honneth, A. (1996). *The struggle for recognition. The moral grammar of social conflicts*. Cambridge: Polity Press.

Maturana, H. (1990). The biological foundations of self-consciousness and the physical domain of existence. In: N. Luhmann et al. (eds), *Beobachter. Konvergenz der Erkenntnisttheorien?* München: Wilhelm Fink Verlag.

Melkman, E., Mor-Salwo, Y., Mangold, K., Zeller, M. & Benbenishty, R. (2015). Care leavers as helpers: Motivations for and benefits of helping others. *Children and Youth Services Review*, 54: 41–68. http://dx.doi.org/10.1016/j.childyouth.2015.05.004

Merrill, B. & West, L. (2009). *Using biographical methods in social research*. London: Sage. http://dx.doi.org/10.4135/9780857028990

Mezirow, J. (1991). *Transformative dimensions of adult learning*. New York: Wiley & Sons.

Mezirow, J. (2012). Learning to think like an adult. Core concepts of transformation theory. In: Taylor, E., Cranton, P. & Associates (eds), *The handbook of transformative learning. theory, research, and practice*. San Francisco: Jossey-Bass.

Morgan, R. (2006, 2008, 2011). *Children's care monitor: Children on the state of social care in England Reported by the Children's Rights Director for England*. London: Ofsted.

Naldini, M. & Saraceno, C. (2008). Social and family policies in Italy: Not totally frozen but far from structural reforms. *Social Policy Administration*, 42(7): 733–48.

Pandolfi, L. (2015). *Costruire resilienza: Analisi e indicazioni per l'accompagnamento educativo in uscita delle comunità per minori*. Milano: Guerini.

Rosina, A. (2015). NEET. *Giovani che non studiano e non lavorano*. Milano: Vita e Pensiero.

Stein, M. & Munro, R. (2008). *Young people's transitions from care to adulthood*. London: Jessica Kingsley.

Thoburn, J. (2010). Toward knowledge-based practice in complex child protection cases: A research-based expert briefing. *Journal of Children's Services*, 5: 9–24. https://doi.org/10.5042/jcs.2010.0114

Varela, F., Thompson E. & Rosch E. (1991). *The embodied mind: Cognitive science and human experience*. Cambridge, MA: MIT Press.

Van Dijk, T.A. (1980). *Discourse studies and education*. http:// www.discourses. org/OldArticles/Discourse%20studies%20and%20education.pdf

West, L. (2016). *Distress in the city. Racism, fundamentalism, and a democratic education*. London: Trentham Books.

West, L. & Carlson, A. (2007). *Claiming space: An in depth auto/biographical study of a local Sure Start project*. Canterbury, UK: CCCU/CISDP.

12. What Game Are We Playing? Narrative Work that Supports Gamblers

Micaela Castiglioni and Carola Girotti

Micaela Castiglioni and Carola Girotti place the official narrative and counter-narrative of gambling in the broader context of modern-day society and adult play before describing two Italian initiatives to support gamblers to shed their addiction, through psychosocial means. One of these, the self-help Gamblers Anonymous group, particularly uses narrative approaches to help members publicly tell and re-frame their own life stories in order to see themselves differently and therefore to resist a return to addiction.

This chapter examines one of the dominant narratives in which we are immersed, one which equates the flexibility, uncertainty and continuous change characterizing contemporary adulthood with the potential to continuously reinvent the self. This type of narrative, at least in the Italian context, can easily slide into a narrative rhetoric that serves the logic of the market and to the consequent commercialization of all that belongs to 'the human'. The ground is ripe to sideline the alternative, the unique and diverse narratives of individual adults who each bear specific needs, anxieties, fears, fragilities, etc., born precisely of the constant mutability to which today's personal and professional lives are subject. Are these two alternative ways of narrating the present? The outcome is undoubtedly a confused and confusing narrative in which fragility can easily turn into varying degrees of vulnerability, potentially leading some adults to adopt risky behaviours.

https://doi.org/10.11647/OBP.0203.12

In this complex and problematic scenario, among the types of experience that receive inadequate attention is that of playing games in adulthood, particularly the phenomenon of gambling that has become increasingly widespread over the past ten years, its all-pervasiveness and appeal making it difficult for individuals to give it up. This chapter establishes a framework through which to consider forms of adult play and explores both the official narrative of gambling — what John (2017, p. 4) terms a shared 'set of values' that is often a 'constitutive activity of social media' in contemporary society — and its more invidious counter-narrative that is rarely foregrounded.

In What Place and in What Timeframe?

T he current political-economic-institutional and sociocultural contexts are shaping a complex globalized society characterized by uncertainty and risk, in which adults often find themselves beset by fragility, anxieties and problems leading them to become vulnerable and unstable (Bauman, 2000/1999; Beck, 2000; Sennett, 1999). In Bauman's (2006) view, our social life today — differently to the past — is characterized by instability, whereby situations and events are subject to sudden and unforeseeable changes, and by existential uncertainty on the part of individuals whose identities are fragmented and complex as a result. Life paths, both professional and personal, are marked by an excess of flexibility, insecurity and vulnerability, with inevitable implications for relationships and exchanges among adult subjects in everyday life contexts (Bauman, 2000/1999, 2003; Sennett, 1999). The bonds among individuals are fluid and inconsistent; there is a lack of sharing, concern, respectful recognition and emotional investment, and relationships dominated by consumerism (Bauman, 2000/1999) are mainly aimed at instrumentally achieving personal gain over the short term (ibid.).

Time and space have also been affected (Giddens, 1990) in that traditional spaces are being taken over by other spaces. Giddens (ibid., p. 18) observed that:

> In premodern societies, space and place largely coincided, since the spatial dimensions of social life are, for most of the population, dominated by presence — by localized activity. Modernity increasingly

tears space away from place by fostering relations between absent others, locationally distant from any given face-to-face interaction.

Similarly, our experience of time is being impacted by the availability of rapid and long-distance virtual connections (Bauman, 2000/1999; Giddens, 1990) that reflect the characteristic traits of electronic telecommunications in which sequentiality and linearity have been substituted by networks, nodes and links (Margiotta, 2005). The time spent today with one's family, at work, with friends, etc., is becoming increasingly rushed and fragmented (Sennett, 1999; Bauman, 2000/1999). Like Illich (1996), we see ourselves 'imprisoned in the age of speed' and 'harried' by the experience of it, and when talking with professionals find that they too are 'self-imprisoned by the certainty that speed encompasses everything' not always remembering that it 'needs proper control'.[1] Hence, the organizational, economic, political-institutional dimensions of contemporary lives are pervaded by the will and the pretension to optimize and control all that we do, accompanied by the feeling that we never have enough time.

The French philosopher Paul Virilio (2008)[2], in Armitage & Bishop, 2013, p. 204) has argued that our society is dominated by the dictatorship of speed, which is based on the principle: 'if time is money, speed is power'. A similar view was put forward by German sociologist Hartmut Rosa[3] (see Rosa, 2013), who has proposed the concept of 'social acceleration', understood as that typically Western phenomenon whereby the speed made possible by technology is transferred to every aspect of our social lives. This places the contemporary individual adult in a permanent state of anxiety and relativism given that all truths, certainties, and beliefs are destined to disappear, squashed out of existence by a consumer society whose sole aim is to enjoy the present moment. Bauman (2000/1999, p. 22) states: 'Abandon all hope of totality, future as well as past, you who enter the world of fluid modernity'.

---

1 Paper delivered on 8 November 1996 at Doors of Perception, Netherlands Design Institute of Amsterdam in a session on 'Speed? What speed?' with Sebastian Trapp and Matthias Rieger. Later published in J. Millar & M. Schwarz (eds) (1998). *Speed: Visions of an accelerated age*. London: Photographers' Gallery.

2 In 'Itineraries of the Catastrophe', an interview with Sylvère Lotringer.

3 Coined in German in 2005, as *Beschleunigung*, later translated as *social* acceleration.

Being Adults Today

Within the dominant performative narrative of the 'culture of the present moment' and the 'rush culture' which taken together undermine the most intimate dimensions of personality and behaviour, it is imperative to enjoy the here and now, viewed as the only possible antidote to emptiness and boredom (Kimura, 2005), as well as uncertainty. The adult who is immersed in this 'chaotic ecstasy' (Bauman, 2000/1999) experiences time as present (Sennett, 1999), with no yesterday or tomorrow, lacking in depth. Hence, there is no time for 'sedimentation' or 're-elaboration' of events (Jedlowski, 2002, p. 38), nor time for welcoming and cultivating plans (Bauman, 2000/1999, 2003; Sennett, 1999). Life is based on the 'instantaneous'. The life stories of adult individuals appear to be emptied of diachronic identity, that is to say, continuity, as well as lacking in narrative identity based on inner dialogue (Stanghellini, 1997).

This seems to be the official narrative — alluded to earlier — in which we are immersed and which tells our story. And in all of this, what is the relevance of playing games? And what has play got to do with discourse? Before answering these questions, let us first take a brief look at the phenomenology of play and games.

Adulthood and Play

Man has always engaged in play; games have always offered a privileged and protected ground to men and women of all historical periods and ages. Modes of play may have changed, some playthings may have changed, yet play is just as crucial for human beings today as it was in ancient times.[4] There is nothing negative in our encounter with play. Play would appear to be in contrast with work, as an activity that is both entertaining and relaxing, and which individuals can engage in as they want, for social rather than for economic gain. Hence playing games is a human activity that is a source of great

---

4   Play is much written about and here we draw on Italian versions of the classic works of Johan Huizinga (originally publishing in Dutch in 1938, in English in 1949 and later, Italian in 1946/2013); of Eugene Fink (a German, publishing originally in 1957, in Italian in 2008); of Roger Caillois (originally publishing in French in 1958, 1961 in English).

pleasure, amusement and gratification. On this theme Roger Caillois (2013, p. 5) has observed that:

> The word play inevitably implies an atmosphere of relaxation or enjoyment, it evokes an activity that is not subject to constructions, but which also lacks real-life consequences [...] at each new repetition of a game, even if they were to go on playing it for their whole lives, the players would encounter the same conditions as the first time. This fundamental gratuitousness of play is precisely the factor that most greatly detracts from its status. And at the same time, it is the factor that allows us to engage in play with the utmost carefreeness and that keeps it separate from productive activity. Play has no outcomes in real life.

Play appears to be a sort of interlude that allows adults to take a break from their work, transporting them into a dimension that is carefree and liberated from their usual commitments, both personal and professional, thereby becoming a real need for the human being. It is about activity and Eberle (2014, p. 231) believes that it has 'resisted definition mainly because it is difficult to render dynamic relationships into language'. Nevertheless, after discussing the topic at length with a colleague, Stuart Brown, he offers the following:

> Play is an ancient, voluntary, 'emergent' process driven by pleasure that yet strengthens our muscles, instructs our social skills, tempers and deepens our positive emotions, and enables a state of balance that leaves us poised to play some more. (ibid., p. 231)

The crucial role of play in human existence also has to do with the fact that it frees subjects' minds from external influences, bringing to the fore their most instinctive, emotional and intimate dimension, given that: 'Man [...] is only fully a human being when he plays' (Friedrich, 1975).

Although play may be viewed as unproductive and without real-life consequences, at the imaginary level it functions as a sort of training for dealing with the risks and unpredictability of society, hence it represents a primary need: 'You can deny, if you like, nearly all abstractions: justice, beauty, truth, goodness, mind, God. You can deny seriousness, but not play' (Huizinga, 2014/1938). This is particularly true of play that is not purely intentional and structured (such as 'board games'), but which takes the form of a metaphorical place of experimentation with the self, exchange with the other and socialization. In Caillois' (2013, originally 1958) view, play is an activity that is freely engaged in, limited only by the rules of the game; it is isolated from the surrounding context because it originates and is carried out within spatial and temporal boundaries that are agreed from the outset; play is uncertain in that it is possible to be the loser; it is unproductive in that it does not produce wealth; it is regulated by ad hoc rules; and finally, it is fictitious and unreal in that it bears no real-life implications.

Huizinga, in *Homo Ludens* (2002 edition), draws on his anthropological studies of play and ritual to argue that play, far from being marginal to culture, is actually a cultural antecedent. If we view culture as a markedly human characteristic, since animals too engage in play, play must necessarily precede culture. To back up this argument, Huizinga analysed what he refers to as the 'great archetypal activities of human society', that is to say, primary categories such as language, myth and religious worship, noting how these are woven into play:

> In the making of speech and language the spirit is continually sparking between matter and mind, as it were. [...] Behind every abstract expression, there lie the boldest of metaphors, and every metaphor is a play on words. Thus in giving expression to life, man creates a second poetic world alongside the world of nature. Or take myth. This too is a transformation of the outer world, only here the process is more elaborate and ornate than is the case with individual words. Primitive man seeks to account for the world of phenomena [...] In all the wild imaginings [...] a fanciful spirit is playing on the borderline between jest and earnest. Or finally let us take ritual. Primitive society performs its sacred rites [...] in a spirit of pure play truly understood. (ibid., p. 7)

On this basis, Huizinga feels justified in adding to *homo*, in addition to the labels *sapiens* and *faber*, also *ludens*, in reference to the crucial role of play in the birth of culture and society. Play still, today, fulfils both an essential biological function and a critical social purpose in terms of contributing to establishing and maintaining bonds between individuals. Culture and play represent a place in which it is possible to detach from real everyday life, a space in which to interpret, re-elaborate and signify experience. Huizinga also proposed that in different human societies, play takes different forms and is engaged in for different purposes: as sacred ritual, as a medium for learning, or as a creative process underpinning poetic, graphic or musical expression, and so on. He also emphasizes the importance of rules in defining the boundaries of the game. These rules are typically inflexible and must be closely followed in order to temporarily create an imaginary micro-world. Fairness is thus a key requirement that cannot be violated in order to maintain the illusion on which play is based, without revealing the game's intrinsic fragility.

This early and rich reflection on play by Huizinga paved the way for other authors such as Eugen Fink who, in 1957, published his *Oasi del gioco*, in which he proposed that play is generally accepted in human societies but accorded marginal status. Acknowledging its entertaining and light side, Fink (1968)[5] viewed play as a space for detaching from the seriousness and responsibility of life. He admits that:

> Play is thought of more or less as frivolous and pleasurable nonsense, as a carefree sojourn in the airy realm of phantasy and sheer potentialities, as an escape from unyielding reality to a dream-utopia. [...] As long as we continue naively using the popular antitheses of 'work-play,' 'frivolity-seriousness' and the like, we will never grasp the ontological meaning of play. (p. 19)

But argues that: 'play is a basic existential phenomenon' (p. 19) that 'is not subordinate to the ultimate purpose served by all other human activity' (p. 21) and that if we try to make it so it is 'perverted and has become merely a means to an end' (p. 21).

In Fink's view, all human action is underpinned by the desire to achieve *eudaimonia* (Greek for happiness), by constantly searching for meaning, as we make our way along our path towards a happy future, for which we perceive the present as the time in which to prepare and plan. Play, on the other hand, transcends this logic:

> In contrast with the restless dynamism, the obscure ambiguity and relentless futurism of our life, play is characterized by calm, timeless 'presence' and autonomous, self-sufficient meaning — play resembles an oasis of happiness that we happen upon in the desert of our Tantalus-like seeking and pursuit of happiness. (p. 21)

This statement implies that the purpose of play is not to ensure a happy future but is contained in itself. Hence, play is a standalone practice that strengthens our ties with the present. According to Fink, play cannot be compared or contrasted with the phenomena of our daily lives, but receives, represents and reinterprets them. Another scholar of play,

---

5   Fink's 1957 work was translated by Ute and Thomas Saine and published by Yale University Press, see Fink, Saine & Saine (1968) in reference list for this chapter.

Gregory Bateson (1987) defined it as a form of meta-communication, given its power to attribute figurative and symbolic, as opposed to literal, meaning to our actions and words, thereby taking fiction to a higher level than reality and viewing it as something that already exists as latent potential.

Alea and *Agon*

Returning once more to the work of Caillois (of 1958), play may be divided into two opposite and antagonistic categories: *Paidia* and *Ludus*. *Paidia* is play that is spontaneous, free, chaotic and anarchic, while *Ludus* is based on institutionalized rule, and the object of participation is to overcome an obstacle that has been deliberately created for the purposes of the game. Caillois also divided games into further categories, of which *Alea* and *Agon* are relevant here.

Alea describes games whose outcome does not depend on the skill of the player but exclusively on chance. Hence, one's opponent is not another player but destiny: players only need to wait to find out what fate has decided for them. This category includes games that are highly passive in nature, in which competence has no bearing on the result: for example, roulette, lotteries and scratch cards. *Alea* contrasts with the games in the *Agon* category, which require players to participate responsibly and draw on different kinds of ability, and whose categorical imperative is precisely that of not abandoning oneself to one's fate. *Agon* demands patience, concentration, constant training and the subject's will to determine, insofar as possible, the outcome of the game. In sum, *Alea* involves waiting for fate to decide on and execute its moves, while *Agon* exalts and leads us to exercise, and put to the test, our own physical and/or mental skills, encouraging perseverance and preparation.

There are games however in which *Alea* and *Agon* are both present, giving rise to a third category, in which the human player is both a passive subject waiting to know his or her fate and at the same time called to actively prepare, participate, and attempt to overcome difficulties; such games demand both luck and skill, which contribute to the final outcome in equal measures.[6]

---

6   This paragraph is attributed to Carola Girotti, Assistant Lecturer in Adult Education and Lifelong Learning at the University of Milano-Bicocca, Italy.

Narrative and Counter-Narrative

A s we have just seen, the dimension of play is of key importance to the demanding adult lives of today. Nevertheless, we need to be aware of another side to play, the dangerous side, that poses risks for adults who engage in it and can even become a form of illness: gambling.

> [...] if one's encounter with an object is fatal and therefore transformational, it may be defined, according to how the encounter develops, as a 'drug object' or 'object of passion'. (Bignamini, 2006)

Gambling is an exciting form of entertainment that provides a diversion from everyday life; however, it also represents the illusion of change and players' lack of confidence in their ability to be effective in their lives. The illusion of easy winnings and overinvestment in gambling leads subjects to lose their awareness that they are certain to lose. It is no coincidence that in periods of economic recession and depression, when consumption is slow and traditional economic sectors contract, the gambling market flourishes. Governments anxious to boost tax revenue frequently contribute to this state of affairs by promoting gambling and thereby selling dreams to their most 'hopeless' citizens (Fiasco, 2001).

In the contemporary social context, described at the start of this chapter, gambling in all its forms finds fertile ground. It does not require any determination, effort, practice, responsibility or skill, and so individuals passively pin their hopes on it, on the mirage of a sudden stroke of good luck, of magically finding themselves in the lap of luxury and wealth, without any struggle to achieve it. Gambling makes the contemporary dream *par excellence* seem attainable — if only for an instant — the dream, that is to say, of obtaining the maximum benefit with the minimum sacrifice, giving the player the illusion of being highly effective.

This illusory contemporary narrative of 'access to everything' and 'everything at once' that 'speaks to us' and 'acts in us' (Bauman, 2012) contains a sub-narrative — fuelled by advertising and other communication media — that frames gambling as an opportunity to make one's fortune and be successful without the need for effort or sacrifice. However, these same media, in a form of narrative schizophrenia, demonize gambling, warning adults and young people — its potential consumers — against its dangers.

Against this backdrop, the phenomenon of gambling has become increasingly widespread over the past ten years, with increases in both the number of gaming halls and the levels of internet gambling. This has had negative side-effects at the social level, causing addiction and leading gamblers into debt. The all-pervasiveness and appeal of gambling makes it difficult for individuals to give it up. Hence, we believe it to be of vital importance that this counter-narrative be brought to the fore so that it may become one of the 'discourses we live by', prompting adults to re-turn to playing games in the sense of re-discovering the re-creational and positive functions of play, and helping them to identify new forms of play for entertainment, relaxation, and socialization purposes. And consequently, to re-discover and re-signify their own adult identities, thereby recovering their sense of self and self-esteem.

Educational Narrative in Care with an Educational Component

G ambling addiction is an illness and as such must be treated via appropriate rehabilitation and educational programmes. In Italy, SerT and Giocatori Anonimi (Gamblers Anonymous, GA) are two organizations that play a key role in educating adults, via narrative tools, to rediscover the positive aspects of playing games. More specifically, the programmes run by these organizations aim to help individuals de-construct both received and original (i.e., subjective, autobiographical and inner) narratives.

SerT

S erT was set up by local health boards as the main public health service offering recovery programmes for those affected by legal (e.g., alcohol) and illegal (e.g., cocaine, heroin) substance abuse/addiction and compulsive behaviours. In recent years, this service — where present — has also begun to work with individuals who are pathologically addicted to gambling even in the absence of an addiction to substances. There are currently 550 SerT in operation in Italy, on average one per health district. SerT guarantee anonymity to their clients, but in the case of minors, parents or guardians must be involved. No medical prescription is required to avail oneself of the service, which is totally free of cost. The service is offered on the same conditions to both Italian citizens and foreign residents who are members of the national health service. SerT employ a range of specialists with expertise in the treatment of addictions, such as doctors, nurses, professional educators, psychologists and social workers, who after fully evaluating the client's physical and mental health, define individual courses of therapy and monitor them periodically according to both medical and psychological criteria. A course of therapy offered by a SerT has a defined start and finish date. The SerT team agrees a timeframe with the client, in the space of which it should be possible for the patient to come to terms with his or her addiction and learn how to cope with it. Hence, the service's goal is to help subjects to overcome their addiction by enabling them to deal with it independently, without creating a further form of dependence whereby they begin to rely on the support of the service, but simply offering them tools that might help them to break their compulsive habits.

Giocatori Anonimi (Gamblers Anonymous, GA)

G A is a fellowship of men and women who have issues with compulsive gambling and who share their experience and strength with one another with a view to solving their common problem and helping others to recover from a gambling problem. Members of GA commit to continue to share their experiences and feelings with their group even when they have achieved 'sobriety', to reduce their risk of having a relapse and to provide support to new members and those who are still struggling with their gambling issues. The recovery programme offered by GA is more educational than clinical in nature and is based on narrative educational tools. The Association follows the model of the self-help group that has been successfully applied by the original American organization. GA has developed a twenty-item questionnaire (see below) that can help gamblers to discern if their addiction is such that they should ask the association for help.[7] This self-report instrument is simple and quick to complete, and a gambler

---

7   For online questionnaires visit http://www.gamblersanonymous.org/ or www. giocatorianonimi.org

may respond to the items unassisted, anonymously and in the privacy
of his or her own home.

The GA Questionnaire

1. Have you ever lost time from school or work due to gambling?
2. Has gambling ever made your home life unhappy?
3. Has gambling damaged your reputation?
4. Have you ever felt remorse after gambling?
5. Did you ever gamble to get money with which to solve financial difficulties?
6. Has gambling caused a decrease in your ambition?
7. After losing do you feel you must return as soon as possible and win back your losses?
8. After winning do you have a strong urge to return and win more?
9. Have you ever gambled until your last euro was gone?
10. Have you ever borrowed to finance your gambling?
11. Have you ever sold anything to finance your gambling?
12. Have you ever been reluctant to use gambling money for other expenditures?
13. Has gambling made you careless about the welfare of yourself or your family?
14. Have you ever gambled for longer than you had planned?
15. Have you ever gambled to get away from worries or difficulties?
16. Have you ever committed or considered committing an illegal act to finance gambling?
17. Has gambling ever caused you to have difficulty sleeping?
18. Have disappointments or frustrations ever given you the urge to gamble?
19. Have you ever felt the urge to celebrate any good fortune by a few hours of gambling?
20 Have you ever considered suicide as a result of your gambling?

Author translation of questionnaire freely available @ www.giocatori.anonimi.org

Statistical evidence indicates that educational programmes based on the
self-help model that allow participants to orally share and compare their
self-narratives and personal experiences can be highly effective. Such
an approach ensures that the individual gambler does not feel judged
by the other members of the group, whose experiences are similar and
who can therefore understand the associated problems and challenges.
This narrative approach helps members to tell their own individual
stories and the consequences that addiction has had on their private
and professional lives. They are encouraged to focus on their strengths
and on the strategies that they can deploy to deal with their gambling
problem. Another aspect that helps participants to open up and share
their stories with the group is the fact that their privacy and anonymity is
guaranteed. Ultimately what emerges is a joint narrative that offers new
perspectives on the self and on the experience of gambling/gaming/
playing games in adulthood: a sort of counter-narrative that stands as
an alternative to official narratives, which are reified in ways that are
ambivalent and therefore anti-educational.

Narrating a Counter-History

We wish to emphasize the importance of narrative research in shaping, containing and communicating meaning, not only in relation to the focus of this chapter but relative to all the themes addressed throughout the volume. Specifically, it is our aim to draw attention to the educational value and care inherent in the narrative healthcare outlined above.

Each of us, from the earliest months of life, internalizes a 'script' (Berne, 2001/1961) that is functional to ensuring our survival. The newborn baby discovers that crying elicits the intervention of its carers to alleviate its suffering, and thereafter continues to have recourse to this strategy every time it finds itself in need. This script is pre-verbal, pre-narrative and, we might say, a successful and 'adaptive' script that is generated in the encounter between stimuli internal to the child and stimuli from the external environment (Cosso, 2013). Later, speech will replace crying, but as the child grows he or she will continue to draw on scripts, though these will gradually increase in number and complexity (ibid.). 'Adaptive' scripts will be weighed up against 'transgressive' scripts, as Bruner (1992) called them, which may also be understood as emancipatory scripts: particularly during all the key transitions, foreseen and unforeseen, that we will go through in the course of our life trajectories (Cosso, 2013).

From an epistemological perspective closer to that informing this book, which draws on the structuralism of Foucault and narrative psychodynamics, we might say that narratives that are official, dominant, authoritative and collective — but not on this account intrinsically or automatically endowed with real or tolerable meaning (Pineau & Le Grand, 1993) — must necessarily encounter, and frequently clash with, the original and generative narratives of which each individual is the more or less conscious bearer. If this fails to occur, the subject will end up being excessively narrated by 'other discourses' and the 'discourses of others' (ibid.) in the form of beliefs, values, viewpoints and even ambivalent and manipulative discourses. As we have seen in relation to gambling, failure in this regard will lead to the loss of self, understood as the loss of oneself and of one's deepest and most personal sense of self.

As is so well expressed by Foucault in *The Order of Things* (1967), discourse is driven by power yet itself exercises a form of power that may be either coercive or emancipatory. According to the French philosopher, the subject is 'spoken' by discursive practices situated within specific political-institutional and socio-cultural paradigms or systems. These discursive practices determine whether factors that limit and/or afford possibilities to the subject are 'speakable' or 'unspeakable'. This is why, in situations of vulnerability bordering on full-blown mental illness, such as forms of gambling addiction, the individual needs to have access to educational approaches of the narrative kind, which prioritize narrative, using it to facilitate the co-construction — with a practitioner or group — of a counter-narrative or counter-history. This will allow the individual to recompose his or her life story and to deviate from a previously internalized and excessively inflexible script of self that rhetorically reflected the requirements of the external social context. Within this newly defined life trajectory, play will remain a key source of liberation, gratification, and regeneration but will imply the acceptance of responsibility for self and others and compliance with the rules.

References

Armitage, J. & Bishop, R. (eds) (2013). *Virilio and visual culture.* Edinburgh: Edinburgh University Press.

Bateson, G. (1987). A theory of play and fantasy. In: *Steps to an ecology of mind: Collected essays in anthropology, psychiatry, evolution and epistemology.* Northvale: Jason Aaronson.

Bauman, Z. (2000). *Liquid modernity.* Cambridge: Polity Press. [*Modernità liquida.* Roma-Bari: Laterza, 2012].

Bauman, Z. (2006). *Vita liquida.* Roma-Bari: Laterza.

Beck, U. (2008). *Costruire la propria vita.* Bologna: Il Mulino.

Berne, E. (2001/1961). *Transactional analysis in psychotherapy.* London: Souvenir Press.

Bignamini, E. (2006). Psicopatologia delle dipendenze da sostanze: Suggestioni per pensarla. In: *Dal fare al dire.* Cuneo: PUBLIEDIT Edizioni e Pubblicazioni Sas.

Bruner, J. (1992). *La ricerca del significato. Per una psicologia del sociale.* Torino: Bollati Boringhieri.

Callois, R. (2013/1958/1961). *I giochi e gli uomini, la maschera e la vertigine.* Milano: Bompiani.

Cosso, A. (2013). *Raccontarsela. Copioni di vita e storie organizzative: l'uso della narrazione per lo sviluppo individuale e d'impresa.* Milano: Lupetti.

Eberle, S.G. (2014). The elements of play: Towards a philosophy and a definition of play. *Journal of Play*, 6(2): 214–33.

Fiasco, M. (2001). Aspetti sociologici, economici e rischio criminalità. In: Croce M., Zerbetto R. (eds), *Il gioco e l'azzardo. Il fenomeno, la clinica, la possibilità d'intervento.* Milano: Franco Angeli.

Fink, E., Saine, U. & Saine, T. (1968). The Oasis of Happiness: Toward an Ontology of Play. *Yale French Studies: Game, Play, Literature*, 41: 19–30. [Trans, from Fink, E. (1957) *Oase des Glücks.*]

Foucault, M. (1967). *Le parole e le cose.* Milano: Rizzoli.

Friedrich, S. (1975). *Lettere sull'educazione estetica dell'uomo.* Roma: Armando.

Giddens, A. (1990). *The consequences of modernity.* Cambridge: Polity Press in association with Blackwell Publishing.

Huizinga, J. (2014/2002/1949 in English, 1938 in Dutch). *Homo ludens*, Ils 86. Abingdon: Routledge.

Jedlowski, P. (2002). *Memoria, esperienza e modernità.* Milan: FrancoAngeli.

John, N.A. (2017). *The Age of Sharing.* Cambridge: Polity Press.

Illich, I. (1996). *Speed? What speed?* http://thackara.com/mobility-design/speed-what-speed-prisoners-of-speed-by-ivan-illich-part-3-of-3/

Kimura, B. (2005). *Scritti di psicopatologia fenomenologica.* Roma: Fioriti.

Margiotta, A. (2005). *Passaggi di pensiero.* Besa: Nardò.

Pineau, G. & Le Grand, J.L. (1993). *Le storie di vita.* Milano: Guerini e Associati.

Sennett, R. (1998). *L'uomo flessibile.* Milano: Feltrinelli.

Stanghellini, G. (1997). *Antropologia della vulnerabilità.* Milano: Feltrinelli.

Photo by Tom Perkins, CC-BY 4.0

IV.

DISCOURSES WE WORK AROUND: MANAGING CONSTRAINING CIRCUMSTANCES

C hapters in this section address situations that the individuals cannot change but can — or have to — find ways of dealing with if they are to have agency in life or in work. These chapters explore how groups and individuals engage with the constraints and (with differing degrees of success) strive to 'outwit' constraining discourses, to achieve outcomes other than those commonly anticipated, or make the discourses work in their interests. There are chapters from Scandinavia: one from a Danish perspective, considering the difficulties faced when an individual is released from prison; another focusing on dilemmas within the upper secondary school in Sweden. A chapter from Colombia offers little-heard views on the progress towards inclusion in the university system; and a chapter from Poland gives a glimpse of local resistance to those in power, as adult educators strive to empower adult students to understand how to find the underlying meanings in policies and texts they wish to challenge.

In 'A Danish Prisoner Narrative: The Tension from a Multifaceted Identity During Re-Entry to Society'(Ch13), Charlotte Mathiassen carries out narrative research with a male offender moving from prison via a halfway house to independent living, after serving a sentence for murder. This is a nuanced narrative that focuses on much more than the offence, and the reader becomes aware that the man at the centre of the study has to deal with multiple and complex issues. On the one hand, he must face the social stigma of imprisonment and his dependence on social workers due to the disruption of home, work and family patterns that otherwise might have provided support; on the other, he has also to work around the problems stemming from an underlying mental health condition. Even small decisions, like whether or not to enrol on an educational course, represent a challenge.

Following a period of political upheaval in Colombia, a country from which the Eurocentric listener seldom hears authentic 'voices', Miguel González González examines the dilemmas that beset diversity/homogeneity and inclusionary/exclusionary policies and practices. In this chapter, 'Inclusion and Exclusion in Colombian Education, Captured Through Life Stories' (Ch14), he uses interviews with academics to reveal the barriers to change within education, showing, too, how new and positively intended policies often impose standard approaches that unintentionally reduce diversity, building even greater obstacles for staff and students to work around.

Next, in 'Navigating Grades *and* Learning in the Swedish Upper Secondary School Where Neoliberal Values Prevail' (Ch15), Patric Wallin examines students' cultural behaviour and their everyday routines during practical exercises in chemistry laboratories. He seeks to better understand how they interact and communicate and their attitudes to asking teachers for help when they need it. Swedish students believe that to do so might affect their final grades and consequently their chances to progress to university, because their teachers, who also assess them, could deem them needy. Consequently, they deny themselves the support from which they might benefit, a paradox that teachers and students need ways to address. There is a further paradox in that they turn instead to their peers, contradicting the view that neoliberal societies normatively foster individualism.

In the final chapter of this section (Ch16), 'Adult Education as a Means to Enable Polish Citizens to Question Media Coverage of Political Messages', Marta Zientek draws attention to the processes that underpin the formation of a national identity. Poland is undergoing a period of instability and unrest, its people unable to challenge political groups effectively as they lack a platform from which to confront rhetoric. Marta is helping adult students to find ways to engage discursively and to work around the political messages that hold the country in thrall, through a course in communication. Here we get a glimpse of a project still unfolding in turbulent times.

Altogether we have four very different explorations of why and how the individual and the group can withstand, manage, even work around, regimes and policies that they find challenging. The researchers are all working in contexts where the situation is volatile, although the extent and impact of this varies considerably. The projects are at different stages of advancement — Marta's is still developing as she writes about it; Miguel's is completed and he is already poised to see what happens next; Charlotte's current research intervention is complete but not the ex-offender's adjustments; in Sweden, Patric is anticipating further educational reform.

Individually, the chapters connect with others in the book. Charlotte's prisoner's tale is partly mirrored in Linda Cooper's account of British ex-offenders (Ch23) but also resonates with issues in Khum Raj Pathak's work on punishment discourses (Ch9); Miguel González González's chapter connects to those with an educational theme but, thematically, with the explorations of diversity in section five (Chs17–20), as well as Laura Mazzoli Smith's chapter that relates to both diversity and higher education (Ch25); Laura's work resonates with Patrick Wallin's chapter, too; Marta's chapter can be read alongside that of Linden West and Alan Bainbridge (Ch3), which also deals with difficult political and cultural situations, although her context and disciplinary background are very different.

13. A Danish Prisoner Narrative
The Tension from a Multifaceted Identity During (Re-)Entry to Society

Charlotte Mathiassen

Charlotte Mathiassen explores the transition of a prisoner who has committed murder, from prison, to halfway house, to rehabilitation in society, in order to show how incarceration affects the individual. She is seeking better ways to support such transitions, ways that could help the prisoner develop a new sense of agency and self-worth.

This chapter recounts Nick's story as he tries to get a grip on life after six years of incarceration, focusing on his experiences as he moves from prison to a halfway house and later from the halfway house to his own apartment. Nick was forty-three years old when I met him. He had served part of his sentence for manslaughter in a high-security (closed) prison and was in the process of moving to the halfway house. As this chapter illustrates, Nick experienced increasing unrest and de-habilitation. This markedly restricted his everyday living and being, even though his physical incarceration was lessened. Nick's experiences challenge a major rehabilitative and societal ambition, namely, to integrate former prisoners into society through education and work. Furthermore, it sheds light on the way that, after prolonged imprisonment, shame, guilt and stigma can heavily influence the route back into society.

The empirical method was qualitative. We (Nick and I) succeeded in three extended dialogues over one-and-a-half years and some follow-up phone calls a year after his release. I analysed the material to search

https://doi.org/10.11647/OBP.0203.13

for personally meaningful narratives and found both contradictions and tensions, agreeing with Bosworth and colleagues (2005) that:

> Prisoners are not numbers. They are living, breathing people with personalities, characteristics, likes, and dislikes. In the current penal climate, as more and more people are locked up all the time, this simple observation is all too often forgotten. (2005, p. 251)

I insisted on taking a point of departure in the prisoner's first-person perspective as closely as I could. As Farrant (2004) described in her article on life story research with men who have served time in prisons, the dialogues between Nick and I were beset with contradictions and complexity and they had emotional effects on both of us.

Prisoners Going Home, or...?

We know from research that the process of re-entry is often difficult (Keene, Smoyer & Blankenship, 2018; Maruna, 2000; Olsen, 2017; Petersilia, 2003; Riggs & Cook, 2015; Seigafo, 2017) and for different reasons. Often prisoners experience challenges due to poor education, poverty, unemployment, homelessness, psychological and health problems, marginal positions or exclusion resulting in what Keene, Smoyer and Blankenship (2018) term 'stigmatized identities associated with their incarceration' (2018, p. 799). Furthermore shame, guilt and challenges in coming to terms with their past contribute to some prisoners' difficulties (Bhatti, 2010; Mathiassen, 2016) as do the lack of ties to a close social community, for instance, a supportive family (Brunton-Smith & McCarthy, 2016).

Different research explores 'what works' in relation to reducing recidivism rates (i.e., offenders' return to crime) (Cook et al, 2015; Hicks, 2004) but the answer to that question is far from simple (Cook et al, 2015; Travis et al, 2014). Time in prison is painful for several prisoners and this does not seem to help matters (Listwan et al, 2013). Petersilia's belief in 2003 that: 'How we plan for inmates' transition to free living — including how they spend their time during confinement, the process by which they are released, and how they are supervised after release — is critical to public safety' (Petersilia, 2003, p. 3), still holds. So does her point that people who have committed criminal acts need incentives to change, which necessitates 'a supervised transition plan' (Petersilia, 2003, p. 75), although the different prison experiences will determine the specific resources 'necessary for successful re-entry' (Anonymous & Dombrowsky, 2010, p. 477). For example, mentally ill prisoners who do not receive help risk harming other people or themselves (Seigafo, 2017).

Conditions in Danish and Nordic prisons are different from those in American prisons and the release processes differ too (Aaltonen et al, 2017; Scharff Smith & Ugelvik, 2017). The preparation for release while the prisoner is still in prison, as well as the follow-up during his or her transition to a less restricted conduct of life, however, are important in both traditions, to try to minimize the risk of reoffending or other negative consequences.

The main character in this chapter, Nick, struggled to adjust to life after prison. In several ways, he seemed to experience anxiety, maybe as a consequence of a societal stigmatizing discourse and practice around ex-prisoners like himself. Tyler and Slater (2018, p. 724) argue that if the focus is only on 'individualized stories of disclosure and recovery, sociological questions about the causes of mental distress are frequently airbrushed out of the picture'. However, the point of departure in my analysis is to acknowledge the societal dimension to the challenges Nick faces and to reveal this through his different versions of parts of his story.

Setting the Scene

N ick committed a single serious violent crime and the victim died of his injuries. A forensic psychiatrist diagnosed Nick to be within the spectrum of severe personality disorder. Therefore, he served his sentence in a special prison facility that employed more psychiatrists and psychologists than is the norm in Danish prison facilities, because the majority of prisoners had diagnoses within the spectrum of severe personality disturbances and the professional approach is that they need treatment.

In Denmark, for 'cases' like Nick, the key professional intent is to reach a forensic psychological and psychiatric understanding of the mind of convicts who have committed serious crimes. However, in this chapter I adopt a different theoretical approach, trying to understand what is at stake in lives like his.

Life-Project

Anthropological psychology, which draws on both existential and phenomenological thinking was one theoretical cornerstone of this research (Bertelsen, 1994; Mathiassen, 2009) and the concept of the 'life-project' was central, capturing the point of view that a person always strives and projects him or herself into the future. The individual directs him or herself in a manner whereby both the past and the present influence the process of direction. During this process, the actual life setting continually influences the person and the person influences the actual life setting. Time, place and person are intertwined and reciprocity and fluidity characterize the way life is established and progresses, which in some respects corresponds with the fundamentals in Ollman's (2015) theoretical thinking, which will be presented later in this chapter. Therefore, one can argue that recollection of the past and expectations of the future influence how the individual strives and projects him or herself while maintaining that individuals strive and project themselves in an intimate and inseparable relation to the life setting directing them.

Nick's story will serve as a 'case' to illustrate the adjustments potentially faced by long-term prisoners who are in the process of being released from — and releasing themselves from — a physical, psychological and existential incarceration in prison. I shall focus on analysing how the context, Nick's experiences in prison and beforehand, and his expectations for the future must all be included in an attempt to understand what is at stake in his life. Time is a crucial part of this. While conducting the dialogues with Nick, I was concerned that not only were his descriptions of whether or not to participate contradictory and conflicting, but so were other parts of his stories. I will analyse and discuss some of these contradictions, which seem to be present both in Nick's stories of his own conduct in life and of the different attempts to assist him to see the possibility of a range of actions other than arrest.

Constructing the Stories

B ecause I designed the research by following the anthropological psychological stance, the starting point in our dialogues was: 'Please, tell me about what is important to you, in your present life' (life project and engagement).

I began in the present, in the here and now, to get an impression of what was important right now (engagement). Therefore, the present was one central anchor point in time in Nick's meaning-making (Bruner, 2004). Furthermore, I asked him about his eventual dreams, hopes and wishes for the future (life project). Finally, I urged him to describe his way of living before imprisonment. In our dialogues Nick moved between different episodes, times and activities and we covered the present, the future and the past.

The individual life project as it develops is intimately connected to the actual conditions, situations and locations — including other people, discourses and activities. I therefore urged Nick to describe how he experienced staying in *this* prison among *this* group of prisoners. Like Farrant (2014) before me, I did the research with 'a clear commitment to take us deep into the heart of the prison experience' (2014, p. 463).

We explored the experience of being a prisoner in the institution of prison from different angles and over several years. How did Nick experience the demands from the psychologist? the governor? the other prisoners? What were the possibilities of exercise? of getting some peace to concentrate on school? Was it possible to have a friend in prison? Nick mostly took the lead in the conversations, but sometimes, just to be sure that I understood his story, I explored the themes he raised further. At times his narrative was very difficult to follow, due partly to peculiar sentence constructions and word usage but also because of the contradictions in Nick's stories. In several ways, our conversations lived up to Jewkes' (2014) characterization of criminology: 'Criminology is about the dramatic, tragic, visceral, and emotive' (2014, p. 388). This, I hope, will become apparent over the following pages.

Contradictory Relations in Nick's Story

Nick explained that he participated in this research to enable people to gain insight into prisoners' experiences of release from a physical prison, a view in line with that expressed by Bosworth and colleagues (2005) who summarized the reasons for prisoners being co-researchers as ones that '...go well beyond purely instrumental factors to include complex affective issues that concern agency and hope' (2005, p. 256). Nick seemed dually motivated; keen to 'open the window' into prison life and an individual prisoner's experiences, but also to broaden his seemingly minimal experience of agency through such participation. Simultaneously, Nick underlined that he wanted to tell his story but also that he did not want to 'enter the limelight'. To put it another way, Nick appeared rather reserved, almost scared, of being 'visible and recognized'.

Ollman (2015) argues that: 'Changes and relations are the basic building materials of the "bigger picture"' (2015, p. 10). He is a proponent of the philosophy of internal relations and has written extensively on Marx. Ollman insists on an understanding of matters in which the focus is on processes and relations rather than on phenomena that exist separately and are only 'externally' connected. In other words, disconnection and separate things do not exist; processes do, and are constantly interacting with other processes. At the same time, all human activity focuses on something, which is still a part of and thereby not separated from the whole. Abstraction is necessary for the process of understanding a whole and complex matter. Inspired by Ollman, I understand Nick's wanting to be visible and non-visible at the same time as a contradictory relation.

Farrant (2014), drawing on Heidegger and the concept of unconcealment, argued that storytelling and stories make ourselves and the other come to life. By sharing stories, the sharers come to life. During our dialogues, Nick tried to engage and participate and move beyond his invisible life in prison, but he also became increasingly worried about the potential consequences of our contact. Stated in more analytical terms, the contradiction or tension between his engagement and worries increased during the years of our contact. The question became one of how to understand this contradiction or at least tension in Nick's description and story. Maybe Nick, by meeting up, by telling his story to me, slowly discovered how difficult it was for him to move towards being a citizen outside of prison. The materiality of life and the challenges of life outside of prison became increasingly evident and more difficult to handle. As Farrant (2014) found with other prisoners, Nick displayed some but not all of his often contradictory and multifaceted stories of self.

Let me now turn to the part of Nick's life-story in which the challenges intensified because he moved from the prison to the halfway house. This move was both a physical move and an existential and social move. Preparation began during the last part of Nick's incarceration in prison and the process continued after the concrete move from prison cell to halfway house. Ongoing contact between prison staff and those in the halfway house demonstrated that procedures followed good practice, as did Nick's involvement, since he was able to present his wishes and expectations for the future.

Leaving Prison

Having completed six years of imprisonment when he left the closed prison, Nick expected to finish his sentence in the halfway house. This was theoretically possible due to his 'calm and well behaved' behaviour in prison and, of course, the length of his served sentence.[1] From prison, Nick made plans to attend a school for adults in the ordinary school system once he was settled in the halfway house. This was mandatory because he wanted to go to university to become an engineer. Nick did attend school in prison but experienced problems concentrating, a common experience among prisoners and ex-prisoners. He had had to force himself to complete his programme of self-study.

Nick had also insisted on having an ordinary job within the prison and was fully capable of working full-time apart from the time he spent on his self-study. Nick described his everyday life as rather routinized (Holzkamp, 2016). Furthermore, although Goffman's description of the total institution can be criticized for being ahistorical and for ignoring the questions of political ideology and power (Slater & Tyler,

---

1   See Schartmueller (2018) for a comparison of the release processes in Denmark, Finland and Sweden.

2018) I shall argue that the way Nick and other prisoners described the organization and regulation of their everyday life in prison echoes several of Goffman's points. Nick described his everyday life in mundane terms: getting up when the guards knocked at the door, getting ready for the day, making breakfast in the kitchen.[2] He started and finished work at the same time every day. After work, he jogged every day and in general, he kept himself apart, avoiding engagement with the social communities among the prisoners.

When Nick moved to the halfway house, the prison routines disappeared. He had to kick-start his life again, a huge challenge. He described the other prisoners' behaviour as disturbing and irresponsible and claimed that they did not respect other people. Nevertheless, his immediate relief and optimism at the prospect of new and different possibilities and relative 'freedom' rapidly diminished after he left the closed prison. During the next few months, Nick became increasingly depressed and his hopes and plans for his future education slowly deteriorated, even though the preparations made in anticipation of his release held good: he had a home, the possibility of attending school, and other people to interact with even though they all were ex-prisoners. We must consider why this should be the case.

You Wrap Yourself In

T he clearest goal and 'life project' in the stories that Nick shared with me was to attend school with the ambition of entering university. However, Nick found it a huge challenge to be in school with people who had no prison experience. As I said at the outset, there seemed to be contradictions in the way he directed himself towards life, other people and himself.

Several activities at school centred on presenting oneself to one's new classmates. This may challenge the shyest among us, but most people manage it without further ado. Sometimes people conceal aspects of their lives and histories and may have conflicted views when determining what to tell and what to keep private. To refer back to Ollman, this activity is part of a bigger whole, and its relation to the whole influences

---

2   Prisoners self-cater in Denmark. They buy food in a grocery store in the prison and prepare their own meals.

how the activity proceeds. Ex-prisoners do not have a complete choice as to how, and in which directions, their return to or reintegration into society goes. Societal discourses about, for instance, 'the criminal', 'the monster', or 'the deviant', influence prisoners' self-narratives (Farrant, 2014), so the identity of prisoners and ex-prisoners can be understood as one constructed in relation to such societal discourses.

Stigma, meaning 'the situation of the individual who is disqualified from full social acceptance' (Goffman, 1986/1963, preface), is the point of departure in my understanding of the processes of 'othering' that take place in our society when it comes to groups of 'outcasts', groups of 'human waste' (to borrow from Zygmunt Bauman, 2003). Ex-prisoners sometimes end up in such groups when the processes of stigmatization rule, not least those prisoners who have committed serious and violent crimes towards children and women. Processes of stigmatization and discrimination are social. Following Parker & Aggleton (2003), these processes are related to power and domination:

> [...] stigma is linked to the workings of social inequality and to properly understand issues of stigmatization and discrimination [...] requires us to think more broadly about how some individuals and groups come to be socially excluded, and about the forces that create and reinforce exclusion in different settings. (2003, p. 16)

Nick experienced difficulties and challenges during his release and his attempts to participate in different societal and institutional arrangements. Nick described both his release in general and his entering school in this way:

> You wrap yourself up ... try not to enter the limelight ... you become extremely vulnerable when you get released ... because there is no defence at all.

I have already explained that Nick wanted both anonymity and the chance to tell his story in a way that offered a real insight into the challenges that face prisoners on leaving prison. Drawing on Ollman, I argued that contradictions emerged in Nick's stories and that it challenged Nick to handle the tension these contradictions caused. Eventually, this proved too much for Nick and he ended up breaking our contact, telling me that he felt he was getting too much attention. As Nick said he wanted to 'wrap himself up'; he felt vulnerable and lacked the means to defend himself. He did not want anybody to reveal any details about him or the manslaughter for which he had served time and he stated this on several occasions, reinforcing his sense of discomfort about what could happen, the possibility of others confronting him with his acts and showing their condemnation. The fear of stigmatization is clearly present, and as I discussed elsewhere (Mathiassen, 2009), Goffman's explanation of stigma suggests there is a process of self-stigmatization underpinning the tension when Nick oscillates between trying to participate in societal and social arrangements and retreating into isolation out of fear.

I interpret Nick's intentions and his feeling of being 'without defence' as closely linked to his attempts to approach and handle guilt and shame as 'his', to take ownership of his crime. Nick behaved in a seriously violent manner towards a young person in a period of his life characterized by substance abuse, personal and relational chaos, jealousy and stress. The young person died of the injuries and Nick, periodically, still seems desperate and unable to believe that he could have committed this serious crime. Therefore, I argue that he may still be going through the process of accepting the knowledge that he has killed a youngster, incorporating it into his self-understanding. In line with Farrant's (2014) points (and drawing on Heidegger), I argue that talking to me assisted the phenomenon to come to life, and Nick to come to life, too. This means that Nick is becoming conscious of the part of him that, under specific circumstances, lost control and beat up another human being so violently that the young person died of the injuries. Thus, the tension I mentioned above is not only one that has developed because of the societal condemnation and exclusion that permeates our relational and institutional arrangements, but also because of Nick's existential struggle. Other research, with and about people convicted of murder or manslaughter, describes similar struggles (Leer-Salvesen, 1991; Wright, Crewe & Hulley, 2017).

The Potentiality of Condemnation

When Nick told me about the reason for his incarceration, he repeatedly oscillated between consternation about what happened on the day of the assault, and a firm belief about it.

Int.:   You cannot help thinking about it?

Nick: It is present all the time. Because, just walking down the street, somebody might recognize you and shout: 'Wow, there he is, that monster'. Such thoughts are always present.

Int.:   Do they refer to the victim?

Nick: It is, well, ... acting the way I did. ... Right, which you can describe in so many ways, right? It is unbelievable, how could that happen? I have never understood how it could actually end that wrong. I have never been able to comprehend and possibly never will. We were so close ... so many positive experiences ... honestly I do not comprehend. ... how could I — that evening — explode so heavily? I do not ... because I had decided that everything should be okay.

Int.:   Nevertheless, it went completely wrong?

Nick: Yes, unbelievable.

Nick did not deny his acts but seemed to struggle with the fact that he actually did them, that within himself he had the capacity to lose control so thoroughly and with such devastating consequences. In a way, he exposed a contradiction and complexity through his story, one that revealed different sides of his self-understanding. Drawing on Tyler & Slater (2018), one could argue that the potentiality (Agamben, 1999) of condemnation, of stigma, which emerges in social settings as a relation, made Nick conceal parts of his story and parts of himself from others, and thereby the potentiality of stigma functioned as a form of power. In turn, this underlines the standpoint that stigma is more than a relational phenomenon which can be handled individually and discursively. Stigma has a social and political function as power, which Tyler and Slater (2018) argue is a form of governmentality (2018, p. 729).

Paradoxically, although Nick criticized it persistently, the prison possibly afforded protection and a bolster against both ordinary life in society and the condemnation and stigma beyond the prison walls. Once released, Nick was no longer one among several who had committed serious and violent criminal acts. In prison, everybody was serving time because they had done something that was socially unacceptable. They shared the ambition that after imprisonment and release they would be able to live a life without committing new criminal acts. When Nick entered the social scene outside prison, he lost the security that came with being among likeminded people, which, I argue, is a significant aspect of his feelings of vulnerability, of being 'without defence'. Nick, therefore, distanced himself from situations where other people could confront him with his past as a prisoner — his criminal act, but also with his present situation — his actual life in a halfway house.

In attempting to conceal his history and his current way of life, Nick also distanced himself from the potential benefits of social and institutional participation. Again, I noticed complex contradictions in Nick's story. He remained rather isolated because he feared what he was also longing for, namely social and interpersonal relations. As Nick said:

> Well, if you are part of a circle of friends you are a part of each other's life [...]. You might have a close friend with whom you share confidentiality. You trust each other. You have a mutual relationship. Here I am in no-man's land. The people I am around, they are in the same situation as I am. Additionally, the staff who are at work.

Nick explained several times that he longed for a confidential relationship and he speculated that I had a close friend whom I trusted. He longed to be part of a relationship like that but his sentence 'Here I am in no-man's land' shows that he is not achieving this, instead experiencing a sense of disconnection.

Returning again to the concept of potentiality (Agamben, 1999), one could argue that Nick was able to imagine what could happen in the social and relational sphere. He expected his classmates to condemn him, which would make him need protection. Therefore, he never invited anyone to engage in an open conversation but protected himself by never actively participating in the social life of the class. I understand this as his acting on the potentiality of condemnation, for when I asked Nick if anybody had commented on, or said anything in relation to, his incarceration and his crime of manslaughter, his answer was a definite 'no'. Thus, I believe that Nick's way of handling his life was influenced by self-stigmatization, according to Goffman's original understanding of stigma as relation.

It is not inconceivable that it might be possible to access some kind of social community after committing manslaughter. There may be ways to find and join groups; some form of social membership available for ex-offenders. Why then did Nick seem so resistant to engage in the potentiality of a social life instead of choosing isolation? We should consider if the social and political dimension of stigma, stigma as governmentality, could fully explain it. When Nick served time in the closed prison, he lived primarily on his own. He did not want to mingle with other prisoners. He seemed to understand himself as a 'different kind' compared to the other prisoners. He seemed to need distance, perhaps because he had not yet found it possible to 'take responsibility' for his act because he could not fully comprehend that he was able to harm a minor. Nick, it seems, experienced contradiction between his (ideal) self-understanding and the reality that he killed somebody. Thus it appears relevant to ask: what were the possibilities for him to take responsibility and still to be able to live within society?

Secrets and Shame

Nick saw an in-house psychologist once a week in prison. This consultation was intended to help him try to engage differently with life compared to the way he lived before his criminal act; to help him to come to terms with himself and his deed; and, finally, to provide assistance throughout the process of leaving prison. People who serve long sentences in this particular prison must agree to engage in psychological and/or psychiatric treatment so Nick experienced an element of pressure to participate in such treatment before he could hope for release.

Nick did not appear ready for 'group therapy' or other intrusions on his privacy, nevertheless it can be argued that individual psychotherapy may have contributed to his sense of secrecy and confusion as to whether his thoughts and feelings about his act should be kept private. Indeed, it can be argued that the praxis of privacy fuelled Nick's deliberate dissemblance and deception around who he was (and is) and what he did. This accords with criticism of the partial use of Goffman's concept of stigma, the dangers of 'schooling the stigmatized to better manage their stigmatized difference' (Tyler & Slater, 2018, p. 729) without acknowledging the individualizing and de-politicizing aspects.

Physical Reactions

A fter his release from prison, Nick felt increasingly sick. Nick described having pneumonia and depression, which he argued was an effect of his release.

Int.:   You were depressed?

Nick: Yes, I was! Bluntly speaking I was. Definitely! I cannot recall ever having been as far down as I have been during this. It really got me by surprise. I ask myself, 'why do I experience this'?

Int.:   And why is that so?

Nick: Well, according to other people that I have talked to, I am not a unique case. Many people who end up in ... who have been in a closed system and then suddenly get out ... in a halfway house or the like... they suddenly get ... they get a downturn...

Nick compared his situation to that of other ex-prisoners and thereby seemed to normalize his own reactions. He took a break from school and struggled to get well. The societal arrangements contributed to his unrest and restricted way of living during release. To some extent, the official system — the different social workers and the absence of cooperation between the prison and the halfway house — contributed to the problems that Nick faced.

According to Nick's account, there appears to have been a contradiction between the educational plans he made and visions he had in cooperation with the in-house prison social worker and the approach within the social-welfare system after he moved to the halfway house. He explained that the municipal social workers preferred to find him a job rather than support his educational project. He experienced his one conversation with a municipal social worker as a 'psychological test'. She posed 'a lot of stupid questions' and asked him whether he was intelligent. Nick described this as degrading and regretted that he had answered the questions at all.

When I listened to Nick's story, I got the impression that problems were caused by both system failure and a personal inability to handle the challenges. He was convinced that 'they' wanted him to work, but at the same time told me that the municipal social worker had agreed to support part of his elementary education begun in prison. The process and the situation were chaotic, with several different persons and institutions involved 'in him'. There seemed to be contradictory, perhaps even conflicting principles in the professional approaches to Nick's educational plans. Furthermore, he experienced a shift from the prison staff, whom he felt endorsed his plans and perspectives, to the municipal employees whom he felt to be in opposition to his wishes. Nick said that the new professionals pushed him too much:

> People do not see how difficult it is for me sometimes. [...] It might be positive that people push you but I do not feel ready yet. It is as if they reckon no matter what you touch you can do it.

Nick believed that he gave other people the impression that he was capable of more than he really was. He thought the picture they held of him contradicted his own experience of himself. Neither the expectations of the social workers, school and prison, nor the societal arrangements, corresponded with Nick's own. As I understood him, Nick saw this schism as feeding his sense of being unable to progress: 'I cannot fly to the moon', he told me towards the end of our contact. In other words, to describe participating in the planned education/ schooling as overwhelming would be an understatement. All the other pupils had a longer history at school and were acquainted with the rules and routines and engaged in the social life there; whereas for Nick the experience was one of being new, of being a stranger, of being insecure in all respects, in life *and* in school.

Listening to Nick's story, it seemed to me that the obvious solution would be to contact the social worker in prison because she best knew him and his 'case', but Nick refused. Nick felt that he should behave decently towards the social worker in the halfway house and wait for her to return from sick leave, even though the prison social worker might be able to help him immediately. This contradiction in Nick's story puzzled me. Why was he acting against his own interests with regard to education? Was he trying to nourish that part of his self-image that was compliant and decent? Could he do this in parallel with his despair over the way the social system was failing him?

Nick seemed to be experiencing a dilemma. How could he protect his own interests and at the same time acknowledge others' rights to conduct their own lives? One could argue that he was in a desperate social situation because the prison social worker, someone who could help him, was physically far away. Conversely, the halfway-house social worker was sick but close by, and he desperately needed an ally close by. He was also lonely and needing a friend. The powerful municipal social worker was available but paid little attention to his interests or wishes. Nick himself talked of a lack of understanding of his marginal and fragile position — and I believe that this, in association with his experience of the potentiality of condemnation and his tendency towards self-stigmatization, added to the sense of stigmatization, in Goffman's usage of the term. His sense of fragility confirmed his reservations about social engagement and encouraged his isolated and depressive ways of living and being. These processes were not separate, rather reciprocal and mutually reinforcing and, as already mentioned, became intertwined with the secrecy surrounding his criminal act.

To refer back to the 'what works' discussion earlier in the chapter, I had found evidence that rehabilitating the individual via programming and therapy alone is insufficient. Such an approach may even confuse as it both assists and stigmatizes the individual. Furthermore, as Nick's story illustrates, the societal and institutional conditions are crucially important in determining the success of an individual's route back into society.

Time Passed

S everal months had passed. Nick was still in the halfway house, and his longing for a real friend and for genuine social relations still troubled him as they did in the prison and on release. However, he had several times experienced that his classmates did not condemn him, and this seemed to assist him in adjusting to life outside of prison. Nonetheless, the challenges of release still dominated Nick's life story:

> I am not very positive towards the future. ... Damn — only problems... it feels like everything falls apart!

Nick still found it difficult to form relationships with other people and his negative expectations, informed by his earlier experiences, were still dominant. In Nick's opinion, the social services had collectively failed to understand his need for what I would characterize as 'a calm and secure zone of development'. He seemed to experience the normal school system as too demanding (and confronting?) to be able to participate in it. The distance between the secure and routinized life of the prison and the challenging and very different school life in everyday society seemed to be too testing for him during the process of transition. The contrasts and contradictions between prison and life outside seemed too encompassing.

Nick described a cessation in his progress towards a more liberated existence: 'It is disappointing that you do not get the things done. ... That you... you... know where you actually have the possibilities'. He considered returning to the type of job he had before incarceration and giving up school altogether.

Released

A year later Nick had moved to his own apartment. He received rehabilitation money to complete his education but in the same type of school he had attended several years earlier. Still he blamed the system for having failed him. He obtained advice from a psychologist with whom he met regularly and still had plans to attend university. He seemed to be moving towards learning to participate in social communities: 'I am too reserved... I do not direct myself towards participating in a social way in society', he said, with the aim of improving.

In our last conversation, Nick stated quite clearly that he might be able to influence his own conditions — his own development. Guided by Dreier (2008), I understand his purpose as slowly gaining a sense of control over his own conditions, for he described himself as becoming clearer when communicating his needs and interests rather than just being a victim or a prisoner in, and of, his own life. This was not just a personal decision but closely connected to his slowly changing living conditions and activities. His progress seemed to be supported by his increasingly settled educational route and the expansion of his economic space. When I talked to Nick several months after he ceased formal contact, he told me that he 'had done something concrete' to diminish his anxiety and shame. He told me that after this action, which had been 'tough', he felt 'relieved'. Nick did not want to elaborate on what he had done but regardless, 'this' also seemed to have supported his move toward a more liberated living and less incarcerated learning.

Leaving the Scene

N ick's life story demonstrated that time is an important factor following release after imprisonment for severe violent criminal acts. Using a life-story-oriented approach and getting close to the lived and living experiences of prisoners and ex-prisoners can reveal details of great importance to rehabilitation programmes. This is especially so when the research discovers contradictions and challenges and offers ways to make such dilemmas comprehensible. The forensic approach focusing on individual pathology is only one dimension of a complex task. Rehabilitation has to take place within restrictive societal and institutional arrangements that are heavily loaded with suppressive and productive power structures, and a framework of societal condemnation and exclusion of the wicked and unwanted.

It seems necessary to acknowledge the objective challenges that prisoners and ex-prisoners experience and to insist on a greater understanding of the insufficiency of handling the processes of stigma individually and socially. 'Today, I am back on the job market, and, without a license to practice law, still face rejection based upon my criminal record', writes the anonymous author (Anonymous & Dombrowski, 2010, p. 481). This quotation illustrates how, although an individual may do his or her utmost to participate in reintegrating themselves in society after imprisonment, social and societal conditions often create invincible obstacles for the individual who tries to become a citizen after doing a long stretch inside. I hope that Nick's life story will contribute to the dissemination of this insight by serving as more than an individualized story of disclosure. Rather, it offers a rigorous way to address both the individual and structural questions that are relevant to the lives of prisoners and ex-prisoners. Whilst I acknowledge that this is only one of several possible approaches — and indeed may be used in conjunction with some of the others — I believe that narrative accounts enable a deep questioning and interpretation of the reality of life after prison and therefore serve a useful purpose in developing our understanding of the needs of the ex-offender if he or she is to fully re-enter the community. Thus, it plays a role in supporting equality and diversity in everyday society.

References

Aaltonen, M., Skardhamar, T., Nilsson, A., Andersen, L.H., Bäckman, O., Estrada, F. & Danielsson, P. (2017). Comparing employment trajectories before and after first imprisonment in four Nordic Countries. *British Journal of Criminology*, 57: 828–47. https://doi.org/10.1093/bjc/azw026

Agamben, G. (1999). *Potentialities: Collected essays in philosophy*. Palo Alto, CA: Stanford University Press.

Anonymous & Dombrowski, K. (2010). Re-entry: A guide to success? *Dialectical Anthropology*, 34(4): 477–81.

Bauman, Z. (2003). *Wasted lives: Modernity and its outcasts*. Cambridge: Polity Press.

Bertelsen, P. (1994). *Tilværelsesprojektet det menneskeliges niveauer belyst i den terapeutiske proces*. København: Dansk Psykologisk Forlag.

Bhatti, G. (2010). Learning behind bars: Education in prisons. *Teaching and Teacher Education*, 26: 31–36.

Bosworth, M., Campbell, D., Demby, B., Ferranti, S.M. & Santos, M. (2005). Doing prison research: Views From inside. *Qualitative Inquiry*, 11(2): 249–64. https://doi.org/10.1177/1077800404273410

Bruner, J. (2004). Life as narrative. *Social Research*, 71(3): 691–710.

Brunton-Smith, I. & McCarthy, D.J. (2017). The effects of prisoner attachment to family on re-entry outcomes: A longitudinal assessment. *The British Journal of Criminology*, 57(2): 463–82. https://doi.org/10.1093/bjc/azv129

Cook, P., Kang, S., Braga. A.A., Ludwig, J, & O'Brien, M.E. (2015). An experimental evaluation of a comprehensive employment-oriented prisoner re-entry program. *Journal of Quantitative Criminology*, 31(3): 355–82. https://doi.org/10.1007/s10940-014-9242-5

Farrant, F. (2014). Unconcealment: What happens when we tell stories. *Qualitative Inquiry*, 20(4): 461–70. https://doi.org/10.1177/1077800413516271

Goffman, E. (1986/63). *Stigma. Notes on the management of spoiled identity*. New York: Simon & Shuster.

Hicks, J. (2004). Upon re-entry: Prison-based preparedness leads to community based success. *Corrections Today*, 66(6): 104–13.

Holzkamp, K. (2016). Conduct of everyday life as a basic concept of critical psychology. In: Scraube, E. & Højholt, C. (eds), *Psychology and the conduct of everyday life*. Hove, UK: Routledge.

Jewkes, Y. (2014). An introduction to 'doing prison research differently'. *Qualitative Inquiry*, 20(4): 387–91. https://doi.org/10.1177/1077800413515828

Keene, D.E., Smoyer, A.B. & Blankenship, K.M. (2018). Stigma, housing and identity after prison. *The Sociological Review Monographs*, 66(4): 799–815.

Leer-Salvesen, P. (1991). *Etter drabbet: samtaler om skyld og soning*. Oslo: Kimære.

Listwan, S.J., Sullivan, C.J., Agnew, Cullen, F.T. & Colvin, M. (2013). The pains of imprisonment revisited: The impact of strain on inmate recidivism. *Justice Quarterly*, 30(1): 144–68. https://doi.org/10.1080/07418825.2011.597772

Maruna, S. (2001). *Making good: How ex-convicts reform and rebuild their lives*. Washington, DC: American Psychological Association.

Mathiassen, C. (2009). Imprisoned in existence: A question of self-stigmatization? *Proceedings Volume*. Concord, ON: Captus Press.

Mathiassen, C. (2016). Nothingness: Imprisoned in existence — excluded from society. In: Bang; J. & Winter- Lindqvist, D. (eds), *Nothingness*. New Brunswick, NJ: Transaction Publishers.

Olesen, A. (2017). Released to the 'battlefield' of the Danish welfare state: A battle between support and personal responsibility. In: Scharff Smith, P. & Ugelvik, T. (eds) *Scandinavian penal history, culture and prison practice: Embraced by the welfare state?* Basingstoke: Palgrave Macmillan. https://doi.org/10.1057/978-1-137-58529-5

Ollman, B. (2015). Marxism and the philosophy of internal relations; or, how to replace the mysterious 'paradox' with 'contradictions' that can be studied and resolved. *Capital & Class*, 39(1): 7–23. https://doi.org/10.1177/0309816814564128

Parker, R. & Aggleton, P. (2003). HIV and AIDS-related stigma and discrimination: A conceptual framework and implications for action. *Social Science & Medicine*, 57: 13–24. https://doi.org/10.1016/S0277-9536(02)00304-0

Petersilia, J. (2003). *When prisoners come home: Parole and prisoner reentry*. Oxford: Oxford University Press.

Riggs, S. & Cook, C.L. (2015). The shadow of physical harm? Examining the Unique and Gendered Relationship Between Fear of Murder Versus Fear of Sexual Assault on Fear of Violent Crime. *Journal of Interpersonal Violence*, 30(14): 2383–409. https://doi.org/10.1177/0886260514553117

Scharff Smith, P. & Ugelvik, T. (eds) (2017). *Scandinavian penal history, culture and prison practice. Embraced by the welfare state?* Basingstoke: Palgrave Macmillan. https://doi.org/10.1057/978-1-137-58529-5

Schartmueller, D. (2018). How long is life? Comparing the processes of release for life-imprisoned offenders in Denmark, Finland, and Sweden. *European Journal on Criminal Policy and Research.* https://doi.org/10.1007/s10610-018-9388-z

Seigafo, S. (2017). Inmate's right to rehabilitation during incarceration: A critical analysis of the United States correctional system. *International Journal of Criminal Justice Sciences*, 12(2): 183–95. https://doi.org/10.5281/zenodo.1034656

Travis, J., Western, B. & Redburn, F.S. (2014). *The growth of incarceration in the United States: Exploring causes and consequences.* Washington, DC: National Academies Press.

Tyler, I. & Slater, T. (2018). Rethinking the sociology of stigma. *The Sociological Review Monographs*, 66(4): 721–43. https://doi.org/10.1177/0038026118777425

Wright, S., Crewe, B., & Hulley, S. (2017). Suppression, denial, sublimation: Defending against the initial pains of very long life sentences. *Theoretical Criminology*, 21(2): 225–46. https://doi.org/10.1177/1362480616643581

14. Inclusion and Exclusion in Colombian Education, Captured Through Life Stories

Miguel Alberto González González

Miguel Alberto González González reports on a narrative study of adult educators in Colombia that seeks their views of the dichotomies of inclusion/exclusion and diversity/homogeneity within their society and presents the evidence within a thematic analysis of key factors. The choice of subject and the commentary itself reveal the researcher's desire to take an emancipatory stance.

This chapter is drawn from part of a research project that took place between 2015 and 2016, which sought to investigate the diversity/homogeneity and inclusionary/exclusionary dichotomies within Colombian education. Colombia is a country where ethnic, environmental, and cultural diversity is manifest and it is just beginning to become aware of this. Hence, social exclusion is one of its greatest problems as legislation and many other alternative proposals are insufficient to address diversity and inclusion.

This leads us to ask ourselves: what are the factors underpinning inclusion and diversity in Colombia? They are partly consequences of internal wars, partly due to international pressures as global attitudes to the human condition are undergoing major realignments that are only just beginning to be understood in Colombian society. The saving grace is that these aspects of human life are already partially addressed through a superficial awareness that change must happen. However, the country faces significant difficulties in implementing change, as the government has neither the financial resources nor adequate infrastructure to work with, or change, inequalities in the distribution of wealth, or to support those who are economically marginalized within society and therefore facilitate greater inclusion.

Furthermore, education is the sector that best understands this great spectrum of diversity and inclusion, but there are not enough organizational and cognitive frameworks in place to confront either the chains of corruption or the relentless waves of internal violence that may never be entirely controlled or ended. In any case, it is necessary to move from an idea of diversity as a singular focused goal, towards an acceptance that diversity itself is complex, with its own diverse strands. We must likewise move away from a notion of inclusion as a unified concept towards an understanding that inclusion is multi-faceted. Hence, it is often more accurate to use these terms in the plural; within this text I discuss these strands further and intentionally refer to diversities, inclusions, exclusions and homogenizations on occasion.

Profound Interests

Given the powerful position of education, it cannot be isolated from the problem of addressing diversity; the more education is homogenized, the more diversity and plurality become hidden, with greater educational exclusion increasing the risk of segregation, and consequently, of real and symbolic violence. Having said that, the greatest challenge the country faces in the educational field is to make practical inroads into achieving authentic inclusion and diversity. To establish these notions as legal precepts or conceptual ideas is not enough; following the cessation of armed conflict it needs to be made manifest in civil practices.

When we consider the Colombian context, this raises many key questions we need to ask ourselves. What do we ask of diversity? What do we want to do with inclusion? What concerns us about homogenization? By what criteria do we understand exclusion? How useful is it to legislate for diversity and inclusion? These questions are not solved through theory alone; intuition and social practices may also offer some answers.

Moreover, the resurgence of right-wing religious and political groups, who are willing to sacrifice their lives to enforce their demands, emanates from an ill-executed diversity and from exclusionary, even humiliating, inclusion programs, even though politicians tell us the opposite. Without a doubt, it is the political field that carries the greatest responsibility when thinking about the diverse and diversity. As Hannah Arendt (2005, p. 93) points out there is diversity within political systems but individual differences are lost in the need to form alliances that can exert power:

> Politics deals with the coexistence and association of different men. Men organize themselves politically according to certain essential commonalities found within or abstracted from an absolute chaos of differences.

What she calls an 'absolute chaos of differences' involves disagreement, but not necessarily war as often happens in Colombia. We now know that the chaos of not understanding diversities — in this case, religious and ethical — has made us into agents of destruction, akin to predators in attacking those who are different. Colombian politicians need a better understanding of how to foster coexistence and association among their fellow citizens if the country is to serve the needs of all its people.

Methodology

This chapter is based on a qualitative research project, which, in the field, focused on the collection of the life histories of a number of Colombian academics. Since the data was collected as stories it was later subjected to narrative analysis following Polkinghorne's recommendations (Polkinghorne, 1995). Since it is based on life histories, the study sits within the world of philosophical interests and their variants: the interpretative tradition. As Bulloogh and Pinnegar (2001, p. 15) clarify (referring to Hamilton, 1998):

> Self-study researchers stand at the intersection of biography and history. The questions self-study researchers ask arise from concern about and interest in the interaction of the self-as-teacher-educator, in context, over time, with others whose interests represent a shared commitment to the development and nurturance of the young and the impact of that interaction on self and other.

This is where I stand, for life histories and self-reports are fundamental to the research process that made this text possible.

Narratives carry us into spatial, temporal, mental, formal and pragmatic dimensions. After addressing criticisms of its tentative nature, like Prince's (1982, p. 4) view that narrative is 'a hedging device, a way to avoid strong positions' (surely useful when dealing with volatile situations), Ryan (2007, p. 24) explores its semiotic status, claiming that:

> Most narratologists agree that narrative consists of material signs, the discourse, which convey a certain meaning (or content), the story, and fulfil a certain social function.

In this research, the social function is to recognize the theoretical and practical forms in which diversity, inclusion, exclusion and homogenization in Colombian education are activated.

A Brief Overview of Education in Colombia

B efore focusing on the research aims and findings, it may be beneficial to provide a broader view of the state of education in the country, as there have been considerable improvements since the movement toward peace began, fuelled since 2002 by a commitment to an 'education revolution'. An OECD report on the state of Antioquia (OECD, 2012) details both policy change and national statistics and those relating to university education are summarized here. Constitutionally, the country provides free compulsory education from 5–15 and since 2012 it has been free through to grade 11, the final year, removing a significant early barrier to university entrance except that substantial numbers of students drop out before they reach, or during, grade 11. In 2010, the Colombian population included 8,442,000 young people aged 15–24 but 15.2% of these had not completed secondary education and were no longer studying, 27.1% were still in secondary education, and 23.8% had left school without enrolling in tertiary education. Only 2% entered and graduated at the tertiary level, a very low figure indeed. Scores are rising in international assessment tests — but is this enough?

Tertiary education is considered a 'cultural public service, inherent to the social ends of the state' (OECD, 2012, p. 161) regulated by Law 30 (1992) and can be undertaken in universities, university institutions, institutes of technology and specialized professional technical institutions. Colombia therefore offers a variety of different types of provision with varying levels of state control, as is often the case elsewhere. To address the length of time that students take to complete degrees, as well as poor retention rates, the State is making resources and support available in the form of loans to those in financial difficulty, and regional projects to provide tutoring and tracking. Perhaps more relevant to this study, however, is to note the 2011 proposals to reform Law 30, to introduce a 'stronger quality assurance system' and 'expand capacity and efficiency' (OECD, 2012, p. 91), effectively to privatize education. These reforms led to extensive, non-violent — and successful — student protest throughout 2012 (Vamoscaminando, 2012) and were withdrawn. However, Law 1740, adopted in December 2014, was set to bring in change, raising new concerns at the start of our research process and making me even more determined to document the situation before change occurred again. Now, to the research itself.[1]

Findings from the Research

T urning to the research data, the intention is to present a thematic analysis to consider the homogeneity-diversity and inclusion-exclusion processes, in part to examine how the dichotomies work against each other. Thus, we look at each dichotomy and subsequently at the practices that support or exemplify each element, drawing upon relevant literature and research data to support many of the points.

Homogenizations-Diversities in Colombian Education

T here is nothing more paradoxical than investigating homogenizations and diversities in Colombian education; the discourse is often contradictory and views forcefully expressed.

> They want us to homogenize and suppress diversity through globalizing exercises, to adjust to PISA tests; that is homogenization

says a teacher from Cartago (Colombia). This teacher's deepest complaint relates to the dominant focus on good results in international

---

1   The author has translated text from Spanish to English.

testing: it is as if they only prepare students to perform to these standards, rather than for life itself. As another professor from Armenia (Colombia) states:

> Here, rules are made for curriculum frameworks; teachers have to conform to the national standards provisions that are responses to international impositions, and every time, there is less autonomy for the country and schools.

Another teacher speaks more strongly:

> Educational leaders talk about inclusion because they accept children and young people into institutions, but they forget that there are no spatial adaptations to shelter them or even a school restaurant in operation.

And this inadequate provision is further exemplified by another teacher, who explains:

> The State speaks about educational inclusion, but it is rhetorical; a very high percentage of high school graduates cannot access higher education because of a real lack of offer. Is that inclusion and respecting diversity? Or is it selling false truths?

We have scandalous data when we study the different uptake of tertiary education across different socio-economic groups. In 2011, fifty-three per cent of young people from the country's richest quintile went into higher education compared to just nine per cent of those in the poorest quintile (OECD, 2016). What kind of inclusion does that represent for Colombian high-schoolers?

Equality of opportunity is so poor in Columbia that it can almost be deemed unsuccessful; however, similar problems occur across the globe, some more extreme, some less so, for inequality seems to affect nearly the entire human race. In a detailed critique of the American Coleman report, *Equality of Educational Opportunity* of 1966, Bowles and Levin (1968, p. 23) pointed out over fifty years ago how issues of equality are 'some of the most difficult questions that our society faces' and this claim was still relevant in 2017; progress is very slow.

Some homogenizations may surprise us, but they are practised within Colombian academic life every day. The difficulties, when thinking about diversity, are: first, to establish what is different, and in the first instance, is this something important; and in the second instance, to understand what is deficient, as we often fail to notice situations others encounter. We also position diversity as external, often believing, as Skliar (2002, p. 20) claims, that: 'Diversity is not us: it is the others'. It is as if, when we value the diverse, we apply it beyond ourselves, seeing it as 'other'. This distancing makes it easy for us to talk about diversity, but to act in ways that encourage homogenization. One of the teachers' comments reflect this clearly:

> We ask students to adapt to the institution, the teachers, and the academic demands, and we ask everyone for flexibility. And I, as an educating subject, am I flexible?

Homogenizations

When homogenization is applied to the social sciences, in this case, to education, there is a kind of imposition; we implement a variety of methodologies to establish unifying criteria in a group of people. This makes it easier for the institutional control of systems, and, in this sense, education promotes homogenizations in the curriculum: similarity of spaces (identical classrooms), schedules, uniforms for schoolchildren, legislation, evaluations, speeches, arrival times, and, in stressing accreditation as a goal, the need to get a diploma. In general, we can find temporal, spatial, and socio-cultural homogenizations.

A unified curriculum: The emergence of an inclusive curriculum is of concern in every context. As UNGEI (2010, p. 17) suggests, we should continually ask ourselves:

> Is the curriculum sensitive to gender, cultural identity, and diversity? Review the curriculum to identify selected equity and inclusion issues such as gender and ethnic stereotyping.

To set formal curricula is a recent initiative in Colombia. We are inexperienced and have sought to establish a universal treatment believing that if everybody studies within the same conditions, we can hypothesize that they are included.

> Why should I lie? Here in the university and in the school where I perform, students must accept a curriculum imposed on them, we include them in compulsory programs, whilst they almost have no freedom to choose,

explains a teacher in Armenia (Colombia). According to her story, we find an intolerant curriculum, a curriculum of conformity.

Similar spaces: Classrooms are similar in all the educational facilities; any differences are not very significant. Over time, variations may be introduced, but nevertheless, the spatial design is often repeated and fatiguing to work in. There is little creativity in classroom design in Colombia, and as we progress through the educational hierarchy, the spaces become less generous:

> Students usually refer to university classrooms as cages; that can tell us how boring they are,

says a professor from Pereira. Students are going from a classroom to a cage; what logic of space organization underlies such a trend?

The same schedule: In primary and secondary schools the typical day stretches from 7am to 12pm and from 12pm to 6pm. In some cases, there is a continuous school day, i.e., the hours are extended from 8am to 5pm without any improvements in the restaurants, libraries and sports venues. As for university training, the scheduling is deplorable; the distribution of lectures requires the student to be on campus the whole day, thereby foregoing any job opportunities.

> Students must bear with up to six hours between one seminar and the next one. It is typical in a Colombian university to abuse students' time, which for sure neither facilitates spaces for work, nor improves the unemployment rates,

says a professor from Manizales (Colombia).

Uniforms for schoolchildren: Many training institutions, both private and public, have uniforms for their primary and secondary students. Even in some universities, there are uniforms for certain academic programmes such as psychology or medicine:

> In my school we wear blue pants and a white shirt, and for P.E. we wear blue entirely,

says a high school principal, then clarifies:

> I think they can be oppressive, however, there are very poor students who, if it weren't for this uniform, they would've had a very bad time

with their peers just because of not having a variety of clothing or certain brands.

Educational legislation: There is universal legislation for education, so although each school can organize its own Individual Educational Plan, the freedom to do this is constrained by the bodies that control education. As a teacher from Manizales explains:

> My school has a fantastic IEP, we have developed it with the intervention of teachers, parents, students, and the community; now, what we don't have, is enough financial resources to deploy it.

Identical methods of evaluation for both men and women: A schoolteacher says:

> I'm not sure whether women learn differently from men, but it's true that many women under pressure start crying and men are ready to perform.

This is not unique to Colombia, according to the European Commission (2010, p. 12):

> It seems that important efforts are being made to integrate gender and gender equality as themes or cross-cutting elements in the school curricula in the European countries.

Yet there are very detailed brain studies that make it clear that the functioning of male and female brains *is* different. Isn't it about time to reconsider whether generalized and generalizing evaluations have validity?

These are just some of the elements that promote homogenization; students lining up to study like shoppers queuing to find bargains to save money; and teachers need to be mindful of these elements when thinking about diversities and inclusions, when meeting with students. The 'shopping centers' that so many educational institutions are operating as, seem to be the new concentration camps, the new sites for homogenization (González, 2016a).

It is necessary, too, to re-examine how our teachers are being trained, i.e., some receive no training, no updates on diversity and equality, not even any information about inclusive education:

> Here we are brought children with difficulties and we are not prepared so that we can attend to them, but the Ministry homogenizes and imposes its forced inclusion criteria,

says a teacher. She also emphasizes the insufficiency of teacher training
to show would-be teachers how to attend to young people and help
them to solve their problems, as many of them are suffering from social
problems that the state fails to address; problems that require joined-up
action, but only get isolated responses.

Diversities

D iversity appears in many organizational forms, which correspond
to the biological, sensorial, cultural and social as well as to diversity
of expression. As an example, cultural diversity alone can comprise
religious, ideological, linguistic, political, legal, and ethical aspects;
gastronomic diversity; aesthetic diversity within literature, music,
architecture, painting, sculpture, and movies; diversity of language,
knowledge, and wisdom (González, 2016b).

Cultural diversity has only been addressed in legal terms since the
Universal Declaration on Cultural Diversity was adopted in Paris in 2005.
This helps to explain why thinking about diversities in terms of what
makes sense and what scope there is for action is socially immature;
hence the difficulties and the limited socio-political initiatives to clarify
this.

Authentic diversity seeks to empower the subject (in this case the
student), enabling him/her to know how s/he is now, and how s/he
feels today:

> Some students enter school having many learning difficulties, and very
> few teachers are interested in knowing what's going on; also the content
> flows over the subject,

says a professor from Armenia (Colombia), raising another question:
what sort of diversity do we teach if we have forgotten the student? As
explained in González (2015a, p. 66): a diversity that is 'more human,
closer, and less humiliating' is important, as he who is humiliated will
be ready to humiliate; misdirected frustration leads to paths of violence.

Exclusions-Inclusions in Colombian Education

I n many public sectors, and especially in education, efforts have been
made to draw attention to extreme forms of exclusion, but in some

cases, policies fail to clarify the distinctions between inclusion, exclusion, and integration, which makes it difficult to improve practice. Berruezo (2006, p. 182) explains that:

> The term inclusion is opposed to exclusion, just as that of integration is opposed to segregation. Perhaps the difference between integration and inclusion is a matter of nuances, but although school integration meant the incorporation of all people into the education system, inclusion requires that within that system, they are treated as subjects with full rights.

The reality is that a person or social group can be included, but not integrated, that is, not enabled to feel part of something bigger, their needs not recognized in the policies that call for their inclusion.

Exclusions

Unresolved symptoms of exclusion hide beneath the surface of life. As Tezanos states (1999, p. 12): 'Social exclusion implies, at its root, a certain dual image of society, in which there is an integrated sector, and an excluded one'. In Colombia, there are complete communities that have been excluded and forgotten by the state; some groups that — in this, the twenty-first century — are only just beginning to be provided with basic public services and a rudimentary system of justice. In education, at least, there has been progress to ensure free primary and secondary schooling and the institutions to support this.

Racial factors: Racial characteristics refer to physical differences, like skin colour, eyes, body shape. In Colombia, as elsewhere, there are many students who are discriminated against, and effectively excluded due to their skin colour or style of hair, because they do not resemble those of the teacher or the group in general.

Ethnic factors: Ethnicity refers to customs and the cultural environment. Although stereotypes around ethnicity are contested (Telles & Bailey, 2013), some believe that Black and Indigenous Peoples are more careless, less motivated, and that therefore, the responsibility for their poverty lies in their own abandonment.

> In my university we know that Blacks [sic] are happy at parties and
> care little to progress, to improve the conditions of their communities;
> Indigenous people are intelligent, but shy and usually retire having only
> reached mid-career status; these and other conditions mean that they are
> excluded by their racial status,

explains a professor from Armenia. In making such claims, he is creating
a symbolic space to abandon working with certain groups because of
their racial status. This is nothing more than exclusion, and there is
some evidence (albeit in a study of Peru) that such prejudices may be
more marked among intellectuals, some of whom appear to despise
mestizaje (miscegenation), while among the working classes it can be
deemed 'empowering' (De la Cadena, 2005, p. 23; in Telles & Bailey,
2013, p. 1590).

Economic factors: Education is also classified as public and private, and
only those who have the economic capacity to do so can access the latter:

> Private education can afford better teachers, and almost always better
> wages; that is where young people who do not do well in public
> education gain access; they're expensive, not everyone can study there,
> not even many teachers' children,

explains a teacher from Armenia (Colombia).

Political factors: This is where Colombia, although a single country,
turns into many countries. Although there are two major political
groupings, liberal and conservative, their leadership is dynastic. In a
process of family succession, the children of elected presidents take
office themselves.

Exclusion happens when someone is excluded or silenced because
their views don't match those of the powerful. Educators often retain
beliefs about the best ways to teach, regardless of whether these suit the
students they are teaching. Reflecting on her own education, a teacher
explains how:

> As a student, I suffered from discrimination, that is, exclusion, because I
> didn't agree with my English teacher, with her teaching methodology. I
> got expelled from the course and I failed it; there was another classmate
> who was treated the same, but in maths.

If such abuses are evident within the discourse around language and mathematics teaching, does this not suggest similar, even more dangerous discourses around racial, political or religious differences?

Lack of innovation: Students or teachers who are not innovative are usually excluded or moved elsewhere. The most dramatic twenty-first-century demand is for innovation and creativity; this is what Nussbaum (2010, p. 53) refers to when she states that:

> A second issue in business is innovation, and there are reasons to suppose that liberal arts education strengthens the skills of imagining and independent thinking that are crucial to maintaining a successful culture of innovation.

However, that which appears a virtue ends up being a problem, one that has invaded education at all levels, leading to the exclusion of those who are supposedly neither innovative nor creative.

Quotas in educational institutions: Exclusion is not only enacted through admission policies, it is also present in application processes for maintenance, subsistence, transport, and other funding support that poorer students need to access and to stay in education. Colombia reflects the Latin American stereotype, as Hevia (2005, p. 2) shows:

> The marginalized population groups' schooling levels are lower than the national averages, and in terms of schooling and literacy inequalities are perceived between rural and urban areas, among the populations with higher and lower percentages of Indigenous people, among Black and White people, among men and women.

Forced displacement: Statistics on forced migration published by the United Nations (UNHCR, 2016) make chilling reading, and Colombia is mentioned specifically.

The study found that three countries produce half of the world's refugee population. Syria, with 4.9 million people; Afghanistan, with 2.7 million and Somalia, with 1.1 million, have expelled more than half of the refugees who are under UNHCR's mandate worldwide. On the other side, Colombia, with 6.9 million people; Syria with 6.6 million, and Iraq, with 4.4 million, are those with the largest populations of internally displaced people.

When families are displaced, children and school-aged children are the most affected. As a school principal says:

> I've had some students, many of whom are displaced; that's painful, one doesn't know how to face their physical needs and their psychological problems, and although we have some support, it is insufficient.

Corruption: Perhaps one of the most dramatic ways to exclude in Colombia is corruption. The number of minor victims of corruption is unbearable. We read in *El Heraldo* (2016): 'With these two new victims, the number of children who died this year of the same causes is 83'. Surely, a country that, as a consequence of corruption, leaves its children to die, is a country without a conscience? Why then, should it be interested in developing the potential of its people? For what would it be educating them?

Envy: Envy is one of those emotions that leads us to places of tyranny towards the other. 'There is a lot of envy among the students and, of course, among the teachers,' writes a teacher. Envy usually happens among the students; whatever their age or class, they exclude a partner from play or an academic activity because they are envious of this student. Professors, too, sometimes express envy, due to differential treatment or salary disparity between the different teacher ranks.

Hatred: In the world in general, hatred seems to be something that has been inculcated, but in Colombia it seems to be a deep-seated part of everyday life.

Disgust: This human reaction is quite frequently seen in Colombian educational establishments, leaving a child out of a group because of their physical appearance, their odour or their secretions.

Fear: In a country that has experienced such widespread warfare, it is understandable that individuals, families or social group are excluded out of fear. Society is wary if your past is unknown, and for many displaced students this wariness is something they encounter daily.

Low academic performance: Students with learning difficulties and those reluctant to learn are often excluded from many activities; they are often the first to be excluded when prizes are to be distributed.

Negligence: Negligence, from those obliged to act and those expected to demand their rights, can both lead to exclusion.

Trends to assess students and classify them are clearly forms of exclusion. Categorizing students as normal-abnormal, committed-noncommitted, studious-neglectful disenfranchises many. So we have seen how exclusion can be spatial and/or temporal, due to silent or radical behaviour, by rank or social position, and enacted through the imposition of seemingly universal schedules in education.

Inclusions

I s inclusion a matter of equality and equity? What are the factors that create inclusion? As Rosano (2008, p. 57, author's translation) explains, 'inclusive education is constituted as the right to equal recognition and a similar quality of education for all, and values the different views of girls and boys'. Yet if recognition is precarious, if recognition is unknowing, it can slide into exclusions and forgetfulness. Nominal inclusion can have the opposite effect when it removes flexibility.

Legislation and inclusion: To be able to unify and include by means of laws, national decrees or local norms is to hold a stake in one the most powerful positions there is. But such actions need to be approached with care, as the outcomes may be problematic, causing 'complications'. As an executive in Manizales (Colombia) points out:

> Here we have a complication: it is mandatory that institutions accept students with different psychological and physical difficulties, alongside those who do not have them, and in the same classrooms.

Inclusion through academic schedule: In theory everybody fits equally into an academic schedule but these unify time and place but not reality.

> We are all assigned the same hours, regardless of whether we have other difficulties or not, they include us without being asked, in the institutionalized agendas,

says a professor. The schedule is modern society's great invention. It programmes and wedges people into time slots, shoehorns society into corners, because time costs money (González, 2015b). Remember that a schedule unifies times and spaces for both students and teachers.

Evaluative inclusions: There are so many criticisms of evaluation that adding another one almost sends us into orbit. Nevertheless, many evaluative traditions are a means to exclude as they do not always even measure knowledge, but rather each teacher's own interests or the external intentions set for international measurement systems.

> To pose a single question, create a questionnaire for all, is to exclude many learning forms, and especially, it facilitates the teacher's path because he does not need to devote much time on grading, which is confused with evaluation,

explains a university executive in Pereira (Colombia).

Forced inclusion: 'The way in which the groups are integrated in the classroom does not reflect students wishes, but [panders] to some people's whim or to computer distribution software', reiterates a teacher in Manizales (Colombia). This is a clear example that inclusion in a particular study group is not voluntary, but forced; there have been known cases where it is mandatory to attend a religious rite, a cultural act, or a sporting event, contradicting what Giné (1998, p. 40) states when he insists that inclusion:

> ...is fundamentally to do with the fact that all students are accepted, recognized in their singularity, valued and able to participate in school according to their capabilities. An inclusive school is, therefore, one that is offering all its students the educational opportunities and the necessary support (curricular, personal, material) for their academic and personal progress. (Author's translation)

Forced inclusion is evident when a student is forced to join a work group and to converse with a group of peers; but it is also present when a group of professors have to accept public policies that they do not like.

In Colombia, the population is classified by social strata from one to six. The estates one to three are those with economic difficulties who constantly struggle to survive, while strata four to six have to pay higher taxes to finance the public services provided to the others. As a consequence, some people are reluctant to admit their social stratum. Although this is a form of inclusion with worthy political and social ends, this is forced. People have no choice and cannot opt out.

Shame: This is the reaction of certain social groups or economic powers when, harassed by the press or another social group, they decide to include others not through conviction but through shame, to avoid further criticism.

Human sympathy: This is an example of authentic inclusion, inclusion arising from a deep interest in belonging and to helping the 'other' to be recognized. In Colombian education, cases are known of people including students by helping them to acquire school supplies, food and transport out of human sympathy rather than convenience.

Social justice: This occurs when, convinced that there are people and social groups who are disadvantaged because of their geographical location or for cultural reasons, decisions are taken to make programmes of social inclusion. Such an act of justice is a type of response toward the improvement of the 'other'.

Environmental relevance: In the face of environmental threats, excluded social groups may be invited to participate in projects to protect or improve environmental conditions and this is also a form of inclusion.

Redistribution of economic resources: Although this is a fairly recent global development, there are philanthropic billionaires making decisions to redistribute their profits to benefit vulnerable social groups, and already there are some examples in Colombia. Many peasants now own land they can cultivate. For example, in 2014, Law 1728, 'Norms for the distribution of vacant land to poor families for social and productive purposes', enabled a small-scale, but significant, redistribution of economic resources.

Academic achievement: Following the myth of Pygmalion, teachers often more readily institute extracurricular activities for students with good academic performance.

Compassion: There are many ways to feel pity and compassion, and such inclusion was evident in the data. 'I accepted a child who did not know anything about maths because it hurt me' [not to help him], explained a teacher from Cartago, Valle del Cauca, Colombia.

Guilt: Carelessness in carrying out an activity can create critical situations or difficulties for other people, and there are cases where this leads to the inclusion of certain social groups not as a political option but to assuage guilt.

Inclusion in the education system requires this to be accepted across the board, but in the first instance by the teachers, the ones who have to live with it. There is no doubt that 'if teachers do not have a positive attitude towards educational inclusion, it is very difficult, if not impossible' (author's translation of Cedeño, 2006, p. 7). A teacher can obey an academic order or adhere to politically or culturally forced inclusion, but they can also include people through consensus, following the lead of the individuals to be included, respecting their wishes.

From a linguistic ideal, it is a challenge to get closer to what is being asked, for example, as the UN (2008, p. 5) states:

> An inclusive school is one that has no selection mechanisms or discrimination of any kind, and which shapes its functioning and pedagogical plans to integrate students' diversity, thus, favouring social cohesion, which is one of the purposes of education. (Author's translation)

To be truly inclusive, schools require an educational system that abandons selection and is open to the local community. They need to play a formative rather than an evaluative role in children's education. In what way and when will we understand this in Colombia?

Some Alternatives for Thinking About Diversities and Inclusions in Education

Among the many options offered by teachers to promote inclusions and diversities are: redirecting economic resources, advanced teacher training, controlling corruption, abandoning political radicalisms, enhancing the ideals of democracy, and giving a central place to aesthetics.

Teachers must insist on restoring horizontal communication to address diversity and inclusion. NCSE (2011, p. 28) states that:

Communication in the school community is conducted in modes, language and format(s) appropriate to the requirements of pupils with special educational need and their parents/guardians.

Teachers should emphasize the necessity for having a greater knowledge of the local, national, and global socio-cultural realities. This makes demands on teachers to read more widely and to find openings that respect differences without meddling with universal discourses, as Frederickson and Cline (2002, p. 32) claim:

Ethnic and cultural differences represent important dimensions of diversity along which differences in the ways individuals interpret their worlds may be identified and environmental influences may vary.

Teachers need to recognize that the basic principles of diversity centre on having the same opportunities within difference, living together rather than competing, freeing rather than controlling, building confidence against overconfidence, and restoring empathy.

Conclusions

Inclusiveness and diversity, however unlikely it seems, appear to make many people nervous, including teachers:

...until they were asked, the professors were not aware of the fact that they had been feeling fear. They recognize that fear is a lifestyle and therefore, they not only teach it but also generate and manage it. (González 2014, p. 355)

Diversities and inclusions are quite vulnerable. Whose project is inclusion and diversity? Which powers benefit from convincing us to be plural, diverse and inclusive? To face these questions about diversity requires conscious thought in order not to subject others to someone else's personal criteria; not to humiliate others when they do not wish to be included, or to place ourselves beyond the languages of power that insist on diversity. Gimeno (1999, p. 2) states that:

Diversity (and also inequality) are normal manifestations among human beings, even of social facts, of cultures, and in individuals' responses to classroom education. (Author's translation)

Diversity may be more or less visible, but it is as normal as life itself, and you have to get used to living with it and working within it. Teachers, executives, and administrative staff need to know more about others who are different: Why do we want to change the other?

We have media powers that tell us where, when, and what to want, how to dress, what to study, what to read, who to hate; therefore, even, what to think.

The gaps between 'what it is', 'what it should be', and 'what it must be', are more visible in countries with wars, with corruption, with insufficient norms that protect the underprivileged. Indeed, when we look at the diversities/homogenizations, at the inclusions/exclusions, we find what seems to be an insurmountable distance between the concrete and the abstract, between the first economic world countries and the rest. Whatever options are chosen among the many put forward to improve attitudes and action around inclusion and diversity — all of them with a unique north — the human being is to be projected as an end, never as a means.

References

Arendt, H. (2005). *The promise of politics*. New York: Shocken Books.

Bulloogh, R. & Pinnegar, S. (2001). Guidelines for quality in autobiographical forms of self-study. *Educational Researcher*, 30(3): 13–21. https://doi.org/10.3102/0013189X030003013

Berruezo, P. (2006). Educación inclusiva en las escuelas canadienses. Una mirada desde la perspectiva española. *Revista Interuniversitaria de Formación del Profesorado*, 20(2): 179–207.

Bowles, S. & Levin, H.M. (1968). The determinants of scholastic achievement: An appraisal of some recent evidence. *The Journal of Human Resources*, 3(1): 3–24.

Cedeño, F. (2006). *Congreso Internacional de Discapacidad en Medellín*. http://www.mineducacion.gov.co

Comisión Europea (2010). *Diferencias de género en los resultados educativos: Medidas adoptadas y situación actual en Europa*. Agencia Ejecutiva en Ámbito Educativo, Audiovisual y Cultural, Bruselas. https://doi.org/10.2797/48598

De la Cadena, M. (2005). Are Mestizos hybrids? The conceptual politics of Andean identities. *Journal of Latin American Studies*, 37: 259–84. https://doi.org/10.1017/S0022216X05009004

El Heraldo (2016). *En la Guajira otros dos niños muertos.* http://www.elheraldo.co/la-guajira/otros-dos-ninos-muertos-por-desnutricion-en-la-guajira-311170

Frederickson, N. & Cline, T. (2002). *Special education needs inclusion and diversity.* Buckingham: Open University Press.

Gimeno S.J. (1999). La construcción del discurso acerca de la diversidad y sus prácticas. *Aula de Innovación Educativa,* 82: 73–78.

Giné, C. (1998). ¿Hacia dónde va la integración? *Cuadernos de Pedagogía,* 269: 40–45.

González, G., M.A. (2014). Metáforas y paradojas de los miedos en los sujetos docentes. Revista Latinoamericana de Ciencias Sociales. *Niñez y Juventud,* 12(1): 355–70. https://doi.org/10.11600/1692715x.12121052013

González, G., M.A. (2015a). Learning in violent contexts. Dialogues war. *Global Journal for Research Analysis,* 4(3): 60–67.

González, G., M.A. (2015b). *Tiempos intoxicados en sociedades agendas. Sospechar un poco del tiempo educativo.* Bogotá: Ediciones desde Abajo.

González, G., M.A. (2016a). *Un preludio de sorderas.* Bogotá: Oveja Negra.

González, G., M.A. (2016b). *Aprender a vivir juntos. Lenguajes para pensar diversidades e inclusions.* Buenos Aires: Noveduc.

Hevia, R. (2005). *Politicas educativas en atención a la diversidad cultural, Brasil, Chile, Colombia, México y Perú.* Santiago de Chile: UNESCO.

Ley 1728 (2014). *Normas de distribución de terrenos baldíos a familias pobres con fines sociales y productivos.* Bogotá: Agencia Prensa Rural.

NCSE (National Council for Special Education) (2011). *Inclusive education framework: A guide for schools on the inclusion of pupils with special educational needs.* http://ncse.ie/publications-overview

Nussbaum, M. (2004). *Hiding from humanity: Disgust, shame, and the law.* New Jersey: Princeton University Press.

Nussbaum, M. (2010). *Not for profit.* New Jersey: Princeton University Press.

OECD (2012). *Antioquia, Colombia: OECD Review of higher education in regional and city development.* Paris: OECD Publishing. http://www.oecd.org/education/Antioquia.pdf

OECD (2016). *Education in Colombia, Reviews of National Policies for Education.* Paris: OECD Publishing. https://www.oecd-ilibrary.org/education/education-in-colombia_9789264250604-en

Polkinghorne, D.E. (1995). Narrative configuration in qualitative analysis. *International Journal of Qualitative Studies in Education,* 8(1): 5–23

Prince, G. (1982). *Narratology: The form and functioning of narrative.* Berlin: Mouton.

Rosano, S. (2008). *El camino de la inclusión educativa en punta hacienda (comunidad campesina de la sierra andina ecuatoriana)*. http://dspace.unia.es/bitstream/handle/10334/34/0050_Rosano.pdf

Ryan, M.L. (2007). Toward a definition of narrative, In: Herman, D. (ed), *The Cambridge Companion to Narrative*. Cambridge: Cambridge University Press.

Skliar, C. (2002). *¿Y si el otro no estuviera ahí? Notas para una pedagogía (improbable) de la diferencia*. Buenos Aires: Miño y Dávila.

Telles, E. & Bailey, S. (2013). Understanding Latin American Beliefs about Racial Inequality. *American Journal of Sociology*, 118(6): 1559–95. https://doi.org/10.1086/670268

Tezanos, J.F. (1999). *Tendencias en desigualdad y exclusión social*. Madrid: Editorial Fundación Sistema.

UN (or Organización de la Naciones Unidas para la Educación, la Ciencia y la Cultura) (2008). *La educación inclusiva: el camino hacia el futuro, una breve mirada a los temas de educación inclusiva: aportes a las discusiones de los talleres*. http://www.ibe.unesco.org/fileadmin/user_upload/Policy_Dialogue/48th_ICE/CONFINTED_48_Inf_2__Spanish.pdf

UNGEI (2010). *Equity and inclusion in education*. Washington: World Bank. http://www.ungei.org/resources/files/Equity_and_Inclusion_Guide.pdf

UNHCR (or ACNUR) (2016). *El desplazmiento forzado en el mundo*. http://www.acnur.org/noticias/noticia/el-desplazamiento-forzado-en-el-mundo-bate-su-cifra-record/one

Vamoscaminando (2012). *Colombia: Students organize against Law 30*. https://vamoscaminando.wordpress.com/2012/01/04/colombia-students-organize-against-law-30/

15. Navigating Grades *and* Learning in the Swedish Upper Secondary School Where Neoliberal Values Prevail

Patric Wallin

Patric Wallin's research in a Swedish secondary school context explores the problem that conflicting paradigms (neoliberalism and student-centred learning) cause students. They need guidance as they want high grades for university entrance but avoid asking teachers for help for fear that they may appear less competent. Paradoxically, students develop mutual support strategies that counterbalance the competitive individualism engendered by neoliberal practices.

This chapter examines the practices through which a cohort of Swedish upper-secondary pupils manage their learning processes to avoid the possibility of their teachers doubting their study abilities. It explains how, in contemporary Sweden, a country where the outlook is increasingly neoliberal, university places are competitively awarded, creating concern among students that asking for support might mark them as unsuitable for university entrance. The research uses in-class observations and focus-group interviews to establish how two classes of students actually manage this dilemma and finds an interesting paradox — that the student practices potentially create both negative and positive consequences for their success. By seeking teacher approval rather than teacher assistance they cut themselves off

https://doi.org/10.11647/OBP.0203.15

from an established effective form of academic support, but by turning to their own resources and discussing their studies with their fellow students, they improve their capacity to learn independently and work in a group of peers, important skills for higher-level study and for working life. Thus, the competitive practices common in neoliberal economies actually encourage the students to work cooperatively even as they strive to attain the high levels of success needed to guarantee a place in a prestigious university, at least in the context of natural science education, when carrying out laboratory work within the discipline of chemistry. This study is limited in scope in terms of subject coverage, but this context was chosen because the more practical format of such work offers opportunities to observe students learning though action rather than see them being taught didactically and thereby makes student-teacher interaction an option rather than a prerequisite.

The Broader Context of the Research

I n response to a rise in neoliberal ideology and practices, educational landscapes all over the world have changed in profound ways during the last few decades (Connell, 2013). The influence of markets and businesses on education has greatly changed the language used in education, and as Giroux (2002, p. 426) pointed out 'one consequence is that civic discourse has given way to the language of commercialism, privatization, and deregulation.' It is through the emphasis on the free market and market-driven agendas that neoliberalism reshapes education, with the aim to increase its efficiency and promote individualism, competition, and consumption in society (Harvey, 2005). In Scandinavia, these changes are particularly present in upper-secondary and higher education. As in other western cultures, examples of this in the higher-education sector include the conceptualization of students as consumers (Molesworth et al, 2009), the increasing importance of rankings (Hazelkorn, 2011) and the emphasis on university branding (Chapleo, 2011). These changes, together with the high number of students applying for higher education, have strongly affected university admission processes.

In order to be admitted to a higher-education institution in Sweden, one first needs to fulfil the general requirements by completing upper-secondary school with a certain number of pass grades, and secondly to go through a selection process (Universitets- och högskolerådet, 2017). The selection process matches the fixed number of places for undergraduate study in Sweden to the applying students. There are two main selection criteria: grade point average (GPA) from upper secondary school and the results from the Swedish Scholastic Assessment Test (sweSAT) (Löfgren, 2005). The GPA is calculated from all grades in upper-secondary school (three years) and ranges from one to twenty; in addition, up to two point five merit points can be earned by reading qualifying courses (Universitets- och högskolerådet, 2017). The sweSAT, on the other hand, is a standardized multiple-choice test given twice a year to allow people to improve their chances to be admitted to the university programme of their choice. The number of places assigned through each selection criteria differs from university to university, but at least a third should be distributed by GPA and a third by sweSAT. The remaining places can be distributed through selection criteria designed by each institution, or by extending the places for GPA- and sweSAT-based selection (Universitets- och högskolerådet, 2017).

In 2016, fifty-seven per cent of all undergraduate programs in Sweden had more than one application per available place. However, there are large variations in popularity and number of applications among different disciplines, programmes, and universities. This leads to large differences in the results applicants need in their GPA or sweSAT scores in order to be accepted. Certain universities are much more prestigious than others and have much higher entry requirements, even though the formal degree that students receive at the end is the same. University admission has become a double-sided competition where students compete to be accepted into prestigious universities, and universities compete for the 'best' students (Olssen & Peters, 2005).

Neoliberalism also has a large impact on upper-secondary education in Sweden (Symeonidis, 2014). From the strong tradition of a welfare state with a centralized education built on democratic and egalitarian values, Swedish education has since the late '90s become one of the most decentralized and market-orientated education systems in the world (Lundahl et al, 2013). The stronger emphasis on the ability to choose freely between schools, in combination with a simultaneous intensification of testing, has created a situation where the student population has become increasingly segregated and the importance of a school's status is rising. At the same time, reforms have tried to promote student-centred education at all levels, with the aim to encourage students to actively define problems and approaches and thus engage in self-regulated and lifelong learning (Ambrose et al, 2010), rather than trying to find the right answer (Sjöberg, 2011). The literature strongly supports the view that teaching approaches that focus on encouraging students to ask their own questions and develop their own inquiries help students to couple theory and practice, as well as build deeper and more holistic conceptual models of the subject area (English & Kitsantas, 2013; Hmelo-Silver, 2004; Madhuri et al., 2012; Zacharia, 2003). Students become curious, independent and motivated learners through less directed teaching processes, not through the default position where students fear to ask their teacher questions.

The Disciplinary Context for the Research

The study focuses on student engagement in laboratory exercises in natural science as these are practical classes that are often seen to provide opportunities for independent learning (Elliott et al, 2008). Despite this claim, laboratory exercises are often reduced to expository lessons that require the students only to follow a specific set of instructions without much reflection and independent inquiry: students' and teachers' time for meaningful, conceptually driven inquiry is often seriously limited, because the technical and inflexible details of the task consume most of their time and energy (Hofstein & Lunetta, 2004).

Recent reforms of upper-secondary education in Sweden aim to overcome this problem and highlight the importance of student-driven inquiry (Skolverket, 2016). For chemistry education, this reform means changes to the curriculum, as well as the way chemistry is taught and assessed in schools. The aim is to create a stronger alignment between the students' laboratory and theoretical work, as well as to promote student-centred inquiries during the laboratory work. To achieve this aim, it is emphasized that chemistry education should provide students with opportunities to acquire five key competences: knowledge of concepts, models, theories and practices in chemistry and understanding of how these evolve; the ability to analyse and answer questions related to the subject as well as to identify, formulate and solve problems, and to reflect on and evaluate their chosen strategies, methods and results; the ability to plan, implement, interpret and present experiments and observations, and to handle chemicals and equipment; knowledge of the importance of chemistry for the individual and society; and the ability to use knowledge in chemistry to communicate with society rather than just internally within the sector.

How this reform will be perceived by students and teachers, and how it will impact on classroom practices in an educational landscape that focuses strongly on grades and assessment is not yet known. However, in light of these changes, it is interesting to take a closer look at how young adults prepare for the transition between upper-secondary school and higher education. Although the departure point for this study is the chemistry laboratory, this context enables us to start to see glimpses of more general and fundamental aspects of the educational system that influence students. In observing and interviewing students in upper secondary schools in Sweden, I explore what factors influence young adults' approaches to learning, what role university admission policies play, and how neoliberal discourses in education influence what happens in practice.

The Local Context of the Research

The research contexts for this study are two municipal upper-secondary schools in the Gothenburg area of Sweden. Both schools have relatively high minimum entry qualification requirements in the form of grades due to a competitive demand for places, and similar student populations, with a majority of students aiming to continue their education at universities afterwards.

The departure points for this study are the practices within the chemistry laboratory and to make these more visible it was decided to introduce a new technique, a change in instructional design. Pictorial instructions were prepared for eight different chemistry laboratory exercises (Rundberg & Sandström, 2016), originally to explore how these instructions would influence students' collaborative approaches. It quickly became clear that the change itself had very little immediate effect on students' interactions and working approaches. However, the pictorial instructions served as a trigger to stimulate students to evaluate, access, and think about their own actions and approaches, thereby making deeper beliefs and values more accessible in the interviews.

Empirical data was collected through classroom observations (six classes) and focus-group interviews (twelve groups). For the observations, a qualitative unstructured approach was used that focused on the whole class, the overall impression of the students' work in the laboratory, and their social interactions. The aim was to better understand and interpret students' cultural behaviour and their everyday routines during the laboratory exercises as they occur by focusing on emerging patterns within the students' actions (Mulhall, 2003). All the individual notes from the observations were written as a storyline soon after the event, to fully profit from the immersive experience of observing the students in action.

Using the observations as a starting point to define areas of interest, the focus-group interviews were used to gain more in-depth information about students' experiences and viewpoints regarding the emerging topics (Ritchie & Lewis, 2003). The aim of the interviews was to better understand why different types of phenomena occur, to explore the students' reasoning, and to see school life from their perspective (Legard et al, 2003). Through the use of focus-group interviews, it was possible to capitalize on communication between students in order to stimulate memories and reflections on experiences, as well as to explore cultural values and procedures that are shared by the members of the group (Mack et al, 2005). All students participating in the interviews gave their written informed consent to be part of the research study. Interviews lasted between forty-five and seventy minutes, and all were audio recorded and transcribed soon after the event.

All material was analysed together using an inductive data analysis approach to capture emergent categories (Ritchie & Lewis, 2003). In the first step, the data was read and listened to multiple times before it was deconstructed into units of meaning by pulling out quotes and passages of interest. Afterwards, units of meaning were used to construct categories that captured emergent topics of importance in the data. At later stages of this iterative process of deconstruction and construction, literature was used to provide an additional perspective and departure point for analysis of the data. The aim was to let the data speak for itself and explore the situation from the students' perspective. In this way, it was possible to discover underlying reasons and actual effects, not only anticipated ones.

The Findings of the Research

T he initial classroom observations make it possible to see how students act and interact in class during their chemistry laboratory exercises. It is through these observations that one can better understand and interpret the students' cultural behaviour and their everyday routines.

The Centrality of Tests

F rom the observations, it became clear that the students' actions, interactions, and foci are not bounded by the chemistry laboratory exercises but extend to other areas. One group (group three) recurrently discussed an upcoming test in another course and tried to prepare and rehearse for that test at the same time as undertaking their chemistry laboratory work, as below.

Observation in Class One: Group Three Activity

Time: 25 min. Group three worries about a test that they will have later today and talk about it for a long time. They look into their books — not their chemistry books, but the book needed for the test later.

Time: 45 min. After working a little bit more on their chemistry laboratory exercise, group three has returned to talking about the upcoming test.

Time: 60 min. Group three is revising and trying to prepare as well as possible for the test.

Commentary: This shows how the students constantly need to adjust and manage their priorities and seem to have developed strategies to use their time most efficiently. At the same time, this means that they divert their attention from engaging in and learning from the class they are in right now, and instead think ahead to the next test that they need to take.

Observation in Class Five: Group Four Activity

Time: 35 min. Group four starts to talk about a biology exam, which they will have later today. They involve some other groups and soon the discussion is about oral and written exams in more general terms.

Commentary: Here, the prominent role of tests and exams is further illustrated by the way students not only talk about the content of a test and what they need to know but engage in more general discussions about exams and testing practices.

Using these observations as a starting point, issues around grades and tests were explored in more detail during the focus-group interviews in order to better understand the students' perspectives. I was keen to take a closer look at why grades play a central role in how these young adults approach different learning situations and education as a whole, and what consequences this might have. When asked directly about the importance of grades, the single most important factor that students talk about is their importance in enabling them free choice of university and study programme after school.

Interviewer:Why do you think you are focusing so much on the exams?

Anders:One wants to have good grades or so...

Maria:Yes, that's the way it is.

Interviewer:Why do you want to have good grades?

Maria:Because... because we want to come in [at the university] where we want and... and there is a lot of pressure in our class as well...

It is not necessarily that the students know exactly what they want to do after school, but they want to have high grades in order to be able to choose without restrictions. They do not want to be the only ones who are unable to choose.

Uncertainty About Assessment Practices

While grades play a central role for the students, they are not really sure about how they are formed. The students know that tests have a big influence on their grades, but also that their performance in class plays an important role. It is this second aspect that students are most unsure about. This uncertainty on how their work in class is assessed influences the students and shapes the strategies that they use when interacting with the teacher.

The students say that they constantly feel they are being observed and assessed by their teacher, and this makes them afraid to do something wrong. They actually try to minimize their contact with the teacher. They try to draw as little attention as possible to themselves and avoid any interactions with the teacher that might suggest that they do not understand:

> I do not really know how we are assessed on the laboratory work. [...] You do not want to ask too much because then you might show that you do not understand [...]. You do not want to do the wrong thing because the practical work is being assessed as well. (Peter)

The students focus on doing things correctly and executing all their experimental work according to the instructions that they have. They feel that this makes them less vulnerable and gives the teacher fewer opportunities to be critical about their work, for they feel that assessment is omnipresent, and that they are watched continuously:

> I know that the teacher assesses this, the laboratory work is still a part of the grade. [...] [For] me it's important that the execution is right because that's what I know the teacher is assessing. I also think that it is important for me to do the right thing and to think right because I know the teacher might not tell you 'Now I'm assessing you' but I know they still do it. (Clara)

Through such strategies the students try to minimize the risk of an unfavourable assessment, even though they do not know how they are assessed. This uncertainty is challenging for the students and leaves them in doubt about what they are supposed to learn and what they should know already.

Hiding Among Peers

This avoidance of the teacher establishes a learning vacuum, and incidentally deprives the students of a formal 'more experienced' other from whom they could potentially learn a great deal. An interesting topic that emerged from the interviews is how the students try to fill this void. To whom do the students pose their questions? How do they learn to conceptualize their questions? To what extent do they know what they need to ask about?

Their fears foreground reputation over learning. First and foremost, the students are cautious about asking the teacher questions. They carefully consider if they should ask and what impression that will give the teacher:

> I get a little bit like this: 'should I ask the teacher, will he think that it is good that I ask or will he just, oh she really does not understand'. (Anna)

The students do not want to risk the teacher finding out that they do not know something that they should be familiar with already by asking a wrong question. Being *viewed* as knowledgeable takes priority over *being* knowledgeable.

Yet the students feel the need to ask someone and one approach that they use is to ask the other students instead of asking the teacher. In this way, they can discuss their thoughts and ideas with each other and avoid being assessed by the teacher. The students also experience this as being much easier and more practical, as they sit around large tables with other students:

> [When we work at the same table as other groups,] one can always discuss fairly easily with each other without having to run around the room in order to find someone who knows what you want to know. (Julia)

It is by helping each other that the students try to reduce the need to ask the teacher. There is, perhaps, an irony here that neoliberal practices that foster competition and individualism lead to a situation where students work collectively in order to protect their academic reputations. Their need to show their teacher that they are competent causes them to turn to their peers when they need help and support. This can be a useful learning strategy, fostering discussion and debate, but could also go wrong. It seems that to risk making the *same* mistakes is less threatening than standing out from the crowd or drawing attention to any personal gaps in knowledge or understanding.

Dissatisfaction with Their Own Approaches

I t becomes clear from the interviews that, despite developing a range of protective and coping strategies, the students are not necessarily satisfied with the situation they find themselves in when asked to reflect upon it. Some students expressed dissatisfaction, recognizing that their approaches are focusing only on grades and tests, and that they are actively choosing these strategies over the ones that they believe would help them to learn better, and this is a source of regret:

> It is a bit sad that all our focus is on what we need to learn for the test, but that is what always happens. We have to [learn it], not because it is part of the course or the topic that we are exploring at the moment but because 'we have to know this exercise because it will be on the test'. (Tim)

Other students talk about their expectations and how disappointed they are by the discrepancy between how things *should* and *do* work at school. One of the students explained that she had looked forward to gaining a greater understanding of things when she started upper-secondary school, but finds not much has changed from her previous school experience:

> Before I started upper secondary school, I thought 'once I am in high school, I will work in the chemistry laboratory and run experiments, but I will not only see and do stuff, but I will understand why'. However now that I am here, it feels like I still do not understand why; I still just do it without really understanding what really happens when I do it, but that would be the interesting part. (Isabella)

Going beyond their own strategies and expectations, some students also expressed more general dissatisfaction with the constant assessment during classes and explain they are struggling to find a balance between focusing on grades and focusing on learning. This is demanding for the students and often limits their desire to engage in exciting challenges. The opportunities for learning that the chemistry laboratory work offers for the students are quickly transformed into stressful situations once the students consider how their performances might affect their grades:

> On one hand you think that it is a little bit fun. At least I think that problems are fun to solve. So, in that regard it can be fun but on the other

hand you get really stressed by the situation. Maybe not by the laboratory work by itself but by everything thing around it, like if a teacher walks past and thinks 'what ARE you doing?'. (Daniel)

Although the students describe their dissatisfaction with their own approaches in the interviews and explain how they are aware of the problems their strategies have for their own learning, they do not propose any alternatives or know how they can change the situation.

Linking the Findings to the Broader Context

Both interviews and observations provide insights into how students approach school and what shapes their learning experiences. To reiterate, there is a strong focus on grades amongst the students in this study, a shared belief that grades are important to be able to choose a university freely, and a desire to be prepared, at the level of formal requirements, for the transition from school to university. At the same time however, the students do not really know how they are assessed and evaluated, which leads to missed learning opportunities as they are afraid to make mistakes or ask for help from the teacher. Furthermore, they describe their dissatisfaction with the situation they find themselves in and criticize their own strategies and approaches to learning. By observing the students and listening to them, it becomes possible to unveil the side effects of the current system of university entry requirements and admission processes, as well as the paradox that neoliberal ideology has created in education, as I will discuss below.

The Neoliberal Educational Discourse

The importance of grades, test scores, and merit in society and in the university admission process is a strong influence on young adults (Alon & Tienda, 2007), especially on the population of high-performing students that were part of this study. With the increasing interest in and focus on education and the contemporary theme of lifelong learning (Fejes, 2009), university admission policies, amongst other things, play an increasingly important role in the educational discourse as they regulate the entry into higher education.

It is in the transition phase between upper-secondary and higher education that university admission policies become a central element in students' lives, as they restrict their possibilities on a formal level. Education becomes instrumentalized as a 'tool for keeping career paths open' (Låftman et al, 2013, p. 933) and contributes to young adults conceptualizing their lives as projects that they actively build and evaluate with the aim of having a successful career (Wyn et al, 2015).

At the same time, there is a desire to change teaching approaches and put a stronger emphasis on student-centred learning. The recent reform of upper secondary chemistry education (Skolverket, 2016) highlights the importance of student-driven inquiry and self-regulated learning. Student-centred learning aims to help students to grow through meaningful interactions with other people (Shor, 1996) and become self-regulated learners who value learning and education (Boekaerts & Corno, 2005; Clark, 2012). However, neoliberal ideology overshadows this process of self-development and growth by focusing on the isolated individual and enforcing tests and control mechanisms upon students and teachers. The focus on individualism in neoliberal discourses means that everyone is responsible for their own success, but also that the ones that do not succeed are failures and this is their own fault (Harvey, 2005; Symeonidis, 2014). Eventually, this leads to the problem that 'students are learning how to pass exams and not how to work together or how to appreciate learning in itself' (Symeonidis, 2014, p. 34). Instead of framing self-regulated and lifelong learning as a personal and intellectual growth, it is often reduced to its importance and value for future careers (Fejes, 2009; Jarvis, 1999).

Contributing to the Discourse

There is an irony that, through the learning strategies and approaches they adopt, the students I worked with actually contribute to the neoliberal discourse and uphold the importance of grades, as they themselves constantly relate to and emphasize them. Rather than opposing these pressures, the students develop strategies that are adapted to the system and that enable them to manage being in their current position. This appears similar to findings from other studies that have looked at students' approaches to learning in different contexts and situations after Marton's and Säljö's (1976a; 1976b) seminal work in this area. Students are conforming to what Connell (2013, p. 110) described as a key feature in the neoliberal education landscape:

> Under neoliberal rule, education is displaced by competitive training, competition for privilege, social conformity, fear and corruption, while protest and rational alternatives are marginalized.

It is the students' desires for social conformity and to fit in with their peers that influence their discourse about learning and education. Due to the emphasis on conformity, the focus shifts from the experienced to the desired or anticipated. It is not only previous experiences on a local and personal level that shape students' strategies for learning and their educational decisions, but the way society and institutions describe, communicate, and incentivize learning on a more systematic and societal level. As Giroux (2002, p. 426) pointed out:

> Market forces have radically altered the language we use in both representing and evaluating human behaviour and action. [...] No longer defined as a form of self-development, individuality is reduced to the endless pursuit of mass-mediated interests, pleasures, and commercially produced lifestyles.

The students live in a world where they are constantly exposed to advertisements that shapes their imagination of what a happy or successful life looks like (Jhally, 1987, 2003) and strive to achieve this. However, the picture might be more nuanced, at least among the students in this study.

Contradictory Discourses

We have seen that the students are dissatisfied with their current situation even as they contribute to a neoliberal educational discourse. They express the sadness and helplessness they associate with their own focus on grades and assessment, but see no opportunity to change anything. They feel a desire to focus on learning and understanding and would like their education to challenge their thinking, but recognize, realistically, that they need good grades to get into university. They describe their wish to work around the current neoliberal educational discourse and bring back the joy of learning by engaging with the topics in their courses but daren't risk breaching current practices. In other words, the students wish for a revitalization of education as a place for intellectual growth (Magolda, 2007; Olssen & Peters, 2005), where they can engage in critical discussions, develop independent thinking, and experience learning as an activity worth pursuing for its own sake.

Arguably, the education system should facilitate young adults' transition from looking to authority figures, like teachers, to provide relevant knowledge and information towards a desire to take responsibility for their own and society's future development by engaging in critical discussions and democracy (King & Kitchener, 1994; Magolda, 1992). Young adults need to have the opportunity to develop a self-authoring mindset: 'the internal capacity of a student to define his/her own belief system, identity, and relationships' (Magolda, 2007, p. 69).

From the interviews, it is clear that students would like their education to be different but seem to lack the necessary tools to critique the system and boundary conditions that create the situation that they are in. Neoliberal ideology has led to an educational system where students only know how to conform. It has reduced the ability of students to critique the system itself by isolating individuals and minimizing critical discussions (Harvey, 2005). Neoliberal discourse maintains, as Fischman (2009, p. 5) pointed out, that 'schools should be apolitical institutions, implementing scientifically verified "best practices" which will be assessed through standardized testing'. Instead of educating to create critical and democratic citizens, the focus has shifted towards educating consumers that function in the workplace (Giroux, 2002).

In emphasizing the qualification function of education, neoliberal discourses focus on the acquisition of knowledge, skills, and dispositions that qualify students to *do* something (Biesta, 2009), leading students to miss important parts of their educational experience (Olssen & Peters, 2005), and the students in this study sensed that this was the case. Whether they fully grasped the socio-political framework lay beyond the boundaries of my research, but they are situated in a context where core skills and a strong emphasis on individualism, competition, and assessment are publicly valued over the socializing function of education that helps students to become part of a socio-cultural context and grow as people (Giroux, 2002; Harvey, 2005).

For teachers, it is difficult to challenge this situation as 'the problems of the education system have been laid at the door of teachers while their capacity for finding solutions has been taken away' (Gunter, 2001, p. 144). Like their students, teachers are pulled in opposing directions. They are expected to create meaningful learning environments, at the same time as their professional autonomy is constantly reduced by standardization, testing, and surveillance in a neoliberal educational landscape (Connell, 2013; Olssen & Peters, 2005). Current university admission policies further complicate the situation, as schoolteachers cannot deny the importance of grades, but still want to encourage students to learn in order to gain a deeper understanding. While this creates tensions for teachers (Sjöberg, 2011), the young adults are also left alone to figure out how to best navigate through this system, and what priorities to choose (Symeonidis, 2014) and it is in this 'space' that the students find their own ways of working.

Circumventing the Discourse

Where the neoliberal values clash with educational ones the students have to find a means of resolution, and they do so, albeit in an unpredictable fashion. We have seen that the students have a strong focus on grades and a desire to be prepared for the transition from school to university but at the same time they do not really know how they are assessed and feel constantly observed by the teacher. While the students contribute to the neoliberal discourse themselves in their desire to achieve high grades, they also describe their dissatisfaction with the situation they find themselves in and criticize their own strategies and approaches to learning. Yet, in their desire not to appear 'needy' to the teachers, the students are developing collaborative ways of working together that, in part, undermine the isolation and competitive nature of a neoliberal educational system; an interesting paradox and a reminder that these cooperative practices could be shaped to support an alternative learning style if the teachers were part of the process rather than bypassed.

Final Remarks

I f students and teachers were to engage in dialogues they might, together, find ways to work around the dominant neoliberal discourse on education. Student dissatisfaction presents an opportunity for change. Listening to the young adults in this study and understanding their struggles in the educational system in more detail is an important step to be able to better help future students in the transition from schools to universities and to provide them with the tools to look beyond the current way that education works. It is in the students' struggles that learning opportunities are lost and the joy for learning is damaged, at a time when lifelong learning, critical citizenship, and democratic values are needed more than ever. There is a need for further research, particularly to examine the learning processes within other disciplines and contexts, in order to better understand how this life phase is influenced by predominant neoliberal discourses.

The voices of young adults, as well as teachers, need to be heard and listened to. Education is an integral part of any democratic society and more research is needed to document how the educational landscape is currently undermined by neoliberalism and how students and teachers manage the situation to find ways forward, to mobilize their resistance to the negative consequences of current neoliberal education discourses.

Acknowledgments

I would like to thank all the students that participated in this study, and their teachers for opening their classrooms. I am also in great debt to Lisa Rundberg and Erica Sandström who have been part of this project. Furthermore, I would like to thank Tom Adawi, Jens Kabo and Liselott Aarsand for interesting discussions during the study and the preparation of this book chapter, and the editors for their thoughtful comments.

References

Alon, S. & Tienda, M. (2007). Meritocracy in higher education. *American Sociological Review*. 72: 487–511.

Ambrose, S.A., Bridges, M.W., DiPietro, M., Lovett, M.C., & Norman, M.K. (2010). *How learning works: Seven research-based principles for smart teaching*. San Francisco, CA: Jossey-Bass.

Biesta, G.J.J. (2009). On the weakness of education. *Philosophy of Education Yearbook (US)*: 354–62.

Boekaerts, M. & Corno, L. (2005). Self-regulation in the classroom: A perspective on assessment and intervention. *Applied Psychology*, 54(2): 199–231. https://doi.org/10.1111/j.1464-0597.2005.00205.x

Chapleo, C. (2011). Branding a university: Adding real value or 'smoke and mirrors'? In: Molesworth, M., Scullion, R. & Nixon, E. (eds), *The marketisation of higher education*. London: Routledge. https://doi.org/10.1080/02672 57X.2011.614734

Clark, I. (2012). Formative assessment: Assessment is for self-regulated learning. *Educational Psychology Review*, 24(2): 205–49. https://doi.org/10.1007/s10648-011-9191-6

Connell, R. (2013). The neoliberal cascade and education: An essay on the market agenda and its consequences. *Critical Studies in Education*, 54(2): 99–112. https://doi.org/10.1080/17508487.2013.776990

Elliott, M.J., Stewart, K.K. & Lagowski, J.J. (2008). The role of the laboratory in chemistry instruction. *Journal of Chemical Education*, 85(1): 145–49. https://doi.org/10.1021/ed085p145

English, M.C. & Kitsantas, A. (2013). Supporting student self-regulated learning in problem- and project-based learning. *Interdisciplinary Journal of E-Learning and Learning Objects*, 7(2): 128–50. https://doi.org/10.7771/1541-5015.1339

Fejes, A. (2009). Fabricating the lifelong learner in an age of neoliberalism. In: Simons, M., Olsson, M. & Peters, M. (eds), *Re-reading education policies: A handbook studying the policy agenda of the 21st century*. Rotterdam, NL: Sense Publishers. https://doi.org/10.1163/9789087908317

Fischman, G. (2009). Introduction. In: Hill, D. (ed), *Contesting neoliberal education: Public resistance and collective advance*. New York: Routledge. https://doi.org/10.4324/9780203893067

Giroux, H. (2002). Neoliberalism, corporate culture, and the promise of higher education: The university as a democratic public sphere. *Harvard Educational Review*, 72(4): 425–64. https://doi.org/10.17763/haer.72.4.0515nr62324n71p1

Gunter, H.M. (2001). *Leaders and leadership in education*. London: Paul Chapman Publishing.

Harvey, D. (2005). *A brief history of neoliberalism.* New York: Oxford University Press. https://doi.org/10.1111/j.1467-9655.2008.00525_38.x

Hazelkorn, E. (2011). *Rankings and the reshaping of higher education: The battle for worldwide excellence.* New York: Palgrave MacMillan.

Hmelo-Silver, C.E. (2004). Problem-based learning: What and how do students learn? *Educational Psychology Review,* 16(3): 235–66. https://doi.org/10.1023/B:EDPR.0000034022.16470.f3

Hofstein, A. & Lunetta, V.N. (2004). The laboratory in science education: Foundations for the twenty-first century. *Science Education,* 88(1): 28–54. https://doi.org/10.1002/sce.10106

Jarvis, P. (1999). Global trends in lifelong learning and the response of the universities. *Comparative Education,* 35(2): 249–57.

Jhally, S. (1987). *The codes of advertising: Fetishism and the political economy of meaning in the consumer society.* New York: Routledge.

Jhally, S. (2003). Image-based culture: Advertising and popular culture. In: Dines, G. & Humez, J.M. (eds), *Gender, race, and class in media.* London: Sage.

Låftman, S.B., Almquist, Y.B. & Östberg, V. (2013). Students' accounts of school-performance stress: A qualitative analysis of a high-achieving setting in Stockholm, Sweden. *Journal of Youth Studies,* 16(7): 932–49. https://doi.org/1 0.1080/13676261.2013.780126

Legard, R., Keegan, J. & Ward, K. (2003). In-depth interviews. In: Ritchie, J. & Lewis J. (eds), *Qualitative research practice: A guide for social science students and researchers.* Thousand Oaks, CA: Sage.

Löfgren, K. (2005). *Validation of the Swedish university entrance system: Selected results from the VALUTA-project.* Sweden: Umeå.

Lundahl, L., Arreman, I.E., Holm, A.S., & Lundström, U. (2013). Educational marketization the Swedish way. *Education Inquiry,* 4(3): 497–517. https://doi.org/10.3402/edui.v4i3.22620

Mack, N., Woodsong, C., MacQueen, K.M., Guest, G., & Namey, E. (2005). *Qualitative research methods: A data collector's field guide.* North Carolina, USA: Family Health International.

Madhuri, G. V., Kantamreddi, V.S.S. & Prakash Goteti, L.N.S. (2012). Promoting higher order thinking skills using inquiry-based learning. *European Journal of Engineering Education,* 37(2): 117–23. https://doi.org/10.1080/03043797.2 012.661701

Magolda, M.B.B. (2007). Self-authorship: The foundation for twenty-first-century education. *New Directions for Teaching and Learning,* 2007(109): 69–83. https://doi.org/10.1002/tl.266

Marton, F. & Säljö, R. (1976a). On qualitative differences in learning: I — Outcome and process. *British Journal of Educational Psychology,* 46(1): 4–11.

Marton, F. & Säljö, R. (1976b). On qualitative differences in learning: II — Outcome as a function of the learner's conception of the task. *British Journal of Educational Psychology*, 46(2): 115–27.

Molesworth, M., Nixon, E. & Scullion, R. (2009). Having, being and higher education: The marketisation of the university and the transformation of the student into consumer. *Teaching in Higher Education*, 14(3): 277–87. https://doi.org/10.1080/13562510902898841

Mulhall, A. (2003). In the field: Notes on observation in qualitative research. *Journal of Advanced Nursing*, 41(3): 306–13. https://doi.org/10.1046/j.1365-2648.2003.02514.x

Olssen, M. & Peters, M.A. (2005). Neoliberalism, higher education and the knowledge economy: From the free market to knowledge capitalism. *Journal of Education Policy*, 20(3): 313–45. https://doi.org/10.1080/02680930500108718

Ritchie, J. & Lewis, J. (2003). *Qualitative research practice: A guide for social science students and researchers.* London: Sage.

Rundberg, L., & Sandström, E. (2016). *A students' perspective on pictorial instructions.* Gothenburg, Sweden: Chalmers University of Technology.

Shor, I. (1996). *When students have power: Negotiating authority in a critical pedagogy.* Chicago, IL: The University of Chicago Press.

Sjöberg, L. (2011). Vygotskij goes neoliberal. *Utbildning & Demokrati*, 20(2): 49–72.

Skolverket (2016). *Kemi kurs och ämnesplan (Gymnasieskola)*: 1–7. http://www.skolverket.se/forskola-och-skola/gymnasieutbildning/amnes-och-laroplaner/rel

Symeonidis, V. (2014). Learning in the free market: A critical study of neoliberal influences on Sweden's education system. *International Journal of Educational Policies*, 8: 25–39.

Universitets- och högskolerådet (2017). *Platsfördelning och urval.* https://www.antagning.se/sv/Ta-reda-pa-mer-/Platsfordelning-och-urval/

Wyn, J., Cuervo, H. & Landstedt, E. (2015). The limits of wellbeing. In: Wright, K. & McLeod, J. (eds), *Rethinking youth wellbeing.* Singapore: Springer.

Zacharia, Z. (2003). Beliefs, attitudes, and intentions of science teachers regarding the educational use of computer simulations and inquiry-based experiments in physics. *Journal of Research in Science Teaching*, 40(8): 792–823. https://doi.org/10.1002/tea.10112

16. Adult Education as a Means to Enable Polish Citizens to Question Media Coverage of Political Messages

Marta Zientek

Marta Zientek offers a rhetorical exposition of the political system in Poland, and shows how an adult education course provided a space to analyse and reflect on the veracity of the messages put out by the dominant governing party. Course members critically examined the speeches of a political leader to see how linguistic devices were employed to attract public support

This chapter reports on a Polish research project that seeks to understand the processes that underpin the formation of a national identity. This is timely. When a country is experiencing broad social change and political unrest, interest in such matters is prominent; incidents awaiting investigation abound in both the media and society. The project adopts a Participatory Action Research (PAR) methodology and this enabled me to work with a group of fifty adult learners who enrolled on a political discourse course at a Polish university. The course, based within an English Philology department, was led by tutors and/or enrolled students who have a background in linguistic and speech communication; studies that equip them to analyse texts for their overt and more covert meanings. Thus, a collective decision was made to use Critical Discourse Analysis (CDA) (Fairclough, 1993)

https://doi.org/10.11647/OBP.0203.16

to examine discursive constructions of meaning and the social biases embedded in politicians' language — written and spoken. CDA was used in tandem with Foucault's writings to keep notions of power clearly in mind throughout. The students' engagement with CDA was thorough and, seemingly, for life. Foucault aroused their interest mainly because his name is appropriated (as well as misappropriated) by the world of political discourse studies. Their university course — of a year's duration — provided students with a safe space in which to do their analyses in a supported educational context, an idea informed by an earlier action research course established by academics in Sussex, England (Pettit, 2010).

Before looking further at the actual research and its findings, I present an overview of the contemporary Polish political context and its social manifestations to enable the reader to better understand the significance and relevance of this PAR project. This is followed by a discussion and partial application of Foucault's discourses on power, before the chapter addresses the methodological frameworks in more detail to show why CDA, PAR, Frames of Reference (FoR) and Metaphorical Analysis (MetA) offered an appropriate framework. The research process is described, and its outcomes are discussed in general terms before four specific examples of political text analysis are presented to demonstrate the nature of the course activity and how the frameworks were applied to actual political messages found in the media.

The Research Context

The Political Situation in Poland

P oland has undergone many changes since the political elections in 2015 when the far-right populist Polish Law and Justice Party (Prawo i Sprawiedliwość, PiS) won both the presidential and parliamentary elections (Lachaise, 2017). PiS was founded in 2001 by twin brothers, Jarosław and Lech Kaczyński (Marcinkiewicz & Stegmaier, 2017). It is closely aligned with powerful Catholic fundamentalists who provide the party with a broad and stable base of electoral support, and whose members campaigned with a promise to crack down on corruption and crime (Marcinkiewicz & Stegmaier, 2017). The Law and Justice Party won overwhelming support from a large number of Poles, as it offered a rudimentary welfare system and a vision of a large and powerful state (Adekoya, 2017), but for both the elite and the inhabitants of Poland's larger and more developed cities, the election result came as a shock. Supporters of the more liberal Committee for the Defence of Democracy (Komitet Obrony Demokracji, KOD) organize regular public protests that were, and are, attended by thousands of citizens (Lachaise, 2017), but to little effect.

Despite these protests and significant international pressure (Lachaise, 2017), the PiS leader has steadily passed laws to reform education, the labour market and the judiciary, which some believe to be eroding Poland's democratic system of government, sometimes challenging the constitution (Wiewiora, 2018). Such actions are said to have created a 'rupture in society' (Hachaud, 2017); a state of 'political crisis' (Lachaise, 2017) that is subject to 'blatant manipulation' in the press (Lachaise, 2017).

Although Polish people continue to be pro-EU, PiS offers a different vision of what this means, one that is White, Catholic and traditional (Adekoya, 2017). This less progressive stance is not acceptable to all nationals and some have chosen to leave the country and settle elsewhere. But for others, often the less educated, the communitarian approach that PiS deploys provides a sense of security, being both 'emotionally reassuring' and financially beneficial (Adekoya, 2017). The President, Andrzej Duda, is described as 'young, charismatic, media savvy, and unashamed of allowing his faith' (Mazurczak, 2015) and many Polish citizens find these qualities attractive.

The Contemporary Scene

In contemporary Poland there are many social agents who reject the biases and symbolic power evident in the daily newspapers and TV interviews. Currently, many Polish citizens are motivated to analyse political speeches and media interviews with politicians in order to be better informed and more able to voice their objections to issues they don't agree with. Some seek to challenge the propaganda that all positive social changes stem from the PiS and any economic problems arise from the activities of their political opponents when in power during the previous seven years of governance. Indeed, rumours and claims of wrongdoing are commonplace (see Lachaise, 2017).

As ever, adult education offers opportunities to become better informed, but many adult learners face problems when they try to put down roots within the space of the 'new and only' right-wing political discourse, presented by the PiS. They have no platform from which to voice their opinions, and the course referred to in this chapter compensates for this in some small part as it enabled adult learners to examine some of the processes by which those in power maintain their following, and to question the metaphorical, and, in their view, often oppressive language used in public gatherings and the media.

Polish Political Discourse: A Foucauldian Analysis

In Foucauldian terms, discourse is presented not only as utterances but also as ways of thinking and sense-making, shaping human actions under given circumstances, interplays and interrelations among discourse actors and, finally, describing the acts and results of arranging signs and material objects (Foucault, 1977). Moreover, discourses can be treated as practices; the discourse-practitioners' customs, which exclude or include political opponents, render some ideas important and others invisible and meaningless (Foucault, 2003). What is more, discourses create and re-create knowledge and power simultaneously. Their effects are spread through the actions of different members of the community who share common ways of thinking, doing and being.

The discursive practice within a discourse community can be seen as normative, formulating 'truths' about what is appropriate thought, speech or action and devaluing the ways of thinking held by those who challenge these values through political dialogue or disputes (Foucault, 1972). The politicians in power use their control strategically to make further claims on citizens, taking this power to themselves, rather than viewing it as both cause and consequence of their dominance; thus, they destabilize transhistorical accounts, effectively rewriting history to suit themselves. According to Foucault, the function of discourse is not to conceal certain truths; it is simply that through its ontogenetic functions it constructs the worlds we live by and establishes the notions of truthfulness that we as communities of learners need to work within (Foucault, 1972). The multiplication of its usage reflects the multiplication of its public spheres of practice. Power is generated through the activities of political leaders and their rivals, but we should be mindful that even though individual subjects become powerless in the sense that they become tied to a normalized ideal, they also subscribe to this position in accepting the conditions of control and the views of knowledge so generated. People from the 'audience' are engaged in their own regulation: they place themselves under the authority of others in order to listen to the 'political truths' and to be familiar with powerful issues. When they see themselves to be under a power that is based on right, they feel themselves to be self-actualized individuals. They regard themselves as powerful and conscious in the way they articulate their political opinions (Foucault, 1977) when, in reality, they actually have become the subjects of political domination.

In Poland, the discipline in right-wing politics is mostly visible in the gatherings of political followers in Krakowskie Przedmieście Street, in front of the President's Palace, and during other political meetings. Disciplinary power is exercised on the body and souls of political supporters of the right-wing PiS. It apparently increases the power of individuals as it renders them more energetic and forceful. Encouraged to become louder and noisier, they amplify their actions to be more aggressive and soldier-like (similar to basic training within the military). Power is generated through the political discourse of the leaders of the right-wing party and emerges among groups of other people — their followers — even as these followers are (consciously) manipulated to bring them (unconsciously) under political control.

Discourse analysis, following a Foucauldian approach, can enable a supportive process of change, as students work through issues they perceive to be problematic, deconstructing texts and exploring normative assumptions. Students can be encouraged to use Foucault's guidelines to deeply analyse political discourses and examine how they can be enforced through language choice. They can focus on the processes of categorization and interpretation of the political language in the Polish press and TV interviews, interrogating the dominant political frames and disrupting the further promotion of unquestioned activities shaped by the right-wing party. Through presenting a discursive analysis and encouraging the students to adopt similar approaches, the course leader can point out the skill with which the party leaders marshal their followers. It can be demonstrated how a following is maintained through certain forms of ideological discourse, such as highlighting how *'our* good things' now apply, and how these contrast with *'their* bad things', through denigrating the activities of past political rivals and insinuating that the prospective unknown people who may challenge in the future will be unsuitable.

Political leaders often use communicative and interactive practices to gain control over their audience and to consolidate shared views through reference to 'bad things'. Circumstances like the treatment of refugees, or their 'bad' religious intentions, are invoked, often just to build an imaginary common enemy. Such political practice not only involves power, it also represents an abuse of power to enable what we may call 'domination'. More specifically, power is so used to imply an (illegitimate) influence; false discourses are expounded to make others believe in the things that serve the interests of the political leader. Such illegitimate power may be enforced through pictorial means, through religious guidelines, and even supported by the mass media (currently governed by those in power). This kind of negative persuasion, which has bolstered political discourse through the power of oppressive language, can be disseminated in local communities where people lack the specific knowledge that might be used to resist this illegitimate manipulation. Well-known examples in contemporary Poland include the governmental and mass-media discourses around the Pro-Democracy Movement (KOD) and discourses about immigrants. Contexts are obfuscated, blurred, lost within political jargon. In differing circumstances, through political or religious persuasion which may be formally legitimate but is actually ethically negative, recipients are more or less manipulated to believe or do what is deemed appropriate. In making this claim, there are several crucial criteria. One is that people are being acted upon against their fully conscious will and interests, and another, that these processes are not fully visible, but concealed through issues like a fear of unconscious enemies or even simply through eloquence or political politeness. When truly visible, such objectives are clearly in the best interests of the manipulator, usually one of the political leaders, not the people on whom they are imposed.

The Methodological Framework

Why Foucault?

Informed by Foucault's views on power (Foucault, 1977), colleagues and I considered the courses of action we could undertake that might overturn the system of domination that has grown up around and through contemporary Polish political discourse. The answer we came up with was to organize a course, one which would give students the opportunity to analyse the language of political discourse. The course could provide students with the insights necessary to understand its oppressive character by enabling in-depth investigation and interpretation of the language of the right-wing political leaders. Given the enslaving tendencies of all thought, all interpretation, all language used and all discourse, adult learners who took the course would be clearly prepared to confront and oppose political demands. In deconstructing political discourse, students would not merely illuminate the background to political power, but also feel more empowered because, aside from absolute passivity, opposition is the only choice that they have, the only response possible. Thus they are following Foucault's (1985) suggestion that by opting for a form of permanent revolution, one that is continual and persistent in its pursuit of a political ideal and an ordered society, they are creating a community that is conscious of political manipulation and sees through the fake jargon used by those in power.

Why Critical Discourse Analysis?

In a seminal paper on Critical Discourse Analysis, Fairclough (1993, p. 135) offers a definition that aptly sums up why this is an appropriate methodology for researching political speeches. He describes CDA as an approach that:

> [...] aims to systematically explore often opaque relationships of causality and determination between (a) discursive practices, events and texts, and (b) wider social and cultural structures, relations and processes; to investigate how such practices, events and texts arise out of and are ideologically shaped by relations of power and struggles over power; and to explore how the opacity of these relationships between discourse and society is itself a factor securing power and hegemony.

In a later paper, Fairclough (2015, p. 6) reminds us that discourse includes 'representations of how things are and have been' — a process that relates to how political leaders denigrate past leaders' activities, and 'imaginaries — representations of how things might or should be'. Polish leaders have recourse to imaginaries when they offer the people a picture of an idealized society, whether honest or contrived. Fairclough also informs us (ibid., p. 12) of three main forms of critique: ideological (the traditional pursuit of the social relations of power); rhetorical, where the focus is persuasion; and strategic critique, which considers how groups of social agents seek to change societies in specific directions. All three types have relevance for the current project but Fairclough believes that it is the last mentioned, strategic, that assumes 'a certain primacy in periods of major social change' and this exemplifies our intentions in establishing the university course and my ensuing research project.

Why Participatory Action Research?

A team of academics in Sussex in the United Kingdom established a Master's course in participation, power and social change that sought to 'facilitate the learning of action research as a way of working for change, embedded in practice' (Pettit, 2010) by encouraging its participants to become aware of their own learning processes and how these connected with elements of social change. Theoretically the course drew on Reason's (1994) triadic model of integrated learning at individual, group and community levels, as did the course that was set up in Poland. Like Pettit and colleagues, we too asked ourselves: 'How can change agents develop the concepts, skills, awareness and capacities they need to generate knowledge and action with others in participatory ways?'.

Participatory Action Research (PAR) was described in the Pettit article as a useful tool. It is one equipped to take up the challenge presented by this 'bad' situation by drawing upon the rich liberating tradition of the adult education movement, its passionate commitment to equality and justice, and the practical skills to investigate reality in order to transform it. As an adult educator, I have found a natural fit between PAR and my understanding of the community development concept as a guide for creating community as a space for mutuality and freedom; an inclusive and safe place to analyse the political language of our main representatives. For me, PAR is a form of resistance to all forms of control that limit our freedom to pursue a reasoned, compassionate, committed and democratic knowledge base. It can be an antidote to oppressive forces of the PiS president. This is in keeping with our tradition of liberation in the adult education movement, which provided fertile ground for PAR.

Research Methods/Frameworks

Frames of Reference

Druckman (2009, p. 2) distinguishes between frames in communication (often used in politics and the media) and frames in thought, which are 'construed as consisting of the dimensions on which one bases his/her evaluation of an object', and can be either emphasis frames (that offer substantively distinct considerations of say, importance, issue or value) or equivalency (or valence) frames, that 'typically involve casting the same information in either a positive or negative light' according to Levin, Schneider and Gaeth (1998, p. 150). All these types have potential relevance for this research project.

Furthermore, Druckman introduces 'availability' and Pan and Kosicki's (2001) notion of 'framing potency' (which relates to 'the persuasiveness or effectiveness of the frame'), two factors that can be used to describe the 'strength' of a frame (p. 4), which are also important considerations in regard to this research. Also relevant is his explanation (attributed to Kinder and Sanders, 1996, p. 164) that 'frames lead a double life' for they are both 'interpretative structures embedded in political discourse' (referred to as rhetorical weapons) and 'cognitive structures that help individual citizens makes sense of the issues' (an idea that aptly captures their effect on the audience).

Thus, FoR are perceived as relevant concepts in political discourse and other political communication practices. Understanding which frames are used to define specific issues in a specific context is a clue that helps one to be well-informed in a political world. It is also a real challenge for the researchers, thanks to the volume of text data, the dynamic nature of language and the variance in applicable frames across issues.

A political discourse functions as a means of linguistic adaptation and realizes various pragmatic effects. Communication in a political environment is a dynamic process of mutual recognition of each other's motivation, and its functions are many and diverse. According to Bayley (2004) political discourse is not only one of the mirrors reflecting the tendencies of discursive and social development but also one of the tools endowed by language to enable political users to satisfy their communicative needs in the short term of mass-media effect and in the longer political term in contributing to survival, an outcome of successful adaptation. Linguistic choices are made dynamically and are negotiable; the discursive texts of politicians vary greatly in terms of complexity.

There are many issue-specific frames that span policy issues. As Henderson (1994) states, we can focus on economic frames (the costs, benefits or financial implications of an issue to the individual, family, community or the economy as a whole). Alternatively, politicians may adopt morality frames (a perspective that is compelled by religious doctrine or interpretation, duty, honour or any other sense of social responsibility), or draw on notions of fairness and equality or inequality frames (applying laws and/or punishment to control individuals or groups). Politicians may manipulate through rhetoric to seemingly 'balance' the rights or interests of one individual or group compared to another; or use security and defence frames to protect the welfare of a nation (sometimes from a threat that is not yet manifest). Moreover, they assume the importance of safety and quality-of-life frames and these are strongly connected to policies that determine an individual's wealth, mobility, access to resources, ease of day-to-day routines, access to healthcare and whether communities thrive.

Otieno (2016) claims that political discourse is full of different speech actions, which can be seen to have a direct, relevant impact on political communication through truth claims, commands and requests, promises and blaming, and these can be especially visible in certain contexts and will vary with conditions such as the power or status of the politician and the style of language used. In fact, the role of the speaker — the politician as an authoritative narrator or a decisive actor — is crucial.

Language as Metaphor

Henderson (1994) describes metaphor as the 'use of language in which what is said is not literally what is meant' and explains that it is this 'almost understood but not quite' quality that creates the tension that makes it forceful (pp. 344/5). It provides 'imaginative power to create meaning' and in so doing can 'shape and extend what can be said through comparisons and associations' to provide 'emotional impact' and to paint strong verbal pictures of ideas (p. 354/6). Thus, metaphors are a key tool for political figures. Indeed, it is important to reflect not only on what is actually said but also that which is left out. As Henderson (p. 357/8) stresses, 'a rhetorical awareness of what it is that is being suppressed by the metaphor can be as important as an understanding of what is being expressed'; both strategies can mislead or clarify, create false hope or realistic expectations, confusion or understanding, and this is easily manipulable.

People use their knowledge of actions and emotions to build both complexity and understanding within the fields of politics, science and economics. Cameron (2003) and Carston (2010) both stress the importance of metaphors to the cognitive re-evaluation that took place in the twentieth century, and both analyse the *ad hoc* nature of concept construction in fields like the environment and socio-economic space, and their relevance to the field of education and the positive or negative mental images of contemporary adult learners. Their separate narratives build on Lakoff and Johnson's (1980, p. 153) work, and the notion that 'metaphor is primarily a matter of thought and action, and only derivatively a matter of language'. They acknowledge that the human mind has the ability to conceptualize abstract ideas in terms of sensitive and particular experiences and widen the range of interests that humans can structure through metaphor. Their approach to metaphors in everyday life clearly connects with theories of framing both in the field of public communication and in the scientific area of economic acts and the decision-making process.

In relation to frames, individual metaphorical expressions become features in conceptual maps that link generic thematic domains. These serve as sources of meaning: source domains (for instance, 'crisis' and 'good change') link to abstract target domains (for example, 'society' or 'economy'). Lakoff and Johnson (1980) identified three kinds of metaphorical concept that correspond to types of non-metaphorical concept:

1. orientational metaphors give concepts a *spatial* orientation (for example, the only correct way to make progress is by walking forwards);

2. ontological metaphors enable us to create bounded categories from things that are not discrete entities, in effect to *contain* them (for instance, social change, the Polish nation, the economy, are all container metaphors);

3. structural metaphors allow us to *transfer* structures associated with one concept to shape the way we understand another (for example, if we say that the economic crisis is a war, we can apply terms like fight, beat, blow up to embellish our discussion of the economy in ways that will be understood by others).

The Research Framework

The PAR project was based on a course that lasted one academic year, but course scheduling limited the time frame to one academic term, within which six cycles of research were planned. The aim of this research was for students to gain the ability to identify and describe different types of meaning using a linguistic, semantic and pragmatic methodology within a framework of political discourse. Moreover, students would study and discuss a range of methodological articles that would then enable them to discuss and critically analyse contemporary political material of national significance to Poland. The student participants decided to analyse the texts and contexts of the leader of the right-wing party currently in power, his speeches and interviews as leader presented on television news broadcasts or in daily newspapers. They chose, particularly, to take material from the programme '*Warto rozmawiać*' ('It is worthwhile to talk'), broadcast on TVP 1 (national government television), as well as selected articles published in '*W sieci*' ('Network'), a weekly online magazine.

Additionally, the co-researchers (the adult learners who participated in the university project) suggested tracking the tone within each section of text in a political speech. They focused on linguistic devices such as figurative speech and metaphors, including some rhetoric and persuasive political pathos. Overall, it was decided to categorize sections of text as positive, negative or neutral in tone but acknowledged that such classification was subjective and would vary according to the issue being studied and the individual researcher's viewpoint. However, through carrying out a pilot — the collective analysis of the immigration codebook — the group were able to establish some basic ground rules for effective categorization.

The Research Process

T he adult learners were teachers in their mid-forties from small towns in western Poland who enrolled at university to gain new professional qualifications, following PiS reforms to the educational system. They chose the course on political discourse from a number on offer to them and were well aware of the bigger political picture. They wanted to gain more theoretical knowledge of rhetoric and biases and sought to co-create a safe learning space in which to study these issues. They were highly motivated, well organized and could cooperate together in the project's tasks, aware of the need to ground them in an understanding of specific political contexts. Furthermore, they wanted to improve their translation skills. Indeed, I found their collective driving force gave the action research project impetus, helping me to complete the project within the timeframe of the academic course.

The research started propitiously, with the adult learners finding in Foucault's work an appropriate theoretical framework for the analysis and interpretation of the data. Their encounter with Foucault's theorizing on the constitution of the subject not only shaped their way of thinking during the next steps of the research, but it also allowed them to sort the voluminous corpus of data they had gathered into a manageable structure. In this respect, the Foucauldian perspective already described and the use of PAR and more specific methods evolved in tandem, each supporting the other.

The students needed to gel as a group in order for the course to be seen as a safe space, so it was reassuring for them to find that they all strongly disagreed with the negative attitudes expressed towards contemporary problems around migration and refugees' lack of status in Poland when they carried out their pilot study. They felt that immigrants and refugees were portrayed in an unsympathetic manner, so those with immigrants as in-laws were particularly disappointed or upset when reading this political discourse.

Rooted in Foucault's analytic approach to social processes of knowledge construction, our study and research examined the process of national identity construction as revealed in a series of practices within the context of adult learning and formal education. Several stages of data analysis were undertaken to make sense of formal adult education practices, and how they reveal students' construction of their national selves. Foucault's theorizing on the constitution of the subject was integral to a critical reading of the data, an iterative process where both I and my students — the adult learners — were moving back and forth through emerging themes and patterns.

Our application of Foucault's theories meant that the process of national identity construction in the context of education was viewed as neither a passive reproduction of dominating structures, nor a manifestation of free will, but as the constant interplay between the two, revealed through a set of practices during the course. This approach to the analysis of socio-political processes is articulated by Foucault as the interplay of various technologies and was conceptualized in our study as the interplay of structure and agency.

Students, the adult learners who participated in the research, agreed that the effectiveness of the politician's frames depends on the mass public's reaction to his claims. But, in turn, the successful communication of a frame depends on whether the politician's claims and arguments reach the mass public. Thus, the students sought to establish how this well-known right-wing leader transmitted rhetoric directly to a national audience through the major television network and the extent to which he chose words, arguments, and symbols favourable to his political position and likely to resonate among members of the mass public, gathered in the street. Students wanted to know how language was used strategically to strengthen public support.

A related line of work maintains that a political actor forges connections between issues and other ideas by developing joint frames of reference in the communication process. To analyse this requires close observation of the words, emotional phrases, images, and styles of presentation that a speaker uses when relaying information to another. In our analysis we found that the leader disseminates ideas by building frames of reference, selecting and highlighting events or issues, and making connections among them so as to promote a particular interpretation, evaluation and, finally, solution.

The power of frames of references rests not simply on the issues or values the politician mentions, but more concretely on the words used. As language is crafted to link policy issues to supportive values and political ideas, we can examine the usage of strategic terms and the associations between them. Above all, when frames are used to change media coverage and create or maintain massed public support, the character of the communication strategies will be manifest in the structure of the rhetoric. If the media and general political discourse mirrors the structure of the frames in communications, this demonstrates success in communicating a frame regardless of the whether the media values or disagrees with the ideas. It is easy to imagine that journalists might challenge rather than praise issue frames, and such unfavourable coverage would likely limit a frame's effectiveness in affecting public opinion. However, such negative coverage would still be consistent with successful communication, because any coverage foregrounds the leader's ideas and political concepts, establishing their place within the mass public's mindset.

The adult learners who participated in this action research speculated that the right-wing political leader would use many rhetorical devices (such as persuasion, metaphors, and repetitions) in the practice of manipulation. What is more, they perceived that the use of symbolic and imaginative language would be emotive, successfully stirring up the feelings of the audience to magnify any negative images towards their political opponents and their former acts of governance. The learners, therefore, determined to study the linguistic tools available to the leader and, consequently, to study the political discourses to see how language was used and what devices enabled it to play an oppressive or coercive role.

Research Outcomes

Metaphors of Crisis and Social Change

The research found that in Poland, the politicians and political leaders did indeed construct their political visions through metaphorical devices, suggesting that such rhetorical and figurative resources are, in consequence, relevant, perhaps essential, to politico-economic thought. Tensions between abstraction and concreteness, intuition and logical thinking, form cornerstones when developing the ability to establish connections with society, particularly with a public audience. From this perspective, metaphors are very useful tools for the improvement of 'economic storytelling', promoting notions of economic success without implementing solid financial strategies or sociological devices of measurement.

In both 'national' TV coverage and the daily press, the adult learners easily identified specific structural metaphors and spheres of meaning that function as source domains and, furthermore, established their visible association to a variety of target domains held by the PiS. When presenting news about their opponents and, indeed, EU organizations, crisis metaphors are frequently employed. Some examples include: 'one giant scandal'[1] in reference to the Polish judiciary (see Rzeczpospolita, February 2017); 'a new big hate attack'[2] in a speech to those gathered in front of the Presidential Palace in Warsaw to mark the 85th anniversary of the Smolensk disaster (see Niezalezna, May 2017); 'a life of constant threat and control'[3] discussing the threat of terrorism (see wGospodarce, June 2017); and 'Warsaw has reached the bottom'[4] at the PiS regional convention in Warsaw (see onet, September 2018).

Many of the examples of figurative speech, as in those cited above, addressed the issue of universality through the use of conceptual metaphors and an undertone that was consistently pejorative. Most focused chiefly on promoting the 'right' social change, and on repairing a 'ruined' Poland after taking hold of the 'steering wheel' to drive through the political minefield.

---

1   *Rzeczpospolita* is a legal daily newspaper website.
2   *Niezalezna* (meaning Independent) is a Polish news website.
3   *wGospodarce* is a professional news portal.
4   *onet* is a much-cited web portal.

As well as these conventional studies of the media's use of economic crisis and social change metaphors, some adult learner-researchers paid attention to the visual representation of conceptual metaphors, which portrayed government decisions as emergency measures needed to rebuild a 'ruined Poland after the elections' or the 'EU crisis'. Here, too, the portrayal of crisis unquestioningly indicated what was right and what was not right in the latest political decisions that were made by former political leaders, and included hints of concerns around Europe.

Examples from the Research

I n keeping with the fair-use rule, we present analyses of short excerpts from texts here and point out that, as part of the course, these excerpts have been translated from Polish into English. However, even such short excerpts contain a significant range of linguistic attributes that imbue political discourse with the power to muster followers.

Text One

'Change will not come if we wait for some other time. We are the ones we've been waiting for. We are the good change the Polish nation seek.'
    Jarosław Kaczyński, leader of the PiS, establishing the 'Good Change' slogan of the 2015 election.

Kaczyński talked about just one thing, *change*. This shows that focusing on a single message reinforces it and makes it memorable. The speech informed the audience that this change was good and that it was the thing that they sought. Yet the prospective change was left to the imagination; change was merely a linguistic metaphor connected to something new and better; something that would bring the audience 'a better political world'.

Persuasive pathos was used as a rhetorical device to appeal to the audience's emotions, to trigger an emotional response, too. The passage of time was introduced, to present a strong argument for the necessity of making the decision to change a very fast one. The metaphor of time was very persuasive, demonstrating a formidable effort to convince the audience.

Like many politicians, the leader tried to influence his audience, to convince them that his party is the one that everyone is looking for. He does this by linking to the change metaphor: *'we are the good change'* that Poland needs. There is an implication that anyone seeking a good change will find it within *this* political party rather than others and the language used expressed great confidence that *this* political party embodied the good change that Poles have waited for. Anaphora in repetition was used both to attract people's attention, '*We are* the ones... *We are* the good change', and to further reinforce the message.

It should also be noted that this speech appears to paraphrase — and thus to nationalize — Barack Obama's campaign speech of 5 February 2008: *'Change will not come if we wait for some other person or if we wait for some other time. We are the ones we've been waiting for. We are the change that we seek'*.[5] The similarity raises questions of intentionality. Was this merely a lack of originality, an unintended adoption of ideas in the public domain? Was it a deliberate borrowing of a rhetorically attractive claim, even an attempt to take on a cloak of 'justice' despite different political leanings? Or was it simple coincidence?

Text Two

'If you are walking down the right path and you are willing to keep walking, eventually you will make progress.'
   Jarosław Kaczyński, April 2017, Wikiquote from the Smolensk meetings.

Kaczyński advised the audience to walk down the right path and to continue walking in that direction in order to make progress. The meaning of the metaphor *'the right path'* was unequivocal without giving detail, being only as informative as was necessary to express certainty. This was a clear, brief and orderly political discourse.

The metaphor of the only *'right path'* as the *'right course and trodden way to follow'* has deep roots in the Old Testament's historical records, its description of the people who were moving forward thanks to God's guidance. Moreover, such words were very relevant to contemporary concerns because they imply a *clear* route to progress, demonstrating

---

5   Post-nominating contests, Chicago Illinois, USA, 5 Feb 2008, In: *Barack Obama: Quotes to live by*. London: Carlton Books, 2019, p. 6.

persuasive reasoning. The excerpt used repetition to enforce its message. The text was eloquent and this, itself, is one of the most prominent, political weapons, as leaders well know. We felt that this excerpt was trying to *convince* the Polish audience that the ruling party represents the right path, the one that should be followed by all others.

As with text one, this excerpt also reflects a speech of Barack Obama's, again raising questions as to whether this was deliberate and if so, for what purpose? On the internet, the attribution to Obama is recurrent but the actual speech not specified. It is claimed that 'If you're walking down the right path and you're willing to keep walking, eventually you'll make progress' was part of the Farewell address in Chicago Illinois on 10 January 2017 (see *Barack Obama: Quotes to live by*. London: Carlton Books, 2019, p. 79) but this has proved difficult to verify.

Text Three

'Our opponents are troublemakers. They are just trying to get legitimate power again. It is obvious, when they speak to us they show their treacherous mugs [faces]. We can clearly see their manipulation. The Pro-Democracy Movement is an example of the political minority held by our opponents.'
Jarosław Kaczyński, April 2017, from the Smolensk meetings.

The language of this speech was more oppressive in tone, probably intended to undermine the opposition. Political opponents were denigrated when their faces were referred to as 'mugs', their civic leaders as power-seeking and manipulative, which implies insincerity. Not only does such language feel oppressive and arrogant but there appears to be little concern that it may come across in this way. Such behaviour implies self-confidence, a certainty that one's words will be appreciated by the audience and will neither destabilize one's leadership nor disturb one's legitimate political position. Indeed, 'we can clearly see' implies a position of superiority.

The orator positioned the opponents' intentions as bad ones, even treacherous ones, and emphasized that they no longer held legitimate power. He also suggested to the audience that his opponents were politically marginalized, unable to return to power. If these opponents were to be insincere towards the people, they might be willing to rule again but they are not necessarily interested in the good of Poland in the future.

It is not spelt out in the excerpt quoted here, but it is relevant to note that claims that the opponents are 'treacherous' commonly relate to the premise that public protest damages the country's public image, creating a negative perspective of Poland within the field of the European Parliament and European Commission, and indeed the wider world.

Text Four

'Communists and thieves, all of Poland is laughing at you.'
Jarosław Kaczyński, at the pro-government counter-protests, Sunday
13 December 2015, Warsaw, cited in *Wroclow Uncut*, 14 December 2015.

These comments were directed at those who participated in the public demonstrations to protest against one of the contested reforms, the de-legalization of the rights of the Constitutional Court; we believe that they disclosed a neglectful attitude towards political changes in the legacy of direct election to the Court.

Analysis of the speech lays bare an attempt to convince political supporters that their opponents are aligned with the 'bad' things that date from communist times, so they cannot be treated as true political rivals. The credibility of the protestors has been undermined by calling them 'thieves' because in Polish society the communists are viewed as criminals, bandits and robbers who were willing to sell Poland for 'red cents' and whose behaviour and greedy attitudes were compared to Judas, the treacherous disciple. Thus, by excluding the untrustworthy, the phrase 'all of Poland' implied that everyone else (deemed trustworthy, in contrast, irrespective of their different characteristics and origins) stood united with the ruling party that legitimately held power.

Overall, we have shown that the Polish leader used several different types of rhetorical device to deliver his messages. It is apparent in the excerpts that he favours the persuasive appeal of ethos and pathos. In addition, there is an imaginative use of language in his political discourse and a reliance on a type of repetition, anaphora. Thus, the texts appeal to the audience's opinions and attitudes through the use of manipulative power and strive to keep the communication process effective.

Conclusion

The length of time at university and the environment within which the course took place crucially impacted on the success of this project, enabling adult learners to open up and offering them powerful opportunities to experience real learning. Given the potential fragility of the space for political debate, experiential learning and learning-by-doing are key factors in enabling the critical analysis of political discourse and the oppressive political language that is presented in the mass media in Poland.

These adult learners follow the social changes and the rumours of economic crisis in Poland every day, but they can now observe the reality with conscious intent and do not easily agree with the rhetoric, or get drawn in by the sometimes seemingly empathetic style of 'the only right, national' TV. As researchers, adult learners established their own right to disagree and to create concepts that embrace diversity and acknowledge multiple perspectives. They are able to address different levels of society simultaneously through the research: the national, the local, the trans-local and the global, in which change is relegated to what is excluded or included in the national context. They, the adult researcher-learners, are the best equipped to grasp the nuances of political complexity. They have become a cutting-edge group of young social scientists, able to present their points of view without hesitation. On the political stage, their role is that of spectators, individuals who listen closely to political discourses and interviews with the leading politicians.

Yet, to borrow a phrase from Shakespeare's *As You Like It*, if 'All the world's a stage, and all the men and women merely players', we should consider if it is the politicians who are 'merely players'. Is it the leaders who are continually acting, albeit without screenplays or scripts of acceptance and tolerance; seemingly forgetful that their 'lines' should be about the future of the country, the pursuit of a flourishing economy and plans for positive social change? This is not best achieved by commenting on the folly of the past and relying on linguistic devices that capitalize on people's fear of the unknown to maintain political power.

That Polish society has radically changed of late goes without saying, but it is seldom truly acknowledged. Poland is sometimes labelled as the nation without a memory, or more accurately by certain Polish sociologists as a 'society of non-remembrance' (Czyżewski in Czyżewski, Kowalski & Piotrowski, 2010) or 'society which is addicted to seduction' (Kowalski in Czyżewski, Kowalski & Piotrowski, 2010). However unfortunate, the past, and our memory of the past, is ever present; close analysis reveals it to be clearly visible in the prevalence of crisis metaphors and clearly demonstrable in the adult learners' reflections and viewpoints. Their greater awareness of political falsities and realities is manifest in many ways, demonstrating the value of both the university course on political discourse and the participatory action research project. As with the English course, in Poland we challenged the 'conventional views of policymaking [that] usually see "research" as a specialized activity which makes objective data and analysis available' to those in power (Pettit, 2010) and agree with Pettit (ibid., p. 820) that:

> Knowledge, policy and practice are co-created through an emergent process of action and learning, often including some form of critical reflection and reappraisal of the norms, values, and assumptions by which we make sense of things, as well as an understanding of how these are shaped by power.

References

Adekoya, R. (2017). Why Poland's Law and Justice Party remains so popular. *Foreign Affairs*. https://www.foreignaffairs.com

Bayley, P. (2004). *Cross-cultural perspectives on parliamentary discourse*. Amsterdam/ Philadelphia: John Benjamins. https://doi.org/10.1075/dapsac.10

Cameron, L. (2003). *Metaphor in educational discourse*. London: Continuum.

Carston, R. (2010). Metaphor: Ad hoc concepts, literal meaning and mental images. *Proceedings of the Aristotelian Society*, 110(3): 200–350. https://doi.org/10.1111/j.1467-9264.2010.00288.x

Czyżewski, M., Kowalski, S. & Piotrowski, A. (2010). *Rytualny chaos. Studium dyskursu publicznego*. Warszawa: Wydawnictwo Akademickie i Profesjonalne.

Druckman, J.N. (2009). What's it all about? Framing in political science. In: Keren, G. (ed), *Perspectives on framing*. New York: Psychology Press. https://doi.org/10.4324/9780203854167

Fairclough, N. (1993). Critical discourse analysis and the marketization of public discourse: The universities. *Discourse & Society*, 4(2): 133–68.

Fairclough, N. (2015). *Critical discourse analysis*. https://balticpractice.hse.ru/data/2015/04/13/1094925608/Critical%20discourse%20analysis_THEORY_FAIRCLOUGH.pdf

Foucault, M. (1972). *The archaeology of knowledge and the discourse on language*. London: Tavistock.

Foucault, M. (1977). *Discipline and punish: The birth of the prison*. London, Penguin.

Foucault, M. (1985). *The history of sexuality, 2: The use of pleasure*. New York: Pantheon.

Foucault, M. (2003). Society must be defended. Lectures at the College de France, 1975–76. (Trans. M. Bertani & A. Fontana). New York: Picador.

Hachoud, M. (2017). Search for a lost culprit. *Duel Amical!* http://duelamical.eu/en/articles/political-situation-poland

Henderson, W. (1994). Metaphor and economics. In: Backhouse, R.E. (ed), *New directions in economic methodology*. London: Taylor & Francis.

Heron, J. & Reason, P. (2001). Power and knowledge. In: Reason, P. & Bradley, H. (eds), *Handbook of action research: Participative inquiry and practice*. London: Sage.

Kaczyński, J. (2017). Wikiquote. https://pl.wikiquote.org/wiki/Jaros%C5%82aw_Kaczy%C5%84ski

Kinder, D.R. & Sanders, L.M. (1996). *Divided by color: Racial politics and democratic ideals*. Chicago: University of Chicago Press.

Lachaise, F. (2017). Towards the end of liberal democracy. *Duel Amical!* http://duelamical.eu/en/articles/political-situation-poland

Lakoff, G. & Johnson, M. (1980). *Metaphors we live by*. Chicago: University of Chicago Press.

Levin, I.P., Schneider, S.L. & Gaeth, G.J. (1998). All frames are not created equal. *Organizational Behavior and Human Decision Processes*, 76 (November): 149–88.

Mazurczak, F. (2015). Poland's presidential election and the future of Catholicism. *Crisis Magazine*, 14 October. https://www.crisismagazine.com/2015/polands-presidential-election-and-the-future-of-european-catholicism

Marcinkiewicz, K. & Stegmaier, M. (2017). Poland appears to be dismantling its own hard-won democracy. *The Washington Post*, July 21. https://www.washingtonpost.com/news/monkey-cage/wp/2017/07/21/poland-appears-to-be-dismantling-its-own-hard-won-democracy/

Niezalezna (2017). *Jarosław Kaczyński at the celebration of the Smolensk monthly: There will be monuments and there will be truth*, niezalezna.pl, 10 May 2017. https://pl.wikiquote.org/wiki/Jarosław_Kaczyński (English translation, Google).

Onet (2018). Jarosław Kaczyński: Warsaw has reached the bottom, onet.pl, 22 September 2018. https://pl.wikiquote.org/wiki/Jarosław_Kaczyński (English translation, Google).

Otieno, R.F. (2016). Metaphor in political discourse: A review of selected studies. International *Journal of English and Literature*, 7(2): 21–26. https://doi.org/10.5897/IJEL2015.0856

Pan, Z. & Kosicki, G.M. (2001). Framing as a strategic action in publication deliberation. In: Reese, S.D., Gandy, O.H. & Grant, A.E. (eds), *Framing public life*. Hillsdale: Erlbaum.

Pettit, J. (2010). Learning to do action research for social change. *International Journal of Communication*, 4: 820–27.

Reason, P. (1994). Three approaches to participatory inquiry. In: Denzin, N. & Lincoln. S. (eds), *Handbook of qualitative research*. Thousand Oaks, CA: Sage.

Rzeczpospolita (2017). *J. Kaczyński: Polish judiciary is a gigantic scandal*, rp.pl, 10 February 2017. https://pl.wikiquote.org/wiki/Jarosław_Kaczyński (English translation, Google).

Szczerbiak, A. (2017). Explaining the popularity of Poland's Law and Justice government. *EUROPP — European Politics and Policy, London School of Economics*, 26 October blog. http://blogs.lse.ac.uk/

wGospodarce (2017). *Jarosław Kaczyński: War is being waged against Europe*, wgospodarce.pl, 4 June 2017. https://pl.wikiquote.org/wiki/Jarosław_Kaczyński (English translation, Google).

Wiewióra, M. (2018). Polish judicial deform: Chapter of the Supreme Court. *Duel Amical!*, February 27. http://duelamical.eu/en/articles/new-act-supreme-court-poland

Photo by Tom Perkins, CC-BY 4.0

V.

DISCOURSES THAT EXPLORE OR REVEAL DIVERSITY: FACING CHOICE AND CHANGE

I n this section, chapters examine issues that arise when people move away (physically or emotionally) from their county or culture of birth and attempt to, and have to, manage disparate worldviews. The chapters are not about the migration processes but disruptions to normative cultural behaviours and expectations. Indeed, the third chapter, from Denmark, is a narrative of religious conversion rather than locational change, and the first, from Germany, is about an individual balancing autonomy against obedience to her parents' wishes. The second is a study using biographical approaches to examine the needs of migrants to England who have low-level literacy, and the fourth is a creative project to explore migration through the collaborative production of a documentary film.

In 'Examining a Kazakh Student's Biographical Narrative and the Discourses She Lives By' (Ch17), Rob Evans presents an interesting account of a young Kazakh women studying in Germany and learning to balance her own emancipatory needs with her family's desire for her to conform to traditional norms. Rob's approach is one of talk-in-action and, quite apart from his skilful interpretation of the shared texts, offers a good example of conversational analysis (CA) in practice, within a Foucauldian framework. He presents excerpts from his narrative interviews to demonstrate the CA process, intertwining method, examples, narrative and theorization to sculpt an integrated whole that does his participant justice.

Monica Mascarenhas's chapter, 'The Needs of Low-Literate Migrants When Learning the English Language' (Ch18), offers an insider account of research into the lives of migrants attending a college English course, to see if such teaching could be made to better suit the needs of learners as the present system is ineffective, although utilitarian. She collects the life stories of a number of migrants and realizes that if teachers were able to focus on the individual there would be much greater opportunity to enable language learning. Importantly, she finds that those with limited prior literacy, lack the necessary grasp of concepts, contexts and literate thinking necessary to be able to learn English, rendering the classes ineffective and highlighting the need for change.

Simone Rasmussen's study, 'Uncovering Habitus in Life Stories of Muslim Converts' (Ch19), uses a Bourdieusian framework (habitus) to look in detail at the lives and beliefs of two young Danish women who chose to convert to Islam without previous religious affiliation. It thus introduces a different strand into the field of conversion, where earlier work identifies converts as commonly moving between radical Christianities to orthodox Islamic branches. For Simone's participants, the reasons appear to be more individualized and quite complex, but both women seek inner peace and links to a nurturing community.

In 'Participatory Approaches in Critical Migration Research: The Example of an Austrian Documentary Film' (Ch20), Annette Sprung looks critically at the construction of the migrant in adult education and considers the researcher's role in reproducing or challenging problematic categories. The research project is multi-layered. Its focus is the collaborative production of a documentary film featuring migrant adult educators, but the process is then subject to group reflection, the filmmakers questioned to determine their sense of 'othering' the film's subjects. Together these processes made visible aspects affecting diversity that are hard to capture in more generalized investigations.

As a group, these chapters offer insights into displacements (physical and emotional) that are not commonly explored, and the detailed individualized data sheds lights on some of the issues that are commonly disrupting political stability in Europe and beyond. They are sympathetic nuanced accounts that seek understanding, and the researchers make considerable efforts to reveal difference without casting those from different background as 'other' in ways they are not. In Evans' case the method is an interactive one, in Sprung's case both her role and her views are structured into the project. Mascarenhas, as a former English Language tutor for her participants, and as someone who has successfully and frequently moved between different languages and cultures, is also able to offer an account that is partially shaped by an insider's perspective, whereas Rasmussen is using an outsider's perspective to observe people's choices anew.

Within the book as a whole, there are clear links with the work in the next section where authors discuss interventions to support diversity, particularly the chapters by Chan (Ch21), Ylitapio-Mäntylä & Mäkiranta (Ch22), and Oikarinen-Jabai's work (Ch27) with young adults with a Muslim background is very relevant and is also a creative project. Like Brayshaw & Granville's film project (Ch24), their creative approaches may provoke new ideas when read alongside Sprung's work. Those who read Mascarenhas's chapter because of its focus on language learning may be interested in the discussions of talk-in-action in the Evans chapter (Ch17) and Breton's study of language use and storying in the care sector (Ch2).

17. Examining a Kazakh Student's Biographical Narrative and the Discourses She Lives By

Rob Evans

Rob Evans offers excerpts from the story of a Kazakh girl who is trying to straddle two cultures but feels disloyal when criticizing her family's actions. He uses Conversation Analysis (close listening and transcriptional devices) to catch and demonstrate nuanced meanings and sets these processes in a strong theoretical and methodological framework.

The starting point of this chapter was a question about the conceptual frameworks that bound people's thoughts and actions and how these matter to a global society. In connection with biographical research, this meant asking about the relationship between the real-life narratives that researchers collect and the commonly held discourses we live by. Do our narratives merely reflect these discourses, or do they shape our acceptance of them? Do our stories transform understandings and potentially change our — and others' — ways of living?

This chapter will take a 'low-inference' approach (following Seale, 1999) using an extract from an unstructured interview narrative to question the discourses evident within the narrative, one closely heard and transcribed, read and examined. To do this, an approach to talk-in-interaction derived from Conversation Analysis (Silverman, 1998) is followed. Briefly, Conversation Analysis (CA) is a method of close analysis of talk, based on detailed and accessible transcripts on which

https://doi.org/10.11647/OBP.0203.17

added symbols record the conversational structures not heard as words, as shown below.

xx::	Word-lengthening, drawl	Xx=xx	Rapid run-ons from word to word
(.)	Pauses (audible breaks in flow of speech)	(1.0)	Pause (timed to nearest second)
hh	Out-breaths/laughter	.hh	In-breaths
°xxx°°	Quiet speech	+xxx++	Rapid speech
(xxx)	Indistinct speech	XXX	Loud, excited speech
(ESp)	Embedded speech = speech of others	Pro / MO	Prosodic device / Modality

In this chapter I employ a talk-in-interaction approach to the analysis of stretches of conversational discourse that is able to synthesize, on the one hand, the attention of CA practice to the close detail of the work done by people in interaction and, on the other, the elements of interdiscursivity arising from the fact that close interpersonal interaction is simultaneously unfolded within, not just one, but a whole set of overlapping and intersecting communicative contexts. This approach to interview talk enables us to ask questions about contrasting discourses emerging in narratives; to consider, too, the origins of dominant discourses, their irruption into narratives, their unfolding, the weight they exert on interaction and daily life choices, their application to lives and to our research. To this end, although I draw from a series of discursive-narrative biographical interviews with young adults in university education, for reasons of space I will consider only parts of one of these interviews. The interview with a Kazakh student, I hope to show, presents talk-in-interaction which will help to address the above questions.

Aylin

Aylin (the student chose this interestingly 'un-Kazakh' name herself) is in her early twenties. She had recently completed her Bachelor's degree in international management at a German university where I interviewed her. She was born in Moscow of Kazakh parents, a construction engineer and a philologist who both studied in Russia. She speaks Kazakh and Russian, and moved from Moscow to Astana at the age of nine, the first in her family to live in the Kazakh capital. The interview ranged across Aylin's childhood memories of life in Moscow, the trees, parks, and colours of Astana. In Moscow she lived close to Red Square and attended a 'very good school' (School No. 1131). She recalled her parents' fear after an encounter once, before her ninth birthday, with Russian skinheads (*britogolovye*) armed with sticks. She connected this memory with the removal of all her family's Kazakh acquaintances back to Kazakhstan at around the same time. Astana and her schooldays were characterized by her early assumption of responsibility in the home, practically managing the household (her elder sister was 'more interested in clothes and things') and looking after her younger brother while her busy parents worked. She changed schools seven times in this period. The interview, it transpired, was taking place at a crucial moment in her life, as she was about to return home to Kazakhstan, where her future would be decided. Her wish was to continue her studies with an MA in another German city. The wish of her family, she said, was that she should remain in Kazakhstan to marry. This is what Aylin said:

Extract One: I'm Going Back to Kazakhstan

1	I'm going back to Kazakhstan (.) I don't really want	Modality/ Loss
2	to but I guess I have to (.) because (1) uhmm (1) my	of agency
3	parents want me to go back and g- =and it's time and	Hedge/
4	I'm allowed only to marry a Kazakh guy=maybe I	Hedge/ Othered
5	can find one here but it's hh	agency
6	hh	Amusement
7	.............................I KNOW	Pro
8	SOMETIMES the guys (1.0) it's not like hhh I hhh	Hedge/Othered
9	can marry them	discourse

Extract 1: I'm going back to Kazakhstan

The discomfort Aylin feels in broaching this subject seems to jump off the inadequate printed page. This short extract already shows evidence of serious discomfort (1–2), dis-preferred topics and strong hedging (2, 3, 4–5), and the reluctance to put items of her narrative into words. Strong loss of agency is hearable here and this is partly mitigated by transferring agency to others (parents) and force of circumstances (it is time).

The 'modality' of much of the language (i.e., the relative significance of necessity — 'have to'; desire, reluctance or will — 'want to'; possibility or ability, freedom or restriction — 'can', 'allowed to'; and intention / decision / obedience — 'am going back') is striking and seems to demonstrate the many-layered-ness, the ambivalence and the liquidity of Aylin's short account. There is prosaic telling (we can term it 'naked saying' of things), and there is an enormous pregnancy of word-choice. The verb 'want' is used contiguously, for example, to express diametrically opposed notions; undesired submission against the imposition of force (ll. 1–3). In this context, the othered-discourse of the parents breaks into Aylin's talk and 'want me to get married' is repaired to 'I'm allowed only to' (for repair, see Gülich & Mondada, 2008, pp. 61–65). Her loss of agency shifts from 'I' to 'they' to an accepted fact, and the repeated, known, unquestioned social discourse of her background moves to occupy the foreground of her narrative.

Stripped Text, Language Resources

To present this 'complaint', I have used an unadorned stripped form of text (no punctuation, no sentence structure, no intentional 'correction' of language). Aylin uses English, which she speaks very well. She refused implicitly to speak Russian, though I do well enough. I make no attempt to convey pronunciation, yet there is some attempt to communicate obvious features of pitch, speed, loudness and quietness, breathing and laughter, hesitation and silence. The discussion of the transcript is focused on description of what is 'there' (what was heard there and then transcribed) and on features such as modality, repair/hedging, prosody, and voice (embedded speech).

As I have pointed out elsewhere (Evans, 2016, pp. 229–30), the plurilingual conduct of research relationships can guarantee linguistic detail that can render the ethnographic description denser in meaning. Contrasting or shared language is clearly part of the complexity of the interdiscursivity that the interview establishes. However, speaking the language of the dominant cultural discourse, English, sets in motion, too, 'self-authoring' in the foreign code (Auer, 1998; Duszak, 2002), as well as code-switching, which remains inaccessible to the listener and must, as Pavlenko points out, be taken into account when evaluating narrative contents and intentions (Pavlenko, 2007, pp. 171–75).

Regarding the making and use of transcripts, Atkinson and Heritage showed long ago that they are 'research activities' (Atkinson & Heritage, 1984, cited in Silverman, 1997a, p. 27). Thus, the decision to opt for a particular level of detail in the reproduction of the spoken interview, or the omission of detail, represents the fundamental level of analysis chosen (Gülich & Mondada, 2008, pp. 21–22, 30–34; Ochs, 1979). Likewise, the analysis of timing, volume, intonation, stress, and prosody, which are understood to be essential products and producers of interaction and co-construction of meaning (Szczepek Reed, 2011; Günthner, 1997).

Aylin also gave me two photographs. The first shows a pair of adults with a baby on a sunny day. The adults are young, late twenties or early thirties perhaps, around 1994. They are dressed formally, smartly: the man (thin, looking seriously into the camera) in a double-breasted suit, shirt and tie; the woman, slim, elegant in a black top and skirt, smart short hair, serious gaze; the child, round in a thick layer of covers, a white ball with a small round face. Behind the couple showing off their child — St Basil's Cathedral, Red Square, Moscow — definitely the place to be photographed, still, in post-Soviet Russia. The other photo is of Aylin at a McDonalds birthday party, it seems: a child, open-mouthed, mesmerized by something going on out of frame. Where, in this sparse mixture of narrated events, a jumble of bare facts and geography, is discourse located? How can we pinpoint, recognize, follow, question it; understand how it is working?

Starting from a Blank Space with Michel Foucault

Since the much-cited 'linguistic turn', discourse has passed through many forms in qualitative research focused on language or language-near interaction. As with so many other concepts, discourse is often used in a very loose fashion and can describe anything from a limited exchange of utterances between speakers — as in classroom discourse (Maybin, 1994); service exchanges and customer-salesperson talk (Drew & Heritage, 1992); specific professional / academic / discipline 'codes' (medical, legal discourse, etc.); or the overarching chains or sequences of language (semiotic sequences, language in all conceivable forms, codes, linguistic, visual, symbols, practices) that in relation to one another (interdiscursivity) offer or impose conceptual frameworks — to the 'big packages' (Sacks, 1992b, pp. 354–59) of cultural and political narratives, which is the understanding of discourse adopted in this chapter.

Interdiscursivity in interaction (co-constructing meaning and sharing language) and relational employment or appropriation of discourses in biographical narratives (Mason, 2004; Mishler, 2006) can be seen as enacting the tension between structure and agency that resides in the culturally constituted social practices that massively determine individual and collective interaction. The agency of the individual always has more, or less, access to accumulated layers of experience that represent more resources of experience than can be 'used' at any one time, yet they go to create a kind of intuitive sense of an own biography, that is self-referential and remains 'porous', transforming and being transformed in ongoing interactions, given that it arises precisely from interdiscursive interaction. The individual's potential to respond to, and to shape, discourse can be seen as drawing on biographical resources, 'biographicity' in Alheit's words (Alheit, 2006, p. 5). The narrative of the young adult presented in this chapter is evidence of the porosity between ubiquitous discourses of discipline, of love, of family, of learning, ambition, obedience, resignation, but equally within a melting of scenes, geographies, zones of comfort and zones of menace, and so on.

To begin to focus on what is discourse, then, it may help to turn first to Foucault, the Foucault of *The Archaeology of Knowledge* (1969), who took stock of what he had achieved in the 'sixties with the clinic and madness and turned to ask how knowledge, how the history of thought and ideas can be conceived. His attempt, full of precautions, 'hobbling' and 'feeling its way' (Foucault, 1969, p. 28) provides a usefully uncertain starting point for considering the notion of discourse.

Discussing the history of ideas and thought and knowledge and the sciences, Foucault says he is attempting to speak from an *'espace blanc'*, that is, a 'blank space' (Foucault, 1969, p. 29). His first job is to accomplish a *'travail negatif'*, a bit of negative work, to free himself and his analysis from all notions that tend to anchor, immovably fix, ideas in solid continuities. Mentalities, the spirit, tradition, custom — all are assigned a *'communauté de sens'* (a community of sense), a symphony of resemblances, mirrorings and repetitions that lend them overwhelming authority (1969, p. 33). To sweep away these anchored certainties, he writes:

> We have to question these ready-made syntheses, these bundles of ideas that one commonly assumes without any examination at all, these connections that are recognized as given before the game starts; it is necessary to debunk these obscure forms and forces with which we habitually tie together the discourses used by people [...]. (Foucault, 1969, p. 34) (Author's translation)

If we can manage to view our work from this blank space Foucault urges us to occupy, we have to see how we can 'feel the pulse', 'catch a glimpse' of the discourse that is, true, 'always there'. We must catch it, Foucault argues, where it irrupts, repeatedly, in acts, in decisions, in, for us most urgently, a story, a statement, an aside, an admission, an accusation, in the middle of an interview moment. Thus, he says, we must:

> Be ready to catch each moment of discourse in the moment of its irruption; in the very moment of its appearance, and in that dispersion in time that allows it to be repeated, known, forgotten, transformed, effaced down to the last traces, gone, far from all view [...]. (Foucault, 1969, p. 39, author's translation)

We turn now to Aylin again.

Extract Two: I Don't Know How to Explain That

E xtract two is dominated throughout by Aylin's repeated work of self-repair, that is, her starting, stopping, re-starting, correcting and her changes of direction in telling her story. There are many possible reasons for this. The narrative itself is difficult. She may believe it is difficult to understand. She may think the interviewer will condemn or reject the things she is telling, the people she is talking about, her thoughts, her decisions. She cannot tell her story without exposing her parents, her family, to criticism from a person she knows, but who has no knowledge of them — or of her, in fact. Thus, there are many examples of self-repair and hedging, as she seeks a path between 'tellability' (Sacks, 1992b, p. 16), comprehension, truth, respect and coherence (Linde, 1993).

Aylin's knowledge / understandings / forgettings / reasonings are recorded on the right of the extracts as epistemic language. These record epistemic claims as well as claims to ignorance. Both may be understood as statements about agency or its loss. Prosodic devices here (e.g.,

1	A yeah quite conservative (3.0) yeah (.) so (.) I	Self-repair attempt
2	(2.0) ACTually they SAY:: I find find some	← ESp
3	Kazakh boy in Kazakhstan I could move	
4	ANYWHERE hhhh but if he has to be a	← Pro
5	Kazakh guy (2.0) ja (.) but (.) they want they	Self-repair
6	want us to keep the tradITIONS so that we	
7	don't forget our la::nguage and yeah I think	
8	that's why (3.0) because they think that=now	
9	HERE I started forgetting our traditions and	← Pro/MO Epistemic
10	uhm I don't practice our language and uhm I'm	
11	becoming more:: uhm (.)	
12	RE: european	
13	A: ja↓ they	Rejection of other
14	want (2.0) they want me to stay like like uhm	discourse
15	ohh (4.0) like a as a (.) uhhh=how to say that	Self-repair/Hedging
16	hhh a good Kazakh GIRL hehehe I don't know	Hedging / Pro
17	how to say that and	Epistemic
18	RE what would you say	
19	in Russian or in Kazakh or	
20	A I don't know how to	Epistemic
21	explain that how to express myself they just	
22	wANT me to remain that uhh (5.0) they want	
23	me TO BE A GOOD EXAMPLE OF A	Other discourse / Pro
24	KAZAKH GIRL↓ ja (.) ja (.) that's what I	Repetition of the
25	mean who learn the traditions=the	criticisms above
26	language=who will take care o:f uhmm	Hedge
27	hhparents hh of her husband ya↓	Othered discourse
28	RE: I understand	
29	that is that attractive for a 22 year old?	
30	A: yah↓ (.) maybe I just forgot how it is there	Epistemic
31	uhm (.) I don't know (.) I=just WANT to do	Hedge/Pro/MO
32	what my parents want me to do I WANT to	Others' discourse/own
33	stay here	discourse
34	RE why?	
35	A: but if they're against I don't want °°to	MO Pro
36	disobey°° (.) because it's hard to (.) to	←Irruption
37	(R: I understand	
38	yeah)	
39	A: be against them ohh everybody will say oh	Pro
40	she's a BAD GIRL	ESp

Extract 2: I don't know how to explain that

louder speech, ll. 4, 9, 16, 23–24) can serve a number of purposes. In these cases, they seem to be moments in which Aylin imposes her own position, signals her stance or standpoint. This is a kind of 'breakout', surrounded as these bursts of energy or emotion are by difficulties in finding words and a discomfited wrestling with possible clarifications.

The prosodic device serves to bolster her position, but also functions spatially, in an acutely interactive fashion: she underlines her immediate physical presence, and her utterance is agentive (first person) and knowledgeable, if also often desperate (ll. 17, 21).

It seems plausible that Aylin's claims that she is unable to explain the family discourses around marriageability and ethnic exclusivity (ll–15–17, 20–24) are, in part, other-oriented. She hesitates to share the words of her family with an outsider of different age, gender, ethnic origin, experience and knowledge. Likewise, her unease when explaining the traditional duties of the daughter-in-law (ll. 26–27) are framed in hedges, delivered breathlessly and at a rush. Much of the distress in Aylin's narrative is thus evidently lived as distress with the narrative and difficulty with the listener.

Finally, the irruption of the discourse of her extended family, of the distant, threateningly foreign and discernibly hostile world of her past — she speaks of traditions, of having forgotten them, of the family wanting her to stay as she was before — is heard as embodied fatality, lived and expressed as necessity and inevitability (ll.35–36) and spoken in an almost awed quietness of voice. The horror of being, of being found to be, disobedient, is spoken with hearable difficulty. Aylin, it seems, is reluctant to express an alternative to what she says she is facing. The different layers of experience contained in this short extract permeate each other and this biographical porosity is reflected in the complexity of the diverse discursive strands of the narrative and their incomplete meanings as heard.

To approach Aylin's biographical narrative and attempt to unravel and comprehend the hardly understood, tacitly understood, seemingly understood discursive textures in her account, and to encompass the traces — forgotten, transformed, known, repeated, effaced — of the discourses so obviously at work, we must, as has already been demonstrated, 'fix' the tools we intend to use.

Ontological and Epistemological First Things

Right from the start, the question of what count as 'facts' (i.e., the ontological view of research undertakings) needs to be clarified. If the biographical interview is seen as a key to open some kind of door

Discourses We Live By

into the thinking of subjects and thereby release a flood of thoughts and utterances about things and feelings, times and events, etc., then the data analysis will be occupied with sifting and separating out what was simply 'said'. The researcher may step back and present the words, the things said. She or he may interpret them in his or her own words. 'Objective' facts — a curriculum vitae, a birth certificate, an army record, a medal, a prize, a wedding photo — may be employed to justify a distanced interpretation of the said (Fuchs-Heinritz, 2000, pp. 265–67; Rosenthal & Fischer-Rosenthal, 2000, pp. 460–61).

Alternatively, the data are seen as constituted in the interview process jointly and as a process. The talk is not analysed as 'facts' or 'examples', rather the speech as interaction. The construction of dialogic talk in the interview is analysed. The interview is then no longer a 'realist' instrument for looking at the grittiness of something 'out there', but at the narrative construction of biographical experience, a learning biography.

Seen in this way, the research interview accesses stories or narratives through which people describe their world (Silverman, 2000). This approach sees talk as evidence of the joint generation by interviewer and interviewees of plausible accounts of the world. The interview is employed less as a 'collection' containing the objective data that the realist view commonly assumes to be 'out there', than as a sensitive space, in which the linguistic repertoires or methods which people draw upon in constructing accounts in interactive encounters can unfold (Seale, 1998, pp. 212–15).

The epistemological aspect of this change of perspective means that the interactive features of the data are highlighted. We cannot know in any final way what people are thinking, what Aylin is thinking, but we can follow how interviewees are positioned and position themselves in discoursal fashion in the course of the continually changing contexts of the interview. For around and beyond the immediate action of the talk, the narration, the conversation, there is a context of relations, exerting their influence on the conjoint work of the interaction.

If my research question, or one of them, here is — why does Aylin speak of 'obedience'? What does this mean for her? — I am assuming that (such) discourses ('obedience') are involved in the make-up (are core components) of social life and that they are somehow knowable through research; it is possible to generate (local) knowledge about, and evidence of them. The language of the talk allows us to hear Aylin's distress in narrating a difficult story.

The above research question poses questions about the influence of discourse on learning biographies as well as the influence of a learning biography on discourse practices. Evidence of such influence is sought in the practical accomplishment — within the interactive setting of the research interview — of narrative discourses of self and learning. This qualitative research draws out a number of significant features from the interactional talk in the context of the research interview. Various aspects of the talk of respondents are examined:

- the employment of coherent narratives;

- the construction of learning biographies;

- the organization of discourses of learning both within and in opposition to dominant discourses;

- the employment of own and others' discourse in meaning-making and in doing;

- the employment of membership-category information to ground discoursal self in talk, i.e., membership of community, family, ethnic belonging, professional practice, identification with, and recognition of, other values, notions, and so on (Baker, 1997; Lepper, 2000).

If the 'real world' to which my explanations will frequently refer is a 'reference to the organized activities of everyday life' and the phenomena that I will be participating in and investigating in the course of my research can be seen as 'an ongoing accomplishment of the concerted activities of daily life' the accomplishment of which are 'ordinary, artful' and known and used by members of society (Garfinkel, 1967,p.vii), then it follows that my research methodology must serve the purposes of this theoretical approach to 'reality'. To be more exact, the methods arising from the research perspective I adopt must be able to generate ontologically stable data around the research questions I formulate. There should, then, be a theoretical and methodological fit between the overarching model of social experience I am advancing — social interaction is accomplished in artful, common-sense fashion, involving accounts that combine particulars of the social and cultural practices of individuals as well as their diffusely interactional practices (Silverman, 1997b, p. 114) — and the methods of data collection and data analysis I have opted to use.

To reduce this to a 'really useful' way of seeing our interest in practice in specific settings, I recall Harvey Sacks' famous 'this-and-that', which he applied to the work of the Chicago school of ethnography of the 1930s. The relevance of the works of the Chicago sociologists, he suggests, 'is that they do contain a lot of information about this and that. And this-and-that is what the world is made up of' (Sacks, 1992a, p. 27).

To approach 'this-and-that', I can draw upon a series of 'ontological components' as proposed by Jennifer Mason (1996, pp. 11–12) that may form the aspects of social reality that a piece of research sets out to explain; the following are directly relevant:

- interactions, situations, social relations;
- social or cultural practices;
- stories, narratives, biographies;
- identity, self;
- understandings.

These research components broadly represent practices and are all facets of 'doing being ordinary' (Sacks, 1992b, pp. 215–21). All of these data sources can be taken as sources of 'naturally occurring talk'; none of them are a simple 'window' onto the world (Seale, 1998, p. 215), none the mere 'registration' of realities ignoring the context and the history of their coming about that Bourdieu criticizes (Bourdieu, 1980, pp. 87–88).

Creation of Discoursal Meaning and Self in Interaction

Deborah Tannen (Tannen, 1993a), in her work on 'frames' and 'framing devices' — in which she draws in part on the work of Erving Goffman on frame analysis — contributes a further insight into the structure of autobiographical talk when she writes of 'structures of expectation' and their role in 'verbalization in the telling of oral narratives' (Tannen, 1993b, p. 15). These structures of expectation — tacitly understood meanings in spoken interaction about what is meant — establish a common-sense basis of understanding, characterized, to use Goffman's definition, by 'normatively residual ambiguity' (Goffman, 1981, p. 11). Tannen herself is stressing here the play of commonly held cultural 'structures of expectation' in individual interaction (Tannen, 1993a, p. 16). Ambiguity, however, and incompleteness characterize the life history and biographical narrative. The individual is understood to have access to a range of discourses. This range may seem endless, yet Foucault points out that:

> The field of discursive events [...] is always the finite and currently limited sum of mere linguistic sequences that have been formulated; they can be innumerable; they can, by their sheer mass, surpass any possibility of being recorded, memorized or read: they constitute nevertheless a finite entity. (Foucault, 1969, pp. 41–42, author translation)

This enormous resource is available to us in the lives and words of others, in temporally and spatially structured reservoirs of own and other experience. At the same time, life stories are essentially occupied with the necessity to synchronize disparate levels of experienced time and practices (Alheit, 1983, p. 189). The cyclical, routine, repeated character of the everyday offers security and provides sets of 'frames' for communication and interpretation. Linde also points out how other peoples' stories (related in reported speech, embedded and 'layered' in the telling) become 'own' stories through a process of appropriation or conversion (Linde, 1993, p. 35). The discontinuous and unfinished state of the oral narrative is embodied therefore in the discourse(s) employed by the narrator. Goffman's concept of 'embedding' describes this aspect of the speaker's 'self'. Embedding makes it possible to 'enact' numerous voices over space and time in interactive frames such as the narrative interview (Goffman, 1981, p. 4). For the development of 'own' discourses within an emergent learning biography, the 'enacted' words of others — 'embedded speech' — are central for contextualizing own discourse, and they can serve as a powerful (and fateful) way of grounding own positions within larger discourse.

Extract Three: Everybody Was Against Me

1	A: yah ↓ (.) maybe I just forgot how it is there	Epistemic
2	uhm (.) I don't know (.) I=just WANT to do	Hedge/Pro/MO
3	what my parents want me to do I WANT to	Others' discourse/o
4	stay here	discourse
5	RE: why?	
6	A: but if they're against I don't want °°to	MO / Pro
7	disobey °° (.) because it's hard to (.) to	← Irruption
8	RE: understand yeah	
9		
10	A: be against them ohh everybody will say oh	Pro
11	she's a BAD GIRL	← ESp
12	RE: you've been under that kind of pressure?	
13	in the family?	
14	A: I WAS under that pressure yeah because I	
15	had (.) a boyfriend? from Singapore? and	
16	THEY	
17	RE: here?	
18	A: yeah that was	
19	HERE yeah but I think I was quite young silly	MO of place
20	and mayBE:: I was hoping I don't know I think	Hedge/Epistemic
21	that I wanted to TRY I think I wanted to try	MO/Epistemic
22	and then they were all the whole family they	
23	were (.) were just (.) and I don't want to	Hedge / resolution
24	experience that again (2.0) they said oh she is	ESp
25	such a bad (1.0) girl oh my (.) god they were	
26	saying bad things about me and (.) I didn't it	
27	didn't feel nice yeah it did it didn't feel nice=so	
28	EVERYbody was SO=they really=my	Self-repair
29	grandpa rents my uncles everybody was against	
30	me so (.) I was crying and crying and crying	
31	and (1.0) yah=so I don't want to go through	Resolution
32	that again I don't want to disobey them again	Resolution
33	(.) because I TRIED to:: (.) somehow	Pro
34	disobEY? so to say? but (.) I can't do that (.) I	
35	found that out can't do that so it's really	
36	hard =ESPECIALLY BECAUSE I'M A GIRL	Resolution/Pro

Extract 3: Everybody was against me

I n this last extract, in which we hear about Aylin's family conflict that has ended with her submission to the pressure exerted upon her from her distant yet patently powerfully vocal family, events are put in some order (ll. 22–30), the climax of the account is reached, and Aylin's new evaluation of her position results in her resolution (for now) of the conflict (ll. 31–32). Aylin is at pains to explain herself, yet the epistemic markers in the transcript point to continuing unease in taking up a firm position ('I was hoping I don't know I think that I wanted to...' ll. 20–21). Uncertain modality ('maybe', 'wanted to TRY' ll. 20–21) and non-agentic knowledge claims characterize her position in Germany ('HERE', l.19). Her freedom of choice and her ability to decide things in Germany are redefined and subordinated to the 'whole family' and its claims.

It is interesting how Aylin foregrounds the crisis by accounting for her sense of self-doubt, suggesting youth and silliness as a possible reason for her underestimation of the gravity of her 'transgression'. The hedging and cautious use of epistemic verbs suggest also, no doubt, that this 'silliness' is an afterthought. For she emphasizes very clearly that she most definitely tried to find another way for herself (l. 21). Having foregrounded her narrative in this way, she is able to fend off, to some extent, criticism of her return to obedience, should it be offered. To reinforce this, the resolution of the conflict or 'evaluation' is offered before the climax of the crisis, or 'complicating action' (for these categories, see Labov, 1999). The outcome precedes the cause and shapes the point of the narrative as it is to be understood by the 'other' ('I don't want to experience that again', ll. 23–24). Further, as can be seen, this resolution is added again as Aylin's frame for the whole crisis (l. 34). This may mean that Aylin submits, returns to the fold of obedience. Just as much, however, it demonstrates how the force of the past, breaking into Aylin's present, is able to exert a strong structuring rectification, and in the process, it produces an obviously ambivalent transformation of her understanding of her position, but a transformation certainly.

There is submission in her words. There is also resistance and greater clarity about things. And some suggestion of a different Aylin ('I found that out can't do that so it's really hard=ESPECIALLY BECAUSE I'M A GIRL', ll- 34–6).

The Structured and Structuring Force of Discourse, Habitus and Practice

B ourdieu, in *Le Sens pratique* (Bourdieu, 1980) goes to some lengths to spell out the difficult but necessary — and uneasy — relationship between the shaping forces of structure and agency, or habitus and practice, as he calls them. He proposes a 'system of structured and structuring dispositions that is constituted in practice and which is always oriented towards functions of practice'. (Bourdieu, 1980, p. 87) Bourdieu argues that habitus — which I understand in a simple way to be sets of discourses about life, behaviour, self, opinion, etc., coagulated into seemingly fixed and socially definable practices — is made up of 'systems of durable and transposable dispositions which are structured structures predisposed to function as structuring structures', and which for all their structured-ness and massive shaping force on behaviours and feelings, plans and dreams, play out in time and space in an apparently orchestrated fashion 'without being the product of the organizing action of the conductor of the orchestra' (Bourdieu, 1980, pp. 88–89). The parameters within which biographical resources, for example, are slowly, incrementally gathered and used, re-used, often not used (because unusable at any given time and only 'usable' in retrospect) and stories, narratives of their use or possible meaning are developed and communicated, are limiting and limited, but limitless, too. Regarding the languaged forms of discursive interaction, Foucault makes the important point — which is useful, here, to throw a light on the many-layered workings of biographical 'background knowledge' and the structuring force of 'unlived life' (Alheit, 2006, p. 5) — that an utterance (languaged interaction) 'is always a [discoursal] event that neither language nor meaning can ever totally encompass and exhaust' (Foucault, 1969, p. 43).

On the shaping and shaped-ness of discourse, Fairclough, too, writes that 'On the one hand, discourse is shaped and constrained by social structure in the widest sense and at all levels [...] On the other hand, discourse is socially constitutive'. Discourse, he continues, 'is a practice not just of representing the world, but of signifying the world, constituting and constructing the world in meaning' (Fairclough, 1992, p. 64).

Vying Contexts
and the Co-Construction of Discourse

C ontext, therefore, is centrally important here and Fairclough's framework for analysing discourse offers a degree of useful complexity because it distinguishes between various contexts of 'discoursal action'. Fairclough proposes the following hierarchy: actual discourses / types of discourse / orders of discourse (Fairclough, 1989, p. 29). This hierarchy can be useful with the kind of talk encountered in Aylin's story. The immediate experience of the interview context for those involved is acutely interactive. The interaction includes the time, the physical space and the participants' relationship to this space and to each other (organizationally, socially) within the space, as well as the joint accomplishment of meaning in interactive talk. Further, the interview is embedded in a much larger interactive context, including the institutional character of the research interview and its organization, and sequences of interaction between researcher and respondents over longer time periods. Such interpersonal contexts may involve questions of access and familiarity, as well as linguistic, idiomatic, local, political or ideological discourses of communication, which are expected, accepted, unconsciously employed, or imposed. The 'long sequences' of personal experience that are narrated create, in their turn, the context at this level. These long sequences of experience-in-talk develop and are tested, are tried, rejected, repaired, and begun again and make up the work of meaning-making for which the interview provides a framework. Finally, we have the larger context of social discourses, the social context in which the participants and the institutions involved interpret their roles and positions (see, for the hierarchy of discourse, Fairclough, 1989, pp. 26–27).

Some Ending Words

So, to briefly return to Aylin, to where she was left in her distress and her dilemma, the aim was to try and start from a kind of methodological scratch once again. A line in T. S. Eliot's poem *The Love Song of J. Alfred Prufrock* (1917) seems to aptly capture Aylin's — and the researcher's — situation. In this poem, after listing all the endless, disparate, desperate things, seen, done, heard, felt, after all this 'and so much more?' the speaker resigns: 'It is impossible to say just what I mean!' (Eliot, 1954, p. 15). The job facing me as I approach Aylin's story, her language (choices), her own grasp of the many significances of the discourses she is tapping into, with her story of a possible arranged marriage, discussed in an interview in an emotional space between a

post-industrial university city in eastern Germany and an extended
family in Kazakhstan, and 'so much more!', demand that I recognize
that it is impossible to say all I, all she, means. And that is, of course, still
a glaring understatement of the situation. But we start from this point,
and we pick ourselves up and always start all over again.

Bourdieu, as so often, provides encouragement:

> Embodied life history, rendered natural and thus forgotten because
> natural, habitus is the active presence of the entire past of which it is itself
> the product: from this it confers on practices their relative independence
> in relation to the external determination of the immediate present. This
> autonomy is that of the enacted and active past which — working like
> accumulated capital — produces the stuff of history from history and
> thus assures permanence in change which makes the individual agent *a
> world in the world*... (Bourdieu, 1980, p. 94, author's italics and translation)

And that is Aylin.

The coda of the story, of disobedience paid for with accusations and
tears, shame and fear of rejection, has since metamorphosed into the
lead-in to a new narrative, yet to be attempted. An email arrived from a
German metropolitan university with the words 'still not married' and
an emoticon. ☺

References

Alheit, P. (1983). *Alltagsleben. Zur Bedeutung eines gesellschaftlichen
'Restphänomens'*. Frankfurt/New York: Campus Verlag.

Alheit, P. (2006). *'Biografizität' als Schlüsselkompetenz in der Moderne. Paper
presented at the Universität Flensburg Tagung: Das Leben gestalten. Biografisch
lernen — biografisch lehren.* http://www.abl-uni-goettingen.de/aktuell/
Alheit_Biographizitaet_Schluessel_Flensburg-2006.pdf

Atkinson, J.M. & Heritage, J. (eds) (1984). Structures of social action (Cambridge:
Cambridge University Press); cited in Silverman, D. (1997). *Discourses of
Counselling. HIV Counselling as Social Interaction*. London: Sage.

Auer, P. (ed) (1998). *Code-switching in conversation. Language, interaction and
identity.* London/New York: Routledge.

Baker, C. (1997). Membership categorization and interview accounts. In:
Silverman, D. (ed), *Qualitative research. Theory, method and practice*. London:
Sage.

Bourdieu, P. (1980). *Le sens pratique*. Paris: Les Éditions de Minuit.

Drew, P. & Heritage, J. (eds) (1992). *Talk at work. Interaction in institutional settings.* Cambridge: Cambridge University Press.

Duszak, A. (ed) (2002). *Us and others. Social identities across languages, discourses and cultures.* Amsterdam/Philadelphia: John Benjamins.

Eliot, T.S. (1954). *Selected poems.* London: Faber & Faber.

Evans, R. (2016). Life is normal in Donetsk: Narratives of distant conflicts and young adults' learning biographies. In: Formenti, L. & West, L. (eds), *Stories that make a difference. Exploring the collective, social and political potential of narratives in adult education research.* Lecce: Pensa.

Fairclough, N. (1989). *Language and power.* London: Longman.

Fairclough, N. (1992). *Discourse and social change.* Cambridge: Polity Press.

Foucault, M. (1969). *L'archéologie du savoir.* Paris: Gallimard.

Fuchs-Heinritz, W. (2000). *Biographische Forschung. Eine Einführung in Praxis und Methoden.* Wiesbaden: Westdeutscher Verlag.

Garfinkel, H. (1967). *Studies in ethnomethodology.* Cambridge: Polity Press.

Gülich, E. & Mondada, L. (2008). *Konversationsanalyse. Eine Einführung am Beispiel des Französischen.* Tübingen: Max Niemeyer Verlag.

Günthner, S. (1997). Complaint stories. Constructing emotional reciprocity among women. In: Kotthoff, H. & Wodak, R. (eds), *Communicating gender in context.* Amsterdam: John Benjamins.

Labov, W. (1999). The transformation of experience in narrative. In: Jaworski, A. & Coupland, N. (eds), *The discourse reader.* London/New York: Routledge.

Lepper, G. (2000). *Categories in text and talk. A Practical Introduction to categorization analysis.* London: Sage.

Linde, C. (1993). *Life stories. The creation of coherence.* New York /Oxford: Oxford University Press.

Mason, J. (1996). *Qualitative researching.* London: Sage.

Mason, J. (2004). Personal narratives, relational selves: Residential histories in the living and telling. *The Sociological Review,* 52: 162–79. https://doi.org/10.1111/j.1467-954X.2004.00463.x

Maybin, J. (1994). Children's voices: Talk, knowledge and identity. In: Graddol, D., Maybin, J. & Stierer, B. (eds), *Researching language and literacy in social context.* Clevedon: Multilingual Matters.

Mishler, E. (2006). Narrative and Identity: The double arrow of time. In: De Fina, A., Schiffrin, D. & Bamberg, M. (eds), *Discourse and identity.* Cambridge: Cambridge University Press. https://doi.org/10.1017/CBO978 0511584459.003

Ochs, E. (1979). Transcription as theory. In Ochs, E. & Schieffelin, B.B. (eds), *Developmental pragmatics*. New York: Academic Press.

Pavlenko, A. (2007). Autobiographic narratives as data in applied linguistics. *Applied Linguistics*, 28: 163–88. https://doi.org/10.1093/applin/amm008

Rosenthal, G. & Fischer-Rosenthal, W. (2000). Analyse narrativ-biographischer Interviews. In: Flick, U., Von Kardoff, E. & Steinke, I. (eds), *Qualitative Forschung*. Reinbek: Rowohlt Taschenbuch Verlag.

Sacks, H. (1992a). *Lectures in conversation, I*. Oxford: Blackwell Publishing.

Sacks, H. (1992b). *Lectures in conversation, II*. Oxford: Blackwell Publishing.

Seale, C. (1998). Qualitative interviewing. In: Seale, C. (ed), *Researching society and culture*. London: Sage.

Seale, C. (1999). *The Quality of Qualitative Research*. London: Sage.

Silverman, D. (1997a). *Discourses of counselling. HIV counselling as social interaction*. London: Sage.

Silverman, D. (ed) (1997b). *Qualitative research. Theory, method and practice*. London: Sage.

Silverman, D. (1998). *Harvey Sacks. Social Science and Conversation Analysis*. London: Sage.

Silverman, D. (2000). *Doing qualitative research. A practical handbook*. London: Sage.

Szczepek Reed, B. (2011). *Analysing conversation. An introduction to prosody*. Basingstoke: Palgrave Macmillan.

Tannen, D. (ed) (1993a). *Framing in discourse*. Oxford: Oxford University Press.

Tannen, D. (1993b). What's in a frame? Surface evidence for underlying expectations. In: Tannen, D. (ed), *Framing in discourse*. Oxford: Oxford University Press.

18. The Needs of Low-Literate Migrants When Learning the English Language

Monica Mascarenhas

Monica Mascarenhas considers language-teaching provision for migrants to Britain, its instrumentality, its universality and its oblivion to their backgrounds, concerns, losses, and aspirations. A former language lecturer, she collected the life stories of students with low-level or no literacy in their home languages in order to seek ways to better motivate them to learn. She finds that fundamental changes are needed if such teaching is to be effective.

'Inside I want to scream, but I can only whisper; I am too weak... I want everyone to hear me. I want to give my scars a voice!'

'When I can read and write all the letters, I will be a lawyer! I will go back and help all the people in my country.'

'I was enslaved, but my children will be free!'

'I cannot help my children with their homework; they already know more than I do, so I pretend I am busy...'

'I was an 'untouchable'. Now I am invisible!'

'My parents constantly told me I was not clever, so I had to work hard from the age of five to help pay for my brothers and sisters' education.'

'I was brought up in a brothel. They always told me that pretty girls don't need to go to school.'

https://doi.org/10.11647/OBP.0203.18

And this is how this chapter begins — but not how the story ends. This is a never-ending story. Here is a glimpse of what is happening in the background, when some migrants want to access education and make a living in the UK.

Successive UK governments have funded ESOL[1] courses because they want migrants to integrate into society, but I suggest that these, often utilitarian, courses impose a restricted language that enables low-level employment rather than grasping the needs of immigrants and motivating them to play a full and active role as citizens. As a former Language teacher in an English Further Education[2] (FE) College I became increasingly aware that courses constrained rather than enabled students; I was therefore determined to undertake qualitative research to examine why this was the case.

With twelve students who had enrolled on my courses in the past, I carried out detailed in-depth interviews, sometimes in English, sometimes in their European language of choice, seeking to find out what motivated them to learn English and also what motivated them more generally. Using a life history approach, I asked about their early life experiences, their move to the UK and their life here, engendering open conversations by prefacing each prompt with the simple phrase 'Tell me about...'. The participants were keen to talk and brought in pictures, photographs and drawings to support their accounts. I gathered a wealth of material that illuminated the reasons why they decided to immigrate, and what has happened to them since. These I presented as 'stories' to allow them an impact that transcends the often hesitant, repetitive, even harrowing, narratives that we pieced together, together. However, I kept true to the emotions expressed and used the participants' words whenever possible to provide authenticity and give a strong and powerful voice to a group of people whose stories often go unheard.

---

1   English for Speakers of Other Languages.
2   Within the UK and Ireland, FE colleges provide courses for post-compulsory learners other than the traditional higher education degree. These often lead to skills-based and/or vocational qualifications.

When Language Teaching Walks Past Language Learning

In this chapter I focus on aspects of some of the stories from my research, but also on the role of language learning in supporting migrants' new lives, for I found in the study that those who had not achieved full literacy in their country of origin needed to learn how to learn before they were ready to learn a new language. This is an element that is not currently recognized within ESOL provision, which follows set guidelines intended to make it both efficient and effective. In contrast, the stories I excavated clearly demonstrate a need for 'artful' language teaching, teaching that takes into consideration the learners' cultural and personal experiences and tries to add meaning, relevance, authenticity and purpose to their lives. We need to take the learners' individual histories, their private dreams, their hopes and fears, their desires and aspirations into account if we are to be able to teach them to express themselves in English and enable them to communicate fully in a new language. Basic vocabulary and phrases intended to enable low-paid work are not enough if migrants are to make meaningful social and economic contributions within their countries of choice.

The twelve participants (ten women and two men) are adult immigrants to England (aged twenty-five to fifty-plus) who have left a variety of countries and contexts to settle in the UK. To protect their identities, they have been allocated a pseudonym, from a list of precious stones, e.g., Amethyst, Jade, Quartz, etc.

To contextualize my study, I investigated different aspects of learning. In addition to the formal learning experienced in the classroom, Griff Foley (2004) identified three additional dimensions to be important for adults: non-formal, informal and incidental. *Formal* education is the most familiar form of learning in Western societies. It is organized by institutions, it follows a set curriculum, is highly regarded and is recognized in the form of certificates or grades. *Non-formal* education has a temporal element to it, adding another dimension to learning. Foley (2004, p. 4) talks about a 'one-off or sporadic' method of instruction, which occurs mostly when people need to learn a skill for a purpose, such as how to operate a whiteboard, a projector or a machine. Indeed, in a study of formal and non-formal learning in language acquisition,

Sarah Eaton (2011) explores the skills transferred from a mother to a child as she passes on language knowledge to her young child, prior to school age, without having to explain about grammar structures.

Informal learning occurs 'when people consciously try to learn from their experience' (Foley 2004, p. 4). This can be done, for example, in classroom discussions, meetings, consultations and reviews. Similar ideas were proposed in an article by the Linguistic Integration of Adult Migrants (LIAM) on the Council of Europe Portal, but — in my opinion misguidedly — the ideas were seen as an innovative response to enabling cost-effective learning at a time when large numbers of refugees are moving around the world:

> ...in the short term it makes much better sense, and is certainly more affordable, to involve volunteers in the organisation of social activities that promote non-formal and informal language learning. If appropriately designed and efficiently implemented, such activities can provide migrant learners with a sound basis for participating in formal language courses at a later stage if that is judged to be desirable or necessary. (LIAM, 2018)

However well intended, this approach is not equipped to cater for the needs of those who have never been in education, those who do not have a concept of number, those who cannot see the purpose of writing and are not used to attending organized opportunities for learning.

Informal learning is less valued than formal learning in Western societies because it is unstructured and hard to control, but both are valid forms of learning, and deserve equal recognition. Informal learning can happen anywhere and anytime throughout one's life, and so it did for the twelve participants in this study. Nevertheless, current emphasis on policies and formal, classroom-based, ESOL practices seldom cater for experiential learning.

Fourthly, *incidental* learning, again undervalued, is constant and ongoing throughout our lives. It is not planned; it just happens. We are continually learning from our everyday activities, jobs and family. However, as powerful as this learning is, it may also be disempowering. Foley claims that incidental learning 'may be constructive or destructive [...] if there is learning, there is also non-learning [...] people can fail to learn or resist learning' (Foley, 2004, p. 5). In the current UK education system, some learners resist learning in order to preserve a sense of identity; some fail to see the value of what they are learning. Yet others see the learning journey as a no-win situation, and study participants often voiced this view, reminding me that educators need to be aware of their power to enable or disable learners.

Pertinently, Morrice (2014) reminds us of the need to explore the ever-expanding socio-cultural environments and learning processes. In terms of learning experiences, the world is no longer fragmented by physical borders or oceans. Travelling is no longer prohibitively expensive. Budget airlines facilitate movement of people and cultural exchanges. Money is also easily transferred around the world, facilitating other experiences, including numeracy and financial literacy skills. In the current climate of international migration, such developments are highly important. Nowadays, migrants engage in transnational communication facilitated by modern technology. Migrants can keep in touch with their relatives in their country of origin and in other countries too. They can exchange learned experiences and information, enabling 'receivers' to extend their existing knowledge repertoires. A common example of this is how stories, songs or even recipes are exchanged and disseminated around the world. Migrants who travel a long way to their destination, sometimes on foot and risking their lives, become exposed to a variety of learning episodes. Whether positive or negative events, travel experiences are invaluable learning in one way or another (Alenius, 2016).

During my conversations/interviews with the twelve participants it became evident that what is missing is not the certification, but the acknowledgement that for migrants to perform life tasks there was substantial learning somewhere along the way. For example, Sapphire mentions knowing how to clean her house, make her own clothes and cook for the family, but does so without having any certificates to confirm her extensive abilities. According to Crystal, her father was a competent professional, functioning at a high level in their country of origin, but he is currently deemed poorly skilled and illiterate in the UK. Quartz tells us that he used to build houses and make furniture and was proud of his manual skills. In the UK he is functioning at a basic level (Pre-Entry I), is currently on probation and looking for work. His low literacy skills disable him from obtaining the certificates necessary to prove that he is an experienced and competent craftsman, so he is unemployed and deskilled by the process of trying to acquire this certification.

It is crucial to understand that these skilled people, who were able to cope with life in extraordinary circumstances, are being demoted due to the misconception of what it is to be considered skilled. Failing to link experiences to skills may be leading to this limited perception of learning. A participant who travelled to the UK 'country by country' for months (Crystal), overcoming many challenges along the way, is now thought to be incompetent due to her lack of literacy skills. This is at best short-sighted. Indeed, Skills for Life courses do not mean that, on completion, the student is skilled for life, possibly even the opposite. Unless existing skills are acknowledged and built upon, newly acquired skills may sit in a vacuum. Informal, non-formal or incidental learning, and skills acquired through a variety of experiences, have a high cognitive value. In a world of multimedia, the more information becomes informal, the more learning can become seamless, almost without borders.

The Meaning(s) of Literacy

L iteracy is a 'core component of the right to education' according to the Universal Declaration of Human Rights (UNESCO, 2013, p. 17), yet although it is clearly of 'critical importance' for development, it was not clearly part of the Millennium Development Goals (UNESCO, 2013, p. 19). Globally, literacy privileges those who possess it, and in countries that are highly literate, it stigmatizes those who do not (ibid., p. 20). Illiteracy is still seen as an illness needing to be cured. Being able to read and write and work with numbers is 'an essential requirement for active participation in society' (ibid., p. 17). However, a more recent report provides us with a clear message: 'Investing in the education of those on the move is the difference between laying a path to frustration and unrest, and laying a path to cohesion and peace' (UNESCO, 2019, p.iii).

The debate around literacy is by no means new. In 1970, Paulo Freire succinctly conceptualized literacy as reading the world as well as the word. Freire

> ...saw the power of literacy as a way of reflecting back to learners their own lived experiences, not in a direct and immediate way but

systematised and amplified through dialogue, as part of educational process. (Goodman et al., 2003, p. 94)

Many years on, and the definition of the term literacy is still subject to discussion; still controversial, as opinions differ on what its meaning entails. Indeed, what it means to be literate, and what literacy is, are concepts in constant debate. Definitions of literacy still seem to be based around the ability to read and write 'appropriately' or to an acceptable level determined by the current standards. Nonetheless, it is not known what level this requires. Certainly, it is highly subjective (Cambridge Assessment Report, 2013).

In my conversations with Crystal she told me that she was perceived as a 'good student', who knew 'all the letters of the alphabet', which was highly regarded in her country of origin and very useful to her family as she could write shopping lists for her mother and help her father with reading his correspondence. However, once she arrived in the UK, those skills were taken for granted and Crystal was expected to access a more comprehensive range of skills to be considered literacy-competent.

In practice, there has to be a great deal more to literacy than just being able to read and write. Acknowledging multiple literacies and knowing the wider perspectives that offer plausible explanations for the variety of views on 'illiteracy' would be a good place to start. Brian Street (1995), for example, offered a perspective on social literacies that bypasses the great divide between literacy and illiteracy. Indeed, Street advocates for the view that literacies are multiple and, consequently, that their uses are situated in multiple social contexts. However, this also means that literacies and their contexts may indisputably be associated with ideology and power. Conceptualizing literacy as an autonomous and universal skill is nothing but a power exercise (Street, 1995).

Focusing more locally, Foley argued in 2004 that a new learning paradigm is in order, one that 'links learners to the environment in which learning takes place' (Foley 2004, p. 19). This makes sense, as learning occurs in many contexts and if such links are overlooked, teachers will miss opportunities to expand and build on those valuable prior learning experiences.

However, the macro- and micro-levels are inevitably interdependent and Hamilton and Hillier (2006) articulate these connections in their discussions of both the manipulation of social policy by the powerful and the role of agency within and below this level. Stories from the participants in my study make the dissonance between what policy offers and what people need very evident, and the mismatch very visible. The current placing of ESOL under the umbrella of Skills for Life distances ESOL even further from its core purpose and the paucity of provision is exacerbated by poor funding. At the policy level, migrants are being supported to learn English; at the practical level this often fails to happen, and the policymakers are unaware of, or do not choose to recognize this gap. This is where my study sits, as it captures the reality of these courses from an ESOL student's perspective, giving those accessing English-language teaching a voice to be heard. Despite ample evidence for the support of multiple literacies, literacy is still often perceived and taught as a skill: a subject that can be learned and tested against whatever current literacy strategy is in place at the time.

Literacy Practices

It becomes apparent that the preference for seeing literacy as literacies, in the plural form, is an approach inclusive of many literacy abilities; literacies as social practices for a variety of social purposes. Literacy cannot be seen as a stand-alone skill and it is indeed closely linked to context. Literacy practices change as one makes sense of them and as one applies informal learning to everyday life (Barton, 2006). It does involve skills, and participants described some that they possess, but these are rarely recognized in cultures that privilege formal schooling. During the interviews, participants assured me that they have some valuable skills. Some are able to recognize icons and identify the purposes of letters coming home from their children's school, without knowing how to read. Similarly, they go shopping and are able to identify the products they want. Crystal writes shopping lists for her mother, and Jade cooks for her children and neighbours, showing that she can follow basic recipes, using her skills as a social practice. Participants also appear to be able to use their mobile phones without any difficulties. Opal uses the pictures on her mobile phone to keep memories alive; Amethyst uses Skype to speak to her children, knowing what to do when asked to turn 'on' and 'off', 'log in', submit a 'password' etc. However, such knowledge seems to be overlooked and disregarded.

The participants in the study may have no or low literacy skills according to the current standards set in the UK, but they were capable of some truly remarkable achievements along their life-paths. They were able to make difficult journeys to get to the UK in search of better opportunities. They managed to run a household and bring up their children effectively when they functioned in societies where literacy is perceived differently but their practices seen to have little value. In the UK and the developed world generally, it is imperative that these existing literacy skills be recognized and seen as useful to the pursuit of lifelong learning (Hamilton & Barton, 2013).

It is surprising that illiteracy is viewed so negatively when you consider that a sixth of the world's population is still unable to read and write, but nevertheless appear to function well (Roser & Ortiz-Ospina, 2018). But as long as literacy is viewed as a skill that must be acquired, the gap between skilled and unskilled people will carry on widening, with 'ins' (literate) and 'outs' (illiterate), to the detriment of the latter. This negativity creates a sense of isolation, a feeling that was reported by all the twelve participants in my study, and one with serious implications for both social integration and individual self-esteem. Indeed, Emerald, Jade, Opal, Quartz and Sapphire all reported that isolation had led them to become demotivated and depressed.

Known Learning Needs of the Non-Literate

An important factor in enabling language and literacy acquisition by non-literates is the acknowledgement that the mother tongue is vital as a prerequisite for the acquisition and development of literacy in a second language (Grabe, 2009).

A UNESCO report (UNESCO, 2014) stresses the importance of multilingual education and promotes mother-tongue instruction as a starting point. The report suggests that it is not about using one language or the other but observing the continuum and bridging the two languages. In addition, developing literacy in the mother tongue needs to be seen as a prerequisite for developing second-language literacy. To achieve this, teachers would need specialist training in other languages but also in multicultural awareness.

In a study of how illiterate adults learn Swedish as a second language, Elmeroth (2003) points out how difficult it is to learn a target language in isolation. The refugees in her study were living under hostile conditions in a camp, with no access to Swedish-speaking people, and this made it difficult for them to learn the language. To be living a parallel life within the same country, with no contact with its native population, is a marginalizing process and one likely to lead to ill feelings towards the 'other' on both sides. But such isolation can occur without internment; some of the participants in my research clearly lacked opportunities for meaningful contact with English people. Language learning is limited by isolation, and, equally importantly, lack of language leads to further isolation, presenting difficulties in integrating into a new community, as was the case in Tshabangu-Soko and Caron's (2011) study of non-literate adult African refugees. Choi and Ziegler (2015) agree. In a multicultural study of three multilingual countries (Luxemburg, Canada and Belgium) they found being able to speak the language is one of the most important aspects of integration in a host country.

Social isolation contributes to unemployment, poverty and poor health, too, and the lack of consideration of native-language literacy was one of the elements identified as a barrier to learning by Tshabangu-Soko and Caron (2011), alongside the short length of the programmes. Both these elements were also mentioned during the interviewing process in my study. It is undoubtedly difficult to establish meaningful links when ESOL courses are only ten weeks long, which is currently the case for some ESOL-for-work courses. Furthermore, without bridging one's own language with the new language, the ten weeks may not even touch the core of the task. To become literate is not a straightforward enterprise in which one smoothly progresses from being illiterate to semi-literate and then, magically, literate. This venture has many different layers, different paths and many players, all pulling from different directions. How to deal with illiteracy is not a new 'problem' and there is clearly an established culture of what is to be considered acceptable, useful, or not, on behalf of ESOL learners, that is, at best, faulty. Indeed, I would argue that within the field of ESOL we still live in a hostile environment as literates have a superior status conferred on them; a passport to enter an elite that wields power over those who cannot read or write. This is unfortunate when the literacy acquisition of non-literate immigrants is one of the most challenging tasks currently facing ESOL education (Choi & Ziegler, 2015).

Becoming literate builds on other knowledge, understanding and skills. Many non-literate learners have never been to school; some are not even aware that the purpose of reading is to extract meaning. They do not know how to begin — text orientation, top or bottom, left or right; or the association between symbols and objects — and lack the basic 'learning blocks' that enable reading and writing (Benseman, 2014). They also need to learn to process information differently, requisites for successful learning usually acquired through formal schooling (Bigelow & Schwarz, 2010). In Benseman's New Zealand study, ESOL classes had both teachers and bilingual tutors, recognizing that the mother tongue plays a role in other language learning. Choi and Ziegler (2015) also see home languages as important, their use empowering for learners. In addition, they recommend the use of modern technology, mobile phones and other ICT devices. Relationships matter, too, and teachers need to be patient, respectful and approachable; 'human' (Benseman, 2014, pp. 100–01). Such views are supported by the UNESCO report of 2014.

Opportunities to radically change the lives of non-literate immigrants are limited. They lack the characteristics and experiences that would enable them to challenge the systems in their new countries. They are unable to change what is available to them in terms of policy and educational systems, no matter how hard they try, and often know it. But for some their lack of knowledge allows aspirations bordering on fantasy. Amber, for example, expressed a wish to become a lawyer in order to help others who are in a similarly disadvantaged position in her country of origin. The thought of helping boosts her self-esteem and gives her learning a noble meaning for her. She values 'having knowledge' and all the benefits that education could bring to her life but still lacks the knowledge base to achieve her ambitions. As Freire (1970) proposed in his concept of 'conscientizacao', people need to become aware and critical of their situation for any changes to occur; they must understand their own place in the world as well as its external manifestations.

However, this is not to suggest that aspirations are unimportant. Indeed, Mezirow's theory of Transformative Learning developed in

1997 (influenced by the liberating ideas of both Freire and Habermas in the 1970s), views hope and education as intrinsically connected for learners to change rather than relying on society to make changes. If a 'vocabulary for hope' were embedded in the ESOL curriculum instead of 'vocabulary for work', learners might achieve far beyond what is laid down for them. Instead they face unknown situations, maybe hostility and isolation, and often learners fear that they might have to negotiate a way into a different identity; one that they do not know much about (Pilarska, 2014). When the new language is seen as the route to change, learners may block out learning in order to self-protect: another potential problem that educators need to acknowledge. Indeed, my study drew attention to a number of factors that go beyond the general discourses surrounding non-literate learners.

Further Insights into the Needs of Non-Literate Students

A s their former teacher I was surprised to find how limited the students' articulacy was when discussing everyday situations. On a daily basis, in the classroom, they seemed competent ESOL speakers, but soon I realized that this was a veneer. They were competent at finding effective strategies to convey meaning and this was only apparent on analysis. It became even more evident when I translated interviews carried out in Portuguese into English. Despite using their native language, many participants could not express themselves with the levels of fluency I expected. Topaz, for example, repeatedly used the same phrases in order to convey meaning; and Cromley's Report for the UK National Institute for Literacy (2000) offers a possible explanation for this, which is important.

> Even though adults have been alive longer than children, they may have had 'one year repeated forty times' rather than 40 years' experience. Despite their family, job, and other adult experiences, many adult literacy students have small vocabularies (about 15% larger than a 5th grader's vocabulary). Children's vocabularies after about 5th grade grow mostly from what they read, not from hearing new words, but adult literacy students have never read much. Basically, adult literacy students use the same small spoken vocabulary as when they were 11 or 12. (Cromley, 2000, p. 188)

There was a remarkable difference between the language used by the literate and non-literate. The semi-literate showed some use of abstract reasoning in their interviews, whereas the non-literate used language soaked only in their practical experiences. For example, Crystal was able to illustrate her experiences by using words that showed her ability to evaluate her experiences: 'Since I grow up, I am a foreign!' Whereas Quartz merely settled for giving his children names from fairy tales (Cinderella, Princess Diana, Doctor — as first names), to give them an instant 'good start in life'.

Moreover, none of the participants seemed to have an effective learning strategy for acquiring literacy. I suspected that there would be initial difficulties adapting to classroom practices of learning as they had not experienced language learning this way before. For instance, Opal had difficulty in holding a pencil. Nor could she understand why she should have to sit down for two hours rather than get up or go for a drink whenever she felt like doing so. However, the difficulty went far beyond that; the struggle was also within the learning itself. They lacked an understanding of the concept of learning and found it difficult to understand what the processes were, instead finding their own methods and alternative learning objectives. Participants mentioned copying and memorizing random texts out of context. They reported numerous experiences of being taught without learning. As might be expected, these mostly resulted in a loss of faith in education, low self-esteem and frustration.

In my field notes I captured a number of different conceptualizations of what makes a person literate and noted that for some, who reported functioning quite effectively without literacy, the unrealistic expectations of the current educational system seemed totally unreasonable. As a child, Turquoise did not accept the need for learning in order to write letters, as all of her family lived nearby: she could talk to them. Perhaps this view demonstrates a lack of adequate awareness of the need to learn how to learn at a basic level, and this is not just from the learners' perspective — her childhood teacher failed to see the inappropriate nature of the task for Turquoise and modify it. Inevitably perhaps, these expectations translate into poor outcomes, making social mobility virtually impossible (Reay, 2012).

Collectively, the interviews drew attention to other disadvantages that stemmed from a lack of childhood education. Children who attend school learn about the world, seasons, basic geography, science and numbers, and acquire a range of general knowledge. It rapidly became evident that an adult who has never been in education has considerable gaps in all those learning blocks that are usually taken for granted. In turn, this poses a further difficulty in understanding the themes presented in the curriculum as a means of learning the language for day to day matters. It is difficult to learn numbers if you have no concept of numbers or counting. One of the participants (Onyx) is a cook and he measures his ingredients 'by eye'. He has developed a competent strategy, which enables him to achieve a high level of proficiency in his field without knowing how to count, even in his own language. The concept of counting will have to be introduced prior to teaching him numbers, and even contemplating teaching him how to spell number names at this stage would be pointless. However, and perhaps unwittingly, it is common practice for courses to jump straight to more sophisticated aspects of learning without first ensuring and consolidating students' understanding of the basics.

There was a map of the world in the room where participants were interviewed and only two of the twelve participants (Crystal and Ruby) were even roughly aware of the location of their home country. Others (Amber, Emerald, and Opal) said that it was not on that map, and some (Amethyst, Jade, Sapphire, and Topaz) asked to look at the back of the map because they could not find it on the front. Turquoise and Quartz were not even interested in looking at the map, and a couple of the students were surprised to find out what 'the blue bit' meant. Onyx did not understand it to represent water, and Topaz was unaware of the portrayal of sea: 'What a huge river!' This foundational knowledge is not directly related to literacy, but its absence is significant as it is vital to becoming fully literate in societies where such understandings are taken for granted. Such basic gaps must be recognized and addressed when teaching adults who have never been through any educational system. Simpson claims that in formal educational spaces, representing the world through maps is often equated to a good knowledge of geography (Simpson & Gresswell, 2012). If you have never been to school, this knowledge may not have been acquired.

Experiences become the lenses through which we see the world (Manen, 2016). Experiences in childhood affect how we feel and behave as an adult. Teachers will play a vital role in facilitating a change from a solely experiential to an educated perspective, so now we consider what the study implies for teachers who seek to support migrants, particularly the low- and non-literate, to learn a strange language in an unfamiliar setting.

Issues for Teachers to Consider

A t the outset, we must remember that students are not *tabulae rasae*. They arrive in the classroom with an abundance of life and learning experiences. In his exploration of the value of lifelong learning, Field (2006) reminds us of the importance of encouraging learners to apply this to other contexts throughout the life-course. Such experiences provide teachers with a wealth of 'starting points' on which to develop and build. To give just one example: this was clearly the case for Opal, whose story, like many others, is shocking when revealed. Opal was seldom parted from her mobile phone and the interview disclosed that it held her pictures of her twelve-year-old daughter, who was killed by a bomb while playing outside their house prior to migration. Opal's teachers did not even know about this; they omitted to enquire into the reasons for an old and damaged mobile phone being so important to her. They were unaware that Opal was battling with profound grief and unlikely to access English through standard teaching activities. They missed significant opportunities to empathize with Opal but also to develop her literacy skills. She could have been encouraged to make a scrapbook, future-proofing the photos from loss through technological failure and giving her the chance to keep some of her precious memories alive by writing about them: a meaningful learning exercise.

Importantly, teachers need to take care to respect their cultural heritage when teaching an alien language to migrants. As we have seen, the migrants' experiences may extend far beyond those of many of the teachers of English who take on the role of English-as-a-Second-Language educators, often in ways that are inconceivable in a Western cultural context. The committed ESOL teacher may, without even realizing it, be cast in a similar role to that of an A&E[3] practitioner, assessing the immediate problem, patching people up and sending them on their way. Unlike the situation for healthcare staff, there are few if any more specialized services to which the ESOL learner can be directed, certainly in terms of educational rather than social support.

So teachers hold a huge responsibility in their hands. They are the mediators who can build bridges, bringing notions of identity, languages and cultures together. They are tasked with reviving learning, self-esteem, confidence, integration, aspiration and hope. Teachers cannot cure but have the potential to minimize some of the casualties they work with. Yet, frequently their efforts are frustrated by the contexts within which they work.

Conclusions from the Study

B etter practices towards migrant learners need to be established at all levels of influence, in policy, in educational institutions, in the curriculum and by the teachers who work directly with them. Despite the differences among ESOL learners, a 2006 NIACE inquiry found that provision was still generic and may be unlikely to change as a 'one size fits all' approach was still prevalent in the compulsory sector in 2016, a decade later, according to Sir Michael Wilshaw, Head of Ofsted and Chief Inspector of Schools (Weale, 2016). Yet, strategies that start from the learners' perspective would be more likely to reach the low-literacy learner (Pitt, 2005). ESOL is far more than just learning a language (NIACE, 2006): Brookhaven National Laboratory claims the intention of 'Educating the world, one person at a time' on their ESOL webpage (BNL, 2019). Indeed, a recent report on the accessibility of provision for ESOL learners, and their progression, states that 'two of the main barriers were access to suitable childcare arrangements, and the existing literacy levels of potential learners' (Higton et al., 2019, p. 12).

There remains a great deal to be done at the policy level, particularly following the migration 'crisis' (Henley, 2018) from 2015 to 2018, now declared officially over but leaving a legacy of 'structural problems' (Rankin, 2019). Opportunities for learning without pressure to achieve universal targets are required and this would be at odds with the current

---

3   Accident & Emergency hospital department.

UK government's views on educational evaluation. Students' needs are subsumed within generic expectations, outcomes channelled to support the world of work, turning both teachers and learners into pawns in a game with alien rules — and condemned to failure. But teachers need opportunities to get to know and understand their students and this has time and cost implications at higher levels.

Many hindrances to learning begin with the barriers that the institution poses to the learners and dissonance between participants' cultures and Western assumptions. The lack of understanding of the background of the learners restricts the possibilities of reaching them. Failing to acknowledge the value of lifelong learning and/or the value of learners' previous incidental, informal and non-formal learning experiences creates a bigger gap between learners and their learning trajectory. I had taught, personally, many of the students I later researched, and was keen to help them flourish despite the limitations of contemporary ESOL provision. But I knew very little about them as people until I took the time, later, to interview them individually. Had I possessed this knowledge earlier, there are many ways that my ESOL classes could have embraced their motivations, improved their lives, and enabled them to integrate happily into British society.

Within colleges, action is necessary to address insensitive and ineffective teaching methods and resources. More positively, measures could be put in place to encourage teaching approaches in tune with the individual learners and their needs, and this may mean a broader curriculum. My research raises the possibility that there is a need to teach a wider range of subjects around the subject of ESOL literacy and numeracy, prior to teaching literacy itself. These include the teaching of strategies for learning, such as thinking and transferring existing skills into new ones. There is also a need to include the prior learning experiences of the learners, be they incidental, non-formal or informal. In missing school, participants have also missed access to a range of knowledge that was not available in their everyday home settings. Recognizing this helped me to understand that we cannot teach a subject out of context. Literacy is best viewed as multiple literacies instead, as it develops within a wide variety of contexts and domains.

The overall findings of my study show the magnitude of the task to be accomplished. This small-scale project shows how every participant is unique, and so are their needs, experiences, hopes and aspirations. It became clear from the interviews that teaching does not always equate to learning. As teachers, there is a lot that can be done to contribute to the success of low-literate learners. The findings direct educators to find out where the students are coming from rather than simply what stage they are at. Learners come to the classroom with a wealth of knowledge acquired throughout life. New learning needs to add and build on their existing knowledge, social practices and skills, so provision needs to be flexible. Learners must have a voice in curriculum development and delivery, and it should be relevant to them. Accessing learning, even when they are allowed to and do attend classes, has proven to be a difficult task for all the participants. A modicum of understanding about other cultures and their peoples would go a long way to making learning more probable. Learners need to be helped to live in another culture without having to relinquish their existing identities. They should not be 'schooled' to become someone they are not. Teachers need to give learners the power to reject what is not in their best interests and the space to decide what not to learn.

These findings provide a significant record of the experiences of a group of people who are still being affected by discourses that further limit their access to education. These discourses portray a picture of oppression and exclusion. They show little or no sympathy towards aspiration or hope. There is a lack of coherence between the generic aspirations for equality of government policy and the actual provision for low- or no-literacy learners. Learners do not have access to the cultural capital of British society and as a result are doomed to remain at the periphery of the society they are meant to be integrating with. The strong and increasingly negative views on immigration and immigrants subtly infiltrate all areas. For participants in my research, this lack of coherence perpetuates the very cycle that the government espouses to be fighting.

Yet alternatives are possible. My study makes a methodological contribution to future work with non-literate learners because it reveals that, in addition to their use as a research method, narrative interviews could be a useful teaching method to use with ESOL learners. Storytelling paves the way to learning. It unlocks potential and enables the learner to learn creatively. Telling your own story frees thinking and enables previous experiences to take a positive turn, constructing new paths. Voicing their feelings was very important to all participants. They reported feeling empowered and were unanimous in being grateful for the opportunity to tell their stories. Narrating their stories has helped learners in this study make sense of their experiences and prioritize events as they saw fit, to make learning fit for their own purposes. They reported a sense of relief after telling their story, suggesting that a narrative approach offers an opportunity to engender feelings of wellbeing, and may help learning, talking and living in the UK to become more positive for newcomers.

Through sharing life stories, the teacher and student would be enabled to focus on the real social and linguistic learning opportunities that might encourage the student to participate and contribute fully to British society with joy and pleasure. Moreover, although this sounds utopian, in maintaining the students' bonds with the past, we might take a small step towards supporting the achievement of a more integrated global culture.

References

Alenius, P. (2016). Informal learning processes of migrants in the civil society: A transnational perspective. *European Journal for Research on the Education and Learning of Adults,* 7(1): 41–55. https://doi.org/10.3384/rela.2000-7426.rela9072

Barton, D. (2006). *Literacy: An introduction to the ecology of written language,* 2nd edn. Oxford: Wiley-Blackwell Publishing.

Benseman, J. (2014). Adult refugee learners with limited literacy: Needs and effective responses. *Refuge,* 30(1): 93–103. https://refuge.journals.yorku.ca/index.php/refuge/article/view/38606

Bigelow, M. & Schwarz, R. (2010). *Adult English language learners with limited literacy.* Washington, DC: National Institute for Literacy.

BNL (Brookhaven National Laboratory) (2017). *English for speakers of other languages webpage.* https://www.bnl.gov/esol/

Cambridge Assessment (2013). *What is literacy? An investigation into definitions of English as a subject and the relationship between English literacy and being literate: A research report commissioned by Cambridge Assessment.* http://www.cambridgeassessment.org.uk/images/130433

Choi, J. & Ziegler, G. (2015). *Literacy education for low-educated second language learning adults in multilingual contexts: The case of Luxembourg.* Multilingual Education. https://doi.org/10.1186/s13616-015-0024-7

Cromley, J. (2000). *Learning to think, learning to learn: What the science of thinking and learning has to offer adult education.* London: National Institute for Literacy.

Eaton, S. (2011). *Family literacy and the new Canadian: Formal, non-formal and informal learning: The case of literacy, essential skills and language learning in Canada.* https://eric.ed.gov/?id=ED522574

Elmeroth, E. (2003). From refugee camp to solitary confinement: Illiterate adults learn Swedish as a second language. *Scandinavian Journal of Educational Research*, 47(4): 431–49.

Field, J. (2006). *Lifelong learning and the new educational order.* Stoke on Trent: Trentham Books.

Foley, G. (2004). *Dimensions of adult learning: Education and training in a global era.* Maidenhead: Open University Press.

Freire, P. (1970). *Pedagogy of the oppressed.* New York: Continuum.

Grabe, W. (2009). *Reading in a second language: Moving from theory to practice.* New York: Cambridge University Press.

Goodman, S., Lillis, T., Maybin, J. & Mercer, N. (2003). *Language, literacy and education: A reader.* Stoke on Trent: Trentham Books with the Open University Press.

Habermas, J. (1978). *Knowledge and human interests.* London: Heinemann.

Hamilton, M. & Barton, D. (2013). *The texts of everyday life: Public and private identities in vernacular literacy practices.* Los Angeles: Sage.

Hamilton, M. & Hillier, Y. (2006). *Changing faces of adult literacy: Language and numeracy, a critical history.* Stoke on Trent: Trentham Books.

Henley, J. (2018). EU migration crisis: what are the key issues? *The Guardian*, 27 June. https://www.theguardian.com/world/2018/jun/27/eu-migration-crisis-what-are-the-issues

Higton, J., Sandhu, J., Stutz, A., Patel, R., Choudhoury, A. & Richards, S. (2019). *English for speakers of other languages: Access and progression, DFE-RR918. CFE Research for DfE.* https://assets.publishing.service.gov.uk/government/uploads/system/uploads/attachment_data/file/811750/English_for_speakers_of_other_languages.pdf

LIAM (Linguistic Integration of Adult Migrants) (2018). *Formal, non-formal and informal learning. Council of Europe Portal.* https://www.coe.int/en/web/lang-migrants/formal-non-formal-and-informal-learning

Manen, M. van (2016). *Researching lived experience: Human science for an action sensitive pedagogy* (2nd edn). Abingdon: Routledge. https://doi.org/10.4324/9781315421056

Mezirow, J. (1997). Transformative learning theory: Theory to practice. In: Cranton, P. (ed), *New directions for adult and continuing education*, 74 (Summer). San Francisco, CA: Jossey-Bass Publishers.

Morrice, L. (2014). The Learning migration nexus: Towards a conceptual understanding. *European Journal for Research on the Education and Learning of Adults*, 5(2): 149–59. https://doi.org/10.3384/rela.2000-7426.rela9044

NIACE (National Institute of Adult Continuing Education) (2006). *More than a language... Final report of the committee of inquiry on English for speakers of other languages* (ESOL), Chaired by Derek Grover. Leicester: NIACE.

Pilarska, A. (2014). Self-construal as a mediator between identity structure and subjective well-being. *Current Psychology Journal*, 33(2): 130–54. https://doi.org/10.1007/s12144-013-9202-5

Pitt, K. (2005). *Debates in ESOL teaching and learning*. Abingdon: Routledge.

Rankin, J. (2019). EU declares migration crisis over as it hits out at 'fake news'. *The Guardian*, 6 March. https://www.theguardian.com/world/2019/mar/06/eu-declares-migration-crisis-over-hits-out-fake-news-european-commission

Reay, D. (2012). What does a socially just educational system look like: Saving the minnows from the pike. *Journal of Education Policy*, 27(5): 587–99. https://doi.org/10.1080/02680939.2012.710015

Roser, M. & Ortiz-Ospina, E. (2019). *Literacy*. Published online at OurWorldinData.org. https://ourworldindata.org/literacy

Simpson, J. & Gresswell, R. (2012). ESOL learners online: New media as a site of identity negotiation. In: Tett, L., Hamilton, M. & Crowther, J. (eds), *More powerful literacies*, 2nd edn. Leicester: NIACE.

Street, B. (1995). *Social literacies: Critical approaches to literacy in development, ethnography and education*. Harlow: Pearson Education.

Tshabangu-Soko, T.S., & Caron, R.M. (2011). English for Speakers of Other Languages (ESOL): Improving English language acquisition for preliterate and non-literate adult African refugees. *Journal of Immigrant & Refugee Studies*, 9(4): 416–33.

UNESCO (2013). *2nd Global report on adult learning and education: Rethinking literacy*. Hamburg: UNESCO Institute for Lifelong Learning. https://unesdoc.unesco.org/ark:/48223/pf0000222407

UNESCO (2014). *Multilingual education: Why is it important? How to implement it?* http://unesdoc.unesco.org/images/0022/002265/226554e.pdf

UNESCO (2019). *Global education monitoring report: Migration, displacement and education; building bridges, not walls*. http://bit.ly/2019gemreport

Weale, S. (2016). One size fits all systems, *The Guardian*, 18 January. https://www.theguardian.com/education/2016/jan/18/one-size-fits-all-system-lets-down-less-academic-pupils-warns-ofsted-chief

19. Uncovering Habitus in Life Stories of Muslim Converts

Simone R. Rasmussen

Simone R. Rasmussen discusses the stories of two young Danish women who decided to become Muslims, attracted to the ethos of care for all that was apparent in a non-radicalized community. She shows how their narratives reflect but contrast with established work that claims that those accustomed to strong doctrines within Catholicism and Protestantism find it easy to convert to Islam but choose stricter branches of the faith.

Conversion accounts have always been the key source to understand the processes of conversion. The main question asked by conversion researchers has therefore been: how best to approach the accounts to be able to understand the convert's motives and individual experiences, rather than gaining a fixed story that reflects how the senior followers of a particular religion wish it to appear (Beckford, 1978; Hindmarsh, 2014; Snow & Machalek, 1984; Taylor, 1976; Warburg, 2007). I believe that by taking a narrative approach to these accounts we gain a fuller picture of the conversion and a better understanding of the individual's motives, rather than focusing on the conversion itself.

Through a narrative approach (Polkinghorne, 1988, 1995; Kim, 2016) and an analysis that draws on Bourdieu's notion of habitus (Bourdieu & Wacquant, 1992), it is my aim in this chapter to examine the life stories of two Danish converts to Islam who, previously, were non-religious. I am interested to see if these converts draw on forms of habitus similar to those of previously religious converts, who were the focus of other earlier studies (Shanneik, 2011; Roy, 2004).

https://doi.org/10.11647/OBP.0203.19

In 2011, Yafa Shanneik wrote an article based on her findings from the narratives of twenty-one female converts from Catholicism to an orthodox branch of Islam. Her research examined how Catholicism was present in the converts' lives before their conversion to Islam. She found that the converts who participated in her study had what could be described as a Catholic habitus (Inglis, 1988). According to Shanneik it was this Catholic habitus that drew the converts towards the religious strand of Salafi Islam, a strand that is known to be particularly strict and dogmatic in relation to adherence to scriptures (Shanneik, 2011; Wiktorowicz, 2006). Shanneik argues that Salafi Islam was particularly appealing for the previously Catholic converts because it draws on the same structures and dispositions as the Catholic habitus.

In her article, Shanneik refers to Olivier Roy, who has drawn similar conclusions about converts from radical Protestantism. Olivier Roy's research showed how radical Protestants also seem to be drawn to Salafi Islam when they choose to convert to Islam. He states that the radicalization, which is often linked to Salafi Islam, should not be seen as a sudden shift in the convert's worldview, but as a continuation of the convert's previous religious habitus (Roy, 2004).

Through their research, Roy and Shanneik seem to have identified a connection between having previously had a strict dogmatic religious habitus, whether Protestant or Catholic, and being drawn towards Salafi Islam. I will follow their analytical path but in a slightly different way, namely by examining previously non-religious individuals who convert, to study their perception of Islam and to see whether a similar continuation of habitus can be established. Before introducing the stories, I briefly explain the Bourdieusian approach to habitus as a sense of rationality, being a result of the internalization of external structures that make us who we are (Bourdieu & Wacquant, 1992); our individual worldviews, practices and understandings. Bourdieu claimed that, from their habitus, individuals develop dispositions that shape how they exist in the world. Habitus tend to reproduce itself even if the contexts change (Bourdieu, 1977). Therefore, in this chapter I will pay attention to the structures glimpsed in the converts' narratives, to ask: are the converts' dispositions, moulded throughout their lives, reproduced in the religious life they live in today? In other words: has the habitus found a habitat (Bourdieu, 2000)?

A word is also needed about the history of conversion research, as this topic is significant to the final discussion on discourses. Historically, the discipline of conversion research was started by the American Psychologist Society in the early eighteenth century. The psychological angle to the subject was widely researched and conversion was viewed from a range of different psychological theories and perspectives. Most psychological conversion research viewed religious conversion to be a result of an existentialist or traumatic crisis that the individual had experienced earlier on in life, and therefore conversion was understood as a break with an unsatisfactory past (Damsager & Mogensen, 2007b). The American psychologist Lewis R. Rambo (1993) presented one of the best-known theories of conversion. He argued that we should view conversion as having seven stages: context, crisis, quest, encounter, interaction, commitment and consequences (Rambo, 1993, s.17). Later a broader spectrum of academics, in disciplines such as anthropology and sociology, began researching the subject and one can argue that the most important shift in the research of conversion is to be found in how the convert is viewed. Damsager and Mogensen (2007b) show how the research of conversion changes from viewing the convert as a passive victim who is searching to escape the past, to viewing the converts as co-players who actively turn towards the new religious environments and who also seem to contribute to those environments.

I interviewed two Danish converts who did not describe themselves as religious before their conversion. In the following section you can read their stories.

Aisha's Story — An Aspiration to Find Inner Peace

Aisha is a twenty-seven-year-old woman who grew up in a nuclear family as the oldest of three siblings. Her mother works as a self-employed alternative practitioner, who helped her clients cleanse their bodies and spirits to either make or keep them healthy. Aisha's mother very much believed in the association of the bodily and spiritual world, and patients came to her when the world's doctors had given up on them. Aisha's father was a well-known ceramic artist, but he only worked in Aisha's early childhood. They lived in a single-family house in a Copenhagen suburb with a garden — small enough to feel safe but big enough to play hide-and-seek in. Aisha and her family lived in the same family home until she moved away to live on her own. Even though Aisha moved away from home, she never lived very far away from her family; she stayed in the vicinity, near enough to drop by for a meal or a cup of coffee. Aisha's family is small; her grandparents died early and there were some conflicts between her parents and her aunt, so they did not stay in contact with her. Aisha does not remember the conflicts but says that she never lacked adults or meaningful relations in her childhood. She enjoys family-like relationships with some of her mother's best friends, whom she calls aunts. It means a lot to Aisha's family to have a strong bond within the family and they value being able to spend time together in the holidays and at weekends.

The family were vegetarians, or at least almost; sometimes they ate lamb because it was her father's favourite food, but they never ate pork or beef. Aisha remembers how her friends in school stared at her packed lunch because it was full of tofu and other meat substitutes, and when she ate at her friends' houses, they found it very odd that she did not eat meat. She attended a Rudolf Steiner school until ninth grade, and she describes it as a cultural shock to face the non-Steiner educational system when she attended upper-secondary school. She had never had to deal with grades in her years at the Rudolf Steiner school and suddenly she was evaluated in terms of a number — a single number to describe everything about her. One of the things she loved the most about the Rudolf Steiner school was the 'attestation' each student was given every second year. The attestation was a two-page document recording the student's social, artistic, methodological and academic development. Looking back Aisha does not think that the Rudolf Steiner school supported her sufficiently well in academic terms, but she believes that the teaching there was significantly important for the development of a pupil as a whole person. Aisha finished upper-secondary school but worked for more than five years afterwards before attending a vocational training school, where she is studying now. Aisha is not sure if the long gap between upper-secondary school and her present studies stems from her academic struggles to get through upper-secondary school, but she does know that she is not a fan of the Danish educational system and its monotonous focus on professional competence.

When it comes to religion, Aisha describes her family as cultural Christians. They celebrated Christmas, as most Danish families do, and they had a creative Easter tradition, where they painted eggs and decorated an Easter tree. The traditions centred around one thing, namely being together as a family and having a good time together. Her parents were baptized and confirmed as Christians — in the Lutheran Church, confirmation is the symbolic affirmation of the baptism. They were also married in the Church, but neither Aisha nor her siblings were baptized. Her parents always said that they would not make that choice for her, but they would support whatever choice she decided to make. They said that the most important thing they could teach her was to be good to the people and things around her. Aisha considers that her parents had some sort of faith and she knows that her mother believes in angels and some kind of spiritual world.

Aisha's father was ill most of Aisha's life and died when Aisha was twenty-two years old. He was in and out of hospitals for most of her life and therefore she learned at an early stage to take responsibility for herself and her younger siblings. She describes her father as a positive and happy man. His illness was something that was just there, something that they sometimes had to face, but it was never a predominant part of their lives.

At the time of her father's death, Aisha lived in her own apartment and worked as a sales coordinator in a fairly large company. She spent her spare time hanging out with her friends, attending fitness classes, shopping and travelling. She describes how she found herself entrenched in a repetitive daily pattern: she got up in the morning, went to work, worked, left work, went to the gym, came back, ate supper, and went to bed. She just longed for the vacation so she could travel, or a weekend so she could hang out with her friends at the café. She felt herself to be living in a void. Sometimes the emptiness could be filled with travelling and shopping, but before she knew it, the feeling was back, and another trip or shopping spree was needed. After her father's death, she started a spiritual pursuit to find out what might have happened to him after he died. She started her search with Christianity, but never found satisfactory answers. She started discussing the issue with her friends — among these were also Muslim friends — and this was the start of her exploration of Islam. One year later, she converted;

two years later, she started wearing a headscarf; and three-and-a-half years later, she changed her name.

Today Aisha is married to Martin, who is also a Muslim convert. They met through mutual friends after they had both converted. Aisha spends her time attending Islamic teachings in the mosque, having conversations with new converts, aspiring to become a Muslim teacher and to be the best Muslim she can be. To her, Islam is about inclusiveness, spirituality and aspiring to be a good and faithful person. When she talks about Islam to new or potential converts, she tells them that Islam is divided into three parts: faith, rituals and spirituality — and to be a good Muslim you must possess all three. She tells them that it makes no sense to pray if you do not have the right intentions and it makes no sense to do things that hurt other people.

Aisha prays five times a day; she wears a headscarf; she goes to the mosque at least once a week; she does not eat during the day during Ramadan; but on Christmas Eve she gathers with her family to celebrate. However, her intention on Christmas Eve is to be a good daughter and have a nice time with her family, which is easily combined with her Islamic faith, since Islam is all about being kind and treating other people well. She has found inner peace in her search to be a good Muslim, and in her inner journey, which she started with her conversion to Islam.

Laura's Story — A Peaceful and Normal Childhood, But...

Laura is twenty years old and she lives in a Copenhagen suburb with her mother, father and younger sister. Laura is a very beautiful girl who knows how to make her hair fall perfectly. She has this beautiful long curly dark hair and her makeup is spotless and looks really natural. Her upbringing was peaceful and, she says, completely normal — but she has an older cousin, Kevin, who is an alcoholic and now suffers from alcohol-related dementia. Laura and her family live in a little red terraced house, with a beautiful enclosed garden where Laura and her younger sister often sit and enjoy the sun or play cards. Laura recalls summer mornings when her mother did her daily yoga and meditation in the garden before the rest of the house woke up. Laura's mother has a spiritual side and loves to explore this by engaging in meditation in her spare time. Laura's father works as an administrator in the local municipality, while her mother is a teacher at the local school. They have lived in the same house for as long as Laura can remember and, to her, the house is the epitome of love and comfort. Laura has a large family; grandparents, cousins, uncles and aunts, who are all a part of her childhood memories. As a minor negative, Laura remembers that her parents told her that Kevin was often drunk, but actually, she did not spend much time with him and does not really remember him.

As a child, Laura attended many leisure time activities because this was very important to her mother, who believed that this was a good way to support children's development. Laura was especially fond of activities where she could express herself through her body and came to love singing and dancing. All in all, Laura comes from a very typical Danish nuclear family. It was a family maxim that there was no reason to engender disagreement because this might be hurtful to other people, so they were never allowed to discuss either religion or politics at the dinner table.

Laura's educational pathway was very straightforward. She went to the local public school and after her graduation she attended upper-secondary school. Now she is in her first year at university studying religion. School was never hard for her. She was no straight-A student, but she did well in most disciplines and had energy left over to participate in the social activities and hang out with her classmates. Laura's first interaction with religion, she recalls, was when she attended a weekly confirmation class at the local vicarage. Danish young people commonly go to such classes during seventh or eighth grade prior to confirming their baptism at a church ceremony. Laura never really gave much thought to what confirmation was beyond presents and a nice celebratory party. She does, however, remember a particular episode relating to confirmation class. On one occasion, one of her classmates — the only Muslim in her class — stood outside the vicarage waiting for the class to finish and the pastor asked the students what that Muslim boy was doing there and why he came to her house. Laura found the pastor's hostile attitude strange and unnecessary; the Muslim boy was their friend and he was just standing there waiting quietly.

However, once confirmation was over, Laura's social life became more sophisticated, a time of parties and drinking, and Laura certainly recalls taking part in these activities with her friends. Laura's life at that time consisted of school, fitness, friends, work and nights out in town with mojitos and beers. Laura dated a non-practising Muslim boy for a couple of months in ninth grade — but this was just a flirtation. In tenth grade, she started in a new class and came to make new friends. One of these was a Muslim girl who went to Islamic teachings once a week. Out of curiosity and because she wanted to spend time with her, Laura attended the teachings with her new friend. Here she got her first knowledge of Islam and its relationship to other religions and she found this very exciting. She was introduced to stories that they had never talked about or discussed in her family and to a forum where it was allowable to ask questions. When some of her other Muslim friends heard that she attended these classes, they made fun of her, saying: 'You could never be Muslim'. Laura was offended — who were they to judge her?

When she started upper-secondary school, she attended religious studies classes and the first year was horrible. There were no believers in her class, to her knowledge, and she found the dialogue about religion and especially Islam very demeaning. Her teacher directed them to a Salafi webpage and asked them to find answers to their questions on Islam there. Laura felt offended. In her second year, she had a new teacher, and this is where Laura first started to consciously reflect on religion. There was a moment, when she was sitting in a bus looking at the sunrise, when she was suddenly sure that there was something bigger than herself. During her second year in upper-secondary school Laura felt as if she was experiencing an identity crisis. Some days, after reading about Islam throughout the night, she felt ready to convert, but the next night she was out drinking mojitos, dancing and worrying about other people's opinions. This went on for almost a year and she spent long nights studying Islam. During her final exams Laura and one of her Christian friends decided to cut down on drinking and help each other withstand the pressure from the crowd when they went out with their classmates. Now she really wanted to convert and she fully accepted that she would not drink alcohol from that point.

She prayed in her own way for comfort when her last exam came around, and she did well. After her graduation she decided now was the time, although she still faced the fear that she did not know enough about Islam and was also afraid of her family's reaction. Laura joined numerous groups on Facebook to look for help and one Friday night in July, she said the Shahada — the Islamic confirmation of faith — aloud in her room. The day after she said her Shahada the family went on a summer camping trip together and Laura decided not to tell anyone before she had her official conversion. For months after the holiday, she sought an official conversion and searched the internet extensively for help. She was never afraid to contact people, because she was sure that they would give her a good reception if they were Muslims.

She had to look for a long time before she found someone who represented the 'pure' Islam that she sought; an Islam without hidden social or political agendas. She used her gut feeling to navigate safely through the websites. On finding an organization that represented her beliefs, she gave up the Facebook groups, and in November 2015 she said her Shahada in front of an Imam. She describes it as calm, peaceful and very much in line with her perception of Islam — a spiritual comfort zone in which she finds peace of mind and where the primary focus is to be good and respectful towards other people.

Laura wanted to tell her family right away, but she was afraid of what they would say. She felt terrible about keeping such a secret from them but one evening, three weeks after her official conversion, her mother jokingly asked her if she had converted to Islam. Laura looked her mother in the eye and nodded, after which her mother exclaimed 'you just did not do that' and they both started crying.

Laura still navigates instinctively among the different Islamic branches. She also decided not to wear a headscarf because she wants to be a good daughter — of whom her parents can be genuinely proud. She says that if it was only about her, then she would probably wear a scarf, but it is not only about her and she would never put her parents in a position where other people would think that they are bad parents just because she wants to wear a headscarf and make a public statement that she is Muslim.

What Kind of Muslim Are You?

N ow, I will analyse the life stories through the concept of habitus as formulated by Bourdieu. To do this, I have chosen three focal points from the converts' lives before their conversion and three focal points from their lives as Muslims. I chose these focal points because they recur often in the interviews with Aisha and Laura, but also because comparable statements recur in similar interviews I did with other converts.

Life Before Islam

T he focal points highlighted in this section are spirituality, respect for difference, and being good.

Spirituality

Spirituality is very much present in both of the converts' lives from an early point. Aisha's mother works as an alternative practitioner, believes in angels and tells her children that they must not lie because they will get black spots on their hearts and have inner diseases. Throughout her life, Aisha has been heavily confronted with the innerness of wellbeing, as she states:

> People come to my mother, when all the world's doctors have been in contact with them, and they still feel bad; then my mother helps them get better.

In the way that Aisha talks about it, there is an implicit acceptance that inner balance is the answer to physical wellbeing. That illness can be cured or treated through inner balance is beyond doubt to Aisha.

Looking at Laura's life, spirituality is not explicit as it is in Aisha's case, but it is still present. Her mother practised meditation and yoga regularly throughout Laura's childhood and Laura remembers watching her mother find peace and practising relaxation through meditation. What is especially interesting concerning spirituality in Laura and Aisha's examples is that spirituality is the only part of Islam that their mothers accept and both Aisha and Laura use the 'language' of their childhoods to explain Islam to their mothers. Aisha states that:

I remember once, I talked to my mother of a lecture I attended in the mosque. It was about inner peace, which is a part of Islam I pay great attention to, and when we talked, she said, 'that is what I always told you, when you where children'.

Or as Laura says:

Once I told my mother that she could view the prayer as a five-times-a-day break, where I have time with God and myself — just like meditation. Now she does the same, not five times a day, but still. I tell myself that she got it from me.

Respect for Difference

Respect for difference is also fairly dominant in the stories of these two converts, although in different ways. Laura always saw herself as part of the norm in the neighbourhood she grew up in, and Aisha always felt a bit different because of the way the family lived. Laura states that 'I felt so sad, when they talked like that...' when she refers to how her classmates in upper-secondary school referred to religious people. She did not feel offended because she did not see herself as religious at that time, but she felt sad, because she thinks that: '...it is beautiful when we are different and when people find something that makes them happy'.

Aisha always felt a bit different in her childhood. She did not eat what her classmates ate, she went to a school other than the local one, and she had a lot of responsibility because of her father's illness. Consequently, when she left the Steiner School she did everything she could to be like her peers. She started to live a life like her friends: trips to cafés, travel, expensive shopping and workouts. However, the lifestyle of her friends did not satisfy her, and now she does not mind being different. But she also respects that other people might look at it differently. As she states, when referring to her family's reaction to her new Muslim name:

I respect that they use my old name, because that is natural to them and I have to respect that they view Islam and my change of name differently than I do.

Being Good

Being good is the third, and, in my opinion, most dominant principle of the two converts' lives. Aisha was not baptized because her parents thought that their children should decide for themselves and Aisha chose not to be baptized when she got older. When Aisha asked her parents why she was not baptized, they replied: 'It does not matter; the most important thing is to be good to yourself and others'.

In Laura's case, the goodness is reflected in her respect for other people and their choices. More than once, she talks about episodes in her childhood when she felt sad that people were treated badly, as when the pastor spoke unkindly about the Muslim boy waiting for the confirmation class to finish. Laura probably reacted to the pastor's remarks because she comes from a home where they were taught to be quiet rather than cause a row or be unkind, where contentious topics were banned at dinner time to ensure a cheerful atmosphere with room for everybody.

I group these three focal points in what I call a *humanistic habitus*. My definition is based on a rather literal meaning of the word, namely that one cherishes the individual's right to be and think as he or she wants to, and that no individual has the right to harm or judge others. Furthermore, my definition implies that most of what is needed to live a satisfying life is found inside the human being and can be reached by striving for inner calm and balance.

A Muslim Life

As in the previous section, I also found three focal points in Laura and Aisha's perceptions of Islam and descriptions of themselves as Muslims. These are *Ihsan*, *respect*, and *who am I to judge?*

Ihsan

Ihsan can be translated as beneficence or perfection and refers to a Muslim's duty to search for perfection in the worship of Allah. Laura and Aisha often refer to this term during our conversations. Aisha describes how it is a part of an important Hadith — Hadith Jibril. In Islam, Hadith refers to the collections of sayings and anecdotes attributed to the Prophet Muhammed and his contemporaries, and the Hadith literature ranks, alongside the Quran, as the fundamental scriptures of Islam. Aisha describes this Hadith as an account of the foundations of Islam and its three parts, faith, rituals and spirituality, with Ihsan representing the last of these, spirituality. Both Laura and Aisha pay great importance to this aspect of Islam and refer to the inner journey that their conversion set in motion, and which they find is not evident in the lives of all Muslims. Laura notes that 'some people tend to forget the spirituality' and Aisha makes a similar point:

> Many Muslims completely removed the spiritual part... it is all about faith and actions... this is why so many terrible things happen between different Islamic groups.

Both Aisha and Laura were in contact with different Islamic branches at the start of their conversion and they both attended teachings in various Islamic groups. Both describe how they navigated instinctively through these different interpretations and understandings of Islam. Aisha states that 'once I attended a teaching and it felt so cold' and Laura even found herself unable to recognize Islam in one teaching she attended. About that specific teaching she says, 'that is not the Islam I read about'. When asked to say more about that Islam she answers 'you know, pure Islam without hidden agendas', and when asked to describe the teachings she attends now she states: 'there is no political aim. It is just Islam'. From Aisha and Laura's perspectives, Islam in many ways characterizes an individual faith powered by an inner spiritual movement to achieve goodness through worship. Laura explains it clearly by stating; 'to me, Islam is my comfort zone'.

Respect

Respect is clearly fundamental to their perceptions of themselves as Muslims. Aisha describes herself as becoming more tolerant after she converted. She especially remembers how she used to have big rows with her sister before she converted, and how she now tries to remember that there are reasons why they disagree, and that Aisha should respect those reasons. Respect also plays an important role in how Aisha and Laura continue to be a part of the Christian traditions, which are a big part of their family lives. Laura and Aisha both continue to celebrate Christmas as they did before they converted. They do that out of respect for their families and because, according to them, it is an Islamic virtue to be as good and inclusive as possible towards other people. Provided their intention is to be good and loving family members, they see nothing wrong in participating in the Christmas celebration. There is no conflict with their Islamic faith in being beneficent and respectful family members at Christmas; they are actually being virtuous Muslims.

Laura believes it is very important for a Muslim to respect her parents and to be honest. Therefore, she had found the three weeks between her conversion and telling her parents very difficult: 'as a Muslim it is so wrong to lie to your parents, but I was so afraid of what they would say'.

Although they do a lot to be respectful towards other people, Laura and Aisha do not always feel their respect for the choices of others is requited. Laura, for instance, is not convinced that her parents would be able to be genuinely proud of her if she decided to wear a headscarf.

Who Am I to Judge?

'*Who am I to judge?*' is a phrase used by both Laura and Aisha throughout the interviews, and they both say more than once that no human can judge another. They may disagree on other people's readings of the Quran and they can state that 'this is not how I view Islam', but they never talk about right or wrong. When they talk about actions conducted by other Islamic groups, e.g., IS — the militant organisation, Islamic State — they either say 'I don't see how they read this' or 'it is not in line with my perception of Islam', but neither Aisha nor Laura talks about misinterpretations or misreading when referring to other Islamic groups. This is especially interesting when I compare this study to that of Shanneik (2011) as *haram* (forbidden) and *halal* (allowed) are very much present in the accounts of the former Catholic converts.

I find that it is possible to make connections between the *humanistic habitus* I found in Laura and Aisha's upbringing, and their present perceptions of Islam and themselves as Muslims. I find that spirituality becomes a recurring theme and that much of what they say about Islam revolves around an inner journey between themselves and Allah, which unfolds through their intentions and actions. Inspired by Olivier Roy (2004), I will refer to this as *humanistic Islam.*

Humanistic Islam; Spirituality and Beneficence

T he term Humanistic Islam captures a perception of Islam that Olivier Roy endorses in his book *Globalised Islam* (2004). When studying Islam in the West, he saw tendencies towards a more spiritually oriented and individualized Islam. He states that 'spiritualisation accompanies the individualisation of religion' and that 'salvation is as much a matter of worldly things as it is heavenly ones' (Roy, 2004, 191, 190–91). Roy argues that it is important not to see this as a new Islamic branch, because these values are very much present in earlier Muslim traditions, too. The new thing, he argues, is the relationship between haram and halal:

> Norms are reformulated in terms of values, and are subsequently 'negotiable', meaning that the issue is not to follow the letter but the spirit of the law. (Roy, 2004, 190)

Instead of strictly sticking to the descriptions of haram and halal, the norms tend to be more fluid and adjustable and this is very much in line with Laura and Aisha's perceptions of Islam, particularly the way they construe participation in the Christian Christmas tradition as a way of performing an Islamic virtue — goodness and respect for others. Through their intentions to be faithful Muslims, they reformulate norms in terms of values, and follow the spirit of the law when practising their Islamic faith.

Another example of the spiritualization and individualization of faith lies in the way Laura and Aisha navigated between the different Islamic branches they became acquainted with. If they do not feel comfortable with the teachings or find the style of Islam in a particular mosque poorly aligned with their own perceptions, they search elsewhere rather than adapting their beliefs to fit the specific Islamic milieu. This is significant when one considers that these women are converts and might be expected to accept the practices of the first Islamic branch they encountered after their conversion, which in Laura and Aisha's cases were both Salafi-oriented branches, which they found cold and lacking in spirituality. It seems that Laura and Aisha both held clear expectations of what Islam is and how it should feel either before or immediately after conversion, which makes them able to navigate instinctively. It is reasonable to argue that these converts lean on their habitus after their conversion, as shown in the discussion of focal points, and also in their ability to use feelings and instincts to make sense of the Islamic context.

The Continuation of Habitus in Conversion

Both Shanneik (2011) and Roy (2004) described the attraction of Salafi Islam for previously religious converts as a continuation of the converts' previous religious habitus in a new religious environment. My analysis of previously non-religious converts reveals a similar process, but not to Salafi Islamic branches, for the converts found these too strict, cold and forgetful of *Ihsan* (spirituality). For Aisha and Laura, Islam offers an inner feeling of individual judgement, a means of spiritual self-development rather than a scripture to be taken literally, and this style of Islam — what Laura terms 'pure' Islam — is more in keeping with their former habitus.

It is clear, both in relation to the previously religious converts studied by Shanneik (2011) and Roy (2004), and the previously non-religious converts presented here, that previous habitus somehow determines where the converts end up placing themselves in their new religious field. Using a Bourdieusian terminology (Bourdieu, 1973) there seems to be an exchange of capitals between the secular social space in which Laura and Aisha are brought up and their new religious social space. Habitus, whether religious or not, seems to play an important role when looking at converts' choices during the conversion process. It seems that the converts draw on accustomed worldviews, practices and understandings — habitus — when they convert.

Discourses We Live By

There is a further point that arises from my study that I consider worthy of discussion. It relates to Laura and her cousin Kevin, the alcoholic. His history of alcohol abuse plays an interesting role in her story, because her reference to it offers a link with earlier theoretical discourses held by conversion researchers. Earlier, I cited works by

Rambo (1993) and Damsager and Mogensen (2007b) that described how conversion research has been heavily influenced by psychology, and conversion was for a long time viewed in terms of breaking out of an unsatisfactory childhood or in other ways related to crises or traumas. Although this perspective is now largely replaced by a more agentive one, I noticed, during the interviews with Laura, Aisha and other converts, that they all in some way circle around this perception, so I have chosen to look further into Laura's example to clarify why this might be so.

When I first ask her to tell me about her life, she says that she grew up in a typical nuclear family, but that she has an older cousin, Kevin, who has a drinking problem. Throughout the interview, she keeps coming back to Kevin even though she almost never saw him as they had little contact with that part of the family — not because of his drinking. Despite this, Kevin keeps turning up in the story, and the story begins to circle around alcohol in general. Even when she describes her decision to convert, the story centres around alcohol and she almost describes the conversion as a choice between alcohol and becoming a Muslim. She tells me that she was surprised how easy it was to stop drinking, although she previously said that she never really drank much alcohol.

Submitting her story to further narrative analysis, I find no evidence that Kevin played any crucial role in her life. She never speaks of experiences with him and yet he is almost the first person she mentions when asked to talk about her life. I surmise that she habitually connects Kevin's drinking problem to her conversion to Islam, perhaps to justify this to herself, maybe to justify it to others. It appears that she may be consciously or unconsciously adopting a commonly held conversion discourse — that of an escape from or break with something traumatic or unsatisfactory. This is particularly interesting as Laura emphasises that her parents' parenting was good and caring. She more than once states that she had a very happy childhood and that she does not want people to think badly about her parents because she converted to Islam. It is difficult for me to corroborate my suggestion that Laura's experience of Kevin's alcohol abuse is not a substantial part of her conversion — not a causal factor but an explanatory device — but I do believe that this is a likely interpretation. When I look at the way it is presented in her story and how the story is created around this experience, compared to other more general experiences, it appears that her experience with her alcohol-demented cousin fits into the conversion story rather than being a root cause.

As I said, this focusing on a possible problem is visible in many of the interviews I carried out and this suggests that the converts in this study may be living by a discourse on conversion that draws on understandings created by previous research and seemingly embedded within society. I argue, too, that the understandings that underpin this discourse serve to justify the converts' choices when they are explaining these within their local communities.

Perhaps we should pay greater attention to discourses, read more widely, and ask broader questions when dealing with a group of people who live by a discourse so heavily discussed as Islam is now. Otherwise, we may merely end up verifying previous research instead of conducting new work. My study demonstrates that the situation is extremely complex and that earlier theories need to be continually re-considered as they may continue to play a role in real lives even when no longer seen as paramount: historical perspectives and commonly held discourses slow the pace of change, whether this process acts consciously or unconsciously on the individual and society.

References

Beckford, J.A. (1978). Accounting for conversion. *The British Journal of Sociology*, 29: 249–62.

Bourdieu, P. (1973). The three forms of theoretical knowledge. *Social Science Information*, 12: 53–80.

Bourdieu, P. (1977). *Outline of a theory of practice*. Cambridge: Cambridge University Press.

Bourdieu, P. (2000) *Pascalian meditations*. Cambridge: Polity Press.

Bourdieu, P. & Wacquant. L. (1992). *An invitation to reflexive sociology*. Cambridge: Polity Press.

Damsager, J.H.M. & Mogensen, M.S. (eds) (2007a). *Dansk konversionsforskning*, Højbjerg: Univers.

Damsager, J.H.M. & Mogensen, M.S. (2007b). Konversionsforskning — Videnskabelige vinkler på studiet af fænomenet og begrebet religiøs konversion. In: Damsager, J.H.M. & Mogensen, M.S. (eds), *Dansk konversionsforskning*. Højbjerg: Univers.

Hindmarsh, B. (2014). Religious conversion as narrative and autobiography. In: Rambo L.R (ed), *The Oxford handbook of religious conversion*. Oxford: Oxford University Press. https://doi.org/10.1093/oxfordhb/9780195338522.001.0001

Inglis, T. (1998). *Moral monopoly: The rise and fall of the Catholic Church in modern Ireland*. Dublin: University College Dublin Press.

Kim, J.-H. (2016). *Understanding narrative inquiry: The crafting and analysis of stories as research*. Thousand Oaks, CA: SAGE

Rambo, L.R. (1993). *Understanding religious conversion*. New Haven: Yale University Press.

Roy, O. (2004). *Globalised Islam: The search for a new Ummah*. London: C. Hurst.

Shanneik, Y. (2011). Conversion and religious habitus: The experiences of Irish women converts to Islam in the pre-Celtic Tiger era. *Journal of Muslim Minority Affairs*, 31: 503–17. https://doi.org/10.1080/13602004.2011.630859

Snow, D.A., & Machalek, R. (1984). The sociology of conversion. *Annual Review of Sociology*, 10(1): 167–90.

Taylor, B. (1976). Conversion and cognition: An area from empirical study in the microsociology of religious knowledge. *Social Compass*, 23: 5.

Polkinghorne, D.E. (1988). *Narrative knowing and the human sciences*. New York: State University of New York Press.

Polkinghorne, D.E. (1995). Narrative configuration in qualitative analysis. *International Journal of Qualitative Studies in Education*, 8(1): 5–23.

Warburg, M. (2007). Fra konversionsberetninger til konversionsanalyser — kildeproblemer og fortolkningsstrategier. In: Damsager, J.H.M. & Mogensen, M.S. (eds), *Dansk konversionsforskning*. Højbjerg: Univers.

Wiktorowicz, Q. (2006). Anatomy of the Salafi movement. *Studies in Conflict & Terrorism*, 29: 207–39. https://doi.org/10.1080/10576100500497004

20. Participatory Approaches in Critical Migration Research

The Example of an Austrian Documentary Film

Annette Sprung

Annette Sprung discusses a participatory research project that created a documentary film about the experiences of migrants working as adult educators in Austria, and then analyses this collaboratively to consider issues of stereotyping and 'otherness' from multiple perspectives.

S ocial change due to migration has become a topical issue for many scientific disciplines. The number of pertinent research activities has significantly increased against the background of the large-scale refugee movements to European countries since summer 2015 (Eurostat, 2017) and was enhanced as migration became a key factor in political developments around the globe. Powerful discourses such as those on 'belonging', representation and 'othering' shape the debate. Individuals' biographies and identities are viewed through the prism of ascriptions and discourses of differentiation, with research often contributing to the construction of certain images of the 'other'. It is therefore necessary to analyse and reflect on the way in which we look at such phenomena in scientific contexts. The related question of representation is a well-known topic in social sciences and cultural studies and has been debated intensely under the slogan of the 'crisis of representation' (Berg & Fuchs, 1999; Marcus & Fischer, 1991). I will refer to it against the background of specific power relations in migration societies.

https://doi.org/10.11647/OBP.0203.20

The aim of this chapter is to explore critical aspects of migration research in adult education by reflecting on the construction of 'the migrant', the phenomena of representation and othering and the role (and responsibility) of researchers in reproducing or deconstructing problematic categories, which ultimately also shape the political and public discourse. Furthermore, appropriate methodologies of research and dissemination — such as participatory research and artistic approaches — are discussed in order to explore possibilities for deconstructing hegemonic discourses. My perspective is inspired by postcolonial studies and critical migration research (e.g., Bhabha, 1994; Mecheril, 2016).

As a concrete example, I will present the case of a documentary film, which I produced, together with Klaudija Sabo, a cultural scientist, filmmaker and adult educator. The film portrays (or in other words, represents) experiences and strategies of professionals with migrant biographies in adult education, but also provides a (self) reflection on othering by questioning the role of the filmmakers and their way of dealing with the narratives. Consequently, it is not only interesting to look at the product as such, the film; but also to discuss the processes of concept development and film production, where we tried to lay open the 'illusionary' character of documentary filmmaking. The role of the filmmaker is set as an analogy to the role of the researcher and should thus inspire discussion on a variety of aspects.

The film was created within the wider framework of a participatory research workshop, with a group of migrant adult educators as co-researchers. The setting of self-directed research workshops was one of several efforts to cross the border which is often constructed between a (White, hegemonic, academic, etc.) 'we' and the (migrant) 'other'. The workshops were part of a transdisciplinary research project (2012–2014), which analysed the representation and access of people with migrant biographies to professions in the field of adult/continuing education in Austria. The findings from other segments of the project have already been presented in earlier publications (Kukovetz, Sadjed & Sprung, 2014; Sadjed, Sprung & Kukovetz, 2015).

Representation and the Construction of 'Migrants'

The Challenge of Representation

C ritical migration research deals with different meanings of 'representation'. Firstly, there is the communicative dimension of representation, related to the way in which we depict something/ somebody, for example in research (who talks about whom? in which way? etc.); this is a well-known point of reflection in social sciences and cultural studies. Secondly, representation in the political sense points to the question of defending one's interests and making one's own positions and claims heard. It can be realized as direct or indirect representation. Relevant questions in the migration context are: What opportunities for self-representation in political participation are given? Who is legitimated to speak out as a proxy? Whose voices are heard? (Kukovetz, Sadjed & Sprung, 2014, p. 53ff.). Moreover, we use the term 'representation' when we talk about equality in participation and access to resources.

The practice of speaking for or about others makes hierarchical social structures apparent. In many countries, current forms of migrant representation in public or scientific spaces are still dominated by external representation by members of the majority society (Sprung, 2011). In these scenarios, the perspectives of the individuals, groups and communities of minorities remain largely unconsidered; the voices of migrants tend to remain unheard. A lack of representation can be identified in diverse spheres of society, for example regarding the visibility of migrants in the media (Bleich, Bloemraad & de Graauw, 2015) or their opportunities for political participation (Chaudhary, 2016).

The crisis in terms of the representation of others constitutes an especially important challenge for research, which has been discussed — not only in terms of migration but also more generally — since the 1990s (Berg & Fuchs, 1999; Marcus & Fischer, 1991). One central idea from these debates points to the need for academics (and in the concrete field I would like to add, White academics) to reflect on their privileged position to speak, and the related power of their interpretations. A common answer to the problem is to promote self-representation of minoritized groups as commonly occurs in politics, social life and science. From a critical viewpoint, it also has to be stated that representation always means the proxy or the depiction of a special group and thus automatically creates a categorization and, as a result, homogeneity within this group (Broden & Mecheril, 2007, p. 12).

Representation and social justice can be seen as central ideas of the theoretical framework of our research: addressing the question of representation of underprivileged groups is a basic condition for an inclusive society. In this sense representation is part of a concept of justice that aims for an equal participation in all economic, social, cultural and political resources (Fraser, 2008; Perko & Czollek, 2007). The equal access of citizens with migration biographies to the field of education is a constant topic of political and social contestation. The exclusion of migrants can also be identified in the scientific field and in adult education (Broden & Mecheril, 2007; Sprung, 2011).

The Migrant as the Other

Representations are always connected to power relations (Broden & Mecheril, 2007). This has been shown, for example, in cultural and postcolonial theories, through a critical reflection on practices of external representation, which generates knowledge about others (Castro Varela & Dhawan, 2004; Said, 1991; Spivak, 2010). Critical migration research consequently has to consider the phenomenon of 'othering'. Research can contribute and point to discrimination and to barriers that avoid equal representation of minoritized groups. At the same time, migration research — as well as education — often reproduces the categories on which exclusion is based.

The construction of the migrant as 'other' tackles diverse groups in different ways. Beside historically passed-on images of the other, the socio-economic disparities have proven to be one of the strongest lines of differentiation between and within various migrant communities. In many European countries the descendants of low-skilled labour migrants, who were needed and recruited as a cheap labour force in the 1960s and 1970s, could not achieve significant upward social mobility. This is also partly caused by their stigmatization and their lack of symbolic capital as an expression of social recognition and power (Bourdieu, 2005; Gächter, 2012). Nowadays, stigmatization and stereotyping often takes place by means of attributes like 'refugee', 'Muslim' etc. and are linked, for example, to attributions like threatening, violent, backward, etc. A public discourse on 'migrants', which is currently influenced and highly instrumentalized by political forces such as the far right (but also other groups), in reality mostly addresses only specific groups and countries of origin. Racist and anti-Muslim politics have contributed significantly to recent electoral successes of extreme right parties in several countries.

An undifferentiated and negative stereotyping of migrants in public is presumably one reason why many people are reluctant to identify with or talk about their migration biography, and often even hide their origins if possible. This attitude became quite evident in our research outcomes, especially when we interviewed members of the so-called second generation who work in adult education. It must be stated that even just addressing subjects as 'migrants' in research brings about the risk of re-inscribing the practices of othering and, as a further consequence, of discriminating against individuals. It is therefore understandable that we had difficulty in finding interviewees, especially amongst the second generation. By way of summary, Vina Yun (2011) aptly observes that the 'post-migrant' subjectivity is characterized by a self-conception that questions conventional, ethnic-nationally defined identities and instead develops a new vocabulary of belonging. Consequently, critical migration research has to pay attention and to find ways to give space to articulate these self-conceptions, which might extend and transcend the predefined, rigid categories that the majority society tends to offer.

The demand for such spaces of self-representation within a research context was a central aspect in our project. Which is why, in addition to reflecting on these issues theoretically throughout the whole project, we also tried to find appropriate methodological approaches to involve migrants and their knowledge beyond addressing them as interviewees.

Methodologies: Participatory Research and Artistic Approaches

For the research workshops the core team of three researchers (which was also 'mixed' in terms of origin) invited seven people with migrant biographies to participate. We involved individuals who had a professional background in adult education and/or research and who had grown up in Austria, but still shared some experiences of being ascribed as 'others' (for example, because of wearing a headscarf or certain physiognomic attributes). They were remunerated for their participation in the workshops, which took place over one year. All group members were included in an interactive communication process to make decisions on topics and methods, dissemination, etc. The group finally decided to conduct five sub-projects in teams of two, of which the film production was one. Nevertheless, the whole group came together regularly to discuss critically the work of the single sub-teams. The film, which will be described in more detail below, portrays careers of adult educators with migrant backgrounds and picks up the question of representation — implicitly and explicitly.

Through the workshops, we aimed to open up a space for representation of migrants in research as a general goal. Furthermore, we wanted to create opportunities to bring diverse perspectives and voices into a dialogue. Finally, we aimed to include different modes of knowledge within a non-hierarchical perspective, such as embodied knowledge, which is usually seen as not being equal to academic knowledge. Research workshops invite people, whose circumstances and strategies are being explored, to engage (Bergold & Thomas, 2010). They aim to integrate target groups into the entire research process, including decision-making. Research workshops not only open a multi-perspective space for research but imply at the same time a collective learning process (Pilch Ortega & Sprung, 2010; Willis, Jost & Nilakanta, 2007). Similar to approaches of action research, they have an exploratory character and employ the use of qualitative methods. In general, communicative research processes entail hierarchical relations in regard to different forms of knowledge and speaking positions, which has to become an integrated point of critical reflection.

Based on a critique of objectifying research methods and following the desire to encourage social change through research (including making unheard voices of minoritized groups heard), researchers have been looking for alternative approaches since the 1970s. Participatory concepts, especially in the social sciences, are connected with the history of social movements and emancipatory struggles (Freire, 1970; Hall, 1992). 'Participatory Action Research', or PAR, aims to encourage actors to engage in changing the circumstantial/structural conditions of their own lives. Another important idea of PAR is to 'redefine the relationship between researchers and the participants in a non-hierarchical manner' (Glassman & Erdem, 2014, p. 215). Glassman and Erdem show that origins of PAR include anticolonial movements as well as feminist ideas (Joyappa & Martin, 1996) and other perspectives. Referring to anti- or postcolonial theories suggests analogies between colonialism and traditional paradigms of scientific research, where the researchers ('data-owners') are in power and use (or exploit?) the researched as their resources to draw profit from them (ibid., p. 15). Some participatory approaches are connected to the development of action-research, which was founded by Kurt Lewin in the 1940s (Reason & Bradbury-Huang, 2008). But not all concepts of action-research — especially the earlier ones — deal explicitly with marginalized people or aim necessarily at emancipatory goals (Glassmann & Erdem, 2014). Additionally, there are particular developments in different scientific contexts. German-speaking action-research, for example, made strong references to a Marxist analysis of capitalism and was geared towards a wider political impact than anything Lewin had done (Unger, 2014, p. 15).

I have been exploring the potential of PAR for migration research in diverse settings over the past fifteen years. These processes led to highly interesting and differentiated experiences and results (Pilch-Ortega & Sprung, 2010). But the approach of 'insider research' also implicates questionable assumptions, for example, because it reconstructs 'the migrant' once more and reproduces problematic understanding of group belonging (Nowicka & Cieslik, 2014). A critical debate about the (dichotomist) insider-outsider divide in migration research suggests a more differentiated view on positionality. One has to be aware that insider-outsider divides are often a relational construction and that a migrant biography does not necessarily cause a different perspective; moreover, there are other intersectional aspects that might play a role (Carling, Erdal & Ezzati, 2014).

Another idea behind the project under discussion was to use artistic approaches, which are often connected with participatory research. Some reference points to Artistic Research (Knowles & Cole, 2008; Peters, 2013) or Performative Social Sciences (Denzin, 2001) can be found. Artistic or Arts-Based Research (ABR) is mostly situated within the qualitative inquiry tradition. The term was first coined in 1993 (Wang, et al., 2017). ABR follows the idea that arts could be useful to gain a deeper understanding of human action and social conditions. It became popular especially for researchers who feel committed to contribute to social change (Savin-Baden & Wimpenny, 2014). Therefore, ABR often deals with minoritized groups, for example via theatre work or analyses of artistic products such as paintings or film material. Most approaches aim to link different modes of knowledge as well, following a political, emancipatory goal and engaging community members in diverse action. In the field of Performative Social Science, artistic approaches are seen as methods to help in answering the research questions, but also to disseminate the results to a broader public. Performative Social Sciences highlight spontaneous moments of insight, which elicit awakening and a change of perspective. They should facilitate the analysis of underlying, unconscious dynamics of social situations by opening up spaces beyond the cognitive and rational (Battisti & Eiselen, 2008). From my point of view, artistic approaches have great potential to unearth tacit knowledge, and also to speak diverse 'languages', which helps to address different people in terms of participation. Many issues can be made understandable in a special way because diverse dimensions of perception (just like emotional ones) are inspired.

'On the Other Side of the Desk' — a Documentary Film

Idea and Concept

E mbedded in the research workshops, Klaudija Sabo and I worked out a concept for a 30-minute documentary film. The production process lasted about 15 months. As we had no extra financial resources, we handled the whole production on our own. The other workshop participants contributed by engaging in on-going discussions about the script, the choice of protagonists, the *mise-en-scène* and especially the question of how to deal with the tension between representation and the problem of othering. The title of the film, 'On the Other Side of the Desk', reflects a quotation from a scene in the film: an adult educator told us about the empowering effects that migrant participants experience when there is a migrant in the teaching position, and she expressed this as being 'on the other side of the desk' (i.e., the teachers' desk).

To open up a space for self-representation in the context of the research topic we invited adult educators with migrant biographies to tell us their individual career stories (in an interview setting), and also to share their expert view on diversity in adult education in general. The narrations covered issues such as the motivation for their career choice, influential factors and people in their lives, individual strategies and the meaning of the migrant biography as cultural capital and/or as a disadvantage. We tried to enable a mostly free and self-directed narration. The film would be released later on to present research outcomes to a broader public and to institutions involved in adult education. We finally invited four people (two men, two women) to participate in the film. They had diverse family backgrounds (in terms of origins, social and educational status) and worked in different fields and positions in adult education. To give an example, the parents' education level ranged from university professor to illiterate labourer. By selecting such socio-demographic characteristics, we also wanted to consider some intersectional aspects.

In the first part of the film, the protagonists are shown individually telling their stories against a black background. A 'talking heads' format was decided after long discussions in the research workshop. We wanted to put the subject at the centre, and no other factors should deflect from their (verbal and non-verbal) narration. We were aware that there is no 'neutral' background, but in the end, we decided for the colour black as aesthetic and technical aspects also played a role. For the first part of the film, cuttings from the four interviews were edited along thematic lines. In the second part of the film we show a cinema screening room where the four protagonists sit together with the filmmakers and discuss the draft version (rough cut) of the film, which they had just watched for the first time. The cinema room points to the idea of the film as a reflection about itself. While we discussed the first screening critically, the camera was again in operation and generated new material. An important point at this stage was that we, as filmmakers, stepped into the scene and became visible. Thus, we explicitly put our role (and power) as constructors of images and assertions up for discussion.

Potential and Challenges of the Medium

A central idea we wanted to deal with in the film was to reflect on the phenomenon of othering — we also wanted to question the medium in this respect. What is described in theory and numerous studies had also been confirmed in our empirical findings: adult educators with migrant biographies often have to struggle with ethnic/racist ascriptions or simply a general 'otherness' (Bhabha, 1994; Said, 1991). The diverse ways of dealing with ascriptions and discrimination range from total denial of one's origin up to creative ways for using migration-related experiences and embodied knowledge for career advancement (Sadjed, Sprung & Kukovetz, 2015).

Because of its visual and acoustic dimensions, the medium of film allows self-representation in a wider and more direct sense in comparison to a written depiction (usually written by the researcher). On the other hand, it is clear that visual media are often used to generate stereotypes — not least about 'migrants'. A film project therefore can — potentially — be a chance to promote alternative images and question usual (hegemonic) patterns of perception.

There are several analogies between research and filmmaking. The director of a film choses the topic and decides on questions and perspectives. The material — be it interview transcripts or film — is edited by her/him and the team. Finally, the presented results are always a construction — created by the researcher or the filmmaker. According to critical migration studies, research often contributes to reproducing images of 'otherness'. The researcher, just like the filmmaker, usually holds the more powerful position and creates meanings (Koch, 1992). In particular, documentary film pretends to be a representation of 'reality' (maybe another analogy, to the sciences). We therefore felt challenged to find an appropriate methodology to make our film a reflective space and to lay open the illusionary character of the medium. Basically, we reference the movement of *Cinéma Verité*, which was developed in the 1960s (Beyerle, 1997; Nichols, 1991). In particular, we drew inspiration from the film 'Chronique d'un été' (Chronicle of a Summer, 1960), produced by the sociologist Edgar Morin and the anthropologist and filmmaker Jean Rouch. This film also involved the protagonists in the process and engaged the filmmakers as part of the story. Morin and

Rouch aimed to make visible the fictional character of documentary film, breaking with conventional approaches within the genre in these times. Questions of authenticity could thus be reconsidered.

What does this mean for our concept? Even if positioning the camera directly in front of our speakers, giving space for free narration and leaving out props or symbols — it was still us, the filmmakers, who finally edited the material and designed the story through our own lenses. To set up a corrective procedure, we had the idea of inviting the protagonists to join us in a cinema for a common screening of the rough cut with a follow-up discussion. With a collective reflection upon our product, we tried to create a participatory space, which had different functions: firstly, the status of the protagonists and the power relations within the process was to undergo a shift.

The protagonists were invited to criticize, correct or confirm the interpretations, which we had suggested, after having gained a more distanced perspective on their own dialogue. The group make-up was to support this process. Secondly, they also had the opportunity to comment on our role as filmmakers and we decided together how to develop the script and how the discussion should be included in the final version. Thirdly, we thought that a debate in the group would bring up new perspectives on the subject of the film — this was definitely the case.

Here is just one example: after having watched the film together, one of the protagonists criticized the omission of negative experiences and aspects of discrimination in the film. He had the impression that we had just shown a 'happy story' about four successful migrants. This statement opened up an interesting debate because we learned that some of the protagonists could not even remember that they had been asked explicitly about experiences of discrimination. In fact, with one exception, they never told us that they had had any bad experiences. They thus started to reflect in the group setting on the reasons for their not talking about negative stories, while the message of mainly positive career development seemed somewhat erroneous to them now when watching the film from a more distanced position. Subsequently we had an exciting discussion on dealing with discrimination and on strategies to counter victimization. Within this discussion the influence and intersection of race, class and gender clearly emerged. These sequences play an important role in the second part of the final version of our film.

In general, the protagonists felt very well represented. Furthermore, they appreciated the process as a chance to reflect on their respective biographies and especially on their methods of dealing with and representing their migration backgrounds. I would say that the process of realizing the described documentary film was not finished with the final cut but when it was premiered at the closing conference of the research project. Around 100 stakeholders from the field of Austrian adult education watched the film at a cinema screening and engaged in a public discussion with the protagonists who, in responding to the audience directly, were able — once more — to be in a position of power when sharing their narrations.

Conclusion

O ur aim in producing a documentary film was to create a concise summary of the overall research outcomes, open a space for representation and critical reflection on migration and adult education research and also to establish an alternative mode of disseminating research findings to the broader public. The film should contribute to the aim of Participatory Action Research to intervene in present discourses about migrants by making their voices heard and, at the same time, to reflect critically on the related problems. Looking at the feedback we have received for the film so far, it can be supposed that many people felt inspired to develop new and more differentiated perspectives on the topic; viewers emphasized that they had perceived the speakers as competent and self-determined agents and that they had discovered nuances that might have stayed invisible in a conventional research report. The film was also honoured with the Ludo-Hartmann-Preis — an Austrian scientific award for research work in the field of adult education — in 2015.

Nevertheless, a permanent critical reflection is necessary, because every approach produces new constructions and implicates certain problems. Therefore, a project like the present one can never actually be seen as 'completed'. The research workshops had essentially supported the whole process by providing input, evaluating suggestions, offering critical feedback and challenging the filmmakers to share and expound upon their own intentions, images and positions. Generally, it can be stated that self-representation of migrants or specific groups does not necessarily deconstruct images of the other but could also be an essentializing practice and lead to a sort of 'authentication' of the 'other' voices. This opens up again the question of ascriptions as well as the question of legitimate representation (Broden & Mecheril 2007, p. 20). The research workshops were, therefore, also defined as a space in which to reflect on these challenges and dilemmas. Aside from the concrete sub-project, the film; the research workshops encouraged all participants to reflect on their thoughts, identities, responsibilities — not least on how we can directly contribute to social change. Our methodology presents an opportunity to articulate forms of resistance against common representations and research practices, and to find a language which supports a critical discourse for migration research.

References

Battisti, M. & Eiselen, T. (2008). Insights through performative approaches, *Forum: Qualitative Social Research*, 9(2), Art.44. http://www.qualitative-research.net/index.php/fqs/article/view/378/823

Bhabha, H. (1994). *The location of culture*. London: Routledge.

Berg, E. & Fuchs, M. (eds) (1999). *Kultur, soziale Praxis, Text. Die Krise der ethnographischen Repräsentation*. Frankfurt am Main: Suhrkamp.

Bergold, J. & Thomas, S. (2010). Partizipative Forschung. In: Mey, G. & Mruck, K. (eds), *Handbuch Qualitative Forschung in der Psychologie*. Wiesbaden: VS. https://doi.org/10.1007/978-3-531-92052-8_23

Beyerle, M. (1997). *Authentisierungsstrategien im Dokumentarfilm. Das amerikanische Direct Cinema der 60er Jahre*. Trier: WVT.

Bleich, E., Bloemraad, I. & de Graauw, E. (2015). Migrants, minorities, and the media: Information, representations, and participation in the public sphere. *Journal for Ethnic and Migration Studies*, 41(6): 857–73. https://doi.org/10.108 0/1369183X.2014.1002197

Broden, A. & Mecheril, P. (2007). Migrationsgesellschaftliche Re-Präsentationen: Eine Einführung. In: Broden, A. & Mecheril, P. (eds), *Re-Präsentationen. Dynamiken der Migrationsgesellschaft*. Düsseldorf: IDA.

Bourdieu, P. (2005). *Die verborgenen Mechanismen der Macht: Schriften zu Politik und Kultur 1*. Hamburg: VSA.

Carling, J., Erdal M.B. & Ezzati, R. (2014). Beyond the insider-outsider divide in migration research, *Migration Studies*, 2(1): 36–54. https://doi.org/10.1093/migration/mnt022

Castro Varela, M. & Dhawan, N. (2004). Horizonte der Repräsentationspolitik — Taktiken der Intervention. In: Ross, B. (ed), *Migration, Geschlecht und Staatsbürgerschaft. Perspektiven für eine antirassistische und feministische Politik und Politikwissenschaft*. Wiesbaden: VS.

Chaudhary, A.R. (2016). *Transnational politics and immigrant political participation in Europe*. Working Papers, No. 127. International Migration Institute (IMI), University of Oxford. https://www.imi.ox.ac.uk/publications/transnational-politics-and-political-integration-among-migrants-in-europe

Denzin, N.K. (2001). The reflexive interview and a performative social science, *Qualitative Research*, 1(1): 23–46.

Eurostat (2017). *Asylum statistics*. http://ec.europa.eu/eurostat/statistics-explained/index.php/Asylum_statistics

Fraser, N. (2008). From redistribution to recognition? Dilemmas of justice in a 'Postsocialist' age. In: Seidmann, S. & Alexander, J. (eds), *The new social theory reader*. Abingdon: Routledge.

Freire, P. (1970). *Pedagogy of the oppressed*. New York: Continuum.

Gächter, A. (2012). Kaum beachtet: Bildungszugewinne der Jugend gegenüber der Elterngeneration. *Working Paper Migration and Social Mobility*, 28. Vienna: ZSI. http://www.zsi.at/users/153/attach/p28_12_bmukk2.pdf

Glassman, M. & Erdem, G. (2014). Participatory action research and its meanings: Vivencia, Praxis, Conscientization. *Adult Education Quarterly*, 64(3): 206–21. https://doi.org/10.1177/0741713614523667

Hall, B. (1992). From margins to center? The development and purpose of participatory research. *The American Sociologist*, 23: 15–28.

Joyappa, V. & M.D. (1996). Exploring alternative research epistemologies for adult education: Participatory research, feminist research and feminist participatory research. *Adult Education Quarterly*, 47(1): 1–14.

Knowles, G. & Cole, A.L. (2008). *Handbook of the arts in qualitative research. Perspectives, methodologies, examples, and issues*. Thousand Oaks, CA: Sage.

Koch, G. (1992). *Die Einstellung ist die Einstellung. Visuelle Konstruktionen des Judentums*. Frankfurt: Suhrkamp.

Kukovetz, B., Sadjed, A. & Sprung, A. (2014). *(K)ein Hindernis? Fachkräfte mit Migrationsgeschichte in der Erwachsenenbildung*. Wien: Löcker.

Marcus, G.E. & Fischer, M.J. (1991). *Anthropology as cultural critique: An experimental moment in the human sciences*. Chicago: University of Chicago Press.

Mecheril, P. (ed) (2016). *Handbuch Migrationspädagogik*. Weinheim: Beltz.

Nichols, B. (1991). *Representing reality. Issues and concepts in documentary*. Bloomington: Indiana University Press.

Nowicka, M. & Cieslik, A. (2014). Beyond methodological nationalism in insider research with migrants. *Migration Studies*, 2(1): 1–15. https://doi.org/10.1093/migration/mnt024

Perko, G. & Czollek, L.C. (2007). Diversity in ausserökonomischen Kontexten: Bedingungen und Möglichkeiten der Umsetzung. In: Broden, A. & Mecheril, P. (eds), *Re-Präsentationen. Dynamiken der Migrationsgesellschaft*. Düsseldorf: IDA.

Peters, S. (ed) (2013). *Das Forschen aller. Artistic Research als Wissensproduktion zwischen Kunst, Wissenschaft und Gesellschaft*. Bielefeld: Transcript.

Pilch-Ortega, A. & Sprung, A. (2010). Forms of self-representation of migrants in public and scientific spaces. In: Lucio-Villegas, E. (ed), *Transforming/researching communities*. El Masnou: Diálogos.

Reason, P. & Bradbury-Huang, H. (2008). *The Sage handbook of action research. Participative inquiry and practice*. Los Angeles: Sage.

Sadjed, A., Sprung, A. & Kukovetz, B. (2015). The use of migration-related competencies in continuing education. Individual strategies, social and institutional conditions. *Studies in Continuing Education*, 37(3): 286–301. https://doi.org/10.1080/0158037X.2015.1066768

Said, E. (1991). *Orientalism*. London: Penguin Books.

Savin-Baden, M., & Wimpenny, K. (2014). *A practical guide to arts-related research*. Rotterdam: Sense Publishers. https://doi.org/10.1007/978-94-6209-815-2

Spivak, G.C. (2010). Can the subaltern speak? In: Morris, R (ed), *Can the subaltern speak? Reflections on the history of an idea*. New York: Columbia University Press.

Sprung, A. (2011). *Zwischen Diskriminierung und Anerkennung. Weiterbildung in der Migrationsgesellschaft*. Münster: Waxmann.

Unger, H. (2014). *Partizipative Forschung. Einführung in die Forschungspraxis*. Wiesbaden: Springer VS.

Wang, Q., Coemans, S., Siegesmund, R. & Kannes, K. (2017). Arts-based methods in socially engaged research practice: A classification framework. *Art Research International: A Transdisciplinary Journal*. 2(2). https://doi.org/10.18432/R26G8P

Willis, J.W., Jost, M. & Nilakanta, R. (2007). *Foundations of qualitative research: Interpretive and critical approaches*. Thousand Oaks, CA: Sage.

Yun, V. (2011). F.A.Q. 'Zweite Generation'. Über Herkunftsdialoge, doppeltes Anderssein und 'Belonging'. Ein Kommentar. www.migrazine.at: online magazine von migrantinnen für alle, 2 [*Migrazine*, 2/2011]. http://www.migrazine.at/artikel/faq-zweite-generation#2%20

Photo by Tom Perkins, CC-BY 4.0

VI.

DISCOURSES TO SUPPORT DIVERSITY: PROJECTS THAT EMPOWER

C hapters in this section, like some of those in section V, discuss projects whose key aim is to support diversity. However, the focus moves away from contemporary migration and religion to marginalized groups. There are two chapters that consider some of the consequences of historical large-scale migrations — colonization — as their focus is on ways to support and protect Indigenous peoples; in Canada, and in South Africa. Another chapter, tells and analyses the stories of two female ex-military in Britain, collected as part of a project to provide support for former soldiers who struggle to adjust to civilian life and commit offences. The fourth chapter is a multi-faceted narrative around a performative approach to encouraging agency in senior citizens in England.

In 'Decolonizing and Indigenizing Discourses in a Canadian Context' (Ch21), Adrienne Chan offers an historical overview and clear explanations of decolonization and indigenization, an area in which she has worked for several decades. She describes how she engages with the discourses of power within the University to make changes to curricula and teaching and then describes and analyses a research project intended to prevent suicide in Aboriginal youth by building their resilience. This is a community-based project, developed organically with members of the Aboriginal community.

In 'Embedding Feminist Pedagogies of Care in Research to Better Support San Youth in South Africa' (Ch22), Outi Ylitapio-Mäntylä and Mari Mäkiranta, consider how holding feminist pedagogies but functioning within a neoliberal academic environment requires researchers working in non-Western contexts to re-think their assumptions and approaches. They discuss the issues relating to research in a large group where many of the collaborators scarcely know each other — maybe never meet — and make a plea for a caring ethos that sensitively recognizes the needs of the project participants rather than the power struggles of the transnational research project and its organizers.

For the women in Linda Cooper's chapter, 'From Defender to Offender: British Female Ex-Military Re-joining Civilian Society' (Ch23), the educational element was a practical one; learning to fight alongside their male compatriots and to live a communal life, held together by camaraderie and tension. The two women interviewed as part of a larger support project come from different generations, but both found adjustment to civilian life very difficult on leaving the Armed Forces and sank into (minor) criminal activities linked to mental health problems, and one case a level of alcohol dependence. Their experiences demonstrate how a radical change of lifestyle can leave people bewildered and with inadequate coping strategies, issues the larger project will seek to address. As women in, and leaving, the British military they represent a group that is traditionally marginalized and still a minority.

Teresa Brayshaw and Jennifer Granville's chapter, 'UK Senior Citizens Learn Filmmaking as a Creative Pathway to Reflection and Fulfilment' (Ch24), is styled to echo the processes that underpin their work and includes the QR code for the actual film produced so that you can view it for yourself. Theirs is an active and visual medium, so rather than present a traditional linear text, we worked with them to develop a multi-stranded chapter whose stages reflect those of filmmaking, introducing visual prompts when possible. Instead of a literature review there is a pictorial representation of key phrases relating to gerontology. The chapter starts with a 'script' and uses emails to tell the story as it developed, being honest about the problems rather than creating a polished overview that smooths away any conflict or confusion.

Together these chapters explore elements of diversity, focusing on those in society whose needs have gone unnoticed in the past. They vary considerably in style, with two very reflective pieces, followed by one that focuses on life stories and their analysis, and one retelling a performative initiative — a film — using the format of film production.

To readers who start with section VI, we direct you to the previous section (Chs17–20) where the focus is on migrants, and especially to Sprung's chapter (Ch20) which discusses a collaborative project intended to explore how the 'different' becomes 'othered'. This section will also resonate with Mascarenhas's chapter (Ch18) in section V: Cooper's ex-military offenders experience disorientation and alienation similar in impact if not in detail to the migrants Mascarenhas studies. Cooper's participants' stories also resonate with the Danish male ex-prisoner in Mathiassen's chapter (Ch13), although in the latter case mental health problems probably pre-dated the crimes. Brayshaw and Granville's chapter represents our joint attempt to create an open dialogue that demonstrates their processes but also captures the difficulties that academics who work in non-traditional fields have to overcome. It is an open-ended collage and readers who also turn to the performative works of Formenti and colleagues (Ch11), Sprung (Ch20) and Oikarinen-Jabai (Ch27) will see that these narratives have neither simple journeys nor final endings — but may, like the above studies, work towards an end product — stories, a film, an exhibition.

21. Decolonizing and Indigenizing Discourses in a Canadian Context

Adrienne S. Chan

Adrienne S. Chan describes her role, when working in Canada, to embed decolonized perspectives and better include Indigenous peoples within community. The funded study uses collaborative ventures to facilitate greater awareness of assumptions and difference and promote greater cultural awareness between groups and within institutions.

In Canada, we have been engaged in a discourse of 'indigenizing' as a means of addressing our work and relations with Aboriginal and Indigenous peoples, or the First Peoples of Canada. In particular, many educational institutions have taken up the discourse of indigenizing as a part of their mandate. In this chapter, I describe the ways in which the discourse is complex, and the approaches taken by a research team to begin to address some elements of decolonization and indigenization. At the core of the discussion and debates are the ways in which individuals and groups have divergent ways of speaking about these contested and binary discourses.

Indigenizing is a process of prioritizing the social and cultural contexts of Indigenous peoples into curriculum, practices (Yishak & Gumbo, 2015), structure, and everyday discourses (Van Wyk, 2002), particularly in a country which is immigrant settler based. Indigenization may also refer to Aboriginal peoples with reference to other countries such as, South Africa; and 'Africanization' with respect to the curriculum and to promote culture (Obanya, 1999). Our project can be viewed as an 'indigenous project' (Smith, 2012, p. 147), one which centres identity

https://doi.org/10.11647/OBP.0203.21

and cultural action with Indigenous peoples. Indigenization is therefore considered within a post-colonial context (Findlay, 2000) and, in an educational context, challenges accepted dominant knowledge and discourses (Todorova, 2016).

Decolonization is 'a process which engages with imperialism and colonialism at multiple levels' (Smith, 2012, p. 21). It invokes an examination of hegemony, our participation in colonialism as immigrants and settlers, and the dissolution of traditional forms of institutional power. For Aboriginal and Indigenous peoples, I suggest it is a troubling discourse that often examines a painful, colonized history. For educational institutions, decolonization is particularly complex and problematic since it challenges the way in which we teach, conduct research, and relate to each other as colleagues and with students. Decolonizing research requires a shift from the power of the researcher to the self-determination (Smith, 2012) of the communities in which research is conducted. It is a term that is used in examining empire (Pollath, 2018) and, while institutions are not empires, they do represent a political realm that can challenge the sovereignty of administrations and suggest returning governance to peoples who were subjects of colonization (Crossen, 2017).

As a concept, decolonization, has been present in my work for several decades; ever since my doctoral studies when I engaged in narratives with Indigenous women, who worked as advisors and counsellors in the university system, and their stories. Smith (2012) influenced my work and my thinking about decolonization research, which is critical to my examination of self as a non-Indigenous person who is a Canadian as a result of migration. The narratives of my research were also part of my examination of my own relationship with Indigeneity. The theme of colonization was a strand that wove through the narratives of my work and signalled the complex and historical nature of the past, which was still a part of the present in the everyday workings of the women and in their positions in the university. Decolonization can be, in and of itself, a concept that is difficult for settlers to examine. I use the term settlers, as, due to its colonial past, Canada is viewed as a settler nation, a country of immigrants. Moreover, the hegemony of colonization has given Canada a legacy of genocide and a host of economic, political, health, and social issues.

In recent years, there have been numerous initiatives putting indigenization at the centre of change, and as a contrasting, but potentially corresponding, approach to the legacy of colonialism. Some of these discussions have compelled academics and communities to begin and continue to grapple with the ideals and notions of decolonization for it requires an adherence to certain understandings of the impact of colonialism. Taiaiake Alfred describes colonialism as:

> ...best conceptualized as an irresistible outcome of a multigenerational and multifaceted process of forced dispossession and attempted acculturation — a disconnection from land, culture, and community — that has resulted in political chaos and social discord. (Alfred, 2009, p. 52)

From the age of Empire, we have been subject to colonialism, dispossession, and colonial legacies.

Background

There are two foundational documents that provide context for indigenization and decolonization: The Royal Commission on Aboriginal Peoples Report (Canada, Erasmus & Dussault, 1996) and the Truth and Reconciliation Commission Report (TRC, 2015). Both documents refer to the tragic history of Canadian treatment of Aboriginal and Indigenous peoples. The 1996 Royal Commission on Aboriginal Peoples Report was one of the pivotal documents broadly circulated to bring historical and contemporary issues to the attention of the Canadian public and into the Canadian education system, and thus required some sectors to attend to the effects of colonialism. There were many levels of Canadian government, and requisite bureaucracies that had, to this point, been allowed to avoid, obfuscate, and ignore, the need to address the impact of colonialism and bring forward a decolonization agenda. The Commission report is important in terms of timeline and provides a context of the work Canada has, and has not, completed in over two decades.

This Royal Commission began their work in 1991, and held 178 days of public hearings, visited 96 communities, consulted many experts, commissioned multiple research studies, and reviewed numerous past inquiries and reports. The Commission stated that Canada is a country that stands for 'peace, harmony, and justice', and that the policy of assimilation had violated these central tenets. The Commission also asserted that we must continue to pursue justice to address the historical injustice and genocide. Aboriginal peoples had limited life chances; their lives were compromised by a history that continues to result in a lower life expectancy, more illness, human, health, and social issues are common (e.g., family dysfunction, alcohol abuse, poor water and sanitation systems, poverty). Aboriginal peoples have had a lower rate of high school completion, and of adults attending colleges and universities. There was and continues to be an over-representation in the child welfare and prison systems of Aboriginal peoples.

The efforts of decolonization can be significant when justice is a fundamental value behind the work. Thus, the history of colonization and the work of decolonization are tied to the examination of the power of the colonizer and the legacy of that power, in which we are still entrenched. Park (2015, p. 21) argues that within 'the context of settler colonialism, the goal of transitional justice must be decolonisation'. The history of settler colonialism was consistent with assimilation and the elimination of Aboriginal and Indigenous peoples, their culture and practices. Park further argues that transitional justice includes the grieving of the deaths of Indigenous peoples, and to do this means to mobilize politically. Death and genocide are political events that cannot be ignored. Corntassel and Bryce (2012) make a case that decolonization and restitution are inextricably linked. It is therefore necessary for us to take up the decolonization project and consider compensation as a necessary part of transformation. This engagement requires recognition from the state and state systems that support national goals and policies.

The Truth and Reconciliation Commission (TRC, 2015) reported nineteen years after the Royal Commission. Like the Royal Commission work, the process of the TRC involved hosting national events, gathering documents and statements about residential schools and their legacy, funding truth and reconciliation events at the community level, recommending commemoration initiatives to the federal government for funding, establishing a research centre for records and documents, and submitting a report with recommendations. The Commission received over 6,750 statements from survivors of residential schools,[1] members

---

1   Residential schools became policy in 1876, whereby thousands of children were
     taken from their homes and separated from their parents and families for long

of their families, and other individuals who shared their knowledge of the residential school system and its legacy (2015, 26). The Commission report made 94 recommendations as Calls to Action. These focused on numerous areas including child welfare, education, language, health, justice, reconciliation, settlement agreements, and apologies. At the core of the TRC Report is the necessity to act in the name of justice and equity. While both the Truth and Reconciliation Commission and the Royal Commission emphasize colonialism and decolonization, little reference is made to 'indigenization', although it may be implied.

Indigenization can be described as the process of infusing Aboriginal/ Indigenous knowledge and perspective into the structural layers of an institution (Camosun College, 2019). This means that Indigenous knowledge is not marginal but central to the work of the institution. Indigenization may take a culturalist perspective, where the multiple cultures, languages, broader worldviews and practices are its main focus. For some proponents, indigenization is seen as less political than decolonization. For others, indigenization and decolonization are part of the same political and educational project. The work of indigenization has been established within a wider move to indigenize the academy, addressing the curriculum, courses, pedagogy, hiring practices, the physical spaces on campus, resources, research activity, to centre Indigenous practices more assertively in the university, and recruit and sustain Indigenous or Aboriginal students in post-secondary education. A Canadian publication, *University Affairs*, noted: 'some universities had already recognized a need to put Indigenous cultures, histories, languages and knowledge on a new footing within the academy,' and 'in the end, indigenization is not a series of tickable boxes, but a process moving at a different pace in each community that has taken it up' (MacDonald, 2016).

Indigenization plans and strategies are taken up within an inclusive framework for the academy — a worthy approach, although not without contentious aspects. Inclusion in the university system has had historical challenges with regard to the culture of the institution (Chan, 2005). Institutional culture is a complex system of values and

---

periods of time. The schools were established for the purpose of eliminating culture and language, as a part of Canada's policy of assimilation. Many students were abused physically, mentally, and sexually while in the schools. The last residential schools closed in the 1960s.

behaviours, thereby making any changes multi-layered and difficult. Culture shifts in any institution are difficult and political, requiring an examination of the values and assumptions within the institution (Schein, 1997), and may be strongly contested (Suransky & van der Merwe, 2016). While there is no universal agreement, indigenization generally seeks to create a new culture within the academy. This culture fosters understanding and promotes content that is based on history, heritage, and cultural pedagogy. In this new culture, there is a recognition of the centrality of Indigenous curricula and content for and with Indigenous peoples — thereby suggesting that all Canadian students should engage in awareness of Indigeneity. One of the goals of indigenization in universities is the aspiration to be more productive in supporting Indigenous students to succeed. To achieve this, universities need to create an academy that values and embraces our Indigenous peoples and recognizes that many of us live and work on the unceded territories of Indigenous peoples. This process therefore requires a shift in institutional culture; a central step to achieving indigenization. Universities are required to engage in transformational work in order to achieve indigenization, to set goals to create and foster a new, shared value system. A move away from individual or small group values to shared ones will be of wider benefit to the institution (Adams, Martin, & Boom, 2018), but such change requires a willingness to deal with difficult issues and controversies.

In my own work, the tension between decolonization and indigenization is relevant and pronounced. Decolonization and indigenization are both personal and institutional. It has become essential to me as a non-Indigenous person who works in the academy and in the community that I focus on both processes and examine both discourses. This work includes engaging with others to create a movement of culture change. If we do not examine both discourses, we are at risk of only seeing one perspective, of lacking the fuller spectrum and contexts of how to succeed. I suggest that this view is similar to the debates that surround multiculturalism and anti-racism. Multicultural approaches have tended to engage in a pluralistic and cultural approach, 'Critical multiculturalism' has been more political, and anti-racism engages in cultural debates and the discourses of power. In my work, I believe it is necessary to engage with the discourses of power and the hegemony that have created inequality, marginalization, and resistance (Chan, Dhamoon, & Moy, 2014). We engage with the uses of power in the curriculum, the classroom, and in the institution as we all play a role in this power dynamic, whether it is acknowledged or not. Foucault (1980), as we know, asserts that power is a circulating force that exists in all of the corridors of our mind, thought, and in our everyday interactions.

The relationship between decolonization and indigenization is complex. There are many principles that educators subscribe to that are more difficult to adhere to. Siu, Desai, and Ritskes (2012, p.ii), for example, suggest: 'Decolonization does not exist without a framework that centers and privileges Indigenous life, community and epistemology'. In my own university, there are articulated goals for meaningful collaboration, dialogue, engagement; to increase capacity; to create a culturally safe environment and develop responsive programs. (UFV, Indigenizing the Academy, 2012). While these goals are embraced, there has been less discussion of decolonization within this framework. Notably, many of us will assert that decolonization is pivotal to the success of indigenization.

The Study

The purpose of our research and our research team was to build resilience among Aboriginal youth as a means of suicide prevention, by engaging in activities focused on their association with the land and cultural identity. Building resilience was identified within the context of understanding the nature of strength and capacity, and connection to the land. The idea of place (i.e., the land) and belonging is considered key to identity within Indigenous cultures (Neville et al, 2014; writing on Australia). A good deal of research indicates that the community, the family and individual resiliency are protective measures against suicide (Dion Stout & Kipling, 2010; Kirmayer et al., 2011).

The research objectives were to develop an Indigenized research process; to create a knowledge library (sítel-basket) of First Nations or Indigenous land-based resiliency; and to develop and support a youth resilience strategy in collaboration with Seabird Island Band. Seabird Island is a recognized band within the context of First Nations. It is located in Agassiz, British Columbia, Canada, is situated on the unceded

territory of the Stó:lō peoples, and has a self-governance system under
an elected Chief and Council, its own school, services, and health unit.

The research objectives were developed through a lengthy
consultative and collaborative process; the people in the Band were
engaged in the discussions from the time the team was conceiving
designs for the project. Thus, resiliency is something that we wanted
to identify and build from. As a researcher working in the academy,
this also brings the work I am doing into the university discussions and
debates — an essential element to ground the university in the reality
of community work. The research team was committed to the research
being community based and community driven.

In our research we initially used the term First Nations but later
preferred Indigenous. First Nations is a term used to describe Aboriginal
peoples of Canada who are neither Métis nor Inuit. Aboriginal is
broader, referring to the first inhabitants of Canada: First Nations, Inuit,
and Métis peoples. Indigenous is a term used to encompass a variety
of Aboriginal groups. It is most frequently used in an international,
transnational, or global context. Indigenous peoples can be used to
refer broadly to peoples of long settlement and connection to specific
lands, ones who have been affected negatively by industrial economies,
displacement, and settlement of their traditional territories by other
peoples (Indigenous Corporate Training Inc, n.d.). Aboriginal and
Indigenous are often used interchangeably. For the purposes of this
chapter, the term Indigenous will refer more specifically to aspects of
identity and culture.

The process of the research was developed in an organic way because
of the nature of the relationships with the community, but with the
key goal focus on suicide prevention at the primary level. The work
with the Band, the Elders, and the Band youth workers at the site of
the community were pivotal, necessary, and always acknowledged.
Permission was given, by the Chief, the Band, and their own research
council, for us to work on this project with and for them. We worked with
the Band to develop a Guiding Group, comprised of Elders, community
members, and a youth worker. The Group provided essential direction
and feedback. This meant that at any given point, our activities might
change to ensure participation and understanding, and that the research
would be community- rather than researcher-driven.

Funding constraints required that at least two researchers came from the University: one named as the principal investigator and one to be an emerging scholar. In order to be true to the community and to the values behind Indigenous research, our team was comprised of two researchers who were Indigenous, paired with two researchers who were not Indigenous. Thus, one of the community researchers and one of the university researchers were Indigenous and I was one of the non-Indigenous researchers. This partnership gave us a strong working relationship with four primary investigators as researchers. It forged new relationships for us that provided us with remarkable insights and collective thinking. The idea of working in this collaborative way is part of two-eyed seeing (Martin, 2012), which allows us to benefit from two worldviews (two pairs of eyes) and does not privilege Western perspectives.

Our work as researchers is historicized by trauma, pain, and the weakened social and economic fabric of these Indigenous communities. Suicide is acknowledged as one of the results of the devastation of Indigenous communities (Royal Commission on Aboriginal Peoples, 1995). This context has set the stage for suicide and related mental health challenges in our communities. Acknowledging trauma and the legacy of colonialism, our team worked with community partners with a focus on the prevention of harm. The cultural narratives of Indigenous peoples were, and are, paramount to working with communities. We believe that the stories of the people were instrumental in reshaping lives and futures, important as youth suicides were a regular occurrence. The precepts of primary prevention are to engage in healthy work with the youth so our objectives were focused on building (potentially reconnecting) identity, reclaiming culture, and engaging in activities and dialogue that promoted healthy ways of being, through a number of activities: our work as a team; the processes, struggles, and discussions we had about decolonization and indigenizing; working with the Band; engaging in activities with youth.

All of these activities would be documented through field notes, minutes, and recordings. The documentation with youth would mainly occur in stories that the youth could tell, but also documentation of the experiences on the land (e.g., video, audio). Focus groups and community consultations were a part of the data collection process, but we did not use these terms, as they are antithetical to Indigenous processes and research. The privileging of language, how we named things and how we discussed them, was all part of our learning and developing work.

At an early stage in the research, I became aware of the tension between decolonization and indigenization. Indigenous Research Methods (IRM) require a commitment to decolonization, to doing no further colonial harm, and strengthening Indigenous ways of knowing. Our methodology was to be guided by Indigenous ways of knowing and principles. IRM refer to principles that privilege a worldview consistent with Indigenous knowledge and writings. One of our goals was to indigenize the team, and our methodology required that we should not privilege the objectives of the work over the needs of the peoples we were working with. The premise was that while we were conducting research and had research goals, our work with people was paramount and took primacy. The relational process was key to our work and needed us to have an understanding of the nature of the complexities we were drawn to.

With my team members, I became responsive and respectful to the project — never forgetting four Indigenous principles that we drew from and committed to: friends working together; reciprocity; everything is connected — land, air, water, fire, spirit, creatures; and 'looking back is looking forward'. The principles were developed in consultation with Elders on our research team. We returned to the principles regularly to remind ourselves of the commitments we had made. Elders, youth, and youth workers were engaged as part of the research team. This was one small step to the decolonization and indigenization process. Central to the team was the issue of having voice at all levels of the research, including individuals who had been rendered voiceless by history. Our research team meetings were always evolving. Agendas for meetings had to change as issues arose, and we had to respect the developing nature of the work. The core research team members were consistently present, but some members moved away from the team. When new members joined, we revisited the principles and process that we were engaged in; it was a recursive, reflective process.

My own position as part of the academy, and as a non-Indigenous person was one of tension: I claim my racial heritage as Chinese, which I believe provides me with some understanding. I have my own experiences of colonialism and racism as a third generation Canadian. Nonetheless, I was challenged to see myself through the eyes of others many times. This necessitated an understanding that being part of the academy meant being a part of the institutional problem of colonization. This issue would arise repeatedly during the course of the research. I was challenged to consider my role as a researcher, to be true to the principles of the work, and continuously reflect on my words and actions as a non-Indigenous person. Such tensions and challenges were part of the lived experiences within the research project and continue to inform my work in the university.

Centrality or Things Falling Apart

I offer two examples that represent different themes in my work: 'Learning about decolonization methodology and Indigenous Research Methods'; and 'The warrior and the outsider'. These are considered before discussing attempts to achieve a decolonized mind (wa Thiong'o, 1986).

Learning About Decolonizing and Indigenous Research Methods

In order to ground ourselves in decolonizing methodology and Indigenous Research Methods, we had a facilitator, external to the team, work with us in order to begin working through the issues of decolonizing, indigenizing, and challenging our assumptions. From the beginning of our work, all of our meetings took place at Stó:lō Nation (Chilliwack, BC), either in the Elders meeting room, or in the Gathering Place. We would sit in a circle, and we would begin with an acknowledgment of the land and territory. To acknowledge the place and space, is to be grounded in knowing where we are, how we come to be on this land, and how we come to be engaged in this work, and in the gathering of partners and collaborators. The facilitator worked with us for two days in the Gathering Place. On the first day we spent together in workshop, we were asked to unpack the notions of research and what we know. Researchers in our team, Elders, students, and witnesses participated in the sessions. Within Indigenous cultures and practices, it is common to have witnesses observe and participate in sessions and provide us with feedback at the end of the day. The two days allowed us to continue our process of building trust and sharing our experiences. There were concerns that this process should not recolonize people; that self-determination, resilience, and healing are all part of the work we must be engaged in.

It was late in the morning of the first day when discussions took place that acknowledged that indigenizing could not take place without decolonization. An example of this was the notion of a knowledge basket (sítel-basket). We came into the research believing that we had to find and fill a knowledge basket. As discussions moved forward, we were asked to consider that we each already had a basket, and some elements of knowledge in our basket. In particular, Indigenous members of our team would have special knowledge, but certainly all of us had something. This salient point underlined how we had been unaware of our own knowledge, stemming from the colonial past. This was particularly important for some Indigenous participants in the workshop, who had historically been told that their knowledge did not count because, as Foucault (1980) claims, recognized knowledge is part of the power-knowledge nexus (Foucault, 1980) and central to our epistemological beliefs. In future meetings, we came to better understand the role of the knowledge-keepers: the community members and Elders, part of the process of decolonization.

It is within the power-knowledge nexus that one of the frictions lies between decolonization and indigenization. While decolonization and indigenization are not binary, they can be seen as separate. The idea of indigenizing ourselves as researchers requires us to examine our place in the colonialism spectrum. Corntassel and Bryce (2012) suggest that decolonization and restitution are elements of the transformation of our relationships with Indigenous peoples. This can only be achieved if we acknowledge our actions, goals, and relationships. Our research had the potential to transform our relationships and play a significant role in decolonizing by virtue of acknowledging Indigenous knowledge. This was, and is, a personal journey that must be taken with intention and with relationships. The process of building the research team required us to be reflective of what we know and what we think constitutes knowledge.

The Warrior and the Outsider

As a non-Indigenous person, I may be viewed as an outsider and part of the colonizing discourse. The notion of outsider was strongly felt in the decolonizing and Indigenous Research Methodology workshop, where I was accused (I do not use this word lightly), of being part of the establishment of colonialism and therefore unable to participate in the work of decolonization as long as I worked in a university. The person who challenged me in this way was a self-proclaimed warrior. In the moments when I was blamed as a colonizing agent, I understood the pain of being isolated. I could never know what the warrior thought or felt, I only heard the words. The sting of the lashing directed at me evoked a defensive position on my part. This took some time for me to understand and absorb. At the end of the day I had to debrief and reflect, at length, with one of my fellow researchers. My commitment to a decolonizing discourse calmed me, but my feelings of being attacked complicated my ability to move forward at the time. Ultimately this exchange helped me consider whether or not I can work with Indigenous peoples as someone who is inside the university. It also reaffirmed the need to examine my part in the colonial past and present. My reflections gave me a pause to return to a belief that it is possible for me to be an ally, a collaborator, without being from the nation or race, and without myself being a warrior. These types of questions and self-examination are an important and necessary part of working in Indigenous community-based research.

Indigenous people often use the term: 'all my relations', for as Wilson (2008) states, relationships do not merely shape reality, they are the reality of Indigenous life and Indigenous research. For Wilson, Indigenous epistemology is the formation of ideas through relations. In the moments of exchange I experienced with the warrior, however threatened I felt, he was telling me something about relations. It was important for me to understand the nature of relationships with Indigenous peoples in more than one way. After two days in the workshop, I felt that the warrior's position was less strident towards me, although this was never directly stated. He was at the workshop to learn as well, and to examine decolonization. Perhaps we had, in a microscopic way, begun to build a relationship.

Being an ally is a possible strategy to link decolonization to indigenization. As with culture change, becoming an ally is linked to values and reflective examination (Chung, 2016). Becoming an ally also requires a fundamental belief that people who do not have the same experiences can support us and our work. In this way, it is possible that White people can be allies in working with people of colour in the work of anti-racism and anti-oppression. Similarly, I argue that there is room for non-Indigenous people to be allies with Indigenous peoples — but not always. Kowal (2015, p. 95) suggests that it is possible for White people who are anti-racists to work with Indigenous peoples and they can come to understand the generational trauma that is part of the legacy of colonization and racism.

The path to collaboration can be disturbing, just as the journey to decolonization has its difficulties. The research required an examination of my role with the team. I offered to withdraw from the project if my co-researchers thought there was no place for me. This was explicitly discussed at a team meeting. The feelings and thoughts that arose out of the incident with the warrior will not be forgotten. I imagine I represented many things to him, and perhaps he did not even 'see me' for who I was. However, the ability to decolonize is a high ideal. In retrospect, I believe the warrior was true to his beliefs through his own work. I continue to work with the research team and they have affirmed my participation.

The conceptions of warrior, outsider, and allies are pertinent to indigenizing and decolonizing work within the university. Within an established institutional culture, change will require an examination of insiders and outsiders, who is willing to leave and who stays, and who advocates for change, as well as a consideration of values and behaviours. Allies must be cognizant of power and be aware of who have a voice and are heard. All of these elements are part of the commitment to indigenization and decolonization.

Decolonizing the Mind

Language is tied to land through story. Strength [is there] when learning language and strength for ancestors, too. (Youth participant, N21L)

I n his seminal work on decolonizing the mind, Ngũgĩ wa Thiong'o (1996), makes a compelling argument about language and culture. Ngũgĩ contends that language is both an instrument for empire-building as well as a potential counter narrative and tool of resistance for those who have been colonized. As part of our research, we spent much time seeking the words and phrases in Halq'emeylem, which is the language of the Stó:lō peoples. This was done and normalized, in order to respect and acknowledge the powerful role of language as it forms an important part of identity. At the beginning of the research team meetings we began with a Halq'emeylem prayer (i.e., acknowledgement) that came from the Elders, important as language is symbolic. Although only a part of the work, it is representative of what the colonizers stole from a generation of peoples through assimilation. The act of using Halq'emeylem words can indeed be an act of defiance, and respect. Indeed, our work with youth referenced the use of language, and re-learning the traditional language.

As with language, place (i.e., the land) and belonging are considered key to identity (Neville, Oyama, Odunewu, & Huggins, 2014). For this work, the research was place-based and on the land: we worked with the youth in their territory. There was never a question about where the meetings or the work would take place; it was always at a Stó:lō meeting place or on the territory of the Band. This can be interpreted as decolonizing because of the power based in the territory. It can also be interpreted as indigenizing by placing the Stó:lō peoples and their culture at the centre of the work.

The nature of academic work is often situated in the university, and the requirement to reach out to Indigenous peoples was fundamental to our success. In our research and work with Indigenous communities, we rarely asked Elders to come to us. As much as possible, we went to their sites, and paid them the respect that was their due. However, there is a potential contradiction for the academy. The university acknowledges the land and that it is unceded territory. Nevertheless, the university is situated on that land. In the work of committees and curriculum, there is sometimes an expectation that Elders are to come to the university. This remains an unresolved tension between the ideals of decolonization and indigenization.

Concluding Thoughts

I n this chapter, I have argued and put forward challenging ideas that have been part of my epistemological and personal evolution about decolonization and indigenizing. Acknowledging the colonial past is part of a step to creating a change in our work with and for Indigenous peoples. To be of value, such decolonization work must be accepted by non-Indigenous people and a trajectory established that we work towards, as allies. Research can create such alliances. I acknowledge that a good deal of our discourse in the research focused on decolonization rather than indigenization because the power-knowledge relationship continues to be at the centre of the work. Orientalism (Said, 1978) made it possible to see and to treat peoples who were not Western as 'other'. Decolonizing and indigenizing research means acknowledging the possibility of othering — and working to prevent the objectification of people and their knowledge. This principle is the place where researchers have the opportunity to build relations and act in respectful or reciprocal ways. The dimensions of power in the Western nations made orientalism possible, and it is therefore important to recognize the role of power in domination and othering. As an academic, someone who is engaged in knowledge, I have learned from these relationships. I am responsible for acknowledging power and the place of power in the research. Indigenous Research Methods attempts to address this responsibility but indigenizing as a broad activity has much work to do. The power of language, knowledge, how we name ideas and concepts and how we discuss them continues to be a necessary part of our work, within the research, with the community, and with the university.

In examining and attempting to address colonialism and the legacy it has left, Corntassel and Bryce (2003) suggest that the discourse of Indigenous rights has its limits. Seeking to recover the land and some form of justice is only part of the struggle. As Park (2015) claims structural justice must occur before we can achieve decolonization. We must address systems, policies, and land claims, and make fundamental shifts in ways of thinking: decolonizing thought.

The work of this research is both personal and social (Evans, 1993). It is also institutional and gives us pause to think about how we can indigenize our university. Indigenous ways of knowing and decolonizing knowledge are central to the work of indigenizing. I continue to contend that indigenizing cannot take place without decolonization. In indigenizing our research methods, we must take into account decolonization and the elements of power that exists in the research relationship. If those who work towards indigenization accept and understand the role of place and power, then it may not be necessary to use the word decolonization but this must remain at the heart of indigenizing work. Indigenization in isolation is unlikely to succeed.

While focusing on Aboriginal and Indigenous peoples, this chapter has implications for researchers working with other marginalized groups and communities. The history, oppression and continued marginalization of Indigenous peoples are key elements to our work and the recognition that we live in the present day through the context of our history. The context of our history shapes how we tell our stories and the ways in which we communicate with each other. From my experience and vantage point, Indigenous peoples have much to teach us about community, valuing Elders and family, and how to listen to each other. The unrecognized elements of our own colonization, and the colonization of other peoples, are also ever-present social and political forces in this work.

Acknowledgement

This research was made possible by funding from the Canadian Institutes Health Research Grant #33785.

References

Adams, R., Martin, S.M. & Boom, K. (2018). University culture and sustainability: Designing and implementing an enabling framework. *Journal of Cleaner Production*, 171(1): 434–45. https://doi.org/10.1016/j.jclepro.2017.10.032

Alfred, T. (2009). Colonialism and state dependency. *Journal of Aboriginal Health*, 5(2): 42–60. https://doi.org/10.3138/ijih.v5i2.28982

Camosun College website (2019). *What is indigenization.* http://camosun.ca/about/indigenization/

Canada, Erasmus, G. & Dussault, R. (1996). *Report of the Royal Commission on Aboriginal Peoples*. Ottawa: The Commission. https://www.bac-lac.gc.ca/eng/discover/aboriginal-heritage/royal-commission-aboriginal-peoples/Pages/final-report.aspx

Coulthard, G.S. (2007). Subjects of empire: Indigenous peoples and the 'Politics of Recognition' in Canada. *Contemporary Political Theory*, 6(4): 437–60.

Chan, A.S. (2005). Policy discourses and changing practice: Diversity and the university college. Higher Education, 50(1): 129–57. https://doi.org/10.1007/sl0734-004-6351-3

Chan, A.S., Dhamoon, R. & Moy, L. (2014). Metaphoric representations of women of colour in the academy: Teaching race, disrupting power. *Borderlands*, 13(2). www.borderlands.net.au

Chung, S. (2016). The morning after Canada's Truth and Reconciliation Commission report: Decolonisation through hybridity, ambivalence and alliance. *Intercultural Education*, 27(5): 399–408. https://doi.org/10.1080/14675986.2016.1240497

Corntassel, J. & Bryce, C. (2012). Practicing sustainable self-determination. Indigenous approaches to cultural restoration and revitalization. *Brown Journal of World Affairs*, 8(11): 151–62.

Crossen, J. (2017). Another wave of anti-colonialism: The origins of Indigenous internationalism. *Canadian Journal of History*, 52(3): 532–59. https://doi.org/10.3138/cjh.ach.52.3.06

Dion Stout, M. & Kipling, G.D. (2003). *Aboriginal people, resilience and the residential school legacy*. Ottawa: The Aboriginal Healing foundation.

Evans, M. (1993). Reading lives: How the personal might be social. *Sociology*, 27(1): 5–13.

Findlay, L. (2000). Always Indigenize! The radical humanities in the postcolonial Canadian university. *Ariel: A Review of International English Literature*, 31(1–2): 307–26.

Foucault, M. (1980). *Power knowledge*. New York: Pantheon Books.

Galliford, M. (2012). Travels in 'becoming-Aboriginal': Research reciprocating between anecdotes and theory. *Critical Arts: A South-North Journal of Cultural & Media Studies*, 26(3): 402–23. https://doi.org/10.1080/02560046.2012.705463

Indigenous Corporate Training Inc. (n.d.) *Indigenous peoples: A guide to terminology*. Port Coquitlam, BC. https://www.ictinc.ca/indigenous-peoples-a-guide-to-terminology

Kirmayer, L.J., Dandeneau, S., Marshall, E., Phillips, M.K. & Williamson, K.J. (2011). Rethinking resilience from Indigenous perspectives. *Canadian Journal of Psychiatry*, 56(2): 84–91.

Kowal, E. (2015). Time, Indigeneity and White anti-racism in Australia. *The Australian Journal of Anthropology*, 26(1): 94–111. https://doi.org/10.1111/taja.12122

Kumar, M. (2009). Aboriginal education in Canada: A post-colonial analysis. *Alternative*, 5(1): 42–57. https://doi.org/10.1177/117718010900500104

MacDonald, M. (2016). Indigenizing the academy. *University Affairs*. https://www.universityaffairs.ca/features/feature-article/indigenizing-the-academy/

Martin, D.H. (2012). Two-eyed seeing: A framework for understanding Indigenous and non-Indigenous approaches to Indigenous health research. *Canadian Journal of Nursing Research*, 44(2): 20–42.

Neville, H.A., Oyama, K.E., Odunewu, L.O. & Huggins, J.G. (2014). Dimensions of belonging as an aspect of racial-ethnic-cultural identity: An exploration of Indigenous Australians. *Journal of Counselling Psychology*, 61(3): 414–26. https://doi.org/10.1037/a0037115

Obany, M. (1999). *The dilemma of education in Africa*. Dakar: UNESCO. https://unesdoc.unesco.org/ark:/48223/pf0000118058

Park, A. (2015). Settler colonialism and the politics of grief: Theorising a colonizing transition justice for Indian residential schools. *Human Rights Review*, 16(3): 273–93. https://doi.org/10.1007/s12142-015-0372-4

Pollath, M. (2018). Revising island decolonization: The pursuit of self-government in Pacific island polities under US hegemony. *Island Studies Journal*, 13(1): 235–50. https://doi.org/10.24043/isj.46

Royal Commission on Aboriginal Peoples (1995). *Choosing life: Special report on suicide among Aboriginal peoples*. Ottawa: Government of Canada. http://data2.archives.ca/rcap/pdf/rcap-459.pdf

Said, E. (1978). *Orientalism*. London: Routledge & Kegan Paul.

Schein, E.H. (1997). *Organizational culture and leadership*, 2nd edn. San Francisco, CA: Jossey Bass.

Sium, A., Desai, C, & Ritskes, E. (2012). Towards the 'tangible unknown': Decolonization and the Indigenous future. *Decolonization: Indigeneity, Education & Society*, 1(1): I–XIII.

Smith, L.T. (2012). *Decolonizing methodologies: Research and Indigenous peoples*, 2nd edn. London: Zed Books.

Suransky, C. & van der Merwe, J.C. (2016). Transcending apartheid in higher education: Transforming an institutional culture. *Race, Ethnicity and Education*, 19(3): 577–99. https://doi.org/10.1080/13613324.2014.946487

Thomas, N., Bystydzienski, J. & Desai, A. (2015). Changing institutional culture through peer mentoring of women STEM faculty. *Innovative Higher Education*, 40: 143–57. https://doi.org/10.1007/s10755-014-9300-9

Todorova, M. (2016). Co-created learning: Decolonizing journalism education in Canada. *Canadian Journal of Communication*, 41: 673–92. https://doi.org/10.22230/cjc.2016v41n4a2970

TRC (2015). *Honouring the truth, reconciling for the future: Summary of the final report of the Truth and Reconciliation Commission of Canada.* Winnipeg: TRC.

University of the Fraser Valley (2012). *Indigenizing the academy.* Abbotsford, BC: University of the Fraser Valley.

Van Wyk, J. (2002). Indigenous knowledge systems: Implications for natural science and technology teaching and learning. *South African Journal of Education*, 22(4): 302–12.

wa Thiong'o, N. (1986). *Decolonising the mind. The politics of language in African literature.* London: James Currey (Nairobi: Heinemann).

Wilson, S. (2008). *Research as ceremony.* Halifax, NS: Fernwood Publishing.

Yishak, D. & Gumbo, M. (2015). A stand-alone blended or restructured indigenisation approach to curriculum? A critical perspective. *International Journal of African Renaissance Studies*, 10(1): 60–82. https://doi.org/10.1080/18186874.2015.1050215

22. Embedding Feminist Pedagogies of Care in Research to Better Support San Youth in South Africa

Outi Ylitapio-Mäntylä and Mari Mäkiranta

Outi Ylitapio-Mäntylä and Mari Mäkiranta discuss how to make sensitive interventions across cultural divides with a focus on the San people of Africa. In line with feminist practices, they outline how a caring ethos can protect the individual from some of the challenges customary within a neoliberal society but reveal that this is hard to achieve within a multi-nation collaborative project where value bases differ.

In the course of our academic careers, we have organized several international art-based workshops exploring the meanings of places, childhood memories and cultural sustainability, among other themes. In these workshops, we have been interested in people's life histories, gender studies and pedagogical developments with multidisciplinary connections to education and art research (Mäkiranta & Ylitapio-Mäntylä, 2019). This chapter stems from our latest collaboration on a European-Union-funded participatory development project with young people; an international and intersectoral research study involving the San youth living in Indigenous communities in South Africa and Namibia.

Participatory Development with the Youth, or PARTY, was a four-year (2015–2019) EU Horizon 2020 project led by Professor Satu

https://doi.org/10.11647/OBP.0203.22

Miettinen of the University of Lapland. It aimed to support the San people to plan their own services through a four-stage process based on the Double Diamond model proposed by the British Council in 2004/5 and developed further in association with eleven global firms. This model helps people to *discover* a problem, *define* it, and — moving towards solution — to *develop* plans in order to *deliver* desired outcomes. For PARTY, the stages were interpreted as helping people to *identify* their beliefs and values by collecting their stories; build a *shared vision* of what is needed and wanted; *plan ways to resource* this vision; and then to *activate* changes. In the terms of the research, these are stages of self-awareness, participation, evolution and action (Pierandrei, et al, 2018, p. 5). The methodological framework is underpinned by earlier theoretical and research activity on service design (see Miettinen & Koivisto, 2009), and the EU funding provided an opportunity for a group of researchers from Finland, Italy, UK, Namibia and South Africa to collaborate to put innovative service design ideas into practice. Their aim was to develop a tool book as a practical manual for carrying out such collaborative work with marginalized groups and, in the first instance, to assist in reducing unemployment and alienation, and associated poverty and social unrest, among the San people. (More detail is available on the PACO website[1] and in Miettinen, et al., 2018).

The San project involved youth aged thirteen to twenty-four years old who were living in poor neighbourhoods and either marginalized or facing the risk of becoming marginalized, but our work was focused on eighteen- to twenty-four-year-olds. We were involved early in the project when the collaborators were still getting to know each other and finding ways of shared working, holding a workshop at a cultural centre for San people, related to curriculum planning. However, this chapter is not about the project itself but about the experience of participating at the early stages of a collaborative project, which made significant demands on researchers like ourselves. Rather than focus on an actual workshop we use the workshop as a channel to consider possibilities for supporting diversity. We ask: what kinds of challenges arise when researchers meet Indigenous young people and try to support diversity? Our theoretical framework relates to feminist pedagogies and neoliberal discourses in academia. Through this combination, we demonstrate

---

1   http://www.pacollaborative.com/our-project/

how productivity, efficiency and competition as neoliberal values affect our work and how we as feminist researchers can create the space for responsible encounters with Indigenous people.

Feminist pedagogies draw attention to researcher — participant relationships, the use of experiences in teaching and learning processes and the importance of hearing all voices in a teaching situation. A reflective feminist researcher listens with compassion and is keenly interested in participants' stories (Chilisa & Ntseane, 2010). We aim to consider how to encourage collaborative co-construction of knowledge and non-hierarchical work, which appreciates varied experiences and knowing (see Sharp et al., 2007). Moreover, the emergent question is how to reflect issues of diversity (Markowitz, 2005). This can be challenging because we live in a neoliberal era that emphasizes internationalization. Other reasons include the need for external funding, the lack of time and space for ethical meetings with research participants, the need for slow thinking (stopping and taking the time to see and hear others) and the possibility of failure (Carpintero, 2017). A further challenge is that theoretical developments nearly always occur in the cities and the global North. The issues relevant for the rural South can be marginalized in the world's economy of knowledge (Connell, 2014). Additionally, a difficulty in studying Indigenous settings is that researchers learn the procedures, ethics and practicalities of research from a Western perspective. If Western researchers approach people from different cultures from these perspectives this can lead to problematic dynamics, meetings and relations between Indigenous and non-Indigenous people (McGloin, 2016).

The Space for Collective Knowing

We met the San youth in March 2016 in the Western Cape, South Africa, through an organization that arranges training and education for them, in this case the workshop on curriculum planning, which aimed to assist the mapping of learning outcomes for the organization's courses and pedagogy. Our preliminary work included collaborating with the participants and discussing how the curriculum would support their future. The idea was that teachers and students could continue developing their courses after our workshops.

However, the collaboration was not mutual, for, as Western researchers, we constructed the situations around the rules *we* had learned, but the San youth found these difficult to relate to. This disjuncture does not mean that we should reject all the theoretical and the methodological contributions we have learned (Smith, 1999). Rather, as feminist researchers, we should lead ourselves and others to ask different kinds of questions with an *analytical* effort (Naskali, 2013).

During the workshop, we photographed, video-recorded and observed the informants and facilitators, the communication situations and spaces and the materials produced. Positioning ourselves as observers while the participants worked, allowed us to witness the interactions among the people, the social space of the workshop and the participants' voices. However, Western tradition has a tendency towards cohesion (unity of belief) or dichotomy (this or that) which feminist research has criticized (Naskali, 2013). Cultural mingling, even 'conflict', is necessary to shake up Western philosophical traditions, value sets, understandings and expectations and engender discussions about different kinds of cultural values. Those who subscribe to the Western intellectual tradition need to examine how academic philosophies and practices ignore, marginalize and exclude others (Kuokkanen, 2008). Conventional Western-based methods and scientific research approaches pay little attention to, and thereby restrict other activities and practices, like customs and traditions. They overlook the importance of folklore, songs, dances or symbolic cultural artefacts common in the Indigenous world (Chilisa & Ntseane, 2010). When the pace of interaction follows Western practices, the product-oriented and fast-moving academic context that is the norm leaves no space for slow thinking, for reproducing new ways of knowing together. Yet as researchers, we should also recognize our need for some time to think, analyse, ponder, read and write. As Rogowska-Stangret (2018) states, Western-based methods relate to the Foucauldian approach of neoliberalism, one that describes the relations and institutions, their power structures and modes of subjectification in the contemporary and effective academic world, and this can be a problem when transplanted to other contexts.

During the workshop, we faced a frustrating situation that demonstrated this problematic aspect of neoliberal values: insufficient time was allowed for us to achieve our goals. Under neoliberalism, the academic world becomes a servant of the economy. Researchers, as well as teachers, are forced to produce knowledge with a market value (Byrne, 2017) and to do so efficiently. We felt that we did not have enough time to share our experiences and knowledge together or to build a space for dialogical educational practices with the San youth. As Merrill (2005) explains, dialogical feminism can offer the possibility of hearing the voices of 'others'. This can further lead to an awareness of the structures behind our habits and practices, such as how we are guided by neoliberal values of effectiveness.

Grace and Gouthro (2000) discuss feminist pedagogies as positional, occurring when we use personal histories, knowledge, locations and experiences in the learning process. Learning is always a subjective experience; however, when a group of people gather to learn, it is also viewed as collective. A person is not only an individual but also a member of both public and private communities; 'I am always part of a we' (Griffiths, 2006, p. 389). This association contrasts with the notion of individualism that is emphasized in contemporary society and academia. When we meet others in a public or a private community, such encounters include opportunities to share knowledge and perhaps to form communities of practice (Wenger, 2015). 'We' is also a troubled word. As Naskali (2013, p. 33) states, 'the problematic nature of presuming who "we" are and justifying "us" becomes visible when the dominant culture defends the rights of "we" in a nationalist sense'. For instance, some African feminists prefer to use the term womanism instead of feminism because the latter word is related to Western philosophies (Chilisa & Ntseane, 2010).

Notably, learning needs knowledge, which is always contextually bound to a specific time and place. In feminist research, it is important to ask how knowing is intertwined with the knower and who the knower is (Naskali, 2013). Therefore, knowledge is never static but constantly reconstructed. It does not only comprise theories and concepts; it is also connected to a material basis and bound with different ways of knowing, different places and times (Naskali, 2013). In learning processes, such as our workshop, knowledge produced in specific contexts is deconstructed and reconstructed through discussions. It is important to enhance critical thinking skills to enable participants to view knowledge from different perspectives. This aim can be achieved by developing discussion techniques and working with others, by reflecting on the phenomena, asking questions and increasing skills in theorizing and reflecting (Vogel, 2002) but this requires sufficient time for people to truly benefit.

Through its activities, the workshop drew attention to knowledge creation as a process (something you do), not a product (something you did). Because knowledge was constructed in a collaborative and collective way in the teaching situation, it could not be deemed value neutral. Rather, it is understood as political (Lempiäinen & Naskali, 2011) and able to provide a framework to engage in raising consciousness, as well as a space to discuss, share ideas and hear multiple stories of life (see also Merriam, Caffarella, & Baumgartner, 2007). The goals of feminist pedagogies are to develop critical thinking and connect students to their learning, by using their experiences and skills as resources to enable a better understanding of the social and political aspects of everyday activities (Vogel, 2002; Weiler, 2001). Some people have stronger positions than others from which to shape political outcomes and are able to exercise more power over whose perspectives are heard and recognized (DeLaet, 2012). Feminist pedagogies stress that the learning process and meetings with participants are always political and conflictual, but that we can build shared knowledge (Costa & Mendel, 2017; Grace & Gouthro, 2000). We need to rethink our actions and make a transition from *what* to *how* we do them; thus, we should refute individuality and trace modes of individuation, which, in Jungian terms, is the process of making personal and collective unconscious views more apparent in order to better develop the individual personality (Rogowska-Stangret, 2017).

As knowledge is embedded in time and place, in diverse social agencies and certain methodologies, we claim that supporting diversity requires slow thinking, time and space to hear political voices as expressions of identities. It also demands that people produce knowledge in collaboration and occasionally in different ways than are common in Western academia and within specific disciplinary methodologies (see also Connell, 2014; Smith, 1999).

Managing Power

W orking with the San community, we noticed that, as researchers, we need to understand that different human groups can hold values that differ considerably from our own. Even if we learn to know one another and reflect on our respective positions, power relations are still present. As researchers, we need to be constantly aware that we might make presumptions and even false assumptions by being blind and deaf to important insights and voices (Hesse-Biber & Piatelli, 2012). Thus, we should remember that we can never fully be either insiders or outsiders in a research process (Hesse-Biber & Piatelli, 2012). Hierarchies and power relationships are always present when researchers and participants meet each other. Even though an encounter may be intimate, researchers are still performing a professional role and this can be formal, maintaining distinctive boundaries that keep researcher and participant apart. Nonetheless, positioning can alter during meetings. This raises the question of who has power. Specifically, who is in a position to express personal values? Whose voice is heard? How does power emerge in the processes of a project? It is important that researchers understand the nature of power in a relationship and recognize that it is never stable.

During our Participatory Development with the Youth project, we became conscious of the complexity of our position and started to suffer the effects of institutional pressures (Carpintero, 2017), power structures and demands for speedy but effective outcomes. Although we understood the project's high-level aims, we found that we were unable to operationalize them well enough as they made little allowance for local circumstances. It is hard to avoid the market orientation that seems to be a fundamental element of projects that sit within a huge transnational cluster, where researchers do not even know all the people with whom they must co-operate (Brunila, 2011). We faced an uncomfortable situation — a need to achieve specific goals without the resources to do this adequately.

For us, committed to feminist methodologies, a sensitive encounter with those we study is one that avoids exploiting or harming human subjects and understands the power differential between the researchers and the participants. The strategies underpinning feminist pedagogies involve protecting the participants by trying to create a safe space in which the project unfolds and generate opportunities for empowerment (Burgess-Proctor, 2015). However, being appreciative and respectful is more than merely verbalizing an accepted opinion but also a way to act. It involves making space for different voices and encouraging critical thinking to ensure that respect is actualized (Costa & Mendel, 2017).

Reflexivity is a self-critical tool that helps researchers explore how the shape of a theoretical position and collaboratively produced knowledge can be studied. With a communal process, it is necessary to consider the structural, political and cultural backgrounds of both researchers and participants. Reflexivity increases engagement and participation in the study process and fosters both a less hierarchical and a more ethical study (Hesse-Biber & Piatelli, 2012). Feminist researchers pay attention to reflexivity, which necessitates questioning and understanding how the researchers' social backgrounds, assumptions and feelings influence the research processes (Hesse-Biber, 2012).

Overall, we argue that, in feminist pedagogies, diversity is supported when we perceive participants as subjects rather than objects and recognize that a subject is always in relationship with others; also, that social reality is polarized and thus often conflicting. It is important to reflect on the researchers' positions and focus on how they encounter the participants. Careful reflection includes an understanding of our own culture and background. It is important to realize from which culture 'we' are encountering other cultures (Lykke, 2010). Reflection also requires a discussion of the epistemology of positioning so that the contexts of domination and freedom can be taken into account (Costa & Mendel, 2017). Distancing ourselves helps us negotiate our positionality as researchers and recognize the shifting nature of power relations (Hesse-Biber & Piatelli, 2012). It is also vital to consider the research subjects' right to self-determination. Such practices take time and cannot be rushed to meet deadlines.

Caring in a Neoliberal Context

P ower is present in all encounters and communications, including caring situations. Caring means doing the very best for the other in the relationship between the carer and the cared-for. Feminist pedagogies emphasize caring as an important factor in the learning process. It refuses commonly acknowledged views of the teacher as 'knowing' and the student as 'unknowing'. Hence, teaching is a bottom-up (rather than a top-down) knowledge exchange (Luke, 1996), to create a nurturing atmosphere and close contact between the students and the teacher (Vogel, 2002). If the participants are involved in the development of the whole project, this helps reduce hierarchy, force, disrespect and indifference (Costa & Mendel, 2017). Such aims are often difficult to put into practice, especially when researchers have insufficient time for meetings with participants and are thus less able to develop trust. It is always a challenge to create a safe learning situation because of self-disclosure and vulnerability (Kishimoto & Mwangi, 2009) and time restraints make it difficult to address such issues.

Under neoliberalism, we have no time to care for others, or even ourselves, within academia. As researchers, we inhabit a publish-or-perish culture with no time to stop, to read and discuss and be present in the moment (Carpintero, 2017). Education is market oriented under neoliberalism, with learning a personal duty (Brunila, 2011). It is 'old-fashioned' to stop and learn together. Additionally, in a society where living well is an individual 'project', people are expected to be perennially busy, engaged in building their everyday lives but available to fulfil the requirements of the market (Brunila, 2011).

Despite these pressures, feminist teachers are highly involved and engaged in their work. They feel the pressure to be caring teachers who are committed to their students (Lempiäinen & Naskali, 2011). The practices of teaching create different kinds of emotional knowledge between caregivers and care receivers, but there are also similarities. Thus, teachers need to understand how emotion operates through responsibility and how it is connected to emotion in caring practices. Teachers should ask critical questions, about how this is, or can be, achieved. It is also important to recognize and to challenge the emotional burden of duties assigned to marginalized people who have to adapt to decisions made by the privileged (Zempylas, Bozalek, & Shefer, 2014). Even in academia, under neoliberalism, professionals are aware that responsibilities can be taken away because 'money talks' and there are not enough resources to maintain the quality of academic work (Carpintero, 2017).

Overall, as feminist researchers, we claim that caring is an important step towards supporting people. It needs responsiveness, respect and attentiveness, which means that a caring person pays attention to others' needs and reacts to them with sympathy and understanding. Responsiveness ensures that the cared-for people understand the requests made to them. Respect in caring maintains the idea that teachers are sensitive to those whom they support (Ylitapio-Mäntylä, 2013). Therefore, a caring ethos could support all participants in developing their everyday lives together without marginalization.

Caring can be related to the use of life stories. Producing life stories makes it possible to acquire experiences, which helps researchers hear other voices and visualize the world of the unknown. However, it can be dangerous to narrate stories about people from other cultures if research continues to legitimize views of Western discourses and disciplines (Smith, 1999). When using life stories, diversity is always present, especially when studying Indigenous people. Diversity is embedded in our different stories and the web of our world. However, the concept of diversity has become a 'brand' with marketing appeal in the commercial world, receiving a very different treatment to that which is traditional within academia, which should be a place where differences are welcomed (Ahmed, 2009). In social communities, difference is often a source of hierarchical power and control (Naskali, 2013). When Indigenous people become involved in the academic world and face Western approaches, the task often becomes one of determining difference (Kuokkanen, 2008) rather than making a political impact on their lives. The emphasis is on collecting stories of 'difference' (Naskali, 2013) and through 'telling' these, the difference is also reconstructed. Instead, when listening to life stories of marginalized people, the narratives need to be interpreted, not just heard. Indeed, marginalized people's life stories can be contrary to expectations (Ahmed, 2009). When researchers analyse such stories, they produce new knowledge that has the possibility to change the subjects' lifeworlds (Naskali, 2013).

Conclusions

I n this chapter, we have examined the kinds of challenges that arise when researchers meet Indigenous young people. Additionally, we have asked what kinds of challenges emerge when we aim to support diversity. When people teach and learn together with those from different backgrounds, there are challenges in working with complex and multiple value sets, varying theories of knowledge, uncertain power structures and hierarchies. Therefore, it is important to support everyone who takes part and to study the processes that enable the participation to be meaningful. A reflective touch is needed, especially when studying people from other cultures. We need to fully understand that different human groups can have divergent values and standards. As Western academic researchers, we have learned specific disciplinary methodologies, which can make us, if not blind, not fully aware of different ways of knowing.

As Naskali (2013) established, there are similarities between feminist and Indigenous epistemologies. Particularly, critique and problematization are significant matters in the knowledge process: it is important to make an unknown and unseen world visible, to deconstruct dichotomies and reveal hierarchies. However, feminist epistemologies focus on and emphasize gender as important in the analysis of someone's experiences (Naskali, 2013). When research is about Indigenous people, the methodological tools may be different and should be considered carefully and be designed to resonate with the participants' worlds. This requires time for sensitive preparation before the fieldwork. Furthermore, the study should have a values and 'other' orientation rather than an action-oriented aim.

Overall, we argue that when meeting people from different cultures, supportive action is required to uncover tacit power structures, as well as the political and personal influences on learning and teaching processes. As feminist researchers we were concerned to ensure that people listened to each other with respect and to promote an ethos where emotions and feelings could safely be expressed. At times, when relationships appeared hierarchical and conflict arose, this caused us to question our efficacy and doubt our own credibility. To create supportive spaces requires time; time to collectively reorganize and sustain meaning in everyday situations, with all the participants included equally in the study process. The point is to make everyone feel important and valued by creating sensitive settings where people care for themselves and others.

References

Ahmed, S. (2009). Embodying diversity: Problems and paradoxes for Black feminists. *Race, Ethnicity and Education*, 12(1): 41–52. https://doi.org/10.1080/13613320802650931

Burgess-Proctor, A. (2015). Methodological and ethical issues in feminist research with abused women: Reflections on participants' vulnerability and empowerment. *Women's Studies International Forum*, 48: 124–34. https://doi.org/10.1016/j.wsif.2014.10.014

Brunila, K. (2011). The projectisation, marketization and therapisation of education. *European Educational Research Journal*, 10(3): 421–32. https://doi.org/10.2304/eerj.2011.10.3.421

Byrne, D. (2017). Teaching and researching women´s and gender studies in post-apartheid South Africa. *Gender and Research*, 18(1): 113–29. http://dx.doi.org/10.13060/25706578.2017.18.1.352

Carpintero, E.C. (2017). (No) time to care and responsibility: From neoliberal practices in academia to collective responsibility in time crisis. In: Revelles-Banevente, B.& González Ramos A.M. (eds), *Teaching gender. Feminist pedagogy and responsibility in times of political crisis*. Abingdon: Routledge.

Chilisa, B. & Ntseane, G. (2010). Resisting dominant discourses: Implications of Indigenous, African feminist theory and methods for gender and education research. *Gender and Education*, 22(6): 617–32. https://doi.org/10.1080/09540253.2010.519578

Connell, R. (2014). Rethinking gender from the South. *Feminist Studies*, 40(3): 518–39.

Costa, R. & Mendel, I. (2017). Feminist science literacy as a political and pedagogical challenge: insights form a high school research project. In: Revelles-Banevente, B. & González Ramos, A.M. (eds), *Teaching gender: Feminist pedagogy and responsibility in times of political crisis*. London: Routledge. https://doi.org/10.4324/9781315204161

DeLaet, D. (2012). Interrogating 'They': A pedagogy of feminist pluralism in the international relations classroom. *International Studies Perspectives*, 13(3): 254–69. https://doi.org/10.1111/j.1528-3585.2012.00479.x

Design Council (2005). *A study of the design process — The Double Diamond*. https://innovationenglish.sites.ku.dk/model/double-diamond-2/

Grace, A.P. & Gouthro, P.A. (2000). Using models of feminist pedagogies to think about issues and directions in graduate educate for women students. *Studies in Continuing Education*, 22(1): 5–28.

Griffiths, M. (2006). The feminization of teaching and the practice of teaching: Threat or opportunity?'. *Educational Theory*, 56(4): 387–405. https://doi. org/10.1111/j.1741-5446.2006.00234.x

Hesse-Biber, S.N. (2012). Feminist research: Exploring, interrogating and transforming the interconnections of epistemology, methodology and method. In: Hesse-Biber S.N. (ed), *The handbook of feminist research: Theory and praxis*. Thousand Oaks, CA: Sage.

Hesse-Biber, S.N., & Piatelli, D. (2012). The feminist practice of holistic reflexivity. In: Hesse-Biber S.N. (ed), *The handbook of feminist research: Theory and praxis*. Thousand Oaks, CA: Sage. https://dx.doi.org/10.4135/9781483384740.n1

Kishimoto, K. & Mwangi, M. (2009). Critiquing the rhetoric of 'safety' in feminist pedagogy: Women of color offering an account of ourselves. *Feminist Teacher*, 19(2): 87–102. https://dx.doi.org/10.1353/ftr.0.0044

Kuokkanen, R. (2008). What is hospitality in the academy? Epistemic ignorance and the (im)possible gift. *Review of Education, Pedagogy, and Cultural Studies*, 30(1): 60–82. https://doi.org/10.1080/10714410701821297

Lempiäinen, K. & Naskali, P. (2011). Feminist researchers learning to teach: A Finnish case of university pedagogy in women's studies. *Women's Studies International Forum*, 34(3): 195–205. https://doi.org/10.1016/j. wsif.2011.01.008

Luke, C. (1996). Feminist pedagogy theory: Reflections on power and authority. *Educational Theory*, 46(3): 283–302. https://doi.org/10.1111/j.1741-5446. 1996.00283.x

Lykke, N. (2010). *Feminist studies: A guide to intersectional theory, methodology and writing*. New York: Routledge. https://doi.org/10.4324/9780203852774

McGloin, C. (2016). Critical allies and feminist praxis: Rethinking dis-ease. *Gender and Education*, 28(7): 839–50. https://doi.org/10.1080/09540253.2015 .1129055

Mäkiranta, M. & Ylitapio-Mäntylä, O. (2011). Researching personal images and multiple voices: The methodological questions of ethics and power. *International Journal of Education Through Art*, 7(3): 221–32. https://doi. org/10.1386/eta.7.3.221_1

Mäkiranta, M. & Ylitapio-Mäntylä, O. (2013). Care and emotional looking in memory-based photographs. In: Keskitalo-Foley, S. Naskali, P. & Rantala, P. (eds), *Northern insights: Feminist inquiries into politics of place, knowledge and agency*. Rovaniemi: Lapin Yliopistokustannus.

Mäkiranta, M. & Ylitapio-Mäntylä, O. (2019) Art-making process as a tool for social change: A case study of an animation 'A short story about feminism in Russia'. In: Brusila, R., Mäkiranta, M. & Nikula, S. (eds), *Visual thinking: Theories and practices*. Rovaniemi: Lapin Yliopistokustannus.

Markowitz, L. (2005). Unmasking moral dichotomies: Can feminist pedagogy overcome student resistance?. *Gender and Education*, 17(1): 39–55. https://doi.org/10.1080/0954025042000301294

Merriam, S.B. Caffarella, R.S. & Baumgartner, L.M. (2007). *Learning in adulthood: A comprehensive guide*. San Francisco: John Wiley & Sons.

Merrill, B. (2005). Dialogical feminism: Other women and the challenge of adult education. *International Journal of Lifelong Education*, 24(1): 41–52. https://doi.org/10.1080/026037042000317338

Miettinen, S. & Koivisto, M. (eds) (2009). *Designing Services with Innovative Methods*. Helsinki, Finland: University of Art and Design Helsinki. https://mycourses.aalto.fi › Reading 1 and 6 ServiceDesign_Ebook-3_H

Miettinen, S., Tang, T., Remotti, S., Delfino, E., Brutto, F, Dammann, J., & Alonso, S. (2018). Service design tools for stakeholder dialogue and youth empowerment in Africa. In: Collina, L. (ed) (2018). *To Get There: Designing Together, Cumulus Conference Proceedings Series 03/2018, Paris*: pp. 492–506. https://www.cumulusassociation.org/cumulus-conference-proceedings-paris-2018-to-get-there-designing-together/

Naskali, P. (2013). Rethinking positionality: Universalism and localism in contact. In: Keskitalo-Foley, S., Naskali, P. & Rantala, P. (eds), *Northern insights: Feminist inquiries into politics of place, knowledge and agency*. Rovaniemi: Lapin Yliopistokustannus.

Pierandrei, F.M., Remotti, S.,Tang, T., Kuria, S.C. & Anfossi, S. (2018). *Service design tools to engage marginalised youth in San Communities of Southern Africa*. Paper for Service Design Proof of Concept, Politecnico di Milano, 18–20 June 2018. http://www.pacollaborative.com/wp-content/uploads/2018/07/ServDes2018_paper_78.pdf

Rowowska-Stangret, M. (2017). Sharing vulnerabilities: Searching for 'unruly edges' in times of the neoliberal academy. In: Revelles-Banevente, B. &. González Ramos, A.M (eds), *Teaching gender: Feminist pedagogy and responsibility in times of political crisis*. Abingdon: Routledge.

Sharp, E.A., Bermudez, J.M., Watson, W. & Fitzpatrick, J. (2007). Reflections from the trenches: Our development as feminist teachers. *Journal of Family Issues*, 28(4): 529–48. https://doi.org/10.1177/0192513X06297473

Smith, L.T. (1999). *Decolonizing methodologies: Research and Indigenous peoples*. London: Zed Books Ltd.

Vogel, K.J. (2002). Feminist pedagogy and international studies. In: Howie, G. & Tauchert, A. (eds), *Gender, teaching and research in higher education. Challenges for the 21st Century*. Farnham: Ashgate.

Weiler, K. (2001). Rereading Paolo Freire. In: Weiler, K. (ed), *Feminist engagements: Reading, resisting, and revisioning male theorists in education and cultural studies.* New York: Routledge.

Wenger, E. (2015). *Communities of practice: A brief introduction.* https://wenger-trayner.com/wp-content/uploads/2015/04/07-Brief-introduction-tocommunities-of-practice.pdf

Ylitapio-Mäntylä, O. (2013). Reflecting caring and power in Early Childhood Education: Recalling memories of educational practices. *Scandinavian Journal of Educational Research*, 57(3): 263–76. https://doi.org/10.1080/00313831.2011.637230

Zembylas, M., Bozalek, V. & Shefer, T. (2014). Tronto's notion of privileged irresponsibility and the reconceptualisation of care: Implications for critical pedagogies of emotion in higher education. *Gender and Education*, 26(3): 200–14. https://doi.org/10.1080/09540253.2014.901718

23. From Defender to Offender
British Female Ex-Military Re-Joining Civilian Society

Linda Cooper

Linda Cooper considers the problems that the ex-military experience when returning to civilian life. She examines the narratives of two female former soldiers who have committed offences, unable to sustain a productive role in the 'real' world where individuals have to create their own structures and relationships if they are to take control of their lives.

T he notion of belonging is a key tenet of life in the UK Armed Forces. Yet the issues surrounding the loss of this camaraderie are often under-estimated when soldiers transition out of the Army and into civilian life. Difficulties are faced by personnel when moving from a job that encompasses one's self-identity — i.e., a Soldier in the Army — to re-negotiation back into a regular job in society and the family home — becoming 'just' an ordinary citizen. Whilst the majority of people who leave the Armed Forces transition successfully into civilian life, there is a significant minority that do not. For many veterans — defined by the Ministry of Defence (MOD, 2011) as somebody who has served at least one day in Her Majesty's Armed Forces — adjustment can be difficult. This chapter tells the stories of two women who created successful careers in the British Army and, importantly, found a real sense of belonging, as women in a male dominated workplace. Only on leaving the Military did they struggle to re-adjust to a civilian, feminized identity and both women found themselves arrested and in the criminal justice system (CJS). For these

https://doi.org/10.11647/OBP.0203.23

women, the Army offered a practical educational experience that was formative; their stories reveal how their lifestyles were shaped by their sense of belonging in the Armed Forces, its loss on their return to civilian life and the re-building of their female, civilian selves.

This chapter stands apart from the mainstream literature on veterans as its focus is on female ex-Soldiers who offended, and it is well-documented that male veterans significantly constitute the veteran offender population (Fossey et al., 2017). Thus, the stories offer some original insights into the problems that women face when returning to civilian life. However, before I engage with the actual narratives and the discourse within which they are embedded, I should explain the broader context for the study. The opportunity to interview these two female veterans arose as my research team (the Veterans & Families Institute for Military Social Research at Anglia Ruskin University) was commissioned to undertake an independent study of a one-year pilot intervention programme running in the East of England, the first stage of a larger initiative, Project Nova.

Project Nova was set up in 2013 to fill a void in support for veterans in the criminal justice system, specifically at the point of arrest. It is a novel and unique initiative funded by FiMT, the Forces in Mind Trust and delivered by RFEA (the Forces Employment Charity) and Walking with the Wounded. Team members will both guide veterans who offend through the criminal justice system and help them to develop practical strategies and coping skills, post-arrest. The service is staffed with support workers who are part of the military community, which is key to encouraging offender management.

The pilot itself was intended to highlight the difficulties that veterans face and its focus was support work with a number of veterans facing criminal charges, including the two females whose stories are central to this chapter. Our task was to evaluate the pilot intervention, and to do this we carried out a mixed methods study that involved interviews with veterans, members of the Project Nova team and a Police officer. In this chapter I will focus on two key findings from the veterans' interviews: firstly, the specific difficulties that the two women faced when adjusting to a civilian lifestyle and secondly, how their stories reflect the wider issues that confront veterans during resettlement, particularly those who are female (and much-less commonly discussed in the literature). In carrying out these analyses I shall draw on discourses of identity.

Identity is a difficult concept to define, as there are various constructions and meanings, which are determined by shared characteristics. Doing this in the context of the Military is made more complex by the way that discourses of diversity are cloaked beneath a masque of solidarity, not surprising as common attitudes, consensus, collaboration and coordination are essential for collective survival in hostile circumstances. Lawler (2008) suggests identity is a combination of sameness and difference, for instance, soldiers in the Army will have shared understandings, but they will have unique differences: age, relationship status, family formation. For the purposes of this chapter, I wish to explore the intensity of shared understanding and identities that exist during military service and the difficulty of adjusting to individual civilian, social norms. I consider how differing identities and traits mean that although for those leaving the Army the transition process is the same, it is negotiated differently by every individual.

The institutional nature of the Armed Forces instils a sense of social membership, a community with a shared social identity (Gibson & Condor, 2009). Condor, Gibson and Abell (2006) assert that institutions are more than a category of people, rather a hybrid of community, environment and the wider societal system. The close-knit living and working conditions in the Armed Forces, often in extreme and harsh surroundings, can mean friendships become more than familial-like in the degree of attachment, providing the strong bonds necessary in such a working environment. They are important for survival in combat and can have positive mental health benefits (Hinojosa & Hinojosa, 2011). Woodward and Jenkings (2011) consider these relationships to be similar to kinship, due to deeply personal shared identities and encounters. This sense of empowerment through friendships, kinships and mutual experiences creates memories of lifelong bonds that are frequently broken or left behind following transition, ties rarely continue into civilian life.

For male soldiers there appears to be a good fit between self-identity and occupation. According to Savage, Bagnall and Longhurst (2001), working class men normatively gain a positive sense of self-identity through engagement with certain forms of physically intensive employment and, in terms of demographics, a significant number of those who enlist come from low socio-economic backgrounds (MOD,

2016). It is yet too soon to be sure how women who are employed in the same environment will shape and re-shape their identities as it was only in 2014 that the Women in Close Combat Review (MOD, 2014), meant that women could serve on the front line and engage in combat, and only in July 2016 that women in most areas of the Armed Forces were given equal workplace rights. However, although their experiences are similar, their personal needs differ from those of their male counterparts (Burkhart and Hogan, 2015). As Secretary of State in December 2015, Theresa May was swift to allay fears that women in principally male environments could be problematic for unit cohesion, but it should be noted that she also voiced the need for further research on the physical challenges and differing health needs of a female cohort (MOD, 2016), and we shall see in the interview material that the problems women face on leaving the Army also need focused attention. Indeed, the evidence is that it is no longer possible to neatly separate 'work' and the 'personal' as, perhaps, it was in the past.

Lawler (2008) recognizes that work can no longer be considered a social field purely aimed at gaining an income. It is now understood to be a place of personal fulfilment, where this is visible in terms of progression, success and failure in the workplace. But employment in the Armed Forces is not a 'regular job' which creates a further layer of identity risk, for as Lawler (ibid.) also argues, the self-esteem we encounter through success in the workplace may not be equally regarded by those who lack insight into a specific job. This ambivalence is particularly true for the Military, which research has shown to be open to misinterpretation (Gibson & Condor, 2009). Gibson and Condor found that to civilians, members of the Armed Forces are viewed as obedient government servants and the Military is by its nature, a disciplined, hierarchal environment, driven by the need for mutual dependency, often for real life survival. Yet they found that, for soldiers, it is not obedience but loyalty that is paramount as they support their colleagues and serve their country. Loyalty is a powerfully emotive characteristic, and it is not difficult to see how this creates bonds and ties that will be sundered on leaving active service, exacerbating the difficulties of adjustment to civilian life.

In Foucauldian terms, the Military overtly acts as a disciplinary force (Foucault, 1991/1975) through the setting of rules and regulations, punishment when these are broken, and an adherence to strict hierarchies of command. Yet, it also covertly demands fealty from those who serve, through engendering feelings of camaraderie, allegiance and loyalty towards peers, which induces continual self-surveillance in its members lest they 'let the side down'. Thus, power is both a hidden and direct discourse controlling all aspects of daily life in the Military, likely to leave a void when people enter civilian society and find they have to make their own choices; have to care, fully, for their own wants; need to set their own boundaries if they want a routine to shape their days and a behavioural code to live by.

Understanding the Veteran CJS Landscape

There is a lack of robust data on veterans in the criminal justice system, an absence of historical statistical information, and little known about specific cohorts, including female veterans (Albertson et al., 2015). Indeed, the last approximation of veterans in prison, dates from 2009, when it was estimated at 2,820 offenders, or 3.5% of the prison population, although anecdotally, this figure is considered to be larger in real terms (Howard League, 2011). This is not a large number in percentage terms, but not to be sanctioned when it is considered that these offenders have played a significant in role in serving and defending their country.

Since this pilot study was carried out, the Philips Review of veterans in the criminal justice system (commissioned in 2014) has proposed a package of measures to identify and support veterans when entering, serving and leaving prison. As a consequence, since January 2015, every prisoner going through the custody process is asked if they have ever served in Her Majesty's Armed Forces. Other key recommendations of the Review (Phillips, 2014) included the need for veteran-specific programmes, transitional support at the end of a prison sentence and a targeted approach to reducing recidivism, including help for offenders' families. In 2015, the government began a process of reform for rehabilitation following release from prison through private companies. This was found to be 'putting the public at risk' necessitating a return of offender monitoring to the National Probation Services (Dearden, 2019). However, at the time of carrying out the pilot study, matters were less clear-cut. Indeed, the review was a consequence of sustained concern voiced by a number of key bodies, starting as early as 2007 with a report in Military Medicine (van Staden et al., 2007), and sustained by the Howard League (2011); the Kings Centre for Military Health Research (MacManus & Wessely, 2011; MacManus et al., 2012, 2013, 2014); often aided by academic articles (Treadwell, 2010; Taylor et al., 2012; Bray et al., 2013; Murray, 2013; and Albertson et al., 2015). It is in this context that Project Nova was established. But we now turn to the women themselves to hear their stories and examine the discourse that shapes their lives. They are, of course, given pseudonyms to protect their identities: Anna and Beth.

The Women's Stories

Anna is 46 years of age. Her father was in the Army and so she was raised as a Service child, with many changes of schools and homes when he was re-stationed. She served for ten years in the Women's Royal Army Corps, with numerous tours in Germany, Bosnia and Ireland and left to pursue marriage and a civilian lifestyle, so this was a definite choice. She had plans for the future and a new and relational context, into which to relocate. However, longer term, the relationship broke down and following a family bereavement and other employment related issues, she was arrested for theft (shoplifting), but no further action was taken, demonstrating that mental health issues were seen to underpin her actions.

Beth is younger, only 29 years old, so she and Anna represent different generations of Army personnel. Beth was one of the first women to work as a draughts person in the Royal Engineers and served for six years from the age of 16, including two tours of Afghanistan. Like Anna, she left to develop an existing personal relationship, but this came to an end soon after she discharged from the Army. She decided to go travelling to compensate for her loss and during her travels, began to struggle with her alcohol and mental health issues. She was later arrested for criminal damage to commercial buildings and issued with community service.

I undertook ten interviews with Project Nova clients and Anna and Beth were the only two female Nova clients at that time. In line with my ethical approval through Anglia Ruskin University, we met in the

Project Nova Hub and I was accompanied at all of the interviews by a Nova Support Worker, in case the clients needed emotional support during the meetings. In fact, both interviews needed to be stopped when they became upset and needed help whilst re-living elements of their stories. After a break, and agreement they were fine, I continued with a set of semi-structured questions and the interviews covered their pre-Service histories, Service life, post-Service and arrest details. The Project Nova Hub is a functional, no-frills office space, providing veterans with the opportunity to drop in and meet with Nova workers. We held individual, one-off interviews, both lasting approximately two hours. Further data were collected through a battery of questions asked by Nova Officers during their initial telephone conversation with their clients. This data does not form the scope for this chapter but can be found in the final Report (Fossey et al., 2017).

Both Anna and Beth talked of having happy childhoods, raised in homes by both parents and siblings, without problem or difficulty. Although Anna moved around with her father's re-stationing and attended many schools, she reflected on her childhood with good memories. Beth too had a 'normal' childhood. Both of them talked of having an adventurous, out-door living nature, which is a key attribute of military personnel. Crowley and Sandhoff's (2017) research with female veterans suggests that those who refer to themselves with masculine attributes such as 'tomboy' believe they will be able to relate better to men. In this respect, both participants fitted this characteristic really well; both women were able to work effectively in a male dominated workplace:

> Mum and Dad were really disappointed, they wanted me to go to university and be a nurse, I was just more of a tomboy, I had an insatiable amount of energy. (Anna)

> I was quite adventurous and I like sport and challenge, so I sort of went down that route. (Beth)

Whether women need to display masculine characteristics in order to achieve success whilst in Service is disputed in the literature. Crowley and Sandhoff (2017) believe it to be necessary for them to be respected and be 'one of the lads' but Woodward and Jenkings (2011) note that the acquisition of a military identity is grounded in military capabilities and skill sets and not in personal attributes.

Beth was actually the first female in her Squadron to undertake what had formerly been a male only role, therefore, being a female in a previously male dominated space was a significant factor in her account and she states this clearly on several occasions but does not always see this in a positive light:

> I was the only female engineer there, so I had to do more, like the tests were more intense, like to lift further or carry heavier. I was the only girl there throughout the training. You've got to be one of the lads, you can't be a woman really [...] For the lads to be able to respect you, you need to be able to fit in. (Beth)

Anna and Beth displayed attributes of being strong women during their time in Service, including several tours in theatres of war. However, this 'fitting in' and being in a hyper masculine environment was at the cost of their femininity. Negra (2009) uses the notion of choice dilemmas to understand the emotional and practical options women face when trying to attain a work/life balance. However, Beth joined the Army at 16 and was still a very young woman discovering her adult, feminine self when posted to austere work environments. Further, it is clear from her narrative that in trying to 'fit in with the lads' and undertaking life or death situations, she felt the loss of her teenage, feminine identity.

> I just feel like I had my whole teenage hood taken away from me really being a girl, because you're not allowed to do the girly things that normal girls enjoy, like straightening your hair or putting your make-up on. So you do lose a lot of your femininity. It took me ages to become a woman and get my femininity back. (Beth)

Cooper and colleagues (2017) discuss the notion of push/pull factors shaping the pressures faced by Service personnel. They recognize that at some point when joining the Armed Forces, there is a need to integrate completely into the military way, in order to thrive in such an environment. New recruits are detached from their civilian identity and are embedded into a military lifestyle. At some stage, however, the need for the regular things in life, including a home, family or normal working hours in a Service person's career pushes them back to wanting attributes of a civilian way of life, and this can be the catalyst for leaving the Army. Smith and Rosenstein (2017) have further found that although there appears to be greater gender balance between military careers and family life, Armed Forces personnel are still leaving due to the impact of Service on their families, demonstrating positive rather than negative reasons for leaving the Army. The push/pull factors are evident in Anna and Beth's narratives. In Anna's case particularly, age considerations may have made this more urgent. In Beth's, her partner-to-be had also experienced Army life — another way in which their situations differed. Both of the participants romanticized their return to civilian life, with a desire to settle down, be 'looked after', and to start a family:

> My boyfriend had just proposed and I was wanting to settle down and have a family and not be part of an institution anymore. I wanted my own identity with kids and a dog and a house and catch up on family life. I couldn't think of anything more that the Army could offer me that I'd find interesting [...] Being a civilian was all new and exciting, getting rid of all the Army uniform and that institution. I wasn't in a rush to do anything, I just wanted to find my feet. (Anna)

> I didn't want to go back, I didn't want to do another operational tour [...] I was engaged to a guy who was also in the Army and he left. He persuaded me to leave and we'd get married and he'd look after me. (Beth)

More recently, there has been a great deal of support for Serving personnel undergoing the resettlement process offered by the Careers Transition Partnership (CTP, 2018) but the type and level of support is dependent on the length of service and the individual's motivation to seek guidance. Findings from the evaluation of Project Nova (Fossey et al., 2017) indicate that among veterans seeking help is problematic: they have a perceived sense of weakness and loss of pride when asking for help for themselves. Anna and Beth were aware of the advice available to them, but like many who are in the period of transition, neither engaged beyond the basic levels of support, assuming they would cope with the practical demands of resettlement back into civilian life.

Ashcroft (2014) acknowledges that most veterans transition well and without problem. However, for Anna and Beth, the return to civilian life was more difficult than they had anticipated. As well as negotiating the practical elements of finding work, housing and settling into completely different lifestyles, they also had to adjust to the loss of camaraderie and the complete change in social attitudes and values. Bergman and colleagues (2014) refer to the movement back into civilian life as a reverse culture shock, where the veteran is required to undo their military norms of hierarchy, uniformity and rigidity and mould into civilian ways. The loss of belonging is evident in these narratives, both in terms of personal relationships and their ways of living.

> It's a shock to the system. I think they (veterans) find it very hard to try and relate to how the outside world works outside of the Army [...] It was a case of take each day as it comes, breathe, find your feet and see where you go. (Anna)

> I just felt lost. I didn't feel like I had any friends. I didn't have much support [...] I couldn't get any proper work, it was just whatever I could fit in. It was just making new friends, just feeling like you don't fit in as well. Just different mentality, different attitude on life, different ways of thinking. Just totally feeling like you don't belong anywhere. (Beth)

> The girls that I served with, I don't really speak to anymore. I haven't got any buddy systems. The Army was a lot more social. (Beth)

There is an assumption that family will act as the main support system for veterans in transition. Both Anna and Beth left the Military to start a life with their partners. However, this support network was lost when both of their relationships broke down. Anna relied on her elderly parents, but her mother died soon after she left the Army, causing further distress and difficulty. Beth went travelling around the world on her own, but soon had to return to the UK when she began to present with mental health issues, on top of her anti-social drinking behaviour. The issues of mental health and alcohol addiction were considered by both of them to be the catalyst for their offending behaviour:

> I think I got down to about 8 stone. My hair was falling out in clumps and I didn't have a scrap of clothing [...] I was in a daze. I was walking around and I was there for about two and a half hours picking up stuff, then I just walked out of the store. The store detective came out and the alarms went off. (Anna)

> I became really withdrawn. I didn't want to be anywhere. I didn't know where I felt safe. When I came back from Afghan I was drinking heavily. I would definitely link the drinking to my military service [...] like after a Friday afternoon you're ordered to parade to the bar and if you're not there then you get in trouble. (Beth)

Interestingly, Higate (2003) argues that the masculine practices within the military culture are tenacious and continue into civilian life after leaving the forces and Beth certainly had significant alcohol-related problems on her resettlement. Yet emotion and dependency are seen as feminine traits that are considered signs of weakness and further prevent veterans from seeking help (Cooper et al., 2016; Fossey et al., 2017) and these, too, appear to have played a role in both narratives.

Conclusion

Anna and Beth's narratives describe the stories of two women who moved into a predominantly masculine environment, gained strong collegiate attachments and adapted their lifestyles to thrive within a military environment. In order to achieve in their chosen work roles, these women adopted masculine traits, necessary for the difficult environment in which they operated, and gained individual success. On leaving the Military, it was necessary for Anna and Beth to re-adapt again back into civilian norms. The difficulty both women found during the transition period, along with personal and mental health issues, culminated in their arrests. It is important to remember that offending is no greater in the veteran cohort than it is within the civilian population and that military service is not a pre-requisite for offending behaviour (MacManus & Wessely, 2011). Moreover, there are numerous, extraneous factors why people commit crime. Those who have committed crime are more likely to have been on a criminal trajectory prior to their military service and crucially, therefore, there is a need to examine pre-enlistment behaviours when considering motives for those in the CJS.

For Anna and Beth, however, life just 'got in the way' for they had not committed offences either prior to joining or during their time in the Army. Thus, their experiences highlight how a radical change of lifestyle can be sufficient to 'knock' a person off balance, turning them from active and effective defenders of the realm into needy and vulnerable offenders instead. For these two women, in particular, Project Nova has been a necessary support and signposting system to help them back onto their feet and demonstrates the importance of systems that can tailor support to meet the needs of the individual. At the time of the interviews, Anna and Beth were seeking help and slowly returning to some sense of a 'normal' life. Since the time of the study, Project Nova has been rolled out to support veterans across nineteen counties within the UK. It, therefore, has the potential to help much greater numbers of former soldiers to find their way back into 'normal' society. However, in becoming a universal service for ex-military personnel in the CJS who need help in adjusting to civilian life, it must take care neither to neglect its clients' diverse needs nor too closely parody the protective, if controlling, ethos of the Army that they are leaving. The ex-soldiers, male or female, need a set of discourses to live by that help them achieve an effective balance between independence and dependence if they are to avoid isolation and the poor mental health this engenders and, instead, form new, lasting and rewarding reciprocal relationships.

Acknowledgements

Project Nova project was funded by FiMT; the Project evaluation supported by staff at the RFEA.

References

Albertson, K., Irving, J. & Best, D. (2015). A social capital approach to assisting veterans through recovery and desistance transitions in civilian life. *The Howard Journal*. 54(4): 384–96. https://doi.org/10.1111/hojo.12138

Ashcroft, M. (2014). *The veterans transition review*. http://www.veteranstransition.co.uk/vtrreport.pdf

Bergman, B., Burdett, H. & Greenberg, N. (2014). Service life and beyond — institution or culture? *RUSI Journal*. 159(5): 60–68. https://doi.org/10.1080/03071847.2014.969946

Bray, I., O'Malley, P., Ashcroft, S., Adedeji, L. & Spriggs, A. (2013). Ex-military personnel in the criminal justice system: A cross sectional study. *The Howard Journal*. 52(5): 516–26. https://doi.org/10.1111/hojo.12027

Burkhart, L. & Hogan, N. (2015). Being a female veteran: A grounded theory of coping with transition. *Social Work in Mental Health*. 13: 108–27. https://doi.org/10.1080/15332985.2013.870102

CTP (Career Transition Partnership) (2018). *Career Transition Partnership*. https://www.ctp.org.uk/

Condor, S., Gibson, S. & Abell, J. (2006). English identity and ethnic diversity in the context of UK constitutional change. *Ethnicities*, 6(2): 123–58. https://doi.org/10.1177/1468796806063748

Cooper, L., Caddick, N., Godier, L., Cooper, A. & Fossey, M. (2016). Transition from the Military into civilian life: an exploration of cultural competence. *Armed Forces & Society*, 44(1): 156–77. https://doi.org/10.1177/0095327X16675965

Cooper, L., Caddick, N., Godier, L., Cooper, A., Fossey, M. & Engward, H. (2017). A model of military to civilian transition: Bourdieu in Action. *Journal of Military, Veteran and Family Health*. http://dx.doi.org/10.3138/jmvfh.4301

Crowley, K. & Sandhoff, M. (2017). Just a girl in the Army: US Iraq war veterans negotiating femininity in a culture of masculinity. *Armed Forces & Society*, 43(2): 221–37. https://doi.org/10.1177/0095327X16682045

Dearden, L. (2019). Government renationalises supervision of criminals in major U-turn after Chris Grayling's probation 'failure'. *Independent*, 16 May 2019. https://www.independent.co.uk/news/uk/home-news/criminal-probation-privatise-chris-grayling-offenders-taxpayer-a8915791.html

Foucault, M. (1991/1975) *Discipline and punishment: The birth of the prison*. London: Penguin.

Fossey, M., Cooper, L., Godier, L. & Cooper, A. (2017). *Project Nova: A pilot study to support veterans in the criminal justice system. Final report*. http://www.fim-trust.org/wp-content/uploads/2017/04/Project-Nova-Report.pdf

Gibson, S., & Condor, S. (2009). State institutions and social identity: National representations in soldiers' and civilians' interview talk concerning military service. *British Journal of Social Psychology*, 48: 313–36. https://doi.org/10.1348/014466608X349496

Higate, P. (2003). 'Soft clerks' and 'hard civvies': Pluralizing military masculinities. In: Higate, P. (ed), *Military masculinities: Identity and the state*. Westport: Praeger.

Hinojosa, R. & Hinojosa, M. (2011). Using military friendships to optimize post-deployment reintegration for male Operation Iraqi Freedom/Operation Enduring Freedom veterans. *Journal of Rehabilitation Research and Development*, 48(10): 1145–58. https://doi.org/ 10.1682/JRRD.2010.08.0151

Howard League for Penal Reform. (2011). *The Howard League for Penal Reform, report of the inquiry into former armed service personnel in prison*. https://d19ylpo4aovc7m.cloudfront.net/fileadmin/howard_league/user/pdf/Publications/Report_of_the_Inquiry_into_Fromer_Armed_Service_Personnel_in_Prison.pdf

Lawler, S. (2008). *Identity: Sociological perspectives*. Cambridge: Polity Press.

MacManus, D. & Wessely S. (2011). Why do some ex-armed forces personnel end up in prison? *British Medical Journal (Editorial)*, 342, d3898. https://doi.org/10.1136/bmj.d3898

MacManus, D. & Wessely S. (2013). Veteran mental health services in the UK: Are we headed in the right direction? *Journal of Mental Health*, 22(4): 301–05. https://doi.org/10.3109/09638237.2013.819421

MacManus, D., Dean, K., Iversen, A., Hull, L., Jones, N., Fahy, T., Wessely, S. & Fear, N. (2012). Impact of pre-enlistment antisocial behaviour on behavioural outcomes among UK military personnel. *Psychiatry Epidemiology*, 47: 1353–58. https://doi.org/10.1007/s00127-011-0443-z

MacManus, D., Fossey, M., Watson, S. & Wessely, S. (2015). Former Armed Forces personnel in the criminal justice system. *The Lancet Psychiatry*, 2(2): 121–22. https://doi.org/10.1016/S2215-0366(14)00095-9

MacManus, D., Jones, N., Wessely, S., Fear, N., Jones, E. & Greenberg, N. (2014). The mental health of the UK Armed forces in the 21st century: Resilience in the face of adversity. *Journal of the Royal Army Medical Corps*, 160: 125–30. https://doi.org/doi:10.1136/jramc- 2013-000213

Ministry of Defence (2011). *The Armed Forces Covenant*. https://www.gov.uk/government/uploads/system/uploads/attachment_data/file/49469/the_armed_forces_covenant.pdf

Ministry of Defence (2014). *Interim report on the health risks to women in close combat roles*. https://assets.publishing.service.gov.uk/government/uploads/system/uploads/attachment_data/file/536381/20160706_ADR006101_Report_Women_in_Combat_WEB-FINAL.PDF

Ministry of Defence (2016). *Women in close combat review*. https://assets.publishing.service.gov.uk/government/uploads/system/uploads/attachment_data/file/389575/20141218_WGCC_Findings_Paper_Final.pdf

Murray, E. (2013). Post-army trouble: Veterans in the criminal justice system. *Centre for Crime and Justice Studies*, 94: 20–21. https://doi.org/10.1080/09627251.2013.865497

Negra, D. (2009). *What a girl wants? Fantasizing the reclamation of the self in post feminism*. Abingdon: Routledge.

Phillips, S. (2014). *Former members of the Armed Forces and the criminal justice system: A review on behalf of the Secretary of State for Justice*. https://www.gov.uk/government/uploads/system/uploads/attachment_data/file/389964/former-members-of-the-armed-forces-and-the-criminal-justice-system.pdf

Savage, M., Bagnall, G. & Longhurst, B. (2001). Ordinary, ambivalent and defensive: Class identities in the northwest of England. *Sociology*, 35: 875–92. https://doi.org/10.1177/0038038501035004005

Smith, D., & Rosenstein, J. (2017). Gender and the Military profession: Early career influences, attitudes and intentions. *Armed Forces & Society*, 43(2): 260–79. https://doi.org/10.1177/0095327X15626722

Taylor, J., Parkes, T., Haw, S. & Jepson, R. (2012). Military veterans with mental health problems: A protocol for a systematic review to identify whether they have an additional risk of contact with criminal justice systems compared with other veteran groups. *Systematic Reviews*, 1(53): 1–9. https://doi.org/10.1186/2046-4053-1-53

Treadwell, J. (2010). Counterblast: More than casualties of war? Ex-military personnel in the criminal justice system. *The Howard Journal*, 49(1): 73–77. https://doi.org/10.1111/j.1468-2311.2009.00598.x

Van Staden, L., Fear, N., Iversen, A. & French C. (2007). Transition back into civilian life: A study of personnel leaving the UK Armed Forces via 'military prison'. *Military Medicine*, 172(9): 925–30. https://doi.org/10.7205/MILMED.172.9.925

Woodward, R. & Jenkings, K. (2011). Military identities in the situated accounts of British military personnel. *Sociology*, 45(2): 252–68. https://doi.org/10.1177/0038038510394016

24. UK Senior Citizens Learn Filmmaking as a Creative Pathway to Reflection and Fulfilment

Teresa Brayshaw and Jenny Granville

Teresa Brayshaw and Jenny Granville offer a non-conventional treatment of a project that supports seniors to engage in collaborative film making. Their performative approach is fairly radical and, in keeping with this, the chapter is multi-faceted. It includes a transcript of the film and its QR code to enable you to view it yourself, feedback from viewers, elements from a conference presentation and selections from the email exchanges between and among editors and academics that illustrate the difficulties when different views collide.

'Never to get lost is not to live, not to know how to get lost brings you to destruction, and somewhere in **the terra incognita in between** lies a life of discovery'. (Rebecca Solnit)

Jenny: Hi Teresa, we've been asked to contribute a chapter to a book based upon our research and the Senior Moments Performance we presented in Copenhagen.

Teresa: Brilliant Jenny — but we only have a performance script and that's not really going to tell our story or communicate how we make practice as research.

Jenny: Yes, you're right. We need to think about capturing liveness on the page — should we make a film instead? We could send them a QR code...

https://doi.org/10.11647/OBP.0203.24

SIX WEEKS LATER....

Editors: 'Your Film is lovely... but we really need a paper too!'

We set out to find 'the terra incognita in between', our writing processes mirroring those we use in filmmaking — but first the context!

The PROPOSAL

In the spirit of creativity and compromise a text is created to re-interpret a visual and auditory experience into a verbal and readable format that challenges the common conventions around what constitutes a book chapter. Rather than offer a single narrative account, the chapter is poly-vocal — episodic in structure — gathering together multiple evidences to reveal, and emulate, the collaborative processes and provocations in both filmmaking and chapter-writing. The idea here is to offer the reader an experience that mirrors the critical and creative multi-modal process we, the researchers, used in the making and disseminating of our work. The ten stages of 'production' in this book chapter include overviews of the 'Senior Moments' presentations and the 'Cinage' (a blend of cinema and ageing) project which led to their creation; feedback from academics who have seen versions of the research in live and mediated forms that capture the audience reaction; some of the email exchange with the editors of this book to give a taste of the difficulties in crossing research borders; the lead up to the creative process; a QR code for the film itself and an annotated description of the script; which together capture many of the research questions and methodologies employed in the development of the project, and makes our actions properly visible. As a coda we look back on the experience and forward to future plans and point out the sources that influenced our work.

The PITCH: Presenting Senior Moments

Our research project comprises the creation of a body of work under the name of CINAGE, addressing ageing as a felt experience, narratives of loss, the telling of personal stories by older people through the creative practice of scriptwriting and filmmaking and the challenges of designing intergenerational learning spaces within a UK university context. The research outcomes of this project, and the dissemination of the practice as research, have been delivered variously through performative lectures, letters, conference papers, journal articles, film screenings and live performances.

The live papers entitled *Senior Moments — Reflections on the Cinage Project*, have been presented at a number of international conference and festival contexts, in the form of tightly structured, but seemingly spontaneous, performative conversations.[1] These performances presented in sometimes very formal academic contexts have served to find new ways to foreground practice as research, to propose different models of reader engagement with research processes and to play with the 'performer/audience' possibilities inherent in the live contexts through a disruption of the usual conventions of conference presentations.

SYNOPSIS: What *is* the CINAGE Project?

It is a research project initially funded by The European Commission's Grundtvig Lifelong Learning programme as a response to the huge increase in the number of older people in Europe, brought about by the success of public health policies and socio-economic development. The pilot project, in 2014–2015, involved four partner countries — the UK, Italy, Slovenia and Portugal. Originally composed of interlinked activities, engaging older people with critical analysis of European cinema and practical filmmaking experience, CINAGE at Leeds Beckett University has further developed the methodology by exploring autobiographical

---

1   Different versions of the research process have been presented under the title of *Senior Moments: Reflections on the CINAGE project and collaborative advances* at The Association for Education & Ageing (AEA) in association with ForAge network; International Conference on Learning in Later Life; Theory, Policy and Practice: Open University Milton Keynes April 2016 — and subsequently published in the International Journal of Education and the Arts; ELOA (Network on Education and learning of Older Adults) Conference; Ageing in A Multi-Cultural World — individual and social contexts of learning, Wroclaw Poland 2016; *'LeBeMe'* — Leeds Beckett Interdisciplinary Media Research Conference, January 2017; ESREA (European Society for Research on the Education of Adults) Life Histories and Biography Network Conference: 'Discourses We Live By', Copenhagen, March 2017.

narrative filmmaking and memory, as central storytelling techniques. CINAGE also forms part of the lifelong learning process by enabling active ageing through learning new skills and working not only with senior learners, but intergenerationally.

The success of the pilot led us, in the School of Film, Music and Performing Arts, to open up to further cohorts of CINAGE in 2015/16 and 2016/17 and, in 2017, the introduction of 'CINAGE: Live', a brand new pilot course offering over 60s the opportunity to devise, develop and perform a contemporary piece of theatre that addressed issues at the heart of their lives. CINAGE has also led to Leeds Beckett University becoming established as the first Age Friendly University in England and has acted as a springboard for a number of graduating participants continuing their filmmaking learning journeys, including two CINAGE alumni studying on our MA Documentary programme, another CINAGE student on our MA Filmmaking programme and yet another studying for his PhD. CINAGE demonstrates lifelong learning in content and in practice.

REVIEWS: The Essence of CINAGE, Captured in Audience Feedback

A udiences who have seen us present our material have been perturbed and made to think anew, so we have included some of their written feedback to help you, the current reader, to better grasp the nature of our work. We offer several examples below.

From Professor Rob Evans, Magdeburg University, Germany after the ESREA (European Society for Research on the Education of Adults) Life Histories and Biography Network Conference: 'Discourses We Live By', Copenhagen, March 2017:

I have had the pleasure and the privilege to watch Teresa and Jenny in action twice and it has been an interesting experience, and one wholly out of the ordinary — at least (and this is the important bit) in spaces where the model of communication and interaction is certainly more staid, more 'measured', more predictable.

Teresa and Jenny's dialogued presentation succeeds by applying something of a V-effect that persistently subverts the measured scientific discourse model of the presentation by allowing personal, intimate, immediate asides and conversation to break into the content. Their paced, tense, unsettling dialogue shifts between a more distancing account of their research and their irruptions of irreverence, candour and vulnerability.

Teresa and Jenny, in this adaptable performance (I noted the practical and theoretical nuances worked into the two performances before two different researcher audiences) took their audience by surprise, unsettled and challenged them. The first time around, in Poland, I was taken aback when they started; taken by surprise by their back-and-forth worried, worrying dialogue of uncertainty and diffidence. There is something wrong, I thought, and saw that (and felt strongly) the rest of the room was on the verge of shifting uncomfortably on their seats, waiting for a rescue, some safe exit from this seemingly wrong-stepped beginning as the two of them questioned each other's readiness and ability to carry on at all. As it dawned on me that this was being performed and that this was turning into their theme — being and getting lost, finding oneself perhaps — unease was instantly replaced by appreciation and increasing involvement.

The plot is a provocation, intriguing and involving. Solidly founded in impressive practice, at an artisanal level of skill that strikes the listener/watcher immediately — these are skilful performers acting with obvious and infectious commitment — and with clear and equally convincing, challenging theoretical grounding. This is an emotional experience. This is a challenging experience. You come out of it ready to talk, to debate, laugh and cry. All at once, if possible.

From Jayne Raisborough, Professor of Media, Leeds Beckett University, UK at the 'LeBeMe', Leeds Beckett Interdisciplinary Media Research Conference, January 2017:

J ust settling into my conference-ready mode — leaning back in my chair, pen idling in my hand, mind gently gazing and then — what the heck was happening? Feeling bit awkward, feeling panic of the loss I think I see in front of me. Should I intervene? Should the chair? Pen thrown down, sitting up, anxious, awkward and then — thank god! Warmth, comfort, humour and a layering of complexity and richness blankets the room. This isn't a paper to take notes from, this is a paper that flicks the senses, gets the nerves jangling and reminds me of the very real material and affective dimensions of age.

From Dr Lynne Hibberd School of Cultural Studies, Leeds Beckett University, UK:

The most interesting thing about this session was the way it was delivered, as a scripted but seemingly spontaneous discussion. This made it feel really alive and discursive (rather than a 'finished' piece of research which always feels a bit definite, fixed and authoritative), also emotionally vibrant (researchers as real people with feelings rather than detached objective observers or facilitators), and like a starting point. I loved it.

From Mike Spence, New Technologist and Games Designer at ELOA (Network on Education and learning of Older Adults) Conference: Ageing in A Multi-Cultural World — individual and social contexts of learning, Wroclaw Poland, 2016:

The biggest hook to this brave maverick performance of research is the elegant ease in which Jenny and Teresa segued an improvisation into the presentation from the status quo. It beautifully confounded the audience into questioning if the presentation had started at all. Is this a mistake? Should someone intervene? The audience is asking themselves questions and shuffling uneasily in their seats when the research team hits them with a smooth, swift delivery of conventional backstory and reference to legitimize the free direction the performers can take to artistically, articulately and elegantly delivering powerful messages for the reviewers to take away with them. It certainly gave me confidence in using fictional narrative to illustrate scientific data in a dynamic method.

DEVELOPMENT: The Process of CINAGE, Captured in the 2017 ESREA Conference Presentation

Teresa: 'Taking back the meaning of being lost in creative practice and Higher Education is really important — it's a political act, that we as academics and practitioners are reclaiming in this project — maybe in order to feel at home in ourselves?'

Jenny: The formal name for the project is Cinage — cinema for active ageing, but those of us running it used the shorthand of 'teaching filmmaking to old people'! The goals were to find ways to get older people to learn. The actual outcome of this project was a series of short films but the real learning was in facing up to the realities of ageing as a felt experience. We started by asking them to describe their experience of ageing… So, then our job was to find a way to expand the question of ageing to encompass autobiographical stories as a field of creative possibilities rather than an experience of deficiency and loss.

Teresa: I worked in exactly the same way as I work with undergraduate, MA and PhD students — with a series of proposals and exercises which I know from experience, will develop creative encounters encouraging risk-taking, problem-solving, personal discovery, failure, flexibility and fun.

As a Feldenkrais[2] practitioner I understand that in order for any and all learning to take place — novelty and curiosity have to be excited in the nervous system. I taught the group some *Awareness through Movement* lessons.

I was surprised by the openness of the group to try things out — to have a go — to play without the usual anxiety around meaning and end-gaining that is now so prevalent throughout undergraduate educational contexts. Of course, the levels of experience and expertise in the group were tremendous but nevertheless — I was particularly impressed by the quality of engagement in the proposal made which

---

2   'An educational method focusing on learning and movement, which can bring about improved movement and enhanced functioning'. See http://www.feldenkrais. co.uk/what.html

directly addressed the questions of 'where am I now?', 'where am I going?', 'where have I been?'.

Letter to Cinage Students: In creative practice, we are very accustomed to material and ideas and interventions emerging from live encounters, which involve people moving and working in the moment. We are trained in and trust the opportunities that present themselves when improvising — which is in truth the art of 'making it up as you go along'. This practice of being in a place of uncertainty is also a constant reminder that 'not knowing' and 'being lost' are parts of any narrative process and I welcome both with open arms.

I *know* that the 'letters to your 16-year-old selves' are a way of accessing an approach to autobiographical writing, which connects you to previous, and future versions of yourselves and others.

I also *know* that outcomes are only part of any learning and growing process, and that the experiences of being in the moment, of getting into flow, of playing around and of putting oneself in the environment where novelty and discovery abound, enables us to connect to different versions of our present self. A self that is flexible, open to changing direction and persuasion and position (physically, intellectually, emotionally, perceptually) and also a self that finds pleasure in an embodied understanding of the differences between a 'human doing' and a 'human being'.

Those spaces, wherever we find them, that enable us to connect with ourselves and others in ways that take us away from our habits offer the potential for us to develop new movements in our brain, in our physiology, in our experiences, in our memories and also in our imaginations.

DEVELOPMENT HELL: Finding a Modus Vivendi for Publication (the Hard Bit), Email Exchanges Between Editors and Authors

Authors to Editors (22/01/18)

Hi Marianne and Hazel,

I am excited to send you, via WeTransfer, the first draft of our 'chapter', which is, in fact, a film based on the paper/presentation that we delivered in Copenhagen.

Given the slightly experimental and performative nature of our paper, we wanted to mirror that in the way we present the material and have been experimenting with the form (film) being used to reflect the content (older people making films and our response as researchers). We are proposing that when the reader turns to our chapter in the book — entitled 'Senior Moments; Reflection on the CINAGE project' — instead of text, they will find a QR code (or URL). This will take them to the short film I am sending you below.

I do hope that this experimental format will be something you feel able to embrace. Please do let us know your thoughts as soon as possible so we can make adjustments if necessary.

With all good wishes,

Jenny and Teresa

Editor to Editor:

Ed 1   Can we do that?
Ed 2   Difficult I think! The publisher is expecting a normal book not alternative media — Why can't they just write a normal paper! Hmm! Will have to think about this...
Ed 2   ... So sorry to have sounded off. I have managed to download and watch the film which is lovely but not enough alone.

Editor to Authors (22/01/18)

Dear Jenny and Teresa

Your film is lovely and it would be great to put an URL (and a QR if we can) in the book but we really need a paper too as our commitment to the publisher is for a 6–7000 word text that explores some of the discourses that you are examining in your work. This is what we suggest in our editorial role:

- That you include a complete (but annotated to explain significant visuals) transcript — perhaps with a cast list to explain the key characters including yourselves and with added scenic descriptors and reference to the publications you display.

- That this starts with a brief overview of the discourses around ageing in Western society: the early view that learning capacity disappeared and brain power declined with age; the trend of treating the elderly as a 'drain' on society, a medical and social problem and institutionalizing them; the more recent view supported by scanning, etc. that active engagement staves off even prevents dementia and any others you see appropriate.

- We assume that you have the sources for this to hand (surely the books were more than props!) — but shout if not — Hazel has vague recollections of teaching an Education and Ageing Society course and might be able dig out some material if that would help.

- That you set the really interesting ideas you have about all-age universities and real educational experiences that your work supports against a brief overview of contemporary educational discourse: the dominant outcomes-based educational ideologies and also the decimation of adult education, dire this millennium (again do you have material to hand?).

Would this work for you? We hope so!

BW, Marianne and Hazel

Author to Author (22/01/18)

Hi Jenny

I think unfortunately there is a real misunderstanding of our work and the forms we work and communicate in here. I think, in the kindest possible way, we extricate ourselves from this project given the amount of publications we are involved with (my own book is nearing completion) and apologize to Hazel and Marianne for this miscommunication. I honestly thought that given the feedback on our paper in situ that there was an understanding of what we were about — but neither of these two saw the paper — and clearly think that the books are 'props' and that we have chosen to present in this form because we cannot write in an academic way. Let's focus our energy upon what is actually important — and live the discourses — what say you?

Alternatively — we could do as they ask — and in the process DIE!

Teresa

Retrospective Editorial comment (01/07/18)

It was more a case of 'we want your contribution as your work so clearly challenges normative discourses but are not sure you have the time, energy, inclination to add some of the more mundane stuff that is traditionally expected in a book chapter'. We were hinting that we would do some of this work to secure the contribution, if necessary, trying NOT to sound patronizing — we failed — probably should have just said this outright!!

Author to Editor (25/01/18)

Hi Hazel and Marianne,

We think that, unfortunately, there is a real misunderstanding of our work and the forms we work and communicate in. We are primarily 'practitioners' who, whilst working on topics that are alive in academia such as 'discourses we live by' and 'active ageing', choose to investigate them as part of our overarching research question, which is how to remain practitioners and present our work and outcomes in a form which reflects our research techniques and process.

Our 'paper' was deliberately constructed as a 'live' performative encounter — and you can see from the attached feedback to various versions of this — that the 'learning' and 'impact' of what we perform prioritizes the form over the content. The knowledges and research that we are interested in are often embodied and tacit (know how). They sometimes swim against the often-dominant cultural tides, which position explicit knowledge (know what), certainty, goal setting and achievement as markers of excellence. This is why we spent a lot of time making this film.

Of course, this is a currently massive debate in the area of the arts and the Academy with the development of practice-based PhDs. In the USA this argument has long been over with the introduction of the MFA [Master of Fine Arts] — which recognizes the practice as the research with its own place in the Academy. That is why we specifically chose to present in this way — not because we cannot or do not want to write an academic treatise, but because we have to develop our practical and applied research methodologies.

Your suggestion that we explain our research in writing with introduction, contextualization etc., is something that we do not want to do since our work is practice as research and this would reduce and sideline our practice and research to illustration within a logocentric discourse. We feel that elements you suggest, such as '...really interesting ideas you have about all-age universities and real educational experiences that your work supports...' are adequately expressed and explored in the film and do not need covering again, in text.

We would, though, be happy to complete your suggestion that we include an annotated version of our presentation/script ... and a full bibliography of the publications referred to and displayed.

If you do not feel that the film, plus annotated version, is sufficient or appropriate for your book, then although we are really very sorry to let you down, we will have to withdraw from the project.

We look forward to hearing from you,

With all good wishes,

Jenny and Teresa

Editor to Editor:

This might work...

Editors to Authors (25/01/18)

Hi Jennifer and Teresa

We hear what you are saying and think that your suggestion may work — please just give us a little time to look at the elements together in more detail.

Certainly, it was not our intention to reject your methods — merely to suggest something that seemed more viable after watching the film, as we did not think our publisher would accept a QR code alone.

Perhaps one question we will be asked is where the film is stored, and can you guarantee that it would be available to readers for the lifetime of the book? (This may not be a concern but it would be good to know about this before we talk with the publisher more formally later in the process of publication). So, could you give us this information please (or explain how it works!). And the transcript when available.

Remember that we are not as accustomed to your way of working as you are (so have to negotiate and ask questions!) but this does not mean we are not interested or supportive. We were very keen to have the workshop at the conference because it is 'different' from the normative papers and stimulating... and forward-looking! You are disrupting discourses (on ageing, education and academic publishing probably!) and we DO want that — just not sure quite how to cope with it!

Simply, we have to make sure this will all work and meet everyone's needs and expectations, so we are glad that you have come back to us with a compromise solution that may do this. Will be in touch again when we have had time to think further (or if we have more questions!)

Meanwhile, all the best,

Marianne and Hazel

Author to Author (25/01/18)

Wow! Result (of sorts)

X –

Author to Editors (06/02/18)

Hello Marianne and Hazel

Sorry to have delayed replying...Teresa and I have talked and think we have a plan! We are teaching and in meetings all day today, so I will write to you further tonight with some details of what we are thinking and see whether you think it could work

With all good wishes

Jenny

Editors to Authors (19/02/18)

Dear Teresa and Jenny

Have now had time to think constructively and collate all the material we have from and about you.

Would you accept a series of edited 'snapshots' from the email exchanges as an introduction to your material: paper, annotated script and bibliography?

This would explain what you are about, and your need to persuade a traditional audience (us!) to think afresh without being the kind of didactic introduction that you dislike (we think...hope!) so prepares the reader for what comes next.

Does this take us forward? Or at least keep the door ajar for further discussion?

We hope so!

Best wishes,

Marianne and Hazel

Author to Editors (19/02/18)

Hi Marianne and Hazel.

I haven't spoken to Jenny about this but think it's actually really interesting. We should of course in the spirit of transparency also send you (maybe?) the email correspondence J and I had in response to your 'perhaps you could actually write a paper! After all the books are surely more than props!' email, before Jenny sent the final version, so that the 'emotional' exchange so prevalent in all our attempts to make this work is as present as it can be to the reader/audience. I'll see if there is anything useful here — I'm hopefully seeing Jen tomorrow so will hear her view then — in the meantime genuine thanks for propping that door!

Respect

Teresa

PRODUCTION: Psyching up for Performance

T: Right Jenny are you ready?

J: Yes — I AM — I'm ready

T: I'm not

J: What do you mean — you're here, I'm here, they're here — let's go

T: Go where Jenny — I'm lost

J: I don't know — let's work it out as we go along

T: What you mean improvise?

J: Yes — you're a performer, a theatre maker — you're trained in the art of making things up as you go along.

T: And you're a film maker, and over 60 — so are well placed to understand how to age well and understand that life stories and autobiographies are too often taken for granted.

J: So — let's begin by remembering what is important, what has been important on this project — by telling our personal stories, because if we know anything it's that in studies exploring ageing and senescing and gerontology — that personal narratives of 'living in time' remain unexplored.

T:	Ok—what has our current practice of making film and performance with people over 65 got to do with discourses we live by?

J:	If we know anything from our experience as teachers in Higher Education of students of all ages and levels — it's that life stories and autobiographies are too often taken for granted.

T:	Ok — so we know that as researchers on this project there is a need to develop a deeper understanding of what it means to 'live in time' — and from that understanding develop an art of ageing — we are narrative practitioners — sharing the importance of narrative practices — and we do have this script that we're reading now — in fact we've got so many versions of it ... SHOULD WE START?

SCREENING: Lights/Camera/Action, Watch SENIOR MOMENTS — REFLECTIONS ON THE CINAGE PROJECT

See the film itself @ http://eprints.leedsbeckett.ac.uk/4775/ or use the QR code below.

Allow 13 minutes for viewing.

SCREENPLAY: Research Film Annotation to CINAGE 'SENIOR MOMENTS'

00:00–01:28

It is a film theory trope that the first scene in a film tells you what the story of the film is. Somehow the writer needs to find a way to encompass the theme and approach during that opening sequence. In working on the basis that the CINAGE film is research, the authors worked to include every element of their creative practice into the body of the work. The use of a vintage TV screen to frame the opening scene is a way of visually, and possibly subliminally, referencing the notion of 'age'. The screen represents a working object, useful and familiar — but no longer valued except as a curiosity and relegated to something that is 'out of date', 'quaint', 'old'. The choice of a vintage TV screen is a creative use of an artefact that is, of course, perfectly serviceable and contributes a unique style and quality, just because it is old. It has much to offer, on its own terms. Thus, we introduce the overarching theme of the CINAGE projects.

This scene was recorded prior to the writing of the script for the Discourses We Live By, Copenhagen conference. The authors were still researching and deciding their approach and wanted to indicate that out of the many studies of different aspects of gerontology, a mass of terms and ideas have emerged.

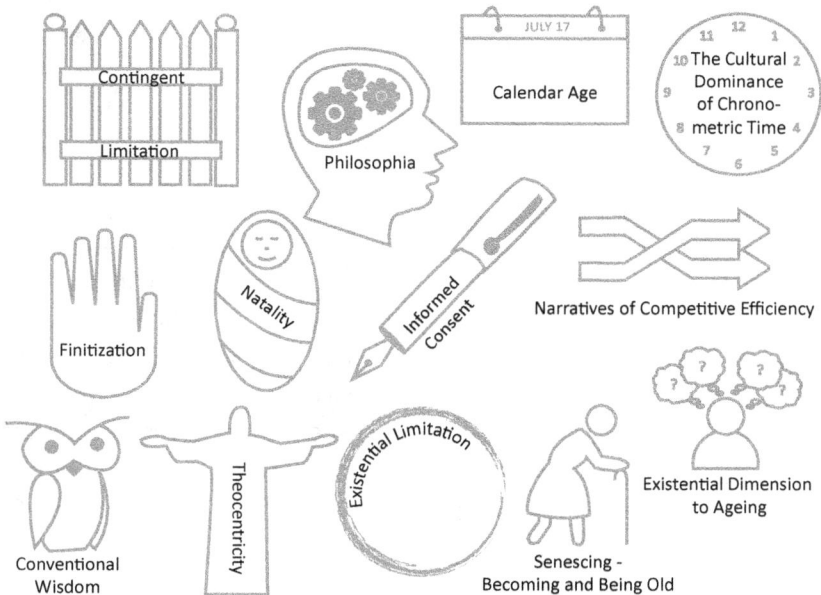

continued overleaf ...

... continued from previous page

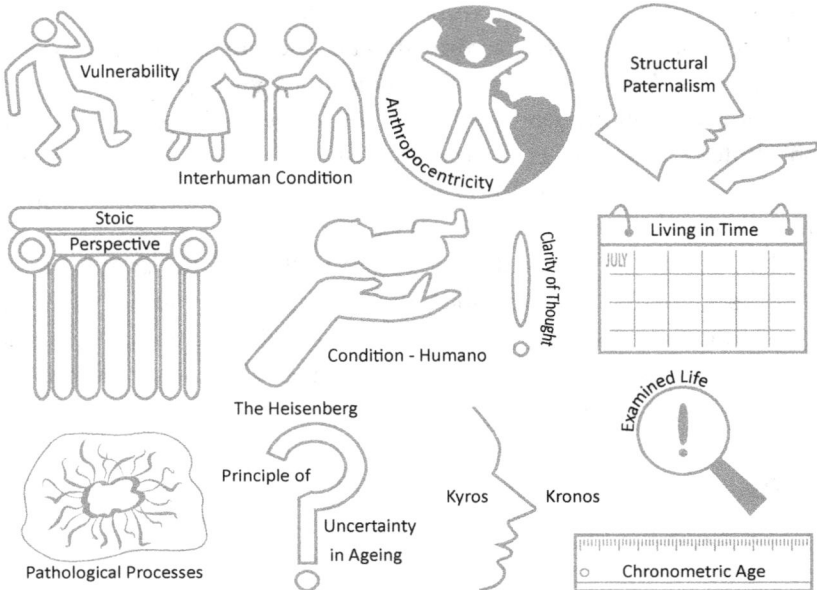

Vulnerability

Interhuman Condition

Anthropocentricity

Structural Paternalism

Stoic Perspective

Clarity of Thought

Living in Time

JULY

Condition - Humano

Examined Life

The Heisenberg

Pathological Processes

Principle of

Uncertainty in Ageing

Kyros

Kronos

Chronometric Age

However, grappling with these theories may not be the only way to study and understand the issues and questions they raise. The exchange of terms is an acknowledgement of these approaches and studies, but the playful method of delivery, tells the audience that their research is not going to be defined or restricted to the application of those notions, but rather using these as a frame of reference.

And, in fact, the authors in their initial scoping exercise, identified a range of additional terms and theories listed below, which, although not directly quoted in this film, provided reference points as the project developed (see next page).

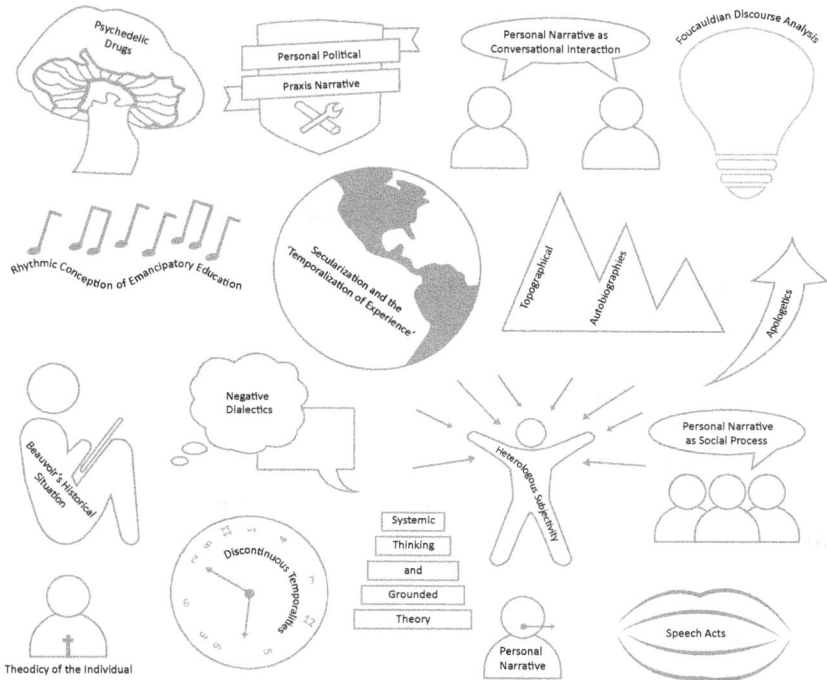

01:23–01:27

CINAGE - Lights, Camera, Action

This is the animated logo used for the CINAGE project films. CINAGE was a Grundtvig multilateral project, supported by the EU Lifelong Learning Programme and was composed of interlinked activities resulting in the production of a learning package, for use by adult educators, and aimed at empowering older people towards achieving a more active ageing. All twelve films made by the four partners, Portugal, Italy, Slovenia and the UK can be found on YouTube https://www. youtube.com/user/cinageproject.

01:29

'If we knew what we were doing it wouldn't be called research would it' (Einstein)

This statement, sometimes attributed to Einstein, was used as a slide in the live paper presentation and points to a creative research process that acknowledges the Uncertainty Principle.

01:29–01:30

We decided to deliver our presentation as a series of letters — during the course of the project, we had written notes and thoughts and reflections to one another, partly as a way of figuring out what would come next and partly to help Teresa 'catch up' with the history of the project, as she only came to it after we had been working on the pilot for over three years.

The images that we use in this segment illustrate the kind of challenges that the participants faced — for example, from 01:50–01:53 the scene of children sitting in front of blue fabric in the studio, is the shooting of the live action for the animated 'blue screen' film, 'Papiyon Vole', which was a very difficult technical challenge.

01:30–02:00

The outcomes from the second cohort of CINAGE students, were four films:

PAPIYON VOLE - based on the memories of a 65-year-old Martinique immigrant and how she could pass on important stories about her heritage to her grandson.

DO NOT DISTURB - a 'carry on' style comedy set in an old people's home looking at the desire to stay young and the stories we tell ourselves that allow us to believe in the fantasy of agelessness.

STORMY WEATHER - the story of two sisters, one dying and the other finding a way to come to terms with her impending loss.

SWANS ARE NOT THE ONLY BIRDS - examining the loss experienced in old age.

Each of the participants in the CINAGE project were supported in writing a film script based on a personal narrative, and the group subsequently selected four of these scripts which then entered into the full development and production process.

02:06–02:11

Moments taken from pre-production on the films made by the second cohort of CINAGE in 2016.

02:11–02:36

In our conference presentation in Copenhagen, we chose to use our emails to one another, discussing the project as we experienced it, because these emails embody the personal voice and thus mirror the autobiographical narratives of the films.

02:36

'We all feel safer when we know where we are going, but creative processes also require us to let ourselves get lost, to force ourselves into leaving the safety of the map behind so that we can surprise ourselves with what we find' (Teresa Brayshaw). This, and other quotations, ideas and thoughts, were part of the PowerPoint conference presentation, but as we have the tools of playing with images, as filmmakers, this floating text is an alternative way of offering these snippets to the audience.

02:36–03:11

Teresa is reflecting upon her first workshop with the 2016 CINAGE participants and the images were those shot during that workshop.

03:00–03:04

When Teresa attributes 'When All Else Fails — Dance' to Beckett she is, of course, paraphrasing Estragon in order to make her point.

03:11–03:21

These ten seconds are an illustration of manipulating the images and facts in order to visually support the words being spoken. Teresa talks about 'working with a series of proposals, exercises, which I know from experience will encourage creative encounters, encouraging risk taking, problem solving....' however, the images for these ten seconds are not of the CINAGE 2016 participants, but are from a workshop we ran at the Copenhagen 'Discourses we Live By' conference, in which we delivered some of the methodology to colleagues.

03:24–04:07

The images take us back to the 2016 CINAGE participants and a quotation from Solnit (A Field Guide to Getting Lost) appears on the screen. This is a visual representation of the layering of ideas and references that would be cited in a written 'paper'. It gives the film audience an opportunity to savour the idea of 'getting lost' whilst remaining with the story Teresa and Jennifer are telling about the CINAGE project.

04:10–06:46

Teresa introduces the idea of 'writing a letter to your 16-year-old self'. We wanted to find a way to communicate to the film's audience, the powerful impact the exercise had on the participants, so invited three of them to come into the studio and read their letters. The beauty of film is that one doesn't need to hear them in their totality — well-chosen moments edited for pace and pathos, illustrate the process.

06:46–06:49

Teresa is a qualified Feldenkrais practitioner and creates learning environments which support embodied knowledge. The positioning at this point in the film of the quotation 'When you know what you are doing you can do what you want' by Moshe Feldenkrais, returns us to the thematic enquiry around notions of certainty, knowledge and the exploration of wisdom which were key research questions during the development process.

06:49–07:08

The images here are again taken from the workshop in Copenhagen where this time the conference participants also co-produced a creative response to one of the original CINAGE films — 'Swans are not the only

Birds'. This both evidences the application of the research methodology and further disseminates the outcomes. As Teresa states '...when these texts are shared, exchanged and bartered with, written over and written through and offered up to the collective writing process...there is the potential for some new and meaningful collective outputs'.

07:08–07:32

The images that accompany Jennifer's description of her teaching experience with older people as 'students' is accompanied by images of the 2016 cohort in the process of making their films.

07:33–07:39

Here, Jennifer mentions her advocacy for making the University a space that is available and accessible to older people.

07:39–08:09

This section describes the success of the project in terms of its inter-generational collaboration. The impact of the two age groups working together as a team provided unexpected, and rich, research opportunities as well as offering valuable experiential learning for our undergraduate students.

08:09–08:20

Since this film was made, Leeds Beckett University has become the first 'Age Friendly University' in England.

08:20–09:04

Because we are first and foremost creative practitioners, we did not want to focus solely on summative evaluations. We felt it necessary to share our own autobiographical narratives and learning experiences through phenomenological methodology.

09:06–09:49

Teresa explores the idea and concept of creativity, how it affects us and how that translates and works in a creative practice. i.e., filmmaking.

09:49–09:57

Teresa reflects upon her ideas concerning creativity and as she muses on 'imagination' we are transported via a Blue Screen studio to an animated world as remembered and imagined by our 65-year-old, Martinique participant who wrote 'Papiyon Vole'!

09:58 - end

Terry Waddington, our oldest participant at 87, reads lines from works authored by T.S. Eliot, Bob Dylan, Sting, Robert Frost, Dante and Robert Browning as the trailer plays for the three original UK CINAGE films — 'Swimming Pool', 'Trapped' and 'Know Thyself'.

POST-PRODUCTION: Reflecting on the Processes, Excerpts from the ESREA (2017) Presentation

Jenny: I have had to find ways to deliver material to students who are hungry to learn but terrified about whether they can tackle something so difficult and outside of their experience. This part has been my major learning curve. In fact, of course, they have so much to offer in comparison to the usual undergraduate, richness of experience, humility, excitement and no sense of entitlement...as a result I have become a passionate advocate of making the university a space that is available and accessible to older people. The undergraduate students who have worked on the film crews making the older peoples' films have told me that this has been the best experience of their time at film school.

They were given respect for what they knew, loved being able to teach and lead, and learned to respect these old people who turned up at 6:00 in the morning and worked full days to 10 at night with energy and commitment to make their films. All those involved last year are clamouring to work on this year's films.

To work without assessment, with no agenda or learning outcomes other than to pass knowledge on, to share expertise, to give opportunity for self-expression and to find new ideas to develop...my own practice has become more reflective and I feel as though I have found a rich area for practice and research... certainly for as many years as I have left!

Teresa: I was surprised by the openness of the group to try things out — to have a go — to play, without the usual anxiety around meaning and end-gaining that is now so prevalent throughout undergraduate educational contexts. Of course, the levels of experience and expertise in the group were tremendous but nevertheless — I was particularly impressed by the quality of engagement in the proposal made which directly addressed the questions of 'where am I now?', 'where am I going?', 'where have I been?'.

I think I know where I'm going and what the next stage of my story is. Jan Baars in his book *Ageing and the art of Living* says ... 'In order to develop a more meaningful culture of ageing — a culture with more respect for the personal identity of aging individuals, is to pay more attention to the different stories that emerge from their reflected experiences.'

So, with this in mind — in the next stage of Cinage Live — I'm going to make a theatre show with the new senior's group about BREXIT — and then I'm going to tour it around Europe. It will be a piece which platforms their voices and opinions and tells the story of why the over 65s in the UK were more than twice as likely as the under 25s to have voted to leave the EU.

Maybe then, through this process, I myself will begin to reconcile the shame, disappointment and deep sense of loss I still feel for the upcoming generation, as a result of the decisions/actions of many of our seniors.

And — for so many reasons — as a teacher, as a mother, as an artist, as a human being — I need to do this practice — this research... In order to understand and process this deep sense of loss — I need to get lost — again!

In her book, *A Field Guide to Getting Lost,* Rebecca Solnit explores the territory of losing something we care about, losing ourselves, losing control. Losing anything is about the familiar falling away, getting lost is about the unfamiliar appearing.

At the start of this chapter we favoured Solnit's highly evocative assertion that: 'Never to get lost is not to live, not to know how to get lost brings you to destruction, and somewhere in the terra incognita in between lies **a life of discovery**'.

We determined to seek the 'terra incognita in between', choosing to live a 'a life of discovery', and are set to continue along that route as are our elderly companions. Join us!

CREDITS: A Bibliography of Texts that Supported the CINAGE project

Baars, J. (2012). *Ageing and the art of living.* Baltimore, MD: The John Hopkins University Press.

Bannerman, C., Sofaer, J. & Watt, J. (eds) (2006). *Navigating the unknown: The creative process in contemporary performing arts.* London: Middlesex University Press.

Beringer, E. (ed) (2010). *Embodied wisdom: The collected papers of Moshe Feldenkrais.* Berkeley, CA: North Atlantic Books.

Bogart, A. (2001). *A director prepares.* Abingdon: Routledge.

Bogart, A. (2007). *And then, you act: Making art in an unpredictable world.* Abingdon: Routledge.

Galliano, J. (ed) (2011). *Dear me: A letter to my sixteen-year-old-self.* New York: Atria Books.

Galliano, J. (ed) (2011). *Dear me: More letters to my sixteen-year-old-self.* London: Simon & Schuster.

Garr, L. (2015). *Becoming aware.* Carlsbad, CA: Hay House.

Heddon, D. (2008). *Autobiography and performance.* Basingstoke: Palgrave Macmillan.

Karpf, A. (2014). *How to age.* Basingstoke: Palgrave Macmillan.

O'Malley, S. (2016). *Advice from my 80-year-old-self.* San Francisco, CA: Chronicle Books.

Read, A. (1995). *Theatre and everyday life: An ethics of performance*. Abingdon: Routledge.

Solnit, R. (2006). *A field guide to getting lost*. Edinburgh: Cannongate Books.

Zaporah, R. (1995). *Action theatre: The improvisation of presence*. Berkeley, CA: North Atlantic Books.

Zuckerman, A. (2008). *Wisdom*. New York: Harry N. Abrams.

Photo by Tom Perkins, CC-BY 4.0

VII.

DISCOURSES THROUGH A SELF-REFLEXIVE LENS: THOUGHTS FROM RESEARCHERS

This final section comprises chapters in which there is a strong element of reflexivity in the examination of discourses within a particular context. We have an account from the UK in which the author reflects on the mechanisms that encouraged her to transcend family expectations and go to university, before using this experience to examine wider participation in higher education. Then another chapter in which the travel is reversed: what starts as a study of schooling for excluded students in the UK becomes a reflective account of the benefits of using a journal during research, not just as a means of recording events, but as a means to interrogate one's own views and understanding during the research process. A third chapter from Finland discusses a collaborative project to support citizens with a Muslim background. In so doing, it offers an insider view of the challenges encountered in handling a creative and transdisciplinary research process that will be of particular interest to those aspiring to join funded projects. Section seven (and the book) ends with a personal overview of a lifetime spent in narrative research from an eminent and recently retired Danish academic. We think this makes a fitting coda.

In 'Diversifying Discourses of Progression to UK Higher Education Through Narrative Approaches' (Ch25), Laura Mazzoli Smith reflects how her teenage reading of Iris Murdoch's novels made her aware that it was possible to challenge social expectations rather than conform to them. This enabled Laura to create an agentive personal counter-narrative to overcome family tradition, go to university, and follow an academic career. Seeing herself as an early example of 'wider participation' and the Murdoch novels as what Raymond Williams terms 'resources of hope' she considers how, by creating and disseminating a diversity of stories that capture individual's learning journeys, we could encourage a broader range of students to apply to university and democratize the system.

In the chapter, 'Using Journaling and Autoethnography to Create Counter-Narratives of School Exclusion in Britain' (Ch26), Helen Woodley describes how she initially sought to give excluded pupils a voice, in the hope that she could put their views to policy-makers and, consequently, convince them to make appropriate adjustments to decisions that affect such pupils. As part of the process, Helen was also exploring ways to collect data without disrupting class activities. This led to her choosing to write field notes, then to more reflective writing and eventually to journaling. Initially this was a way of recording, reflecting and analysing in narrative form but it became a means of self-discovery. Her chapter offers insights into the way this method can be adopted by others.

In, 'Reflections on a Creative Arts Project to Explore the Resilience of Young Adults with a Muslim Background in Finland', Helena Oikarinen-Jabai (Ch27) offers a detailed and candid account of the reality of involvement in a participatory project that is a collaboration across disciplinary boundaries. Both researchers and participants held different priorities and the creative nature of the project further widened the scope for interpretation. The author offers interesting insights into the processes of bringing the project to conclusion in a successful exhibition and also conveys the issues that were important to participants with a Muslim background (captured, for example, in this appellation).

'Discourses, Cultural Narratives, and Genre in Biographical Narratives: A Personal Overview' (Ch28) offers a fitting coda to the chapters in this book. Marianne Horsdal shares insights developed over a long career in narrative research and explains her own choice of cultural narratives as an alternative framework to discourses.

The chapters in this section have a joint coherence in their focus on reflection and reflexivity but also relate well to other contributions in the book. A degree of reflection is common within narrative and life history research; in this book, also in the chapters by Dyson (Ch1), by Middleton (Ch8), Pathak (Ch9), Mascarenhas (Ch18), Sprung (Ch20), Chan (Ch21), Ylitapio-Mäntylä and Mäkiranta (Ch22), and in the conversations captured in Brayshaw and Granville (Ch24). Readers of Mazzoli Smith may find Sheridan's study of progression in an Irish University useful (Ch10); those reading Woodley's account of pupil exclusion should be mindful that this represents the next stage, if preventative work in schools such as the Nurture groups that Middleton examines (Ch8), fails to turn behaviour around. They may also like to look at Etta's story in Dyson (Ch1) that is also about Pupil Referral Units. Readers of Oikarinen-Jabai may wish to look at the other texts that describe creative interventions, the chapters by Sprung (Ch20), and Brayshaw and Granville (Ch24).

All four chapters in this final section demonstrate the usefulness of reflexivity through either academic deliberation and/or in practice. Importantly, they link reflexivity to external research themes demonstrating how individualized thinking and writing can inform the interpretation of material about others. In effect, the authors are using reflexivity to question their own thinking and in writing reflexively are making internal processes visible, either with a broad gaze, like Horsdal, or through a more focused lens. They are trusting the reader to accept their once private thoughts respectfully even when he or she disagrees with what is said. This position of trust seems an appropriate endpoint for a collection of chapters in a book that holds diversity and respect for others as core values.

25. Diversifying Discourses of Progression to UK Higher Education Through Narrative Approaches

Laura Mazzoli Smith

Laura Mazzoli Smith considers widening participation in higher education in the light of Williams' notion of resources of hope. Taking an autoethnographic approach, Laura demonstrates how her reading of Iris Murdoch as a young person facilitated her own entry into higher education. Through understanding Murdoch as someone who challenged orthodox worldviews, she found the confidence to develop a personalized counter-narrative to allow her to break with family tradition and open up new pathways of progression.

'…there are in fact no masses, but only ways of seeing people as masses'. (Williams, 1989, p. 11)

This chapter commences from the critique of how some research and practice with marginalized or disadvantaged learners utilizes an impoverished and generalized discourse of individualistic capacities — such as aspirations, motivation and self-esteem — to explain educational 'success' or 'failure'. It is a chapter focused on correcting what can be the rigid discourse of widening participation to higher education through appeal to the idea of 'resources of hope', in the words of Raymond Williams, which sits outside of an abstracted set of concepts that are now axiomatic in the field. It is a chapter drawing on

https://doi.org/10.11647/OBP.0203.25

biographical methods as a critical/emancipatory approach in opposing the reductions of the dominant discourse, by seeking to understand how one or more counter-discourses may help people to think beyond the one that predominates. It is a chapter, too, where I reflect on personal experiences in order to better understand some of the issues around widening participation as a concept and practice, an aim and/or an achievement, drawing on my longstanding interest in stories as both research tools and outcomes.

The discourse of widening participation has a number of unintended consequences. It promotes binaries, simplistic models of success versus failure, or aspiration versus lack of aspiration (Taylor, 2008) and employs deficit discourses, which position non-traditional entrants to higher education as 'other' (Burke, 2002; Walker, 2003). The discourse contains value judgements, such as in the 'civilizing' function of higher education in shaping democratic, inclusive societies (Archer, 2003); and draws on stereotypes of different groups (Taylor, 2008). Indeed the seminal phrase 'raising aspirations', in use almost universally in the discourse of widening participation in England, has itself been critiqued as being a largely misconceived conception, since a focus on low aspirations is not the problem *per se* — rather realizing aspirations is the issue when successive barriers are to be faced (Carter-Wall & Whitfield, 2012; Cummings et al., 2012). The paucity of aspirations may then be what significant others read into the behaviours and narratives of marginalized youth, but research into these narratives and lived experiences conveys a more complex picture of aspirations that are successively — and arguably rationally — reconfigured in the face of challenges and lack of recognition (Cummings et al., 2012).

This chapter will articulate these critiques through the deployment of reflexivity in biographical methods to investigate and make available what is referred to in this chapter as counter-discourses. In the first and main example, I employ auto-ethnography to situate myself within such spaces and access what were for me resources of hope — constitutive of a particular counter-discourse — in navigating an unconventional route into higher education. This has the benefit of changing the power dynamic from those instances when the researcher remains abstracted from the structures of feeling that such discourses engender, as in much widening participation research.

The terminology of discourses and counter-discourses is in use here to identify the role of language in shaping social relations and the social world (Tamboukou & Livholts, 2015). The approach could also be termed a form of cultural discourse analysis situated wholly within the reflexive positioning of the researcher in the first example. It draws on Burr's (2003) socio-constructionist premises of epistemology in taking a critical stance towards taken-for-granted knowledge (here the discourse of student progression and widening participation); the historical and cultural specificity of knowledge (here within the micro-specificities of the life worlds of researcher and student respectively); knowledge as sustained by social processes (that is as socially constructed); and knowledge and social action as coterminous (here demonstrated by what counter-discourses enable in the way of social action). Burr describes truth as a discursive force for the production of knowledge about what it is possible to say and, in this example, I explicitly interrogate how different truths about social identities and relations may be productive of counter-discourses producing different forms of knowledge. In asking students to explore how they shape self in storied form, as part of my own research, I was led inadvertently to reflect on this same question in relation to a similar point in my life.

Conceptualizing counter-discourses as 'resources of hope' offers an enriched, complex web of potentialities that should be central to widening participation work and which could provide a better framework from which to work towards the diversification and shifting of discourses that constrain, dominate or hurt, however inadvertently. This could reorient the framing of the problem, from strategies done 'to' students, for example to raise their aspirations/attainment, to resources, both individual and collective, from which they can draw hope and work around dominant cultural representations. This research aims to uncover discursive resources that work to enable young people to think around those that dominate (because we know that this is the case for some — those that 'succeed against the odds'), that create a cultural image of success, which employ the binary of the achieving/ aspiring student and the likelihood of failure for others from the 'wrong' backgrounds. This chapter will demonstrate how through reflective biographical work we can see examples of the counter-discourses that enable new socio-cultural structures of experience to arise. I am therefore interested in employing discourse as a vehicle for both constraining and enabling critical change processes for individual learning (Evans, 2013).

A focus on available discourses of progression to higher education should also produce a shift away from the individualization of perceived 'lacks' to a focus on relationships and socio-cultural representations. This is another way of saying that we should attend more closely to how individuals create culture and society through access to discourse and not primarily to how culture shapes individuals in both structural and discursive ways in widening participation work. It is this bottom up cultural creation and appropriation by individuals that I am interested in with respect to higher education discourses of progression throughout the life course. Understanding how individuals adopt and shape particular stories from the discourses available to them is a challenge for widening participation research, not least because, as I will demonstrate through an auto-ethnographic piece of work, these processes are not necessarily immediately obvious.

Both 'having voice' and also 'finding a voice' are then part of the problematic *status quo* with respect to which learners are routinely dissuaded from accessing, or even conceiving of, higher education. The reflective, retrospective element elaborated here may be problematic for approaches focused on an objective version of the 'truth,' as I will suggest that the meaning of counter-discourses that facilitate new representations may sometimes only become available on reinterpreting past events through later understandings and insights. Counter-discourses may, we could say, work at a deeper, or less conscious level, and as such be less amenable to interrogation in the present.

This chapter, finally, is oriented in the values-based perspective that supporting learners to higher education at any time of life is a good thing, not because this choice is routinely the best one for everyone, but because choices may have been restricted through lack of access to knowledge of and support for diverse routes through learning and it is important to strive to ensure meaningful choice exists here, particularly in a climate of high tuition fees, as is now the case in England. (This is notwithstanding the fact that all choice is adaptive to the extent that contextual framing is a given, as discussed well in the context of widening participation by Bridges, 2005, for instance.) It is also based on a number of suppositions about identity and narrativity, particularly work around the notion of identity capital and articulating a narrative of the self (Warin, 2015).

Narratives of Learning Take Many Forms, and Diversity Matters

'We must emphasise not the ladder but the common highway, for every man's ignorance diminishes me, and every man's skill is a common gain of breath'. (Williams, 1989, p. 15)

As Raymond Williams speaks about culture as ordinary (1989), the remit and creation of us all, so we must see diverse discourses about higher education and lifelong learning as ordinary — although not always accessible to us all. I do not mean ordinary in the sense of unexceptional (although a previous research participant articulated with great passion how he would not have succeeded against the odds were he to believe himself doing something extra-ordinary, (Mazzoli Smith & Laing, 2016), but ordinary primarily in the sense of ubiquitous and necessary. A hegemonic discourse of university access, the ultimately successful student climbing successive rungs of the ladder, from which other 'non-traditional' discourses are deviations, marginalizes an array of deeply significant, plural and diverse stories, yet these are often unrecognized as such, or not thought to be significant if they are not about progression in learning in some explicitly causal way.

In writing about and researching the dominant discourse on widening participation to higher education, I found myself unexpectedly accessing for the first time a personal resource of hope on my own journey to higher education, which I will argue functioned as a counter-discourse to the dominant cultural trope of the successful student. Whilst the specificity of my story is likely to differ from others, some theoretical generalizations suggest ways in which we in the research community can support the diversification of discourses of widening participation, by drawing on more varied methods than usually pertain in the field, to explore how resources of hope can manifest in counter-discourses, which help us 'work around' those that dominate.

In my case, I reflect on how the novels of Iris Murdoch provided me with narratives of new and diverse structures of feeling before, and throughout, my higher education years. Through reflective analysis I now understand these to have been functioning as a counter-discourse, a way of thinking beyond and so undermining the dominant, narrow, discourse of student success and progression, despite the fact that the novels are not explicitly about this. Auto-ethnography is not an approach that I had previously used, but it became the default method to describe this systematic reflective analysis of a period of my own personal experience, which had returned to the present as I engaged with analogous periods in my research participants' lives. The self-conscious and socially conscious nature of this act was neither planned, nor initially welcome. The resulting small auto-ethnographic study is therefore a reflection on this period of my life, as the process by which I analysed how my participants were able to access counter-discourses led to a self-reflexive analysis of how I, too, had done so. I argue that these varied counter-discourses served a similar functional purpose in diversifying the discourse about educational progression that was predominant.

The Novels of Iris Murdoch: Thinking Beyond a Narrow Discourse of Success

Iris Murdoch (1919–1999) was an Anglo-Irish novelist and philosopher, author of some twenty-six novels focused on the key themes of morality, relationships and the unconscious, as well as plays, poetry and philosophy. Iris Murdoch's many novels hold within them narratives of flawed, neurotic, complex and contradictory characters living and learning in a multitude of ways: the successful, wealthy psychoanalyst paid to alleviate the trauma of others, busily committing incest at weekends; the successful writer in his seaside retreat quietly enslaving his long lost love; the postulant nun and schizophrenic, passionately in love with the failed priest who leads her lay religious community. On the face of it the particularities of these contexts bore no relation to my own, yet nonetheless between the ages of 16 and 21 these novels enabled me to connect with diverse structures of emotion, thought and action, taking me far beyond my own context and enabling a wider imaginary of other lives and the structures of feeling that these opened up. Murdoch was pre-eminent at evoking the inner world of fantasy, projection and delusion, whilst celebrating a diverse range of ordinary foibles and eccentricities in her characters. As her biographer Peter Conradi says:

> One source of positive pleasure in the bizarrerie offered by her plots comes from our sense that, as Murdoch has often averred, people are secretly much odder, less rational, more often powered by obsession and passion than they outwardly pretend or know, and that the novelist is revealing such secrets in creating her (imaginary) people. (Conradi, 1989, p. 6)

In writing about the dominant discourse of progression to higher education in my research, I came to reflect on how Murdoch's novels constituted for me in their imaginary worlds a discourse that countered the institutional educational discourses that tended to the conservative and the rhetorical, ill-defined recourse to 'realizing potential' or 'aiming higher' for instance in order to achieve 'success'. In their holding together of these individual eccentricities and foibles in the ordinary and quotidian, Murdoch's novels introduced me to a multiplicity of ways to succeed and fail — often at the same time — which ran so counter to the hegemonic discourse of the successful student and a linear, rational trajectory of university progression that I felt subject to. The educational discourses during those years felt overpowering yet were narrow. In struggling to stay on track and epitomize the successful student, the only alternative to not doing so felt like failure.

The method I embarked on involved a self-reflexive re-reading of Murdoch's novels, whilst writing about resources of hope as counter-discourses for other students. This auto-ethnographic analysis positioned Murdoch's novels as a resource of hope I drew on, in the form of both introducing and legitimating diverse discourses of progress through life. Whilst a sociological understanding of these novels would be as a form of cultural capital (Bourdieu, 2011), imparting a rich set of cultural values and meanings otherwise not accessible to me, I argue that this is not an adequate explanation, as the concept of cultural capital fails to engage with the subjective experience of objective possibilities (West, 2014). A psycho-social approach would suggest that these novels helped me to work and think around the tyranny of the simplified, narrow discourse of successful progression that I felt constrained by. The richness of Murdoch's characters and plots, in contradistinction to what was my narrow socio-cultural context and the equally narrow messages of what educational success meant and for whom, provided me with not only models, but more crucially structures of feeling that could enable me to imagine difference and contradiction as other than failure.

In this retrospective narrative of my youthful, somewhat obsessive relationship to Murdoch's *oeuvre* and its role as a resource of hope, I would suggest that an important element was the unconscious juxtaposition of the glossy pictures of university undergraduates on prospectuses — the successful student — with Murdoch's array of eccentric and earnest protagonists, muddling through chaotic lives, and prey to contingencies which they tried, but routinely failed, to control. Graham (2013), utilizing Foucault, describes the constitutive effect of brochure images, marking out the 'ideal' student as a dividing practice. Without diversity, these images take on substantial power, creating megaliths of the mind, likely to leave many young people and adults feeling inadequate.

I now look back on how Murdoch's characters' vulnerabilities and aberrances likely constituted a resource of hope by enabling me to think beyond the boundaries of highly prescribed, singular identities and expectations of a particular kind of success, and therefore failure, to a more diverse array of lived lives. The 'success discourse' and related images of the 'good' student construe such young people as rational, self-governing, autonomous and empowered. Murdoch's novels abound with characters that are driven by irrational desire, repeatedly failing to self-govern, who depend — often fatally — on others and who are prey to contingency. Yet, simultaneously, they were often accomplished in their career and the development of their intellect, reflecting explicitly on matters philosophical as ends in themselves, and in so doing subverting the discourse of instrumental educational outcomes or narrow models of success against which I was straining.

Arguably the widening participation discourse of 'aiming higher' and 'realizing potential' carries a particular moralizing force. Murdoch's novels are full of characters who attempt to moralize and coerce the world, but for which they often pay a high price, while the hedonists get off altogether more lightly, another reason a young person may well have taken pleasure in these novels. Murdoch's characters' lives are given to disjuncture and rupture, as they create, or have foisted upon them, the shocking or the unforeseen in life, particularly those who are most earnest to control and preordain. The critic Lorna Sage commented that Murdoch's plots were a 'device for humiliating those who wish to contain experience or abstract from it' (in Conradi, 1989, p. 99). I took great delight in such irreverent narratives and I now reflect on how they gave me permission to question those who attempted to control and preordain my future through a discourse of making use of one's talents and aiming 'high' in a linear, narrow route to higher education progression as the foremost measure of success for a young person after leaving school. I have found similar concerns articulated by some of the widening participation students I have worked with, interviewed both in order to understand non-traditional routes to higher education (Mazzoli Smith & Laing, 2016) and about what constitutes fairness in education (Mazzoli Smith et al., 2017).

The Importance of Diverse Structures of Feeling and Social Imaginaries for Widening Participation

M y interpretation from this auto-ethnographic study is that these novels were read and reread in part because they offered a way of working through and thinking around the contradiction that successful students are made to feel if they don't aspire to a particular pathway and/or feel they are failing. What may well have been provided was a way in which to learn to live with this perceived contradiction. The dichotomy often articulated by students in distress — aiming to conform, or being expected to, or thought to conform to the empowered self-regulating student, whilst feeling the opposite — inevitably produces anxiety. I suggest that diverse discourses of progression to higher education throughout the life course could militate against anxiety borne of nonconformity to some ideal as portrayed through narrow discourses of student success. Through the personal tutor system within the university, for instance, students have told me that they have resisted applying for extensions to assignments or temporarily suspending studies, even when they have had strong medical evidence to do so, because this is not what 'successful' students do.

My experience as a researcher leads me to argue that we fail to see with adequate sensitivity the implications of positioning young people as both lacking in various capitals — social, cultural, emotional — alongside promoting a narrow discourse of success in widening participation activity. What is often read as an individual deficit could also be read as a discourse deficit in terms of narrow vision, and over-simplification. The data with which we structure our knowledge of young people as marginalized or disadvantaged, alongside the methodologies that we then employ to solve the problems that follow, too often eclipse what may actually be significant resources of hope to a young person, or indeed any person. I suggest that these may come in the form of counter- or diverse discourses, which if recognized and/or promoted as such, could support working around the structural and discursive barriers that too often become unassailable.

Such counter-discourses may provide a means to imagine, accept and recognize the self as complex and contradictory, yet crucially without the evocation of intolerable anxiety, which we know many students experience. The argument of this chapter is that the promotion of diverse discourses in various fields — here widening participation — may be a functional vehicle through which we can promote this perspective and facilitate how we can live with complexity and contradiction that at other times can threaten to overwhelm or limit. This may in turn help students who face multiple challenges to live with an imaginary of possible versions of student progression beyond narrow ideals.

Re-Description and Diversification

R ichard Rorty's philosophical work informs the supposition that the imaginary can play an important role in shaping identities and achievements. Rorty (1989) argued that human solidarity is not to be achieved through willed, individual self-creation and self-reflection, but through imagination and novels, for instance, which let us 're-describe ourselves'. He spoke about self-knowledge not as a process of discovery, but as one of creation. Rorty discusses Proust and Nietzsche, for whom, he says, there is nothing more powerful than self-re-description and he talks about how only other human beings can propose languages for us to speak — on his view, truth is made, rather than found. Yet the framework in which much widening participation work happens is largely positivistic, focusing on how language gets at the truth, rather than how it creates it, which could be construed as one of its *de facto* limitations. In Iris Murdoch's novels I was provided with a novel language for re-description and simultaneously warned about the pitfalls of seeing one description — in one dominant discourse — as a final truth about self, place, and others. Rorty's view of the need for equal opportunities for self-creation is therefore highly pertinent to this chapter and yet this is of course not a normal part of what we mean when we talk about equal opportunity in education. This chapter is intended to highlight how taken-for-granted and likely un-recognized and under-theorized such opportunities may well be.

As has been said, Murdoch routinely challenges her characters through her plots and those that come away less scathed are those, often, who can hold conflicting emotions and thoughts together. Those who desire wholeness and completeness, which she often associates with moral hubris and the desire for goodness, flounder. In her philosophical writings, such as *Against Dryness* (1961), Murdoch does not argue for a choice between realism and myth, but for a dialectic or mediation between them. In her novels I found such a dialogue between forms of life and modes of thought, which in repeat re-reading, provided me with access to structures of feeling that would have helped allay anxiety. Murdoch's characters therefore provided a way of militating against the outcomes of the cognitive dissonance that must result for many students who become invested in narrowly conceived educational discourses about success. Freeman says that:

> ...in becoming aware of the ways in which we are determined and in considering alternate modes of living our lives than the ones bequeathed us, we denature and demystify the established order of selfhood itself, thus paving the way for different stories to be told. (Freeman, 2015, p. 186)

I did not ask whether there was any truth in the actions of Murdoch's characters, but in what possible worlds these actions could be true, the very fact of which altered the range of my own possible worlds. If, increasingly, learning and educational achievement are tightly bound to particular models of 'the good student' (Taylor, 2008) in a narrow range of possible worlds, then a version of freedom for me was found in the highly wrought depictions of adult learning and development that continued alongside, in spite of and sometimes in virtue of, personal failings.

Accessing Diverse Narratives of Progression as a Means of Diversifying the Dominant Discourse

A main concern of this chapter is that we need to find more and better ways of researching, understanding and promoting how individuals not only counter the narrowing of opportunities for self-creation in an increasingly performative educational landscape (Ball, 2012) and in the face of a narrow dominant discourse of higher education progression, but also our own prejudices and lacunae in recognizing these in our own lives and in those of others. The last section of the chapter sets out several examples, which demonstrate how this may be possible through alternative methodologies and what challenges there are inherent in these, not least that the focus on care leavers as marginalized in some of these studies serves to confirm this position even as it seeks to ameliorate it.

Recent life history work with care-experienced adults (Duncalf, 2010) demonstrates how a synchronic research perspective can itself negate or obscure diverse and complex patterns of progression through education and lifelong learning, here with respect to what care-experienced adults were doing later in their lives than is often the focal point. When research views learning lives diachronically, these care leavers were not so likely to be out of education, but rather were accessing education at different points in their lives, in different ways to what a perspective at age eighteen would reveal. It was argued that lifelong learning for care leavers was possible only when more basic support needs were first met (Maslow & Herzberg, 1954), something I heard directly from care leavers on a panel at a National Network for the Education of Care Leavers event in London in 2015. Hence accessing education later in life, when other needs had been met, was more likely to be the case than at age eighteen. In this example a diachronic research perspective offers more diverse narratives not only *of*, but also *for* this particular group and can provide support for thinking beyond the dominant discourses of care leavers' relative failure in education when measured at a single point in time. As one of the participants in a previous research project said to me, knowing the statistics on educational progression for care leavers as a teenager made him feel backed into a corner, but these statistics were of course for progression to higher education at one point in life only and therefore unnecessarily restrictive if seen as a single end-point (Mazzoli Smith & Laing, 2016).

So, a relevant issue here is whether the politics of hope is connected to the idea of epistemic justice. Fricker (2007) says that one can be harmed in one's capacity as a 'knower' by virtue of a marginalized status and if so, are structural determinants implicated in the availability of resources of hope, in either implicit and tacit, or more explicit ways? Are diverse discourses of progression to higher education more available to some young people and adults than to others, both literally and in terms of what they can convey? Does democratizing knowledge through diversifying discourses mitigate the impact of this? I want to suggest that the answer to these questions is yes.

One way of attempting to deliberately democratize or widen a narrow discourse about university progression and widening participation is through the use of the digital medium to share stories. I will mention two projects designed to change and diversify stories through horizontal dialogues, which bypass professional mediation, but in different ways. One is an app, *Inspire Me!*, designed as a vehicle to inspire, advise and mentor care leavers in an exogenous way by The National Institute of Adult Continuing Education. The other, *Changing Stories*, is a project at Newcastle University, with aims of democratizing who has the power to speak, through utilizing varied life stories and narrative learning to diversify the over-arching discourse of successful student progression to higher education.

Inspire Me! enables young people in care to access aspects of the life stories of young adults who were themselves care-experienced. These are unlikely to be lengthy life histories, rather they are designed as short fact-filled pieces providing young people in care with information and so provide some of the mentoring they may be missing out on in their everyday experiences. It is ostensibly about raising aspirations through the provision of knowledge from the very people who benefitted from it themselves and went on to succeed against the odds. *Changing Stories* is a portal for current university students of all ages to tell their own digital story of getting to university and becoming a student, in an unmediated way, i.e., using their own words, videos or images. This project aspires to put students at the heart of a widening participation intervention, but also takes account of critiques of widening participation work, which suggest that higher education institutions are necessarily, at times, part of the very cultures of elitism from which disadvantaged students feel themselves excluded, hence the stories are to be hosted on institutional sites to mitigate this. A literature review on widening participation to higher education had as one of its key findings that 'higher education students and other positive role models can make a significant contribution to delivery of information, advice and guidance interventions' (Moore et al., 2013, p. 5). Yet I would suggest that this has to happen in such a way that removes the likelihood of hegemonic 'good student' discourses (Taylor, 2008).

Students are invited to share with others their journey to and through higher education, in order to expose others to multitudes of ways to learn and progress in education, which encompass varied failures and varied successes, these being defined by the students themselves. Narrow discourses of success do not of course always fit even those supposedly 'entitled' to higher education, the middle-classes, those with cultural capital, the right postcode and parents who have been to university. Moreover, diverse narratives can challenge the notion of 'kinds' and 'types', recalling the quote by Raymond Williams at the start of this chapter, and simple stories of success or assumptions about end points in learning lives. Diverse discourses of this kind would potentially bring with them much needed recognition of diverse forms of knowledge, experience and learning potential; 'learners can bring diverse forms of capital into universities and via good enough recognition, claim space for self, agency, and social justice' (West, 2014, p. 80). Access to diverse stories that make contradiction not only possible but normal and bearable, could function for others as resources of hope, analogous to what I accessed through the novels of Iris Murdoch as a young person.

Goodson's (2010) conception of narrative learning and action potential drives this conception of narrative capital. By default, these narratives will be oriented towards action potential because of the context in which they are generated (progressing to higher education) and towards diversity both between and within narratives. The aim of *Changing Stories* is that personal stories can contribute to public, political (counter) discourses. Goodson argues that 'strategies to facilitate narrative learning are currently unexplored and hence underdeveloped' (2010, p. 132) and an approach like *Changing Stories* and similar others that have begun to appear in higher education institutions, could provide a learning resource to test and utilize narrative learning as a widening participation tool.

The expectation is not just that these narratives will communicate realist events in a transparent way but will perhaps more importantly constitute a varied array of learning journeys, making available many more possible imaginary worlds than are usually known to prospective students. A narrative is generally purposive, moving towards an ending and, in this sense, I am taking the critical humanist perspective of an optimistic view of narrative learning, 'posing narrative as a means to recuperate individual and social agency' (Andrews et al., 2002, p. 7). Jacobs (2002) is one of many authors writing on narrative to state that civil society must contain public spaces for constructing alternative narratives and that these introduce new perspectives through narrative creation, or put a different way, provide the opportunity for counter- or diverse discourses that enable thinking around those that predominate. In our recent chapter (Mazzoli Smith & Laing, 2016), such transformative learning spaces were discussed, where the telling of varied life stories created new horizons of possibility for others. Yet it is striking how few such spaces are available through institutional forums, especially for prospective students.

Conclusion: Narrative Imagination and Discourse

'...the revelation of the diversity of individual world-views, of the plurality of ethical life-worlds, of deviance, fluidity and irony, is itself a liberation in the context of ubiquitous frameworks of social institutionalism proclaiming behavioural and moral homogeneity'. (Rapport, 2010, p. 21)

Rapport is here reflecting on the conflicted nature of fieldwork and the limitation of one's own vantage-point, and the moral benefits that result from putting into comparative perspective societal roles and beliefs, however partial the overall study may be. He also draws on Ricœur in reflecting on how far individuals know themselves and are known by others through the stories that they and others tell about themselves. Rapport draws on this idea of 'narrative identity' for ethical advantage, claiming that it is of benefit for people to recognize that individual, group and cultural level identities are not fixed and this stance may make us more able to accommodate the stories of others. He goes on to say that the stories of others may make it more possible for us to imagine their lives (as in fiction, for me with Iris Murdoch's characters) as 'we might extend a generosity towards our own stories [...] not being rigid in our conception of them' (Rapport, 2010, p. 22). Again, it is this openness to fluidity and thinking/working around the rigidity of dominant discourses, not only in widening participation but arguably in much of education today, which may be a resource of hope for others, too.

Diversifying the discourses of student progression through sharing widely narratives of progressing to higher education across the life course draws heavily on the concept of narrative imagination, that 'the way we see the world is only one way amongst infinite possibilities' (Andrews, 2014, p. 27). Nussbaum (1997) says that narrative imagination is necessary to transport an individual into the frame of meaning of another person whose life circumstances are different, which gives us the tools to decipher meaning from another's perspective. Going back to Murdoch's narratives, these different perspectives expand the horizon of the possible: 'Through exercising our narrative imagination, we increase our awareness of the choices available to us' (Andrews, 2014, p. 110).

Narrative imagination thus depends on access to narratives that not only diversify but unseat, transgress and liberate us from hegemonic stories and discourses, de-centring the idea of centralized knowledge. This way of displacing central knowledge and discourses makes ideology visible (Burke, 2002), hence the importance of *Changing Stories* being hosted on higher education websites and platforms. More diverse narratives of pathways to higher education and through learning will be of use not only to potential students, but importantly also to those working in higher education, who can engage in a creative re-positioning of the marginalized learner. Such institutional-level reflection is also important and part of a much-needed shift in higher education from a politics of representation of certain groups, to a politics of recognition of more diverse knowledges and identities alongside (Fraser, 2014).

Finally, increased access to diverse narratives of educational progression may also function as a means through which young pupils may be able to develop identity capital (Warin, 2015). Warin demonstrates how particular kinds of discourses and the opportunities made available in privileged families foster the construction of a personal sense of self. This may also be fostered through narrative learning, and we should not only see the formation of cultural capital as resulting from the crucible of the family, as the dominant discourse maintains. Walker (2003) refers to how gaining knowledge and constructing successful learner identities should go hand in hand. In this chapter I have advocated the availability of diverse narratives of progression to higher education as well as a better understanding of resources of hope that may function to counter and transgress the dominant narrow discourse, and through recourse to narrative learning, support the development of more agentic learner identities. But this is not to see the learner identity as a fixed or generalizable quality, but rather as a capacity that can be shaped and reshaped anew through articulating and re-articulating a narrative of the self in order to achieve what Walker refers to as 'deep participation and ownership' (2003, p. 176).

References

Andrews, M. (2014). *Narrative imagination and everyday life*. Oxford: Oxford University Press.

Andrews, M., Sclater, S.D., Squire, C. & Treacher, A. (2002). *Lines of narrative: Psychosocial perspectives*. Abingdon: Routledge. https://doi.org/10.1093/acprof:oso/9780199812394.001.0001

Archer, L. (2003). The 'value' of higher education. In: Archer, L., Hutchings, M. & Ross, A. (eds), *Higher Education and Social Class: Issues of exclusion and inclusion*. Abingdon: Routledge.

Ball, S.J. (2012). Performativity, commodification and commitment: An I-spy guide to the neoliberal university. *British Journal of Educational Studies*, 60(1): 17–28. https://doi.org/10.1080/00071005.2011.650940

Bourdieu, P. (2011/1986). The forms of capital. *Cultural theory: An anthology*, 1: 81–93.

Bridges, D. (2005). *Widening participation in Higher Education: The philosopher and the bricklayer revisited*. Paper presented to Philosophy of Education Conference, 1–3 April at the Institute of Education, London.

Burke, P.J. (2002). Towards a collaborative methodology: An ethnography of widening educational participation. *The Australian Educational Researcher*, 29(1): 115–36. https://doi.org/10.1007/BF03219772

Burr, V. (2003). *Social constructionism*. Abingdon: Routledge.

Carter-Wall, C. & Whitfield, G. (2012). *The role of aspirations, attitudes and behaviour in closing the educational attainment gap*. York, UK: Joseph Rowntree Foundation.

Conradi, P. (1989). *The saint and the artist: A study of the fiction of Iris Murdoch*. London: HarperCollins.

Cummings, C., Laing, K., Law, J., McLaughlin, J., Papps, I., Todd, L. & Woolner, P. (2012). *Can changing aspirations and attitudes impact on educational attainment? A review of interventions*. York, UK: Joseph Rowntree Foundation.

Duncalf, Z. (2010). *Listen Up! Adult care leavers speak out*. Manchester: Care Leavers' Association.

Evans, R. (2013). Learning and knowing. Narratives, memory and biographical knowledge in interview interaction. *European Journal for Research on the Education and Learning of Adults*, 4(1): 17–31. https://doi.org/10.3384/rela.2000-7426.rela0092

Fraser, N. (2014). *Justice interruptus: Critical reflections on the 'postsocialist' condition*. Abingdon: Routledge. https://doi.org/10.4324/9781315822174

Freeman, M. (2015). *Rewriting the self: History, memory, narrative*. Abingdon: Routledge.

Fricker, M. (2007). *Epistemic injustice: Power and the ethics of knowing*. Oxford: Oxford University Press.

Goodson, I.F., Biesta, G., Tedder, M. & Adair, N. (2010). *Narrative learning*. Abingdon: Routledge.

Graham, C. (2013). Discourses of widening participation in the prospectus documents and websites of six English higher education institutions. *British Journal of Sociology of Education*, 34(1): 76–93. https://doi.org/10.1080/01425692.2012.692048

Jacobs, R. (2002). Narrative, civil society and public culture. In: Andrews, M., Day Sclater, S., Squire, C. & Treacher, A. (eds), *Lines of narrative — Psychosocial perspectives*. Abingdon: Routledge.

Maslow, A. & Herzberg, A. (1954). Hierarchy of needs. In: Maslow, A. (ed), *Motivation and Personality*. New York: Harper.

Mazzoli Smith, L. & Laing, K. (2016). Creating a transformational space through narrative: Looked after young people tell their life stories. In: Formenti, L. & West, L. (eds), *Stories that make a difference: Exploring the collective, social and political potential of narratives in adult education research*. Milan: Pensa Multimedia.

Mazzoli Smith, L., Todd, L. & Laing, K. (2017). Students' views on fairness in education: The importance of relational justice and stakes fairness. *Research Papers in Education*, 33(3): 1–18. https://doi.org/10.1080/02671522.2017.1302500

Murdoch, I. (1961). Against dryness — A polemical sketch. *Encounter*, 16(1): 16–20.

Nussbaum, M.C. (1997). *Cultivating humanity*. Cambridge, MA: Harvard University Press.

Rapport, N. (2010). The ethics of participant-observation: Personal reflections on fieldwork in England. In: Collins, P. & Gallinat, A. (eds), *The ethnographic self as resource: Writing memory and experience into ethnography*. Oxford: Berghahn.

Rorty, R. (1989). *Contingency, irony, and solidarity*. Cambridge: Cambridge University Press.

Tamboukou, M. & Livholts, M. (2015). *Discourse and narrative methods*. London: Sage.

Taylor, Y. (2008). Good students, bad pupils: Constructions of 'aspiration', 'disadvantage' and social class in undergraduate-led widening participation work. *Educational Review*, 60(2): 155–68. https://doi.org/10.1080/00131910801934029

Walker, M. (2003). Framing Social Justice in Education: What does the 'capabilities' approach offer? *British Journal for Educational Studies*, 51(2): 168–87. https://doi.org/10.1111/1467-8527.t01-2-00232

Warin, J. (2015). Identity Capital: An application from a longitudinal ethnographic study of self-construction during the years of school. *British Journal of Sociology of Education*, 36(5): 689–706. https://doi.org/10.1080/01425692.2013.849565

Williams, R. (1989). *Resources of hope: Culture, democracy, socialism*. London and New York: Verso.

West, L. (2014). When Bourdieu met Winnicott, and Honneth: Bodily matters in the experiences of non-traditional learners. In: Formenti, L., West, L. & Horsdal, M. (eds), *Embodied narratives: Connecting stories, bodies, cultures and ecologies*. Odense: University Press of Southern Denmark.

26. Using Journaling and Autoethnography to Create Counter-Narratives of School Exclusion in Britain

Helen Woodley

Helen Woodley describes an insider study of a pupil referral unit (for excluded children) that challenges the orthodoxies that are commonly attributed to such facilities. She seeks to give the pupils a voice, and thereby to modify the views of the public and policymakers. Helen discovered the power of journaling and autoethnography as methods of data collection and interpretation, and demonstrates their value as research tools.

For many years I was a teacher of pupils with Special Educational Needs (SEN), working in an alternative educational setting with children excluded from mainstream schooling. Consequently, I was keen, when undertaking doctoral research, to find a way to make their voices heard. I was motivated to do this by my personal and professional frustration that these young children were 'done to' rather than 'done with' in the UK education system when decisions were made about their futures. They were not involved in any part of the exclusion process and often not even aware of the discussions surrounding their lives. They were subject to powers beyond their control and their views and opinions were not sought. As my research progressed it became clear that the process of exclusion, and the discourses around it, rested solely with

https://doi.org/10.11647/OBP.0203.26

adults at a national and local level, and were largely informed by beliefs around power and discipline. My research focus shifted to encompass my own learning journey as both academic, researcher and teacher of SEN learners as I realized the power of the ideas and developments captured in my research journals and through autoethnographic writing, and saw how my narratives could sit alongside the discourses from the pupils themselves.

I worked in a unique type of alternative education setting within the UK education system, as I taught young people who had been permanently excluded from their mainstream school, meaning that they are not allowed to return to the school that they have left. They are often permanently excluded for acts of violence and aggression. Therefore, the children I taught were educated not in settings which they or their parents had selected, but ones that had been chosen for them. This lack of selection and personal choice is unparalleled in any other area of the school system for, in every other circumstance, parental views and often pupil views are taken into account. The establishments that the permanently excluded pupils attend may be known as Pupil Referral Units (PRUs) although this term is increasingly falling into disuse as many, including my own setting, prefer to style themselves in a more positive manner using the PRU title as a means of explaining their function rather than as their own self-description. Many of these PRUs are rebranding themselves as Alternative Provision (AP) or simply choosing a name and then discussing their function either in a strap line or on their school websites. In spite of these attempts at a creating a positive self-image, many people continue to refer to such schools as being 'the PRU' due to their familiarity with the term. For the purposes of this chapter I will continue to use the term PRU whilst acknowledging the use of AP as a broader term to include a wider variety of settings.

Dominant Discourses in the Current UK Education System: Power and Discipline

B efore taking a deeper look at the discourses within PRU settings, a wider view of the dominant discourses within the UK education system is necessary. The focus of the majority of discourses in the UK education system at both the macro- and micro-levels, are discourses of power and discipline. Foucault discusses how discipline is a specific type of power and how such disciplines are techniques used for ordering human groups to increase the docility and utility of the people who are subject to being disciplined (Foucault, 1995/1977). When applied to an understanding of the UK education system, one can imagine an environment where questions of power and disciplinary actions are embedded at the very heart of the ethos and philosophy of schools. In this case, the teachers wield power and the pupils are the subjects of their discipline.

Social media is often full of comments and observations on the role of government in judging the effectiveness of schools, the power which the newly created privately run academies have compared to schools run by the local authority, and criticism of the assumed authority which non-teachers may claim they have in dictating how schools should operate. So as much as I can criticize the use of power and discipline towards pupils, it must be framed within a larger discourse about how schools themselves are controlled and maintained. These discussions of power and authority can even be seen within the UK teacher training system where Britzman (1986) discusses how cultural educational myths are taught to trainee teachers leading to a reproduction of such ideas within their classroom practice. This means that each subsequent generation of teachers is brought up within the discourses of power, control and domination held by the preceding generation thereby reproducing, even extending, the narratives held. If one takes the view of PRUs into this stance, then it can be seen how such discourses can continue to influence the viewpoints of schools and teachers and impact upon how they relate to and work with the PRUs in their local authorities.

Another side effect of such discourses at a macro-level is the influence they have upon pupils and teacher relationships including the cultural differences between pupils and teachers (Delpit, 1988). If the macro-level discourses relating to teacher power versus pupil subservience are maintained then this will have a lasting impact on pupils' lives (Uitto & Syrjälä, 2008) and teachers' understanding of their own identities (Sachs, 2001); the relationship of power continues to encourage a hierarchy with learners as the weaker partner. This ultimately leads to a continuing cycle of discourses of power dividing us, which, as Foucault reminds us, is due to their familiarity (Foucault, 1989/1969).

Within UK Government policy, these familiar discourses of teacher power are firmly established and are found within numerous texts that have been published within recent years. In 2012 the Government produced a guide to support schools in understanding their role in the exclusion process. This document refers to 'exclusion [from school] as a sanction' for behaviours exhibited by pupils (DfE, 2012, p. 4) although no specific guidance is given as to what types of behaviour may be deemed to require such a sanction, which leaves the matter open to interpretation by those holding the power in school. A later 2015 Government advisory document discusses the rights of teachers in using physical force with pupils and refers to the ability of staff to 'control' and 'restrain' pupils when needed (DfE, 2015, p. 4). Yet again there is a lack of guidance surrounding the specific circumstances it discusses, which again leaves those in power within each school to define the terms as they see fit. A final example from 2016 is a Government document on behaviour and discipline within schools, which refers to teachers' 'power' and their legal right to use 'punishment' as a tool when needed (DfE, 2016, p. 7). The free and unqualified use of such terms leaves plenty of scope for school leaders to interpret their meaning as they choose and cements the notion that it is the teachers who hold power and authority.

These macro-discourses at a national level have a substantial effect on the micro discourses within individual school settings, specifically in the language of power that they use to describe the gulf in relationship between adults and children. This use of the language of power and discipline is seen across all age ranges and in all types of settings, and they are often found in the school behaviour policies, which are freely available online but which I, nevertheless, choose to leave anonymous when I highlight the point, by presenting three examples from schools within the North East of England. The first is from an 11–18 comprehensive school, which is maintained by the local authority. The school behaviour policy states that, 'no adult may be treated dismissively or unfairly'. The fact that there is no mention of how the pupils must be treated is a reminder that the power and authority remain with the adults in the setting. A similar school has a policy that states that teachers may enforce a 'disciplinary penalty' on pupils. However, such statements are not confined to school policies that refer to older pupils, as one 5–11 primary school states that 'a child can have a maximum total of 18 days seclusion (educated in isolation away from peers) in one academic year'. These are the discourses of power and behaviour management found in mainstream schools, which are subsequently those that are passed onto pupils who are permanently excluded. In the minds of mainstream colleagues, PRUs therefore become the repositories of pupils who have already experienced a lack of power and autonomy and staff working within them who must also exhibit such control and dominion when faced with educating a setting full of excluded pupils; PRUs are often seen by outsiders as places where more power and discipline is used than in mainstream provision.

Discourses on PRUs

Whilst these are the macro- and micro-dominant discourses seen within mainstream schools and the assumption of many about the remit of a PRU, it is crucial to understand how different being educated in, and teaching in, a PRU is, and therefore how different a discourse on power and discipline is possible. Currently, being excluded to a PRU is a school's ultimate sanction and use of power for poor behaviour. The path for the creation of PRUs was laid down in the 1980s allowing the permanent exclusion of pupils from mainstream schools. Currently, there is no uniformity across the UK for how a PRU should function and meet the needs of its pupils. Instead a series of basic principles are laid down:

- The act of permanent exclusion transfers the pupil from the school roll to the care of the local authority.

- Parents have a right of appeal, although their chances of success are slim; they are often confused about the process and trusting of the school's decision (Children's Commissioner Report, 2012, pp. 69–73).

- Unless they can get an exclusion overturned, convince the school to offer a move to a different mainstream school or offer home schooling, the only option is the local area PRU which is regulated at a national level by Ofsted (Ogg & Kaill, 2010).

- PRUs have to offer at least 25 hours of education a week (the national standard for pupils to attend school) but each PRU can decide how these hours are achieved.

- Pupils may attend a PRU on a short-term basis to prevent a permanent exclusion; this is around 3 months but may be up to 9 months.

Many teachers within the UK education system will therefore have heard of a PRU but the discourses surrounding them are often negative. At their conception, PRUs (like APs now) were for a wide range of pupils who, for a number of reasons, could not attend their mainstream school. This might be due to illness or school phobia but PRUs also took pupils who had suddenly arrived in the area and had no named school to attend (Teachernet, 2005). However, the main route into a PRU for most young people was, and is, through permanent exclusion from their mainstream school or the risk of it. Government guidance says that, 'The decision to exclude a pupil needs to be robust, fair and defensible' (DfE, 2011) with subsequent advice requiring it to be 'lawful, reasonable and fair' (DfE, 2013/2015). There is no definition of what these terms mean, and they are therefore open to interpretation by individual schools. This means that some young people can be permanently excluded for rather minor acts such as non-compliance to school rules, compared to others who may be excluded for extreme acts of physical assault or carrying a weapon.

PRUs, then, are often only known by mainstream schools to be the place that their unwanted pupils subsequently attend. That many PRUs are small in size adds to the situation that many mainstream staff never have the opportunity to meet with colleagues who work in alternative education settings as their chances of meeting each other are naturally reduced. Adding to this seclusion is the way that many PRUs develop their own cultural expectations of not being public about who they are or what they do and do not necessarily advertise their services or expertise. This therefore adds to the negative discourses surrounding the provisions, for surely educational establishments filled with unwanted and disagreeable young people cannot be positive or purposeful learning environments. PRUs, therefore, are cast in a dark and negative light. Mainstream schools have a role in this as they often reinforce the negativity of the establishments as a warning to errant pupils before their exclusion is unpreventable.

The mainstream school's responsibility for the excluded pupil ends the moment they start at a PRU. Mainstream schools' legal right to permanently exclude is bound by a responsibility to inform the parents and the governing body of the school correctly and to provide work for the pupil until they start at the PRU. As long as the mainstream school has lawful justification, they are entitled to permanently exclude a pupil and the local authority has a responsibility to provide alternative provision within six days (DfE, 2012).

Discourses in my Former Setting: The Role and Remit of an Individual PRU

As discussed above, each local authority has a PRU or an AP and some have several catering for different ages or needs. How each specific PRU or AP is set up and runs is unique to each individual setting. In my former role, I worked across the entire age range of the provision which caters for children aged five to sixteen. However, when carrying out my doctoral research, I primarily worked with young children aged between five and nine who displayed a range of SEN needs including social, emotional and communication needs. Many were working at an academic level significantly below their peers and had often missed large periods of time away from school due to their behaviour.

Within my former local authority the excluding schools are required to pass on the following information: the form outlining the reason for exclusion (this is where they tick the 'robust', 'reasonable' and 'fair' boxes), a copy of the letter sent to the parents and a very basic outline of the pupil's academic levels and wider needs. Although they were encouraged to share more, this rarely happened, for the act of exclusion and the demonstration of school power ends the relationship in the eyes of many school leaders. It is also important to note that these discourses of power do not solely apply to the pupils; they extend to their parents, who in many cases do not appeal the school's decision to exclude, although they have a legal right to do so. Instead they seem accepting of decisions and narratives put forth by the school about their child; many apparently believe that the school knows best when dealing with their child's needs. The discourses held by staff within the PRU regarding exclusions are often one of frustration with the education system, both for allowing some young people to be excluded for reasons which seem unfair as well as for the execution of power by schools over parents.

In the UK, it is Black males who are at greatest risk of exclusion from school and those whose life chances are most affected by their lack of educational experiences (Andrews & Palmer, 2016). The North East where my PRU was located, due to the smaller numbers of pupils from ethnic minority backgrounds, offers a counter-discourse to the nationwide picture of the type of pupil who is likely to be permanently excluded. Data held by the regional local authorities show that in 2010/2011 in the North East of England, there were 240 exclusions across KS1-4 and of those 220 were recorded as being White British. Therefore, the vast majority of pupils who were excluded in my local area were of White British origins, an alternative paradigm to that which is generally perceived at a macro-level by those in education.

The specific remit of my former PRU was to re-engage these permanently excluded pupils and support them in moving to a new mainstream school. This again offered a different discourse to that generally held by those at both a macro- and micro-level in education who perceive exclusion to be removing such pupils from mainstream schooling. The discourse from the PRU I worked within was one of social engagement, acceptance, and academic progress, as opposed to the need to use power and discipline to control pupils. Pupils largely stayed at the PRU for two terms. However, more complex cases would stay for a full academic year or longer. We offered a broad curriculum with targeted, personalized interventions for those in need. Although making academic progress was often possible, more important was the social and emotional progress that was made. Any academic progress was the positive by-product of a successful placement. Pupils came from across the local authority and the majority were therefore educated outside of their local community when they came to the PRU. Those who lived over two miles away were eligible for free transport in a taxi resulting in many pupils making long journeys. The provision had space for up to 122 young people who were either excluded or at risk of exclusion. However, there was a degree of flexibility given we were the only PRU provision for excluded pupils in the county. This meant that the PRU's ideal staff-to-pupil ratio of 1:4 often became 1:7, and classrooms designed for eight pupils were forced to accommodate fourteen or more. As a consequence, there was less time to give pupils individual support and if there was a behavioural incident staff support was further reduced for its duration. When all the pupils have behavioural concerns, a setting is (and was) often understaffed at such moments.

In summary, the discourses present within the specific PRU I worked in related to power but from a very different perspective. Instead of discussions around the use of power by staff, the focus was on finding ways to empower the young people we were responsible for. These pupils, subjects of power and discipline at their previous schools, often have limited experience in how to be part of the equal and reciprocal relationship we encouraged them to develop with staff. Whilst the use of disciplinary measures was still required, the focus was not to create hierarchy or distance. Instead measures were influenced by principles of restorative justice which seeks to create a new paradigm in contrast to that of retribution (Hopkins, 2002).

Development of my Research Methodology: Becoming a Journaler

Initially, my research plans were very pupil-centred with a focus on trying to understand their perspectives and views of permanent exclusion. I sought answers around how an authentic voice could be found and which methods were useful in supporting SEN learners to share or record their voice for others. I was keen to understand what learners could add to the wider discourse around education in a PRU. During this earliest stage of my research and writing, I found it advantageous to have a notebook readily accessible, as many thoughts and events occurred that I wanted to record. During the research process my notepad developed into a journal, which ultimately led to a change of research direction to include a focus on teacher voice and my own learning experiences, shared through autoethnography.

In the later stages of my research, I began to hear the plurality of identities and voices recorded in my journals, those of myself as teacher, an academic and my own personal thoughts. Ultimately, I realized that autoethnographic accounts allow an insider perspective to be heard, specifically that of a teacher learning, not only about her pupils, but about herself as a professional, as she attempts to counter the macro- and micro- discourses she has heard. It is this combination of teacher's voice and the use of autoethnography that I suggest can offer an alternative way of sharing 'new' discourses around permanent exclusion and the PRU system to challenge those that are already established. Who better to share the discourses of working within a PRU than those employed there?

Journaling as a Method of Recording Teacher Voice and Developing a New Discourse

First Research Journal — Personal Development

So, I turn my focus to the use of journaling as a method of developing personal knowledge and forming new discourses. During the earliest stages of my research, my notebook was simply a lined school textbook belonging to a past pupil with the used pages torn out. This early recording was functional and contained to-do lists, *aide memoires* and scribbled notes. They did not contain any reflection or scaffolding of ideas, lacking what Engin suggests that a teacher's diary should contain (Engin, 2011). However, reading Moon's (1999) book, which details the benefits a learning journal can bring to personal development within higher education, encouraged me to change my approach. I started my first research journal with this line: 'Current pupils I have and my thoughts...' (14.9.12 Research Journal 1).

My journal became a place where I discussed thoughts with myself, including emerging concerns about insider/outside research, especially the problem of sharing my 'voice' whilst maintaining my professional identity:

> What struck me was that field journals played a massive role in her (Lanas, 2011) research. She recorded so much detail. Sometimes beautifully so [...] The researcher was not part of the community and therefore chose to show her emotions with the kids. I am not in that place and I need to act with them as I always have done. Professionalism? Yet dialogue is a two-way street. (16.9.12 Research Journal 1)

However, these moments were rare, and my journal largely focused on my pupils and the insights that I was having about their worlds and voices. As time progressed, I began to ask myself what my motivation for using a journal was. I had started to recognize that my focus had shifted at times to being about my own learning. This was something that I felt uncomfortable with initially:

> I don't think I have found my own voice yet. True, I have only been keeping one since September, but I am yet to find me in it. Maybe I am too conscious of how other people write and what I should write like. It's funny that I am struggling with my own identity in this when I am so interested in the pupils' identity. (4.1.13 Research Journal 1)

Towards the end of that first journal, my writing took a further change in direction, becoming more personal with an increased focus on my own identity and hardly any mention of the pupils at all:

> Candlemas. Thinking back to my time in Chad's Chapel. That world all seems so long ago now yet I am still so fundamentally the same as I was. (2.2.13 Research Journal 1)

At this stage I had not even heard of the term autoethnography and my journals had certainly not been written with the intention of ever sharing them. Yet what they had allowed was a continuation of my own learning both in terms of my knowledge about the pupils and of my own identity. It was this development of my professional voice as a teacher offering a new discourse on working with excluded pupils which became the focus of my second research journal.

Second Research Journal — Development of Teacher Voice

As discussed earlier, the dominant discourses in education in the UK are largely about power and control. However, through my journaling I began to see that there could be a different approach to the power relationship between staff and pupils. My own reflections highlighted that, within my classroom, my use of 'power' was very different to the national cultural climate I was working within and the dominant discourses found in education. I explored my own understanding of my relationship with my pupils, considering whether it was possible to have friendly and loving relationships with pupils. I wondered if the act of working in a PRU had affected my moral compass as a teacher, leading me to view it as a vocation rather than a profession (Buijs, 2005).

I became aware that I was building a counter-discourse to that more commonly accepted:

> Reading about vocation in education. One article by Schwarz (Schwarz, 1999) quotes Huebner (Huebner, 1996) saying that vocation in teaching allows teachers to talk about feelings and themselves — I like! [...] So, after all of that reading, what do I make of teaching as a vocation? I think I am more convinced that it is, yet aware that the way we are judged is a professional one with a set of standards, etc. (3.3.13 Research Journal 2)

Through this learning, I began to feel a sense of frustration that my professional voice, at odds with the dominant discourse of power I encountered on a daily basis, was unheard within the micro-setting of my local area and the macro-setting of the wider educational context within the UK. An example of this frustration was when the local area education department applied new restrictions on the physical support that we could give pupils. For us, physical interventions were not a means of exercising power or controlling behaviour: our rationale was to protect the young person, their peers, and staff from injury. However, the education department in the local area established new rules across all schools. Schools must try a wider range of more punitive measures before physical intervention could be used. Whilst I appreciated that within the mainstream schools this had some value, I believed that this was at odds with the type of setting that I worked in and I was angry that there had been no scope to share my thoughts:

> So my frustration is this. Change management. How this was decided and translated to us was by word of mouth. No discussion. No evaluation. No understanding of the job we do. They want to cut exclusion rates and MIR rates [major incident reports — the use of physical intervention] but the effect on the rest of the pupils' learning is dramatic. (2.5.13 Research Journal 2)

My journals had allowed me to weave my own thoughts with my research and reading on wider issues. They were a tangible record of my own adult learning and my developing voice as a teacher speaking against the dominant discourses of education. Yet they remained private and book bound. This was to change through the use of autoethnography when I realized that I could share my own learning at an academic level by sharing my own narratives in my thesis.

The Use of Autoethnography as a Means of Sharing Teacher Voice and Alternative Discourses

I was actually six months into my research when, having realized that my journals and emerging writing had become really focused on my own learning, I stumbled across autoethnography as a legitimate methodology. It was a chance reading of a text by Moriarty with the title 'Leaving the blood in' (Moriarty, 2013) that made me realize that, without knowing it, I was writing autoethnographically. Moriarty's title summed up all that I felt about my own writing so far. However, I also realized that I had taken on a new battle with a new set of dominant discourses: traditional academia. Moriarty sums this up succinctly:

> I suppose he helped me to believe that I could do it on my own terms but that I had to be realistic about what those terms were in relation to a dominant and oppressive discourse that had thrived for hundreds of years. Let me make it clear: I did not knock down any walls when I completed my thesis but I tried to take part in helping those already at work building the tunnel through, the bridge over and the road around the concrete mass that is conventional academic research. (Moriarty, 2013, p. 75)

Whilst I found some validity in the criticisms of the method as discussed by Delamont (Delamont, 2009), I found a greater wealth of material about the use of autoethnography to share adult experiences of their own learning in an open and accessible way. Although the evocative nature of some of this writing, such as that by Ellis (Ellis, 2004), was not something that I felt professionally comfortable with, I encountered writing by a range of people involved within education. One author who became important for my own research was Clough (Clough, 2002), who wrote about his own experiences as a teacher using fictionalized narratives to protect his professional identity and the identities of the pupils he wrote about. This went beyond simply anonymizing his writing. He created entire scenes and situations that had not necessarily happened in the manner in which he presented them yet contained the 'truth' of the events that had occurred.

Combining both autoethnography and fictionalization in this way enabled me to discuss my learning experiences in my thesis, share my voice as a teacher and show an alternative educational discourse about working in a PRU whilst maintaining the professionalism required of me in my role as a teacher. Specifically relating to discourses of power and discipline, I was able to share my own stories and those of my pupils and show how these relationships can be positive, balanced and shape each other (Clandinin et al., 2006). The voices of insiders, such as practitioner researchers like me, are able to provide an honest and reliable understanding of the impact of educational discourses in PRU settings as well as offering an alternative perspective. There is a wealth of experience and knowledge hidden in classrooms all over the United Kingdom, yet it is largely unseen. However, insider research can achieve an understanding that an outsider might not as successfully achieve (Brannick & Coghlan, 2007) and this is especially true regarding the sharing of discourses from specific settings which may be counter to those at a macro-level.

The Use of Journaling in Education Settings

As previously discussed, my use of a journal grew out of keeping a notebook and was then further influenced by reading academic research (Moon, 1999). I continued to use it beyond the end of my research as I became aware that it was a tool with wider uses. Keeping a journal was not a natural act and was a discipline I needed to learn. As a child, I had repeatedly tried to be an active writer and keep a journal, influenced by prolific writers such as Jane Austen. I was never successful and grew into an adult who assumed that I had nothing worthy of being written about.

After I started to use a journal for my thesis, I began to understand that I had a misconception about what, and who, a journal was for. My doctoral journals were not written to be shared with anyone else but for me alone. I grew to understand that my journal was a 'paper mirror' rather than a document I needed to construct to appease an unknown audience (Hubbs & Brand, 2005). This awareness meant that my writing became free. I was able to write about and discuss challenging subjects. My journal became a safe 'space' where I could write my way through demanding situations — and there were many in a setting that was undergoing cultural change. This space was important: there were often issues that I did not want to discuss with colleagues who, like me, were struggling to protect their own emotional and mental wellbeing.

In the UK, the teaching profession has been subjected to many changes at a macro-level which have impacted upon the micro-level working lives of staff. In 2015, 10% of teachers left the profession (Worth et al., 2015). Many of them cited the negative impact of teaching on their wellbeing and the lack of support for this at a school level (Simon & Johnson, 2015). Journaling enabled me to identify and address issues that were affecting my wellbeing at an early stage. This self-reflection, using my journal as a mirror, meant that I was able to work through some of my concerns, often finding my inner voice an aid in problem-solving (Boden et al., 2006). Keeping a journal enabled me to make sense of my professional life as a teacher and align this to my personal beliefs; to find a degree of security in knowing who I was and being able to maintain this self-belief. In turn, this meant that I was able to understand that the negative experiences I was having at work were not a personal attack but were instead the product of the changing climate within education.

Conclusions

In this chapter I have highlighted the current dominant discourses within the UK education system relating to power and discipline which are punitive in nature and balanced in the favour of the adults in schools. I have shown how these dominant discourses have influenced schools at an individual level through having a direct effect on their behaviour policies and school ethos. I have then shown how a journal, and the space it creates to express voice through autoethnography, can be used as a tool to enable a different discourse; one that counters that which is accepted as the established norm. Staff working in education during periods of cultural change (or personal stress) could effectively use journals to foster a sense of wellbeing.

To maintain the continued development of teacher voices through the use of autoethnography and fictionalized narratives to counter the dominant discourses, is crucial in shaping the education system at a micro- and subsequently macro-level. Current discourses of power and discipline have created a narrative whereby pupils who are permanently excluded and are educated in a PRU are viewed negatively and are seen as both perpetrators of discord and a challenge to the authority and power of adults in schools. Such pupils are seen as requiring disciplinary measures to readdress the power balance. The current discourses also lead to a belief that all adults in education share this hierarchical viewpoint and this allows the discourses to be continually perpetuated.

Current movements within the UK education system which began as grassroots initiatives (such as The Chartered College of Teaching and WomenEd), are beginning to bridge the gap between the discourses from within individual classrooms and those held at both local authority and national levels. However, it is also important to develop the use of teacher voice at an individual level to enable professionals to share their own narratives of experience, some of which may offer a counter-discourse to that which is generally accepted. There is still a lot to be done to strengthen links between the micro-level of individual school development and ethos and macro-level Government policy. It would be beneficial if future research were to map the influence that such personal learning at the micro-level of individual school development and ethos can have at the macro-level of Government policy.

References

Andrews, K. & Palmer, L.A. (2016). *Blackness in Britain*. Abingdon: Routledge.

Boden, C.J., Cook, D., Lasker-Scott, T., Moore, S. & Shelton, D. (2006). Five perspectives on reflective journaling. *Adult Learning*, 17 (1–4): 11–15. https://doi.org/10.1177/104515950601700105

Brannick, T. & Coghlan, D. (2007). In defence of being 'native': The case for insider academic research. *Organizational Research Methods*, 10: 59–74. https://doi.org/10.1177/1094428106289253

Britzman, D. (1986). Cultural myths in the making of a teacher: Biography and social structure in teacher education. *Harvard Educational Review*, 56: 442–57.

Buijs, J. (2005). Teaching: Profession or vocation. *Journal of Catholic Education*, 8 (3): 326–45. http://dx.doi.org/10.15365/joce.0803042013

Children's Commissioner Report. (2012). *They never give up on you: School Exclusions Enquiry*. https://www.childrenscommissioner.gov.uk/wp-content/uploads/2017/07/They-never-give-up-on-you-final-report.pdf

Clandinin, D.J., Huber, J., Huber, M., Murphy, M.S., Orr, A.M., Pearce, M. & Steeves, P. (2006). *Composing diverse identities: Narrative inquiries into the interwoven lives of children and teachers.* Abingdon: Routledge.

Clough, P. (2002). *Narratives and fictions in educational research.* Maidenhead: Open University Press.

Delamont, S. (2009). The only honest thing: Autoethnography, reflexivity and small crises in fieldwork. *Ethnography and Education,* 4: 51–63. https://doi.org/10.1080/17457820802703507

Delpit, L. (1988). The silenced dialogue: Power and pedagogy in educating other people's children. *Harvard Educational Review,* 58: 280–99.

DfE (2012). *Exclusion from maintained schools, academies and pupil referral units.* London: DfE. No longer available but referred to in 2017 update, pp. 3–4: https://assets.publishing.service.gov.uk/government/uploads/system/uploads/attachment_data/file/641418/20170831_Exclusion_Stat_guidance_Web_version.pdf. 2012 regulations: http://www.legislation.gov.uk/uksi/2012/1033/made

DfE (2013/2015). *Use of reasonable force.* London: DfE. https://assets.publishing.service.gov.uk/government/uploads/system/uploads/attachment_data/file/444051/Use_of_reasonable_force_advice_Reviewed_July_2015.pdf

DfE (2016). *Behaviour and discipline in schools — a guide for headteachers and school staff.* London: DfE. https://assets.publishing.service.gov.uk/government/uploads/system/uploads/attachment_data/file/488034/Behaviour_and_Discipline_in_Schools_-_A_guide_for_headteachers_and_School_Staff.pdf

Ellis, C. (2004). *The ethnographic I: A methodological novel about autoethnography.* Walnut Creek, CA: Altamira Press.

Engin, M. (2011). Research diary: A tool for scaffolding. *International Journal of Qualitative Methods,* 10. https://journals.sagepub.com/doi/pdf/10.1177/160940691101000308

Foucault, M. (1989/1969). *Archaeology of knowledge.* London: Routledge.

Foucault, M. (1995/1977). *Discipline and punish: The birth of the prison* (2nd English edn). New York: Vintage Books.

Hopkins, B. (2002). Restorative justice in schools. *Support for Learning,* 17: 144–49. https://doi.org/10.1111/1467-9604.00254

Hubbs, D.L. & Brand, C.F. (2005). The paper mirror: Understanding reflective journaling. *The Journal of Experiential Education,* 28(1): 60–71. https://doi.org/10.1177/105382590502800107

Huebner, D. (1996). Educational foundations for dialogue. *Religious Education.* 91: 582–88.

Lanas, M. (2011). How can non-verbalized emotions in the field be addressed in research? *International Journal of Research & Method in Education*, 34: 131–45. https://doi.org/10.1080/1743727X.2011.578822

Moon, J.A. (1999). *Learning journals: A handbook for academics, students and professional development*. Abingdon: Routledge.

Moriarty, J. (2013). Leaving the blood in: Experiences with an autoethnographic doctoral thesis. In: Short, N.P., Turner, L. & Grant, A. (eds), *Contemporary British Autoethnography*. Rotterdam: Sense.

Ogg, T. & Kaill, E. (2010). *A new secret garden? Alternative provision, exclusion and children's rights*. London: Civitas. http://www.civitas.org.uk/pdf/NewSecretGarden.pdf

Sachs, J. (2001). Teacher professional identity: Competing discourses, competing outcomes. *Journal of Education Policy*, 16: 149–61. https://doi.org/10.1080/02680930116819

Schwarz, G.E. (1999). Teaching as vocation: Enabling ethical practice. *The Educational Forum*, 63: 23–29. https://doi.org/10.1080/00131729808984383

Simon, N.S. & Johnson, S.M. (2015). Teacher turnover in high poverty schools: What we know and can do. *Teachers College Record*, 117(3): 1–36. https://www.tcrecord.org ID Number: 17810

Teachernet (2005). *Guidance for local authorities and schools: Pupil referral units and alternative provision (LEA/0024–2005)*. No longer available but referred to in OFSTED (2007) Pupil referral units, 070019, footnote 2. https://dera.ioe.ac.uk/6542/1/Pupil%20referral%20units%20establishing%20successful%20practice%20in%20pupil%20referral%20units%20and%20local%20authorities%20PDF%20format%29.doc.pdf

Uitto, M. & Syrjälä, L. (2008). Body, caring and power in teacher-pupil relationships: Encounters in former pupils' memories. *Scandinavian Journal of Educational Research*, 52: 355–371. https://doi.org/10.1080/00313830802184517

UNESCO (1994). *The Salamanca statement and framework for action on special needs education*. Salamanca, Spain: UNESCO & Ministry of Education. http://www.unesco.org/education/pdf/SALAMA_E.PDF

Worth, J., Bamford, S. & Durbin, B. (2015). *Should I stay or should I go? NFER analysis of teachers joining and leaving the profession*. Slough, UK: National Foundation for Educational Research.

27. Reflections on a Creative Arts Project to Explore the Resilience of Young Adults with a Muslim Background in Finland

Helena Oikarinen-Jabai

Helena Oikarinen-Jabai discusses her involvement in a participatory project that combines a social science framework and creative methods. She describes how young Finnish women with Muslim backgrounds explored their diverse embodied cultural in-between spaces and sense of belonging by creating artworks as part of the research process. This chapter offers a glimpse of the challenges to be met within an interdisciplinary research project.

In this chapter, I discuss some of the challenges that arose whilst working as a researcher on a project that sought to explore the resilience of young adults from a Muslim background.[1] The project embraced a participatory framework and used arts-based approaches that enabled self-expression. This 'sharing of control' and freedom of form allowed the nature of the project to evolve, creating new understandings of diversity among the participant and associated Muslim communities. It also indirectly captured resilience through the

---

1 The research project, 'Young Muslims and Resilience: A Participatory Study', was based in the Department of Social Research at the University of Helsinki between 2016 and 2018. It was funded by the Kone Foundation, which supports 'bold initiatives in research and art'.

https://doi.org/10.11647/OBP.0203.27

actions and initiatives that ensued and the tensions that arose during the process. For me, it raised many unanticipated issues and my intention, here, is to discuss the challenges of merging performative and arts-based approaches with a more traditional qualitative social studies methodology; a process that left me feeling that I was often 'trapezing between paradigms'.

For me this was not a new experience but a continuation of my earlier research with young people with an immigrant or minority background. Previously, I had clearly shown that participants with a Muslim lineage (specifically a group of young Finnish Somalis) wanted the productions they created during the research process (exhibitions, books, TV and radio documentaries) to challenge existing racial, national, ethnic, gender and religious stereotypes and create new positions for cultural citizenship (see Hua, 2011; Oikarinen-Jabai, 2018). The study I discuss here was therefore a natural progression, offering me a chance to understand better the multiple positionings of young adults (aged 20 to 35) belonging to a religious group that is often demonized in public discussions in Finland and other Western countries (Ernst, 2003; Oikarinen-Jabai, 2018). In this new project, I was to concentrate primarily on working with female participants with differing ethnic, religious and national backgrounds — part of a group that also included five young male participants. Among other outputs, the study resulted in an exhibition, 'Numur — Islam and I' (in Helsinki in 2017, in Turku in 2018) that presented the artworks of eighteen young people, including the five female and five male participants, plus eight artists participating only in the exhibitions. Members of local Muslim youth organizations arranged additional workshops and seminars.

Our methodological background was performative and arts-based, incorporating a specific resilience methodology, devised by Michael Ungar and colleagues (Didkowsky, Ungar & Liebenberg, 2010; Liebenberg & Ungar, 2009). The overall goals and research questions were fairly wide-ranging, but despite this, appeared to steer the research process in ways that caused this diverse group of participants to be categorized in essentialist ways that obscured intersectionality, an outcome I found problematic.

Resilience: The Concept and Ways to Capture It

Though now more broadly applicable, the idea of resilience was originally used in the social sciences, where the concept was generally criticized for being too vague, multidimensional and value-laden (Luthar, Cichetti & Becker 2000). Ungar (2004), a therapist employing a social ecological approach and both solution-therapeutic and system-theoretical thinking, addressed these criticisms by restructuring the concept and deepening its theoretical and methodological underpinnings. This was of particular interest to me, as at the time I was undergoing training in solution-focused therapy. Yet, despite this, I found it problematic to apply the methodology in contexts unconnected to social work or therapy. The resilience method as set out in our research plan, involved each participant taking photographs during a one-week period and researchers videotaping a day in the participants' life. The videos were then to be watched by the research group, who would select a small number of five-minute sections which were deemed to reflect the resilience of the participants. These sections would then be watched and analysed together with the participants, to identify jointly the resilience factors within these sections and, consequently, in the participants' everyday lives.

This kind of methodology may be of benefit in some action research projects, but for our small research group, hours of video filming and subsequent analysis of the material seemed an almost impossible mission. Furthermore, the young adults involved in the research had already found their place in society. They knew their strengths and were familiar with the social structures that supported or rejected their personal decisions. For them, such an approach appeared strange and unattractive. In contrast, being involved in an artistic process would enable them to share their personal experiences and ambiguous questions with the research group and audience, to deepen their own interests and communicate their own visions and views. Moreover, the structured plan was in conflict with arts-based and performative creative approaches, which generally emphasize the process, dialogue, different ways of knowing, potential spaces, transitions and border crossings (Conquergood, 2009; Jungnickel & Hjorth, 2014; Minh-ha, 2011; O'Neill, 2008; Rolling, 2010). This methodological dissonance raised a number of theoretical and practical challenges that we faced during the research project. Though, as I worked primarily with the female participants, I will concentrate mostly on their processes and artworks but first look generally at how the project unfurled.

Researchers and Schedules

As is often the case with collaborative research projects, our study plan was quickly stitched together by people from different fields, backgrounds and life situations. Furthermore, during the research period, the composition of the researchers and participants changed, and this created further unplanned ambiguities around our intentions and actions. There were initially three of us: a project leader and two researchers comprising myself and my colleague (a PhD student from Somalia who was to be supervised by the project leader). A fourth person, a research assistant was hired at an early stage and, being a Muslim herself, used her networks to find the female participants.

My role in the project was mainly to work with female participants and to help my colleague shoot and analyse the videos and data collected with male participants. This colleague planned to conduct observations and interviews at mosques and other Muslim gatherings and events in the Helsinki Metropolitan Area in order to understand the sense of belonging, citizenship, roots of radicalization and resilience factors of young Finnish Muslim men. After that, he would conduct a follow up study with a smaller group of informants using performative, visual and related methods. However, at the beginning of the second year, he decided to abandon his doctoral studies. In late spring, he was replaced by two individuals: a young man who had previously been a participant and a male researcher who was particularly interested in Muslim Youth organizations. An intern was also hired to help in planning the exhibition, so we became a team of six, plus the participants.

By the second year, the female participants had begun working with the art pieces that they wanted to include in the exhibition. However, most male participants were recruited by the former participant — who was now one of the replacement researchers — from the Muslim youth organization to which he belonged. They created photographic material and were interviewed about it as part of the project and were subsequently invited to participate further. However, they only began working with their ideas in the summer and autumn of 2017, so our timings were disparate. Nevertheless, everything was ready by November 2017 for the exhibition at Stoa, the Cultural Centre of Eastern Helsinki, which is located in an area with a multicultural population. In March 2018 the second exhibition took place at the Institute of Migration, in Turku, accompanied by seminars and workshops organized by people from local Muslim youth organizations, so in respect of its public face, the project fulfilled its intentions. But, at the local level, the research activities were more fluid.

In the Field: Modifying Methodological Approaches

I began work with the female participants and found them reluctant to follow the proposed data-collection procedures. Instead of taking photographs over a one-week period, some wanted to choose photos they already had, others wished to extend the process to photograph their forthcoming travels abroad. They disliked the idea of a 'day-in-the-life' video; so, I agreed to film with them in places they found empowering. Thus, the research assistant and I followed those who agreed to participate to locations that they chose: to cafés, their childhood places, schools, museums, mosques or the countryside. These sessions often ended up resembling a deep, non-directive interview. For example, one participant, caring for her new-born baby on her lap, shared her ideas on motherhood, religion, and her own career at a mosque and Shia cultural centre, where her media company also had a studio. I consider that our meeting was empowering for her: it inspired her to continue filming in her free time and create a video-based artwork for the exhibition even if it failed to follow the planned formats.

In the interviews with the female participants, the central themes that arose were gender and sexuality, motherhood, spirituality, relationship to Islam, aesthetics and being in between different ethnic, gender, racial and class identifications and languages. These were also themes that the participants wished to address with their art works for the exhibition, and I became interested in creating an installation on multilingualism, a topic that connected all the participants. Our project had a limited amount of funds allocated to the artistic activities of the participants and researchers, so I sought, and managed to get, extra funding to recruit an art student to our workgroup to help with the video works and recordings. Thus, our team gained a new member.

From the outset, some of the female participants had highlighted the need for the exhibition to show respect for diversity and to allow multiple approaches and various perspectives on religion and many of their artworks touched on gender and diversity issues. Although these themes were evident in the exhibition itself, they were overlooked in the seminars and workshops created around the exhibitions. Moreover, in some cases, the male participants even attempted to limit the female participants' artistic expression. Again, I felt that I was balancing on a trapeze traversing two contradictory positions, as the relative importance of the artwork and other qualitative data was never clearly established in our research team. It remained unclear whether the art constituted core research or it was simply visual or textual co-production alongside more important interview material. Such ambivalence is worth discussing further and touches on a range of historical and ideological positions.

Beyond the Field: Considering the Theoretical Frameworks

Resilience studies are usually conducted in a traditional quantitative and/or qualitative research setting, even if the focus of the analysis is the content co-produced with the participants. Moreover, reporting often concentrates on statistical measures of resilience to develop public health, human wellbeing and social policy (Didkowsky, Ungar & Liebenberg, 2010; Windle, Bennett & Noyes, 2011). Visual methods provide an alternative or complementary approach for use in studies of resilience because they may address problems associated with interviews, such as power imbalances, young participants' lack of engagement in the research process, and language barriers (Didkowsky, Ungar & Liebenberg, 2010). Furthermore, by including the participants' own ideas of construction and representation, images act as a catalyst for transforming thoughts and understandings of self and society (Liebenberg & Ungar, 2009).

Nevertheless, using visual data does not change the methodological limitations of qualitative research, such as its emphasis on written outcomes. Thus, researchers have increasingly employed practice-based performative research, which is experiential both for the participating informants and for the researcher (Haseman, 2006). Practice-based methodology can be enriched by familiar qualitative methods, but research outputs and knowledge claims are most often created through symbolic language, such as creative writing, music, drama, dance, (audio)visual methods and digital media, with little interest in attempting to translate the findings and understandings of practice into numbers (quantitative) and words (qualitative) (Haseman, 2006). Practice-based performative research can be defined as an independent paradigm, emerging from relativist ontology and celebrating multiple constructed realities and interpretative epistemologies where the knower and the known interact, shape and interpret the other. This represents something more than 'the performance turn', which can be understood as a form of emancipatory action through embodied and enacted storytelling (Bauman, 1977; Haseman, 2006).

Maggie O'Neill (2008) combines ethnography and arts into the idea of 'ethno-mimesis', an approach that includes producing fiction and art works, trusting different ways of knowing through the research process and underlining the enthusiasm for practice instead of the problem (see Barone, 2006; Barone & Eisner, 2012; Rolling, 2010; Tolia-Kelly 2007). Borrowing from different narrative, performative and arts-based epistemologies, the performative approach emphasizes practice as a precondition for engagement, and widens understanding of knowledge and data production in the context of the social sciences (Haseman, 2006; Jungnickel & Hjorth, 2014; O'Neill 2008; Rolling, 2010).

Experimental and performative approaches have various roots. Since the 19th century, racialized people have developed academic strategies that lean on embodied and localized ways of knowing and, in this fashion, have criticized the hegemonic standpoints existing in academia (Conquergood, 2009; hooks, 1990). In addition, many philosophers and educators, including Buber (1970/1923), Dewey (2005/1934) and Freire (1970/1968), have emphasized the empowering capabilities of sensuous, narrative and dialogical knowledge in educational settings and human encounters. Since the 1980s, various scholars working in social science or ethnographic and (art)educational fields (such as Barone, 2006; Denzin, 2003; Richardson, 1997) have introduced practices that provide the space to understand knowledge production in wider terms.

Many feminist scholars, especially women belonging to diversified groups or minorities, have created fresh approaches for critically examining the standpoints, power relations and hierarchy hidden in academic theories, methods and reporting (see Anzaldúa & Moraga, 1983; Conquergood, 2009; hooks, 1990). Similarly, many continental feminists, such as Julia Kristeva (1980), Helene Cixous (1993) and Luce Irigaray (2002), have emphasized the superiority of experimental and poetic writing, autoethnographies and fiction for deconstructing language and deepening understanding of social structures and human encounters.

In performance studies, the notion of performativity is often linked to J.L. Austin's (1955) linguistic notion of the speech act as a performance. For instance, according to Judith Butler's constructivist approach, subjectivity is established through repeated performances as a result of pre-existing rigid discourses, such as those of 'gender,' 'race', or 'sexuality' (Butler, 1993; Friedman, 2002). Moreover, Victor Turner's (1967) ideas of betwixt and between have inspired performance and performativity researchers. For Richard Schechner, performance and performativity — understood as intertwined spheres of entertainment, healing, education and ritualizing — are symbolic forms of cultural/ artistic expressions that may expand the distance between the performer and what or who is being represented (Friedman, 2002, Schechner, 1993, p. 20). Post-structuralist Derridean performance can be understood as 'representation without reproduction', where performed living bodies 'are forever cut from what they represent' (Phelan, 1993, pp. 148–49; in Friedman, 2002), or as a bridge between individuals, genres and cultures that may lead us towards the other side of speech and as representations where no narrative can describe the opened boundary between different approaches to sensing the world (Minh-ha, 2011, p. 94).

Yet, the ideological position framing our overall research process remained unspecified and unclear. As a personal construction, I felt that my fieldwork process was supported by the idea of unfinished knowledge (Yuval-Davis, 1997), which allows the simultaneous presence of epistemologically diverse perspectives. Unfinished knowledge is based on Martin Buber's (1970/1923) notion of dialogue, in which 'I' encounters another person not as an objectified 'it' but as part of an interconnected 'I-Thou' relationship, which he also considers the foundation of artistic practice and works of art. Further, 'nomadic inquiry' (St. Pierre, 2005), exploration and writing that departs from representationalism and interpretation, supported the exploration of different intertwined spheres of performance during the material-creation and research process.

The 'potential spaces' and landscapes created within the dialogues and artworks exposed diasporic experiences, multiple senses of belonging and the intersectional practices of differentiation, thereby allowing the fusion of embodied experiences, collected/produced material and different ways of knowing in the research reporting (O'Neill, 2008: Oikarinen-Jabai, 2018). This also allowed the participants' resilience to be approached through embodied intersectional perspectives, where agency and the ability to define their own citizenship and positionings in social, cultural and religious discussions became an important key for appreciating personal empowerment (Oikarinen-Jabai, 2018; Ungar, 2004).

From the Field: Issues Made Visible

Muslims or Young People with a Muslim Background?

A longside the project's theoretical and methodological confusion, the word Muslim in our research title created certain questions and tensions from the outset. Rather than approaching Tatars (the oldest Muslim community in Finland) or first-generation Muslim immigrants, we had mainly contacted second-generation citizens when recruiting our research participants. It transpired that, even among our small group of co-researchers, their relationship to religion differed. For many, religious identity was just one identification intersecting with other important locations or metaphorical spaces of belonging. Indeed, religious traditions, local ways of living and cultural values vary widely between countries with Muslim majorities, as well as between Muslim diaspora communities around the world. Thus, it is somewhat strange to use Muslims as an essential expression for a group of people with such varied backgrounds (see Ernst, 2003), and it is important to avoid further 'othering' the participants (Cooke & Kothari, 2001) when grouping people together in this way. Furthermore, on a stage built like this, researchers may find themselves trapezing between different academic, social, psychological and embodied domains, and they must be careful to avoid strengthening social hierarchies and reproducing the dominant hegemonic agenda (Koobak, 2014).

Diversity of Approach

Working with the female participants reinforced the idea that people with Muslim backgrounds are an extremely heterogeneous ensemble. From the beginning, it was clear that many of the young women were motivated to participate in the study by the issues with which they were struggling at the time, such as career plans, reflections on women's roles and rights, and questions about Queer Islam or cultural citizenship. The young women emphasized pluralist values and critically approached, among other things, questions of gender, belonging and some ethnic and religious customs in their artworks.

One young artist with a textile-design background created an installation called *Sufi-Masa*, which depicts a whirling dervish dancer. Through her work, she brought an important dimension of Islamic spirituality to the research setting (see Figure 27.1).

Another participant used her photographs and poems (and collages based on these works) to explore a queer perspective in an Islamic context, which in Finland, as well as in many other countries, is a sensitive topic inside the Muslim community. A third female participant commented on her belonging/not belonging and the stereotypes and restrictions that she encountered as a young woman with a Somali background in both Finnish society and her ethnic community, through her installation *Inside/Outside the Box*. This installation included a video, shown inside a chamber constructed from black cloth, of her encountering artworks at the Finnish National Gallery and wandering in the cultural landscapes of Helsinki. Outside the gloomy box, she hung photographs presenting places that she found important and empowering in Finland and abroad. The fourth of the female participants I worked alongside, wrote poems expressing her different senses of belonging and cultural citizenship

Fig. 27.1 The installation *Sufi-Masa* (2017). *Source:* Author.

between multiple positions and embodied landscapes, presenting them on a traditional Sudanese cloth embroidered with beads (see Figure 27.2).

A fifth participant discussed her belonging and spirituality by creating a video letter to her daughter. She had already begun filming during the birth of her child and continued over the space of one year by videotaping everyday life, family trips, her work and spiritual life. Furthermore, some photos taken by female participants from my earlier research and photographs, paintings and texts produced by some young

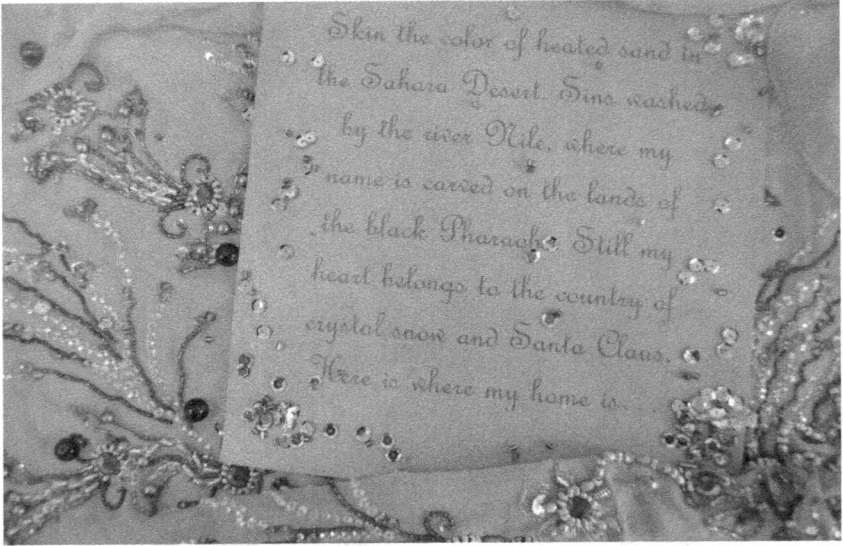

Fig. 27.2 A poem written by a participant. *Source:* Author.

women belonging to a Muslim youth organization were included in the exhibition.

The young men's working process started relatively late. All the participants were active in a Muslim youth organization, and much of the creative work they presented at the exhibition was somehow connected to religion and religious or activist identities. Two of them made videos that were connected to the work of Muslim youth organizations and Islamophobia. One man made digitally produced calligraphy paintings, another produced a series of photographs of the places in Helsinki that were important to him, while a third created little boxes covered with mosaic print that opened like books revealing quotes from, for example, the Quran and Malcolm X. In addition, two other male artists participated in the exhibition, presenting their poems, and, in the case of one, pieces of jewellery inspired by the different traditions and religions in between which he had grown up and exists.

Tensions Within the Group

W hile planning the exhibition, differences over the proposed content created some tensions, both between the participants and among members of the research group. For example, a heated discussion arose about the first suggestion for the name of the exhibition, which involved the word Muslim. Two of the female participants were particularly insistent that they should be introduced as people with a Muslim background — not Muslims — and suggested that the name for the exhibition be 'Numur — Islam and I' (instead of Young Muslims). The word Numur, meaning small tigers, had previously been proposed by some female participants as the basis for the exhibition's logo. Although some of the male participants considered the image of small tigers an inappropriate representation for the exhibition in the current Islamophobic climate, the word was retained in the title.

Another image that provoked impassioned discussions was a photograph taken by one of the female participants, which we had also used as the background image on the research webpage. The photographer had captured her feet as she stood on her prayer mat (see Figure 27.3). When pieces of the photograph were used as part of a mosaic print for the background illustration of the exhibition poster, together with some other excerpts of photographs taken by the female participants, some male participants objected, claiming that the photograph was unsuitable in this context because it depicted naked feet. Thus, the clippings showing feet and prayer items were cut from the final version of the poster.

Fig. 27.3 *My prayer mat*, a photograph taken by a participant. *Source:* Author.

The process of creating the exhibitions became rather chaotic, as nobody really managed the planning and curating, perhaps because so many people were involved. For example, the workshops that had initially been planned around the themes introduced by the female participants never occurred. However, the project assistant and the intern created a guided tour for schools, and this provided an educational dimension to the exhibition. As some of the participants were involved in guiding the student groups around the exhibition, they were able to receive feedback on their artworks and engage in a dialogue with the audience; moreover, some were involved in organizing handicraft workshops for children, alongside the workshops and seminars directed by the local Muslim youth organizations.

Many people attended the opening of the exhibition in Helsinki, including friends of the artists, members of the research group, members of Islamic organizations and local citizens. Nasima Razmyar, one of the deputy mayors of Helsinki and herself a young woman with a Muslim background, gave a moving opening speech. It was apparent that an event like this was significant to many Finnish people having their roots in Islam. In Turku, however, some tensions arose even between different cooperating Muslim youth groups. In the opening ceremony these tensions were apparent when a conservative Imam spoke on behalf of one organization, while two female members of another organization performed pop songs, which were considered impious by the other group.

Leaving the Field: In Which Direction Does the Trapeze Swing?

Katrina Jungnickel and Larissa Hjorth (2014) observe that methods do not remain untouched by practice, rather, they are transformed by the subject and content. This also occurred in our project, which — even by the rather strict methodological limitations imposed upon it — managed to reveal some subjugated realities and provide space for imagination, border crossings and cultural citizenship (Conquergood, 2009; Hua, 2011; St. Pierre, Jackson & Mazze, 2016). Consequently, the exhibition offered a site for a diverse group of young people with Muslim backgrounds to discuss their varied sense of belonging and their relationship to Islam.

The research process itself challenged the divisive epistemology and problem-centred approach defined in the research plan. The methods and goals created for the plan were simultaneously specific and broad, and as such they failed to adequately support the enthusiasm and creativity of the participants and researchers. However, by trusting in the unfinished research process and by travelling the borders where meaning dissipated, a dialogue was opened around the ideas and artworks created and presented by the participants, becoming a kind of nomadic inquiry and transforming the research setting (Haseman 2006; St. Pierre, 2005). For example, the original idea of videotaping a day in the participants' life transpired to be both practically and methodologically problematic. Likewise, the original plan to categorize participants by, for example, their sect, ethnicity, social class, or their own or their parents' occupation appeared strange in a creative research process which wanted participants to explore their sense of belonging (and resilience) by using artistic approaches. Ultimately, for example in the research catalogue, everyone introduced themselves in their own style, and underlying tensions could be found between the lines of these introductions. For instance, the participant dealing with queer perspectives wrote a more poignant text for the second exhibition, expressing her disappointment with patriarchal and dogmatic interpretations of Islam.

Where the Project Leaves the Researcher

I learned a great deal through such a creative research process, and this learning continues. The issues the participants dealt with in their work were inspiring and eye-opening. For example, my perception of Helsinki changed as a consequence of participating with the young Somali woman in making the video that recorded her visit to the Finnish national art collection and in the shadows of Helsinki's cultural monuments and landscapes. Seeing a mosque and Muslim cultural centre through the eyes of a young woman who worked and prayed there, and who wanted to remove the curtain that separated male and female visitors, filled me with admiration for people who give their leisure time to developing such places, which are open to everyone. I also learnt how traditional Kurdish designs are combined with modern styles and became familiar with Sudanese society and customs, life in Lebanese villages, North-African architecture, the Sufi faith and Queer Islam. Furthermore, I heard many stories of resilience told spontaneously.

Perhaps because of these experiences, I was confused when the male participants and members of the participating Muslim Youth organizations began to transform the exhibition into what I interpreted as a presentation of active and even 'pure' religious values. Certainly, the young women's artworks remained part of the exhibition, but somehow their message was 'veiled'. This both reflected and endorsed the problematic positions and expectations arising from living in between Finnish society and their ethnic and religious communities, which many of the participants had discussed at the beginning of the process.

Where the Project Leaves Research

It is unlikely that the female participants followed all the discussions, for example concerning the layout of the poster, as they were not active visitors on the project's Facebook pages. However, for me these incidents raised many questions concerning the positionings of research and researcher and, moreover, the interpretation of visuality and the arts in different Muslim communities. Furthermore, they also led me to consider who had the right to speak for Muslims, especially for young people with a Muslim background, and decide what was correct and appropriate. At the exhibition, it became clear that some Muslim audiences were disturbed by particular artworks. For example, some interpreted *Sufi-Masa* as unorthodox; others were disturbed by a pair of photographs of Imam Hussain's (a founder of the Shia sect) flag, one of which was depicted in rainbow colours; and some could not accept the collage *Face of God*, which presented the idea of God as potentially female.

These questions, in turn, gave rise to others concerning research practices and approaches to organizing exhibitions. For example, is possible negative feedback from audiences a reason to censor the way an art exhibition is presented? Furthermore, should customs concerning art practices and visual culture be adapted differently to suit people with Muslim backgrounds? And finally, are incidents like those I describe unavoidable if researchers listen to different epistemological understandings and become entangled in messy 'rootings' and 'shiftings' (Yuval-Davis, 1997) within the field-research process (Jungnickel & Hjorth, 2014)?

In her essays in *Key writings*, Irigaray (2004) discusses politics, language, art, sensuality, religion and the importance of finding new ways to understand each other in a world where borders are both dissolving and strengthening. In Irigaray's suggestion to let the subject go and accept the limitations of our ability to co-exist with whom or what exceeds us, extends beyond us and remains exterior and foreign to us (ibid., 2004, p. 25), I hear echoes of Buber (1970/1923). In order to create a dialogue, Irigaray underscores the importance of recognizing the difference between the sexes, as Western culture has cultivated the male subject while leaving women without subjectivity. I wonder, could her ideas promote understanding of epistemological and even ontological standpoints concerning the strict division between gender positions — positions which I interpreted as existing behind the specific phenomena discussed in these pages — and help create encounters and transgressions on the borders (Irigaray, 2004, pp. 26–27, Oikarinen-Jabai, 2019).

Unfencing the Field: Embracing Instability and Plurality

James Haywood Rolling writes:

> There is no one set of criteria for judging the artistic quality of a work of arts-based research just as there is no one paradigm for the beauty of a work of art; for some, the beauty of a work of art is in the aesthetics of its forms and the mastery of its techniques, for others, it is in the authenticity and expressiveness of voice, and for still others, in the incisiveness of its social critique. (Rolling, 2010, p. 104)

The same may hold true for research that uses creative methods. In our research, certainly both the researchers and co-researchers had different ideas, not only about methodological inquiries but also about art, its content and its functions. Perhaps the participants from religious organizations considered the project their own in a way that other participants did not. Moreover, their participation probably produced more answers to the questions posed by the original research plan.

Anyhow, the way that different works of art, which — dare I say — even offered varied perspectives and epistemological standpoints on Islam, were presented under the same roof may provoke further discussion inside the community and inspire participants to continue their research and creative artwork.

For me personally, the research has been and, I hope, will remain an eye-opening process, promoting understanding of the multiple realities encountered by different research communities and especially by young women with a Muslim background. Moreover, it is still possible to continue working with the ideas that arose at different stages of the process, including my unrealized plans for a multilingual installation. Research can be conducted in many ways, for example by posing questions about the perception of a phenomenon, explaining that phenomenon through a rich and analytical description of its qualities, or experimenting with the phenomenon in a hands-on intervention that engages with its limits and possibilities (Rolling, 2010). Adopting Deleuze and Guattari's term 'micro-becomings' (1983, p. 70), Rolling (ibid., p. 107) describes how 'Arts-based research practices manifest themselves as poststructural and erosive pathways, flowing over, through, around, and under scientific and social scientific, quantitative, and qualitative epistemologies in a rhizomatic filigree of "micro-becomings"', capturing the flexibility inherent in artistic endeavour.

Maybe it is time to jump from the research trapeze onto a trampoline that may at different times, and in different contexts, fling one in unpredictable directions. Experimental research leaning on performativity, arts and embodied knowledge can take many directions and discover new paths (Pink & Leder Mackley, 2014; Tolia-Kelly, 2007). It was inspirational, therefore, to discover at an international conference in South Africa in June 2017,[2] that resilience researchers in different parts of the world are open to diverse approaches and practise their work by leaning on multiple methodologies, interdisciplinary sources and embodied knowledge. This flexibility encourages further experimentation and engagement with the field and may enable diverse groups within society to be heard and to claim cultural citizenship rights and dignity.

---

2   Pathways to Resilience IV: Global South Perspectives, organized by the Resilience Centre in Cape Town, June 2017.

References

Anzaldúa, G. & Moraga C. (1983). *This bridge called my back: Writings by radical women of colour*. New York: Kitchen Table.

Austin, J. L. (1975/1955). *How to do things with words*. Cambridge, MA: Harvard University Press.

Barone, T. (2006). Arts-based educational research then, now, and later. *Studies in Art Education*, 48(1): 4–8. https://doi.org/10.1080/00393541.2006.1165049 5

Barone, T. & Eisner, E. (2012). *Arts based research*. Los Angeles: Sage.

Bauman, R. (1977). *Verbal art as performance*. Long Grove, IL: Waveland.

Buber, M. (1970/1923). *I and Thou*. Edinburgh: T. & T. Clark.

Butler, J. (1993). *Bodies that matter: On the discursive limits of 'sex'*. Abingdon: Routledge.

Cixous, H. (1993). *Three steps on the ladder of writing*. New York: Columbia University Press.

Conquergood, D. (2009). Performance studies: Interventions and radical research. In: Bial, H. (ed), *Performance studies reader*. New York: Routledge.

Cooke, B. & Kothari U. (2001). The case for participation as tyranny. In: Cooke, B. & Kothari, C. (eds), *Participation: The new tyranny*. London: Zed Books.

Deleuze, G. & Guattari, F. (1983). *On the line*. Los Angeles, CA: Semiotexte.

Denzin, N.K. (2003). *Performance ethnography: Critical pedagogy and the politics of culture*. Thousand Oaks, CA: Sage.

Dewey, J. (2005/1934). *Art as experience*. London: Perigee books.

Didkowsky, N., Ungar, M. & Liebenberg, L. (2010). Using visual methods to capture embedded processes of resilience for youth across cultures and contexts. *Journal of the Canadian Academy of Child and Adolescent Psychiatry*, 19(1): 12–18.

Ernst, C. (2003). *Following Muhammad. Rethinking Islam in the contemporary world*. Chapel Hill, CA: University of North Carolina Press.

Freire, P. (1970/1968). *Pedagogy of the oppressed*. New York: Continuum.

Friedman, S. (2002). 'Border talk', hybridity, and performativity: Cultural theory and identity in the spaces between difference. *Eurozine*. https://www.eurozine.com/authors/susanstanford-friedman/

Haseman, B. (2006). A manifesto for performative research. *Media International Australia Incorporating Culture and Policy*, 118(1): 98–106. https://doi.org/10.1177/1329878X0611800113

hooks, b. (1990). *Yearning: Race, gender and cultural politics*. Boston, MA: South End Press.

Hua, A. (2011). Homing desire, cultural citizenship, and diasporic imaginings. *Journal of International Women's Studies*, 12(4): 45–56. http://vc.bridgew.edu/jiws/vol12/iss4/3

Irigaray, L. (2002). *The way of love*. London: Continuum.

Irigaray L. (2004). *Key writings*. London: Continuum.

Jungnickel, K. & Hjorth, L. (2014). Methodological entanglements in the field: methods, transitions and transmissions. *Visual Studies*, 29(2): 136–45. https://doi.org/10.1080/1472586X.2014.887263

Koobak, R. (2014). Six impossible things before breakfast: How I came across my research topic and what happened next. In: Lykke, N. (ed), *Writing academic texts differently: Intersectional feminist methodologies and the playful art of writing*. New York: Routledge.

Kristeva, J. (1991). *Desire in language*. New York: Columbia University Press.

Liebenberg L. & Ungar, M. (2009). Introduction: The challenges in researching resilience. In: Liebenberg, L. & Ungar, M. (eds), *Researching resilience*. Toronto: Toronto University Press.

Luthar, S., Cichetti, D, & Becker, B. (2000). The construct of resilience: A critical evaluation and guidelines for future work. *Child Development*, 71(3): 543–62. https://doi.org/10.1111/1467-8624.00164

Minh-ha, T.H. (2011). *Elsewhere, within here: Immigration, refugeeism and the boundary event*. New York: Routledge.

O'Neill, M. (2008). Transnational refugees: The transformative role of art? *Forum: Qualitative Social Research*, 9(2): Art. 59. http://nbn-resolving.de/urn:nbn:de:0114-fqs0802590

Oikarinen-Jabai, H. (2018). Young Finnish Somalis exploring their belonging within participatory performative research. In: Davis, K., Ghorashi H. & Smets P. (eds), *Contested belongings: Spaces, practices, biographies*. London: Emerald.

Oikarinen-Jabai, H. (2019). Young Finnish people of Muslim background creating 'spiritual becomings' and 'coming communities' in their art works. *Of Sacred Crossroads — Cultural Studies and the Sacred. Open Cultural Studies*, 2019, 3, 148–60.

Phelan, P. (1993). *Unmarked: The politics of performance*. Abingdon: Routledge.

Pink, S. & Leder Mackley, K. (2014). Re-enactment methodologies for everyday life research: Art therapy insights for video ethnography. *Visual Studies*, 29(2): 146–54. https://doi.org/10.1080/1472586X.2014.887266

Richardson, L. (1997). *Fields of play: Constructing academic life*. New Brunswick, NJ: Rutgers University Press.

Rolling J.H. (2010). A paradigm analysis of arts-based research and implications for education. *Studies in Art Education*, 51(2): 102–14. https://doi.org/10.108 0/00393541.2010.11518795

St. Pierre, E.A. (2005). Writing as a method of nomadic inquiry. In: Denzin, N.K & Lincoln, Y.S. (eds), *The Sage handbook of qualitative inquiry*. London: Sage.

St. Pierre, E.A., Jackson, A.Y. & Mazze, L.A. (2016). New empiricisms and new materialisms: Conditions for new inquiry. *Cultural Studies-Critical Methodologies*, 16(2): 99–110. https://doi.org/10.1177/1532708616638694

Schechner R. (1993). *The future of ritual: Writings on culture and performance*. Abingdon: Routledge.

Tolia-Kelly, D. (2007). Participatory art: Capturing spatial vocabularies in a collaborative visual methodology with Melanie Carvalho and South-Asian women in London, UK. In: Kindon, S., Pain, R. & Kesby, M. (eds), *Participatory action research approaches and methods: Connecting people, participation and place*. Abingdon: Routledge.

Turner, V. (1967). Betwixt and between: The liminal period in Rites de Passage. In: Turner, V. (ed), *The forest of symbols: Aspects of Ndembu ritual*. New York: Cornell University Press.

Ungar, M. (2004). *Nurturing hidden resilience in troubled youth*. Toronto: Toronto University Press.

Windle, G., Bennett, K, & Noyes, J. (2011). A methodological review of resilience measurement scales. *Health and Quality of Life Outcomes 2011*, 9(8): 2–18. https://doi:org/ 10.1186/1477-7525-9-8

Yuval-Davis, N. (1997). *Gender & nation*. London: Sage.

28. Discourses, Cultural Narratives, and Genre in Biographical Narratives
A Personal Overview

Marianne Horsdal

Marianne Horsdal considers different approaches and projects using biographical narrative methods, drawing on a lifetime of experience as an educator and researcher in Denmark. This is a concise but artfully composed account, which is set within a historical and theoretical context.

T he invitation to contribute to this book asked us 'to interrogate the discourses we live by and consider how they are present in cultural narratives, and how they are relevant to the real life contexts of adult education and of people's life histories, and to question to what extent people's accounts are shaped by the understandings already held', and this is what I have done.

During a quarter of a century of research on biographical narratives a significant part of my analysis has been to identify and examine the cultural narratives expressed in the life stories right from the beginning. I rarely use the term 'discourse' in my books and articles on biographical narrative research, but this does not mean that I object to the terms used in the invitation. I only prefer the term cultural narratives in order to distance myself from the theories on narrative, which in the postmodern line of thought only wanted to speak of discourse. In viewing

https://doi.org/10.11647/OBP.0203.28

biographical narratives, also, as a purely linguistic phenomenon, such theorists abstained from any cognitive, embodied or phenomenological approach to the life story narratives.

My immediate answer to the question posed in the invitation is clear: People's accounts of their lives are to a very great extent shaped by understandings which may be termed and analysed as discourses or cultural narratives, that is as understandings already held in the communities and societies in which the narrators interact. What is interesting, however, is the way the cultural narratives or discourses appear in the stories.

Biographical Narratives

When someone is asked to tell about her life — in an interview, in an interpersonal exchange of human curiosity, in a professional setting — the context of the telling is obviously of great significance. We do not tell the same story in different settings, and we do not tell the same story throughout changing times. The context of the narrative has a decisive impact on the discourses we may find in the story.

This, however, does not imply a complete relativism; the context is very important but not the only significant element of the story told. A life story narrative contains cultural, as well as cognitive and corporeal elements, however inseparable. The life story informs the listener about interpretations of self and existence, as memories from the past, expectations of the future, and the experience of the present are conceived, combined and expressed in the moment and context of telling.

The argument that we are confined to or limited by the cultural-symbolic signs available to us is often put forward, and for good reasons, mainly due to the influence of impoverished cultural environments. However, it is a remarkable fact that the human imagination enables unlimited creative and innovative use of culturally and socially inherited symbolic forms. The ongoing production of fiction is a proof of the human aptitude for new creations, just as the fantastic possibility of new musical compositions exists in spite of the fact that they all use the same twelve tones. Limitation of the cultural tools for symbolic expression is a social and cultural issue, not an immanent feature of symbolic representation.

Biographical narratives also contain a mixture of something unique as well as socially and culturally familiar symbolic material; there are remarkably common features. We are a paradoxical mixture of cultural imprints, such as social discourses and features of learned social interactions and, at the same time, we are individually unique human beings due to our corporeal existence in space and time in a cultural environment. Only Siamese twins share an identical path and trajectory throughout life. The rest of us move physically along individual trajectories in space and time although constantly involved in interpersonal relationships of various kinds, which partly determine our interpretations and embodied experiences of our life journey as well as our intentions and actions. Large samples of biographical narratives make the paradox evident. Each story and each human being is unique, and yet stories display so many common traits that similarities are found between many individual stories.

We are narrated from a third person perspective before we ourselves are able to narrate (Kerby, 1991). The world is pointed out to us adorned or burdened with values and significance from the very beginning. During our upbringing we acquire the available cultural tools in richer or poorer degrees, including the words and discourses at our disposal. Even the cognitive parts, our mastery of language and episodic memory, depends heavily on interpersonal interactions.

Whether or not we regard ourselves or others as individual beings is a different matter. Individualism is a major discourse or grand narrative in our Western culture today, which significantly affects our interpretations of self. Whether we regard the other as an individual human being or as a generalized member of a group is another question to be considered (Horsdal, 2012; 2017).

Discourse and Genre

Discourse analysis can be a useful tool in the analysis of biographical narratives. Back in 1998 Ochs wrote a fine chapter on narrative in Van Dijks book, *Discourse as Structure and Process*. A central part of discourse analysis has been the identification of 'floating signifiers' and the tensions between various discourses used to determine the assignment of meaning to concepts such as 'freedom', 'democracy', 'equality', or 'nation'. Discourse analysis thus provides an important tool in critical analysis not least of social media.

As the chapters in Van Dijk's book (and, indeed in the very book that you are reading) demonstrate, discourse may be applied in a way somewhat similar to the term 'genre', as when you talk of a 'narrative discourse' in comparison with a different discursive genre, or as a concept somewhat similar to 'grand narratives' or 'cultural narratives'. But the ambiguity of the concepts may be confusing. You can speak of a narrative genre in comparison with, say, lyrics; and you may speak of the genre of a particular narrative, which may be told as a fairy tale, a *Bildung* novel, or a tragedy. The terms 'discourse' and 'genre' may also signify larger or smaller linguistic units.

As for third term, 'grand narrative', Lyotard (1979) proved to be quite wrong in his claim that 'grand narratives' were extinct. Although the interpretation of the significance of class and other collective frameworks has changed, grand narratives of 'individualism', not to speak of 'growth', are still very much alive.

Personally, I have primarily used the term 'cultural narratives' in my own research, signifying both grand narratives and discourses of various kinds, such as the two grand narratives mentioned above, as well as, say, religious narratives and social political narratives, which are part of people's biographical stories.

Negotiating Meaning

S ome of the hundreds of stories I have collected or analysed show a tendency toward negotiation of meaning between competing discourses, as in the two examples below.

Story 1

Can you force someone to do something — because what will be the result? In a way I feel that when I have finished this education and I am able to do various things and also want to do various things, well, when there are lots of schools missing teachers the problem is that most of the students at the college of education say they may well study there, but they do not want to become teachers. The college works as a jumping-off point for something else. You don't really know what you want — you have tried the university — may be two or three times. This is typical of many of the students at college. What, really do I think myself? What do I want? We...maybe you have an obligation towards society. My father always maintained that.

(Woman, aged 23)

Story 2

On the other hand, I have no doubts as for when we feel fine. Most people feel bad about being alone, and they feel better being part of communities, and when they feel loved and appreciated by other people. That you now and again may want to act selfish, it may be suffocating, and then you want to break out. But I believe we generally feel better in communities. The thing is that what is frightening in our time is also the gift. That we are released from a lot of family ties, religious ties, national ties, ideological ties...the question is to accept that we haven't got those ties you had in different times. Yet while we are so differentiated it is important to have the basic belief that at some point we just want the same things.

(Man, aged 27)

These two young people negotiate an interpretation of self and existence with themselves among several common discourses. The discourse of individuality and variety of choices and 'death of the grand narratives' on the one hand, and a need for relationships and communitarianism on the other.

The open approach to the narrative interview — one in which the story told is the response to one single question: 'Please, tell me about your life from the beginning until we are here today', and where interruptions and redirections by further questions from the interviewer are completely avoided — leads to interviews, and stories, that more often display a negotiation of meaning between a variety of different cultural narratives or discourses (Horsdal, 2016b).

In some research projects this open narrative interview was followed by a more traditional semi-structured interview in which I posed several questions according to the interests of the research. Here, I noticed that the responses to the questions in the semi-structured interview proved to be much more unambiguous and unequivocal compared to the open biographical narrative. In other words, the narrators negotiated meaning in the open biographical narrative, but chose one discourse (that perhaps might be expressed as the 'good interviewee') in the semi-structured interview. Also, a very specific context for the interview might limit the application of various discourses to what was thought most appropriate, thus equivalent to Bruner's argument of rhetorical justifications (Bruner, 1991).

An analytic implication of this is an increasing impact of the relationship between interviewer and interviewee — which, however, is always very important — in a semi-structured interview, colouring the chosen discourses and/or cultural narratives. The more the methodology of the interview procedure supports time for thought, for reflection, for consideration of what to say and how to put it in a relaxed atmosphere, the more negotiations of meaning between different 'voices' and given cultural narratives are expressed in the biographical narrative.

Some commonly held beliefs and widespread discourses, or grand narratives, are present in most biographical interviews. The context of the biographical interview in itself points to an individualistic interpretation of existence and to an emphasized linearity in modern Western life stories. I have in a few cases met other forms, cyclical stories based on the seasons as well as collective conceptions of the person in her relationships of kin or class. Interestingly, the main discourse has changed over recent generations. For those born during the beginning of the 20th century, life was viewed as a common destiny; to their grandchildren, life is viewed as a matter of personal choice.

The biographical reflexivity I am referring to above is in itself a quite dominant cultural narrative in our cultural environment. We ask the questions: 'who am I?' 'who do I want to become'? 'Am I doing the right thing?' 'Making the right choices?'. These are questions that are part of a grand narrative or discourse of: 'life as a project and a matter of personal choice'. Naturally, biographical research on lifelong learning underscored this tendency.

This individual biographical reflexivity so well discussed by Taylor (1989) and Giddens (1990), meaning that individual biographies replaced the cultural narratives of a collective fate ('Such were the conditions for women/small farmers/workers') is nevertheless hardly visible in some biographical narratives.

Biography and Social Context

B iographical reflexivity is mostly found in stories of well-educated, prosperous young people. The two stories presented above come from a project researching biographical learning of active citizens. Stories collected in more impoverished areas beyond the range of possibilities belonging to the middle class rather show an interpretation of existence as a troublesome journey in a rough terrain with few options and a careless resignation to circumstances combined sometimes with some anger and frustration (Evans, 2016; Horsdal, 2016a; 2017). The antagonism between this interpretation of experience and the mainstream dominant discourse of life as a personal project with full control over success or failure may furnish the frustration.

'We don't always get it, as we want', 'Life is no bed of roses', 'This was hard, it was a failure', 'What doesn't kill you, makes you stronger', are some of the expressions commonly heard in a typical life story from someone from a less privileged background.

Narrators belonging to the much older generations often tell us about the hard circumstances they endured, with a certain pride that they managed to have a reasonable life after all. The individual — often quite moderate — success is viewed within a frame of a collective fate of poverty, hard work, gender, social class, illness, etc. Today foreground and background are almost reversed for the less privileged narrators. The discourse of life as an individual project to be achieved is hinted at as a background upon which the actual life conditions seem almost given or fatal. And yet, the personal responsibility for success or failure lurks in the background.

Over many years I have asked my students of education at the university to carry out a narrative interview with someone they know, in order to become more familiar with the methods of biographical research before entering the field. Together we have read and analysed most of those stories in class. This random collection of life stories from my students included a significant number of biographical narratives told by people who had to struggle with very serious problems during their childhoods. Serious neglect, violence, mental illness, abuse of drugs or alcohol make children's and young people's lives difficult:

it can be a major challenge just to survive without deterioration, and without repeating destructive patterns in their own relationships.

Other narrators tell about caring families, secure childhoods and lots of happy memories. However, the most significant issue in the stories I have read, across different backgrounds, is the question of relationships.

Many biographical narratives show relationships as the overall theme of the stories: the relationships within the family between the different members; the relationships in kindergarten, in schools, in neighbourhoods, in sports or other leisure activities, other educational settings and workplaces. Shifts of place or communities of practice, such as the family moving, parents getting divorced, enrolment in a new school etc., entail new challenges within the theme of relationships. Did the narrator manage to make new friends in the new place, did he/ she feel accepted, legitimate in his/her participation, matters. This is significant.

Relationships are the big, big issue, and the feeling of being bullied or excluded seems devastating. Our participation in different communities is valued in the stories according to the kind of relationships they offer or oppose. Even in stories in which working life and career play a significant role in the biography, the relationships within the different workplaces have a heavy impact.

The dependency on good relationships exposes a certain vulnerability, which can be interpreted as connected to the overall discourse on individualism and the 'liberation from', or 'dissolution of' earlier more persistent communities based on necessity. The old collective communities did not question the legitimacy of the wish to be accepted and appreciated for the person you are and for what you can do, to the same extent. You were free to go, but also to be excluded.

I also noticed a tendency to a quite narrow range of social relationships in the stories of less privileged people. Does the outer world seem frightening or hostile? Or, challenging and fascinating? Active citizens have the resilience and extra energy to engage in a larger world, the less privileged tend to care only for their closest relationships. One of the active citizens I interviewed said:

I think it is one of the curses of our time, exactly because we have got so many options, and we'll always feel there is something we haven't time to do. The danger, of course, is that you go to the other extreme and search yourself more than necessary, and then that you turn around and say that you'll only concern yourself with the Danish, or you'll only concern yourself with your family, or you'll only concern yourself with your job and that's it. This is a danger these years, and some people are caught.

(Man, aged 29)

This is clearly a statement from a person who has the freedom of choice and the resources to reach out to a larger range of communities. In contrast, another interviewee, a young woman alone with four children, from a third generation subjected to a succession of violent family relationships, limits her ambitions to the hope that her children do not become mothers at an early age as she has done. Typically, the only person outside her own closest family mentioned in her story is a doctor who treated her when she was sick as a child. How narrow or how spacious is the human lifeworld in which we engage? And what reserves of strength do we need, and have, for this engagement?

In Conclusion

I now take up the question of hope foregrounded at an ESREA Life History and Biography Network conference I attended (Canterbury, 2016), for I hold that the sharing of life story narratives can play a significant role in supporting social harmony. It may, in itself, enhance a view of the other as someone with whom you can identify as well as recognize and accept as a different, unique, and equal person. The paradox between the individual trajectory and the persistent interdependency of humans in society cannot and should not be resolved; just acknowledged. Most certainly narrative competences, enabling individuals to safely negotiate their way round prevailing discourses, are indispensable today in a world full of troublesome, even dangerous, manipulative behaviours.

References

Bruner, J. (1990). *Acts of meaning*. Cambridge, MA: Harvard University Press.

Evans, R. (2016). Life is normal in Donetsk: Narratives of distant conflict and young adults' learning biographies. In: Formenti, L. & West, L. (eds), *Stories that make a difference*. Milano: Pensa MultiMedia Editore.

Giddens, A. (1990). *The consequences of modernity*. Cambridge: Polity.

Horsdal, M. (2012). *Telling lives. Exploring dimensions of narrative*. Abingdon: Routledge. https://doi.org/10.4324/9780203805046

Horsdal, M. (2016a). The intergenerational impact on the experience of learning. In: Formenti, L. & West, L. (eds), *Stories that make a difference*. Milano: Pensa MultiMedia Editore.

Horsdal, M. (2016b). The narrative interview — method, theory and ethics: Unfolding a life. In: Goodson, I. (ed), *The Routledge international handbook on narrative and life history*. Abingdon: Routledge.

Horsdal, M. (2017). *Tilværelsens fortællinger. Tilegnelse og anvendelse*. København: Hans Reitzels Forlag.

Kerby, A. (1991). *Narrative and the self*. Indiana, PA: Indiana University Press.

Lyotard, J.F. (1979). *La condition postmoderne*. Paris: Minuit.

Ochs, E. (1998). Narrative. In: Van Dijk, T. (ed), *Discourse as structure and process*. London: Sage.

Taylor, C. (1989). *Sources of the self: The making of modern identity*. Cambridge: Cambridge University Press.

Photo by Tom Perkins, CC-BY 4.0

Learning from Narratives, Discourses and Biographical Research
An Afterword

Hazel R. Wright and Marianne Høyen

Our Intentions for the Book

The introduction set out our editorial stance as embracing diversity by welcoming chapters with a broad range of content written in a range of styles. We knew that we could end up with 'this-and-that', a little like the Chicago Sociologists, but as Sacks acknowledges, 'this-and-that is what the world is made up of' and can lead to work that is 'worth criticizing' (Sacks, 1992a, p. 27). As our explicit motivation was to be inclusive and open up the possibility of publication to as many researchers as possible, we were prepared to take this risk. We were confident that we would gain some interesting insights and committed to shaping the book into a coherent publication. On reflection, however, we may also have been making a stand against the neoliberal practices constraining higher education, which increasingly limit what gets published and by whom.

A great deal of biographical research is about 'doing being ordinary' (Sacks, 1992b, pp. 215–21), 'attending the world, yourself, others, objects so as to see how it is that it's a usual scene' (p. 218) and this book collects together a good number of everyday narratives of 'life as lived' (Ricœur, 1986a, p. 121). Some chapters will have interested the educated reader as they echo his or her own experiences, but others

https://doi.org/10.11647/OBP.0203.29

enter the lives of those less fortunate in society so bring us into close proximity with the unfamiliar; many occupy positions between these two extremes. But, apart from being interesting stories, what other value derives from a reading of the different chapters? What insights do we gain from looking beyond the information articulated within each chapter?

Before addressing those questions, we need to engage in a little '*travail négatif*' and set aside the content, context and findings from each chapter and 'the connections that are recognized as given before the game starts' (Foucault, 1969, p. 34, translated by Evans). Then, engage in processes that could be termed '*travail positif*', asking in turn: Why does this chapter matter? What is it doing? What do we learn from it? Through such a process it was possible to identify specific themes and then to group them together into meta-themes that we could discuss. Through doing this we found the chapters delivered some unexpected riches, justifying the latitude accorded authors to write as they chose.

Emergent Themes Within the Book

Methodologies

We stated in the introduction that authors were asked to focus on discourses and narratives rather than on describing methodologies, unless these were key foci, nevertheless, some of the chapters offer very clear descriptions and / or exemplar of particular approaches. Dyson's work closely follows the Narrative Inquiry methodology as set out by Jean Clandinin and Michael Connolly (Ch1), exploring the process of thinking *with* rather than *about* stories and providing an explanation of a process that others have used instinctively. Similarly applicable elsewhere, Breton (Ch2) uses a case study to show how the dynamics of biographical inter-comprehension can be harnessed to turn lived experience into expressible content and explains how this could be of benefit in therapeutic education.

Formenti, Galimberti and Ferrari (Ch11) present three alternative ways of writing a life history, one relational to the actual interview, one pursuing a specific interest and one written as fiction. These materials are there to draw on, to study and decide when you might use each style or which one you prefer. A clear account of Conversational Analysis and how to use it appears in Evans' chapter (Ch17), and in chapter 20 Sprung discusses both participatory approaches and the use of a documentary film as a reporting mechanism. Brayshaw and Granville also describe a filmmaking project and their text itself is a collage that both parodies and presents elements of the stages of filmmaking. It also draws attention in a very honest way to the problems encountered by creative researchers when asked to submit written papers; as a result there is a mine of information in chapter 24. Chan (Ch21) provides an insightful discussion around successfully using Indigenous Research Methods (IRM) and there are ideas within this account that are transferable into other work with minority groups. Woodley (Ch26) focuses on a journaling method that developed from her need to reflect and make field notes as her work progressed, while Horsdal (Ch28) contributes to debates around method in clearly describing how differing interview styles provoke narrative responses that are qualitively distinctive. Mazzoli Smith (Ch25) provides a well-sculpted example of reflection and reflexivity in practice that enables her to move from her own experiences to her research participants, seamlessly, and with greater understanding. Together these chapters offer authentic accounts of methods that are far removed from the 'do this, do that' style of many textbooks; as such a wider variety of researchers will find them useful.

Narrative Power

The powerful role played by narrative is clearly visible in many chapters. Dyson's entire chapter (Ch1) is about the strength of narrative and an exploration of how fictional narrative can often capture, even concentrate, the significance of an event or emotion giving it impact and making it memorable long after the narration is complete. Breton (Ch2) discusses how storytelling and writing can make the unsayable 'sayable' and transform patients' relationships to their illnesses, enabling them to gain a greater sense of control. He claims that it also generates understanding of their experience as, 'in articulating and in developing it, it becomes itself' (Ricœur 1986b, p. 62). Castiglioni and Girotta (Ch12) see maturation as dependent upon the impact of official dominant narratives on personal internalized scripts, necessitating adaptation, and also argue the need to develop counter-narratives when life goes askew. Mascarenhas (Ch18) finds that through the creation of stories from interview material she was able see behind some of the horrific situations migrants faced and find meaningful ways in which they could be encouraged to learn English, foregrounding their needs as humans, ahead of governmental aims of making them merely employable.

Family Influences

M ascarenhas also reveals the importance of biographical research in understanding the formative influences in people's lives. Others find significance in objects, events or family: Mazzoli Smith (Ch25), for example, clearly links her life choices to reading Murdoch's novels as a young person. In Høyen and Rasmussen's work (Ch5) family influences relate to professional life; their study quite clearly shows how decisions to teach particular academic subjects reflect family members' affiliation to the sciences or humanities in their working lives. Wright (Ch4) demonstrates how individuals construct their own understandings of nature but shows too that, alongside education and life experiences, family funds of knowledge (Moll et al., 1992) play a part in the development and retention of ideas. Individuals may conceive a personal sense of what nature 'is' but this is shaped by those with whom they have regular contact. Family values can be a source of conflict, too. Evans' chapter (Ch17) conveys in detail the tensions that arise when a young migrant woman wants to go to university whilst her family think marriage a more appropriate choice. Yet for Rasmussen's converts to Islam, the family moderates a new Muslim's beliefs to accommodate their needs — celebrating Christmas, for example.

Researcher Positioning

O ur chapters offer interesting insights into how the researchers position themselves within the study undertaken — many choose research topics where they have the benefits of being an insider researcher. One would assume this was for ease of access but the commitment that resonates in the chapters suggests that the desire to make things better may be more important. Middleton (Ch8) clearly states, 'I wanted to influence policy-making' and Woodley (Ch26), who was working in a setting for excluded pupils, 'was keen to carry out research that might benefit them'. It is evident, too, in the passion with which González González (Ch14) addresses his theme: phrases like 'scandalous data' and 'the number of minor victims of corruption, is unbearable' do not denote detachment. Language, again, demonstrates enthusiastic participation in Sprung's chapter (Ch20). She describes how 'filmmakers, stepped into the scene and became visible' and how she finds a discussion within the project 'exciting'. Researchers are often keen to address power imbalances, too. Zientek (Ch16) even chooses participatory action research because, '[f]or me, PAR is a form of resistance to all forms of control limiting our freedom'. Evans (Ch17) describes data as 'constituted in the interview process jointly', implying that talk-in-action is a democratic research process. Even when not a true 'insider', there may be a parallel association. Chan (Ch21), for example, does not share a cultural identity with her research participants but has an alternative Chinese heritage that 'I believe, provides me with some understanding'. Such links enable empathy.

Researcher Identities

The informality of the biographical research process, with interviews more often resembling conversations than structured processes, draws the researcher into the participant's life even as s/he seeks to draw the story out. We seek to generate trust and expect to be part of the interaction; this is a privilege that we need to be aware of constantly. It can make it difficult to settle for anything less when engaging in other types of project. For Oikarinen-Jabai (Ch27), a transdisciplinary project caused stress, as she was constantly 'trapezing between paradigms', unsure of expectations. This chapter gives a candid account of membership of a large-scale research project which reveals how these can be difficult to co-ordinate and focus. It is interesting to read in Ylitapio-Mäntylä and Mäkiranta's chapter (Ch22) that they, too, found working 'in a huge transnational cluster where researchers do not even know all the people with whom they must cooperate' challenging — their task at odds with their feminist pedagogies. We may wonder if being part of such a process is especially difficult for the biographical researcher who more normatively engages in one-to-one interactions. Ylitapio-Mäntylä and Mäkiranta explain the issue in terms of a clash between the neoliberal expectations of 'busyness' with the need to have 'enough time for meeting with participants', because caring is 'an important factor in the learning process'.

Caring and the Relational Nature of Biographical Research

Together, the chapters in this book reveal the relational nature of researcher/participant engagement when using biographical and narrative methods, something specifically addressed by Horsdal (Ch28). As you move through the book there is a growing sense that the researcher 'cares'; there are no less than sixteen chapters that talk about vulnerability and/or focus on studying vulnerable people. Caring was evident in the earlier discussion of researcher position and is directly raised by Ylitapio-Mäntylä and Mäkiranta in chapter 22. It is central to Breton's chapter (Ch2) in both context and research intention. Bainbridge and West's chapter (Ch3) draws attention to the 'shared humanity' in the WEA classes and the sense 'of belonging' found within fundamentalism, prompting us to think further about the consequences of social isolation and marginalization. Rasmussen's chapter (Ch19) discusses conversion to Islam in a different context and country. The two converts to Islam she interviewed both rejected branches that they found 'cold and lacking in spirituality'. Respectively, they saw Islam as 'about inclusiveness' and as a 'spiritual comfort zone', fundamentalism plays no part, yet their stories testify to the need to belong.

Noddings, in her work on the ethics of care, makes sense of the relational processes we identified within other chapters. Analysing how caring functions, she talks of 'engrossment', the attentiveness of the carer who receives what the cared-for is feeling and saying and undergoes 'motivational displacement'. This manifests in an outflow of energy 'toward the needs and wants of the cared-for', who recognizes this caring and makes some sort of response (Noddings, 2005, p. 2). Thus, she sees caring as essentially relational — clearly its interactive nature carries the potential to strengthen over time. The combination of relationality and insider identity offers a possible additional explanation to why caring is so apparent in these biographical interviews.

Transformational Effects

Our own experience of carrying out biographical interviews is that the participants often find their involvement rewarding, perhaps due to the attentiveness of the interviewer, striving to listen closely, constantly monitoring the exchange to determine when to prompt, when to question, when to affirm and when to simply listen. Some will learn things about themselves or their views that they did not previously realize, in a process akin to that described by Breton (Ch2) who draws attention to 'transformative processes that take place during the activities of wording, meaning-making and storytelling'. The notion of transformation is well-established within education following the works of Freire (1970) and Mezirow (1975) among others, and fits well with the broader theme of changing lives that resonates across many of the chapters. The potential — maybe a need — to change, is embedded in notions of vulnerability already discussed, and is particularly problematic when people are in crisis: the prisoners in Mathiassen's (Ch13) and Cooper's (Ch23) studies, the gamblers in Castiglioni and Girotti's (Ch12) project. It is captured in religious and cultural beliefs in chapters 3, 12, 18, 19 and 27 in particular, and more subtly in Chan (Ch21) as the project around Indigenous peoples is a collaborative one of 'doing with' rather than 'doing to'. As Andrews (2014, p. 27), reminds us narrative imagination offers a way of seeing the world as one of 'infinite possibilities', and this adds a positive note for the resolution of problems.

Empowerment

It is relevant, too, to consider the number of chapters that directly relate to larger-scale emancipatory projects, for Indigenous people in chapter 22 (as well as Ch21), for migrants in chapters 20 and 27, the ageing population in chapter 24, and through educational support in chapter 18. These projects all specifically aim to change lives in some way, and in Zientek (Ch16) we saw how an educational course in Poland specifically aimed to enable citizens to work for change — changing society not just individual lives. In Mazzoli Smith (Ch25), we saw how personal reflection can offer insights that may further change society by supporting the functioning of the UK educational 'widening participation' agenda (Bridges, 2005), something that has proved somewhat difficult to operationalize. Empowerment is an important factor here, but in other chapters participants (students) develop agency despite the educational system. This is apparent in Wallin's study in a Swedish school (Ch15), in the actions of the Kenyan students in Dahl (Ch6) and Sheridan's study of Irish students (Ch 10). Such narratives contrast with that of the Irish adult educators in Bates Evoy (Ch7) who, instead of demanding change, find reward through intrinsic motivation. Poorly enacted empowerment through education can, however, become a source of internal conflict and social challenge, as is visible in Mathiassen's study of an ex-offender (Ch13).

Protected Enclaves

Some authors refer to 'safe spaces', echoing the notion of protected enclaves common within adult education (Boud & Walker, 2002). These phrases imply tutor support to create student opportunities for testing and planning change, and this concept appears in several chapters (2, 8, 12, 13, 16, 20, 24 and 27) but can refer to very different structures. Breton's study reminds us that these may be carefully orchestrated and be established in health settings, too (Ch2). Middleton (Ch8) shows that they may be enclosures within a larger institution (the Nurture group within the school), Zientek (Ch16) that they may be actively established to further the cause of societal change.

Change Agendas and Counter Discourses

The need for change at social level is also apparent in the discussion of counter-productive agendas (chapters 5, 6, 14, 15, 18), and counter-productive practices in Pathak (Ch9). For example, Høyen and Rasmusen (Ch5) discuss an official counter-educational narrative of 'competence' that has turned the gaze away from a 'fundamentally inappropriate' counter-productive division between arts (cultural) and science (natural) subjects. There are a number of other chapters that call for change and suggest possible ways forward. Pathak (Ch9) believes that curbing the use of violent language and reward systems in schools might, in the long-term, challenge the dominance of punitive discourses.

Castiglioni and Girotti (Ch12) endorse the value of narrative in changing internal scripts controlling individual behaviours. Mascarenhas (Ch18) demonstrates how English Language teaching could do so much more to support migrants in taking their place in society. Rasmussen (Ch 19) makes several salient points: Firstly, she calls for a 'greater attention to discourses' and research that asks questions anew rather than simply testing existing beliefs, lest it ends up simply endorsing prevalent views, mindful that her own small study that was hypothesis-free, challenges normative understandings. Secondly, she raises the concern that outdated modes of thinking may actually 'slow the pace of change', important when dealing with issues that divide societies, like religion. In chapter 25, Mazzoli Smith demonstrates how counter-discourses could help people 'to think beyond the one that predominates', and Woodley (Ch26) also hopes that through sharing narratives, professionals may be able to 'offer a counter-discourse to that which is generally accepted' within teaching. Changing the prevalent discourse is a reliable means of embedding a change of culture but may not be easy to achieve.

Education

Finally, and importantly, we turn to the theme of education which underpins all the chapters, if sometimes a little obliquely. In most cases, chapters address *adult* education in some way but with approaches ranging across the spectrum: incidental, informal, non-formal and formal (Foley, 2004), varying in the degree to which they mention pedagogic practices. In terms of sectors, many relate to the tertiary sector, whether higher (for example, 10, 14, 25) or vocational/professional (for example, 1, 5, 6, 7), but a few attach to the compulsory sector (for example, 8, 15, 26). Only a small number of authors were still directly working within a formal adult education sector at the time of writing (for example, 7, 16, 18), an area sorely diminished through successive cuts to purportedly 'non-essential' services (a label we strongly reject). However, their number is boosted by the funded community-based projects (12, 20, 21, 22, 24, 27) where the target audience is adults (or youths as preparation for adulthood), usually from groups that are socially marginalized, giving this work a 'remedial' connotation.

In reality, many chapters straddle these administrative boundaries: Brayshaw and Granville's chapter (24), sits within higher education but serves an adult education purpose in catering for senior citizens; Mazzoli Smith (Ch25) and Woodley (Ch26) closely juxtapose the personal and the professional; with the prisoner narratives the educational element is implicit in Cooper (Ch23), and a tentative plan in Mathiassen (Ch13), and for these and other accounts (4, 11, 17, 19), informal learning is buried within the individual life stories, or discussed from a historical/ philosophical perspective (2, 3, 9, 28). These categorizations are only loosely applied to give an overall sense of coverage, they are indicative rather than definitive. Perhaps one of the outcomes from their application is the reassurance that, despite cuts in adult education provision across Westernized societies, the field continues in alternative ways: through the community project, the individual researcher pursuing an interest or further qualification, or simply fascinated to 'see what is really happening' in a context familiar to them. Perhaps a book like this can serve to keep the flame alive — nourish and promote the importance of education for everyone, endorse a shift away from the focus on test-led schooling from infancy, through to the credentialism and performative ideology that saturates the tertiary sector and neoliberal societies, detracting from the pleasure of 'education for education's sake'. Certainly, when good practice turns students' lives around, as in Sheridan's story of enabling progression after examination failure (Ch10), we see the possibility for hope to have a tangible shape.

Looking Forward

To look ahead, we first return to caring. It is salutary to note Noddings' claim (2005, p. 6) that continual testing 'is largely a product of separation and lack of trust', a sign of a society that makes neither time nor space for caring. Her topic is children's education, but her arguments have wider application. We endorse her claim that when society looks for easy and efficient ways to evaluate complex ideas 'then fear and competition take the place of eager anticipation and shared delight in learning'. Like Noddings (who would have been seventy-six when the paper cited was published) we adult educators need to keep making a stand until things change. Perhaps this book has played a role here and can continue to serve the cause of adult education by demonstrating that there is still some pleasure in teaching, in learning and in examining these processes in action! To embrace Raymond William's conceptualization, may it serve as a 'resource for hope' (Williams, 1989), even a resource for 'educated hope' (Giroux, 2012, p. 38) given its overall focus.

Henry Giroux, in his statements about hope and educated hope, provides us with a fitting framework through which to view the achievements of this book. He sees hope as 'a pedagogical and performative practice' that helps humans to become 'moral and civic agents' and, fittingly, as the:

> [...] outcome of those educational practices and struggles that tap into memory and lived experiences [...] linking individual responsibility with a progressive sense of social change. (ibid., pp. 38–39)

He makes a clear link between pedagogy and performance, agency and work that relates to recall and real life — the fundamental sources for biographical research like ours. Equally relevant is Giroux's description of educated hope as:

> [...] a form of utopian longing, [that][...] opens up horizons of comparison by evoking not just different histories but different futures. Educated hope is a subversive force when it pluralizes politics by opening up a space for dissent, making authority accountable, and becoming an activating presence in promoting social transformation. (ibid., p. 39)

These notions — of lived experiences, 'horizons of comparison', difference, pluralization, dissent leading to change — resonate clearly with the narratives unfolded within this book. In its turn, our book may be viewed as a resource for 'educated hope', for its varied chapters reflect the different strands identified by Giroux. However, other important messages derive *directly* from the research into Discourses We Live By, so we give the final words to three of *our* authors. Firstly, to Horsdal (Ch28) who inheres to 'the sharing of life story narratives [...] a significant role in supporting social harmony'. Secondly, to González González (Ch14) for his explicit reminder that 'the human being is to be projected as an end, never as a means', prompting us to keep the person at the heart of his/her story. And, thirdly, to Mazzoli Smith (Ch25) who points to learner identity as a 'capacity that can be shaped and reshaped anew', thus signalling that educators *can* initiate change — an affirmation that encourages us to renew our efforts. These are surely important messages for a book that foregrounds biographical methods and coalesces around educational themes, presenting them as Narratives of Educational and Social Endeavour.

References

Andrews, M. (2014). *Narrative imagination and everyday life.* Oxford: Oxford University Press.

Boud, D. & Walker, D. (2002). Promoting reflection in professional courses: The challenge of context. In: Harrison, R., Reeve, F., Hanson, A. & Clarke, J. (eds), *Supporting Lifelong Learning, 1: Perspectives on learning.* London: Routledge Falmer.

Bridges, D. (2005). *Widening participation in Higher Education: The philosopher and the bricklayer revisited.* Paper presented to Philosophy of Education Conference, 1–3 April in Institute of Education, London.

Foley, G. (2004). *Dimensions of adult learning: Adult education and training in a global era.* Maidenhead: Open University Press.

Foucault, M. (1969). *L'archéologie du savoir* (The archaeology of knowledge). Paris: Gallimard.

Freire, P. (1970). *Pedagogy of the oppressed.* New York: Continuum.

Giroux, H.A. (2012). When hope is subversive. *Tikkun,* 19(6): 38–39.

Mezirow, J. (1975). *Education for perspective transformation: Women's re-entry programs in community colleges.* New York: Center for Adult Education, Teachers College, Columbia University.

Moll, L., Amanti, C., Neff, D., & Gonzalez, N. (1992). Funds of knowledge for teaching: Using a qualitative approach to connect homes and classrooms. *Theory into Practice,* 31(2), 132–41.

Noddings, N. (2005). *Caring in education. The Encyclopedia of Informal Education,* 7pp online. www.infed.org/biblio/noddings_caring_in_education.htm

Ricœur, P. (1986a). *Du texte à l'action* (From text to action). Paris: Seuil.

Ricœur, P. (1986b). Life: A story in search of a narrator. In: Doeser M.C., Kraay J.N. (eds) *Facts and values.* Martinus Nijhoff Philosophy Library, 19. Dordrecht (Neths): Springer.

Sacks, H. (1992a). *Lectures in conversation,* Vol I. Oxford: Blackwell Publishing.

Sacks, H. (1992b). *Lectures in conversation,* Vol. II. Oxford: Blackwell Publishing.

Williams, R. (1989). *Resources of hope: Culture, democracy, socialism.* London/ New York: Verso.

List of Illustrations

Photo by Tom Perkins, CC-BY 4.0   ii

Photo by Tom Perkins, CC-BY 4.0   xxii

Photo by Tom Perkins, CC-BY 4.0   22

Fig. 2.1   Phases of the passage from experience into language. *Source:*   58
            Breton, 2017a.

Fig. 2.2   Periodization of the experience of the patient between being   62
            given a first diagnosis and having it confirmed.

Fig. 2.3   Expressing experience in a story in sessions of expressing   64
            and writing life histories.

Fig. 2.4   Narrative modes and transformations of experience during   67
            biographical activity.

Photo by Tom Perkins, CC-BY 4.0   114

Photo by Tom Perkins, CC-BY 4.0   206

Photo by Tom Perkins, CC-BY 4.0   284

Photo by Tom Perkins, CC-BY 4.0   378

Photo by Tom Perkins, CC-BY 4.0   460

Photo by Tom Perkins, CC-BY 4.0   544

Fig. 27.1   The installation *Sufi-Masa* (2017). *Source:* Author.   597

Fig. 27.2   A poem written by a participant. *Source:* Author.   598

Fig. 27.3   *My prayer mat*, a photograph taken by a participant.   599
            Source: Author.

Photo by Tom Perkins, CC-BY 4.0   620

Photo by Tom Perkins, CC-BY 4.0   634

Photo by Tom Perkins, CC-BY 4.0

Index

academic performance 115, 126, 148, 151, 175, 189, 226–227, 313, 324, 342, 428, 479, 488, 523, 575

achievement 18, 83–84, 135, 152, 168, 180, 327, 411, 528, 550, 558

action research 353, 450, 589

adult education 73–87, 163–181, 353–373

adult play 269–281

agency 55, 97, 116, 164, 201, 249, 285, 366, 410, 461, 562–563, 595, 628

Alheit, P. 254, 388

Archer, M. 164–182

arts-based research 451, 587–588

aspiration 77, 146, 405, 413, 427, 470, 549, 561

assessment 225–239, 333–348

Austria 445

autoethnography 546, 570, 594

Barthes, R. 5, 34

Bauman, Z. 212, 271–278, 297

becoming 57, 127, 141, 199, 229, 249, 271, 298, 416, 437, 478, 486, 520, 559, 577, 601, 631

belonging 81, 116, 127, 141, 225, 327, 393, 445, 471, 501, 588, 615

Bildung 119–136

biographicity 254, 388

biography 14, 231, 313, 388, 449, 615–616

Bourdieu, P. 143, 228, 394, 397–398, 425

Britain 27, 73, 91, 185, 211, 404, 501, 517, 549, 569

Bruner, J. 8, 28, 188, 222, 230, 281

Caillois, R. 273

Canada 465

care leavers 245–265

caring 13, 77, 102, 441, 462, 492, 591, 616, 626

change 1, 10, 24, 55, 75, 94, 135, 142, 169, 190, 200, 212, 234, 253, 269, 291, 312, 334, 353, 383, 410, 426, 450, 462, 467, 486, 506, 552, 577, 593, 614

Christian beliefs 73–74, 149, 426

CINAGE 517–542

Clandinin, D.J. 9, 29, 189, 582, 622

Colombia 311

community 63, 78, 127, 145, 166, 199, 215, 229, 290, 328, 356, 380, 412, 452, 461, 468, 489, 503, 554, 595, 630

contexts 1, 24, 91, 115, 141, 164, 207, 215, 228, 248, 270, 287, 337, 358, 392–393, 405, 426, 445, 461, 465, 488, 519, 589, 609

Conversation Analysis 383–399

conversion 425–441

Critical Discourse Analysis (CDA) 353

culture 2, 23, 73, 115, 119, 149, 167, 207, 213, 246, 272, 334, 379, 410, 465, 492, 510, 541, 552, 594, 611

curriculum 45, 98, 124, 146, 316, 336, 405, 465, 486, 576

Davies, B. 143, 153

decolonization 465–481

democracy 73–87, 122, 147, 347, 355, 561

Denmark 119, 141, 289, 425, 609

Dewey, J. 30

Dickens, C. 37–38

discourses xi, 1, 74, 91, 115, 126, 141, 200, 207, 211, 238, 245, 281, 285, 293, 323, 337, 354, 383, 414, 427, 445, 461, 465, 486, 503, 526, 545, 550, 569, 594, 609

discrimination 311–329

diversity 2, 82, 128, 164, 227, 257, 286, 311, 373, 380, 453, 461, 486, 503, 556, 587, 621
documentation 473
Druckman, J.N. 361

education 1, 53, 75, 94, 115, 120, 141, 163, 187, 221, 247, 278, 286, 289, 334, 355, 380, 404, 428, 446, 466, 485, 502, 523, 545, 569, 593, 609
employment conditions 163–181
empowerment 256, 492, 503, 628
equality/inequality 311–329, 360, 362, 471
exclusion 11, 117, 144, 192, 251, 286, 298, 311–312, 420, 448, 546, 569
experience 1, 23, 53, 74, 99, 122, 143, 165, 185, 201, 215, 225, 245, 270, 289, 324, 338, 363, 388

failure 117, 182, 207–208, 222, 226, 281, 302, 345, 417, 487, 504, 523, 550, 615
Fairclough, N. 353, 398
family 24, 91, 115, 127, 175, 189, 217, 225, 248, 271, 285, 290, 362, 379, 385, 406, 427, 453, 471, 501, 545, 597, 613, 624
Feldenkrais method 523
feminism 445–456, 485–496, 587–604
fiction 27–46, 257, 455, 554–567, 581, 593, 610
filmmaking 445–456, 517–542
Fink, E. 275
Finland 485, 587
Foley, G. 3, 92, 405
Foucault, M. 11, 33, 142, 144, 212, 281, 354, 388, 571
Frames of Reference 361
France 53
Frank, A.W. 27
Freire, P. 408
fundamentalism 73–87, 354
further education 163–181, 403–420

Gadamer, H-G. 28
gambling 269–281

gender 97, 250, 272, 317, 319, 485, 488–496, 501–512, 588–592, 591–592, 596–599
genre 455, 546, 594, 612
Germany 383
Giddens, A. 135, 271, 614
Giroux, H. 334, 631

habitus 143, 200, 228, 256, 397–398, 425–441
health 55
health education 53–70
heritage 417, 470, 474, 536, 625
higher education 225–239, 549–565
homogeneity 311–329
hope 80, 170, 251, 271, 294, 363, 414, 546, 617
Huizinga, J. 273
humanities v sciences 119–136

identity 1, 68, 116, 133, 146, 164, 179, 229, 245, 272, 286, 297, 317, 347, 353, 394, 407, 432, 465, 501, 541, 552, 578, 595, 626
inclusion 144, 187, 285–286, 311, 469
Indigenous peoples 465–481, 485–496
Indigenous Research Methods 471–481
individualism 75, 135, 286, 334, 489, 611
informal learning 91–110, 269–281, 517–542
insider research 116, 451, 582, 624
institutional narratives 128
institutional regimes 141–157, 226–231, 248, 290, 314, 334, 466, 489, 503, 553
interviews 5, 55, 76, 97, 124, 165, 190, 207, 230, 254, 286, 333, 355, 379, 384, 404, 434, 453, 502, 590, 613
Ireland 163, 225
Iser, W. 28
Islamic beliefs 74–82, 425–441, 587–604
isolation 155, 191, 298, 348, 411, 573
Italy 245, 269

journaling 569–584

Keats, J. 75
Kenya 141–157

Khazakstan 383

language 3, 5, 53, 84, 96, 122, 189, 207, 211, 246, 273, 320, 334, 354, 380, 386, 404, 434, 452, 469, 551, 572, 591, 611
lifespan 84–85
life stories 63–64, 115, 272, 286, 380, 395, 421, 425, 462, 494, 561, 563, 609
literacy 403–420
low-literate people 403–420

marginalization 74, 471, 494, 626
Mason, J. 394
memories 66, 99, 211, 263, 338, 385, 410, 431, 485, 503, 524, 610
mental health 56, 75, 279, 289, 473, 503
metaphor 37, 82–85, 192, 222, 246, 273, 356–358, 363–375
Mezirow, J. 250, 413
Miettinen, S. 486
migrant 214, 358, 379, 404, 446, 462, 465, 536, 588, 624
migration 250, 323, 366, 379, 417, 445, 461
military veterans 501–512
morality 78, 141–157, 212, 362, 554
motivation 85, 164, 192, 221, 253, 362, 419, 453, 509, 549, 579, 621
Murdoch, I. 553–567

Namibia 485
Naskali, P. 488, 490–498
natural world 91–110
negative capability 73–87
neoliberalism 82, 120, 147, 213, 334, 488
Nepal 211
Nurture groups 185–201
Nussbaum, M.C. 38, 323, 564

obedience 217, 386–401
observational methods 333–348
offenders 289–306, 501–512
othering 297, 380, 445–446, 480, 596

participatory action research 353, 450, 456, 625
performative social science 451

personal development 172, 200, 231, 578
Poland 353
Polkinghorne, D.E. 3, 99, 126, 313, 425
power 4, 23, 60, 74, 93, 116, 135, 142, 172, 201, 212, 246, 271, 285, 313, 354, 407, 445, 447, 461, 488, 505, 550, 570, 592, 623
professional identity 133, 148, 170, 578
progression 16, 117, 207, 225–239, 418, 504, 545, 551, 630
punishment 211–222
Pupil Referral Unit (PRU) 39, 569–584

reflexivity 61, 256, 492, 545, 550, 614
rehabilitation 269–281, 289–306, 501–512
relationship(s) 24, 56, 75, 97, 126, 152, 167, 187, 211, 229, 251, 270, 300, 347, 359, 383, 413, 428, 451, 466, 487, 503, 552, 571, 591, 611, 623
religion 24, 73, 108, 129, 255, 425, 461, 591, 629
representation, (self-) 445–456
resilience 187, 461, 546, 587, 616
retention 225–239
rhetoric 211–222, 316, 353–373
Ricœur, J-P. 7, 56, 621
rites of passage 228
Rolling, J.H. 589
Rorty, R. 558
Rushdie, S. 28–37
Russia 383

Sacks, H. 388, 621
school education 91–110, 185–201, 333–348, 569–584
senior citizens 517–542
Snow, C.P. 119–136
South Africa 485–496
special education 176, 185–201, 569–584
spirituality 425–441
stigma 155, 249, 289–291, 297–306, 408, 448
stories 1, 23, 53, 79, 96, 126, 157, 207, 245, 280, 291, 313, 383, 404, 426, 453, 461, 466, 486, 501, 518, 550, 582, 602, 610, 622

storytelling 55, 294, 368, 420, 520, 593, 623

subjectivity 66, 86, 142, 229, 449, 594

suffering 56–60

support 10, 57, 102, 130, 174, 185, 212, 225, 251, 279, 285, 302, 312, 333, 354, 381, 404, 410, 429, 455, 461–462, 486, 502, 537, 545, 552, 572, 601, 627

Sweden 333

teacher education 27–46, 119–136, 141–157

teaching 7, 98, 115, 121, 142, 163, 185, 217, 229, 322, 336, 345, 379, 405, 428, 452, 461, 487, 523, 573, 629

teaching assistants 185–201

therapeutic education 53–70

transgression 397

transition 54, 117, 208, 227, 253, 281, 291, 337, 490, 501, 589

truth 1–20, 27–46, 73–87, 356, 468, 551, 554–562, 581

university admission 333–348

Vermersch, P. 58

violence 74–87, 188, 211–222, 249–251, 258–265, 291–306, 320

voice 3, 126, 153, 185, 216, 230, 249, 286, 349, 355, 386, 403, 447, 474, 487, 504, 537, 546, 552, 569, 603

vulnerability 66, 74, 245, 269, 300, 493, 521, 616, 626

wellbeing 116, 168, 194, 421, 434, 583

widening participation 549–565

Williams, R. 549, 631

workers' education 73–87

workshop 446, 475, 485, 529, 591

About the Team

Alessandra Tosi was the managing editor for this book.

Lucy Barnes performed the copy-editing and proofreading.

Anna Gatti designed the cover using InDesign. The cover was produced in InDesign using Fontin (titles) and Calibri (text body) fonts.

Luca Baffa typeset the book in InDesign. The text font is Tex Gyre Pagella; the heading font is Californian FB. Luca created all of the editions — paperback, hardback, EPUB, MOBI, PDF, HTML, and XML — the conversion is performed with open source software freely available on our GitHub page (https://github.com/OpenBookPublishers).

This book need not end here...

Share

All our books — including the one you have just read — are free to access online so that students, researchers and members of the public who can't afford a printed edition will have access to the same ideas. This title will be accessed online by hundreds of readers each month across the globe: why not share the link so that someone you know is one of them?

This book and additional content is available at:

https://doi.org/10.11647/OBP.0203

Customise

Personalise your copy of this book or design new books using OBP and third-party material. Take chapters or whole books from our published list and make a special edition, a new anthology or an illuminating coursepack. Each customised edition will be produced as a paperback and a downloadable PDF.

Find out more at:

https://www.openbookpublishers.com/section/59/1

You may also be interested in:

Oral Literature in the Digital Age
Archiving Orality and Connecting with Communities
Mark Turin, Claire Wheeler and Eleanor Wilkinson (eds.)

https://doi.org/10.11647/OBP.0032

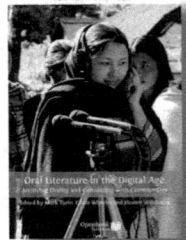

Tellings and Texts
Music, Literature and Performance in North India
Francesca Orsini and Katherine Butler Schofield (eds.)

https://doi.org/10.11647/OBP.0062

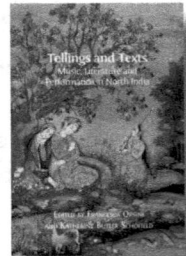

Stories from Quechan Oral Literature
Linguistic work by A.M. Halpern and Amy Miller

https://doi.org/10.11647/OBP.0049

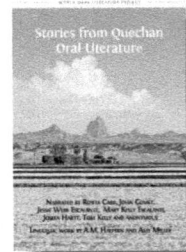

www.ingramcontent.com/pod-product-compliance
Lightning Source LLC
Chambersburg PA
CBHW051945270326
41929CB00015B/2542